Worldwide Acclaim for
THE THIRD WAVE

"A MAGNIFICENT PIECE OF WORK . . . Toffler sweeps across space and time to integrate an astonishing array of information—from family life to microbiology—into a theory of history . . . Lest anyone suspect otherwise, this is a rave review."
—*Washington Post*

"AN EXTRAORDINARY SYNTHESIS . . . Toffler is situated far from all ideology and all scientific prophecy, which gives him a remarkable point of view . . . Read this book: it is invigorating."
—Paris, *Le Figaro*

"A POWERFUL BOOK . . . Alvin Toffler has written another blockbuster . . ."
—London, *The Guardian*

"UNQUESTIONABLY A MAJOR WORK—highly entertaining . . . the strengths of the book are its wide horizons, its ability to synthesize, its riveting argument, its keen insight into new developments and its courageous speculation . . ."
—Zurich, *Neue Zurcher Zeitung*

"TOFFLER HAS IMAGINATION and an ability to think of various future possibilities by transcending prevailing values, assumptions and myths."
—*Associated Press*

"RICH, STIMULATING AND BASICALLY OPTIMISTIC . . . will unquestionably aid many to a greater understanding of [today's] puzzling social changes . . ."
—Toronto *Globe and Mail*

"DESTINED TO BECOME ANOTHER CONTEMPORARY CLASSIC like its predecessor FUTURE SHOCK . . . Toffler has proven again that he is a master . . . a unique author who in less than ten years has produced two books that will become classics, both with fresh ideas, clearly explained."
—*United Press International*

"A PROVOCATIVE GLIMPSE INTO AN EXCITING FUTURE . . . Toffler's sweeping synthesis—a remarkable map of civilization's fragile interdependencies—can be ignored only at our peril . . . THE THIRD WAVE will probably become one of the most talked-about books of the year."
—*Business Week*

"TOFFLER HAS . . . AUTHORITY, AND A VOICE. He renders sharp, unequivocal judgments on today's world and offers nothing less than a vision of tomorrow, 'a new civilization' for mankind . . . THE THIRD WAVE will mesmerize readers, and rightly so."
—*Vogue*

"MUST READING FOR INVESTORS . . . Understanding the concepts and visions of this extraordinary book will be as important . . . in the 1980s as Toffler's earlier seminal work, FUTURE SHOCK, was to an understanding of the 1970s."
—*Financial World*

"A DETAILED BREATHTAKINGLY BOLD PROJECTION of the social changes required if we are to survive . . . Toffler's vision of a democratic, self-sustaining utopia is a brave alternative to recent grim warnings."
—*Cosmopolitan*

"A SEMINAL WORK destined to take its place alongside those fictional crystal balls—Orwell's *1984* and Aldous Huxley's BRAVE NEW WORLD . . . Toffler is no small-scale thinker . . . his book is bursting with ideas."

—*John Barkham Reviews*

"Once you have walked into his version of the future, you may decide never again to whitewash some of the built-in frailties of the real present."

—Toronto *Financial Post*

"Scholarly observers . . . call his synthesis 'original,' a 'grand tableau', and 'courageous' . . . [among] information professionals . . . none we surveyed could think of anyone else who has reached as far or encompassed as much of the new technologies and their impact."

—*Information World*

"It's not very often that a book comes along that shakes up your assumptions about the whole world and how it works. Alvin Toffler's THE THIRD WAVE is that kind of book . . . imaginative and . . . brilliant."

—*Environmental Action*

"A SUPERB STATEMENT . . . no other book known to me would make such a useful resource for any Christian willing to learn."

—*Church Times*

Bantam Books by Alvin Toffler
Ask your bookseller for the books you have missed

THE ECO-SPASM REPORT
FUTURE SHOCK
THE THIRD WAVE

THE
THIRD
WAVE

ALVIN TOFFLER

BANTAM BOOKS
TORONTO · NEW YORK · LONDON · SYDNEY

*This low-priced Bantam Book
has been completely reset in a type face
designed for easy reading, and was printed
from new plates. It contains the complete
text of the original hard-cover edition.*
NOT ONE WORD HAS BEEN OMITTED.

THE THIRD WAVE

*A Bantam Book / published in association with
William Morrow & Co., Inc.*

PRINTING HISTORY

*William Morrow edition published March 1980
5 printings September 1980*

*A Literary Guild Selection October 1979
A Selection of Preferred Choice Bookplan October 1979 and
the Macmillan Book Club May 1980.*

Serialized in Industry Week, *February 1980;* East/West Net-
work, *February 1980;* Across the Board, *March 1980;* Inde-
pendent News Alliance, *March 1980;* Rotarian, *April 1980;*
Mechanix Illustrated, *May 1980;* Reader's Digest, *May 1980;*
Video Review, *May 1980;* Journal of Insurance, *July 1980;*
Reader's Digest (Canada), *August 1980* and Modern Office
Procedures, *September 1980.*

Bantam edition / April 1981

2nd printing ..... April 1981	5th printing .... October 1981
3rd printing ..... April 1981	6th printing .. December 1981
4th printing .. September 1981	7th printing .... August 1982

THE THIRD WAVE also appears in translation:
French (Editions Deneol); *German* (Bertelsmann); *Japanese*
(NHK Books); *Spanish* (Plaza y Janes and Editorial Diana);
Danish (Chr. Erichsens Forlag); *Dutch* (Uitgenerij L.J. Veen);
Hebrew (Am Oved); *Portuguese* (Distribuidora Record); *Serbo-
Croatian* (Jugoslavija); *Swedish* (Esselte Info AB); *Turkish*
(Altin Kitaplar); *Chinese* (Dushu-Peking).

*All rights reserved.
Copyright © 1980 by Alvin Toffler.
Cover art copyright © 1981 by Bantam Books, Inc.
This book may not be reproduced in whole or in part, by
mimeograph or any other means, without permission.
For information address: Bantam Books, Inc.*

ISBN 0-553-22635-5

Published simultaneously in the United States and Canada

*Bantam Books are published by Bantam Books, Inc. Its trade-
mark, consisting of the words "Bantam Books" and the por-
trayal of a rooster, is Registered in U.S. Patent and Trademark
Office and in other countries. Marca Registrada. Bantam
Books, Inc., 666 Fifth Avenue, New York, New York 10103.*

PRINTED IN THE UNITED STATES OF AMERICA

H   16 15 14 13 12 11 10 9 8

FOR HEIDI

Whose convincing arguments helped me decide to write *The Third Wave*. Her tough, tenacious criticism of my ideas and her professionalism as an editor are reflected on every page.

Her contributions to this book extend far beyond those one would expect of a colleague, an intellectual companion, a friend, lover and wife.

Did we come here to laugh or cry?
Are we dying or being born?
>   *Terra Nostra* by Carlos Fuentes

CONTENTS

CONTENTS

INTRODUCTION

In a time when terrorists play death-games with hostages, as currencies careen amid rumors of a third World War, as embassies flame and storm troopers lace up their boots in many lands, we stare in horror at the headlines. The price of gold—that sensitive barometer of fear—breaks all records. Banks tremble. Inflation rages out of control. And the governments of the world are reduced to paralysis or imbecility.

Faced with all this, a massed chorus of Cassandras fills the air with doom-song. The proverbial man in the street says the world has "gone mad," while the expert points to all the trends leading toward catastrophe.

This book offers a sharply different view.

It contends that the world has not swerved into lunacy, and that, in fact, beneath the clatter and jangle of seemingly senseless events there lies a startling and potentially hopeful pattern. This book is about that pattern and that hope.

The Third Wave is for those who think the human story, far from ending, has only just begun.

A powerful tide is surging across much of the world today, creating a new, often bizarre, environment in which to work, play, marry, raise children, or retire. In this bewildering context, businessmen swim against highly erratic economic currents; politicians see their ratings bob wildly up and down; universities, hospitals, and other institutions battle desperately against inflation. Value systems splinter and crash, while the lifeboats of family, church, and state are hurled madly about.

Looking at these violent changes, we can regard them as

isolated evidences of instability, breakdown, and disaster. Yet, if we stand back for a longer view, several things become apparent that otherwise go unnoticed.

To begin with, many of today's changes are not independent of one another. Nor are they random. For example, the crack-up of the nuclear family, the global energy crisis, the spread of cults and cable television, the rise of flextime and new fringe-benefit packages, the emergence of separatist movements from Quebec to Corsica, may all seem like isolated events. Yet precisely the reverse is true. These and many other seemingly unrelated events or trends are interconnected. They are, in fact, parts of a much larger phenomenon: the death of industrialism and the rise of a new civilization.

So long as we think of them as isolated changes and miss this larger significance, we cannot design a coherent, effective response to them. As individuals, our personal decisions remain aimless or self-canceling. As governments, we stumble from crisis to crash program, lurching into the future without plan, without hope, without vision.

Lacking a systematic framework for understanding the clash of forces in today's world, we are like a ship's crew, trapped in a storm and trying to navigate between dangerous reefs without compass or chart. In a culture of warring specialisms, drowned in fragmented data and fine-toothed analysis, synthesis is not merely useful—it is crucial.

For this reason, *The Third Wave* is a book of large-scale synthesis. It describes the old civilization in which many of us grew up, and presents a careful, comprehensive picture of the new civilization bursting into being in our midst.

So profoundly revolutionary is this new civilization that it challenges all our old assumptions. Old ways of thinking, old formulas, dogmas, and ideologies, no matter how cherished or how useful in the past, no longer fit the facts. The world that is fast emerging from the clash of new values and technologies, new geopolitical relationships, new life-styles and modes of communication, demands wholly new ideas and analogies, classifications and concepts. We cannot cram the embryonic world of tomorrow into yesterday's conventional cubbyholes. Nor are the orthodox attitudes or moods appropriate.

Thus, as the description of this strange new civilization unfolds in these pages, we will find reason to challenge the chic pessimism that is so prevalent today. Despair—salable and self-indulgent—has dominated the culture for a decade or more. *The Third Wave* concludes that despair is not only a sin (as C. P. Snow, I believe, once put it), but that it is also unwarranted.

I am under no Pollyannaish illusions. It is scarcely necessary today to elaborate on the real dangers facing us—from nuclear annihilation and ecological disaster to racial fanaticism or regional violence. I have written about these dangers myself in the past, and will no doubt do so again. War, economic debacle, large-scale technological disaster—any of these could alter future history in catastrophic ways.

Nevertheless, as we explore the many new relationships springing up—between changing energy patterns and new forms of family life, or between advanced manufacturing methods and the self-help movement, to mention only a few—we suddenly discover that many of the very same conditions that produce today's greatest perils also open fascinating new potentials.

The Third Wave shows us these new potentials. It argues that, in the very midst of destruction and decay, we can now find striking evidences of birth and life. It shows clearly and, I think, indisputably, that—with intelligence and a modicum of luck—the emergent civilization can be made more sane, sensible, and sustainable, more decent and more democratic than any we have ever known.

If the main argument of this book is correct, there are powerful reasons for long-range optimism, even if the transitional years immediately ahead are likely to be stormy and crisis-ridden.

As I've worked on *The Third Wave* in the past few years, lecture audiences have repeatedly asked me how it differs from my earlier work *Future Shock*.

Author and reader never see quite the same things in a book. I view *The Third Wave* as radically different from *Future Shock* in both form and focus. To begin with, it covers a much wider sweep of time—past as well as future. It is more prescriptive. Its architecture is different. (The perceptive reader will find that its structure mirrors its central metaphor—the clash of waves.)

Substantively, the differences are even more pronounced. While *Future Shock* called for certain changes to be made, it emphasized the personal and social costs of change. *The Third Wave,* while taking note of the difficulties of adaptation, emphasizes the equally important costs of not changing certain things rapidly enough.

Moreover, while in the earlier book I wrote of the "premature arrival of the future," I did not attempt to sketch the emergent society of tomorrow in any comprehensive or systematic way. The focus of the book was on the processes of change, not the directions of change.

In this book, the lens is reversed. I concentrate less on acceleration, as such, and more on the destinations toward which change is carrying us. Thus one work focuses more heavily on process, the other on structure. For these reasons, the two books are designed to fit together, not as source and sequel, but as complementary parts of a much larger whole. Each is very different. But each casts light on the other.

In attempting so large-scale a synthesis, it has been necessary to simplify, generalize, and compress. (Without doing so, it would have been impossible to cover so much ground in a single volume.) As a result, some historians may take issue with the way this book divides civilization into only three parts—a First Wave agricultural phase, a Second Wave industrial phase, and a Third Wave phase now beginning.

It is easy to point out that agricultural civilization consisted of quite different cultures, and that industrialism itself has actually gone through many successive stages of development. One could, no doubt, chop the past (and the future) into 12 or 38 or 157 pieces. But, in so doing, we would lose sight of the major divisions in a clutter of subdivisions. Or we would require a whole library, instead of a single book, to cover the same territory. For our purposes, the simpler distinctions are more useful, even if gross.

The vast scope of this book also required the use of other shortcuts. Thus I occasionally reify civilization itself, arguing that First Wave or Second Wave civilization "did" this or that. Of course, I know, and readers know, that civilizations don't do anything; people do. But attributing this or that to a civilization now and then saves time and breath.

Similarly, intelligent readers understand that no one—historian or futurist, planner, astrologer, or evangelist—"knows" or can "know" the future. When I say something "will" happen, I assume the reader will make appropriate discount for uncertainty. To have done otherwise would have burdened the book with an unreadable and unnecessary jungle of reservations. Social forecasts, moreover, are never value-free or scientific, no matter how much computerized data they use. *The Third Wave* is not an objective forecast, and it makes no pretense to being scientifically proven.

To say this, however, is not to suggest that the ideas in this book are whimsical or unsystematic. In fact, as will soon become apparent, this work is based on massive evidence and on what might be called a semi-systematic model of civilization and our relationships to it.

It describes the dying industrial civilization in terms of a "techno-sphere," a "socio-sphere," an "info-sphere," and a "power-sphere," then sets out to show how each of these is undergoing revolutionary change in today's world. It attempts to show the relationships of these parts to each other, as well as the "bio-sphere" and "psycho-sphere"—that structure of psychological and personal relationships through which changes in the outer world affect our most private lives.

The Third Wave holds that a civilization also makes use of certain processes and principles, and that it develops its own "super-ideology" to explain reality and to justify its own existence.

Once we understand how these parts, processes, and principles are interrelated, and how they transform one another, touching off powerful currents of change, we gain a much clearer understanding of the giant wave of change battering our lives today.

The grand metaphor of this work, as should already be apparent, is that of colliding waves of change. This image is not original. Norbert Elias, in his *The Civilizing Process*, refers to "a wave of advancing integration over several centuries." In 1837, a writer described the settlement of the American West in terms of successive "waves"—first the pioneers, then the farmers, then the business interests, the "third wave" of migration. In 1893, Frederick Jackson Turner cited and employed the same analogy in his classic essay *The Significance of the Frontier in American History*. It is not, therefore, the wave metaphor that is fresh, but its application to today's civilizational shift.

This application proves to be extremely fruitful. The wave idea is not only a tool for organizing vast masses of highly diverse information. It also helps us see beneath the raging surface of change. When we apply the wave metaphor, much that was confusing becomes clear. The familiar often appears in a dazzlingly fresh light.

Once I began thinking in terms of waves of change, colliding and overlapping, causing conflict and tension around us, it changed my perception of change itself. In every field, from education and health to technology, from personal life to politics, it became possible to distinguish those innovations that are merely cosmetic, or just extensions of the industrial past, from those that are truly revolutionary.

Even the most powerful metaphor, however, is capable of yielding only partial truth. No metaphor tells the whole story from all sides, and hence no vision of the present, let alone the future, can be complete or final. When I was a Marxist during my late teens and early twenties—now more than a quarter of a century ago—I, like many young people, thought I had all the answers. I soon learned that my "answers" were partial, one-sided, and obsolete. More to the point, I came to appreciate that the right question is usually more important than the right answer to the wrong question.

My hope is that *The Third Wave*, at the same time that it provides answers, asks many fresh questions.

The recognition that no knowledge can be complete, no metaphor entire, is itself humanizing. It counteracts fanaticism. It grants even to adversaries the possibility of partial truth, and to oneself the possibility of error. This possibility is especially present in large-scale synthesis. Yet, as the critic George Steiner has written, "To ask larger questions is to risk getting things wrong. Not to ask them at all is to constrain the life of understanding."

In a time of exploding change—with personal lives being torn apart, the existing social order crumbling, and a fantastic new way of life emerging on the horizon—asking the very largest of questions about our future is not merely a matter of intellectual curiosity. It is a matter of survival.

Whether we know it or not, most of us are already engaged in either resisting—or creating—the new civilization. *The Third Wave* will, I hope, help each of us to choose.

A COLLISION OF WAVES

1

SUPER-STRUGGLE

A new civilization is emerging in our lives, and blind men everywhere are trying to suppress it. This new civilization brings with it new family styles; changed ways of working, loving, and living; a new economy; new political conflicts; and beyond all this an altered consciousness as well. Pieces of this new civilization exist today. Millions are already attuning their lives to the rhythms of tomorrow. Others, terrified of the future, are engaged in a desperate, futile flight into the past and are trying to restore the dying world that gave them birth.

The dawn of this new civilization is the single most explosive fact of our lifetimes.

It is the central event—the key to understanding the years immediately ahead. It is an event as profound as that First Wave of change unleashed ten thousand years ago by the invention of agriculture, or the earthshaking Second Wave of change touched off by the industrial revolution. We are the children of the next transformation, the Third Wave.

We grope for words to describe the full power and reach of this extraordinary change. Some speak of a looming Space Age, Information Age, Electronic Era, or Global Village. Zbigniew Brzezinski has told us we face a "technetronic age." Sociologist Daniel Bell describes the coming of a "post-industrial society." Soviet futurists speak of the S.T.R.—the "scientific-technological revolution." I myself have written extensively about the arrival of a "super-industrial society." Yet none of these terms, including my own, is adequate.

Some of these phrases, by focusing on a single factor, narrow rather than expand our understanding. Others are static, implying that a new society can come into our lives smoothly, without conflict or stress. None of these terms even begins to convey the full force, scope, and dynamism of the changes rushing toward us or of the pressures and conflicts they trigger.

Humanity faces a quantum leap forward. It faces the deepest social upheaval and creative restructuring of all time. Without clearly recognizing it, we are engaged in building a remarkable new civilization from the ground up. This is the meaning of the Third Wave.

Until now the human race has undergone two great waves of change, each one largely obliterating earlier cultures or civilizations and replacing them with ways of life inconceivable to those who came before. The First Wave of change—the agricultural revolution—took thousands of years to play itself out. The Second Wave—the rise of industrial civilization—took a mere three hundred years. Today history is even more accelerative, and it is likely that the Third Wave will sweep across history and complete itself in a few decades. We, who happen to share the planet at this explosive moment, will therefore feel the full impact of the Third Wave in our own lifetimes.

Tearing our families apart, rocking our economy, paralyzing our political systems, shattering our values, the Third Wave affects everyone. It challenges all the old power relationships, the privileges and prerogatives of the endangered elites of today, and provides the backdrop against which the key power struggles of tomorrow will be fought

Much in this emerging civilization contradicts the old traditional industrial civilization. It is, at one and the same time, highly technological and anti-industrial.

The Third Wave brings with it a genuinely new way of life based on diversified, renewable energy sources; on methods of production that make most factory assembly lines obsolete; on new, non-nuclear families; on a novel institution that might be called the "electronic cottage"; and on radically changed schools and corporations of the future. The emergent civilization writes a new code of behavior for us and carries us beyond standardization, synchronization, and centralization, beyond the concentration of energy, money, and power.

This new civilization, as it challenges the old, will topple bureaucracies, reduce the role of the nation-state, and give rise to semiautonomous economies in a postimperialist world. It requires governments that are simpler, more effective, yet more democratic than any we know today. It is a civilization with its own distinctive world outlook, its own ways of dealing with time, space, logic, and causality.

Above all, as we shall see, Third Wave civilization begins to heal the historic breach between producer and consumer, giving rise to the "prosumer" economics of tomorrow. For this reason, among many, it could—with some intelligent help from us—turn out to be the first truly humane civilization in recorded history.

THE REVOLUTIONARY PREMISE

Two apparently contrasting images of the future grip the popular imagination today. Most people—to the extent that they bother to think about the future at all—assume the world they know will last indefinitely. They find it difficult to imagine a truly different way of life for themselves, let alone a totally new civilization. Of course they recognize that things are changing. But they assume today's changes will somehow pass them by and that nothing will shake the familiar economic framework and political structure. They confidently expect the future to continue the present.

This straight-line thinking comes in various packages. At one level it appears as an unexamined assumption lying behind the decisions of businessmen, teachers, parents, and politicians. At a more sophisticated level it comes dressed up in statistics, computerized data, and forecasters' jargon. Either way it adds up to a vision of a future world that is essentially "more of the same"—Second Wave industrialism writ even larger and spread over more of this planet.

Recent events have severely shaken this confident image of the future. As crisis after crisis has crackled across the headlines, as Iran erupted, as Mao was de-deified, as oil prices skyrocketed and inflation ran wild, as terrorism spread and governments seemed helpless to stop it, a bleaker vision has become increasingly popular. Thus, large numbers of people —fed on a steady diet of bad news, disaster movies, apocalyptic Bible stories, and nightmare scenarios issued by prestigious think tanks—have apparently concluded that today's society cannot be projected into the future because there is no future.

For them, Armageddon is only minutes away. The earth is racing toward its final cataclysmic shudder.

On the surface these two visions of the future seem very different. Yet both produce similar psychological and political effects. For both lead to the paralysis of imagination and will.

If tomorrow's society is simply an enlarged, Cinerama version of the present, there is little we *need* do to prepare for it. If, on the other hand, society is inevitably destined to self-destruct within our lifetime, there is nothing we *can* do about it. In short, both these ways of looking at the future generate privatism and passivity. Both freeze us into inaction.

Yet, in trying to understand what is happening to us, we are not limited to this simpleminded choice between Armageddon and More-of-the-Same. There are many more clarifying and constructive ways to think about tomorrow—ways that prepare us for the future and, more important, help us to change the present.

This book is based on what I call the "revolutionary premise." It assumes that, even though the decades immediately ahead are likely to be filled with upheavals, turbulence, perhaps even widespread violence, we will not totally destroy ourselves. It assumes that the jolting changes we are now experiencing are not chaotic or random but that, in fact, they form a sharp, clearly discernible pattern. It assumes, moreover, that these changes are cumulative—that they add up to a giant transformation in the way we live, work, play, and think, and that a sane and desirable future is possible. In short, what follows begins with the premise that what is happening now is nothing less than a global revolution, a quantum jump in history.

Put differently, this book flows from the assumption that we are the final generation of an old civilization and the first generation of a new one, and that much of our personal confusion, anguish, and disorientation can be traced directly to the conflict within us, and within our political institutions, between the dying Second Wave civilization and the emergent Third Wave civilization that is thundering in to take its place.

When we finally understand this, many seemingly senseless events become suddenly comprehensible. The broad patterns of change begin to emerge clearly. Action for survival becomes possible and plausible again. In short, the revolutionary premise liberates our intellect and our will.

* * *

THE LEADING EDGE

To say the changes we face will be revolutionary, however, is not enough. Before we can control or channel them we need a fresh way to identify and analyze them. Without this we are hopelessly lost.

One powerful new approach might be called social "wave-front" analysis. It looks at history as a succession of rolling waves of change and asks where the leading edge of each wave is carrying us. It focuses our attention not so much on the continuities of history (important as they are) as on the discontinuities—the innovations and breakpoints. It identifies key change patterns as they emerge, so that we can influence them.

Beginning with the very simple idea that the rise of agriculture was the first turning point in human social development, and that the industrial revolution was the second great breakthrough, it views each of these not as a discrete, one-time event but as a wave of change moving at a certain velocity.

Before the First Wave of change, most humans lived in small, often migratory groups and fed themselves by foraging, fishing, hunting, or herding. At some point, roughly ten millennia ago, the agricultural revolution began, and it crept slowly across the planet spreading villages, settlements, cultivated land, and a new way of life.

This First Wave of change had not yet exhausted itself by the end of the seventeenth century, when the industrial revolution broke over Europe and unleashed the second great wave of planetary change. This new process—industrialization—began moving much more rapidly across nations and continents. Thus two separate and distinct change processes were rolling across the earth simultaneously, at different speeds.

Today the First Wave has virtually subsided. Only a few tiny tribal populations, in South America or Papua New Guinea, for example, remain to be reached by agriculture. But the force of this great First Wave has basically been spent.

Meanwhile, the Second Wave, having revolutionized life in Europe, North America, and some other parts of the globe in a few short centuries, continues to spread, as many countries, until now basically agricultural, scramble to build steel mills, auto plants, textile factories, railroads, and food processing plants. The momentum of industrialization is still felt. The Second Wave has not entirely spent in force.

But even as this process continues, another, even more important, has begun. For as the tide of industrialism peaked in the decades after World War II, a little-understood Third Wave began to surge across the earth, transforming everything it touched.

Many countries, therefore, are feeling the simultaneous impact of two, even three, quite different waves of change, all moving at different rates of speed and with different degrees of force behind them.

For the purposes of this book we shall consider the First Wave era to have begun sometime around 8000 B.C. and to have dominated the earth unchallenged until sometime around A.D. 1650–1750. From this moment on, the First Wave lost momentum as the Second Wave picked up steam. Industrial civilization, the product of this Second Wave, then dominated the planet in its turn until it, too, crested. This latest historical turning point arrived in the United States during the decade beginning about 1955—the decade that saw white-collar and service workers outnumber blue-collar workers for the first time. This was the same decade that saw the widespread introduction of the computer, commercial jet travel, the birth control pill, and many other high-impact innovations. It was precisely during this decade that the Third Wave began to gather its force in the United States. Since then it has arrived—at slightly different dates—in most of the other industrial nations, including Britain, France, Sweden, Germany, the Soviet Union, and Japan. Today all the high-technology nations are reeling from the collision between the Third Wave and the obsolete, encrusted economies and institutions of the Second.

Understanding this is the secret to making sense of much of the political and social conflict we see around us.

WAVES OF THE FUTURE

Whenever a single wave of change predominates in any given society, the pattern of future development is relatively easy to discern. Writers, artists, journalists, and others discover the "wave of the future." Thus in nineteenth-century Europe many thinkers, business leaders, politicians, and ordinary people held a clear, basically correct image of the future. They sensed that history was moving toward the ultimate triumph of industrialism over premechanized agriculture, and they foresaw with considerable accuracy many of the changes that the Second Wave would bring with it: more powerful technologies, bigger cities, faster transport, mass education, and the like.

This clarity of vision had direct political effects. Parties and political movements were able to triangulate with respect to the future. Preindustrial agricultural interests organized a rearguard action against encroaching industrialism, against "big business," against "union bosses," against "sinful cities." Labor and management grappled for control of the main levers of the emergent industrial society. Ethnic and racial minorities defining their rights in terms of an improved role in the industrial world, demanded access to jobs, corporate positions, urban housing, better wages, mass public education, and so forth.

This industrial vision of the future had important psychological effects as well. People might disagree; they might engage in sharp, occasionally even bloody, conflict. Depressions and boom times might disrupt their lives. Nevertheless, in general, the shared image of an industrial future tended to define options, to give individuals a sense not merely of who or what they were, but of what they were likely to become. It provided a degree of stability and a sense of self, even in the midst of extreme social change.

In contrast, when a society is struck by two or more giant waves of change, and none is yet clearly dominant, the image of the future is fractured. It becomes extremely difficult to sort out the meaning of the changes and conflicts that arise. The collision of wave fronts creates a raging ocean, full of clashing currents, eddies, and maelstroms which conceal the deeper, more important historic tides.

In the United States today—as in many other countries—the collision of Second and Third Waves creates social tensions, dangerous conflicts, and strange new political wave fronts that cut across the usual divisions of class, race, sex, or party. This collision makes a shambles of traditional political vocabularies and makes it very difficult to separate the progressives from the reactionaries, friends from enemies. All the old polarizations and coalitions break up. Unions and employers, despite their differences, join to fight environmentalists. Blacks and Jews, once united in the battle against discrimination, become adversaries.

In many nations, labor, which has traditionally favored "progressive" policies such as income redistribution, now often holds "reactionary" positions with respect to women's rights, family codes, immigration, tariffs, or regionalism. The traditional "left" is often pro-centralization, highly nationalistic, and antienvironmentalist.

At the same time we see politicians, from Valéry Giscard d'Estaing to Jimmy Carter or Jerry Brown, espousing "conservative" attitudes toward economics and "liberal" attitudes toward art, sexual morality, women's rights, or ecological controls. No wonder people are confused and give up trying to make sense of their world.

The media, meanwhile, report a seemingly endless succession of innovations, reversals, bizarre events, assassinations, kidnappings, space shots, governmental breakdown, commando raids, and scandals, all seemingly unrelated.

The apparent incoherence of political life is mirrored in personality disintegration. Psychotherapists and gurus do a land-office business; people wander aimlessly amid competing therapies, from primal scream to *est*. They slip into cults and covens or, alternatively, into a pathological privatism, convinced that reality is absurd, insane, or meaningless. Life may indeed be absurd in some large, cosmic sense. But this hardly proves that there is no pattern in today's events. In fact, there is a distinct, hidden order that becomes detectable as soon as we learn to distinguish Third Wave changes from those associated with the diminishing Second Wave.

An understanding of the conflicts produced by these colliding wave fronts gives us not only a clearer image of alternative futures but an X ray of the political and social forces acting on us. It also offers insight into our own private roles in history. For each of us, no matter how seemingly unimportant, is a living piece of history.

The crosscurrents created by these waves of change are reflected in our work, our family life, our sexual attitudes and personal morality. They show up in our life-styles and voting behavior. For in our personal lives and in our political acts, whether we know it or not, most of us in the rich countries are essentially either Second Wave people committed to maintaining the dying order, Third Wave people constructing a radically different tomorrow, or a confused, self-canceling mixture of the two.

*   *   *

GOLDBUGS AND ASSASSINS

The conflict between Second and Third Wave groupings is, in fact, the central political tension cutting through our society today. Despite what today's parties and candidates may preach, the infighting among them amounts to little more than a dispute over who will squeeze the most advantage from what remains of the declining industrial system. Put differently, they are engaged in a squabble for the proverbial deck chairs on a sinking *Titanic*.

The more basic political question, as we shall see, is not who controls the last days of industrial society but who shapes the new civilization rapidly rising to replace it. While short-range political skirmishes exhaust our energy and attention, a far more profound battle is already taking place beneath the surface. On one side are the partisans of the industrial past; on the other, growing millions who recognize that the most urgent problems of the world—food, energy, arms control, population, poverty, resources, ecology, climate, the problems of the aged, the breakdown of urban community, the need for productive, rewarding work—can no longer be resolved within the framework of the industrial order.

This conflict is the "super-struggle" for tomorrow.

This confrontation between the vested interests of the Second Wave and the people of the Third Wave already runs like an electric current through the political life of every nation. Even in the non-industrial countries of the world, all the old battle lines have been forcibly redrawn by the arrival of the Third Wave. The old war of agricultural, often feudal, interests against industrializing elites, either capitalist or socialist, takes on a new dimension in light of the coming obsolescence of industrialism. Now that Third Wave civilization is making its appearance, does rapid industrialization imply liberation from neocolonialism and poverty—or does it, in fact, guarantee permanent dependency?

It is only against this wide-screen background that we can begin to make sense of the headlines, to sort out our priorities, to frame sensible strategies for the control of change in our lives.

As I write this, the front pages report hysteria and hostages in Iran, assassinations in South Korea, runaway speculation in gold, friction between Blacks and Jews in the U.S., big increases in West German military spending, cross burnings on Long Island, a giant oil spill in the Gulf of Mexico, the biggest antinuclear rally in history, and a battle between the rich nations and the poor over the control of radio frequencies. Waves of religious revivalism crash through Libya, Syria, and the U.S.; neofascist fanatics claim "credit" for a political assassination in Paris. And General Motors reports a breakthrough into technology needed for electric automobiles. Such disconnected news-clips cry out for integration or synthesis.

Once we realize that a bitter struggle is now raging between those who seek to preserve industrialism and those who seek to supplant it, we have a powerful new key to understanding the world. More important—whether we are setting policies for a nation, strategies for a corporation, or goals for one's own personal life—we have a new tool for changing that world.

To use this tool, however, we must be able to distinguish clearly those changes that extend the old industrial civilization from those which facilitate the arrival of the new. We must, in short, understand both the old and the new, the Second Wave industrial system into which so many of us were born and the Third Wave civilization that we and our children will inhabit.

In the chapters that follow, we return for a closer look at the first two waves of change as a preparation for our exploration of the third. We shall see that Second Wave civilization was not an accidental jumble of components, but a *system* with parts that interacted with each other in more or less predictable ways—and that the fundamental patterns of industrial life were the same in country after country, regardless of cultural heritage or political difference. This is the civilization that today's "reactionaries"—both "left-" and "right-wing"—are fighting to preserve. It is this world that is threatened by history's Third Wave of civilizational change.

THE
SECOND
WAVE

≋ 2

THE ARCHITECTURE
OF
CIVILIZATION

Three hundred years ago, give or take a half-century, an explosion was heard that sent concussive shock waves racing across the earth, demolishing ancient societies and creating a wholly new civilization. This explosion was, of course, the industrial revolution. And the giant tidal force is set loose on the world—the Second Wave—collided with all the institutions of the past and changed the way of life of millions.

During the long millennia when First Wave civilization reigned supreme, the planet's population could have been divided into two categories—the "primitive" and the "civilized." The so-called primitive peoples, living in small bands and tribes and subsisting by gathering, hunting, or fishing, were those who had been passed over by the agricultural revolution.

The "civilized" world, by contrast, was precisely that part of the planet on which most people worked the soil. For wherever agriculture arose, civilization took root. From China and India to Benin and Mexico, in Greece and Rome, civilizations rose and fell, fought and fused in endless, colorful admixture.

However, beneath their differences lay fundamental similarities. In all of them, land was the basis of economy, life, culture, family structure, and politics. In all of them, life was organized around the village. In all of them, a simple division of labor prevailed and a few clearly defined castes and classes arose: a nobility, a priesthood, warriors, helots, slaves or serfs. In all of them, power was rigidly authoritarian. In all of them, birth determined one's position in life. And in all of

21

them, the economy was decentralized, so that each community produced most of its own necessities.

There were exceptions—nothing is simple in history. There were commercial cultures whose sailors crossed the seas, and highly centralized kingdoms organized around giant irrigation systems. But despite such differences, we are justified in seeing all these seemingly distinctive civilizations as special cases of a single phenomenon: agricultural civilization—the civilization spread by the First Wave.

During its dominance there were occasional hints of things to come. There were embryonic mass-production factories in ancient Greece and Rome. Oil was drilled on one of the Greek islands in 400 B.C. and in Burma in A.D. 100. Vast bureaucracies flourished in Babylonia and Egypt. Great urban metropolises grew up in Asia and South America. There was money and exchange. Trade routes crisscrossed the deserts, oceans, and mountains from Cathay to Cálais. Corporations and incipient nations existed. There was even, in ancient Alexandria, a startling forerunner of the steam engine.

Yet nowhere was there anything that might remotely have been termed an industrial civilization. These glimpses of the future, so to speak, were mere oddities in history, scattered through different places and periods. They never were brought together into a coherent system, nor could they have been. Until 1650–1750, therefore, we can speak of a First Wave world. Despite patches of primitivism and hints of the industrial future, agricultural civilization dominated the planet and seemed destined to do so forever.

This was the world in which the industrial revolution erupted, launching the Second Wave and creating a strange, powerful, feverishly energetic countercivilization. Industrialism was more than smokestacks and assembly lines. It was a rich, many-sided social system that touched every aspect of human life and attacked every feature of the First Wave past. It produced the great Willow Run factory outside Detroit, but it also put the tractor on the farm, the typewriter in the office, the refrigerator in the kitchen. It produced the daily newspaper and the cinema, the subway and the DC-3. It gave us cubism and twelve-tone music. It gave us Bauhaus buildings and Barcelona chairs, sit-down strikes, vitamin pills, and lengthened life spans. It universalized the wristwatch and the ballot box. More important, it linked all these things together—assembled them, like a machine—to form the most powerful, cohesive and expansive social system the world had ever know: Second Wave civilization.

THE VIOLENT SOLUTION

As the Second Wave moved across various societies it touched off a bloody, protracted war between the defenders of the agricultural past and the partisans of the industrial future. The forces of First and Second Wave collided head-on, brushing aside, often decimating, the "primitive" peoples encountered along the way.

In the United States, this collision began with the arrival of the Europeans bent on establishing an agricultural, First Wave civilization. A white agricultural tide pushed relentlessly westward, dispossessing the Indian, depositing farms and agricultural villages farther and farther toward the Pacific.

But hard on the heels of the farmers came the earliest industrializers as well, agents of the Second Wave future. Factories and cities began to spring up in New England and the mid-Atlantic states. By the middle of the nineteenth century, the Northeast had a rapidly growing industrial sector producing firearms, watches, farm implements, textiles, sewing machines, and other goods, while the rest of the continent was still ruled by agricultural interests. Economic and social tensions between First Wave and Second Wave forces grew in intensity until 1861, when they broke into armed violence.

The Civil War was not fought exclusively, as it seemed to many, over the moral issue of slavery or such narrow economic issues as tariffs. It was fought over a much larger question: would the rich new continent be ruled by farmers or industrializers, by the forces of the First Wave or the Second? Would the future American society be basically agricultural or industrial? When the Northern armies won, the die was cast. The industrialization of the United States was assured. From that time on, in economics, in politics, in social and cultural life, agriculture was in retreat, industry ascendant. The First Wave ebbed as the Second came thundering in.

The same collision of civilizations erupted elsewhere as well. In Japan the Meiji Restoration, beginning in 1868, replayed in unmistakably Japanese terms the same struggle between agricultural past and industrial future. The abolition of feudalism by 1876, the rebellion of the Satsuma clan in 1877, the adoption of a Western-style constitution in 1889, were all reflections of the collision of the First and Second Waves in Japan—steps on the road to Japan's emergence as a premier industrial power.

In Russia, too, the same collision between First and Second Wave forces erupted. The 1917 revolution was Russia's version of the American Civil War. It was fought not primarily, as it seemed, over communism but once again over the issue of industrialization. When the Bolsheviks wiped out the last lingering vestiges of serfdom and feudal monarchy, they pushed agriculture into the background and consciously accelerated industrialism. They became the party of the Second Wave.

In country after country, the same clash between First Wave and Second Wave interests broke out, leading to political crisis and upheavals, to strikes, uprisings, coups d'état, and wars. By the mid-twentieth century, however, the forces of the First Wave were broken and the Second Wave civilization reigned over the earth.

Today an industrial belt girdles the globe between the twenty-fifth and sixty-fifth parallels in the Northern Hemisphere. In North America, some 250 million people live an industrial way of life. In Western Europe, from Scandinavia south to Italy, another quarter of a billion humans live under industrialism. Eastward lies the "Eurussian" industrial region—Eastern Europe and the western part of the Soviet Union—and there we find still another quarter of a billion people living out their lives in industrial societies. Finally, we come to the Asian industrial region, comprising Japan, Hong Kong, Singapore, Taiwan, Australia, New Zealand, and parts of South Korea and the Chinese mainland, and yet another quarter billion industrial people. In all, industrial civilization embraces roughly one billion human beings—one fourth the population of the globe.*

Despite dizzying differences of language, culture, history, and politics—differences so deep that wars are fought over them—all these Second Wave societies share common fea-

* For the purposes of this book, I shall define the world industrial system, circa 1979, as comprising North America; Scandinavia; Britain and Ireland; Europe, both East and West (except for Portugal, Spain, Albania, Greece, and Bulgaria); the U.S.S.R.; Japan, Taiwan, Hong Kong, Singapore, Australia, and New Zealand. Of course, there are other nations that might arguably be included—as well as industrial nodes in essentially non-industrial nations: Monterrey and Mexico City in Mexico, Bombay in India, and many others.

tures. Indeed, beneath the well-known differences lies a hidden bedrock of similarity.

And to understand today's colliding waves of change we must be able to identify clearly the parallel structures of all industrial nations—the hidden framework of Second Wave civilization. For it is this industrial framework itself that is now being shattered.

LIVING BATTERIES

The precondition of any civilization, old or new, is energy. First Wave societies drew their energy from "living batteries"—human and animal muscle-power—or from sun, wind, and water. Forests were cut for cooking and heating. Waterwheels, some of them using tidal power, turned millstones. Windmills creaked in the fields. Animals pulled the plow. As late as the French Revolution, it has been estimated, Europe drew energy from an estimated 14 million horses and 24 million oxen. All First Wave societies thus exploited energy sources that were renewable. Nature could eventually replenish the forests they cut, the wind that filled their sails, the rivers that turned their paddle wheels. Even animals and people were replaceable "energy slaves."

All Second Wave societies, by contrast, began to draw their energy from coal, gas, and oil—from irreplaceable fossil fuels. This revolutionary shift, coming after Newcomen invented a workable steam engine in 1712, meant that for the first time a civilization was eating into nature's capital rather than merely living off the interest it provided.

This dipping into the earth's energy reserves provided a hidden subsidy for industrial civilization, vastly accelerating its economic growth. And from that day to this, wherever the Second Wave passed, nations built towering technological and economic structures on the assumption that cheap fossil fuels would be endlessly available. In capitalist and communist industrial societies alike, in East and West, this same shift has been apparent—from dispersed to concentrated energy, from renewable to non-renewable, from many different sources and fuels to a few. Fossil fuels formed the energy base of all Second Wave societies.

* * *

THE TECHNOLOGICAL WOMB

The leap to a new energy system was paralleled by a gigantic advance in technology. First Wave societies had relied on what Vitruvius, two thousand years ago, called "necessary inventions." But these early winches and wedges, catapults, winepresses, levers, and hoists were chiefly used to amplify human or animal muscles.

The Second Wave pushed technology to a totally new level. It spawned gigantic electromechanical machines, moving parts, belts, hoses, bearings, and bolts—all clattering and ratcheting along. And these new machines did more than augment raw muscle. Industrial civilization gave technology sensory organs, creating machines that could hear, see, and touch with greater accuracy and precision than human beings. It gave technology a womb, by inventing machines designed to give birth to new machines in infinite progression—i.e., machine tools. More important, it brought machines together in interconnected systems under a single roof, to create the factory and ultimately the assembly line within the factory.

On this technological base a host of industries sprang up to give Second Wave civilization its defining stamp. At first there were coal, textiles, and railroads, then steel, auto manufacture, aluminum, chemicals, and appliances. Huge factory cities leaped into existence: Lille and Manchester for textiles, Detroit for automobiles, Essen and—later—Magnitogorsk for steel, and a hundred others as well.

From these industrial centers poured millions upon endless millions of identical products—shirts, shoes, automobiles, watches, toys, soap, shampoo, cameras, machine guns, and electric motors. The new technology powered by the new energy system opened the door to mass production.

THE VERMILION PAGODA

Mass production, however, was meaningless without parallel changes in the distribution system. In First Wave societies, goods were normally made by handcraft methods. Products were created one at a time on a custom basis. The same was largely true of distribution.

It is true that large, sophisticated trading companies had been built up by merchants in the widening cracks of the old feudal order in the West. These companies opened trade routes around the world, organized convoys of ships and camel caravans. They sold glass, paper, silk, nutmeg, tea, wine and wool, indigo and mace.

Most of these products, however, reached consumers through tiny stores or on the backs and wagons of peddlers who fanned out into the countryside. Wretched communications and primitive transport drastically circumscribed the market. These small-scale shopkeepers and itinerant vendors could offer only the slenderest of inventories, and often they were out of this or that item for months, even years, at a time.

The Second Wave wrought changes in this creaking, overburdened distribution system that were as radical, in their ways, as the more publicized advances made in production. Railroads, highways, and canals opened up the hinterlands, and with industrialism came "palaces of trade"—the first department stores. Complex networks of jobbers, wholesalers, commission agents, and manufacturers' representatives sprang up, and in 1871 George Huntington Hartford, whose first store in New York was painted vermilion and had a cashier's cage shaped like a Chinese pagoda, did for distribution what Henry Ford later did for the factory. He advanced it to an entirely new stage by creating the world's first mammoth chain-store system—The Great Atlantic and Pacific Tea Company.

Custom distribution gave way to the mass distribution and mass merchandising that became as familiar and central a component of all industrial societies as the machine itself.

What we see, therefore, if we take these changes together, is a transformation of what might be called the "technosphere." All societies—primitive, agricultural, or industrial—use energy; they make things; they distribute things. In all societies the energy system, the production system, and the distribution system are interrelated parts of something larger. This larger system is the techno-sphere, and it has a characteristic form at each stage of social development.

As the Second Wave swept across the planet, the agricultural techno-sphere was replaced by an industrial technosphere: non-renewable energies were directly plugged into a mass production system which, in turn, spewed goods into a highly developed mass distribution system.

THE STREAMLINED FAMILY

This Second Wave techno-sphere, however, needed an equally revolutionary "socio-sphere" to accommodate it. It needed radically new forms of social organization.

Before the industrial revolution, for example, family forms varied from place to place. But wherever agriculture held sway, people tended to live in large, multigenerational households, with uncles, aunts, in-laws, grandparents, or cousins all living under the same roof, all working together as an economic production unit—from the "joint family" in India to the "zadruga" in the Balkans and the "extended family" in Western Europe. And the family was immobile—rooted to the soil.

As the Second Wave began to move across First Wave societies, families felt the stress of change. Within each household the collision of wave fronts took the form of conflict, attacks on patriarchal authority, altered relationships between children and parents, new notions of propriety. As economic production shifted from the field to the factory, the family no longer worked together as a unit. To free workers for factory labor, key functions of the family were parceled out to new, specialized institutions. Education of the child was turned over to schools. Care of the aged was turned over to poor-houses or old-age homes or nursing homes. Above all, the new society required mobility. It needed workers who would follow jobs from place to place.

Burdened with elderly relatives, the sick, the handicapped, and a large brood of children, the extended family was anything but mobile. Gradually and painfully, therefore, family structure began to change. Torn apart by the migration to the cities, battered by economic storms, families stripped themselves of unwanted relatives, grew smaller, more mobile, and more suited to the needs of the new techno-sphere.

The so-called nuclear family—father, mother, and a few children, with no encumbering relatives—became the standard, socially approved, "modern" model in all industrial societies, whether capitalist or socialist. Even in Japan, where ancestor worship gave the elderly an exceptionally important role, the large, close-knit, multigenerational household began to break down as the Second Wave advanced. More and more nuclear units appeared. In short, the nuclear family became an identifiable feature of all Second Wave societies, marking them off from First Wave societies just as surely as fossil fuels, steel mills, or chain stores.

THE COVERT CURRICULUM

As work shifted out of the fields and the home, moreover, children had to be prepared for factory life. The early mine, mill, and factory owners of industrializing England discovered, as Andrew Ure wrote in 1835, that it was "nearly impossible to convert persons past the age of puberty, whether drawn from rural or from handicraft occupations, into useful factory hands." If young people could be prefitted to the industrial system, it would vastly ease the problems of industrial discipline later on. The result was another central structure of all Second Wave societies: mass education.

Built on the factory model, mass education taught basic reading, writing, and arithmetic, a bit of history and other subjects. This was the "overt curriculum." But beneath it lay an invisible or "covert curriculum" that was far more basic. It consisted—and still does in most industrial nations—of three courses: one in punctuality, one in obedience, and one in rote, repetitive work. Factory labor demanded workers who showed up on time, especially assembly-line hands. It demanded workers who would take orders from a management hierarchy without questioning. And it demanded men and women prepared to slave away at machines or in offices, performing brutally repetitious operations.

Thus from the mid-nineteenth century on, as the Second Wave cut across country after country, one found a relentless educational progression: children started school at a younger and younger age, the school year became longer and longer (in the United States it climbed 35 percent between 1878 and 1956), and the number of years of compulsory schooling irresistibly increased.

Mass public education was clearly a humanizing step forward. As a group of mechanics and workingmen in New York City declared in 1829, "Next to life and liberty, we consider education the greatest blessing bestowed upon mankind." Nevertheless, Second Wave schools machined generation after generation of young people into a pliable, regimented work force of the type required by electro-mechanical technology and the assembly line.

Taken together, the nuclear family and the factory-style

school formed part of a single integrated system for the preparation of young people for roles in industrial society. In this respect, too, Second Wave societies, capitalist or communist, North or South, were all alike.

IMMORTAL BEINGS

In all Second Wave societies a third institution arose that extended the social control of the first two. This was the invention known as the corporation. Until then, the typical business enterprise had been owned by an individual, a family, or a partnership. Corporations existed, but were extremely rare.

Even as late as the American Revolution, according to business historian Arthur Dewing, "no one could have concluded" that the corporation—rather than the partnership or individual proprietorship—would become the main organizational form. As recently as 1800 there were only 335 corporations in the United States, most of them devoted to such quasi-public activities as building canals or running turnpikes.

The rise of mass production changed all this. Second Wave technologies required giant pools of capital—more than a single individual or even a small group could provide. So long as proprietors or partners risked their entire personal fortunes with every investment, they were reluctant to sink their money in vast or risky ventures. To encourage them, the concept of limited liability was introduced. If a corporation collapsed, the investor stood to lose only the sum invested and no more. This innovation opened the investment floodgates.

Moreover, the corporation was treated by the courts as an "immortal being"—meaning it could outlive its original investors. This meant, in turn, that it could make very long-range plans and undertake far bigger projects than ever before.

By 1901 the world's first billion-dollar corporation—United States Steel—appeared on the scene, a concentration of assets unimaginable in any earlier period. By 1919 there were half a dozen such behemoths. Indeed, large corporations became an in-built feature of economic life in all the industrial nations, including socialist and communist societies, where the form varied but the substance (in terms of organization) remained very much the same. Together these three—the nuclear family, the factory-style school, and the giant corporation—

became the defining social institutions of all Second Wave societies.

And, throughout the Second Wave world—in Japan as well as in Switzerland, Britain, Poland, the U.S., and the U.S.S.R.—most people followed a standard life trajectory: reared in a nuclear family, they moved en masse through factorylike schools, then entered the service of a large corporation, private or public. A key Second Wave institution dominated each phase of the life-style.

THE MUSIC FACTORY

Around these three core institutions a host of other organizations sprang up. Government ministries, sports clubs, churches, chambers of commerce, trade unions, professional organizations, political parties, libraries, ethnic associations, recreational groups, and thousands of others bobbed up in the wake of the Second Wave, creating a complicated organizational ecology with each group servicing, coordinating, or counterbalancing another.

At first glance, the variety of these groups suggests randomness or chaos. But a closer look reveals a hidden pattern. In one Second Wave country after another, social inventors, believing the factory to be the most advanced and efficient agency for production, tried to embody its principles in other organizations as well. Schools, hospitals, prisons, government bureaucracies, and other organizations thus took on many of the characteristics of the factory—its division of labor, its hierarchical structure and its metallic impersonality.

Even in the arts we find some of the principles of the factory. Instead of working for a patron, as was customary during the long reign of agricultural civilization, musicians, artists, composers, and writers were increasingly thrown on the mercies of the marketplace. More and more they turned out "products" for anonymous consumers. And as this shift occurred in every Second Wave country, the very structure of artistic production changed.

Music provides a striking example. As the Second Wave arrived, concert halls began to crop up in London, Vienna, Paris, and elsewhere. With them came the box office and the impresario—the businessman who financed the production and then sold tickets to culture consumers.

The more tickets he could sell, naturally, the more money

he could make. Hence more and more seats were added. In turn, however, larger concert halls required louder sounds—music that could be clearly heard in the very last tier. The result was a shift from chamber music to symphonic forms.

Says Curt Sachs in his authoritative *History of Musical Instruments*, "The passage from an aristocratic to a democratic culture, in the eighteenth century, replaced the small salons by the more and more gigantic concert halls, which demanded greater volume." Since no technology existed yet to make this possible, more and more instruments and players were added to produce the necessary volume. The result was the modern symphony orchestra, and it was for this industrial institution that Beethoven, Mendelssohn, Schubert, and Brahms wrote their magnificent symphonies.

The orchestra even mirrored certain features of the factory in its internal structure. At first the symphony orchestra was leaderless, or the leadership was casually passed around among the players. Later the players, exactly like workers in a factory or bureaucratic office, were divided into departments (instrumental sections), each contributing to the overall output (the music), each coordinated from above by a manager (the conductor) or even, eventually, a straw boss farther down the management hierarchy (the first violinist or the section head). The institution sold its product to a mass market—eventually adding phonograph records to its output. The music factory had been born.

The history of the orchestra offers only one illustration of the way the Second Wave socio-sphere arose, with its three core institutions and thousands of varied organizations, all adapted to the needs and style of the industrial techno-sphere. But a civilization is more than simply a techno-sphere and a matching socio-sphere. All civilizations also require an "info-sphere" for producing and distributing information, and here, too, the changes brought by the Second Wave were remarkable.

THE PAPER BLIZZARD

All human groups, from primitive times to today, depend on face-to-face, person-to-person communication. But systems were needed for sending messages across time and space as well. The ancient Persians are said to have set up towers or "call-posts," placing men with shrill, loud voices atop them to relay messages by shouting from one tower to the next. The Romans operated an extensive messenger service called the *cursus publicus.* Between 1305 and the early 1800's, the House of Taxis ran a form of pony express service all over Europe. By 1628 it employed twenty thousand men. Its couriers, clad in blue and silver uniforms, crisscrossed the continent carrying messages between princes and generals, merchants and money lenders.

During First Wave civilization all these channels were reserved for the rich and powerful only. Ordinary people had no access to them. As the historian Laurin Zilliacus states, even "attempts to send letters by other means were looked upon with suspicion or . . . forbidden" by the authorities. In short, while face-to-face information exchange was open to all, the newer systems used for carrying imformation beyond the confines of a family or a village were essentially closed and used for purposes of social or political control. They were, in effect, weapons of the elite.

The Second Wave, as it moved across country after country, smashed this communications monopoly. This occurred not because the rich and powerful grew suddenly altruistic but because Second Wave technology and factory mass production required "mass-ive" movements of information that the old channels simply could no longer handle.

The information needed for economic production in primitive and First Wave societies is comparatively simple and usually available from someone near at hand. It is mostly oral or gestural in form. Second Wave economies, by contrast, required the tight coordination of work done at many locations. Not only raw materials but great amounts of information had to be produced and carefully distributed.

For this reason, as the Second Wave gained momentum every country raced to build a postal service. The post office was an invention quite as imaginative and socially useful as the cotton gin or the spinning jenny and, to an extent forgotten today, it elicited rhapsodic enthusiasm. The American orator Edward Everett declared: "I am compelled to regard the Post-office, next to Christianity, as the right arm of our modern civilization."

For the post office provided the first wide open channel for industrial-era communications. By 1837 the British Post Office was carrying not merely messages for an elite but some 88 million pieces of mail a year—an avalanche of communications by the standards of the day. By 1960, at about the time the industrial era peaked and the Third Wave began its surge, that number had already climbed to 10 billion. That same year the U.S. Post Office was distributing 355 pieces of domestic mail for every man, woman, and child in the nation.*

The surge in postal messages that accompanied the industrial revolution merely hints, however, at the real volume of information that began to flow in the wake of the Second Wave. An even greater number of messages poured through what might be called "micro-postal systems" within large organizations. Memos are letters that never reach the public communications channels. In 1955, as the Second Wave crested in the United States, the Hoover Commission peeked inside the files of three major corporations. It discovered, respectively, thirty-four thousand, fifty-six thousand, and sixty-four thousand documents and memos on file for each employee on the payroll!

Nor could the mushrooming informational needs of industrial societies be met in writing alone. Thus the telephone and telegraph were invented in the nineteenth century to carry their share of the ever-swelling communications load. By 1960 Americans were placing some 256 million phone calls per day—over 93 billion a year—and even the most advanced telephone systems and networks in the world were often overloaded.

All these were essentially systems for delivering messages from one sender to one receiver at a time. But a society developing mass production and mass consumption needed ways to send mass messages, too—communications from one sender to many receivers simultaneously. Unlike the preindustrial employer, who could personally visit each of his handful of employees in their own homes if need be, the industrial employer could not communicate with his thousands of workers on a one-by-one basis. Still less could the mass merchandiser or distributor communicate with his customers one by one. Second Wave society needed—and not surprisingly invented —powerful means for sending the same message to many people at once, cheaply, rapidly, and reliably.

Postal services could carry the same message to millions— but not quickly. Telephones could carry messages quickly—

---

* The amount of mail provides a good, instant index to the level of traditional industrialization in any country. For Second Wave societies, the average in 1960 was 141 pieces of mail per person. By contrast, in First Wave societies the level was barely a tenth of that—twelve per person per year in Malaysia or Ghana, four per year in Colombia.

but not to millions of people simultaneously. This gap came to be filled by the mass media.

Today, of course, the mass circulation newspaper and magazine are so standard a part of daily life in every one of the industrial nations that they are taken for granted. Yet the rise of these publications on a national level reflected the convergent development of many new industrial technologies and social forms. Thus, writes Jean-Louis Servan-Schreiber, they were made possible by the coming together of "trains to transport the publications throughout a [European-size] country in a single day; rotary presses capable of turning out dozens of millions of copies in several hours; a network of telegraph and telephones . . . above all a public taught to read by compulsory education, and industries needing to mass distribute their products."

In the mass media, from newspapers and radio to movies and television, we find once again an embodiment of the basic principle of the factory. All of them stamp identical messages into millions of brains, just as the factory stamps out identical products for use in millions of homes. Standardized, mass-manufactured "facts," counterparts of standardized, mass-manufactured products, flow from a few concentrated image-factories out to millions of consumers. Without this vast, powerful system for channeling information, industrial civilization could not have taken form or functioned reliably.

Thus there sprang up in all industrial societies, capitalist and socialist alike, an elaborate info-sphere—communication channels through which individual and mass messages could be distributed as efficiently as goods or raw materials. This info-sphere intertwined with and serviced the techno-sphere and the socio-sphere, helping to integrate economic production with private behavior.

Each of these spheres performed a key function in the larger system, and could not have existed without the others. The techno-sphere produced and allocated wealth; the socio-sphere, with its thousands of interrelated organizations, allocated roles to individuals in the system. And the info-sphere allocated the information necessary to make the entire system work. Together they formed the basic architecture of society.

We see here in outline, therefore, the common structures of all Second Wave nations—regardless of their cultural or climatic differences, regardless of their ethnic and religious heritage, regardless of whether they call themselves capitalist or communist.

These parallel structures, as basic in the Soviet Union and Hungary as in West Germany, France, or Canada, set the limits within which political, social, and cultural differences were expressed. They emerged everywhere only after bitter political, cultural, and economic battles between those who attempted to preserve the older First Wave structures and those who recognized that only a new civilization could solve the painful problems of the old.

The Second Wave brought with it a fantastic extension of human hope. For the first time men and women dared to believe that poverty, hunger, disease, and tyranny might be overthrown. Utopian writers and philosophers, from Abbe Morelly and Robert Owen to Saint-Simon, Fourier, Proudhon, Louis Blanc, Edward Bellamy, and scores of others, saw in the emerging industrial civilization the potential for introducing peace, harmony, employment for all, equality of wealth or of opportunity, the end of privilege based on birth, the end of all those conditions that seemed immutable or eternal during the hundreds of thousands of years of primitive existence and the thousands of years of agricultural civilization.

If today industrial civilization seems to us something less than utopian—if it appears, in fact, to be oppressive, dreary, ecologically precarious, war-prone, and psychologically repressive—we need to understand why. We will be able to answer this question only if we look at the gigantic wedge that split the Second Wave psyche into two warring parts.

≈≈≈≈ 3

THE INVISIBLE WEDGE

The Second Wave, like some nuclear chain reaction, violently split apart two aspects of our lives that had always, until then, been one. In so doing, it drove a giant invisible wedge into our economy, our psyches, and even our sexual selves.

At one level, the industrial revolution created a marvelously integrated social system with its own distinctive technologies, its own social institutions, and its own information channels—all plugged tightly into each other. Yet, at another level, it ripped apart the underlying unity of society, creating a way of life filled with economic tension, social conflict, and psychological malaise. Only if we understand how this invisible wedge has shaped our lives throughout the Second Wave era can we appreciate the full impact of the Third Wave that is beginning to reshape us today.

The two halves of human life that the Second Wave split apart were production and consumption. We are accustomed, for example, to think of ourselves as producers or consumers. This wasn't always true. Until the industrial revolution, the vast bulk of all the food, goods, and services produced by the human race was consumed by the producers themselves, their families, or a tiny elite who managed to scrape off the surplus for their own use.

In most agricultural societies the great majority of people were peasants who huddled together in small, semi-isolated communities. They lived on a subsistence diet, growing just barely enough to keep themselves alive and their masters happy. Lacking the means for storing food over long periods,

37

lacking the roads necessary to transport their product to distant markets, and well aware that any increase in output was likely to be confiscated by the slave-owner or feudal lord, they also lacked any great incentive to improve technology or increase production.

Commerce existed, of course. We know that small numbers of intrepid merchants carried goods for thousands of miles by camel, wagon, or boat. We know that cities sprang up dependent on food from the countryside. By 1519, when the Spaniards arrived in Mexico, they were astonished to find thousands of people in Tlatelolco engaged in buying and selling jewels, precious metals, slaves and sandals, cloth, chocolate, ropes, skins, turkeys, vegetables, rabbits, dogs, and pottery of a thousand kinds. *The Fugger Newsletter*, private dispatches prepared for German bankers in the sixteenth and seventeenth centuries, give colorful evidence of the scope of trade by that time. A letter from Cochin, in India, describes in detail the trials of a European merchant who arrived with five ships to buy pepper for transport to Europe. "A pepper store is fine business," he explains, "but it requires great zeal and perseverance." This merchant also shipped cloves, nutmeg, flour, cinnamon, mace, and various drugs to the European market.

Nevertheless, all this commerce represented only a trace element in history, compared with the extent of production for immediate self-use by the agricultural slave or serf. Even as late as the sixteenth century, according to Fernand Braudel, whose historical research on the period is unsurpassed, the entire Mediterranean region—from France and Spain at one end to Turkey at the other—supported a population of sixty to seventy million, of which 90 percent lived on the soil, producing only a small amount of goods for trade. Writes Braudel, "60 percent or perhaps 70 percent of the overall production of the Mediterranean never entered the market economy." And if this was the case in the Mediterranean region, what should we assume of Northern Europe, where the rocky soil and long cold winters made it even more difficult for peasants to extract a surplus from the soil?

It will help us understand the Third Wave if we conceive of the First Wave economy, before the industrial revolution, as consisting of two sectors. In Sector A, people produced for their own use. In Sector B, they produced for trade or exchange. Sector A was huge; Sector B was tiny. For most people, therefore, production and consumption were fused into a single life-giving function. So complete was this unity that the Greeks, the Romans, and the medieval Europeans did not distinguish between the two. They lacked even a word for consumer. Throughout the First Wave era only a tiny fraction of the population was dependent on the market; most people lived largely outside it. In the words of the historian R. H. Tawney, "pecuniary transactions were a fringe on a world of natural economy."

The Second Wave violently changed this situation. Instead of essentially self-sufficient people and communities, it created for the first time in history a situation in which the overwhelming bulk of all food, goods, and services was destined for sale, barter, or exchange. It virtually wiped out of existence goods produced for one's own consumption—for use by the actual producer and his or her family—and created a civilization in which almost no one, not even a farmer, was self-sufficient any longer. Everyone became almost totally dependent upon food, goods, or services produced by somebody else.

In short, industrialism broke the union of production and consumption, and split the producer from the consumer. The fused economy of the First Wave was transformed into the split economy of the Second Wave.

THE MEANING OF THE MARKET

The consequences of this fission were momentous. Even now we scarcely understand them. First, the marketplace—once a minor and peripheral phenomenon—moved into the very vortex of life. The economy became "marketized." And this happened in *both* capitalist and socialist industrial economies.

Western economists tend to think of the market as a purely capitalist fact of life and often use the term as though it were synonymous with "profit economy." Yet from all we know of history, exchange—and hence a marketplace—sprang up earlier than, and independently of, profit. For the market, properly speaking, is nothing more than an exchange network, a switchboard, as it were, through which goods or services, like messages, are routed to their appropriate destinations. It is not inherently capitalist. Such a switchboard is just as essential to a socialist industrial society as it is to profit-motivated industrialism.*

In short, wherever the Second Wave struck and the purpose of production shifted from use to exchange, there had to be a mechanism through which that exchange could take place. There had to be a market. But the market was not passive. The economic historian Karl Polanyi has shown how the market, which was subordinated to the social or religio-cultural goals of early societies, came to set the goals of industrial societies. Most people were sucked into the money system. Commercial values became central, economic growth (as measured by the size of the market) became the primary goal of governments, whether capitalist or socialist.

For the market was an expansive, self-reinforcing institution. Just as the earliest division of labor had encouraged commerce in the first place, now the very existence of a market or switchboard encouraged a further division of labor and led to sharply increased productivity. A self-amplifying process had been set in motion.

This explosive expansion of the market contributed to the fastest rise in living standards the world had ever experienced.

In politics, however, Second Wave governments found themselves increasingly torn by a new kind of conflict born of the split between production and consumption. The Marxist emphasis on class struggle has systematically obscured the larger, deeper conflict that arose between the demands of producers (both workers *and* managers) for higher wages, profits, and benefits and the counter-demand of consumers

---

* The market as a switchboard must exist whether trade is based on money or barter. It must exist whether or not profit is siphoned out of it, whether prices follow supply and demand or are fixed by the state, whether the system is planned or not, whether the means of production are private or public. It must exist even in a hypothetical economy of self-managed industrial firms in which workers set their own wages high enough to eliminate profit as a category.

So overlooked is this essential fact, so closely has the market been identified with only one of its many variants (the profit-based, private-property model, in which prices reflect supply and demand), that there is not even a word in the conventional vocabulary of economics to express the multiplicity of its forms.

Throughout these pages, the term "market" is used in its full generic sense, rather than in the customary restrictive way. Semantics aside, however, the basic point remains: wherever producer and consumer are divorced, some mechanism is needed to mediate between them. This mechanism, whatever its form, is what I call the market.

(including the very same people) for lower prices. The seesaw of economic policy rocked on this fulcrum.

The growth of the consumer movement in the United States, the recent uprisings in Poland against government-decreed price hikes, the endlessly raging debate in Britain about prices and incomes policy, the deadly ideological struggles in the Soviet Union over whether heavy industry or consumer goods should receive first priority, are all aspects of the profound conflict engendered in any society, capitalist or socialist, by the split between production and consumption.

Not only politics but culture, too, was shaped by this cleavage, for it also produced the most money-minded, grasping, commercialized, and calculating civilization in history. One need scarcely be a Marxist to agree with *The Communist Manifesto*'s famous accusation that the new society "left remaining no other nexus between man and man than naked self-interest, than callous 'cash payment.'" Personal relationships, family bonds, love, friendship, neighborly and community ties all became tinctured or corrupted by commercial self-interest.

Correct in identifying this dehumanization of interpersonal bonds, Marx was incorrect, however, in attributing it to capitalism. He wrote, of course, at a time when the only industrial society he could observe was capitalist in form. Today, after more than half a century of experience with industrial societies based on socialism, or at least state socialism, we know that aggressive acquisitiveness, commercial corruption, and the reduction of human relationships to coldly economic terms are no monopoly of the profit system.

For the obsessive concern with money, goods, and things is a reflection not of capitalism or socialism, but of industrialism. It is a reflection of the central role of the marketplace in *all* societies in which production is divorced from consumption, in which everyone is dependent upon the marketplace rather than on his or her own productive skills for the necessities of life.

In such a society, irrespective of its political structure, not only products are bought, sold, traded, and exchanged, but labor, ideas, art, and souls as well. The Western purchasing agent who pockets an illegal commission is not so different from the Soviet editor who takes kickbacks from authors in return for approving their works for publication, or the plumber who demands a bottle of vodka to do what he is paid to do. The French or British or American artist who writes or paints for money alone is not so different from the Polish, Czech, or Soviet novelist, painter, or playwright who sells his creative freedom for such economic perquisites as a dacha, bonuses, access to a new car or otherwise unobtainable goods.

Such corruption is inherent in the divorce of production from consumption. The very need for a market or switchboard to reconnect consumer and producer, to move goods from producer to consumer, necessarily places those who control the market in a position of inordinate power—regardless of the rhetoric they use to justify that power.

This divorce of production from consumption, which became a defining feature of all industrial or Second Wave societies, even affected our psyches and our assumptions about personality. Behavior came to be seen as a set of transactions. Instead of a society based on friendship, kinship, or tribal or feudal allegiance, there arose in the wake of the Second Wave a civilization based on contractual ties, actual or implied. Even husbands and wives today speak of marital contracts.

The cleavage between these two roles—producer and consumer—created at the same time a dual personality. The very same person who (as a producer) was taught by family, school, and boss to defer gratification, to be disciplined, controlled, restrained, obedient, to be a team player, was simultaneously taught (as a consumer) to seek instant gratification, to be hedonistic rather than calculating, to abandon discipline, to pursue individualistic pleasure—in short, to be a totally different kind of person. In the West especially, the full firepower of advertising was trained on the consumer, urging her or him to borrow, to buy on impulse, to "Fly now, pay later," and, in so doing, to perform a patriotic service by keeping the wheels of the economy turning.

THE SEXUAL SPLIT

Finally, the same giant wedge that split producer from consumer in Second Wave societies also split work into two kinds. This had an enormous impact on family life, sexual roles, and on our inner lives as individuals.

One of the most common sexual stereotypes in industrial society defines men as "objective" in orientation, and women as "subjective." If there is a kernel of truth here, it probably lies not in some fixed biological reality but in the psychological effects of the invisible wedge.

In First Wave societies most work was performed in the fields or in the home, with the entire household toiling together as an economic unit and with most production destined for consumption within the village or manor. Work life and home life were fused and intermingled. And since each village was largely self-sufficient, the success of the peasants in one place was not dependent upon what happened in another. Even within the production unit most workers performed a variety of tasks, swapping and shifting roles as demanded by the season, by sickness, or by choice. The pre-industrial division of labor was very primitive. As a result, work in First Wave agricultural societies was characterized by low levels of interdependency.

The Second Wave, washing across Britain, France, Germany, and other countries, shifted work from field and home to factory, and introduced a much higher level of interdependency. Work now demanded collective effort, division of labor, coordination, the integration of many different skills. Its success depended upon the carefully scheduled cooperative behavior of thousands of far-flung people, many of whom never laid eyes on one another. The failure of a major steel mill or glass factory to deliver needed supplies to an auto plant could, under certain circumstances, send repercussions throughout a whole industry or regional economy.

The collision of low- and high-interdependency work produced severe conflict over roles, responsibilities, and rewards. The early factory owners, for example, complained that their workers were irresponsible—that they cared little about the efficiency of the factory, that they went fishing when most needed, engaged in horseplay, or turned up drunk. In fact, most of the early industrial workers were rural folk who were accustomed to low interdependency, and had little or no understanding of their own role in the overall production process or of the failures, breakdowns, and malfunctions occasioned by their "irresponsibility." Moreover, since most of them earned pitiful wages, they had little incentive to care.

In the clash between these two work systems, the new forms of work seemed to triumph. More and more production was transferred to the factory and office. The countryside was stripped of population. Millions of workers became part of high-interdependence networks. Second Wave work overshadowed the old backward form associated with the First Wave.

This victory of interdependence over self-sufficiency, however, was never fully consummated. In one place the older form of work stubbornly held on. This place was the home.

Each home remained a decentralized unit engaged in biological reproduction, in child-rearing, and in cultural transmission. If one family failed to reproduce, or did a poor job of rearing its children and preparing them for life in the work system, its failures did not necessarily endanger the accomplishment of those tasks by the family next door. Housework remained, in other words, a low-interdependency activity.

The housewife continued, as always, to perform a set of crucial economic functions. She "produced." But she produced for Sector A—for the use of her own family—not for the market.

As the husband, by and large, marched off to do the direct economic work, the wife generally stayed behind to do the indirect economic work. The man took responsibility for the historically more advanced form of work; the woman was left behind to take care of the older, more backward form of work. He moved, as it were, into the future; she remained in the past.

This division produced a split in personality and inner life. The public or collective nature of factory and office, the need for coordination and integration, brought with it an emphasis on objective analysis and objective relationships. Men, prepared from boyhood for their role in the shop, where they would move in a world of interdependencies, were encouraged to become "objective." Women, prepared from birth for the tasks of reproduction, child-rearing, and household drudgery, performed to a considerable degree in social isolation, were taught to be "subjective"—and were frequently regarded as incapable of the kind of rational, analytic thought that supposedly went with objectivity.

Not surprisingly, women who did leave the relative isolation of the household to engage in interdependent production were often accused of having been defeminized, of having grown cold, tough, and—objective.

Sexual differences and sex role stereotypes, moreover, were sharpened by the misleading identification of men with production and women with consumption, even though men also consumed and women also produced. In short, while women were oppressed long before the Second Wave began to roll across the earth, the modern "battle of the sexes" can be traced in large measure to the conflict between two workstyles, and beyond that to the divorce of production and consumption. The split economy deepened the sexual split as well.

What we have seen so far, therefore, is that once the invisible wedge was hammered into place, separating producer from consumer, a number of profound changes followed: A market had to be formed or expanded to connect the two; new political and social conflicts sprang up; new sexual roles were defined. But the split implied far more than this. It also meant that all Second Wave societies would have to operate in similar fashion—that they would have to meet certain basic requirements. Whether the object of production was profit or not, whether the "means of production" were public or private, whether the market was "free" or "planned," whether the rhetoric was capitalist or socialist made no difference.

So long as production was intended for exchange, instead of use, so long as it had to flow through the economic switchboard or market, certain Second Wave principles had to be followed.

Once these principles are identified, the hidden dynamics of all industrial societies are laid bare. Moreover, we can anticipate how Second Wave people typically think. For these principles added up to the basic rules, the behavioral code book, of Second Wave civilization.

4

BREAKING THE CODE

Every civilization has a hidden code—a set of rules or principles that run through all its activities like a repeated design. As industrialism pushed across the planet, its unique hidden design became visible. It consisted of a set of six interrelated principles that programmed the behavior of millions. Growing naturally out of the divorce of production and consumption, these principles affected every aspect of life from sex and sports to work and war.

Much of the angry conflict in our schools, businesses, and governments today actually centers on these half-dozen principles, as Second Wave people instinctively apply and defend them and Third Wave people challenge and attack them. But that is getting ahead of the story.

STANDARDIZATION

The most familiar of these Second Wave principles is standardization. Everyone knows that industrial societies turn out millions of identical products. Fewer people have stopped to notice, however, that once the market became important, we did more than simply standardize Coca-Cola bottles, light bulbs, and auto transmissions. We applied the same principle to many other things. Among the first to grasp the importance of this idea was Theodore Vail who, at the turn of the century, built the American Telephone & Telegram Company into a giant.*

---

* Not to be confused with the multinational ITT, the International Telephone & Telegraph Corporation.

Working as a railway postal clerk in the late 1860's, Vail had noticed that no two letters necessarily went to their destinations via the same route. Sacks of mail traveled back and forth, often taking weeks or months to reach their destinations. Vail introduced the idea of standardized routing—all letters going to the same place would go the same way—and helped revolutionize the post office. When he later formed AT&T, he set out to place an identical telephone in every American home.

Vail standardized not only the telephone handset and all its components but AT&T's business procedures and administration as well. In a 1908 advertisement he justified his swallowing up small telephone companies by arguing for "a clearing-house of standardization" that would ensure economy in "construction of equipment, lines and conduits, as well as in operating methods and legal work," not to mention "a uniform system of operating and accounting." What Vail recognized is that to succeed in the Second Wave environment, "software"—i.e., procedures and administrative routines—had to be standardized along with hardware.

Vail was only one of the Great Standardizers who shaped industrial society. Another was Frederick Winslow Taylor, a machinist turned crusader, who believed that work could be made scientific by standardizing the steps each worker performed. In the early decades of this century Taylor decided that there was one best (standard) way to perform each job, one best (standard) tool to perform it with, and a stipulated (standard) time in which to complete it.

Armed with this philosophy, he became the world's leading management guru. In his time, and later, he was compared with Freud, Marx, and Franklin. Nor were capitalist employers, eager to squeeze the last ounce of productivity from their workers, alone in their admiration for Taylorism, with its efficiency experts, piece-work schemes, and rate-busters. Communists shared their enthusiasm. Indeed, Lenin urged that Taylor's methods be adapted for use in socialist production. An industrializer first and a Communist second, Lenin, too, was a zealous believer in standardization.

In Second Wave societies, hiring procedures as well as work were increasingly standardized. Standardized tests were used to identify and weed out the supposedly unfit, especially in the civil service. Pay scales were standardized throughout whole industries, along with fringe benefits, lunch hours, holidays, and grievance procedures. To prepare youth for the job market, educators designed standardized curricula. Men like Binet and Terman devised standardized intelligence tests. School grading policies, admission procedures, and accreditation rules were similarly standardized. The multiple-choice test came into its own.

The mass media, meanwhile, disseminated standardizing imagery, so that millions read the same advertisements, the same news, the same short stories. The repression of minority languages by central governments, combined with the influence of mass communications, led to the near disappearance of local and regional dialects or even whole languages, such as Welsh and Alsatian. "Standard" American, English, French, or, for that matter, Russian, supplanted "nonstandard" languages. Different parts of the country began to look alike, as identical gas stations, billboards, and houses cropped up everywhere. The principle of standardization ran through every aspect of daily life.

At an even deeper level, industrial civilization needed standardized weights and measures. It is no accident that one of the first acts of the French Revolution, which ushered the age of industrialism into France, was an attempt to replace the crazy-quilt patchwork of measuring units, common in preindustrial Europe, with the metric system and a new calendar. Uniform measures were spread through much of the world by the Second Wave.

Moreover, if mass production required the standardization of machines, products, and processes, the ever-expanding market demanded a corresponding standardization of money, and even prices. Historically, money had been issued by banks and private individuals as well as by kings. Even as late as the nineteenth century privately minted money was still in use in parts of the United States, and the practice lasted until 1935 in Canada. Gradually, however, industrializing nations suppressed all nongovernmental currencies and managed to impose a single standard currency in their place.

Until the nineteenth century, moreover, it was still common for buyers and sellers in industrial countries to haggle over every sale in the time-honored fashion of a Cairo bazaar. In 1825 a young Northern Irish immigrant named A. T. Stewart arrived in New York, opened a dry-goods store, and shocked customers and competitors alike by introducing a fixed price for every item. This one-price policy—price standardization—made Stewart one of the merchant princes of his era and cleared away one of the key obstacles to the development of mass distribution.

Whatever their other disagreements, advanced Second Wave thinkers shared the conviction that standardization was efficient. At many levels, therefore, the Second Wave brought a flattening out of differences through a relentless application of the principle of standardization.

SPECIALIZATION

A second great principle ran through all Second Wave societies: specialization. For the more the Second Wave eliminated diversity in language, leisure, and life-style, the more it needed diversity in the sphere of work. Accelerating the division of labor, the Second Wave replaced the casual jack-of-all-work peasant with the narrow, purse-lipped specialist and the worker who did only one task, Taylor-fashion, over and over again.

As early as 1720 a British report on *The Advantages of the East India Trade* made the point that specialization could get jobs done with "less loss of time and labour." In 1776 Adam Smith opened *The Wealth of Nations* with the ringing assertion that "the greatest improvement in the productive powers of labour . . . seem[s] to have been the effects of the division of labour."

Smith, in a classic passage, described the manufacture of a pin. A single old-style workman, performing all the necessary operations by himself, he wrote, could turn out only a handful of pins each day—no more than twenty and perhaps not even one. By contrast, Smith described a "manufactory" he had visited in which the eighteen different operations required to make a pin were carried out by ten specialized workers, each performing only one or a few steps. Together they were able to produce more than forty-eight thousand pins per day—over forty-eight hundred per worker.

By the nineteenth century, as more and more work shifted into the factory, the pin story was repeated again and again on an ever-larger scale. And the human costs of specialization escalated accordingly. Critics of industrialism charged that highly specialized repetitive labor progressively dehumanized the worker.

By the time Henry Ford started manufacturing Model T's in 1908 it took not eighteen different operations to complete a unit but 7,882. In his autobiography, Ford noted that of these 7,882 specialized jobs, 949 required "strong, able-bodied, and practically physically perfect men," 3,338 needed men of merely "ordinary" physical strength, most of the rest could be performed by "women or older children," and, he continued coolly, "we found that 670 could be filled by legless men, 2,637 by one-legged men, two by armless men, 715 by one-armed men and 10 by blind men." In short, the specialized job required not a whole person, but only a part. No more vivid evidence that overspecialization can be brutalizing has ever been adduced.

A practice which critics attributed to capitalism, however, became an inbuilt feature of socialism as well. For the extreme specialization of labor that was common to all Second Wave societies had its roots in the divorce of production from consumption. The U.S.S.R., Poland, East Germany, or Hungary can no more run their factories today without elaborate specialization than can Japan or the United States—whose Department of Labor in 1977 published a list of twenty thousand identifiably different occupations.

In both capitalist and socialist industrial states, moreover, specialization was accompanied by a rising tide of professionalization. Whenever the opportunity arose for some group of specialists to monopolize esoteric knowledge and keep newcomers out of their field, professions emerged. As the Second Wave advanced, the market intervened between a knowledge-holder and a client, dividing them sharply into producer and consumer. Thus, health in Second Wave societies came to be seen as a product provided by a doctor and a health-delivery bureaucracy, rather than a result of intelligent self-care (production for use) by the patient. Education was supposedly "produced" by the teacher in the school and "consumed" by the student.

All sorts of occupational groups from librarians to salesmen began clamoring for the right to call themselves professionals—and for the power to set standards, prices, and conditions of entry into their specialties. By now, according to Michael Pertschuk, Chairman of the U.S. Federal Trade Commission, "Our culture is dominated by professionals who call us 'clients' and tell us of our 'needs.' "

In Second Wave societies even political agitation was conceived of as a profession. Thus Lenin argued that the masses could not bring about a revolution without professional help. What was needed, he asserted, was an "organization of revolutionaries" limited in membership to "people whose profession is that of a revolutionary."

Among communists, capitalists, executives, educators, priests, and politicians, the Second Wave produced a common mentality and a drive toward an ever more refined division of labor. Like Prince Albert at the great Crystal Palace Exhibition of 1851, they believed that specialization was "the moving power of civilization." The Great Standardizers and The Great Specializers marched hand in hand.

SYNCHRONIZATION

The widening split between production and consumption also forced a change in the way Second Wave people dealt with time. In a market-dependent system, whether the market is planned or free, time equals money. Expensive machines cannot be allowed to sit idly, and they operate at rhythms of their own. This produced the third principle of industrial civilization: synchronization.

Even in the earliest societies work had to be carefully organized in time. Warriors often had to work in unison to trap their prey. Fishermen had to coordinate their efforts in rowing or hauling in the nets. George Thomson, many years ago, showed how various work songs reflected the requirements of labor. For the oarsmen, time was marked by a simple two-syllable sound like *O—op!* The second syllable indicated the moment of maximum exertion while the first was the time for preparation. Hauling a boat, he noted, was heavier work than rowing, "so the moments of exertion are spaced in longer intervals," and we see, as in the Irish hauling cry *Ho-li-ho-hup!*, a longer preparation for the final effort.

Until the Second Wave brought in machinery and silenced the songs of the worker, most such synchronization of effort was organic or natural. It flowed from the rhythm of the seasons and from biological processes, from the earth's rotation and the beat of the heart. Second Wave societies, by contrast, moved to the beat of the machine.

As factory production spread, the high cost of machinery and the close interdependence of labor required a much more refined synchronization. If one group of workers in a plant was late in completing a task, others down the line would be further delayed. Thus punctuality, never very important in agricultural communities, became a social necessity, and clocks and watches began to proliferate. By the 1790's they were already becoming commonplace in Britain. Their diffusion came, in the words of British historian E. P. Thompson, "at the exact moment when the industrial revolution demanded a greater synchronization of labor."

Not by coincidence, children in industrial cultures were taught to tell time at an early age. Pupils were conditioned to arrive at school when the bell rang so that later on they would arrive reliably at the factory or office when the whistle blew. Jobs were timed and split into sequences measured in fractions of a second. "Nine-to-five" formed the temporal frame for millions of workers.

Nor was it only working life that was synchronized. In all Second Wave societies, regardless of profit or political considerations, social life, too, became clock-driven and adapted to machine requirements. Certain hours were set aside for leisure. Standard-length vacations, holidays, or coffee breaks were interspersed with the work schedules.

Children began and ended the school year at uniform times. Hospitals woke all their patients for breakfast simultaneously. Transport systems staggered under rush hours. Broadcasters fitted entertainment into special time slots— "prime time," for example. Every business had its own peak hours or seasons, synchronized with those of its suppliers and distributors. Specialists in synchronization arose—from factory expediters and schedulers to traffic police and time-study men.

By contrast, some people resisted the new industrial time system. And here again sexual differences arose. Those who participated in Second Wave work—chiefly men—became the most conditioned to clock-time.

Second Wave husbands continually complained that their wives kept them waiting, that they had no regard for time, that it took them forever to dress, that they were always late for appointments. Women, primarily engaged in noninterdependent housework, worked to less mechanical rhythms. For similar reasons urban populations tended to look down upon rural folk as slow and unreliable. "They don't show up on time! You never know whether they'll keep an appointment." Such complaints could be traced directly to the difference between Second Wave work based on heightened interdependence and the First Wave work centered in the field and the home.

Once the Second Wave became dominant even the most intimate routines of life were locked into the industrial pacing system. In the United States and the Soviet Union, in Singapore and Sweden, in France and Denmark, Germany and Japan, families arose as one, ate at the same time, commuted, worked, returned home, went to bed, slept, and even made love more or less in unison as the entire civilization, in addition to standardization and specialization, applied the principle of synchronization.

CONCENTRATION

The rise of the market gave birth to yet another rule of Second Wave civilization—the principle of concentration.

First Wave societies lived off widely dispersed sources of energy. Second Wave societies became almost totally dependent on highly concentrated deposits of fossil fuel.

But the Second Wave concentrated more than energy. It also concentrated population, stripping the countryside of people and relocating them in giant urban centers. It even concentrated work. While work in First Wave societies took place everywhere—in the home, in the village, in the fields—much of the work in Second Wave societies was done in factories where thousands of laborers were drawn together under a single roof.

Nor was it only energy and work that were concentrated. Writing in the British social science journal *New Society*, Stan Cohen has pointed out that, with minor exceptions, prior to industrialism "the poor were kept at home or with relatives; criminals were fined, whipped or banished from one settlement to another; the insane were kept in their families, or supported by the community, if they were poor." All these groups were, in short, dispersed throughout the community.

Industrialism revolutionized the situation. The early nineteenth century, in fact, has been called the time of the Great Incarcerations—when criminals were rounded up and concentrated in prisons, the mentally ill rounded up and concentrated in "lunatic asylums," and children rounded up and concentrated in schools, exactly as workers were concentrated in factories.

Concentration occurred also in capital flows, so that Second Wave civilization gave birth to the giant corporation and, beyond that, the trust or monopoly. By the mid-1960's, the

Big Three auto companies in the United States produced 94 percent of all American cars. In Germany four companies—Volkswagen, Daimler-Benz, Opel (GM), and Ford-Werke—together accounted for 91 percent of production. In France, Renault, Citroën, Simca, and Peugeot turned out virtually 100 percent. In Italy, Fiat alone built 90 percent of all autos.

Similarly, in the United States 80 percent or more of aluminum, beer, cigarettes, and breakfast foods were produced by four or five companies in each field. In Germany 92 percent of all the plasterboard and dyes, 98 percent of photo film, 91 percent of industrial sewing machines, were produced by four or fewer companies in each respective category. The list of highly concentrated industries goes on and on.

Socialist managers were also convinced that concentration of production was "efficient." Indeed, many Marxist ideologues in the capitalist countries welcomed the growing concentration of industry in capitalist countries as a necessary step along the way to the ultimate total concentration of industry under state auspices. Lenin spoke of the "conversion of *all* citizens into workers and employees of *one* huge 'syndicate'—the whole state." Half a century later the Soviet economist N. Lelyukhina, writing in *Voprosy Ekonomiki* could report that "the USSR possesses the most concentrated industry in the world."

Whether in energy, population, work, education, or economic organization, the concentrative principle of Second Wave civilization ran deep—deeper, indeed, than any ideological differences between Moscow and the West.

MAXIMIZATION

The split-up of production and consumption also created, in all Second Wave societies, a case of obsessive "macrophilia"—a kind of Texan infatuation with bigness and growth. If it were true that long production runs in the factory would produce lower unit costs, then, by analogy, increases in scale would produce economies in other activities as well. "Big" became synonymous with "efficient," and maximization became the fifth key principle.

Cities and nations would boast of having the tallest skyscraper, the largest dam, or the world's biggest miniature golf course. Since bigness, moreover, was the result of growth, most industrial governments, corporations, and other organizations pursued the ideal of growth frenetically.

Japanese workers and managers at the Matsushita Electric Company would jointly chorus each day:

> . . . Doing our best to promote production,
> Sending our goods to the people of the world,
> Endlessly and continuously.
> Like water gushing from a fountain.
> Grow, industry, Grow, Grow, Grow!
> Harmony and sincerity!
> Matsushita Electric!

In 1960, as the United States completed the stage of traditional industrialism and began to feel the first effects of the Third Wave of change, its fifty largest industrial corporations had grown to employ an average of 80,000 workers each. General Motors alone employed 595,000, and one utility, Vail's AT&T, employed 736,000 women and men. This meant, at an average household size of 3.3 that year, that well over 2,000,000 people were dependent upon paychecks from this one company alone—a group equal to one half the population of the entire country when Hamilton and Washington were stitching it into a nation. (Since then AT&T has swollen to even more gargantuan proportions. By 1970 it employed 956,000—having added 136,000 employees to its work force in a single twelve-month period.)

AT&T was a special case and, of course, Americans were peculiarly addicted to bigness. But macrophilia was no monopoly of the Americans. In France in 1963 fourteen hundred firms—a mere ¼ of 1 percent of all companies—employed fully 38 percent of the work force. Governments in Germany, Britain, and other countries actively encouraged mergers to create even larger companies, in the belief that larger scale would help them compete against the American giants.

Nor was this scale maximization simply a reflection of profit maximization. Marx had associated the "increasing scale of industrial establishments" with the "wider development of their material powers." Lenin, in turn, argued that "huge enterprises, trusts and syndicates had brought the mass production technique to its highest level of development." His first order of business after the Soviet revolution was to consolidate Russian economic life into the smallest possible number of the largest possible units. Stalin pushed even harder for maximum scale and built vast new projects—the steel complex at Magnitogorsk, another at Zaporozhstal, the Balkhash copper smelting plant, the tractor plants at Kharkov and Stalingrad. He would ask how large a given American installation was, then order construction of an even larger one.

In *The Cult of Bigness in Soviet Economic Planning*, Dr. Leon M. Herman writes: "In various parts of the USSR, in fact, local politicians became involved in a race for attracting the 'world's largest projects.'" By 1938 the Communist party warned against "gigantomania," but with little effect. Even today Soviet and East European communist leaders are victims of what Herman calls "the addiction to bigness."

Such faith in sheer scale derived from narrow Second Wave assumptions about the nature of "efficiency." But the macrophilia of industrialism went beyond mere plants. It was reflected in the aggregation of many different kinds of data into the statistical tool known as Gross National Product, which measured the "scale" of an economy by totting up the value of goods and services produced in it. This tool of the Second Wave economists had many failings. From the point of view of GNP it didn't matter whether the output was in the form of food, education and health services, or munitions. The hiring of a crew to build a home or to demolish one both added to GNP, even though one activity added to the stock of housing and the other subtracted from it. GNP also, because it measured only market activity or exchanges, relegated to insignificance a whole vital sector of the economy based on unpaid production—child-rearing and housework, for example.

Despite these shortcomings, Second Wave governments around the world entered into a blind race to increase GNP at all costs, maximizing "growth" even at the risk of ecological and social disaster. The macrophiliac principle was built so deeply into the industrial mentality that nothing seemed more reasonable. Maximization went along with standardization, specialization, and the other industrial ground rules.

CENTRALIZATION

Finally, all industrial nations developed centralization into a fine art. While the Church and many First Wave rulers knew perfectly well how to centralize power, they dealt with far less complex societies and were crude amateurs by contrast with the men and women who centralized industrial societies from the ground floor up.

All complicated societies require a mixture of both centralized and decentralized operations. But the shift from a basically decentralized First Wave economy, with each locality largely responsible for producing its own necessities, to the integrated national economies of the Second Wave led to totally new methods for centralizing power. These came into play at the level of individual companies, industries, and the economy as a whole.

The early railroads provide a classic illustration. Compared with other businesses they were the giants of their day. In the United States in 1850 only forty-one factories had a capitalization of 250 thousand dollars or more. By contrast, the New York Central Railroad as early as 1860 boasted a capitalization of 30 million dollars. To run such a gargantuan enterprise, new management methods were needed.

The early railroad managers, therefore, like the managers of the space program in our own era, had to invent new techniques. They standardized technologies, fares, and schedules. They synchronized operations over hundreds of miles. They created specialized new occupations and departments. They concentrated capital, energy, and people. They fought to maximize the scale of their networks. And to accomplish all this they created new forms of organization based on centralization of information and command.

Employees were divided into "line" and "staff." Daily reports were initiated to provide data on car movements, loadings, damages, lost freight, repairs, engine miles, et cetera. All this information flowed up a centralized chain of command until it reached the general superintendent who made the decisions and sent orders down the line.

The railroads, as business historian Alfred D. Chandler, Jr., has shown, soon became a model for other large organizations, and centralized management came to be regarded as an advanced, sophisticated tool in all the Second Wave nations.

In politics, too, the Second Wave encouraged centralization. In the United States, as early as the late 1780's, this was illustrated by the battle to replace the loose, decentralist Articles of Confederation with a more centralist Constitution. Generally the First Wave rural interests resisted the concentration of power in the national government, while Second

Wave commercial interests led by Hamilton argued, in *The Federalist* and elsewhere, that a strong central government was essential not only for military and foreign policy reasons but for economic growth.

The resultant Constitution of 1787 was an ingenious compromise. Because First Wave forces were still strong, the Constitution reserved important powers to the states rather than the central government. To prevent overly strong central power it also called for a unique separation of legislative, executive, and judicial powers. But the Constitution also contained elastic language that would eventually permit the federal government to extend its reach drastically.

As industrialization pushed the political system toward greater centralization, the government in Washington took on an increasing number of powers and responsibilities and monopolized more and more decision-making at the center. Within the federal government, meanwhile, power shifted from Congress and the courts to the most centralist of three branches—the Executive. By the Nixon years, historian Arthur Schlesinger (himself once an ardent centralizer) was attacking the "imperial presidency."

The pressures toward political centralization were even stronger outside the United States. A quick look at Sweden, Japan, Britain, or France is enough to make the U.S. system seem decentralized by comparison. Jean-François Revel, author of *Without Marx or Jesus,* makes this point in describing how governments respond to political protest: "When a demonstration is forbidden in France, there is never any doubt about the source of the prohibition. If it is a question of a major political demonstration, it is the [central] government," he says. "In the United States, however, when a demonstration is forbidden, the first question everyone asks is, 'By whom?'" Revel points out that it is usually some local authority operating autonomously.

The extremes of political centralization were found, of course, in the Marxist industrial nations. In 1850 Marx called for a "decisive centralization of power in the hands of the state." Engels, like Hamilton before him, attacked decentralized confederations as "an enormous step backward." Later on the Soviets, eager to accelerate industrialization, proceeded to construct the most highly centralized political and economic structure of all, submitting even the smallest of production decisions to the control of central planners.

*   *   *

The gradual centralization of a once decentralized economy was aided, moreover, by a crucial invention whose very name reveals its purpose: the central bank.

In 1694, at the very dawn of the industrial age, while Newcomen was still tinkering with the steam engine, William Paterson organized the Bank of England—which became a template for similar centralist institutions in all Second Wave countries. No country could complete its Second Wave phase without constructing its own equivalent of this machine for the central control of money and credit.

Paterson's bank sold government bonds; it issued government-backed currency; it later began to regulate the lending practices of other banks. Eventually it took on the primary function of all central banks today: central control of the money supply. In 1800 the Banque de France was formed for similar purposes. This was followed by the formation of the Reichsbank in 1875.

In the United States the collision between First and Second Wave forces led to a major battle over central banking shortly after the adoption of the constitution. Hamilton, the most brilliant advocate of Second Wave policies, argued for a national bank on the English model. The South and the frontier West, still wedded to agriculture, opposed him. Nevertheless, with the support of the industrializing Northeast, he succeeded in forcing through legislation that created the Bank of the United States—forerunner of today's Federal Reserve System.

Employed by governments to regulate the level and rate of market activity, central banks introduced—by the back door, as it were—a degree of unofficial short-range planning into capitalist economies. Money flowed through every artery in Second Wave societies, both capitalist and socialist. Both needed, and therefore created, a centralized money pumping station. Central banking and centralized government marched hand in hand. Centralization was another dominating principle of Second Wave civilization.

What we see, therefore, is a set of six guiding principles, a "program" that operated to one degree or another in all the Second Wave countries. These half-dozen principles—standardization, specialization, synchronization, concentration, maximization, and centralization—were applied in both the capitalist and socialist wings of industrial society because they grew, inescapably, out of the basic cleavage between producer and consumer and the ever-expanding role of the market.

These principles in turn, each reinforcing the other, led relentlessly to the rise of bureaucracy. They produced some of the biggest, most rigid, most powerful bureaucratic organizations the world had ever seen, leaving the individual to wander in a Kafka-like world of looming mega-organizations. If today we feel oppressed and overpowered by them, we can trace our problems to the hidden code that programmed the civilization of the Second Wave.

The six principles that formed this code lent a distinctive stamp to Second Wave civilization. Today, as we shall shortly see, every one of these fundamental principles is under attack by the forces of the Third Wave.

So, indeed, are the Second Wave elites who are still applying these rules—in business, in banking, in labor relations, in government, in education, in the media. For the rise of a new civilization challenges all the vested interests of the old one.

In the upheavals that lie immediately ahead, the elites of all industrial societies—so accustomed to setting the rules—will in all likelihood go the way of the feudal lords of the past. Some will be by-passed. Some will be dethroned. Some will be reduced to impotence or shabby gentility. Some—the most intelligent and adaptive—will be transformed and emerge as leaders of the Third Wave civilization.

To understand who will run things tomorrow when the Third Wave becomes dominant, we must first know exactly who runs things today.

$$\approx\!\!\approx\!\!\approx 5$$

THE TECHNICIANS
OF POWER

The question "Who runs things?" is a typically Second Wave question. For until the industrial revolution there was little reason to ask it. Whether ruled by kings or shamans, warlords, sun gods, or saints, people were seldom in doubt as to who held power over them. The ragged peasant, looking up from the fields, saw the palace or monastery looming in splendor on the horizon. He needed no political scientist or newspaper pundit to solve the riddle of power. Everyone knew who was in charge.

Wherever the Second Wave swept in, however, a new kind of power emerged, diffuse and faceless. Those in power became the anonymous "they." Who were "they"?

THE INTEGRATORS

Industrialism, as we have seen, broke society into thousands of interlocking parts—factories, churches, schools, trade unions, prisons, hospitals, and the like. It broke the line of command between church, state, and individual. It broke knowledge into specialized disciplines. It broke jobs into fragments. It broke families into smaller units. In doing so, it shattered community life and culture.

Somebody had to put things back together in a different form.

This need gave rise to many new kinds of specialists whose basic task was integration. Calling themselves executives or administrators, commissars, coordinators, presidents, vice-presidents, bureaucrats, or managers, they cropped up in every business, in every government, and at every level of society. And they proved indispensable. They were the integrators.

They defined roles and allocated jobs. They decided who got what rewards. They made plans, set criteria, and gave or withheld credentials. They linked production, distribution, transport, and communications. They set the rules under which organizations interacted. In short, they fitted the pieces of the society together. Without them the Second Wave system could never have run.

Marx, in the mid-nineteenth century, thought that whoever owned the tools and technology—the "means of production"—would control society. He argued that, because work was interdependent, workers could disrupt production and seize the tools from their boses. Once they owned the tools, they would rule society.

Yet history played a trick on him. For the very same interdependency gave even greater leverage to a new group—those who orchestrated or integrated the system. In the end it was neither the owners nor the workers who came to power. In both capitalist and socialist nations, it was the integrators who rose to the top.

It was not ownership of the "means of production" that gave power. It was control of the "means of integration." Let's see what that has meant.

In business the earliest integrators were the factory proprietors, the business entrepreneurs, the mill owners and ironmasters. The owner and a few aides were usually able to coordinate the labor of a large number of unskilled "hands" and to integrate the firm into the larger economy.

Since, in that period, owner and integrator were one and the same, it is not surprising that Marx confused the two and laid so heavy an emphasis on ownership. As production grew more complex, however, and the division of labor more specialized, business witnessed an incredible proliferation of executives and experts who came between the boss and his workers. Paperwork mushroomed. Soon in the larger firms no individual, including the owner or dominant shareholder, could even begin to understand the whole operation. The owner's decisions were shaped, and ultimately controlled, by the specialists brought in to coordinate the system. Thus a new executive elite arose whose power rested no longer on ownership but rather on control of the integration process.

As the manager grew in power, the stockholder grew less important. As companies grew bigger, family owners sold out to larger and larger groups of dispersed shareholders, few of whom knew anything about the actual operations of the business. Increasingly, shareholders had to rely on hired managers not merely to run the day-to-day affairs of the company but even to set its long-range goals and strategies. Boards of directors, theoretically representing the owners, were themselves increasingly remote and ill-informed about the operations they were supposed to direct. And as more and more private investment was made not by individuals but indirectly through institutions like pension funds, mutual funds, and the trust departments of banks, the actual "owners" of industry were still further removed from control.

The new power of the integrators was, perhaps, most clearly expressed by W. Michael Blumenthal, former U.S. Secretary of the Treasury. Before entering government Blumenthal headed the Bendix Corporation. Once asked if he would some day like to own Bendix, Blumenthal replied: "It's not ownership that counts—it's control. And as Chief Executive that's what I've got! We have a shareholders' meeting next week, and I've got ninety-seven percent of the vote. I only *own* eight thousand shares. Control is what's important to me. . . . To have the control over this large animal and to use it in a constructive way, that's what I want, rather than doing silly things that others want me to do."

Business policies were thus increasingly fixed by the hired managers of the firm or by money managers placing other people's money, but in neither case by the actual owners, let alone by the workers. The integrators took charge.

All this had certain parallels in the socialist nations. As early as 1921 Lenin felt called upon to denounce his own Soviet bureaucracy. Trotsky, in exile by 1930, charged that there were already five to six million managers in a class that "does not engage directly in productive labor, but administers, orders, commands, pardons and punishes." The means of production might belong to the state, he charged, "But the state . . . 'belongs' to the bureaucracy." In the 1950's Milovan Djilas, in *The New Class,* attacked the growing power of the managerial elites in Yugoslavia. Tito, who imprisoned Djilas, himself complained about "technocracy, bureaucracy, the class enemy." And fear of managerialism was the central theme in Mao's China.*

Under socialism as well as capitalism, therefore, the integrators took effective power. For without them the parts of the system could not work together. The "machine" would not run.

THE INTEGRATIONAL ENGINE

Integrating a single business, or even a whole industry, was only a small part of what had to be done. Modern industrial society, as we have seen, developed a host of organizations, from labor unions and trade associations to churches, schools, health clinics, and recreational groups, all of which had to work within a framework of predictable rules. Laws were needed. Above all, the info-sphere, socio-sphere, and techno-sphere had to be brought into alignment with one another.

Out of this driving need for the integration of Second Wave civilization came the biggest coordinator of all—the integrational engine of the system: big government. It is the system's hunger for integration that explains the relentless rise of big government in every Second Wave society.

Again and again political demagogues arose to call for smaller government. Yet, once in office, the very same leaders expanded rather than contracted the size of government. This contradiction between rhetoric and real life becomes understandable the moment we recognize that the transcendent aim of all Second Wave governments has been to construct and maintain industrial civilization. Against this commitment, all lesser differences faded. Parties and politicians might squabble over other issues, but on this they were in tacit agreement. And big government was part of their unspoken program regardless of the tune they sang, because industrial societies depend on government to perform essential integrational tasks.

In the words of political columnist Clayton Fritchey, the United States federal government never ceased to grow, even under three recent Republican administrations, "for the

---

* Mao, leading the world's biggest First Wave nation, repeatedly warned against the rise of managerial elites and saw this as a dangerous concomitant of traditional industrialism.

simple reason that not even Houdini could dismantle it without serious and harmful consequences."

Free marketeers have argued that governments interfere with business. But left to private enterprise alone, industrialization would have come much more slowly—if, indeed, it could have come at all. Governments quickened the development of the railroad. They built harbors, roads, canals, and highways. They operated postal services and built or regulated telegraph, telephone, and broadcast systems. They wrote commercial codes and standardized markets. They applied foreign policy pressures and tariffs to aid industry. They drove farmers off the land and into the industrial labor supply. They subsidized energy and advanced technology, often through military channels. At a thousand levels, governments assumed the integrative tasks that others could not, or would not, perform.

For government was the great accelerator. Because of its coercive power and tax revenues, it could do things that private enterprise could not afford to undertake. Governments could "hot up" the industrialization process by stepping in to fill emerging gaps in the system—before it became possible or profitable for private companies to do so. Governments could perform "anticipatory integration."

By setting up mass education systems, governments not only helped to machine youngsters for their future roles in the industrial work force (hence, in effect, subsidizing industry) but also simultaneously encouraged the spread of the nuclear family form. By relieving the family of educational and other traditional functions, governments accelerated the adaptation of family structure to the needs of the factory system. At many different levels, therefore, governments orchestrated the complexity of Second Wave civilization.

Not surprisingly, as integration grew in importance both the substance and style of government changed. Presidents and prime ministers, for example, came to see themselves primarily as managers rather than as creative social and political leaders. In personality and manner they became almost interchangeable with the men who ran the large companies and production enterprises. While offering the obligatory lip service to democracy and social justice, the Nixons, Carters, Thatchers, Brezhnevs, Giscards, and Ohiras of the industrial world rode into office by promising little more than efficient management.

Across the board, therefore, in socialist as well as capitalist industrial societies, the same pattern emerged—big companies or production organizations and a huge governmental machine. And rather than workers seizing the means of production, as Marx predicted, or capitalists retaining power, as Adam Smith's followers might have preferred, a wholly new force arose to challenge both. The technicians of power seized the "means of integration" and, with it, the reins of social, cultural, political, and economic control. Second Wave societies were ruled by the integrators.

THE POWER PYRAMIDS

These technicians of power were themselves organized into hierarchies of elites and sub-elites. Every industry and branch of government soon gave birth to its own establishment, its own powerful "They."

Sports . . . religion . . . education . . . each had its own pyramid of power. A science establishment, a defense establishment, a cultural establishment sprang up. Power in Second Wave civilization was parceled out to scores, hundreds, even thousands of such specialized elites.

In turn, these specialized elites were themselves integrated by generalist elites whose membership cut across all the specializations. For example, in the Soviet Union and Eastern Europe the Communist party had members in every field from aviation to music and steel manufacture. Communist party members served as a crucial grapevine carrying messages from one sub-elite to another. Because it had access to all information, it had enormous power to regulate the specialist sub-elites. In the capitalist countries, leading businessmen and lawyers, serving on civic committees or boards, performed similar functions in a less formal way. What we see, therefore, in all Second Wave nations are specialized groups of integrators, bureaucrats, or executives, themselves integrated by generalist integrators.

THE SUPER-ELITES

Finally, at yet a higher level, integration was imposed by the "super-elites" in charge of investment allocation. Whether in finance or industry, in the Pentagon or in the Soviet plan-

ning bureaucracy, those who made the major investment allo-
cations in industrial society set the limits within which the
integrators themselves were compelled to function. Once a
truly large-scale investment decision had been made, whether
in Minneapolis or Moscow, it limited future options. Given a
scarcity of resources, one could not casually tear out Bessemer furnaces or cracking plants or assembly lines until their
cost had been amortized. Once in place, therefore, this capital
stock fixed the parameters within which future managers or
integrators were confined. These groups of faceless decision-
makers, controlling the levers of investment, formed the super-
elite in all industrial societies.

In every Second Wave society, consequently, a parallel architecture of elites sprang up. And—with local variation—
this hidden hierarchy of power was born again after every
crisis or political upheaval. Names, slogans, party labels and
candidates might change; revolutions might come and go.
New faces might appear behind the big mahogany desks. But
the basic architecture of power remained.

Time and again during the past three hundred years, in
one country after another, rebels and reformers have attempted to storm the walls of power, to build a new society
based on social justice and political equality. Temporarily, such
movements have seized the emotions of millions with
promises of freedom. Revolutionists have even managed, now
and then, to topple a regime.

Yet each time the ultimate outcome was the same. Each
time the rebels re-created, under their own flag, a similar
structure of sub-elites, elites, and super-elites. For this integrational structure and the technicians of power who ruled it
were as necessary to Second Wave civilization as factories,
fossil fuels, or nuclear families. Industralism and the full democracy it promised were, in fact, incompatible.

Industrial nations could be forced, through revolutionary
action or otherwise, to move back and forth across the spectrum from free market to centrally planned. They could go
from capitalist to socialist and vice versa. But like the much-
cited leopard, they could not change their spots. They could
not function without a powerful hierarchy of integrators.

Today, as the Third Wave of change begins to batter at
this fortress of managerial power, the first fleeting cracks are
appearing in the power system. Demands for participation in
management, for shared decision-making, for worker, consumer, and citizen control, and for anticipatory democracy

are welling up in nation after nation. New ways of organizing along less hierarchical and more ad-hocratic lines are springing up in the most advanced industries. Pressures for decentralization of power intensify. And managers become more and more dependent upon information from below. Elites themselves, therefore, are becoming less permanent and secure. All these are merely early warnings—indicators of the coming upheaval in the political system.

The Third Wave, already beginning to batter at these industrial structures, opens fantastic opportunities for social and political renovation. In the years just ahead startling new institutions will replace our unworkable, oppressive, and obsolete integrational structures.

Before we turn to these new possibilities, we need to press our analysis of the dying system. We need to X-ray our obsolete political system to see how it fitted into the frame of Second Wave civilization, how it served the industrial order and its elites. Only then can we understand why it is no longer appropriate or tolerable.

6
THE HIDDEN BLUEPRINT

Nothing is more confusing to a Frenchman than the spectacle of an American presidential campaign: the hot-dog gulping, backslapping, and baby kissing, the coy refusal to cast hat in ring, the primaries, the conventions, followed by the manic frenzy of fund raising, whistle-stopping, speechmaking, television commercials—all in the name of democracy. By contrast, Americans find it hard to make sense of the way the French choose their leaders. Still less do they understand the tame British elections, the Dutch free-for-all with two dozen parties, the Australian preferential voting system, or the Japanese wheeling and dealing among factions. All these political systems seem frightfully different from one another. Even more incomprehensible are the one-party elections or pseudo-elections that take place in the U.S.S.R. and Eastern Europe. When it comes to politics, no two industrial nations look the same.

Yet once we tear away our provincial blinders we suddenly discover that a set of powerful parallels lies beneath the surface differences. In fact, it is almost as if the political systems of all Second Wave nations were built from the same hidden blueprint.

When Second Wave revolutionaries managed to topple First Wave elites in France, in the United States, in Russia, Japan, and other nations, they were faced with the need to write constitutions, set up new governments, and design almost from scratch new political institutions. In the excitement of creation they debated new ideas, new structures. Everywhere they fought over the nature of representation. Who

69

should represent whom? Should representatives be instructed how to vote by the people—or use their own judgment? Should terms of office be long or short? What role should parties play?

In each country a new political architecture emerged from these conflicts and debates. A close look at these structures reveals that they are built on a combination of old First Wave assumptions and newer ideas swept in by the industrial age.

After millennia of agriculture, it was hard for the founders of Second Wave political systems to imagine an economy based on labor, capital, energy, and raw materials, rather than land. Land had always been at the very center of life itself. Not surprisingly, therefore, geography was deeply embedded in our various voting systems. Senators and congressmen in America—and their counterparts in Britain and many other industrial nations—are still elected not as representatives of some social class or occupational, ethnic, sexual, or life-style grouping, but as representatives of the inhabitants of a particular piece of land: a geographical district.

First Wave people were typically immobile, and it was therefore natural for the architects of industrial-era political systems to assume that people would remain in one locality all their lives. Hence the prevalence, even today, of residency requirements in voting regulations.

The pace of First Wave life was slow. Communications were so primitive that it might take a week for a message from the Continental Congress in Philadelphia to reach New York. A speech by George Washington took weeks or months to filter through to the hinterland. As late as 1865 it still took twelve days for London to learn that Lincoln had been assassinated. On the unspoken assumption that things moved slowly, representative bodies like Congress or the British Parliament were regarded as "deliberative"—having the time and taking the time to think through their problems.

Most First Wave people were illiterate and ignorant. Thus it was widely assumed that representatives, particularly if drawn from the educated classes, would inevitably make more intelligent decisions than the mass of voters.

But even as they built these First Wave assumptions into our political institutions, the revolutionaries of the Second Wave also cast their eyes on the future. Thus the architecture they constructed reflected some of the latest technological notions of their time.

MECHANO-MANIA

The businessmen, intellectuals, and revolutionaries of the early industrial period were virtually mesmerized by machinery. They were fascinated by steam engines, clocks, looms, pumps, and pistons, and they constructed endless analogies based on the simple mechanistic technologies of their time. It was no accident that men like Benjamin Franklin and Thomas Jefferson were scientists and inventors as well as political revolutionaries.

They grew up in the churning cultural wake of Newton's great discoveries. Newton had searched the heavens and concluded that the entire universe was a giant clockwork operating with exact mechanical regularity. La Mettrie, the French physician and philosopher, in 1748 declared man himself to be a machine. Adam Smith later extended the analogy of the machine to economics, arguing that the economy is a system and that systems "in many respects resemble machines."

James Madison, in describing the debates that led to the United States Constitution, spoke of the need to "remodel" the "system," to change the "structure" of political power, and to choose officials through "successive filtrations." The Constitution itself was filled with "checks and balances" like the inner works of a giant clock. Jefferson spoke of the "machinery of government."

American political thinking continued to reverberate with the sound of flywheels, chains, gears, checks and balances. Thus Martin Van Buren invented the "political machine" and eventually New York City had its Tweed machine, Tennessee its Crump machine, New Jersey its Hague machine. Generations of American politicians, right down to the present, prepared political "blueprints," "engineered elections," "steam-rollered" or "railroaded" bills through Congress and the state legislatures. In the nineteenth century in Britain, Lord Cromer conceived of an imperial government that would "ensure the harmonious working of the different parts of the machine."

Nor was this mechanistic mentality a product of capitalism. Lenin, for example, described that state as "nothing more than a machine used by the capitalists to suppress the workers." Trotsky spoke of "all the wheels and screws of the bourgeois social mechanism" and went on to describe the function of a revolutionary party in similarly mechanical phrases. Terming it a powerful "apparatus," he pointed out that "as with any mechanism this is in itself static . . . the movement of the masses has . . . to overcome dead inertia. . . . Thus, the living force of steam has to overcome the inertia of the machine before it can set the flywheel in motion."

Drenched in such mechanistic thinking, imbued with an almost blind faith in the power and efficiency of machines, the revolutionary founders of Second Wave societies, whether capitalist or socialist, not surprisingly invented political institutions that shared many of the characteristics of early industrial machines.

THE REPRESENTO-KIT

The structures they hammered and bolted together were based on the elemental notion of representation. And in every country they made use of certain standard parts. These components came out of what might be called, only half facetiously, a universal represento-kit.

The components were:

1. Individuals armed with the vote
2. Parties for collecting votes
3. Candidates who, by winning votes, were instantly transformed into "representatives" of the voters
4. Legislatures (parliaments, diets, congresses, bundestags, or assemblies) in which, by voting, representatives manufactured laws
5. Executives (presidents, prime ministers, party secretaries) who fed raw material into the lawmaking machine in the form of policies, and then enforced the resulting laws

Votes were the "atom" of this Newtonian mechanism. Votes were aggregated by parties, which served as the "manifold" of the system. They gathered votes from many sources and fed them into the electoral adding machine, which blended them in proportion to party strength or mixture, producing as its output the "will of the people"—the basic fuel that supposedly powered the machinery of government.

The parts of this kit were combined and manipulated in different ways in different places. In some places everyone over the age of twenty-one was permitted to vote; elsewhere only white males were enfranchised; in one country the entire process was merely a facade for control by a dictator; in another the elected officials actually wielded considerable power. Here there were two parties, there a multiplicity of parties, elsewhere only one. Nevertheless, the historical pattern is clear. However the parts might be modified or configured, this same basic kit was used in constructing the formal political machinery of all industrial nations.

Even though Communists frequently attacked "bourgeois democracy" and "parliamentarianism" as a mask for privilege, arguing that the mechanisms were usually manipulated by the capitalist class for its own private gain, all socialist industrial nations installed similar representational machines as soon as possible.

While holding forth a promise of "direct democracy" in some far-off post-representational era, they relied heavily in the meantime on "socialist representative institutions." The Hungarian Communist Ottó Bihari, in a study of these institutions, writes, "in the course of election the will of the working people makes its influence felt in the governmental organs called to life by voting." The editor of *Pravda*, V. G. Afanasyev, in his book *The Scientific Management of Society* defines "democratic centralism" as including "the sovereign power of the working people . . . the election of governing bodies and leaders and their accountability to the people."

Just as the factory came to symbolize the entire industrial techno-sphere, representative government (no matter how denatured) became the status symbol of every "advanced" nation. Indeed, even many non-industrial nations—under pressure from colonizers or through blind imitation—rushed to install the same formal mechanisms and used the same universal represento-kit.

THE GLOBAL LAW FACTORY

Nor were these "democracy machines" restricted to the national level. They were installed at state, provincial, and local levels as well, right down to the town or village council. Today in the United States alone there are some five-hundred thousand elected public officials and 25,869 local governmental units in metropolitan areas, each with its own elections, representative bodies, and election procedures.

Thousands of these representational machines are creaking and grinding away in nonmetropolitan regions, and tens of thousands more around the world. In Swiss cantons and French departments, in the countries of Britain and the provinces of Canada, in the voivodships of Poland and the republics of the Soviet Union, in Singapore and Haifa, Osaka and Oslo, candidates run for office and are magically transmuted into "representatives." It is safe to say that more than one-hundred thousand of these machines are now manufacturing laws, decrees, regulations, and rules in Second Wave countries alone.*

In theory, just as each human being and each vote was a discrete, atomic unit, each of these political units—national, provincial, and local—was also regarded as discrete and atomic. Each had its own carefully defined jurisdiction, its own powers, its own rights and duties. The units were wired together in hierarchical arrangement, from top to bottom, from nation to state or region or local authority. But as industrialism matured and the economy grew increasingly integrated, decisions taken by each of these political units touched off effects outside its own jurisdiction, thereby causing other political bodies to act in response.

A decision by the Diet regarding the Japanese textile industry could influence employment in North Carolina and welfare services in Chicago. A congressional vote to put quotas on foreign automobiles could make additional work for local governments in Nagoya or Turin. Thus while at one time politicians could make a decision without upsetting conditions outside their own neatly defined jurisdiction, this became less and less possible.

By the mid-twentieth century, tens of thousands of ostensi-

---

* Apart from governments as such, virtually all the political parties of industrialism, from extreme right to extreme left, routinely went through the traditional motions of choosing their own leaders by vote. Even contests for precinct-level or local cell leadership typically required some form of election, if only for the ratification of choices made from above. And in many countries the ritual of election became a standard part of the life of all sorts of other organizations, from trade unions and churches to Cub Scout packs. Voting became part of the industrial way of life.

bly sovereign or independent political authorities, stretching around the planet, were connected to one another through the circuits of the economy, through vastly increased travel, migration, and communication, so that they continually activated and excited one another.

The thousands of representational mechanisms built out of components of the represento-kit thus increasingly came to form a single invisible supermachine: a global law factory. Now it remains only for us to see how the levers and control wheels of this global system were manipulated—and by whom.

THE REASSURANCE RITUAL

Born of the liberating dreams of Second Wave revolutionaries, representative government was a stunning advance over earlier power systems, a technological triumph more striking in its own way than the steam engine or the airplane.

Representative government made possible orderly succession without hereditary dynasty. It opened feedback channels between top and bottom in society. It provided an arena in which the differences among various groups could be reconciled peacefully.

Tied to majority rule and the idea of one-man/one-vote, it helped the poor and weak to squeeze benefits from the technicians of power who ran the integrational engines of society. For these reasons, the spread of representative government was, on the whole, a humanizing breakthrough in history.

Yet from the very beginning it fell far short of its promise. By no stretch of the imagination was it ever controlled by the people, however defined. Nowhere did it actually change the underlying structure of power in industrial nations—the structure of sub-elites, elites, and super-elites. Indeed, far from weakening control by the managerial elites, the formal machinery of representation became one of the key means of integration by which they maintained themselves in power.

Thus elections, quite apart from who won them, performed a powerful cultural function for the elites. To the degree that everyone had a right to vote, elections fostered the illusion of equality. Voting provided a mass ritual of reassurance, conveying to the people the idea that choices were being made systematically, with machine-like regularity, and hence, by implication, rationally. Elections symbolically assured citizens that they were still in command—that they could, in theory at least, dis-elect as well as elect leaders. In both capitalist and socialist countries, these ritual reassurances often proved more important than the actual outcomes of many elections.

Integrational elites programmed the political machinery differently in each place, controlling the number of parties or manipulating voting eligibility. Yet the electoral ritual—some might say farce—was employed everywhere. The fact that Soviet and Eastern European elections routinely produced magical majorities of 99 to 100 percent suggested that the need for reassurance remained at least as strong in the centrally planned societies as in the "free world." Elections took the steam out of protests from below.

Furthermore, despite the efforts of democratic reformers and radicals, the integrational elites retained virtually permanent control of the systems of representative government. Many theories have been advanced to explain why. Most, however, overlook the mechanical nature of the system.

If we look at Second Wave political systems with the eyes of an engineer rather than a political scientist, we suddenly are struck by a key fact that generally goes unobserved.

Industrial engineers routinely distinguish between two fundamentally different classes of machine: those that function intermittently, otherwise known as "batch-processing" machines, and those that function uninterruptedly, called "continuous-flow" machines. An example of the first is the commonplace punch press. The worker brings a batch of metal plates and feeds them into the machine, one or a few at a time, to stamp them into desired shapes. When the batch is finished the machine stops until a new batch is brought. An example of the second is the oil refinery which, once started up, never stops running. Twenty-four hours a day, oil flows through its pipes and tubes and chambers.

If we look at the global law factory, with its intermittent voting, we find ourselves face to face with a classical batch processor. The public is allowed to choose between candidates at stipulated times, after which the formal "democracy machine" is switched off again.

Contrast this with the continuous flow of influence from various organized interests, pressure groups, and power peddlers. Swarms of lobbyists from corporations and from government agencies, departments, and ministries testify before committees, serve on blue-ribbon panels, attend the same receptions and banquets, toast each other with cocktails in

Washington or vodka in Moscow, carry information and influence back and forth, and thus affect the decision-making process on a round-the-clock basis.

The elites, in short, created a powerful continuous-flow machine to operate alongside (and often at cross purposes with) the democratic batch processor. Only when we see these two machines side by side can we begin to understand how state power was really exercised in the global law factory.

So long as they played the representational game, people had at best only intermittent opportunities, through voting, to feed back their approval or disapproval of the government and its actions. The technicians of power, by contrast, influenced those actions continuously.

Finally, an even more potent tool for social control was engineered into the very principle of representation. For the mere selection of some people to represent others created new members of the elite.

When workers, for example, first fought for the right to organize unions, they were harassed, prosecuted for conspiracy, followed by company spies, or beaten up by police and goon squads. They were outsiders, unrepresented or inadequately represented in the system.

Once unions established themselves, they gave rise to a new group of integrators—the labor establishment—whose members, rather than simply representing the workers, mediated between them and the elites in business and government. The George Meanys and Georges Séguys of the world, despite their rhetoric, became themselves key members of the integrational elite. The fake union leaders in the U.S.S.R. and Eastern Europe never were anything but technicians of power.

In theory, the need to stand for re-election guaranteed that representatives would stay honest and would continue to speak for those they represented. Nowhere, however, did this prevent the absorption of representatives into the architecture of power. Everywhere the gap widened between the representative and the represented.

Representative government—what we have been taught to call democracy—was, in short, an industrial technology for assuring inequality. Representative government was pseudorepresentative.

What we see, then, glancing backward for a moment of summary, is a civilization heavily dependent on fossil fuels, factory production, the nuclear family, the corporation, mass education, and the mass media, all based on a widening cleavage between production and consumption—and all managed by a set of elites whose task it was to integrate the whole.

In this system, representative government was the political equivalent of the factory. Indeed, it *was* a factory for the manufacture of collective integrational decisions. Like most factories, it was managed from above. And like most factories, it is now increasingly obsolete, a victim of the advancing Third Wave.

If Second Wave political structures *are* increasingly out of date, unable to cope with today's complexities—part of the trouble, as we shall see, lies in another crucial Second Wave institution: the nation-state.

A FRENZY
OF
NATIONS

Abaco is an island. It has a population of sixty-five hundred and forms part of the Bahamas lying off the coast of Florida. Several years ago a group of American businessmen, arms merchants, free enterprise ideologues, a Black intelligence agent, and a member of the British House of Lords determined that it was time for Abaco to declare its independence.

Their plan was to take over the island and break it away from the Bahamian government by promising each of the native residents of the island a free acre of land after the revolution. (This would have left over a quarter of a million acres for use by the real estate developers and investors behind the project.) The ultimate dream was the establishment on Abaco of a taxless utopia to which wealthy businessmen, dreading the Socialist apocalypse, might flee.

Alas for free enterprise, the native Abaconians showed little inclination to throw off their chains, and the proposed new nation was stillborn.

Nevertheless, in a world in which nationalist movements battle for power, and in which some 152 states claim membership in that trade association of nations, the U.N., such parodic gestures serve a useful purpose. They force us to challenge the very notion of nationhood.

Could the sixty-five hundred people of Abaco, whether financed by oddball businessmen or not, constitute a nation? If Singapore with its 2.3 million people is a nation, why not New York City with its 8 million? If Brooklyn had jet bombers would it be a nation? Absurd as they sound, such questions will take on new significance as the Third Wave batters

79

at the very foundations of Second Wave civilization. For one of those foundations was, and is, the nation-state.

Until we cut through the foggy rhetoric that surrounds the issue of nationalism, we cannot make sense of the headlines and we cannot understand the conflict between First and Second Wave civilizations as the Third Wave strikes them both.

CHANGING HORSES

Before the Second Wave began rolling across Europe most regions of the world were not yet consolidated into nations but were organized, rather, into a mishmash of tribes, clans, duchies, principalities, kingdoms, and other more or less local units. "Kings and princes," write the political scientist S. E. Finer, "held powers in bits and blobs." Borders were ill-defined, governmental rights fuzzy. The power of the state was not yet standardized. In one village, Professor Finer tells us, it amounted only to the right to collect tolls on a windmill, in another to tax the peasants, elsewhere to appoint an abbot. An individual with property in several different regions might owe allegiance to several lords. Even the greatest of emperors typically ruled over a patchwork of tiny locally-governed communities. Political control was not yet uniform. Voltaire summed it all up: In traveling across Europe, he complained, he had to change laws as frequently as horses.

There was more to this quip than met the eye, of course, for the frequent need to change horses reflected the primitive level of transport and communications—which, in turn, reduced the distance over which even the most powerful monarch could impose effective control. The farther from the capital, the weaker the authority of the state.

Yet without political integration, economic integration was impossible. Costly new Second Wave technologies could only be amortized if they produced goods for larger-than-local markets. But how could businessmen buy and sell over a large territory if, outside their own communities, they ran into a maze of different duties, taxes, labor regulations, and currencies? For the new technologies to pay off, local economies had to be consolidated into a single national economy. This meant a national division of labor and a national market for commodities and capital. All this, in turn, required national political consolidation as well.

Put simply, a Second Wave political unit was needed to match the growth of Second Wave economic units.

Not surprisingly, as Second Wave societies began to build national economies, a basic shift in public consciousness became evident. The small-scale local production in First Wave societies had bred a race of highly provincial people—most of whom concerned themselves exclusively with their own neighborhoods or villages. Only a tiny handful—a few nobles and churchmen, a scattering of merchants and a social fringe of artists, scholars, and mercenaries—had interests beyond the village.

The Second Wave swiftly multiplied the number of people with a stake in the larger world. With steam- and coal-based technologies, and later with the advent of electricity, it became possible for a manufacturer of clothing in Frankfurt, watches in Geneva, or textiles in Manchester to produce far more units than the local market could absorb. He also needed raw materials from afar. The factory worker, too, was affected by financial events occurring thousands of miles away: jobs depended on distant markets.

Bit by bit, therefore, psychological horizons expanded. The new mass media increased the amount of information and imagery from far away. Under the impact of these changes, localism faded. National consciousness stirred.

Starting with the American and French revolutions and continuing through the nineteenth century, a frenzy of nationalism swept across the industrializing parts of the world. Germany's three hundred and fifty petty, diverse, quarreling mini-states needed to be combined into a single national market—das Vaterland. Italy—broken into pieces and ruled variously by the House of Savoy, the Vatican, the Austrian Hapsburgs, and the Spanish Bourbons—had to be united. Hungarians, Serbs, Croats, Frenchmen, and others all suddenly developed mystical affinities for their fellows. Poets exalted the national spirit. Historians discovered long-lost heroes, literature, and folklore. Composers wrote hymns to nationhood. All at precisely the moment when industrialization made it necessary.

Once we understand the industrial need for integration, the meaning of the national state becomes clear. Nations are not "spiritual unities" as Spengler termed them, or "mental communities" or "social souls." Nor is a nation "a rich heritage of memories," to use Renan's phrase, or a "shared image of the future," as Ortega insisted.

What we call the modern nation is a Second Wave phenomenon: a single integrated political authority superimposed on or fused with a single integrated economy. A ragbag collection of locally self-sufficient, sparsely connected economies cannot, and does not, give rise to a nation. Nor is a tightly unified political system a modern nation if it sits atop a loose conglomeration of local economies. It was the welding of the two, a unified political system and a unified economy, that made the modern nation.

Nationalist uprisings triggered by the industrial revolution in the United States, in France, in Germany and the rest of Europe, can be seen as efforts to bring the level of political integration up to the fast-rising level of economic integration that accompanied the Second Wave. And it was these efforts, not poetry or mystical influences, that led to the division of the world into distinct national units.

THE GOLDEN SPIKE

As each government sought to extend its market and its political authority, it came up against outer limits—language differences, cultural, social, geographic, and strategic barriers. The available transport, communication, and energy supplies, the productivity of its technology, all set limits on how large an area could be effectively ruled by a single political structure. The sophistication of accounting procedures, budgetary controls, and management techniques also determined how far political integration could reach.

Within these limits, the integrational elites, corporate and governmental alike, fought for expansion. The broader the territory under their control and the bigger the economic market area, the greater their wealth and power became. As each nation stretched its economic and political frontiers to the utmost, it ran up not merely against these inherent limits but also against rival nations.

To break out of these confines the integrational elites used advanced technology. They hurled themselves, for example, into the "space race" of the nineteenth century—the building of railroads.

In September 1825 a rail line was established that linked Stockton to Darlington in Britain. In May 1835, on the continent, Brussels was tied to Malines. That September in Bavaria the Nuremberg–Furth line was laid. Next were Paris and St. Germain. Far to the east, in April 1838, Tsarkoe Selo was connected to St. Petersburg. For the next three decades or more, railroad workers stitched one region to another.

The French historian Charles Morazé explains: "The countries which were already almost united in 1830 were consolidated by the coming of the railway . . . those still unprepared saw new bands of steel . . . tightening around them. . . . It was as if every possible nation was hastening to proclaim its right to exist before the railways were built, so that it might be acknowledged as a nation by the transport system which defined the political boundaries of Europe for over a century."

In the United States the government awarded vast land grants to the private railroad companies, inspired, as historian Bruce Mazlish has written, by "the conviction that transcontinental roads would strengthen the ties of union between the Atlantic and Pacific coasts." Hammering in the golden spike that completed the first transcontinental rail line opened the door to a truly national market—integrated on a continental scale. And it extended the actual, as distinct from nominal, control of the national government. Washington could now move troops quickly all across the continent to enforce its authority.

What one saw, therefore, in one country after another, was the rise of this powerful new entity—the nation. In this way the world map came to be divided into a set of neat, nonoverlapping patches of red, pink, orange, yellow, or green, and the nation-state system became one of the key structures of Second Wave civilization.

Beneath the nation lay the familiar imperative of industrialism: the drive toward integration.

But the drive for integration did not end at the borders of each nation-state. For all its strengths, industrial civilization had to be fed from without. It could not survive unless it integrated the rest of the world into the money system and controlled that system for its own benefit.

How it did so is crucial to any understanding of the world the Third Wave will create.

8

THE IMPERIAL DRIVE

No civilization spreads without conflict. Second Wave civilization soon launched a massive attack on the First Wave world, triumphed, and imposed its will on millions, ultimately billions, of human beings.

Long before the Second Wave, of course, from the sixteenth century on, European rulers had already begun to build extensive colonial empires. Spanish priests and conquistadors, French trappers, British, Dutch, and Portuguese or Italian adventurers fanned out across the globe, enslaving or decimating whole populations, claiming control of vast lands, and sending tribute home to their monarchs.

Compared with what was to follow, however, all this was insignificant.

For the treasure these early adventurers and conquerors sent home was, in effect, private booty. It financed wars and personal opulence—winter palaces, colorful pageantry, a leisurely workless life-style for the court. But it had little to do with the still basically self-sufficient economy of the colonizing country.

Largely outside the money system and the market economy, the serfs who scraped a bare living from the sunbaked soil of Spain or the misty heaths of England had little or nothing to export abroad. They scarcely grew enough for local consumption. Nor did they depend on raw materials stolen or purchased in other countries. For them life went on, one way or another. The fruits of overseas conquest enriched the ruling class and the towns rather than the mass of ordinary people who lived as peasants. In this sense, First Wave imperialism was still petty—not yet integrated into the economy.

The Second Wave transformed this relatively small-scale pilferage into big business. It transformed Petty Imperialism into Grand Imperialism.

Here was a new imperialism aimed not at bringing back a few trunkloads of gold or emeralds, spices and silks. Here was an imperialism that ultimately brought back shipload after shipload of nitrates, cotton, palm oil, tin, rubber, bauxite, and tungsten. Here was an imperialism that dug copper mines in the Congo and planted oil rigs in Arabia. Here was an imperialism that sucked in raw materials from the colonies, processed them, and very often spewed the finished manufactured goods back into the colonies at a huge profit. Here, in short, was imperialism no longer peripheral but so integrated into the basic economic structure of the industrial nation that the jobs of millions of ordinary workers came to depend on it.

And not just jobs. In addition to new raw materials, Europe also needed increasing amounts of food. As Second Wave nations turned to manufacturing, transferring rural labor into the factories, they were forced to import more of their foodstuffs from abroad—beef, mutton, grain, coffee, tea, and sugar from India, from China, from Africa, from the West Indies and Central America.

In turn, as mass manufacturing grew, the new industrial elites needed bigger markets and fresh outlets for investment. In the 1880's and 1890's European statesmen were unabashedly open about their objectives. "Empire is commerce," proclaimed the British politician Joseph Chamberlain. The French premier Jules Ferry was even more explicit: What France needed, he declared, were "outlets for our industries, exports, and capital." Jolted by cycles of boom and bust, faced with chronic unemployment, European leaders were for generations obsessed by the fear that if colonial expansion stopped, unemployment would lead to armed revolution at home.

The roots of Grand Imperialism were, however, more than economic. Strategic considerations, religious fervor, idealism, and adventure all played a part, as did racism, with its implicit assumption of white or European superiority. Many saw imperial conquest as a divine responsibility. Kipling's phrase, the "White Man's burden," summed up the European's missionary zeal to spread Christianity and "civilization"—

meaning, of course, Second Wave civilization. For the colonizers regarded First Wave civilizations, no matter how refined and complex, as backward and underdeveloped. Rural people, especially if they happened to wear dark skins, were supposedly childlike. They were "tricky and dishonest." They were "shiftless." They did not "value life."

Such attitudes made it easier for the Second Wave forces to justify the annihilation of those who stood in their path.

In *The Social History of the Machine Gun,* John Ellis shows how this new, fantastically deadly weapon, perfected in the nineteenth century, was at first systematically employed against "native" populations and not against white Europeans, since it was considered unsportsmanlike to kill an equal with it. Shooting colonials, however, was thought to be more like a hunt than a war, so other standards applied. "Mowing down Matabeles, Dervishes or Tibetans," writes Ellis, "was regarded more as a rather risky kind of 'shoot' than a true military operation."

At Omdurman, across the Nile from Khartoum, this superior technology was displayed with withering effect in 1898 when Dervish warriors led by the Mahdi were defeated by British troops armed with six Maxim machine guns. An eyewitness wrote: "It was the last day of Mahdism and the greatest. . . . It was not a battle but an execution." In that one engagement twenty-eight British died, leaving behind eleven thousand Dervish dead—392 colonial casualties for every Englishman. Writes Ellis: "It became another example of the triumph of the British spirit, and the general superiority of the white man."

Behind the racist attitudes and the religious and other justifications as the British, French, Germans, Dutch, and others spread around the world, stood a single hard reality. Second Wave civilization could not exist in isolation. It desperately needed the hidden subsidy of cheap resources from the outside. Above all, it needed a single integrated world market through which to siphon those subsidies.

GAS PUMPS IN THE GARDEN

The thrust to create this integrated world market was based on the idea, best expressed by David Ricardo, that the division of labor ought to be applied to nations as well as to factory workers. In a classical passage he pointed out that if

Britain specialized in the manufacture of textiles and Portugal in making wine, both countries would gain. Each would be doing what it did best. Thus the "international division of labor," assigning specialized roles to different nations, would enrich everyone.

This belief hardened into dogma in the generations that followed and still prevails today, although its implications often go unnoticed. For just as the division of labor in any economy created a powerful need for integration and thereby gave rise to an integrational elite, so the international division of labor required integration on a global scale and gave rise to a global elite—a small group of Second Wave nations which, for all practical purposes, took turns dominating large parts of the rest of the world.

The success of the drive to create a single integrated world market can be measured in the fantastic growth of world trade once the Second Wave passed through Europe. Between 1750 and 1914 the value of world trade is estimated to have multiplied more than fiftyfold, rising from 700 million dollars to almost 40 billion dollars. If Ricardo had been right, the advantages of this global trade should have accrued more or less evenly to all sides. In fact, the self-serving belief that specialization would benefit everyone was based on a fantasy of fair competition.

It presupposed a completely efficient use of labor and resources. It presupposed deals uncontaminated by threats of political or military force. It presupposed arm's-length transactions by more or less evenly matched bargainers. The theory, in short, overlooked nothing—except real life.

In reality, negotiations between Second Wave merchants and First Wave people over sugar, copper, cocoa, or other resources were often totally lopsided. On one side of the table sat money-shrewd European or American traders backed by huge companies, extensive banking networks, powerful technologies, and strong national governments. On the other one might find a local lord or tribal chieftain whose people had scarcely entered the money system and whose economy was based on small-scale agriculture or village crafts. On one side sat the agents of a thrusting, alien, mechanically advanced civilization, convinced of its own superiority and ready to use bayonets or machine guns to prove it. On the other sat representatives of small prenational tribes or principalities, armed with arrows and spears.

Often local rulers or entrepreneurs were simply bought off

by the Westerners, offered bribes or personal gain in return for sweating the native labor force, putting down resistance, or rewriting local laws in favor of the outsiders. Once conquering a colony, the imperial power often set preferential raw-material prices for its own businessmen and erected stiff barriers to prevent the traders of rival nations from bidding prices up.

Under such circumstances, it was hardly surprising that the industrial world was able to obtain raw materials or energy resources at less than fair-market prices.

Beyond this, prices were often further depressed in the favor of the buyers by what might be termed "The Law of the First Price." Many raw materials needed by Second Wave nations were virtually valueless to the First Wave populations who had them. African peasants had no need for chromium. Arab sheiks had no use for the black gold that lay under their desert sands.

Where no previous history of trade existed for a given commodity, the price set in the first transaction was crucial. And this price was often based less on such economic factors as cost, profit, or competition than on relative military and political strength. Typically set in the absence of active competition, almost any price was acceptable to a lord or tribal chief who regarded his local resources as valueless and found himself facing a regiment of troops with Gatling guns. And this First Price, once established at a low level, depressed all subsequent prices.

As soon as this raw material was shipped back to the industrial nations and incorporated in final products, the low initial price was, for all intents, frozen in place.* Eventually, as a world price was gradually established for each commodity, all industrial nations benefited from the fact that the First Price had been set at an "a-competitive" low level. For many different reasons, therefore, despite much imperialist rhetoric about the virtues of free trade and enterprise, the Second

---

* Example: Suppose Company A bought a raw material from Colonia for one dollar a pound, then used it to manufacture widgets selling for two dollars each. Any other company seeking to enter the widget market would strive to keep its own raw-material cost at, or below, that of Company A. Unless it had some technological or other edge, it could not afford to pay significantly more for its raw material and still sell widgets at a competitive price. Thus the *initial* price set for the raw material, even if arrived at under the shadow of bayonets, became the base for all subsequent negotiation.

Wave nations profited greatly from what was euphemistically called "imperfect competition."

Rhetoric and Ricardo aside, the benefits of expanding trade were not evenly shared. They flowed mainly from the First Wave world to the Second.

THE MARGARINE PLANTATION

To facilitate this flow, the industrial powers worked hard to expand and integrate the world market. As trade passed beyond national boundaries each national market became part of a larger set of interconnected regional or continental markets and, finally, part of the single, unified exchange system envisioned by the integrational elites who ran Second Wave civilization. A single web of money was woven around the world.

Treating the rest of the world as its gas pump, garden, mine, quarry, and cheap labor supply, the Second Wave world wrought deep changes in the social life of the earth's non-industrial populations. Cultures that had subsisted for thousands of years in a self-sufficient manner, producing their own food supplies, were sucked willy-nilly into the world trade system and compelled to trade or perish. Suddenly the living standards of Bolivians or Malayans were tied to the requirements of industrial economies half a planet away, as tin mines and rubber plantations sprang up to feed the voracious industrial maw.

The innocent household product margarine provides a dramatic case in point. Margarine was originally manufactured in Europe out of local materials. It grew so popular, however, that these materials proved insufficient. In 1907 researchers discovered that margarine could be made out of coconut and palm-kernel oil. The result of this European discovery was an upheaval in the life-style of West Africans.

"In the main areas of West Africa," writes Magnus Pyke, former president of the British Institute of Food Science and Technology, "where palm oil was traditionally produced, the land was owned by the community as a whole." Complex local customs and rules governed the use of the palm trees. Sometimes a man who had planted a tree was entitled to its product for the rest of his life. In some places women had special rights. According to Pyke, the Western businessmen who organized "the large-scale production of palm oil for the manufacture of margarine as a 'convenience' food for the industrial citizens of Europe and America destroyed the fragile and complex social system of the non-industrial Africans." Huge plantations were set up in the Belgian Congo, in Nigeria, the Cameroons, and the Gold Coast. The West got its margarine. And Africans became semi-slaves on huge plantations.

Rubber offers another example. After the turn of the century when automobile production in the United States created a sudden heavy demand for rubber for tires and inner tubes, traders, in collusion with local authorities, enslaved Amazonian Indians to produce it. Roger Casement, the British consul in Rio de Janeiro, reported that the production of four thousand tons of Putumayo rubber between 1900 and 1911 resulted in the death of thirty thousand Indians.

It can be argued that these were "excesses" and were not typical of Grand Imperialism. Certainly the colonial powers were not unrelievedly cruel or evil. In places they did build schools and rudimentary health facilities for their subject populations. They improved sanitation and water supplies. They no doubt raised the living standard for some.

Nor would it be fair to romanticize precolonial societies or to blame the poverty of today's non-industrial populations exclusively on imperialism. Climate, local corruption and tyranny, ignorance, and xenophobia all contributed. There was plenty of misery and oppression to go around long before the Europeans ever arrived.

Nevertheless, once torn out of self-sufficiency and compelled to produce for money and exchange, once encouraged or forced to reorganize their social structure around mining, for example, or plantation farming, First Wave populations were plunged into economic dependence on a marketplace they could scarcely influence. Often their leaders were bribed, their cultures ridiculed, their languages suppressed. Moreover, the colonial powers hammered a deep sense of psychological inferiority into the conquered people that stands even today as an obstacle to economic and social development.

In the Second Wave world, however, Grand Imperialism paid off handsomely. As the economic historian William Woodruff put it: "It was the exploitation of these territories and the growing trade done with them that obtained for the European family wealth on a scale never seen before." Built deep into the very structure of the Second Wave economy, feeding its ravenous need for resources, imperialism marched across the planet.

In 1492 when Columbus first set foot in the New World, Europeans controlled only 9 percent of the globe. By 1801 they ruled a third. By 1880, two thirds. And by 1935 Europeans politically controlled 85 percent of the land surface of the earth and 70 percent of its population. Like Second Wave society itself, the world was divided into integrators and integratees.

INTEGRATION À L'AMÉRICAIN

Not all integrators were equal, however. The Second Wave nations waged an increasingly bloody battle among themselves for control of the emerging world economic system. English and French dominance was challenged in World War I by rising German industrial might. The war's destruction, the devastating cycle of inflation and depression that followed it, the revolution in Russia, all shook the industrial world market.

These upheavals brought on a drastic slowdown in the rate of growth of world trade, and, even though more countries were sucked into the trading system, the actual volume of goods traded internationally declined. World War II further slowed extension of the integrated world market.

By the end of World War II, Western Europe lay in smoking ruins. Germany had been reduced to a lunar landscape. The Soviet Union had suffered indescribable physical and human damage. Japan's industry was shattered. Of the major industrial powers only the United States found itself unharmed economically. By 1946–1950 the global economy stood in such disarray that foreign trade was at its lowest level since 1913.

Moreover, the very weakness of the war-stricken European powers encouraged one colony after another to demand political independence. Gandhi, Ho Chi Minh, Jomo Kenyatta, and other anti-colonialists stepped up their campaigns to oust the colonizers.

Even before the wartime guns stopped firing, therefore, it was apparent that the entire world industrial economy would have to be reconstituted on a new basis after the war.

Two nations took upon themselves the task of reorganizing

and reintegrating the Second Wave system: the United States and the Union of Soviet Socialist Republics.

The United States until then had played a limited part in the Grand Imperial campaign. In opening its own frontier it had decimated the Native Americans and cordoned them off in reservations. In Mexico, Cuba, and Puerto Rico, and the Philippines, Americans imitated the imperial tactics of the British, the French, or the Germans. In Latin America throughout the early decades of this century U.S. "dollar diplomacy" helped United Fruit and other corporations guarantee low prices for sugar, bananas, coffee, copper, and other goods. Nevertheless, compared with the Europeans, the United States was a junior partner in the Grand Imperial crusade.

After World War II, by contrast, the United States stood as the chief creditor nation in the world. It had the most advanced technology, the most stable political structure—and an irresistible opportunity to move into the power vacuum left behind by its shattered competitors as they were forced to withdraw from the colonies.

As early as 1941 U.S. financial strategists had begun to plan for a postwar reintegration of the world economy along lines more favorable to the United States. At the Bretton Woods Conference in 1944, held under U.S. leadership, forty-four nations agreed to set up two key integrative structures—the International Monetary Fund and the World Bank.

The IMF compelled its member nations to peg their currency to the American dollar or to gold—most of which was held by the United States. (By 1948, the United States possessed 72 percent of the whole world's gold reserves.) The IMF thus fixed the basic relationships of the major world currencies.

The World Bank, meanwhile, at first established to provide postwar reconstruction funds to European nations, gradually began providing loans to the non-industrial countries, too. These were often for the purpose of building roads, harbors, ports, and other "infra-structure items" to facilitate the movement of raw materials and agricultural exports to the Second Wave nations.

Soon a third component was added to the system: the General Agreement on Tariffs and Trade—GATT for short. This agreement, again promoted originally by the United States, set out to liberalize trade, which had the effect of making it difficult for the poorer, less technologically advanced countries to protect their tiny fledgling industries.

The three structures were wired together by a rule that prohibited the World Bank from making loans to any country that refused to join the IMF or to abide by the GATT.

This system made it difficult for debtors of the United States to reduce their obligations through currency or tariff manipulation. It strengthened the competitiveness of U.S. industry in world markets. And it gave the industrial powers, and especially the United States, a strong influence on economic planning in many First Wave countries, even after they had attained political independence.

These three interconnected agencies formed a single integrative structure for world trade. And from 1944 to the early 1970's, the United States basically dominated this system. Among nations, it integrated the integrators.

SOCIALIST IMPERIALISM

American leadership of the Second Wave world, however, was increasingly challenged by the rise of the Soviet Union. The U.S.S.R. and other socialist nations portrayed themselves as anti-imperialist friends of the colonial peoples of the world. In 1916, a year before he took power, Lenin had written a slashing attack on the capitalist nations for their colonial policies. His *Imperialism* became one of the most influential books of the century and still shapes the thinking of hundreds of millions around the world.

But Lenin saw imperialism as a purely capitalist phenomenon. Capitalist nations, he insisted, oppressed and colonized other nations not out of choice but out of necessity. A dubious iron law, put forward by Marx, held that profits in capitalist economies showed a general, irresistible tendency to decline over time. Because of this, Lenin held, capitalist nations in their final stage were driven to seek "super-profits" abroad to compensate for diminishing profits at home. Only socialism, he argued, would free colonial peoples from their oppression and misery, because socialism had no built-in dynamic requiring their economic exploitation.

What Lenin overlooked is that many of the same imperatives that drove capitalist industrial nations operated in socialist industrial nations as well. They, too, were part of the world money system. They, too, based their economies on the

divorce of production from consumption. They, too, needed a
market (albeit not necessarily a profit-oriented market) to
reconnect producer and consumer. They, too, needed raw
materials from abroad to feed their industrial machines. And
for these reasons they, too, needed an integrated world
economic system through which to obtain their necessities
and sell their products abroad.

Indeed Lenin, at the very same time he attacked imperialism, spoke of socialism's aim "not only to bring the nations
closer together but to integrate them." As the Soviet analyst
M. Senin has written in *Socialist Integration,* Lenin by 1920
"regarded the drawing together of nations as an objective
process which . . . will finally and ultimately lead to the
creation of a single world economy, regulated by . . . a common plan." This, if anything, was the ultimate industrial vision.

Externally, socialist industrial nations were driven by the
same resource needs as capitalist nations. They, too, needed
cotton, coffee, nickel, sugar, wheat, and other goods to feed
their fast-multiplying factories and their urban populations.
The Soviet Union had (and still has) enormous reserves of
natural resources. It has manganese, lead, zinc, coal, phos-
phates, and gold. But so had the United States, and that
stopped neither nation from seeking to buy from others at
the cheapest possible price.

From its inception the Soviet Union became part of the
world money system. Once any nation entered this system
and accepted the "normal" ways of doing business, it immediately locked itself into conventional definitions of efficiency
and productivity—definitions that were themselves traceable
back to early capitalism. It was compelled to accept, almost
unconsciously, conventional economic concepts, categories,
definitions, accounting methods, and units of measurement.

Socialist managers and economists, exactly like their capitalist counterparts, thus calculated the cost of producing their
own raw materials as against the cost of purchasing them.
They faced a straight "make or buy" decision of the kind
capitalist corporations confront every day. And it soon became apparent that buying certain raw materials on the world
market would be cheaper than trying to produce them at
home.

Once this decision was made, sharp Soviet purchasing
agents fanned out into the world market and bought at prices
previously set at artificially low levels by imperialist traders.
Soviet trucks rolled on rubber bought at prices that were

probably determined *ab initio* by British merchants in Malaya. Worse, in recent years the Soviets (who maintain troops there) paid Guinea six dollars per ton for bauxite when the Americans were paying twenty-three dollars. India has protested that the Russians overcharge them 30 percent on imports and pay 30 percent too little for Indian exports. Iran and Afghanistan received subnormal prices from the Soviets for natural gas. Thus the Soviet Union, like its capitalist adversaries, benefited at the expense of the colonies. To have done otherwise would have been to slow its own industrialization process.

The Soviet Union was also driven toward imperialist policies by strategic considerations. Faced with the military might of Nazi Germany, the Soviets first colonized the Baltic states and made war on Finland. After World War II, with troops and the threat of invasion, they helped install or maintain "friendly" regimes throughout most of Eastern Europe. These countries, more industrially advanced than the U.S.S.R. itself, were intermittently milked by the Soviets, justifying their description as colonies or "satellites."

"There can be no doubt," writes the neo-Marxist economist Howard Sherman, "that, in the years immediately following the Second World War, the Soviet Union removed a certain amount of resources from Eastern Europe without giving equal resources in payment. . . . There was some direct plunder and military reparation. . . . There were also joint companies established with Soviet predominance in control and Soviet exploitation of profits from these countries. There were also extremely unequal trade agreements that amounted to further reparations."

At present there is apparently no direct plunder and the joint companies have disappeared, but, adds Sherman, "There is much evidence that most of the exchanges between the U.S.S.R. and most East European countries are still unequal—with the U.S.S.R. coming out best." How much "profit" is extruded by these means is difficult to determine, given the inadequacy of published Soviet statistics. It may well be that the costs of maintaining Soviet troops throughout Eastern Europe actually outweigh the economic benefits. But one fact is indisputably clear.

While the Americans built the IMF–GATT–World Bank structure, the Soviets moved toward Lenin's dream of a single integrated world economic system by creating the Council for Mutual Economic Assistance (COMECON) and compelling the Eastern European countries to join it. COMECON countries are forced by Moscow not only to trade with one another and with the Soviet Union but to submit their economic development plans to Moscow for approval. Moscow, insisting on the Ricardian virtues of specialization, acting exactly like the old imperialist powers vis-à-vis African, Asian, or Latin American economies, has assigned specialized functions to each Eastern European economy. Only Romania has openly and staunchly resisted.

Claiming that Moscow has tried to turn it into the "petrol pump and garden" of the Soviet Union, Romania has set out to achieve what it calls multilateral development, meaning a fully rounded industrialization. It has resisted "socialist integration" despite Soviet pressures. In sum, at the very time that the United States assumed leadership of the capitalist industrial nations and built its own self-serving mechanisms for integrating the world economic system anew after World War II, the Soviets built a counterpart of this system in the part of the world they dominated.

No phenomenon as vast, complex, and transforming as imperialism can be described simply. Its effects on religion, on education, on health, on themes in literature and art, on racial attitudes, on the psycho-structure of whole peoples, as well as more directly on economics, are still being unraveled by the historians. It no doubt had positive accomplishments to its credit as well as atrocities. But its role in the rise of Second Wave civilization cannot be overemphasized.

We can think of imperialism as the supercharger or accelerator of industrial development in the Second Wave world. How rapidly would the United States, Western Europe, Japan, or the U.S.S.R. have been able to industrialize without infusions of food, energy, and raw materials from outside? What if the prices of scores of commodities like bauxite, manganese, tin, vanadium, or copper had been 30 to 50 percent higher for a period of decades?

The price of thousands of end-products would have been correspondingly higher—in some cases, no doubt, so high as to make mass consumption impossible. The shock of oil price increases in the early 1970's gives only a pale hint of the potential effects.

Even if domestic substitutes had been available, the economic growth of the Second Wave nations would in all probability have been stunted. Without the concealed subsidies made possible by imperialism, capitalist and socialist, Second Wave civilization might well be today where it was in 1920 or 1930.

The grand design should now be clear. Second Wave civilization cut up and organized the world into discrete nation-states. Needing the resources of the rest of the world, it drew First Wave societies and the remaining primitive peoples of the world into the money system. It created a globally integrated marketplace. But rampant industrialism was more than an economic, political, or social system. It was also a way of life and a way of thinking. It produced a Second Wave mentality.

This mentality stands today as a key obstacle to the creation of a workable Third Wave civilization.

9

INDUST-REALITY

As Second Wave civilization pushed its tentacles across the planet, transforming everything with which it came in contact, it carried with it more than technology or trade. Colliding with First Wave civilization, the Second Wave created not only a new reality for millions but a new way of thinking about reality.

Clashing at a thousand points with the values, concepts, myths, and morals of agricultural society, the Second Wave brought with it a redefinition of God . . . of justice . . . of love . . . of power . . . of beauty. It stirred up new ideas, attitudes, and analogies. It subverted and superseded ancient assumptions about time, space, matter, and causality. A powerful, coherent world view emerged that not only explained but justified Second Wave reality. This world view of industrial society has not had a name. It might best be termed "indust-reality."

Indust-reality was the overarching set of ideas and assumptions with which the children of industrialism were taught to understand their world. It was the package of premises employed by Second Wave civilization, by its scientists, business leaders, statesmen, philosophers, and propagandists.

There were, of course, countervoices, those who challenged the dominant ideas of indust-reality, but we are concerned here not with the side currents but with the mainstream of Second Wave thought. On the surface, it seemed, there was no mainstream at all. Rather, it appeared that there were two powerful ideological currents in conflict. By the middle of the nineteenth century every industrializing nation had its sharply defined left wing and its right, its advocates of individualism and free enterprise, and its advocates of collectivism and socialism.

This battle of ideologies, at first confined to the industrializing nations themselves, soon spread around the globe. With the Soviet Revolution of 1917, and the organization of a centrally directed worldwide propaganda machine, the ideological struggle grew even more intense. And by the end of World War II, as the United States and the Soviet Union attempted to reintegrate the world market—or large parts of it—on their own terms, each side was spending huge sums to spread its doctrines to the world's non-industrial peoples.

On one side were totalitarian regimes, on the other the so-called liberal democracies. Guns and bombs stood ready to take up where logical arguments ended. Seldom since the great collision of Catholicism and Protestantism during the Reformation had doctrinal lines been so sharply drawn between two theological camps.

What few noticed, however, in the heat of this propaganda war, was that while each side promoted a different *ideology*, both were essentially hawking the same *superideology*. Their conclusions—their economic programs and political dogmas—differed radically, but many of their starting assumptions were the same. Like Protestant and Catholic missionaries clutching different versions of the Bible, yet both preaching Christ, Marxists and anti-Marxists alike, capitalists and anticapitalists, Americans and Russians marched forth into Africa, Asia, and Latin America—the non-industrial regions of the world—blindly bearing the same set of fundamental premises. Both preached the superiority of industrialism to all other civilizations. Both were passionate apostles of indust-reality.

THE PROGRESS PRINCIPLE

The world view they disseminated was based on three deeply intertwined "indust-real" beliefs—three ideas that bound all Second Wave nations together and differentiated them from much of the rest of the world.

The first of these core beliefs had to do with nature. While socialists and capitalists might disagree violently about how to share its fruits, both looked upon nature in the same way. For both, nature was an object waiting to be exploited.

The idea that humans should hold dominion over nature can be traced at least as far back as Genesis. Nevertheless, it was decidedly a minority view until the industrial revolution. Most earlier cultures emphasized instead an acceptance of poverty and the harmony of humankind with its surrounding natural ecology.

These earlier cultures were not particularly gentle with nature. They slashed and burned, overgrazed, and stripped the forests for firewood. But their power to do damage was limited. They had no great impact on the earth and no need for an explicit ideology to justify the damage they did.

With the coming of Second Wave civilization one found capitalist industrialists gouging resources on a massive scale, pumping voluminous poisons into the air, deforesting whole regions in pursuit of profit, without much thought about side effects or long-term consequences. The idea that nature was there to be exploited provided a convenient rationalization for shortsightedness and selfishness.

But the capitalists were scarcely alone. Wherever they took power, Marxist industrializers (despite their conviction that profit was the root of all evil) acted in exactly the same way. Indeed, they built the conflict with nature right into their scriptures.

Marxists pictured primitive peoples not as coexisting harmoniously with nature but as engaged in a fierce life-and-death struggle against it. With the emergence of class society, they held, the war of "man against nature" was unfortunately transformed into a war of "man against man." The achievement of a Communist classless society would permit humanity to get back to its first order of business once again—the war of man against nature.

On both sides of the ideological divide, therefore, one found the same image of humanity standing in opposition to nature and dominating it. This image was a key component of indust-reality, the superideology from which Marxist and anti-Marxist alike drew their assumptions.

A second, interrelated idea carried the argument a step further. Humans were not merely in charge of nature, they were the pinnacle of a long process of evolution. Earlier theories of evolution existed, but it was Darwin, in the middle of the nineteenth century, brought up in the most advanced industrial nation of the time, who provided scientific underpinning for this view. He spoke of the blind workings of "natural selection"—an inevitable process that mercilessly weeded out weak and inefficient forms of life. Those species who survived were, by definition, the fittest.

Darwin was chiefly concerned with biological evolution, but his ideas had distinct social and political overtones that others were quick to recognize. Thus the Social Darwinists argued that the principle of natural selection worked within society as well, and that the wealthiest and most powerful people were, by virtue of that fact, the fittest and the most deserving.

It was only a short leap to the idea that whole societies evolve according to the same laws of selection. Following this reasoning, industrialism was a higher stage of evolution than the non-industrial cultures that surrounded it. Second Wave civilization, to put it bluntly, was superior to all the rest.

Just as Social Darwinism rationalized capitalism, this cultural arrogance rationalized imperialism. The expanding industrial order needed its lifeline to cheap resources, and it created a moral justification for taking them at depressed prices, even at the cost of obliterating agricultural and so-called primitive societies. The idea of social evolution provided intellectual and moral support for the treatment of non-industrial peoples as inferior—and hence unfitted for survival.

Darwin himself wrote unfeelingly of the massacre of the aborigines of Tasmania and, in a burst of genocidal enthusiasm, prophesied that "At some future period . . . the civilized races of man will almost certainly exterminate, and replace, the savage races throughout the world." The intellectual front-runners of Second Wave civilization had no doubt about who deserved to survive.

While Marx bitterly criticized capitalism and imperialism, he shared the view that industrialism was the most advanced form of society, the stage toward which all other societies would inevitably advance in turn.

For the third core belief of indust-reality that linked nature and evolution together was the progress principle—the idea that history flows irreversibly toward a better life for humanity. This idea, too, had plenty of preindustrial precedent. But it was only with the advance of the Second Wave that the idea of Progress with a capital P burst into full flower.

Suddenly, as the Second Wave pulsed over Europe a thousand throats began to sing the same hallelujah chorus. Leibniz, Turgot, Condorcet, Kant, Lessing, John Stuart Mill,

Hegel, Marx, Darwin, and countless lesser thinkers all found reasons for cosmic optimism. They argued over whether progress was truly inevitable or whether it needed a helping hand from the human race; over what constituted a better life; over whether progress would or could continue ad infinitum. But they all nodded in agreement at the notion of progress itself.

Atheists and divines, students and professors, politicians and scientists preached the new faith. Businessmen and commissars alike heralded each new factory, each new product, each new housing development, highway, or dam as evidence of this irresistible advance from bad to good or good to better. Poets, playwrights, and painters took progress for granted. Progress justified the degradation of nature and the conquest of "less advanced" civilizations.

And once more the same idea ran parallel through the works of both Adam Smith and Karl Marx. As Robert Heilbroner has noted, "Smith was a believer in progress. . . . In *The Wealth of Nations* progress was no longer an idealistic goal of mankind, but . . . a destination to which it was driven . . . a by-product of private economic aims." For Marx, of course, these private aims produced only capitalism and the seeds of its own destruction. But this event in itself was part of the long historical sweep carrying humanity forward to socialism, communism, and an even better beyond.

Throughout Second Wave civilization, therefore, three key concepts—the war with nature, the importance of evolution, and the progress principle—provided the ammunition used by the agents of industrialism as they explained and justified it to the world.

Beneath these convictions lay still deeper assumptions about reality—a set of unspoken beliefs about the very elementals of human experience. Every human being must deal with these elementals, and every civilization describes them in a different way. Every civilization must teach its children to grapple with time and space. It must explain—whether through myth, metaphor, or scientific theory—how nature works. And it must offer some clue to *why* things happen as they do.

Thus Second Wave civilization, as it matured, created a wholly new image of reality, based on its own distinctive assumptions about time and space, matter and cause. Picking up fragments from the past, piecing them together in new ways, applying experiment and empirical tests, it drastically altered the way human beings came to perceive the world around them and how they behaved in their daily lives.

THE SOFTWARE OF TIME

We have seen in an earlier chapter how the spread of industrialism was dependent upon the synchronization of human behavior with the rhythms of the machine. Synchronization was one of the guiding principles of Second Wave civilization, and everywhere the people of industrialism appeared to outsiders to be time-obsessed, always glancing nervously at their watches.

To bring about this time-consciousness and achieve synchronization, however, people's basic assumptions about time —their mental images of time—had to be transformed. A new "software of time" was needed.

Agricultural populations, needing to know when to plant and when to harvest, developed remarkable precision in the measurement of long spans of time. But because they did not require close synchronization of human labor, peasant peoples seldom developed precise units for measuring short spans. They typically divided time not into fixed units, like hours or minutes, but into loose, imprecise chunks representing the length of time needed to perform some homely task. A farmer might refer to an interval as "a cow milking time." In Madagascar, an accepted unit of time was called "a rice cooking"; a moment was known as "the frying of a locust." Englishmen spoke of a "pater noster wyle"—the time needed for a prayer—or, more earthily, of a "pissing while."

Similarly, because there was little exchange between one community or village and the next, and because work did not require it, the units in which time was mentally packaged varied from place to place and season to season. In medieval northern Europe, for example, daylight was divided into equal hours. But since the interval between dawn and sunset varied from day to day, an "hour" in December was shorter than an "hour" in March or June.

Instead of vague intervals like a pater noster wyle, industrial societies needed extremely precise units like hour, minute, or second. And these units had to be standardized, interchangeable from one season or community to the next.

Today the entire world is neatly divided into time zones.

We speak of "standard" time. Pilots all over the globe refer back to "Zulu" time—i.e., Greenwich Mean Time. By international convention Greenwich, England, became the point from which all time differences would be measured. Periodically, in unison, as though motivated by a single will, millions of people set their clocks back or forward an hour, and whatever our inner, subjective sense of things may tell us when time is dragging, or conversely when it seems to be whizzing by, an hour is now a single interchangeable, standardized hour.

Second Wave civilization did more than cut time up into more precise and standard chunks. It also placed these chunks in a straight line that extended indefinitely back into the past and forward into the future. It made time linear.

Indeed, the assumption that time is linelike is so deeply embedded in our thoughts that it is hard for those of us raised in Second Wave societies to conceive of any alternative. Yet many preindustrial societies, and some First Wave societies even today, see time as a circle, not a straight line. From the Mayas to the Buddhists and the Hindus, time was circular and repetitive, history repeating itself endlessly, lives perhaps reliving themselves through reincarnation.

The idea that time was like a great circle is found in the Hindu concept of recurrent *kalpas,* each one four thousand million years long, each representing but a single Brahma day beginning with re-creation, ending in dissolution, and beginning again. The notion of circular time is found in Plato and Aristotle, one of whose students, Eudemus, pictured himself living through the same moment again and again as the cycle repeated itself. It was taught by Pythagoras. In *Time and Eastern Man,* Joseph Needham tells us that "For the Indo-Hellenic . . . time is cyclical and eternal." Moreover, while in China the idea of linear time dominated, according to Needham, "Cyclical time was certainly prominent among the early Taoist speculative philosophers."

In Europe, too, in the centuries preceding industrialization, these alternative views of time coexisted. "Throughout the whole medieval period," writes mathematician G. J. Whitrow, "the cyclic and linear concepts of time were in conflict. The linear concept was fostered by the mercantile class and the rise of a money economy. For as long as power was concentrated in the ownership of land, time was felt to be plentiful and was associated with the unchanging cycle of the soil."

As the Second Wave gathered force this age-old conflict was settled: linear time triumphed. Linear time became the dominant view in every industrial society, East or West. Time came to be seen as a highway unrolling from a distant past through the present toward the future, and this conception of time, alien to billions of humans who lived before industrial civilization, became the basis of all economic, scientific, and political planning, whether in the executive suite of IBM, the Japanese Economic Planning Agency, or the Soviet Academy.

It is worth noting, however, that linear time was a precondition for indust-real views of evolution and progress. Linear time made evolution and progress plausible. For if time were circular instead of linelike, if events doubled back on themselves instead of moving in a single direction, it would mean that history repeated itself and that evolution and progress were no more than illusions—shadows on the wall of time.

Synchronization. Standardization. Linearization. They affected the root assumptions of the civilization and they brought massive changes in the way ordinary people handled time in their lives. But if time itself was transformed, space, too, had to be repackaged to fit into the new indust-reality.

REPACKAGING SPACE

Long before the dawn of First Wave civilization, when our most distant ancestors relied on hunting and herding, fishing, or foraging for survival, they kept constantly on the move. Driven by hunger, cold, or ecological mishaps, pursuing weather or game, they were the original "high-mobiles"— traveling light, avoiding the accumulation of cumbersome goods or property, and ranging widely over the landscape. A band of fifty men, women, and children might need a land area six times the size of Manhattan Island to feed them, or they might trace a migratory path over literally hundreds of miles each year as conditions demanded. They led what today's geographers call a "spatially extensive" existence.

First Wave civilization, by contrast, bred a race of "space misers." As nomadism was replaced by agriculture, migratory trails gave way to cultivated fields and permanent settlements. Rather than roaming restlessly over an extensive area, the farmer and his family stayed put, intensively working their

tiny patch within the larger sea of space—a sea so large as to
dwarf the individual.

By the period immediately preceding the birth of industrial
civilization, vast open fields surrounded each huddle of
peasant huts. Apart from a handful of merchants, scholars,
and soldiers, most individuals lived their lives at the end of a
very short tether. They walked to the fields at sunrise, then
back again at nightfall. They traced a path to church. On
rare occasions they trekked to the next village six or seven
miles away. Conditions varied with climate and terrain, of
course, but according to historian J. R. Hale, "We should
probably not be far wrong if we took the average longest
journey made by most people in their lifetimes as fifteen
miles." Agriculture produced a "spatially restricted" civilization.

The industrial storm that broke over Europe in the
eighteenth century created once again a "spatially extended"
culture—but now on a nearly planetary scale. Goods, people,
and ideas were transported thousands of miles and vast populations migrated in search of jobs. Instead of production
being widely dispersed in the fields, it was now concentrated
in cities. Huge, teeming populations were compressed into a
few tightly packed nodes. Old villages shriveled and died;
booming industrial centers sprang up, rimmed with
smokestacks and furnace fire.

This dramatic reworking of the landscape required much
more complex coordination between city and country. Thus
food, energy, people, and raw materials had to flow into the
urban nodes, while manufactured goods, fashions, ideas, and
financial decisions flowed out. The two flows were carefully
integrated and coordinated in time and space. Within the cities themselves, moreover, a much wider variety of spatial
shapes was needed. In the old agricultural system the basic
physical structures were a church, a nobleman's palace, some
wretched huts, an occasional tavern or monastery. Second
Wave civilization, because of its much more elaborate division of labor, demanded many more specialized types of
space.

Architects, for this reason, soon found themselves creating
offices, banks, police stations, factories, railroad terminals, department stores, prisons, fire houses, asylums, and theaters.
These many different types of space had to be fitted together
in logically functional ways. The location of factories, the
pathways that led from home to shop, the relationships of rail-

road sidings to docks or truck yards, the placement of schools and hospitals, of water pipes, power stations, conduits, gas lines, telephone exchanges—all had to be spatially coordinated. Space had to be as carefully organized as a Bach fugue.

This remarkable coordination of specialized spaces—necessary to get the right people to the right places at the right moment—was the exact spatial analogue of temporal synchronization. It was, in effect, synchronization in space. For *both* time and space had to be more carefully structured if industrial societies were to function.

Just as people had to be provided with more exact and standardized units of time, they also needed more precise and interchangeable units of space. Prior to the industrial revolution, when time was still being sliced up into crude units like pater noster wyles, spatial measures, too, were a mishmash. In medieval England, for example, a "rood" might be as little as sixteen and a half feet or as much as twenty-four feet. In the sixteenth century the best advice on how to arrive at a measured rood was to select sixteen men at random as they walked out of church, to stand them in a line "their left feet one behind the other," and to measure off the resulting distance. Even vaguer terms were used, such as "a day's ride," "an hour's walk," or "half an hour's canter."

Such looseness could no longer be tolerated once the Second Wave began to change work patterns, and the invisible wedge created an ever-expanding marketplace. Precise navigation, for example, became more and more important as trade increased, and governments offered huge prizes to anyone who could devise better methods of keeping merchant ships on course. On land, too, more and more refined measurements and more precise units were introduced.

The confusing, contradictory, chaotic variety of local customs, laws, and trade practices that prevailed during First Wave civilization had to be cleaned up, rationalized. Lack of precision and standard measurement were a daily aggravation to manufacturers and the rising merchant class. This explains the enthusiasm with which the French revolutionaries, at the dawn of the industrial era, applied themselves to the standardization of distance through the metric system as well as time through a new calendar. So important did they deem these problems that they were among the very first items taken up when the National Convention first met to declare a republic.

The Second Wave of change also brought with it a multi-
plication and sharpening of spatial boundaries. Until the
eighteenth century the boundaries of empires were often imprecise. Because vast areas were unpopulated, precision was
unnecessary. As population rose, trade increased, and the first
factories began to spring up around Europe, many governments began systematically to map their frontiers. Customs
zones were more clearly delineated. Local and even private
properties came to be more carefully defined, marked,
fenced, and recorded. Maps became more detailed, inclusive,
and standardized.

A new image of space arose that corresponded exactly to
the new image of time. As punctuality and scheduling set
more limits and deadlines in time, more and more boundaries
cropped up to set limits in space. Even the linearization of
time had its spatial counterpart.

In preindustrial societies straight-line travel, whether by
land or sea, was an anomaly. The peasant's path, the cowpath
or Indian trail, all meandered according to the lay of the
land. Many walls curved, bulged, or went off at irregular
angles. The streets of medieval cities folded in on one another, curved, twisted, convoluted.

Second Wave societies not only put ships on exact
straight-line courses, they also built railroads whose shining
tracks stretched in parallel straight lines as far as the eye
could see. As the American planning official Grady Clay has
noted, these rail lines (the term itself is a giveaway) became
the axis off which new cities, built on grid patterns, took
shape. The grid or gridiron pattern, combining straight lines
with ninety-degree angles, lent a characteristic machine regularity and linearity to the landscape.

Even now in looking at a city one can see a jumble of
streets, squares, circles, and complicated intersections in the
older districts. These frequently give way to neat gridirons in
those parts of the city built in later, more industrialized periods. The same is true for whole regions and countries.

Even farm land began, with mechanization, to show linear
patterns. Preindustrial farmers, plowing behind oxen, created
curvy, irregular furrows. Once the ox had started, the farmer
did not want to stop him and the beast curved wide at the
end of the furrow, forming a kind of S-curve pattern in the
land. Today anyone looking out the window of an airplane
sees squared off fields with ruler-straight plow marks.

The combination of straight lines and ninety-degree angles

was reflected not merely on the land and in the streets but in the intimate spaces experienced by most men and women—the rooms they lived in. Curved walls and non-right angles are seldom found in industrial age architecture. Neat rectangular cubicles came to replace irregularly shaped rooms, and high-rise buildings carried the straight line vertically toward the sky as well, with windows forming linear or grid patterns on the great walls facing the now straight streets.

Thus our conception of and experience of space went through a process of linearization that paralleled the linearization of time. In all industrial societies, capitalist or socialist, Eastern or Western, the specialization of architectural spaces, the detailed map, the use of uniform, precise units of measurement and, above all, the line, became a cultural constant—basic to the new indust-reality.

THE "STUFF" OF REALITY

Second Wave civilization not only built up new images of time and space and used them to shape daily behavior, it constructed its own answers to the age-old question: What are things made of? Every culture invents its own myths and metaphors in an attempt to answer this question. For some, the universe is imagined as a swirling "oneness." People are seen as a part of nature, integrally tied into the lives of their ancestors and descendants, stitched into the natural world so closely as to share in the actual "livingness" of animals, trees, rocks, and rivers. In many societies, moreover, the individual conceives of herself or himself less as a private, autonomous entity than as part of a larger organism—the family, the clan, the tribe or community.

Other societies have emphasized not the wholeness or unity of the universe but its dividedness. They have looked upon reality not as a fused entity but as a structure built up out of many individual parts.

Some two thousand years before the rise of industrialism Democritus put forward the then extraordinary idea that the universe was not a seamless whole but consisted of particles—discrete, indestructible, irreducible, invisible, unsplittable. He called these particles *atomos*. In the centuries that followed, the idea of a universe built out of irreducible blocks of matter appeared and reappeared. In China shortly after Democritus' time, in the *Mo Ching*, a "point" was apparently defined as a line that had been chopped into such short segments that it could no longer be subdivided. In India, too, the theory of the atom or irreducible unit of reality cropped up not long after the time of Christ. In ancient Rome the poet Lucretius expounded the atomist philosophy. Nevertheless, this image of matter remained a minority view, often derided or neglected.

It was not until the dawn of the Second Wave era that atomism became a dominating idea as several streams of intermingling influences converged to revolutionize our conception of matter.

In the middle of the seventeenth century a French abbé named Pierre Gassendi, an astronomer and philosopher at the Royal College in Paris, began arguing that matter must consist of ultra-small *corpuscula*. Influenced by Lucretius, Gassendi became so forceful an advocate of the atomic view of matter that his ideas soon crossed the English Channel and reached Robert Boyle, a young scientist studying the compressibility of gas. Boyle transferred the idea of atomism from speculative theory into the laboratory and concluded that even air itself was composed of tiny particles. Six years after Gassendi's death, Boyle published a treatise arguing that any substance—earth, for example—that could be broken down into simpler substances is not, and could not be, an element.

Meanwhile, René Descartes, a Jesuit-trained mathematician whom Gassendi criticized, contended that reality could only be understood by breaking it down into smaller and smaller bits. In his own words, it was necessary "to divide each of the difficulties under examination into as many parts as possible." Side by side, therefore, as the Second Wave began its surge, philosophical atomism advanced with physical atomism.

Here was a deliberate assault on the notion of oneness—an assault promptly joined by wave after wave of scientists, mathematicians, and philosophers who proceeded to break the universe into even smaller fragments, with exciting results. Once Descartes published his *Discourse on Method*, writes the microbiologist René Dubos, "innumerable discoveries immediately emerged from its application to medicine." In chemistry and other fields the combination of atomic theory and Descartes's atomic method brought startling breakthroughs. By the mid-1700's the notion that the universe consisted of independent separable parts and subparts was itself conventional wisdom—part of the emerging indust-reality.

Every new civilization plucks ideas from the past and reconfigures them in ways that help it understand itself in relationship to the world. For a budding industrial society—a society just beginning to move toward the mass production of assembled machine products composed of discrete components—the idea of an assembled universe, itself composed of discrete components, was probably indispensable.

There were political and social reasons, too, for the acceptance of the atomic model of reality. As the Second Wave crashed against the old pre-existing First Wave institutions, it needed to tear people loose from the extended family, the all-powerful church, the monarchy. Industrial capitalism needed a rationale for individualism. As the old agricultural civilization decayed, as trade expanded and towns multiplied in the century or two before the dawn of industrialism, the rising merchant classes, demanding the freedom to trade and lend and expand their markets, gave rise to a new conception of the individual—the person as atom.

The person was no longer merely a passive appendage of tribe, caste, or clan but a free, autonomous individual. Each individual had the right to own property, to acquire goods, to wheel and deal, to prosper, to starve according to his or her own active efforts, with the corresponding right to choose a religion and to pursue private happiness. In short, indust-reality gave rise to a conception of an individual who was remarkably like an atom—irreducible, indestructible, the basic particle of society.

The atomic theme even appeared, as we have seen, in politics, where the vote became the ultimate particle. It appeared in our conception of international affairs as consisting of self-contained, impenetrable, independent units called nations. Not only physical matter but social and political matter were conceived in terms of "bricks"—autonomous units or atoms. The atomic theme ran through every sphere of life.

This view of reality as composed of organized separable chunks, in turn, fitted perfectly together with the new images of time and space, themselves divisible into smaller and smaller definable units. Second Wave civilization, as it expanded and overpowered both "primitive" societies and First Wave civilization, propagated this increasingly coherent and consistent industrial view of people, politics, and society.

One final piece was missing, however, to complete the logical system.

THE ULTIMATE WHY

Unless a civilization has some explanation for why things happen—even if its explanation is nine parts mystery to one part analysis—it cannot program lives effectively. People, in carrying out the imperatives of their culture, need some reassurance that their behavior will produce results. And this implies some answer to the perennial why. Second Wave civilization came up with a theory so powerful it seemed sufficient to explain everything.

A rock smashes into the surface of a pond. Ripples swiftly radiate out across the water. Why? What causes this event? Chances are that children of industrialism would say, "because someone threw it."

An educated European gentlemen of the twelfth or thirteenth century, in attempting to answer this question, would have had ideas remarkably different from our own. He probably would have relied on Aristotle and searched for a material cause, a formal cause, an efficient cause, and a final cause, no one of which would, by itself, have been sufficient to explain anything. A medieval Chinese sage might have spoken about the yin and yang, and the force-field of influences in which all phenomena were believed to occur.

Second Wave civilization found its answer to the mysteries of causation in Newton's spectacular discovery of the universal law of gravitation. For Newton, causes were "the forces impressed upon bodies to generate motion." The conventional example of Newtonian cause and effect is the billiard balls that strike one another and move in response to one another. This notion of change, which focused exclusively on outside forces that are measurable and readily identifiable, was extremely powerful because it dovetailed perfectly with the new industrial notions of linear space and time. Indeed, Newtonian or mechanistic causation, which came to be adopted as the industrial revolution spread over Europe, pulled indust-reality together into a hermetically sealed package.

If the world consisted of separate particles—miniature billiard balls—then all causes arose from the interaction of these balls. One particle or atom struck another. The first was the *cause* of the movement of the next. That movement was the *effect* of the movement of the first. There was no action without motion in space, and no atom could be in more than one place at one time.

Suddenly a universe that had seemed complex, cluttered, unpredictable, richly crowded, mysterious, and messy, began to look neat and tidy. Every phenomenon from the atom inside a human cell to the coldest star in the distant night sky could be understood as matter in motion, each particle activating the next, forcing it to move in an endless dance of existence. For the atheist this view provided an explanation of life in which, as Laplace later put it, the hypothesis of God was unnecessary. For the religious, however, it still left room for God, since He could be regarded as the Prime Mover who used the cue stick to set the billiard balls in motion, then perhaps retired from the game.

This metaphor for reality came like a shot of intellectual adrenaline into the emerging indust-real culture. One of the radical philosophers who helped set the climate of the French Revolution, the Baron d'Holbach, exulted, "The universe, that vast assemblage of everything that exists, presents only matter and motion: the whole offers to our contemplation nothing but an immense, an uninterrupted succession of causes and effects."

It is all there—all implied in that one short, triumphant statement: the universe is an *assembled* reality, made of discrete parts put together into an "assemblage." Matter can only be understood in terms of motion—i.e., movement through *space*. Events occur in a [linear] succession, a parade of events moving down the line of *time*. Human passions like hatred, selfishness, or love, d'Holbach went on, could be compared to physical forces like repulsion, inertia, or traction, and a wise political state could manipulate them for the public good just as science could manipulate the physical world for the common good.

It is precisely from this indust-real image of the universe, from the assumptions buried within it, that some of the most potent of our personal, social, and political behavior patterns have come. Buried within them was the implication that not only the cosmos and nature but society and people behaved according to certain fixed and predictable laws. Indeed, the greatest thinkers of the Second Wave were precisely those who most logically and forcefully argued the lawfulness of the universe.

Newton seemed to have discovered the laws that pro-

grammed the heavens. Darwin had identified laws that programmed social evolution. And Freud supposedly laid bare
the laws that programmed the psyche. Others—scientists, engineers, social scientists, psychologists—pressed the search for
still more, or different, laws.

Second Wave civilization now had at its command a theory
of causality that seemed miraculous in its power and wide ap-
plicability. Much that hitherto had seemed complex could be
reduced to simple explanatory formulae. Nor were these laws
or rules to be accepted simply because Newton or Marx or
someone laid them down. They were subject to experiment
and empirical test. They could be validated. Using them, we
could build bridges, send radio waves into the sky, predict
and retrodict biological change; we could manipulate the
economy, organize political movements or machines, and
even—so they claimed—foresee and shape the behavior of
the ultimate individual.

All that was needed was to find the critical variable to explain any phenomenon. We could accomplish anything if
only we could find the appropriate "billiard ball' and hit it
from the best angle.

This new causality, combined with the new images of time,
space, and matter, liberated much of the human race from
the tyranny of ancient mumbo jumbo. It made possible triumphant achievements in science and technology, miracles of
conceptualization and practical accomplishment. It challenged
authoritarianism and liberated the mind from millennia of
imprisonment.

But indust-reality also created its own new prison, an industrial mentality that derogated or ignored what it could
not quantify, that frequently praised critical rigor and pun-
ished imagination, that reduced people to oversimplified pro-
toplasmic units, that ultimately sought an engineering solution
for any problem.

Nor was indust-reality as morally neutral as it pretended to
be. It was, as we have seen, the militant super-ideology of
Second Wave civilization, the self-justifying source from
which all the characteristic left-wing and right-wing ideologies
of the industrial age sprang. Like any culture, Second Wave
civilization produced distorting filters through which its
people came to see themselves and the universe. This package
of ideas, images, assumptions—and the analogies that flowed
from them—formed the most powerful cultural system in history.

Finally, indust-reality, the cultural face of industrialism, fitted the society it helped to construct. It helped create the society of big organizations, big cities, centralized bureaucracies, and the all-pervasive marketplace, whether capitalist or socialist. It dovetailed perfectly with the new energy systems, family systems, technological systems, economic systems, political and value systems that together formed the civilization of the Second Wave.

It is that entire civilization taken together, along with its institutions, technologies, and its culture, that is now disintegrating under an avalanche of change as the Third Wave, in its turn, surges across the planet. We live in the final, irretrievable crisis of industrialism. And as the industrial age passes into history, a new age is born.

10

CODA:
THE FLASH FLOOD

One mystery remains. Industrialism was a flash flood in history—a brief three centuries lost in the immensity of time. What caused the industrial revolution? What sent the Second Wave surging across the planet?

Many streams of change flowed together to form a great confluence. The discovery of the New World sent a pulse of energy into Europe's culture and economy on the eve of the industrial revolution. Population growth encouraged a movement into the towns. The exhaustion of Britain's timber forests prompted the use of coal. In turn, this forced the mine shafts deeper and deeper until the old horse-driven pumps could no longer clear them of water. The steam engine was perfected to solve this problem, leading to a fantastic array of new technological opportunities. The gradual dissemination of indust-real ideas challenged church and political authority. The spread of literacy, the improvement of roads and transport—all these converged in time, forcing open the floodgates of change.

Any search for The cause of the industrial revolution is doomed. For there was no single or dominant cause. Technology, by itself, is not the driving force of history. Nor, by themselves, are ideas or values. Nor is the class struggle. Nor is history merely a record of ecological shifts, demographic trends or communications inventions. Economics alone cannot explain this or any other historical event. There is no "independent variable" upon which all other variables depend. There are only interrelated variables, boundless in complexity.

Faced with this maze of causal influences, unable even to

trace all their interactions, the most we can do is focus on those that seem most revealing for our purposes and recognize the distortion implicit in that choice. In this spirit, it is clear that of all the many forces that flowed together to form Second Wave civilization, few had more traceable consequences than the widening split between producer and consumer, and the growth of that fantastic exchange network we now call the market, whether capitalist or socialist in form.

The greater the divorce of producer from consumer—in time, in space, and in social and psychic distance—the more the market, in all its astonishing complexity, with all its train of values, its implicit metaphors and hidden assumptions, came to dominate social reality.

As we have seen, this invisible wedge produced the entire modern money system with its central banking institutions, its stock exchanges, its world trade, its bureaucratic planners, its quantitative and calculating spirit, its contractual ethic, its materialist bias, its narrow measurement of success, its rigid reward systems, and its powerful accounting apparatus, whose cultural significance we routinely underestimate. From this divorce of producer from consumer came many of the pressures toward standardization, specialization, synchronization, and centralization. From it came differences in sexual role and temperament. However we evaluate the many other forces that launched the Second Wave, this splitting of the ancient atom of production $\rightleftarrows$ consumption must surely rank high among them. The shock waves of that fission are still apparent today.

Second Wave civilization did not merely alter technology, nature, and culture. It altered personality, helping to produce a new social character. Of course, women and children shaped Second Wave civilization and were shaped by it. But because men were drawn more directly into the market matrix and the new modes of work, they took on more pronounced industrial characteristics than women, and women readers will perhaps forgive the use of the term Industrial Man to sum up these new characteristics.

Industrial Man was different from all his forerunners. He was the master of "energy slaves" that amplified his puny power enormously. He spent much of his life in a factory-style environment, in touch with machines and organizations that dwarfed the individual. He learned, almost from infancy, that survival depended as never before on money. He typically grew up in a nuclear family, and went to a factory-style school. He got his basic image of the world from the mass media. He worked for a large corporation or public agency, belonged to unions, churches, and other organizations—to each of which he parceled out a piece of his divided self. He identified less and less with his village or city than with his nation. He saw himself standing in opposition to nature—exploiting it daily in his work. Yet he paradoxically rushed to visit it on weekends. (Indeed, the more he savaged nature, the more he romanticized and revered it with words.) He learned to see himself as part of vast, interdependent economic, social, and political systems whose edges faded into complexities beyond his understanding.

Faced with this reality, he rebelled without success. He fought to make a living. He learned to play the games required by society, fitted into his assigned roles, often hating them and feeling himself a victim of the very system that improved his standard of living. He sensed straight-line time bearing him remorselessly toward the future with its waiting grave. And as his wristwatch ticked off the moments, he approached death knowing that the earth and every individual on it, including himself, were merely part of a larger cosmic machine whose motions were regular and relentless.

Industrial Man occupied an environment that would have been in many respects unrecognizable to his ancestors. Even the most elementary sensory signals were different.

The Second Wave changed the soundscape, substituting the factory whistle for the rooster, the screech of tires for the chirruping of crickets. It lit up the night, extending the hours of awareness. It brought visual images no eye had ever seen before—the earth photographed from the sky, or surrealist montages in the local cinema, or biological forms revealed for the first time by high-powered microscopes. The odor of night soil gave way to the smell of gasoline and the stench of phenols. The tastes of meat and vegetables were altered. The entire perceptual landscape was transformed.

So too was the human body, which for the first time grew to what we now regard as its full normal height; successive generations grew taller than their parents. Attitudes toward the body changed as well. Norbert Elias tell us in *The Civilizing Process* that, whereas up to the sixteenth century in Germany and elsewhere in Europe, "the sight of total nakedness was an everyday rule," nakedness came to be regarded as shameful when the Second Wave spread. Bedroom behavior changed as special nightclothes came into use. Eating became technologized with the diffusion of forks and other specialized table implements. From a culture that took active pleasure in the sight of a dead animal on the table came a shift toward one in which "reminders that the meat dish has something to do with the killing of an animal are to be avoided to the utmost."

Marriage became more than an economic convenience. War was amplified and put on the assembly line. Changes in the parent-child relationship, in opportunities for upward mobility, in every aspect of human relations brought for millions a radically changed sense of self.

Faced by so many changes, psychological as well as economic, political as well as social, the brain boggles at evaluation. By what criteria do we judge an entire civilization? By the standard of living it provided for the masses who lived in it? By its influence on those who lived outside its perimeter? By its impact on the biosphere? By the excellence of its arts? By the lengthened life span of its people? By its scientific achievements? By the freedom of the individual?

Within its borders, despite massive economic depressions and a horrifying waste of human life, Second Wave civilization clearly improved the material standard of living of the ordinary person. Critics of industrialism, in describing the mass misery of the working class during the eighteenth and nineteenth centuries in Britain, often romanticize the First Wave past. They picture that rural past as warm, communal, stable, organic, and with spiritual rather than purely materialist values. Yet historical research reveals that these supposedly lovely rural communities were, in fact, cesspools of malnutrition, disease, poverty, homelessness, and tyranny, with people helpless against hunger, cold, and the whips of their landlords and masters.

Much has been made of the hideous slums that sprang up in or around the major cities, of the adulterated food, disease-bearing water supplies, the poorhouses and daily squalor. Yet, terrible as these conditions unquestionably were, they surely represented a vast improvement over the conditions most of these same people had left behind. The British author John Vaizey has noted, "The picture of bucolic yeoman England was an exaggerated one," and for significant numbers the move to the urban slum provided "in fact a dramatic rise in the standard of living, measured in terms of length of life, of a rise in the physical conditions of housing, and an improvement in the amount and variety of what they had to eat."

In terms of health, one need only read *The Age of Agony* by Guy Williams or *Death, Disease and Famine in Pre-Industrial England* by L. A. Clarkson to counteract those who glorify First Wave civilization at the expense of Second. Christina Larner, in a review of these books, states, "The work of social historians and demographers has highlighted the overwhelming presence of disease, pain and death in the open countryside as well as the noxious towns. Life expectancy was low: about 40 years in the 16th century, reduced to the mid-thirties in the epidemic-ridden 17th century, and rising to the early forties in the 18th. . . . It was rare for married couples to have long years together . . . all children were at hazard." However justly we may criticize today's crisis-ridden, misdirected health systems, it is worth recalling that before the industrial revolution official medicine was deadly, emphasizing bloodletting and surgery without anesthesia.

The major causes of death were plague, typhus, influenza, dysentery, smallpox, and tuberculosis. "It is often observed by the sages," Larner writes dryly, "that we have merely replaced these by a different set of killers, but these do leave us till a little later. Pre-industrial epidemic disease killed the young indiscriminately with the old."

Moving from health and economics to art and ideology—was industrialism, for all its narrow-minded materialism, any more mentally stultifying than the feudal societies that preceded it? Was the mechanistic mentality, or indust-reality, any less open to new ideas, even heresies, than the medieval church or the monarchies of the past? For all we detest our giant bureaucracies, are they more rigid than the Chinese bureaucracies of centuries ago, or ancient Egyptian hierarchies? And as for art, are the novels and poems and paintings of the past three hundred years in the West any less alive, profound, revealing, or complex than the works of earlier periods or different places?

The dark side, however, is also present. While Second Wave civilization did much to improve the conditions of our fathers and mothers, it also triggered violent external consequences—unanticipated side effects. Among these was the rampant, perhaps irreparable damage done to the earth's fragile biosphere. Because of its indust-real bias against nature, because of its expanding population, its brute technology, and its incessant need for expansion, it wreaked more environmental havoc than any preceding age. I have read the accounts of horse dung in the streets of preindustrial cities (usually offered as reassuring evidence that pollution is nothing new). I am aware that sewage filled the streets of ancient towns. Nevertheless, industrial society raised the problems of ecological pollution and resource use to a radically new level, making the present and past incommensurable.

Never before did any civilization create the means for literally destroying not a city but a planet. Never did whole oceans face toxification, whole species vanish overnight from the earth as a result of human greed or inadvertence; never did mines scar the earth's surface so savagely; never did hair-spray aerosols deplete the ozone layer, or thermopollution threaten the planetary climate.

Similar but even more complex is the question of imperialism. The enslavement of Indians to dig the mines of South America, the introduction of plantation farming in large parts of Africa and Asia, the deliberate distortion of colonial economies to suit the needs of the industrial nations, all left agony, hunger, disease, and deculturation in their wake. The racism exuded by Second Wave civilization, the forced integration of small-scale self-sufficient economies into the world trade system, left festering wounds that have not yet begun to heal.

However, once again it would be a mistake to glamorize these early subsistence economies. It is questionable whether the populations of even the non-industrial regions of the earth are worse off today than they were three hundred years ago. In terms of life span, food intake, infant mortality, literacy, as well as human dignity, hundreds of millions of human beings today, from the Sahel to Central America, suffer indescribable miseries. Yet it would be a disservice to them to invent a fake, romantic past in our rush to judge the present. The way into the future is not through reversion to an even more miserable past.

Just as there is no single cause that produced Second Wave civilization, so there can be no single evaluation. I have tried to present a picture of Second Wave civilization with its faults included. If I appear on the one hand to condemn it and on the other to approve, it is because simple judgments are misleading. I detest the way industrialism crushed First Wave and primitive peoples. I cannot forget the way it massified war and invented Auschwitz and unleashed the atom to incinerate Hiroshima. I am ashamed of its cultural arrogance and its depredations against the rest of the world. I am sickened by the waste of human energy, imagination, and spirit in our ghettos and barrios.

Yet unreasoning hatred for one's own time and people is hardly the best basis for creation of the future. Was industrialism an air-conditioned nightmare, a wasteland, an unmitigated horror? Was it a world of "single vision" as claimed by the enemies of science and technology? No doubt. But it was far more than that as well. It was, like life itself, a bittersweet instant in eternity.

However one chooses to evaluate the fading present, it is vital to understand that the industrial game is over, its energies spent, the force of the Second Wave diminishing everywhere as the next wave of change begins. Two changes, by themselves, make the "normal" continuation of industrial civilization no longer possible.

First, we have reached a turning point in the "war against nature." The biosphere will simply no longer tolerate the industrial assault. Second, we can no longer rely indefinitely on nonrenewable energy, until now the main subsidy of industrial development.

These facts do not mean the end of technological society, or the end of energy. But they do mean that all future technological advance will be shaped by new environmental constraints. They also mean that until new sources are substituted, the industrial nations will suffer recurrent, possibly violent withdrawal symptoms, with the struggle to substitute new forms of energy itself accelerating social and political transformation.

One thing is apparent: we are at the end—at least for some decades—of cheap energy. Second Wave civilization has lost one of its two most basic subsidies.

Simultaneously that other hidden subsidy is being withdrawn: cheap raw materials. Faced with the end of colonialism and neoimperialism, the high technology nations will either turn inward for new substitutes and resources, buying from one another and gradually lessening their economic ties with the non-industrial states, or they will continue buying from the non-industrial countries but under totally new terms of trade. In either case costs will rise substantially, and the entire resource base of the civilization will be transformed along with its energy base.

These external pressures on industrial society are matched by disintegrative pressures inside the system. Whether we focus on the family system in the United States or the telephone system in France (which is worse today than in some banana republics), or the commuter rail system in Tokyo (which is so bad that riders have stormed the stations and held rail officials hostage in protest), the story is the same: people and systems strained to the ultimate breaking point.

Second Wave systems are in crisis. Thus we find crisis in the welfare systems. Crisis in the postal systems. Crisis in the school systems. Crisis in the health-delivery systems. Crisis in the urban systems. Crisis in the international financial system. The nation-state itself is in crisis. The Second Wave value system is in crisis.

Even the role system that held industrial civilization together is in crisis. This we see most dramatically in the struggle to redefine sex roles. In the women's movement, in the demands for the legalization of homosexuality, in the spread of unisex fashions, we see a continual blurring of the traditional expectations for the sexes. Occupational role-lines are blurring, too. Nurses and patients alike are redefining their roles vis-à-vis doctors. Police and teachers are breaking out of their assigned roles and taking illegal strike action. Paralegals are redefining the role of attorney. Workers, more and more, are demanding participation, infringing on traditional management roles. And this society-wide crack-up of the role structure upon which industrialism depended is far more revolutionary in its implications than all the overtly political protests and marches by which headline writers measure change.

Finally, this convergence of pressures—the loss of key subsidies, the malfunctioning of the main life-support systems of the society, the break-up of the role structure—all produce crisis in that most elemental and fragile of structures: the personality. The collapse of Second Wave civilization has created an epidemic of personality crisis.

Today we see millions desperately searching for their own shadows, devouring movies, plays, novels, and self-help books, no matter how obscure, that promise to help them locate their missing identities. In the United States, as we shall see, the manifestations of the personality crisis are bizarre.

Its victims hurl themselves into group therapy, mysticism, or sexual games. They itch for change but are terrified by it. They urgently wish to leave their present existences and leap, somehow, to a new life—to become what they are not. They want to change jobs, spouses, roles, and responsibilities.

Even supposedly mature and complacent American businessmen are not exempt from this disaffection with the present. The American Management Association finds in a recent survey that fully 40 percent of middle managers are unhappy in their jobs, and over a third dream of an alternative career in which they feel they would be happier. Some act on their dissatisfaction. They drop out, become farmers or ski bums, they search for new life-styles, they return to school or simply chase themselves faster and faster around a shrinking circle and eventually crack under the pressure.

Rooting about in themselves for the source of their discomfort, they undergo agonies of unnecessary guilt. They seem blankly unaware that what they are feeling inside themselves is the subjective reflection of a much larger objective crisis: they are acting out an unwitting drama within a drama.

One can persist in viewing each of these various crises as an isolated event. We can ignore the connections between the energy crisis and the personality crisis, between new technologies and new sexual roles, and other such hidden interrelationships. But we do so at our peril. For what is happening is larger than any of these. Once we think in terms of successive waves of interrelated change, of the collision of these waves, we grasp the essential fact of our generation—that industrialism is dying away—and we can begin searching among signs of change for what is truly new, what is no longer industrial. We can identify the Third Wave.

It is this Third Wave of change that will frame the rest of our lives. If we are to smooth the transition between the old dying civilization and the new one that is taking form, if we are to maintain a sense of self and the ability to manage our own lives through the intensifying crises that lie ahead, we must be able to recognize—and create—Third Wave innovations.

For if we look closely around us we find, crisscrossing the manifestations of failure and collapse, early signs of growth and new potential.

If we listen closely we can hear the Third Wave already thundering on not so distant shores.

THE
THIRD
WAVE

11

THE NEW SYNTHESIS

In January 1950, just as the second half of the twentieth century opened, a gangling twenty-two-year-old with a newly minted university diploma took a long bus ride through the night into what he regarded as the central reality of our time. With his girl friend at his side and a pasteboard suitcase filled with books under the seat, he watched a gunmetal dawn come up as the factories of the American Midwest slid endlessly past the rain-swept window.

America was the heartland of the world. The region ringing the Great Lakes was the industrial heartland of America. And the factory was the throbbing core of this heart of hearts: steel mills, aluminum foundries, tool and die shops, oil refineries, auto plants, mile after mile of dingy buildings vibrating with huge machines for stamping, punching, drilling, bending, welding, forging, and casting metal. The factory was the symbol of the entire industrial era and, to a boy raised in a semi-comfortable lower-middle-class home, after four years of Plato and T. S. Eliot, of art history and abstract social theory, the world it represented was as exotic as Tashkent or Tierra del Fuego.

I spent five years in those factories, not as a clerk or personnel assistant but as an assembly hand, a millwright, a welder, a forklift driver, a punch press operator—stamping out fans, fixing machines in a foundry, building giant dust-control machines for African mines, finishing the metal on light trucks as they sped clattering and screeching past on the assembly line. I learned firsthand how factory workers struggled to earn a living in the industrial age.

127

I swallowed the dust, the sweat and smoke of the foundry. My ears were split by the hiss of steam, the clank of chains, the roar of pug mills. I felt the heat as the white-hot steel poured. Acetylene sparks left burn marks on my legs. I turned out thousands of pieces a shift on a press, repeating identical movements until my mind and muscles shrieked. I watched the managers who kept the workers in their place, white-shirted men themselves endlessly pursued and harried by higher-ups. I helped lift a sixty-five-year-old woman out of the bloody machine that had just torn four fingers off her hand, and I still hear her cries—"Jesus and Mary, I won't be able to work again!"

The factory. Long live the factory! Today, even as new factories are being built, the civilization that made the factory into a cathedral is dying. And somewhere, right now, other young men and women are driving through the night into the heart of the emergent Third Wave civilizaion. Our task from here on will be to join, as it were, their quest for tomorrow.

If we could pursue them to their destinations, where would we arrive? In the launching stations that hurl flaming vehicles and fragments of human consciousness into outer space? In oceanographic laboratories? In communal families? In teams working on artificial intelligence? In passionate religious sects? Are they living in voluntary simplicity? Are they climbing the corporate ladder? Are they running guns to terrorists? Where is the future being forged?

If we ourselves were planning a similar expedition into the future, how would we prepare our maps? It is easy to say the future begins in the present. But which present? Our present is exploding with paradox.

Our children are supersophisticated about drugs, sex, or space shots; some know far more about computers than their parents. Yet educational test scores plummet. Divorce rates continue their climb—but so do remarriage rates. Counterfeminists arise at the exact time that women win rights even the counterfeminists endorse. Gays demand their rights and come charging out of the closet—only to find Anita Bryant waiting for them.

Intractable inflation grips all the Second Wave nations, yet unemployment continues to deepen, contradicting all our classical theories. At the very same time, in defiance of the logic of supply and demand, millions are demanding not merely jobs but work that is creative, psychologically fulfilling, or socially responsible. Economic contradictions multiply.

In politics, parties lose the allegiance of their members at the precise moment when key issues—technology, for example—are becoming more politicized than ever. Meanwhile, over vast reaches of the earth, nationalist movements gain power—at the exact instant that the nation-state comes under intensifying attack in the name of globalism or planetary consciousness.

Faced with such contradictions, how might we see *behind* the trends and countertrends? No one, alas, has any magic answer to that question. Despite all the computer printouts, cluster diagrams, and mathematical models and matrices that futurist researchers use, our attempts to peer into tomorrow—or even to make sense of today—remain, as they must, more an art than a science.

Systematic research can teach us much. But in the end we must embrace—not dismiss—paradox and contradiction, hunch, imagination, and daring (though tentative) synthesis.

In probing the future in the pages that follow, therefore, we must do more than identify major trends. Difficult as it may be, we must resist the temptation to be seduced by straight lines. Most people—including many futurists—conceive of tomorrow as a mere extension of today, forgetting that trends, no matter how seemingly powerful, do not merely continue in a linear fashion. They reach tipping points at which they explode into new phenomena. They reverse direction. They stop and start. Because something is happening now, or has been happening for three hundred years, is no guarantee that it will continue. We shall, in the pages ahead, watch for precisely those contradictions, conflicts, turnabouts, and breakpoints that make the future a continuing surprise.

More important, we will search out the hidden connections among events that on the surface seem unrelated. It does little good to forecast the future of semiconductors or energy, or the future of the family (even one's own family), if the forecast springs from the premise that everything else will remain unchanged. For nothing *will* remain unchanged. The future is fluid, not frozen. It is constructed by our shifting and changing daily decisions, and each event influences all others.

Second Wave civilization placed an extremely heavy emphasis on our ability to dismantle problems into their components; it rewarded us less often for the ability to put the pieces back together again. Most people are culturally more skilled as analysts than synthesists. This is one reason why our images of the future (and of ourselves in that future) are so fragmentary, haphazard—and wrong. Our job here will be to think like generalists, not specialists.

Today I believe we stand on the edge of a new age of synthesis. In all intellectual fields, from the hard sciences to sociology, psychology, and economics—especially economics—we are likely to see a return to large-scale thinking, to general theory, to the putting of the pieces back together again. For it is beginning to dawn on us that our obsessive emphasis on quantified detail without context, on progressively finer and finer measurement of smaller and smaller problems, leaves us knowing more and more about less and less.

Our approach in what follows, therefore, will be to look for those streams of change that are shaking our lives, to reveal the underground connections among them, not simply because each of these is important in itself, but because of the way these streams of change run together to form even larger, deeper, swifter rivers of change that, in turn, flow into something still larger: the Third Wave.

Like that young man who set out in mid-century to find the heart of the present, we now begin our search for the future. This search may be the most important of our lives.

THE COMMANDING HEIGHTS

On August 8, 1960, a West Virginia–born chemical engineer named Monroe Rathbone, sitting in his office high over Rockefeller Plaza in Manhattan, made a decision that future historians might some day choose to symbolize the end of the Second Wave era.

Few paid any attention that day when Rathbone, chief executive of the giant Exxon Corporation, took steps to cut back on the taxes Exxon paid to the oil-producing countries. His decision, though ignored by the Western press, struck like a thunderbolt at the governments of these countries, since virtually all their revenues derived from oil company payments.

Within a few days the other major oil companies had followed Exxon's lead. And one month later, on September 9, in the fabled city of Baghdad, delegates of the hardest-hit countries met in emergency council. Backed to the wall, they formed themselves into a committee of oil-exporting governments. For fully thirteen years the activities of this committee, and even its name, were ignored outside the pages of a few petroleum industry journals. Until 1973, that is, when the Yom Kippur War broke out and the Organization of Petroleum Exporting Countries suddenly stepped out of the shadows. Choking off the world's supply of crude oil, it sent the entire Second Wave economy into a shuddering downspin.

What OPEC did, apart from quadrupling its oil revenues, was to accelerate a revolution that was already brewing in the Second Wave techno-sphere.

131

THE SUN AND BEYOND

In the earsplitting clamor over the energy crisis that has since followed, so many plans, proposals, arguments, and counterarguments have been hurled at us that it is difficult to make sensible choices. Governments are just as confused as the proverbial man in the street.

One way to cut through the murk is to look beyond the individual technologies and policies to the principles underlying them. Once we do, we find that certain proposals are designed to maintain or extend the Second Wave energy base as we have known it, while others rest on new principles. The result is a radical clarification of the entire energy issue.

The Second Wave energy base, we saw earlier, was premised on non-renewability; it drew from highly concentrated, exhaustible deposits; it relied on expensive, heavily centralized technologies; and it was nondiversified, resting on a relatively few sources and methods. These were the main features of the energy base in all Second Wave nations throughout the industrial era.

Bearing these in mind, if we now look at the various plans and proposals generated by the oil crisis we can quickly tell which ones are mere extensions of the old and which are forerunners of something fundamentally new. And the basic question becomes not whether oil should sell at forty dollars per barrel or whether a nuclear reactor should rise at Seabrook or Grohnde. The larger question is whether any energy base designed for industrial society and premised on these Second Wave principles can survive. Once asked in this form, the answer is inescapable.

Through the past half-century, fully two thirds of the entire world's energy supply has come from oil and gas. Most observers today, from the most fanatic conservationists to the deposed Shah of Iran, from solar freaks and Saudi sheikhs to the button-down, briefcase-carrying experts of many governments, agree that this dependency on fossil fuel cannot continue indefinitely, no matter how many new oil fields are discovered.

Statistics vary. Disputes rage over how long the world has before the ultimate crunch. The forecasting complexities are enormous and many past predictions now look silly. Yet one thing is clear: no one is pumping gas and oil *back* into the earth to replenish the supply.

Whether the end comes in some climactic gurgle or, more

likely, in a succession of dizzyingly destabilizing shortages, temporary gluts, and deeper shortages, the oil epoch is ending. Iranians know this. Kuwaitis and Nigerians and Venezuelans know it. Saudi Arabians know it—which is why they are racing to build an economy based on something other than oil revenues. Petroleum companies know it—which is why they are scrambling to diversify out of oil. (One president of a petroleum company told me at a dinner in Tokyo not long ago that, in his opinion, the oil giants would become industrial dinosaurs, as the railroads have. His time frame for this was breathtakingly short—years, not decades.)

However, the debate over physical depletion is almost beside the point. For in today's world it is price, not physical supply, that has the most immediate and significant impact. And here, if anything, the facts point even more strongly to the same conclusion.

In a matter of decades energy may once more become abundant and cheap as a result of startling technological breakthroughs or economic swings. But whatever happens, the relative price of oil is likely to continue its climb as we are forced to plumb deeper and deeper depths, to explore more remote regions, and to compete among more buyers. OPEC aside, an historic turn has taken place over the past five years: despite massive new discoveries like those in Mexico, despite skyrocketing prices, the actual amount of confirmed, commercially recoverable reserves of crude oil has shrunk, not grown—reversing a trend that had lasted for decades. Further evidence, if needed, that the petroholic era is screeching to a halt.

Meanwhile, coal, which has supplied most of the remaining third of the world energy total, is in ample supply, though it, too, is ultimately depletable. Any massive expansion of coal usage, however, entails the spread of dirty air, a possible hazard to the world's climate (through an increase of carbon dioxide in the atmosphere), and a ravaging of the earth as well. Even if all these were accepted as necessary risks over the decades to come, coal cannot fit into the tank of an automobile nor carry out many other tasks now performed by oil or gas. Plants to gasify or liquefy coal require staggering amounts of capital and water (much of it needed for agriculture) and are so ultimately inefficient and costly that they, too, must be seen as no more than expensive, diversionary, and highly temporary expedients.

Nuclear technology presents even more formidable problems at its present stage of development. Conventional reactors rely on uranium, yet another exhaustible fuel, and carry safety risks that are extremely costly to overcome—if, indeed, they ever can be. No one has convincingly solved the problems of nuclear waste disposal, and nuclear costs are so high that until now government subsidies have been essential to make atomic power remotely competitive with other sources.

Fast breeder reactors are in a class by themselves. But while often presented to the uninformed public as perpetual motion machines because the plutonium they spew out can be used as a fuel, they, too, remain ultimately dependent upon the world's small and non-renewable supply of uranium. They are not only highly centralized, incredibly costly, volatile, and dangerous, they also escalate the risks of nuclear war and terrorist capture of nuclear materials.

None of this means that we are going to be thrown back into the middle ages, or that further economic advance is impossible. But it surely means that we have reached the end of one line of development and must now start another. It means that the Second Wave energy base is unsustainable.

Indeed, there is yet another, even more fundamental reason why the world must and will shift to a radically new energy base. For any energy base, whether in a village or an industrial economy, must be suited to the society's level of technology, the nature of production, the distribution of markets and population, and many other factors.

The rise of the Second Wave energy base was associated with society's advance to a whole new stage of technological development. And while fossil fuels certainly accelerated technological growth, the exact reverse was also true. The invention of energy-thirsty, brute technology during the industrial era spurred the ever-more-rapid exploitation of those very fossil fuels. The development of the auto industry, for example, caused so radical an expansion of the oil business that at one time it was essentially a dependency of Detroit. In the words of Donald E. Carr, formerly an oil company research director, and author of *Energy and the Earth Machine*, the petroleum industry became "a slave to one form of internal combustion engine."

Today we are once more at the edge of an historic technological leap, and the new system of production now emerging will require a radical restructuring of the entire energy business—even if OPEC were to fold its tent and quietly steal away.

For the great overlooked fact is that the energy problem is not just one of quantity; it is one of structure as well. We not only need a certain *amount* of energy, but energy delivered in many more varied forms, in different (and changing) locations, at different times of the day, night, and year, and for undreamed-of purposes.

This, not simply OPEC's pricing decisions, explains why the world must search for alternatives to the old energy system. That search has been accelerated, and we are now applying vast new resources of money and imagination to the problem. As a result we are taking a close look at many startling possibilities. While the shift from one energy base to the next will no doubt be darkened by economic and other upheavals, there is another, more positive aspect to it. For never in history have so many people plunged with such fervor into a search for energy—and never have we had so many novel and exciting potentials before us.

It is clearly impossible to know at this stage which combination of technologies will prove most useful for what tasks, but the array of tools and fuels available to us will surely be staggering, with more and more exotic possibilities becoming commercially plausible as oil prices climb.

These possibilities range from photovoltaic cells that convert sunlight into electricity (a technology now being explored by Texas Instruments, Solarex, Energy Conversion Devices, and many other companies), to a Soviet plan for placing windmill-carrying balloons in the tropopause to beam electricity down to earth through cables. New York City has contracted with a private firm to burn garbage as fuel and the Philippine Islands are building plants to produce electricity from coconut waste. Italy, Iceland, and New Zealand are already generating electricity from geothermal sources, tapping the heat of the earth itself, while a five-hundred-ton floating platform off Honshu island in Japan is generating electricity from wave power. Solar heating units are sprouting from rooftops around the world, and the Southern California Edison Company is constructing a "power-tower" which will capture solar energy through computer-controlled mirrors, focus it on a tower containing a steam boiler, and generate electricity for its regular customers. In Stuttgart, Germany, a hydrogen-powered bus built by Daimler-Benz has cruised the city streets, while engineers at Lockheed-California are working on a hydrogen-powered aircraft. So many new avenues are being explored, they are impossible to catalog in a short space.

When we combine new energy-generating technologies with new ways to store and transmit energy, the possibilities become even more far-reaching. General Motors has announced a new, more efficient automobile battery for use in electric cars. NASA researchers have come up with "Redox"—a storage system they believe can be produced for one third the cost of conventional lead acid batteries. With a longer time horizon we are exploring super-conductivity and even—beyond the fringes of "respectable" science—Tesla waves as ways of beaming energy with minimal loss.

While most of these technologies are still in their early stages of development and many will no doubt prove zanily impractical, others are clearly on the edge of commercial application or will be within a decade or two. Most important is the neglected fact that big breakthroughs often come not from a single isolated technology but from imaginative juxtapositions or combinations of several. Thus we may see solar photovoltaics used to produce electricity which will, in turn, be used to release hydrogen from water so it can be used in cars. Today we are still at the pre-takeoff stage. Once we begin to combine these many new technologies, the number of more potent options will rise exponentially, and we will dramatically accelerate the construction of a Third Wave energy base.

This new base will have characteristics sharply different from those of the Second Wave period. For much of its supply will come from renewable, rather than exhaustible sources. Instead of being dependent upon highly concentrated fuels, it will draw on a variety of widely dispersed sources. Instead of depending so heavily on tightly centralized technologies, it will combine both centralized and decentralized energy production. And instead of being dangerously over-reliant on a handful of methods or sources, it will be radically diversified in form. This very diversity will make for less waste by allowing us to match the types and quality of energy produced to the increasingly varied needs.

In short, we can now see for the first time the outlines of an energy base that runs on principles almost diametrically opposed to those of the recent, three-hundred-year past. It is also clear that this Third Wave energy base will not come into being without a bitter fight.

In this war of ideas and money that is already raging in all the high-technology nations, it is possible to discern not two but three antagonists. To begin with, there are those with vested interests in the old, Second Wave energy base. They call for conventional energy sources and technologies—coal, oil, gas, nuclear power, and their various permutations. They fight, in effect, for an extension of the Second Wave status quo. And because they are entrenched in the oil companies, utilities, nuclear commissions, mining corporations, and their associated trade unions, the Second Wave forces seem unassailably in charge.

By contrast, those who favor the advance to a Third Wave energy base—a combination of consumers, environmentalists, scientists, and entrepreneurs in the leading-edge industries, along with their various allies—seem scattered, underfinanced, and often politically inept. Second Wave propagandists regularly picture them as naïve, unconcerned with dollar realities, and bedazzled by blue-sky technology.

Worse yet, the Third Wave advocates are publicly confused with a vocal fringe of what might best be termed First Wave forces—people who call not for an advance to a new, more intelligent, sustainable, and scientifically based energy system, but for a reversion to the preindustrial past. In extreme form, their policies would eliminate most technology, restrict mobility, cause cities to shrivel and die, and impose an ascetic culture in the name of conservation.

By lumping these two groups together the Second Wave lobbyists, public relations experts, and politicians deepen the public confusion and keep the Third Wave forces on the defensive.

Nevertheless, supporters of neither First nor Second Wave policies can win in the end. The former are devoted to a fantasy, and the latter are attempting to maintain an energy base whose problems are intractable—in fact, insuperable.

The relentlessly rising cost of Second Wave fuels works strongly against the Second Wave interests. The skyrocketing capital cost of Second Wave energy technologies works against them. The fact that Second Wave methods often require heavy inputs of energy to eke out relatively small increments of new "net" energy works against them. The escalating problems of pollution work against them. The nuclear risk works against them. The willingness of thousands in many countries to battle the police in order to stop nuclear reactors or strip mines or giant generating plants works against them. The tremendous rising thirst of the non-industrial world for energy of its own, and for higher prices for its resources, works against them.

In short, though nuclear reactors or coal gasification or liquefaction plants and other such technologies may *seem* to be advanced or futuristic and therefore progressive, they are, in fact, artifacts of a Second Wave past caught in its own deadly contradictions. Some may be necessary as temporary expedients, but they are essentially regressive. Similarly, though the forces of the Second Wave may *seem* powerful and their Third Wave critics feeble, it would be foolish to bet too many chips on the past. Indeed, the issue is not whether the Second Wave energy base will be overthrown, superseded by a new one, but how soon. For the struggle over energy is inextricably intertwined with another change of equal profundity: the overthrow of Second Wave technology.

TOOLS OF TOMORROW

Coal, rail, textile, steel, auto, rubber, machine tool manufacture—these were the classical industries of the Second Wave. Based on essentially simple electromechanical principles, they used high energy inputs, spat out enormous waste and pollution, and were characterized by long production runs, low skill requirements, repetitive work, standardized goods, and heavily centralized controls.

From the mid-1950's it became increasingly apparent that these industries were backward and waning in the industrial nations. In the United States, for example, while the labor force grew by 21 percent between 1965 and 1974, textile employment rose by only 6 percent and employment in iron and steel actually dropped 10 percent. A similar pattern was evident in Sweden, Czechoslovakia, Japan, and other Second Wave nations.

As these old-fashioned industries began to be transferred to so-called "developing" countries, where labor was cheaper and technology less advanced, their social influence also began to die out and a set of dynamic new industries shot up to take their place.

These new industries differed markedly from their predecessors in several respects: they were no longer primarily electromechanical and no longer based on the classic science of the Second Wave era. Instead, they rose from accelerating breakthroughs in a mix of scientific disciplines that were rudimentary or even nonexistent as recently as twenty-five years ago—quantum electronics, information theory, molecular biology, oceanics, nucleonics, ecology, and the space sciences. And they made it possible for us to reach beyond the grosser features of time and space, with which Second Wave industry concerned itself, to manipulate, as Soviet physicist B. G. Kuznetsov has noted, "very small spatial regions (say, of the radius of an atomic nucleus, i.e., 10^{-13} centimeters) and temporal intervals of the order of 10^{-23} seconds."

It is from these new sciences and our radically enhanced manipulative abilities that the new industries arose—computers and data processing, aerospace, sophisticated petrochemicals, semiconductors, advanced communications, and scores of others.

In the United States, where this shift from Second Wave to Third Wave technologies began earliest—sometime in the mid-1950's—old regions like the Merrimack Valley in New England sank into the status of depressed areas while places like Route 128 outside Boston or "Silicon Valley" in California zoomed into prominence, their suburban homes filled with specialists in solid-state physics, systems engineering, artificial intelligence, or polymer chemistry.

Moreover, one could track the transfer of jobs and affluence as they followed the transfer of technology, so that the so-called "sun-belt" states, fed by heavy defense contracts, built an advanced technological base while the older industrial regions in the Northeast and around the Great Lakes plunged into lassitude and near-bankruptcy. The long running financial crisis of New York City was a clear reflection of this technological upheaval. So, too, was the stagnation of Lorraine, France's center of steelmaking. And so, at yet another level, was the failure of British socialism. Thus, at the end of World War II the Labour government spoke of seizing the "commanding heights" of industry and did so. But the commanding heights it nationalized turned out to be coal, rail, and steel—precisely those industries being by-passed by the technological revolution: yesterday's commanding heights.

Regions or sectors of the economy based on Third Wave industries boomed; those based on Second Wave industries languished. But the changeover has hardly begun. Today many governments are consciously seeking to accelerate this structural shift while reducing the pains of transition. Japanese planners in MITI—the Ministry of International

Trade and Industry—are studying new technologies to support the service industries of the future. West German Chancellor Helmut Schmidt and his advisers speak of *strukturpolitik* and look to the European Investment Bank to facilitate the move out of traditional mass production industries.

Today, four clusters of related industries are poised for major growth and are likely to become the backbone industries of the Third Wave era, bringing with them, once more, major shifts in economic power and in social and political alignments.

Electronics and computers clearly form one such interrelated cluster. The electronics industry, a relative newcomer on the world scene, now accounts for more than $100 billion in sales per year and is expected to hit $325 billion or even $400 billion by the late 1980's. This would make it the world's fourth largest industry, after steel, auto, and chemicals. The speed with which computers have spread is so well known it hardly needs elaboration. Costs have dropped so sharply and capacity has risen so spectacularly that, according to *Computerworld* magazine, "If the auto industry had done what the computer industry has done in the last 30 years, a Rolls-Royce would cost $2.50 and get 2,000,000 miles to the gallon."

Today, cheap mini-computers are about to invade the American home. By June 1979 some one hundred companies were already manufacturing home computers. Giants like Texas Instruments were in the field, and chains like Sears and Montgomery Ward were on the edge of adding computers to their household wares. "Some day soon," chirruped a Dallas microcomputer retailer, "every home will have a computer. It will be as standard as a toilet."

Linked to banks, stores, government offices, to neighbors' homes *and* to the workplace, such computers are destined to reshape not only business, from production to retailing, but the very nature of work and, indeed, even the structure of the family.

Like the computer industry to which it is umbilically tied, the electronics industry has also been exploding, and consumers have been deluged with hand-held calculators, diode watches, and TV-screen games. These, however, provide only the palest hint of what lies in store: tiny, cheap climate and soil sensors in agriculture; infinitesimal medical devices built into ordinary clothing to monitor heartbeat or stress levels of the wearer—these and a multitude of other applications of electronics lurk just beyond the present.

The advance toward Third Wave industries, moreover, will be radically accelerated by the energy crisis, inasmuch as many of them carry us toward processes and products that are miserly in their energy requirements. Second Wave telephone systems, for example, required virtual copper mines beneath the city streets—endless miles of snaking cable, conduit, relays, and switches. We are now about to convert to fiber optic systems that use hair-thin light-carrying fibers to convey messages. The energy implications of this switchover are staggering: it takes about one thousandth the energy to manufacture optical fiber that it took to dig, smelt, and process an equivalent length of copper wire. The same ton of coal required to produce 90 miles of copper wire can turn out 80,000 miles of fiber!

The shift to solid-state physics in electronics moves in the same direction, each step forward producing components that require smaller and smaller inputs of energy. At IBM, the latest developments in L.S.I. (Large Scale Integration) technology involve components that are activated by as little as fifty microwatts.

This characteristic of the electronic revolution suggests that one of the most powerful conservation strategies for energy-starved high-technology economies may well be the rapid substitution of low-energy Third Wave industries for energy-wasting Second Wave industries.

More generally, the journal *Science* is correct when it states that "the country's economic activity may be substantially altered" by the electronics explosion. "Indeed, it is probable that reality will outstrip fiction in the rate of introduction of new and often unexpected applications of electronics."

The electronics explosion, however, is only one step in the direction of an entirely new techno-sphere.

MACHINES IN ORBIT

Much the same might be said of our ventures into outer space and the oceans, where our leap beyond the classic technologies of the Second Wave is even more striking.

The space industry forms a second cluster in the emerging

techno-sphere. Despite delays, five space shuttles may soon be moving cargo and people back and forth between the earth and outer space on a weekly schedule. The impact of this is as yet underestimated by the public, but many companies in the United States and Europe regard the "high frontier" as the source of the next revolution in high technology and are acting accordingly.

Grumman and Boeing are working on satellites and space platforms for energy generation. According to *Business Week*, "Another group of industries only now is beginning to understand what the orbiter may mean to them—manufacturers and processors whose products range from semi-conductors to medicines. . . . Many high-technology materials require delicate, controlled handling, and the force of gravity can be a nuisance. . . . In space, there is no gravity to worry about, no need for containers, and no problem with handling poisons or highly reactive substances. And there is a limitless supply of vacuum, as well as super-high and super-low temperatures."

As a result, "space manufacturing" has become a hot topic among scientists, engineers, and high-technology executives. McDonnell Douglas offers to pharmaceutical companies a space shuttle device that will separate rare enzymes from human cells. Glass manufacturers are looking at ways of making materials for lasers and fiber optics in space. Space-produced single-crystal semiconductors make earth-made models seem primitive. Urokinase, a blood clot dissolver needed for patients suffering from certain forms of blood disease, now costs $2,500 per dose. According to Jesco von Puttkamer, chief of space industrialization studies for NASA, it could be manufactured in space for less than one fifth that amount.

More important are the totally new products that simply cannot be made on earth at virtually any price. TRW, an aerospace and electronics company, has identified four hundred different alloys that we cannot manufacture on earth because of the pull of gravity. General Electric, meanwhile, has begun the design of a space furnace. Daimler-Benz and M.A.N. in West Germany are interested in the space manufacture of ball bearings, and the European Space Agency and individual companies like British Aircraft Corporation are also designing equipment and products aimed at making space useful commercially. *Business Week* tells its readers that "such prospects are not science fiction and a growing number of companies are deadly serious in pursuing them."

Equally serious, and even more zealous, are the supporters of Dr. Gerard O'Neill's plan for the creation of space cities. O'Neill, a Princeton physicist, has been indefatigably educating the public about the possibilities of building very large scale communities in space—platforms or islands with populations in the thousands—and has won enthusiastic support from NASA, the governor of California (whose state economy is heavily space dependent) and, more surprisingly, from a band of vocal ex-hippies led by Stewart Brand, creator of the *Whole Earth Catalog.*

O'Neill's idea is to build a city in space, bit by bit, out of materials mined on the moon or elsewhere in space. A colleague, Dr. Brian O'Leary, has been studying the possibilities of mining the Apollo and Amor asteroids. Regular conferences at Princeton bring together experts from NASA, General Electric, U.S. energy agencies, and other interested parties to swap technical papers on the chemical processing of lunar and other extraterrestrial minerals and on the design and construction of space habitats and closed ecological systems.

The combination of advanced electronics and a space program that moves beyond terrestrial production possibilities carries the techno-sphere to a new stage, no longer limited by Second Wave considerations.

INTO THE DEPTHS

The push into the depths of the sea provides us with a mirror image of the drive into outer space, and lays the basis for the third cluster of industries likely to form a major part of the new techno-sphere. The first historic wave of social change on earth came when our ancestors ceased to rely on foraging and hunting, and began instead to domesticate animals and cultivate the soil. We are now at precisely this stage in our relationship to the seas.

In a hungry world, the ocean can help break the back of the food problem. Properly farmed and ranched, it offers us a virtually endless supply of desperately needed protein. Present-day commercial fishing, which is highly industrialized—Japanese and Soviet factory-ships sweep the seas—

results in ruthless overkill and threatens the total extinction of many forms of marine life. By contrast, intelligent "aquaculture"—fish farming and herding, along with plant harvesting—could make a major dent in the global food crisis without damaging the fragile biosphere upon which all our lives depend.

The rush to offshore oil drilling, meanwhile, has obscured the possibility of "growing oil" in the sea. Dr. Lawrence Raymond at the Battelle Memorial Institute has demonstrated that it is possible to produce algae with a high oil content, and efforts are under way to make the process economically effective.

The oceans also offer an overwhelming array of minerals, from copper, zinc, and tin, to silver, gold, platinum and, even more important, phosphate ores from which to produce fertilizer for land-based agriculture. Mining companies are eyeing the hot waters of the Red Sea which hold an estimated $3.4 billion worth of zinc, silver, copper, lead, and gold. About 100 companies, including some of the world's largest, are now preparing to mine potato-shaped manganese nodules from the sea bed. (These nodules are a renewable resource, forming at the rate of six to ten million tons per year in a single well-identified belt just south of Hawaii.)

Today four truly international consortia are gearing up to start ocean mining on a multibillion dollar scale in the mid-1980's. One such consortium brings together twenty-three Japanese companies, a West German group called AMR, and the U.S. subsidiary of Canada's International Nickel. A second links Union Minière, the Belgian company, with United States Steel and the Sun Company. The third venture unites Canada's Noranda interests with Mitsubishi of Japan, Rio Tinto Zinc, and Consolidated Gold Fields of the United Kingdom. The last consortium ties Lockheed to the Royal Dutch/Shell group. These efforts, says the *Financial Times* of London, are expected to "revolutionise world mining activities for selected minerals."

In addition, Hoffmann-La Roche, the pharmaceutical company, has been quietly scouring the seas for new drugs, such as antifungal agents and pain-killers or diagnostic aids and drugs that stop bleeding.

As these technologies develop we are likely to witness the construction of semi- or even wholly submerged "aquavillages" and floating factories. The combination of zero real estate costs (at least at present) plus cheap energy produced on the spot from ocean sources (wind, thermal currents, or tides) can make this kind of construction competitive with that on land.

The technical journal *Marine Policy* concludes that "Ocean floating platform technology appears to be inexpensive enough and simple enough to be within the reach of most nations of the world, as well as numerous companies and private groups. At present, it seems likely that the first floating cities will be built by crowded industrial societies for the purpose of offshore housing. . . . Multinational corporations may see them as mobile terminals for trade activities, or as factory ships. Food companies may build floating cities to carry out mariculture operations. . . . Corporations seeking tax havens and adventurers seeking new lifestyles may build floating cities and declare them to be new states. Floating cities may achieve formal diplomatic recognition . . . or become a vehicle for ethnic minorities to achieve their independence."

Technological progress associated with the construction of thousands of offshore oil rigs, some anchored to the bottom but many positioned dynamically with propellers, ballast, and buoyancy controls, are developing very rapidly and laying the basis for the floating city and enormous new supporting industries.

Overall, the commercial reasons for moving into the sea are multiplying so swiftly that, according to economist D. M. Leipziger, many large corporations today, "like homesteaders in the Old West, are queuing up waiting for the starter's pistol to stake out large areas of the ocean floor." This also explains why the non-industrial countries are fighting to guarantee that the resources of the oceans become the common heritage of the human race rather than of the rich nations alone.

If we see these various developments not as independent of one another but as interlinked and self-reinforcing, each technological or scientific advance accelerating others, it becomes clear that we are no longer dealing with the same level of technology on which the Second Wave was based. We are on the way to a radically new energy system *and* a radically new technological system.

But even these examples are small in comparison with the techno-quake now rumbling in our molecular biology laboratories. Biological industry will form the fourth cluster of industries in tomorrow's economy, and may have the heaviest impact of all.*

THE GENE INDUSTRY

With information on genetics doubling every two years, with the gene mechanics working overtime, *New Scientist* magazine reports that "genetic engineering has been going through an essential tooling up phase; it is now ready to go into business." The distinguished science commentator, Lord Ritchie-Calder, explains that "Just as we have manipulated plastics and metals, we are now manufacturing living materials."

Major companies are already in hot pursuit of commercial applications of the new biology. They dream of placing enzymes in the automobile to monitor exhaust and send data on pollution to a microprocessor that will then adjust the engine. They speak of what *The New York Times* calls "metal-hungry microbes that might be used to mine valuable trace metals from ocean water." They have already demanded and won the right to patent new life forms. Eli Lilly, Hoffmann-La Roche, G. D. Searle, Upjohn, and Merck, not to mention General Electric, are all in the race.

Nervous critics, including many scientists, justifiably worry that there is a race at all. They conjure up images not of oil spills, but of "microbe spills" that could spread disease and decimate entire populations. The creation and accidental release of virulent microbes, however, is only one cause for alarm. Completely sober and respectable scientists are talking about possibilities that stagger the imagination.

Should we breed people with cowlike stomachs so they can digest grass and hay—thereby alleviating the food problem by

---

* In *Future Shock*, where I originally touched on some of these matters many years ago, I suggested that we would eventually be able to "pre-design" the human body, "grow machines," chemically program the brain, make identical carbon copies of ourselves through cloning, and create wholly new and dangerous life-forms. "Who shall control research into these fields?" I asked. "How shall the new findings be applied? Might we not unleash horrors for which man is totally unprepared?"

Some readers thought the forecast farfetched. That, however, was *before* 1973 and the discovery of the recombinant DNA process. Today the same anguished questions are being asked by citizen protesters, congressional committees, and by scientists themselves as the biological revolution gains runaway speed.

modifying us to eat lower down on the food chain? Should we biologically alter workers to fit job requirements—for example, creating pilots with faster reaction times or assembly-line workers neurologically designed to do our monotonous work for us? Should we attempt to eliminate "inferior" people and breed a "super-race"? (Hitler tried this, but without the genetic weaponry that may soon issue from our laboratories.) Should we clone soldiers to do our fighting? Should we use genetic forecasting to pre-eliminate "unfit" babies? Should we grow reserve organs for ourselves—each of us having, as it were, a "savings bank" full of spare kidneys, livers, or lungs?

Wild as these notions may sound, every one has its advocates (and adversaries) in the scientific community as well as its striking commercial applications. As two critics of genetic engineering, Jeremy Rifkin and Ted Howard, state in their book *Who Should Play God?*, "Broad scale genetic engineering will probably be introduced to America much the same way as assembly lines, automobiles, vaccines, computers and all the other technologies. As each new genetic advance becomes commercially practical, a new consumer need . . . will be exploited and a market for the new technology will be created." The potential applications are myriad.

The new biology, for example, could potentially help solve the energy problem. Scientists are now studying the idea of utilizing bacteria capable of converting sunlight into electrochemical energy. They speak of "biological solar cells." Could we breed life forms to replace nuclear power plants? And if so, might we substitute the danger of a bioactive release for the danger of radioactive release?

In the field of health, many diseases now untreatable will no doubt be cured or prevented—and new ones, perhaps worse, introduced through inadvertence or even malice. (Think what a profit-hungry company could do if it developed and secretly spread some new disease for which it alone had the cure. Even a mild, coldlike ailment could create a massive market for the appropriate, monopolistically controlled cure.)

According to the president of Cetus, a California company to which many world-famous geneticists are commercially linked, "biology will replace chemistry in importance" in the next thirty years. And in Moscow an official policy statement urges "the wider use of micro-organisms in the national economy. . . ."

Biology will reduce or eliminate the need for oil in the production of plastics, fertilizer, clothes, paint, pesticides, and thousands of other products. It will sharply alter the production of wood, wool, and other "natural" goods. Companies like United States Steel, Fiat, Hitachi, ASEA, or IBM will undoubtedly have their own biology divisions as we begin to shift, over time, from manufacture to "biofacture," giving rise to a range of products unimaginable until now. Says Theodore J. Gordon, the head of The Futures Group, "In biology, once we get started, we'll have to think about things like . . . can you make a 'tissue-compatible shirt' or a 'mammary mattress'—created out of the same stuff as the human breast."

Long before then, in agriculture, genetic engineering will be employed to increase the world food supply. The much-publicized Green Revolution of the 1960's proved, in large measure, a colossal trap for farmers in the First Wave world because it required enormous inputs of petroleum-based fertilizer that had to be bought abroad. The next bio-agricultural revolution aims at reducing that dependence on artificial fertilizer. Genetic engineering points toward high-yielding crops, crops that grow well in sandy or salty soil, crops that fight off pests. It also seeks to create entirely new foods and fibers, along with simpler, cheaper, energy-conserving methods for storing and processing foods. As though to balance off some of its awesome peril, genetic engineering once more holds out for us the possibility of ending widespread famine.

One must remain skeptical of these glowing promises. Yet if some of the advocates of genetic farming are half right, the impact on agriculture could be tremendous, ultimately altering, among other things, relations between the poor countries and the rich. The Green Revolution made the poor more, not less, dependent on the rich. The bio-agricultural revolution could do the reverse.

It is too early to say with confidence how biotechnology will develop. But it is too late to turn back to zero. We cannot undiscover what we know. We can only fight to control its application, to prevent hasty exploitation, to transnationalize it, and to minimize corporate, national, and interscientific rivalry in the entire field before it is too late.

One thing is immutably clear: we are no longer locked into the three-hundred-year-old electromechanical frame of traditional Second Wave technology, and can only begin to glimpse the full significance of this historic fact.

Just as the Second Wave combined coal, steel, electricity, and rail transport to produce automobiles and a thousand other life-transforming products, the real impact of the new changes will not be felt until we reach the stage of combining the new technologies—linking together computers, electronics, new materials from outer space and the oceans, with genetics, and all of these, in turn, with the new energy base. Bringing these elements together will release a flood of innovation unlike any seen before in human history. We are constructing a dramatically new techno-sphere for a Third Wave civilization.

THE TECHNO-REBELS

The magnitude of such an advance—its importance for the future of evolution itself—makes it critically necessary that we begin to guide it. To adopt a hands-off, damn-the-torpedoes approach could spell doom for ourselves and our children. For the power, scale, and speed of the change is like nothing before in history, and our minds are still fresh with news of the near-catastrophe at Three Mile Island, the tragic DC-10 crashes, the hard-to-plug massive oil spill off the Mexican coast, and a hundred other technological horrors. Faced with such disasters, can we permit the development and combination of tomorrow's even more powerful technologies to be controlled by the same shortsighted and selfish criteria used during the Second Wave era?

The basic questions asked of new technologies during the past three hundred years, in both capitalist and socialist nations, have been simple: do they contribute to economic gain or military clout? These twin criteria are clearly no longer adequate. New technologies will have to pass far stiffer tests—ecological and social as well as economic and strategic.

When we look closely at what a report to the U.S. National Science Foundation has called "technology and social shock"—a catalog of technological calamities in recent years—we discover that most of them are associated with Second Wave, not Third Wave technologies. The reason is obvious: Third Wave technologies have not yet been deployed on a grand scale. Many are still in their infancy. Nevertheless, we can already glimpse the dangers of electronic smog, information pollution, combat in outer space, genetic leakage, climatic intervention, and what might be called "ecological warfare"—the deliberate induction of earthquakes, for example, by triggering vibrations from a distance. Beyond this lies a host of other perils associated with the advance to a new technological base.

Under these circumstances it is no surprise that recent years have seen massive, almost indiscriminate, public resistance to new technology. The early period of the Second Wave also saw attempts to block new technology. As early as 1663, London workers tore down the new mechanical saw-mills that threatened their livelihood. In 1676 ribbon workers smashed their machines. In 1710 rioters protested the newly introduced stocking frames. Later, John Kay, inventor of the flying shuttle used in the textile mills, saw his home wrecked by an infuriated mob and ultimately fled England alto-gether. The most publicized example came in 1811 when machine wreckers calling themselves Luddites destroyed their textile machines in Nottingham.

Yet this early antagonism to the machine was sporadic and spontaneous. As one historian notes, many of the cases "were not so much the result of hostility to the machine itself as a method of coercing an obnoxious employer." Unlettered workingmen and women, poor, hungry, and desperate, saw in the machine a threat to their individual survival.

Today's rebellion against runaway technology is different. It involves a fast-growing army of people—by no means poor or unlettered—who are not necessarily anti-technological, or opposed to economic growth, but who see in the uncontrolled technological thrust a threat to themselves and to global sur-vival.

Some fanatics among them, given the chance, might well employ Luddite tactics. It doesn't take much to imagine the bombing of a computer installation or a genetic laboratory or a partially constructed nuclear reactor. One can even more easily picture some particularly hideous technological disaster triggering a witch-hunt for the white-coated scientists who "caused it all." Some demagogic politician of the future may well rise to fame by investigating the "Cambridge Ten" or the "Oak Ridge Seven."

However, most of today's techno-rebels are neither bomb-throwers nor Luddites. They include thousands of people who are themselves scientifically trained—nuclear engineers, bio-chemists, physicians, public health officials, and geneticists as well as millions of ordinary citizens. Again, unlike the Lud-dites, they are well organized and articulate. They publish their own technical journals and propaganda. They file lawsuits and draft legislation, as well as picket, march, and demonstrate.

This movement, often attacked as reactionary, is actually a vital part of the emerging Third Wave. For its members are the leading edge of the future in a three-way political and economic battle that parallels, in the field of technology, the struggle over energy that we have described earlier.

Here, too, we see Second Wave forces on one side, First Wave reversionists on the other, and Third Wave forces struggling against both. Here the Second Wave forces are those who favor the old, mindless approach to technology: "If it works, produce it. If it sells, produce it. If it makes us strong, build it." Imbued with obsolete, indust-real notions of progress, many of these adherents of the Second Wave past have vested interests in the irresponsible application of technology. They shrug off the dangers.

On the other side, we find once more a small, vocal fringe of romantic extremists hostile to all but the most primitive First Wave technologies, who seem to favor a return to medieval crafts and hand labor. Mostly middle-class, speaking from the vantage point of a full belly, their resistance to technological advance is as blindly indiscriminate as the support of technology by Second Wave people. They fantasize about a return to a world that most of us—and most of them—would find abhorrent.

Ranged against both these extremes is an increasing number of people in every country who form the core of the techno-rebellion. They are, without knowing it, agents of the Third Wave. They begin not with technology but with hard questions about what kind of future society we want. They recognize that we now have so many technological opportunities we can no longer fund, develop, and apply them all. They argue, therefore, the need to select more carefully among them and to choose those technologies that serve long-range social and ecological goals. Rather than letting technology shape our goals, they wish to assert social control over the larger directions of the technological thrust.

The techno-rebels have not as yet formulated a clear, comprehensive program. But if we extrapolate from their numerous manifestos, petitions, statements, and studies, we can identify several streams of thought that add up to a new way of looking at technology—a positive policy for managing the transition to a Third Wave future.

The techno-rebels start from the premise that the earth's biosphere is fragile, and that the more powerful our new technologies become, the higher the risk of doing irreversible damage to the planet. Thus they demand that all new technologies be prescreened for possible adverse effects, that dangerous ones be redesigned or actually blocked—in short, that tomorrow's technologies be subjected to tighter ecological constraints than those of the Second Wave era.

The techno-rebels argue that either we control technology or it controls us—and that "we" can no longer simply be the usual tiny elite of scientists, engineers, politicians, and businessmen. Whatever the merits of the antinuclear campaigns that have erupted in West Germany, France, Sweden, Japan, and the United States, the battle against Concorde, or the rising demands for regulation of genetic research, all reflect a widespread passionate demand for the democratization of technological decision-making.

The techno-rebels contend that technology need not be big, costly, or complex in order to be "sophisticated." The heavy-handed technologies of the Second Wave seemed more efficient than they actually were because corporations and socialist enterprises externalized—transferred to society as a whole—the enormous costs of cleaning up pollution, of caring for the unemployed, or dealing with work-alienation. When these are seen as costs of production, many seemingly efficient machines turn out to be quite the opposite.

Thus the techno-rebels favor the design of a whole range of "appropriate technologies" intended to provide humane jobs, to avoid pollution, to spare the environment, and to produce for personal or local use rather than for national and global markets alone. The techno-rebellion has sparked thousands of experiments all over the world, with just such small-scale technologies, in fields ranging from fish farming and food processing to energy production, waste recycling, cheap construction, and simple transport.

While many of these experiments are naïve and hark back to a mythical past, others are more practical. Some reach out for the latest materials and scientific tools and combine them in new ways with old techniques. Jean Gimpel, for example, the historian of medieval technology, has built elegant models of simple tools that might prove useful in non-industrial countries. Some of these combine new materials with old methods. A surge of interest in the airship provides another example—use of a by-passed technology that can now be made with advanced fabrics or materials that give it much greater payload capacity. Airships are ecologically sound and could be used for slow but cheap and safe transport in regions where there are no roads—Brazil, perhaps, or Nigeria. Experiments with appropriate or alternative technologies, especially in the energy field, suggest that some simple, small-scale technologies can be as "sophisticated" as complex, large-scale technologies when the full range of side effects is taken into account and when the machine is properly matched to the task.

The techno-rebels are also disturbed by the radical imbalance of science and technology on the face of the planet, with only 3 percent of the world's scientists in countries containing 75 percent of the global population. They favor devoting more technological attention to the needs of the world's poor, and a more equitable sharing of the resources of outer space and the oceans. They recognize that not only are the oceans and skies part of the common heritage of the race, but that advanced technology itself could not exist without the historic contributions of many peoples, from the Indians and Arabs to the ancient Chinese.

Finally, they argue that in moving into the Third Wave we must advance, step by step, from the resource-wasteful, pollution-producing system of production used during the Second Wave era toward a more "metabolic" system that eliminates waste and pollution by making sure that the output and by-product of each industry becomes an input for the next. The goal is a system under which no output is produced that is not an input for another production process downstream. Such a system is not only more efficient in a production sense, it minimizes, or indeed eliminates, damage to the biosphere.

Taken as a whole, this techno-rebel program provides the basis for humanizing the technological thrust.

The techno-rebels are, whether they recognize it or not, agents of the Third Wave. They will not vanish but multiply in the years ahead. For they are as much a part of the advance to a new stage of civilization as our missions to Venus, our amazing computers, our biological discoveries, or our explorations of the oceanic depths.

Out of their conflict with the First Wave fantasizers and the Second Wave advocates of technology *über alles* will come sensible technologies matched to the new, sustainable energy system toward which we are beginning to reach. Plugging the new technologies into this new energy base will raise to a wholly new level our entire civilization. At its heart we will find a fusion of sophisticated, science-based "high stream" industries, operating within much tightened ecological and social controls, with equally sophisticated, "low-stream" industries that operate on a smaller, more human scale, both based on principles radically different from those which governed the Second Wave techno-sphere. Together, these two layers of industry will form tomorrow's "commanding heights."

But this is only a detail of a much vaster picture. For at the same time that we are transforming the techno-sphere we are also revolutionizing the info-sphere.

DE-MASSIFYING
THE MEDIA

The espionage agent is one of the most powerful metaphors of our time. No other figure has so successfully captured the contemporary imagination. Films by the hundred glorify 007 and his brash fictional counterparts. Television and paperbacks churn out endless images of the spy as daring, romantic, amoral, larger (or smaller) than life. Governments, meanwhile, spend billions on espionage. Agents of the KGB, the CIA, and a score of other intelligence agencies trip over one another from Berlin to Beirut, from Macao to Mexico City.

In Moscow, western correspondents are accused of spying. In Bonn, chancellors fall because spies infest their ministries. In Washington, congressional investigators simultaneously expose the misdeeds of secret agents, American and Korean, while above, the sky itself is filled with spy satellites apparently photographing every inch of the earth.

The spy is hardly new to history. It is worth asking, therefore, why at this particular moment the theme of espionage has come to dominate the popular imagination, throwing even private eyes, cops, and cowboys into the shadow. When we do ask, we immediately notice one important difference between the spy and these other culture heroes: While fictional policemen and cowboys rely on mere pistols or their bare fists, the fictional spy comes equipped with the latest, most exotic technology—electronic bugs, banks of computers, infrared cameras, cars that fly or swim, helicopters, one-man submarines, death rays, and the like.

There is, however, a deeper reason for the rise of the spy.

155

Cowboys, cops, private eyes, adventurers, and explorers—the traditional heroes of print and celluloid—typically pursue the tangible: they want land for cattle, they want money, they want to capture the crook or gain the girl. Not so the spy.

For the spy's basic business is information—and information has become perhaps the world's fastest growing and most important business. The spy is a living symbol of the revolution now sweeping the info-sphere.

A WAREHOUSE OF IMAGES

An information bomb is exploding in our midst, showering us with a shrapnel of images and drastically changing the way each of us perceives and acts upon our private world. In shifting from a Second Wave to a Third Wave info-sphere, we are transforming our own psyches.

Each of us creates in his skull a mind-model of reality—a warehouse of images. Some of these are visual, others auditory, even tactile. Some are only "percepts"—traces of information about our environment, like a glimpse of blue sky seen from the corner of the eye. Others are "linkages" that define relationships, like the two words "mother" and "child." Some are simple, others complex and conceptual, like the idea that "inflation is caused by rising wages." Together such images add up to our picture of the world—locating us in time, space, and the network of personal relationships around us.

These images do not spring from nowhere. They are formed, in ways we do not understand, out of the signals or information reaching us from the environment. And as our environment convulses with change—as our jobs, homes, churches, schools, and political arrangements feel the impact of the Third Wave—the sea of information around us also changes.

Before the advent of mass media, a First Wave child growing up in a slowly changing village built his or her model of reality out of images received from a tiny handful of sources—the teacher, the priest, the chief or official and, above all, the family. As psychologist-futurist Herbert Gerjuoy has noted: "There was no television or radio in the home to give the child a chance to meet many different kinds of strangers from many different walks of life and even from different countries. . . . Very few people ever saw a foreign city. . . . The result [was that] people had only a small number of different people to imitate or model themselves after.

"Their choices were even more limited by the fact that the people they could model themselves after were themselves all of limited experience with other people." The images of the world built up by the village child, therefore, were extremely narrow in range.

The messages he or she received, moreover, were highly redundant in at least two senses: they came, usually, in the form of casual speech, which is normally filled with pauses and repetitions, and they came in the form of connected "strings" of ideas reinforced by various information givers. The child heard the same "thou shalt nots" in church and in school. Both reinforced the messages sent out by the family and the state. Consensus in the community, and strong pressures for conformity, acted on the child from birth to narrow still further the range of acceptable imagery and behavior.

The Second Wave multiplied the number of channels from which the individual drew his or her picture of reality. The child no longer received imagery from nature or people alone but from newspapers, mass magazines, radio and, later on, from television. For the most part, church, state, home, and school continued to speak in unison, reinforcing one another. But now the mass media themselves became a giant loudspeaker. And their power was used across regional, ethnic, tribal, and linguistic lines to standardize the images flowing in society's mind-stream.

Certain visual images, for example, were so widely massdistributed and were implanted in so many millions of private memories that they were transformed, in effect, into icons. The image of Lenin, jaw thrust out in triumph under a swirling red flag, thus became as iconic for millions of people as the image of Jesus on the cross. The image of Charlie Chaplin with derby and cane, or Hitler raging at Nuremberg, the image of bodies stacked like cords of wood at Buchenwald, of Churchill making the V sign or Roosevelt wearing a black cape, of Marilyn Monroe's skirt blown by the wind, of hundreds of media stars and thousands of different, universally recognizable commercial products—the bar of Ivory soap in the United States, the Morinaga chocolate in Japan, the bottle of Perrier in France—all became standard parts of a universal image-file.

This centrally produced imagery, injected into the "mass mind" by the mass media, helped produce the standardization of behavior required by the industrial production system.

Today the Third Wave is drastically altering all this. As change accelerates in society it forces a parallel acceleration within us. New information reaches us and we are forced to revise our image-file continuously at a faster and faster rate. Older images based on past reality must be replaced, for, unless we update them, our actions become divorced from reality and we become progressively less competent. We find it impossible to cope.

This speedup of image processing inside us means that images grow more and more temporary. Throwaway art, one-shot sitcoms, Polaroid snapshots, Xerox copies, and disposable graphics pop up and vanish. Ideas, beliefs, and attitudes skyrocket into consciousness, are challenged, defied, and suddenly fade into nowhere-ness. Scientific and psychological theories are overthrown and superseded daily. Ideologies crack. Celebrities pirouette fleetingly across our awareness. Contradictory political and moral slogans assail us.

It is difficult to make sense of this swirling phantasmagoria, to understand exactly how the image-manufacturing process is changing. For the Third Wave does more than simply accelerate our information flows; it transforms the deep structure of information on which our daily actions depend.

THE DE-MASSIFIED MEDIA

Throughout the Second Wave era the mass media grew more and more powerful. Today a startling change is taking place. As the Third Wave thunders in, the mass media, far from expanding their influence, are suddenly being forced to share it. They are being beaten back on many fronts at once by what I call the "de-massified media."

Newspapers provide the first example. The oldest of the Second Wave mass media, newspapers are losing their readers. By 1973 U.S. newspapers had reached a combined aggregate circulation of 63 million copies daily. Since 1973, however, instead of adding circulation, they have begun to lose it. By 1978 the total had declined to 62 million and worse was in store. The percentage of Americans who read a paper every day also fell, from 69 percent in 1972 to 62 percent in 1977, and some of the nation's most important papers were the hardest hit. In New York, between 1970 and 1976, the three major dailies combined lost 550,000 readers. The *Los Angeles Times*, having peaked in 1973, went on to lose 80,000 readers by 1976. The two big Philadelphia papers dropped 150,000 readers, the two big Cleveland papers 90,000 and the two San Francisco papers more than 80,000. While numerous smaller papers cropped up in many parts of the country, major U.S. dailies like the *Cleveland News*, the *Hartford Times*, the *Detroit Times*, *Chicago Today*, or the *Long Island Press* all fell by the wayside. A similar pattern appeared in Britain where, between 1965 and 1975, the national dailies lost fully 8 percent of their circulation.

Nor were such losses due merely to the rise of television. Each of today's mass-circulation dailies now faces increasing competition from a burgeoning flock of mini-circulation weeklies, biweeklies, and so-called "shoppers" that serve not the metropolitan mass market but specific neighborhoods and communities within it, providing far more localized advertising and news. Having reached saturation, the big-city mass-circulation daily is in deep trouble. De-massified media are snapping at its heels.*

Mass magazines offer a second example. From the mid-1950's on, hardly a year has passed without the death in the United States of a major magazine. *Life, Look,* the *Saturday Evening Post*—each went to its grave, later to undergo resurrection as a small-circulation ghost of its former self.

Between 1970 and 1977, despite a 14 million rise in U.S. population, the combined aggregate circulation of the remaining top twenty-five magazines dropped by 4 million.

Simultaneously, the United States experienced a population explosion of mini-magazines—thousands of brand new magazines aimed at small, special-interest, regional, or even local markets. Pilots and aviation buffs today can choose among literally scores of periodicals edited just for them. Teen-agers,

---

* Some publishers do not consider newspapers to be mass media because many have small circulations and serve small communities. But most papers, at least in the United States, are filled with nationally produced "boilerplate"—news from the AP and UPI wires, comic strips, crosswords, fashions, feature articles—which are largely the same from one city to the next. To compete with the smaller, more localized media the larger papers are increasing local coverage and adding a variety of special-interest sections. The surviving dailies of the 1980's and 1990's will be drastically changed by the segmentation of the reading public.

scuba divers, retired people, women athletes, collectors of antique cameras, tennis nuts, skiers, and skateboarders each have their own press. Regional magazines like *New York, New West, D* in Dallas, or *Pittsburgher,* are all multiplying. Some slice the market up even more finely by both region and special interest—the *Kentucky Business Ledger,* for example, or *Western Farmer.*

With new, fast, cheap short-run printing presses, every organization, community group, political or religious cult and cultlet today can afford to print its own publication. Even smaller groups churn our periodicals on the copying machines that have become ubiquitous in American offices. The mass magazine has lost its once powerful influence in national life. The de-massified magazine—the mini-magazine—is rapidly taking its place.

But the impact of the Third Wave in communications is not confined to the print media. Between 1950 and 1970 the number of radio stations in the United States climbed from 2,336, to 5,359. In a period when population rose only 35 percent, radio stations increased by 129 percent. This means that instead of one station for every 65,000 Americans, there is now one for every 38,000, and it means the average listener has more programs to choose from. The mass audience is cut up among more stations.

The diversity of offerings has also sharply increased, with different stations appealing to specialized audience segments instead of to the hitherto undifferentiated mass audience. All-news stations aim at educated middle-class adults. Hard rock, soft rock, punk rock, country rock, and folk rock stations each aim at a different sector of the youth audience. Soul music stations aim at Black Americans. Classical music stations cater to upper-income adults, foreign language stations to different ethnic groups, from the Portuguese in New England to Italians, Hispanics, Japanese, and Jews. Writes political columnist Richard Reeves, "In Newport, R.I., I checked the AM radio dial and found 38 stations, three of them religious, two programmed for blacks and one broadcasting in Portuguese."

Relentlessly, newer forms of audio communication chip away at what remains of the mass audience. During the 1960's tiny, cheap tape recorders and cassette players spread like prairie fire among the young. Despite popular misconceptions to the contrary, today's teen-agers spend *less,* not more, time with their ears glued to the radio than was the case in the sixties. From an average of 4.8 hours a day in 1967, the amount of radio listening time plummeted to 2.8 hours in 1977.

Then came citizens band radio. Unlike broadcast radio, which is strictly one-way (the listener cannot talk back to the programmer), CB radios in cars make it possible for drivers within a five- to fifteen-mile radius to communicate with each other.

Between 1959 and 1974, only one million CB sets came into use in America. Then, in the words of an astounded official of the Federal Communications Commission, "It took eight months [for us] to get the second million and three months to get the third." CB blasted off. By 1977 some 25 million CB sets were in use, and the airwaves were filled with colorful chatter—from warnings that "smokies" (police) were setting speed traps, to prayers and prostitutes' solicitations. The fad is now over, but its effects are not.

Radio broadcasters, nervous about their advertising revenues, vigorously deny that CB has cut into radio listenership. But the ad agencies are not so sure. One of them, Marsteller, Inc., conducted a survey in New York and found that 45 percent of CB users report a 10 to 15 percent drop in listening to their regular car radios. More significantly, the survey found that over half the CB users listened to both their car radios *and* their CBs simultaneously.

In any case, the shift toward diversity in print is paralleled in radio. The soundscape is being de-massified along with the printscape.

Not until 1977, however, did the Second Wave media suffer their most startling and significant defeat. For a generation the most powerful and the most "massifying" of the media has, of course, been television. In 1977 the picture tube began to flicker. Wrote *Time* magazine, "All fall, broadcast and ad executives nervously peeked at the figures . . . they could not believe what they were seeing. . . . For the first time in history, television viewing declined."

"Nobody," mumbled one astonished ad man, "*ever* assumed that viewership would go down."

Even now explanations abound. We are told the shows are even more miserable than in the past. That there is too much of this and not enough of that. Executive heads have rolled down the network corridors. We have been promised this or that new type of show. But the deeper truth is only beginning to emerge from the clouds of tele-hype. The day of the all-powerful centralized network that controls image production is waning. Indeed, a former president of NBC, charging the three main U.S. television networks with strategic "stupidity," has predicted their share of the prime-time viewing public would drop to 50 percent by the late 1980's. For the Third Wave communications media are subverting the dominance of the Second Wave media lords on a broad front.

Cable television today already reaches into 14.5 million American homes and is likely to spread with hurricane force in the early 1980's. Industry experts expect 20 to 26 million cable subscribers by the end of 1981, with cabling available to fully 50 percent of U.S. households. Things will move even faster once the shift is made from copper wires to cheap fiber optic systems that send light pulsing through hair-thin fibers. And like short-run printing presses or Xerox copiers, cable de-massifies the audience, carving it into multiple mini-publics. Moreover, cable systems can be designed for two-way communication so that subscribers may not merely watch programs but actively call various services.

In Japan, by the early 1980's entire towns will be linked to light-wave cable, enabling users to dial requests not only for programs but for still photographs, data, theater reservations, or displays of newspaper and magazine material. Burglar and fire alarms will work through the same system.

In Ikoma, a bedroom suburb of Osaka, I was interviewed on a TV show on the experimental Hi-Ovis system, which places a microphone and television camera on top of the TV set in the home of every subscriber, so that viewers can become senders as well. As I was being interviewed by the program host, a Mrs. Sakamoto, viewing the program from her own living room, switched in and began chatting with us in broken English. I and the viewing public saw her on the screen and watched her little boy romping around the room as she welcomed me to Ikoma.

Hi-Ovis also keeps a bank of video cassettes on everything from music to cooking to education. Viewers can punch in a code number and request the computer to play a particular cassette for them on their screen at whatever hour they wish to see it.

Though it involves only about 160 homes, the Hi-Ovis experiment is backed by the Japanese government and contributions from such corporations as Fujitsu, Sumitomo Electric, Matsushita, and Kintetsu. It is extremely advanced and already based on fiber optics technology.

In Columbus, Ohio, a week earlier, I had visited Warner Cable Corporation's Qube system. Qube provides the subscriber with thirty TV channels (as against four regular broadcast stations) and presents specialized shows for everyone from preschoolers to doctors, lawyers, or the "adults only" audience. Qube is the most well-developed, commercially effective two-way cable system in the world. Providing each subscriber with what looks like a hand-held calculator, it permits him or her to communicate with the station by push button. A viewer using the so-called "hot buttons" can communicate with the Qube studio and its computer. *Time*, in describing the system, waxes positively rhapsodic, noting that the subscriber can "voice his opinions in local political debates, conduct garage sales and bid for *objets d'art* in a charity auction. . . . By pressing a button, Joe or Jane Columbus can quiz a politician, or turn electronic thumbs down or up on a local amateur talent program." Consumers can "comparison-shop the local supermarkets" or book a table at an Oriental restaurant.

Cable, however, is not the only worry facing the networks.

Video games have become a "hot item" in the stores. Millions of Americans have discovered a passion for gadgets that convert a TV screen into a Ping-Pong table, hockey rink, or tennis court. This development may seem trivial or irrelevant to orthodox political or social analysts. Yet it represents a wave of social learning, a premonitory training, as it were, for life in the electronic environment of tomorrow. Not only do video games further de-massify the audience and cut into the numbers who are watching the programs broadcast at any given moment, but through such seemingly innocent devices millions of people are learning to play with the television set, to talk back to it, and to interact with it. In the process they are changing from passive receivers to message senders as well. They are manipulating the set rather than merely letting the set manipulate them.

Information services, fed through the TV screen, are now already available in Britain where a viewer with an adapter unit can push a button and select which of a dozen or so different data services he or she wants—news, weather, financial, sports, and so forth. This data then moves across the TV screen as though on ticker tape. Before long users will no doubt be able to plug a hard-copier into the TV to capture on paper any images they wish to retain. Once again there is wide choice where little existed before.

Video cassette players and recorders are spreading rapidly as well. Marketers expect to see a million units in use in the United States by 1981. These not only allow viewers to tape Monday's football match for replay on, say, Saturday (thus demolishing the synchronization of imagery that the networks promote), but lay the basis for the sale of films and sports events on tape. (The Arabs are not asleep at the proverbial switch: the movie *The Messenger*, about the life of Muhammad, is available in boxed cassettes with gilt Arabic lettering on the outside.) Video recorders and players also make possible the sale of highly specialized cartridges containing, for example, medical instructional material for hospital staff, or tapes that show consumers how to assemble knockdown furniture or rewire a toaster. More fundamentally, video recorders make it possible for any *consumer* to become, in addition, a *producer* of his or her own imagery. Once again the audience is de-massified.

Domestic satellites, finally, make it possible for individual television stations to form temporary mini-networks for specialized programming by bouncing signals from anywhere to anywhere else at minimal cost, thus end-running the existing networks. By the end of 1980 cable-TV operators will have one thousand earth stations in place to pick up satellite signals. "At that point," says *Television/Radio Age*, "a program distributor need only buy time on a satellite, presto, he has a nationwide cable TV network . . . he can selectively feed any group of systems he chooses." The satellite, declares William J. Donnelly, vice-president for electronic media at the giant Young & Rubicam advertising agency, "means smaller audiences and a greater multiplicity of nationally distributed programs."

All these different developments have one thing in common: they slice the mass television public into segments, and each slice not only increases our cultural diversity, it cuts deeply into the power of the networks that have until now so completely dominated our imagery. John O'Connor, the perceptive critic of *The New York Times*, sums it up simply. "One thing is certain," he writes. "Commercial television will no longer be able to dictate either what is watched or when it is watched."

What appears on the surface to be a set of unrelated events turns out to be a wave of closely interrelated changes sweeping across the media horizon from newspapers and radio at one end to magazines and television at the other. The mass media are under attack. New, de-massified media are proliferating, challenging—and sometimes even replacing—the mass media that were so dominant in all Second Wave societies.

The Third Wave thus begins a truly new era—the age of the de-massified media. A new info-sphere is emerging alongside the new techno-sphere. And this will have a far-reaching impact on the most important sphere of all, the one inside our skulls. For taken together, these changes revolutionize our images of the world and our ability to make sense of it.

BLIP CULTURE

The de-massification of the media de-massifies our minds as well. During the Second Wave era the continual pounding of standardized imagery pumped out by the media created what critics called a "mass mind." Today, instead of masses of people all receiving the same messages, smaller de-massified groups receive and send large amounts of their own imagery to one another. As the entire society shifts toward Third Wave diversity, the new media reflect and accelerate the process.

This, in part, explains why opinions on everything from pop music to politics are becoming less uniform. Consensus shatters. On a personal level, we are all besieged and blitzed by fragments of imagery, contradictory or unrelated, that shake up our old ideas and come shooting at us in the form of broken or disembodied "blips." We live, in fact, in a "blip culture."

"Fiction increasingly stakes out smaller and smaller chunks of territory," complains critic Geoffrey Wolff, adding that each novelist "apprehends less and less of any big picture." In nonfiction, writes Daniel Laskin, reviewing such phenomenally popular reference works as *The People's Almanac* and *The Book of Lists*, "The idea of any exhaustive synthesis seems untenable. The alternative is to collect the world at random, especially its more amusing shards." But the breakup of our images into blips is hardly confined to books or literature. It is even more pronounced in the press and the electronic media.

In this new kind of culture, with its fractured, transitory images, we can begin to discern a widening split between Second Wave and Third Wave media users.

Second Wave people, yearning for the ready-to-wear moral

and ideological certainties of the past, are annoyed and disoriented by the information blitz. They are nostalgic for radio programs of the 1930's or movies of the 1940's. They feel cut off from the new media environment, not merely because much of what they hear is threatening or upsetting, but because the very packages in which information arrives are unfamiliar.

Instead of receiving long, related "strings" of ideas, organized or synthesized for us, we are increasingly exposed to short, modular blips of information—ads, commands, theories, shreds of news, truncated bits and blobs that refuse to fit neatly into our pre-existing mental files. The new imagery resists classification, partly because it often falls outside our old conceptual categories, but also because it comes in packages that are too oddly shaped, transient, and disconnected. Assailed by what they perceive as the bedlam of blip culture, Second Wave people feel a suppressed rage at the media.

Third Wave people, by contrast, are more at ease in the midst of this bombardment of blips—the ninety-second newsclip intercut with a thirty-second commercial, a fragment of song and lyric, a headline, a cartoon, a collage, a newsletter item, a computer printout. Insatiable readers of disposable paperbacks and special-interest magazines, they gulp huge amounts of information in short takes. But they also keep an eye out for those new concepts or metaphors that sum up or organize blips into larger wholes. Rather than trying to stuff the new modular data into the standard Second Wave categories or frameworks, they learn to make their own, to form their own "strings" out of the blipped material shot at them by the new media.

Instead of merely receiving our mental model of reality, we are now compelled to invent it and continually reinvent it. This places an enormous burden on us. But it also leads toward greater individuality, a de-massification of personality as well as culture. Some of us crack under the new pressure or withdraw into apathy or anger. Others emerge as well formed, continually growing, competent individuals able to operate, as it were, on a higher level. (In either case, whether the strain proves too great or not, the result is a far cry from the uniform, standardized, easily regimented robots foreseen by so many sociologists and science fiction writers of the Second Wave era.)

Above all this, the de-massification of the civilization, which the media both reflects and intensifies, brings with it an enormous jump in the amount of information we all exchange with one another. And it is this increase that explains why we are becoming an "information society."

For the more diverse the civilization—the more differentiated its technology, energy forms, and people—the more information must flow between its constituent parts if the entirety is to hold together, particularly under the stress of high change. An organization, for example, must be able to predict (more or less) how other organizations will respond to change, if it is to plan its own moves sensibly. And the same goes for individuals. The more uniform we are, the less we need to know about each other in order to predict one another's behavior. As the people around us grow more individualized or de-massified, we need more information—signals and cues—to predict, even roughly, how they are going to behave toward us. And unless we can make such forecasts we cannot work or even live together.

As a result, people and organizations continually crave more information and the entire system begins to pulse with higher and higher flows of data. By forcing up the amount of information needed for the social system to cohere, and the speeds at which it must be exchanged, the Third Wave shatters the framework of the obsolete, overloaded Second Wave info-sphere and constructs a new one to take its place.

14

THE INTELLIGENT ENVIRONMENT

Many different people of the world believed—and some still do—that behind the immediate physical reality of things lie spirits, that even seemingly dead objects, rocks or earth, have a living force within them: *mana*. The Sioux Indians called it *wakan*. The Algonkians, *manitou*. The Iroquois, *orenda*. For such people the entire environment is alive.

Today, as we construct a new info-sphere for a Third Wave civilization, we are imparting to the "dead" environment around us not life but intelligence.

The key to this revolutionary advance is, of course, the computer. A combination of electronic memory with programs that tell the machine how to process the stored data, computers were still a scientific curiosity in the early 1950's. Between 1955 and 1965, however, the decade when the Third Wave began its surge in the United States, they began to seep slowly into the business world. At first they were stand-alone units of modest capacity, employed chiefly for financial purposes. Soon machines with huge capacity began moving into corporate headquarters and were deployed for a variety of tasks. From 1965 to 1977, says Harvey Poppel, a senior vice president of Booz Allen & Hamilton, the management consultants, we were in the "era of the large central computer. . . . It represents the epitome, the ultimate manifestation of machine age thinking. It is the crowning achievement—a large super-computer buried hundreds of feet beneath the center [in a] bombproof . . . antiseptic environment . . . manned by a bunch of super-technocrats."

So impressive were these centralized giants that they soon

became a standard part of social mythology. Movie makers, cartoonists, and science fiction writers, using them to symbolize the future, routinely pictured the computer as an all-powerful brain—a massive concentration of superhuman intelligence.

During the 1970's, however, fact outraced fiction, leaving obsolete imagery behind. As miniaturization advanced with lightning rapidity, as computer capacity soared and prices per function plunged, small, cheap, powerful mini-computers began to sprout everywhere. Every branch factory, laboratory, sales office or engineering department claimed its own. So many computers appeared, in fact, that companies sometimes lost track of how many they had. The "brainpower" of the computer was no longer concentrated at a single point; it was "distributed."

This dispersion of computer intelligence is now moving ahead at high speed. In 1977 expenditures for what is now called "distributed data processing," or DDP, ran to $300 million in the United States. According to the International Data Corporation, a leading market research firm in the field, this figure will reach a solid $3 billion by 1982. Small, cheap machines, no longer requiring a specially trained computer priesthood, will soon be as omnipresent as the typewriter. We are "smartening" our work environment.

Outside the confines of industry and government, moreover, a parallel process is under way based on that soon-to-be-ubiquitous gadget: the home computer. Five years ago the number of home or personal computers was negligible. Today it is estimated that 300,000 computers are whirring and buzzing away in living rooms, kitchens, and dens from one end of America to the next. And this is before the major manufacturers, like IBM and Texas Instruments, launch their sales drives. Home computers will soon be selling for little more than a television set.

These clever machines are already being used for everything from doing the family taxes to monitoring energy use in the home, playing games, keeping a file of recipes, reminding their owners of upcoming appointments, and serving as "smart typewriters." This, however, offers only a tiny glimpse of their full potential.

Telecomputing Corporation of America offers a service called simply "The Source," which for minuscule costs provides the computer user with instant access to the United Press International news wire; a vast array of stock and commodity market data; educational programs to teach children arithmetic, spelling, French, German, or Italian; membership in a computerized discount shoppers' club; instant hotel or travel reservations, and more.

The Source also makes it possible for anyone with a cheap computer terminal to communicate with anyone else in the system. Bridge, chess, or backgammon players who so desire can play games with someone a thousand miles distant. Users can send private messages to one another or to large numbers of people all at once, and store all correspondence in electronic memory. The Source will even facilitate the creation of what might be called "electronic communities"—groups of people with shared interests. A dozen photo buffs in a dozen cities, brought together electronically by The Source, can converse to their heart's delight about cameras, equipment, darkroom techniques, lighting, or color film. Months later they can retrieve their comments from The Source's electronic memory, by subject, date, or other category.

The dispersal of computers into the home, not to mention their interconnection in ramified networks, represents another advance in the construction of an intelligent environment. Yet even this is not all.

The spread of machine intelligence reaches another level altogether with the arrival of microprocessors and microcomputers, those tiny chips of congealed intelligence that are about to become a part, it seems, of nearly all the things we make and use.

Apart from their applications in manufacturing processes and business generally, they are already embedded, or soon will be, in everything from air-conditioners and autos to sewing machines and scales. They will monitor and minimize the waste of energy in the home. They will adjust the amount of detergent and the water temperature for each washing machine load. They will fine-tune the car's fuel system. They will flag us when something needs repair. They will flick on the clock radio, the toaster, the coffee maker, and the shower for us in the morning. They will warm the garage, lock the doors, and perform a vertiginous variety of other humble and not-so-humble tasks.

Just how far things might go within a few decades is suggested by Alan P. Hald, a leading microcomputer distributor, in an amusing scenario he calls "Fred the House."

According to Hald, "Home computers can already talk, interpret speech, and control appliances. Throw in a few sensors, a modest vocabulary, the Bell Telephone system and your house could talk to . . . anyone or anything in the world." Many obstacles still lie ahead, but the direction of change is clear.

"Imagine," Hald writes. "You're at work, the phone rings. It's Fred, your house. While monitoring the morning news reports for stories of recent burglaries, Fred picked up a weather bulletin warning of pending heavy rain. This jogged Fred's bubble memories to run a routine roof maintenance check. A potential leak was found. Before calling you, Fred phoned Slim for advice. Slim is a ranchstyle home down the block . . . Fred and Slim often shared data banks and each knew they were programmed with an effective search technique for identifying household services. . . . You've learned to trust Fred's judgment, and approve the repairs. The rest is rather straight forward, Fred calls the roofer . . ."

The fantasy is funny. Yet it spookily catches the feel of life in an intelligent environment. Living in such an environment raises chilling philosophical questions. Will machines take over? Can intelligent machines, especially as they are linked together in intercommunicating networks, outrun our ability to understand and control them? Will Big Brother some day be able to tap not merely our telephones but our toasters and television sets, keeping tabs on our every move and mood? How dependent should we allow ourselves to become on the computer and the chip? As we pump more and more intelligence into the material environment, won't our own minds atrophy? And what happens if someone or something pulls the plug out of the wall? Will we still have the basic skills needed for survival?

For each question there are innumerable counterquestions. Can Big Brother really keep tabs on every toaster and TV set, every car engine and kitchen appliance? When intelligence is distributed widely throughout the entire environment, when it can be activated by users in a thousand places at once, when computer users can communicate with one another without going through the central computer (as they do in many distributed networks), can Big Brother still control things? Rather than enhancing the power of the totalitarian state, the decentralization of intelligence may, in fact, weaken it. Alternatively, won't we be smart enough to outfox government? In *The Shockwave Rider*, a brilliant, complex novel by John Brunner, the central character successfully sabotages the efforts of the government to impose thought control through the computer network. Must minds atrophy? As we shall see in a moment, the creation of an intelligent environment could have precisely the opposite effect. In designing machines to do our bidding, can't we program them, like Robbie in Isaac Asimov's classic tale, *I, Robot*, never to harm a human? The verdict is not yet in, and, while it would be irresponsible to ignore such issues, it would be naïve to assume that the cards are stacked against the human race. We have intelligence and imagination we have not yet begun to use.

What is inescapably clear, however, whatever we choose to believe, is that we are altering our info-sphere fundamentally. We are not merely de-massifying the Second Wave media, we are adding whole new strata of communication to the social system. The emerging Third Wave info-sphere makes that of the Second Wave era—dominated by its mass media, the post office, and the telephone—seem hopelessly primitive by contrast.

ENHANCING THE BRAIN

In altering the info-sphere so profoundly, we are destined to transform our own minds as well—the way we think about our problems, the way we synthesize information, the way we anticipate the consequences of our own actions. We are likely to change the role of literacy in our lives. We may even alter our own brain chemistry.

Hald's comment about the ability of computers and chip-studded appliances to converse with us is not as blue-sky as it might seem. "Voice data entry" terminals in existence today are already capable of recognizing and responding to a vocabularly of one thousand words, and many companies, from giants like IBM or Nippon Electric to midgets like Heuristics, Inc., or Centigram Corporation, are racing to expand that vocabularly, simplify the technology, and radically slash the costs. Forecasts for when computers will feel at home with natural language range from upwards of twenty years down to a mere five years, and the implications of this development—on both the economy and the culture—could be tremendous.

Today millions of people are excluded from the job market because they are functionally illiterate. Even the simplest jobs demand people capable of reading forms, on-off buttons, paychecks, job instructions, and the like. In the Second Wave world the ability to read was the most elemental skill required by the hiring office.

Yet illiteracy is not the same as stupidity. We know that illiterate people the world over are capable of mastering highly sophisticated skills in activities as diverse as agriculture, construction, hunting, and music. Many illiterates have prodigious memories and can speak several languages fluently—something most university-educated Americans cannot do. In Second Wave societies, however, illiterates were economically doomed.

Literacy, of course, is more than a job skill. It is the doorway to a fantastic universe of imagination and pleasure. Yet in an intelligent environment, when machines, appliances, and even walls are programmed to speak, literacy could turn out to be less paycheck-linked than it has been for the past three hundred years. Airline reservation clerks, stock-room personnel, machine operators, and repairmen may be able to function quite adequately on the job by listening rather than reading, as a voice from the machine tells them, step by step, what to do next or how to replace a broken part.

Computers are not superhuman. They break down. They make errors—sometimes dangerous ones. There is nothing magical about them, and they are assuredly not "spirits" or "souls" in our environment. Yet with all these qualifications, they remain among the most amazing and unsettling of human achievements, for they enhance our mind-power as Second Wave technology enhanced our muscle-power, and we do not know where our own minds will ultimately lead us.

As we grow more familiar with the intelligent environment, and learn to converse with it from the time we leave the cradle, we will begin to use computers with a grace and naturalness that is hard for us to imagine today. And they will help all of us—not just a few "super-technocrats"—to think more deeply about ourselves and the world.

Today, when a problem arises we immediately seek to discover its causes. However, until now even the most profound thinkers have usually attempted to explain things in terms of a relative handful of causal forces. For even the best human mind finds it difficult to entertain, let alone manipulate, more than a few variables at a time.* In consequence, when faced with a truly complicated problem—like why a child is delinquent, or why inflation ravages an economy, or how urbanization affects the ecology of a nearby river—we tend to focus on two or three factors and to ignore many others that may, singly or collectively, be far more important.

Worse yet, each group of experts typically insists on the primal importance of "its own" causes, to the exclusion of others. Faced with the staggering problems of urban decay, the Housing Expert traces it to congestion and a declining housing stock; the Transportation Expert points to the lack of mass transit; the Welfare Expert shows the inadequacy of budgets for day-care centers or social work; the Crime Expert points a finger at the infrequency of police patrols; the Economics Expert shows that high taxes are discouraging business investment; and so on. Everyone high-mindedly agrees that all these problems are somehow interconnected— that they form a self-reinforcing system. But no one can keep the many complexities in mind while trying to think through a solution to the problem.

Urban decay is only one of a large number of what Peter Ritner, in *The Society of Space,* once felicitously termed "weave problems." He warned that we would increasingly face crises that were "not susceptible to 'cause and effect analysis' but would require 'mutual dependence analysis'; not composed of easily detachable elements but of hundreds of cooperating influences from dozens of independent, overlapping sources."

Because it can remember and interrelate large numbers of causal forces, the computer can help us cope with such problems at a deeper than customary level. It can sift vast masses of data to find subtle patterns. It can help assemble "blips" into larger, more meaningful wholes. Given a set of assumptions or a model, it can trace out the consequences of alternative decisions, and do it more systematically and completely than any individual normally could. It can even suggest imaginative solutions to certain problems by identifying novel or hitherto unnoticed relationships among people and resources.

Human intelligence, imagination, and intuition will continue in the foreseeable decades to be far more important than the machine. Nevertheless, computers can be expected to deepen the entire culture's view of causality, heightening our understanding of the interrelatedness of things, and helping us to synthesize meaningful "wholes" out of the discon-

---

* While we may deal with many factors simultaneously on a subconscious or intuitive level, systematic, conscious thinking about a great many variables is damnably difficult, as anyone who has tried it knows.

nected data whirling around us. The computer is one antidote to blip culture.

At the same time, the intelligent environment may eventually begin to change not merely the way we analyze problems and integrate information, but even the chemistry of our brains. Experiments by David Krech, Marian Diamond, Mark Rosenzweig, and Edward Bennett, among others, have shown that animals exposed to an "enriched" environment have larger cerebral cortices, more glial cells, bigger neurons, more active neurotransmitters, and larger blood supplies to the brain than animals in a control group. Can it be that, as we complexify the environment and make it more intelligent, we shall make ourselves more intelligent as well?

Dr. Donald F. Klein, Director of Research at New York Psychiatric Institute, one of the world's leading neuropsychiatrists, speculates:

"Krech's work suggests that among the variables affecting intelligence is the richness and responsiveness of the early environment. Kids brought up in what might be called a 'stupid' environment—understimulating, poor, unresponsive—soon learn not to take chances. There's little margin for error, and it actually pays off to be cautious, conservative, uninquisitive or downright passive, none of which works wonders for the brain.

"On the other hand, kids raised in a smart, responsive environment, which is complex and stimulating, may develop a different set of skills. If kids can call on the environment to do things for them, they become less dependent on parents at a younger age. They may gain a sense of mastery or competence. And they can afford to be inquisitive, exploratory, imaginative, and to adopt a problem-solving approach to life. All of which may promote changes in the brain itself. At this point, all we can do is guess. But it is not impossible that an intelligent environment could lead us to develop new synapses and a larger cortex. A smarter environment might make smarter people."

All this, however, only begins to hint at the larger significance of the changes the new info-sphere brings with it. For the de-massification of the media and the concomitant rise of the computer together change our social memory.

* * *

THE SOCIAL MEMORY

All memories can be divided into those that are purely personal or private and those that are shared or social. Unshared private memories die with the individual. Social memory lives on. Our remarkable ability to file and retrieve shared memories is the secret of our species' evolutionary success. And anything that significantly alters the way we construct, store, or use social memory therefore touches on the very wellsprings of destiny.

Twice before in history humankind has revolutionized its social memory. Today, in constructing a new info-sphere, we are poised on the brink of another such transformation.

In the beginning, human groups were forced to store their shared memories in the same place they kept private memories—i.e., in the minds of individuals. Tribal elders, wise men, and others carried these memories with them in the form of history, myth, lore, and legend, and transmitted them to their children through speech, song, chant, and example. How to light a fire, the best way to snare a bird, how to lace a raft or pound taro, how to sharpen a plowstick or care for the oxen—all the accumulated experience of the group was stored in the neurons and glia and synapses of human beings.

So long as this remained true, the size of the social memory was sorely limited. No matter how good the memories of the elderly, no matter how memorable the songs or lessons, there was only so much storage space in the skulls of any population.

Second Wave civilization smashed the memory barrier. It spread mass literacy. It kept systematic business records. It built thousands of libraries and museums. It invented the file cabinet. In short, it moved social memory outside the skull, found new ways to store it, and thus expanded it beyond its previous limits. By increasing the store of cumulative knowledge, it accelerated all the processes of innovation and social change, giving Second Wave civilization the most rapidly changing and developing culture the world until then had known.

Today we are about to jump to a whole new stage of social memory. The radical de-massification of the media, the invention of new media, the mapping of the earth by satellite, the monitoring of hospital patients by electronic sensors, the computerization of corporate files—all mean we are recording the activities of the civilization in fine-grain detail. Unless we incinerate the planet, and our social memory with it, we shall before long have the closest thing to a civilization with total recall. Third Wave civilization will have at its disposal more information, and more finely organized information, about itself than could have been imagined even a quarter-century ago

The shift to a Third Wave social memory, however, is more than just quantitative. We are also, as it were, imparting life to our memory.

When social memory was stored in human brains it was continually being eroded, refreshed, stirred about, combined and recombined in new ways. It was active, or dynamic. It was, in the most literal sense, alive.

When industrial civilization moved much of social memory outside the skull, that memory became objectified, embedded in artifacts. books, payroll sheets, newspapers, photographs, and films. But a symbol once inscribed on a page, a photo once captured on film, a newspaper once printed, remained passive or static. Only when these symbols were fed into a human brain again did they come alive, to be manipulated or recombined in fresh ways. While Second Wave civilization radically expanded social memory, it also froze it.

What makes the leap to a Third Wave info-sphere so historically unprecedented a situation: it makes social memory both extensive and active. And this combination will prove to be propulsive.

Activating this newly expanded memory will unleash fresh cultural energies. For the computer not only helps us organize or synthesize "blips" into coherent models of reality, it also stretches the far limits of the possible. No library or file cabinet could think, let alone think in an unorthodox fashion. The computer, by contrast, can be asked by us to "think the unthinkable" and the previously unthought. It makes possible a flood of new theories, ideas, ideologies, artistic insights, technical advances, economic and political innovations that were, in the most literal sense, unthinkable and unimaginable before now. In this way, it accelerates historic change and fuels the thrust toward Third Wave social diversity.

In all previous societies the info-sphere provided the means for communication between humans. The Third Wave multiplies these means. But it also provides powerful facilities, for the first time in history, for machine-to-machine communication and, even more astonishing, for conversation between humans and the intelligent environment around them. When we stand back and look at the larger picture, it becomes clear that the revolution in the info-sphere is at least as dramatic as that in the techno-sphere—in the energy system and technological base of society.

The work of constructing a new civilization is racing forward on many levels at once.

BEYOND MASS PRODUCTION

One day not long ago I drove a rented car from the snow-swathed peaks of the Rocky Mountains down along snaky roads, then across the high plains, and down, down again until I reached the eastern foothills of that majestic mountain range. There in Colorado Springs, under a brilliant sky, I made my way to a long, low building complex that nestled along the highway, dwarfed by the peaks looming behind me.

As I entered the building, I remembered again the factories in which I had once worked, with all their clatter and roar, their dirt, smoke, and suppressed anger. For years, ever since leaving our manual jobs, my wife and I have been "factory voyeurs." In all our travels around the globe, instead of zeroing in on ruined cathedrals and tourist clip joints we have made it our business to see how people work. For nothing tells us more about their culture. And now in Colorado Springs I was once again visiting a factory. I had been told that it was among the most advanced manufacturing facilities in the world.

It soon became clear why. For, in plants like this, one glimpses the latest in technology and the most advanced information systems—and the practical effects of their convergence.

This Hewlett-Packard facility turns out $100 million worth a year of electronic apparatus—cathode-ray tubes for use in TV monitors and medical equipment, oscilloscopes, "logic analyzers" for testing, and even more arcane items. Of the 1,700 people employed here, fully 40 percent are engineers, programmers, technicians, clerical or managerial personnel. They work in a huge, high-ceilinged open space. One wall is a giant picture window that frames an imposing view of Pikes Peak. The other walls are painted bright yellow and white. The floors are light-colored vinyl, gleaming and hospital clean.

The workers at H-P, from clerks to computer specialists, from the plant manager to assemblers and inspectors, are not separated spatially but work together in open bays. Instead of shouting to one another over a machine clatter, they speak in normal conversational tones. Because everyone wears ordinary street clothes there are no visible distinctions of rank or task. Production employees sit at their own benches or desks; so many of these are decorated with trailing ivy, flowers, and other greenery that, from some visual angles, one has the fleeing illusion of being in a garden.

Striding through this facility, I thought how poignant it would be if I could magically lift some of my old mates out of the foundry and auto assembly line, out of the racket, the dirt, the hard bruising manual labor, and the rigidly authoritarian discipline that accompanied it, and transplant them into this new-style work environment.

They would stare in wonder at what they saw. I doubt very much that H-P is a workers' paradise, and my blue collar friends would not be easily fooled. They would demand to know, item by item, the pay schedules, the fringe benefits, the grievance procedures, if any. They would ask whether the exotic new materials being handled in this plant are really safe or whether there are environmental health hazards. They would assume rightly that even under the seemingly casual relationships some people give orders and others take them.

Nevertheless, my old friends' shrewd eyes would take in much that is new and sharply different from the classical factories they knew. They would notice, for example, that instead of all the H-P employees arriving at once, punching the clock, and racing to their work stations, they are able, within limits, to choose their own individual working hours. Instead of being forced to stay in one work location, they are able to move about as they wish. My old friends would marvel at the freedom of the H-P employees, again within limits, to set their own work pace. To talk to managers or engineers without worrying about status or hierarchy. To dress as they wish. In short, to be individuals. In fact, my old companions in their heavy steel-tipped shoes, dirty overalls, and workingmen's caps would find it hard, I believe, to think of the place as a factory at all.

And if we regard the factory as the home of mass production, they would be right. For *mass* production is not what this facility is all about. We have moved beyond mass production.

MOUSE MILK AND T-SHIRTS

It is conventional knowledge by now that the percentage of workers employed in manufacturing in the "advanced" nations has declined in the past twenty years. (In the United States today only 9 percent of the total population—20 million workers—manufacture goods for some 220 million people. The remaining 65 million workers provide services and manipulate symbols.) And as this shrinkage of manufacturing has accelerated in the industrial world, more and more routine manufacturing has been farmed out to the so-called developing countries, from Algeria to Mexico and Thailand. Like rusty used cars, the most backward Second Wave industries are thus exported from the rich nations to the poor.

For strategic as well as economic reasons, the rich nations cannot afford to surrender manufacturing altogether, and they will not become pure examples of "service societies" or "information economies." The image of the rich world living off nonmaterial production while the rest of the world engages in the output of material goods is highly oversimplified. Instead, we will find the rich nations continuing to manufacture key goods—but needing fewer workers to do so. For we are transforming the very way goods are made.

The essence of Second Wave manufacture was the long "run" of millions of identical, standardized products. By contrast, the essence of Third Wave manufacture is the short run of partially or completely customized products.

The public still tends to think of manufacture in terms of long runs, and we do of course continue to turn out cigarettes by the billion, textiles by the millions of yards, light bulbs, matches, bricks, or spark plugs in astronomical quantities. No doubt we will continue to do so for some time. Yet these are precisely the products of the more backward industries rather than the most advanced, and today they account for only about 5 percent of all our manufactured goods.

An analyst in *Critique*, a journal of Soviet studies, notes that while "the less highly developed countries—[those] with a GNP of between U.S. $1000–2000 per capita per annum—concentrate on mass produced manufactures" the "most highly developed countries . . . concentrate on the export of one-off and short-run manufactured goods depending on highly skilled labour and . . . high research costs: computers, specialised machinery, aircraft, automated production systems, high technology paints, pharmaceutical products, high technology polymers and plastics."

In Japan, West Germany, the United States, even in the Soviet Union, in such fields as electrical manufacturing, chemicals, aerospace, electronics, specialized vehicles, communications, and the like, we find the trend toward de-massification well developed. At Western Electric's super-advanced plant in northern Illinois, for example, workers make over four hundred different "circuit packs" in runs that range from a maximum of two thousand a month all the way down to two a month. At Hewlett-Packard in Colorado Springs, production runs as small as fifty to one hundred units are common.

At IBM, Polaroid, McDonnell Douglas, Westinghouse, and General Electric in the United States, at Plessey and ITT in Great Britain, at Siemens in Germany or Ericsson in Sweden, the same shift toward short run and customized products is marked. In Norway the Aker Group, which once accounted for 45 percent of that nation's ship construction, has shifted to the manufacture of off-shore oil equipment. The result: a switch from "series production" of ships to "tailor-made" offshore products.

In chemicals, meanwhile, according to executive R. E. Lee, Exxon is "moving to short runs in fabricated products—polypropylene and polyethelyne in extruded plastics for pipe, sidings, panelling, etc. In Paramins we are doing increasing custom work." Some of the runs are so small, Lee adds, "we call them 'mouse-milk' runs."

In military production most people still think in terms of mass—but the reality is "de-mass." We think of millions of identical uniforms, helmets, rifles. In fact, the vast bulk of what a modern military establishment needs is not mass produced at all. Jet fighters can be produced in runs as small as ten to fifty at a time. Each one of these may be slightly different, depending on purpose and branch of service. And with such small orders, many of the components that go into the planes are usually produced in short runs also.

Thus an eye-opening analysis of Pentagon spending by the number of end-products purchased came up with the finding that, out of $9.1 billion spent on goods for which the number of end items was identifiable, fully 78 percent ($7.1 billion) went for goods produced in lots of under 100 units!

Even in fields where components are still mass-produced in very large quantities—and in some highly advanced industries this is still the case—the components are usually configured to form many different end-products, each of which is in turn produced in short runs.

One need only look at the incredibly diverse vehicles whizzing down an Arizona highway to recognize how the once relatively uniform auto market has splintered into segments, forcing even those technological tyrannosaurs, the auto makers, to back grudgingly into partial customization. The car manufacturers in Europe, the United States, and Japan now mass-manufacture components and sub-assemblies, then plug them together in myriad ways.

At another level, note the humble T-shirt. The shirts are mass-made. But new, cheap fast-heat presses make it economical to imprint designs or slogans on very small batches. The result is a wild flowering of shirts facetiously identifying the wearer as a Beethoven fan, a beer drinker, or a porno star. Autos, T-shirts, and many other products represent a halfway stage between mass and de-massified manufacture.

The step beyond this, of course, is complete customization—the actual manufacture of one-of-a-kind products. And that is clearly the direction in which we are heading: products custom-cut for individual users.

According to Robert H. Anderson, head of the Information Services Department at the Rand Corporation, and an expert on advanced manufacturing: "It will be no harder in the near future to custom produce something . . . than it is to mass produce . . . today. . . . We're beyond the modularization stage where you make a lot of modules and plug them together . . . and we're getting on to the stage of just plain custom production. Just like clothes."

The shift toward customization is perhaps best symbolized by a computer-based laser gun introduced a few years ago into the clothing industry. Before the Second Wave brought mass production, if a man wanted a piece of clothing made he went to a tailor or a seamstress, or his wife sewed it. In any case, it was done on a handcraft basis, to his individual measure. All sewing was essentially custom tailoring.

After the arrival of the Second Wave, we began to manufacture identical clothes on a mass-production basis. Under this system the worker placed one layer of cloth on top of another; he laid a pattern on top; then, with an electric cutting knife he cut around the edges of the pattern and produced multiple, identical cutouts of the cloth. These were then subjected to identical processing and came out identical in size, shape, color, and so forth.

The new laser machine operates on a radically different principle. It does not cut 10 or 50 or 100 or even 500 shirts or jackets at a time. Its cuts *one* at a time. But it acutally cuts faster and cheaper than the mass-production methods employed until now. It reduces waste and eliminates the need for inventory. For these reasons, according to the president of Genesco, one of the largest manufacturers of apparel in the United States, "The laser machines can be programmed to fill an order for one garment economically." What that suggests is that some day even standard sizes may disappear. It may be possible to read one's measurements into a telephone, or point a video camera at oneself, thus feeding data directly into a computer, which in turn will instruct the machine to produce a single garment, cut exactly to one's personal, individualized dimensions.

What we are looking at, in effect, is custom tailoring on a high-technology basis. It is the reinstatement of a system of production that flourished before the industrial revolution—but now built on the basis of the most advanced, sophisticated technology. Just as we are de-massifying the media, we are de-massifying manufacture.

THE PRESTO EFFECT

Several other quite extraordinary advances are transforming the way we make things.

As some industries move from mass to small batch production, others are already moving beyond *that* toward full customization on a continuous-flow basis. Instead of starting and stopping production at the beginning and end of each short run, they are advancing to the point at which the machines can continuously reset themselves, so that the units of output—each one different from the next—stream from the machines in an unbroken flow. In a nutshell, we are racing toward machine customization on a round-the-clock, continuous basis.

Another significant change, as we shall shortly see, brings the customer more directly than ever before into the manufacturing process. In some industries we are only a step removed from a situation in which a customer-company pipes its specifications directly into the manufacturer's computers, which will in turn control the production line. As this practice becomes widespread, the customer will become so integrated into the production process that we will find it more and more difficult to tell just who is actually the consumer and who the producer.

Finally, while Second Wave manufacture was Cartesian in the sense that products were broken into pieces, then painstakingly reassembled, Third Wave manufacture is post-Cartesian or "wholistic." This is illustrated by what has happened to common manufactured products like the wristwatch. Whereas watches once had hundreds of moving parts, we are now able to make solid-state watches that are more accurate and reliable—with no moving parts at all. Similarly, today's Panasonic TV set has half as many parts as the sets of ten years ago. As tiny microprocessors—those miracle chips again—turn up in more and more products, they replace impressive numbers of conventional components. Exxon introduces the "Qyx"—a new typewriter with only a handful of moving parts as against the hundreds in the IBM Selectric. Similarly, a well-known 35mm camera, the Canon AE-1, is now made with 300 fewer parts than the model it superseded. Fully 175 of these were replaced by a single Texas Instruments chip.

By intervening at the molecular level, by using computer-aided design or other advanced manufacturing tools, we integrate more and more functions into fewer and fewer parts, substituting "wholes" for many discrete components. What is occurring can be compared to the rise of photography in the visual arts. Instead of making a picture by placing innumerable daubs of paint on a canvas, the photographer "makes" the entire image at once by pressing a button. We are beginning to see this "presto effect" in manufacturing.

The pattern becomes clear, therefore. Vast changes in the techno-sphere and the info-sphere have converged to change the way we make goods. We are moving rapidly beyond traditional mass production to a sophisticated mix of mass and de-massified products. The ultimate goal of this effort is now apparent: completely customized goods, made with wholistic, continuous-flow processes, increasingly under the direct control of the consumer.

In brief, we are revolutionizing the deep structure of production, sending currents of change through every layer of society. However, this transformation, which will affect the student planning a career, the business planning an investment, or the nation planning a development strategy, can't be understood in isolation. It must be seen in direct relationship to yet another revolution—this one in the office.

THE DEATH OF THE SECRETARY?

As fewer workers in the rich nations have engaged in physical production, more have been needed to produce ideas, patents, scientific formulae, bills, invoices, reorganization plans, files, dossiers, market research, sales presentations, letters, graphics, legal briefs, engineering specifications, computer programs, and a thousand other forms of data or symbolic output. This rise in white-collar, technical, and administrative activity has been so widely documented in so many countries that we need no statistic here to make the point. Indeed, some sociologists have seized on the increasing abstraction of production as evidence that society has moved into a "post-industrial" stage.

The facts are more complicated. For the growth of the white-collar work force can be better understood as an extension of industrialism—a further last surge of the Second Wave—than as a leap to a new system. While it is true that work has grown more abstract and less concrete, the actual offices in which this work is being done are modeled directly after Second Wave factories, with the work itself fragmented, repetitive, dull, and dehumanizing. Even today, much office reorganization is little more than an attempt to make the office more closely resemble a factory.

In this "symbol-factory," Second Wave civilization also created a factorylike caste system. The factory work force is divided into manual and nonmanual workers. The office is similarly divided into "high abstraction" and "low abstraction" workers. At one level we find the high abstracters, the technocratic elites: scientists, engineers, and managers, much of whose time is taken up with meetings, conferences, business lunches, or in dictating, drafting memos, placing phone calls, and otherwise exchanging information. One recent survey estimated that 80 percent of the manager's time is spent in 150 to 300 "information transactions" daily.

At the other level we find the low abstracters—white-collar proletarians, as it were—who, like factory workers throughout the Second Wave period, perform endlessly routine and deadening work. Mostly female and nonunionized, this group can justifiably smile with irony at the sociologists' talk of "post-industrialism." They are the *industrial* work force of the office.

Today the office, too, is beginning to move beyond the Second Wave and into the Third, and this industrial caste system is about to be challenged. All the old hierarchies and structures of the office are soon to be reshuffled.

The Third Wave revolution in the office is the result of several colliding forces. The need for information has mushroomed so wildly that no army of Second Wave clerks, typists, and secretaries, no matter how large or hard-working, can possibly cope with it. In addition, the cost of paper work has climbed so calamitously that a frantic search is underway to control it. (Office costs have swelled to 40 or 50 percent of all costs in many companies, and some experts estimate that the expense of preparing a single business letter can run as high as $14 to $18 when all the hidden factors are taken into account.) Moreover, while the average factory worker in the United States today is supported by an estimated $25,000 worth of technology, the office worker, as one Xerox salesman puts it, "works with $500 or $1000 worth of old typewriters and adding machines, and is probably among the least productive workers in the world." Office productivity has climbed a bare 4 percent over the past decade, and conditions in other countries are probably even more pronounced.

Contrast this with the extraordinary decline in the cost of computers, as measured by the number of functions performed. It has been estimated that computer output has increased 10,000 times in the past fifteen years, and that the per-function cost today is down 100,000-fold. The combination of rising costs and stagnating productivity on the one hand and computer advances on the other make an irresistible combination. The result is likely to be nothing less than a "wordquake."

The main symbol of this upheaval is an electronic device

called the word processor—some 250,000 of which are already at work in U.S. offices. Manufacturers of these machines, including such titans as IBM and Exxon, are bracing themselves to compete in what they believe will soon be a $10-billion-a-year market. Sometimes called a "smart typewriter" or a "text editor," this device fundamentally alters the flow of information in the office, and with it the job structure. It is, however, only one of a great family of new technologies about to deluge the white-collar world.

In Chicago in June 1979, at the convention of the International Word Processing Association, some 20,000 perspiring visitors trooped through an exhibition hall to examine or try out a bewildering array of other machines as well—optical scanners, high-speed printers, micrographic equipment, facsimile machines, computer terminals, and the like. They were looking at the beginning of what some term the "paperless office" of tomorrow.

In Washington, D.C., in fact, a consulting firm known as Micronet, Inc. has brought together the equipment of seventeen different manufacturers into an integrated office in which paper is *verboten*. Any document arriving in this office is instantly microfilmed and stored for computer retrieval later on. This demonstration office and training facility integrates dictating equipment, microfilm, optical scanners, and video terminals into a functioning system. The objective, says Micronet president Larry Stockett, is an office of the future in which "there are no misfiles; marketing, sales, accounting and research data are always up to the minute; information is reproduced and distributed at hundreds of thousands of pages per hour for a fraction of a cent per page; and . . . information is converted back and forth from print to digital to photographic media at will."

The key to such an office of the future is ordinary correspondence. In a conventional Second Wave office, when an executive wants to fire off a letter or memo, an intermediary is called in—the secretary. This person's first task is to capture the executive's words on paper—in a notebook or a typed draft. Next the message is corrected to eliminate errors, and perhaps retyped a few times. After that it is clean typed. A carbon or Xerox copy is made. The original is dispatched to its destination through the mailroom or the post office. The duplicate is filed. Not counting the initial step of composing the message, five distinct sequential steps are required.

Today's machines compress these five steps into one, making the sequential all but simultaneous.

To learn how—and to speed up my own work—I bought a simple computer, used it as a word processor, and wrote the latter half of this book on it. To my pleasure, I found I could master the machine in a single short session. Within a few hours I was using it fluently. After more than a year at the keyboard I am still amazed by its speed and power.

Today, instead of typing a draft of a chapter on paper, I type on a keyboard that stores it in electronic form on what is known as a "floppy disk." I see my words displayed before me on a TV-like screen. By punching a few keys I can instantly revise or rearrange what I have written, shifting paragraphs, deleting, inserting, underlining, until I have a version I like. This eliminates erasing, "whiting out," cutting, pasting, stripping, Xeroxing, or typing successive drafts. Once I have corrected the draft, I press a button, and a printer at my side makes a letter-perfect final copy for me at vision-blurring speeds.

But making paper copies of anything is a primitive use of such machines and violates their very spirit. For the ultimate beauty of the electronic office lies not merely in the steps saved by a secretary in typing and correcting letters. The automated office can file them in the form of electronic bits on tape or disk. It can (or soon will) pass them through an electronic dictionary that will automatically correct their spelling errors. With the machines hooked up to one another and to the phone lines, the secretary can instantly transmit the letter to its recipient's printer or screen. The equipment thus can capture an original, correct it, duplicate it, send it, and file it in what amounts virtually to a single process. Speed increases. Costs go down. And the five steps are compressed into one.

The implications of this compression extend far outside the office. For among other things, this equipment, linked to satellites, microwave, and other telecommunications facilities, makes it possible to end-run that overworked, malfunctioning, classically Second Wave institution, the Post Office. Indeed, the spread of office automation, of which word processing is only a single small aspect, is integrally linked to the creation of "electronic mail" systems to replace the postman and his burdensome bag.

In the United States today, fully 35 percent of total domestic postal volume consists of transaction reports: bills, receipts, purchase orders, invoices, bank statements, checks, and the like. However, a vast amount of mail flows not between individuals but between organizations. As the postal crisis has deepened, more and more companies have sought an alternative to the Second Wave postal system and begun to build pieces of a Third Wave system instead.

Based on teleprinters, facsimile machines, word processor equipment, and computer terminals, this electronic postal system is spreading very rapidly, especially in the advanced industries, and will be given a further tremendous boost by the new satellite systems.

Together, IBM, Aetna Casualty and Surety, and Comsat (the quasi-governmental communications satellite agency) have set up a company called Satellite Business Systems to provide integrated information services to other companies. SBS plans to loft satellites for client firms like General Motors, say, or Hoechst or Toshiba. Together with cheap ground stations located at each company installation, the SBS satellite makes it possible for each company to have, in effect, its own electronic postal system, bypassing in good measure the public postal services.

Instead of transporting paper, the new system moves electronic pulses. Even today, notes Vincent Giuliano of the Arthur D. Little research organization, electronics is the "hot" medium in many fields; it is the electronic impulse that effectuates a transaction, with a paper bill or receipt or statement going out afterward merely to validate it. How long the paper will be needed is a matter of dispute.

Messages and memos move silently and instantaneously. Terminals at every desk—thousands of them in any large organization—flicker quietly as information flows through the system, bouncing up to a satellite and down to an office halfway around the world or to a terminal in an executive's home. Computers link the company's files with those of other companies where necessary, and managers can call up information stored in hundreds of outside data banks like the New York Times Information Bank.

Just how far events move in this direction remains to be seen. The image of the office of the future is too neat, too smooth, too disembodied to be real. Reality is always messy. But it is clear that we are rapidly on our way, and even a partial shift toward the electronic office will be enough to trigger an eruption of social, psychological, and economic consequences. The coming workquake means more than just new machines. It promises to restructure all the human relationships and roles in the office as well.

It will, for a start, eliminate many of the secretary's functions. Even typing becomes an obsolete skill in tomorrow's office, when speech-recognition technology arrives. At first typing will still be necessary to capture the messages and put them in transmittable form. But before long, dictation equipment tuned to the distinctive accents of each individual user will convert the sounds into written words, thus entirely bypassing the typing operation.

"The old technology used a typist," says Dr. Giuliano, "because it was klutzy. When you had a clay tablet, you needed a scribe who knew how to bake clay and chisel marks on it. Writing was not for the masses. Today we have scribes called typists. But as soon as the new technology makes it easier to capture the message, to correct it, store it, retrieve it, send it and copy it, we will do all those things for ourselves—just like writing and talking. Once the klutz-factor is eliminated, we don't need the typist."

Indeed, one dearly held hope of many word-processing experts has the secretary being upgraded and the executive taking on or sharing the typing chore, at least until such time as it is totally eliminated. When I delivered a speech at the International Word Processing convention, for example, I was asked if my secretary uses the machine for me. When I said I typed my own drafts and that, in fact, my secretary could hardly get near my computer/word processor, cheers rang through the room. They dream of a day when the classified section in the newspaper may include ads like:

> WANTED: GROUP VICE PRISIDENT
> Responsibilities include coordinating finance, marketing, product line development in several divisions. Must have demonstrated ability to apply sound management control. Report to Exec. VP, multi-line international company.
> **TYPING REQUIRED.**

Executives, by contrast, are likely to resist sullying their fingertips, just as they resist fetching their own mugs of coffee. And knowing that speech-recognition equipment is around the corner, so that they will be able to dictate and have the machine do all the typing, they will resist learning how to handle a keyboard all the more.

Whether they do so or not, the unevadable fact remains that Third Wave production in the office, as it collides with the old Second Wave systems, will produce anxiety and conflict as well as reorganization, restructuring, and—for some—rebirth into new careers and opportunities. The new systems will challenge all the old executive turfs, the hierarchies, the sexual role divisions, the departmental barriers of the past.

All of this has raised many fears. Opinion divides sharply between those who insist that millions of jobs will simply vanish (or that today's secretaries will mainly be reduced to mechanical slaves) and a more sanguine view widely held in the word processing industry, and expressed by Randy Goldfield, a principal of the Booz Allen & Hamilton consulting firm. According to Ms. Goldfield, secretaries, far from being reduced to mindless, repetitive processors, will become "paraprincipals," sharing in some of the professional work and decision-making from which they have been largely excluded until now. More likely we will see a sharp division between those white-collar workers who move up to more responsible positions and those who move down—and eventually out.

What, then, happens to these people—and to the economy in general? During the late 1950's and early 1960's, when automation first began arriving on the scene, economists and trade unionists in many countries forecast massive unemployment. Instead, employment in the high-technology nations expanded. As the manufacturing sector shrank the white-collar and service sectors expanded, taking up the slack. But if manufacturing continues to shrink, and if office employment is to be put through the wringer at the same time, where will the jobs of tomorrow come from?

Nobody knows. Despite endless studies and vehement claims, the forecasts and the evidence are contradictory. Attempts to relate investment in mechanization and automation to levels of manufacturing employment show what the *Financial Times* of London calls an "almost complete lack of correlation." Between 1963 and 1973 Japan had the highest rate of investment in new technology, as a percentage of value added, of any country in a seven-nation study. It also had the highest growth in employment. Britain, whose investment in machinery was the lowest, showed the greatest *loss* of jobs.

The American experience roughly paralleled that of Japan—technology and new jobs both increasing—while Sweden, France, West Germany, and Italy all showed markedly individual patterns.

It is clear that the level of employment is not merely a reflection of technological advance. It does not simply rise and fall as we automate or fail to do so. Employment is the net result of many converging policies.

Pressures on the job market may well increase dramatically in the years ahead. But it is naïve to single out the computer as their source.

What is certain is that both the office and the factory are destined to be revolutionized in the decades ahead. The twin revolutions in the white-collar sector and in manufacture add up to nothing less than a wholly new mode of production for society—a giant step for the human race. This step carries with it indescribably complex implications. It will affect not only such things as the level of employment and the structure of industry but also the distribution of political and economic power, the size of our work units, the international division of labor, the role of women in the economy, the nature of work, and the divorce of producer from consumer; it will even alter so seemingly simple a fact as the "where" of work.

16

THE ELECTRONIC COTTAGE

Hidden inside our advance to a new production system is a potential for social change so breathtaking in scope that few among us have been willing to face its meaning. For we are about to revolutionize our homes as well.

Apart from encouraging smaller work units, apart from permitting a decentralization and de-urbanization of production, apart from altering the actual character of work, the new production system could shift literally millions of jobs out of the factories and offices into which the Second Wave swept them and right back where they came from originally: the home. If this were to happen, every institution we know, from the family to the school and the corporation, would be transformed.

Watching masses of peasants scything a field three hundred years ago, only a madman would have dreamed that the time would soon come when the fields would be depopulated, when people would crowd into urban factories to earn their daily bread. And only a madman would have been right. Today it takes an act of courage to suggest that our biggest factories and office towers may, within our lifetimes, stand half empty, reduced to use as ghostly warehouses or converted into living space. Yet this is precisely what the new mode of production makes possible: a return to cottage industry on a new, higher, electronic basis, and with it a new emphasis on the home as the center of society.

To suggest that millions of us may soon spend our time at home, instead of going out to an office or factory, is to unleash an immediate shower of objections. And there are many sensible reasons for skepticism. "People don't want to work at home, even if they could. Look at all the women struggling to get *out* of the home and into a job!" "How can you get any work done with kids running around?" "People won't be motivated unless there's a boss watching them." "People need face-to-face contact with each other to develop the trust and confidence necessary to work together." "The architecture of the average home isn't set up for it." "What do you mean work at home—a small blast furnace in every basement?" "What about zoning restrictions and landlords who object?" "The unions will kill the idea." "How about the tax collector? The tax people are getting tougher on deductions claimed for working at home." And the ultimate stopper: "What, and stay home all day with my wife (or husband)?"

Even old Karl Marx would have frowned. Working at home, he believed, was a reactionary form of production because "the agglomeration in one workshop" was "a necessary condition for the division of labor in society." In short, there were, and are, many reasons (and pseudoreasons) for regarding the whole idea as silly.

DOING HOMEWORK

Yet there were equally, if not more, compelling reasons three hundred years ago to believe people would never move *out* of the home and field to work in factories. After all, they had labored in their own cottages and the nearby land for 10,000 years, not a mere 300. The entire structure of family life, the process of child-rearing and personality formation, the whole system of property and power, the culture, the daily struggle for existence were all bound to the hearth and the soil by a thousand invisible chains. Yet these chains were slashed in short order as soon as a new system of production appeared.

Today that is happening again, and a whole group of social and economic forces are converging to transfer the locus of work.

To begin with, the shift from Second Wave manufacturing to the new, more advanced Third Wave manufacturing reduces, as we just saw, the number of workers who actually have to manipulate physical goods. This means that even in the manufacturing sector an increasing amount of work is being done that—given the right configuration of telecommunications and other equipment—could be accomplished anywhere, including one's own living room. Nor is this just a science fiction fantasy.

When Western Electric shifted from producing electromechanical switching equipment for the phone company to making electronic switching gear, the work force at its advanced manufacturing facility in northern Illinois was transformed. Before the changeover, production workers outnumbered white-collar and technical workers three to one. Today the ratio is one to one. This means that fully half of the 2,000 workers now handle information instead of things, and much of their work can be done at home. Dom Cuomo, director of engineering at the Northern Illinois facility, put it flatly: "If you include engineers, ten to twenty-five percent of what is done here could be done at home with *existing* technology."

Cuomo's manager of engineering, Gerald Mitchell, went even further. "All told," he stated, "600 to 700 of the 2,000 could *now*—with existing technology—work at home. And in five years, we could go far beyond that."

These informed "guesstimates" are remarkably similar to those made by Dar Howard, manufacturing manager of the Hewlett-Packard factory in Colorado Springs: "We have 1,-000 in actual manufacturing. Technologically, maybe 250 of them could work at home. The logistics would be complicated, but the tooling and capital equipment would not prevent it. In white collar research and development, if you're willing to invest in [computer] terminals, one half to three quarters could also work at home." At Hewlett-Packard that would add up to an additional 350 to 520 workers.

All told, it means that fully 35 to 50 percent of the entire work force in this advanced manufacturing center could even now do most, if not all, their work at home, providing one chose to organize production that way. Third Wave manufacturing, Marx notwithstanding, does not require 100 percent of the work force to be concentrated in the workshop.

Nor are such estimates found in electronic industries alone or in giant enterprises. According to Peter Tattle, vice-president of Ortho Pharmaceutical (Canada) Ltd., the question is not "How many can be permitted to work at home?" but rather, "How many *have* to work in the office or factory?" Speaking of the 300 employed in his plant, Tattle says: "Fully 75 percent could work at home if we provided the necessary communications technology." Clearly, what applies to electronics and pharmaceuticals also applies to other advanced industries.

If significant numbers of employees in the manufacturing sector could be shifted to the home even now, then it is safe to say that a considerable slice of the white-collar sector—where there are no materials to handle—could also make that transition.

Indeed, an unmeasured but appreciable amount of work is already being done at home by such people as salesmen and saleswomen who work by phone or visit, and only occasionally touch base at the office; by architects and designers; by a burgeoning pool of specialized consultants in many industries; by large numbers of human-service workers like therapists or psychologists; by music teachers and language instructors; by art dealers, investment counselors, insurance agents, lawyers, and academic researchers; and by many other categories of white-collar, technical, and professional people.

These are, moreover, among the most rapidly expanding work classifications, and when we suddenly make available technologies that can place a low-cost "work station" in any home, providing it with a "smart" typewriter, perhaps, along with a facsimile machine or computer console and teleconferencing equipment, the possibilities for home work are radically extended.

Given such equipment, who might be the first to make the transition from centralized work to the "electronic cottage"? While it would be a mistake to underestimate the need for direct face-to-face contact in business, and all the subliminal and nonverbal communication that accompanies that contact, it is also true that certain tasks do not require much outside contact at all—or need it only intermittently.

Thus "low-abstraction" office workers for the most part perform tasks—entering data, typing, retrieving, totaling columns of figures, preparing invoices, and the like—that require few, if any, direct face-to-face transactions. They could perhaps be most easily shifted into the electronic cottage. Many of the "ultrahigh-abstraction" workers—researchers, for example, and economists, policy formulators, organizational designers—require both high-density contact with peers and colleagues *and* times to work alone. There are times when even deal-makers need to back off and do their "homework."

Nathaniel Samuels, an advisory director of the Lehman Brothers Kuhn Loeb investment banking house, agrees. Samuels, who already works at home 50 to 75 days a year, contends that "future technology will increase the amount of 'homework.'" Indeed, many companies are already relaxing their insistence that work be done in the office. When Weyerhaeuser, the great timber-products company, needed a new brochure on employee conduct not long ago, Vice-President R. L. Siegel and three of his staff members met at his home for almost a week until they had hammered out a draft. "We felt we needed to get out [of the office], to avoid the distractions," says Siegel. "Working at home is consistent with our shift toward flexible hours," he adds. "The important thing is getting your job done. It's incidental to us where you do it."

According to the *Wall Street Journal,* Weyerhaeuser is not alone. "Many other companies also are letting their employees work at home," the newspaper reports, among them United Airlines, whose director of public relations allows his staff people to write at home as much as 20 days a year. Even McDonald's, whose lower-rung employees are needed to staff the hamburger grills, encourages home work among some top executives.

"Do you really need an office as such at all?" asks Booz Allen & Hamilton's Harvey Poppel. In an unpublished forecast, Poppel suggests that "by the 1990s, two-way communications capability [will have been] enhanced sufficiently to encourage a widespread practice of working at home." His view is supported by many other researchers, like Robert F. Latham, a long-range planner at Bell Canada in Montreal. According to Latham, "As information jobs proliferate and communications facilities improve, the number of people who may work at home or at local work centres will also increase."

Similarly, Hollis Vail, a management consultant for the United States Department of the Interior, asserts that by the mid-1980's, "tomorrow's word-processing centers" could easily be in one's own home"; he has written a scenario describing how a secretary, "Jane Adams," employed by the "Afgar Company" could work at home, meeting her boss only periodically to "talk over problems, and, of course, to attend office parties."

This same view is shared by the Institute for the Future, which, as early as 1971, surveyed 150 experts in "leading edge" companies dealing with the new information technologies, and spelled out five different categories of work that could be transferred to the home.

Given the necessary tools, the IFF found, many of the present duties of the secretary "could be done from home as well as in the office. Such a system would increase the labor pool by allowing married secretaries caring for small children at home to continue to work. . . . There may be no overriding reason why a secretary could not just as well, in many instances, take dictation at home and type the text on a home terminal which produces a clean text at the author's home or office."

In addition, IFF continued, "Many of the tasks performed by engineers, draftsmen, and other white-collar employees might be done from home as readily as, or sometimes more readily than, from the office." One "seed of the future" exists already in Britain, for example, where a company called F. International Ltd. (the "F" stands for Freelance) employs 400 part-time computer programmers, all but a handful of whom work in their own homes. The company, which organizes teams of programmers for industry, has expanded to Holland and Scandinavia and counts among its clients such giants as British Steel, Shell, and Unilever. "Home computer programming," writes the *Guardian* newspaper, is "the cottage industry of the 1980s."

In short, as the Third Wave sweeps across society, we find more and more companies that can be described, in the words of one researcher, as nothing but "people huddled around a computer." Put the computer in people's homes, and they no longer need to huddle. Third Wave white-collar work, like Third Wave manufacturing, will not require 100 percent of the work force to be concentrated in the workshop.

One should not underestimate the difficulties entailed in transferring work from its Second Wave locations in factory and office to its Third Wave location in the home. Problems of motivation and management, of corporate and social reorganization will make the shift both prolonged and, perhaps, painful. Nor can all communication be handled vicariously. Some jobs—especially those involving creative deal-making, where each decision is nonroutine—require much face-to-face contact. Thus Michael Koerner, President of Canada Overseas Investments, Ltd., says, "We all need to be within a thousand feet of one another."

* * *

THE TELECOMMUTERS

Nevertheless, powerful forces are converging to promote the electronic cottage. The most immediately apparent is the economic trade-off between transportation and telecommunication. Most high-technology nations are now experiencing a transportation crisis, with mass transit systems strained to the breaking point, roads and highways clogged, parking spaces rare, pollution a serious problem, strikes and breakdowns almost routine, and costs skyrocketing.

The escalating costs of commuting are borne by the individual workers. But they are, of course, indirectly passed on to the employer in the form of higher wage costs, and to the consumer in higher prices. Jack Nilles and a team sponsored by the National Science Foundation have worked out both the dollar and the energy savings that would flow from any substantial shift of white-collar jobs out of centralized downtown offices. Instead of assuming the jobs would go into the homes of employees, the Nilles group used what might be termed a halfway-house model, assuming only that jobs would be dispersed into neighborhood work centers closer to employee homes.

The implications of their findings are startling. Studying 2,048 insurance company employees in Los Angeles, the Nilles group found that each person, on average, traveled 21.4 miles a day to and from work (as against a national average of 18.8 miles for urban workers in the United States). The higher up the managerial scale, the longer the commute, with top executives averaging 33.2 miles. All told, these workers drove 12.4 million miles each year to get to work, using up nearly a half-century's worth of hours to do so.

At 1974 prices, this cost twenty-two cents per mile, or a total of $2,730,000—an amount borne indirectly by the company and its customers. Indeed, Nilles found that the company was paying its downtown workers $520 a year more than the going rate in the dispersed locations—in effect, "a subsidy of transportation costs." It was also providing parking spaces and other costly services made necessary by the centralized location. If we now assume a secretary was earning in the neighborhood of $10,000 a year, the elimination of this commuting cost could have permitted the company to hire nearly 300 additional employees or, alternatively, to add a substantial amount to profits.

The key question is: When will the cost of installing and

operating telecommunications equipment fall below the present cost of commuting? While gasoline and other transport costs (including the costs of mass-transit alternatives to the auto) are soaring everywhere, the price of telecommunications is shrinking spectacularly.* At some point the curves must cross.

But these are not the only forces subtly moving us toward the geographical dispersal of production and, ultimately, the electronic cottage of the future. The Nilles team found that the average American urban commuter uses the gasoline equivalent of 64.6 kilowatts of energy to get back and forth to work each day. (The Los Angeles insurance employees burned 37.4 million kilowatts a year in commuting.) By contrast, it takes far less energy to move information.

A typical computer terminal uses only 100 to 125 watts or less when it is in operation, and a phone line consumes only one watt or less while it is in use. Making certain assumptions about how much communications equipment would be needed, and how long it would operate, Nilles calculated that "the relative energy consumption advantage of telecommuting over commuting (i.e., the ratio of commuting energy consumption to telecommuting consumption) is at least 29:1 when the private automobile is used; 11:1 when normally loaded mass transit is used; and 2:1 for 100 per cent utilized mass transit systems."

Carried to their conclusion, these calculations showed that in 1975, had even as little as 12 to 14 percent of urban commuting been replaced by telecommuting, the United States would have saved approximately 75 million barrels of gasoline—and would have thereby completely eliminated the need to import any gasoline from abroad. The implications of that one fact for the U.S. balance of payments and for Middle East politics might also have been more than trivial.

As gasoline prices and energy costs in general rise in the decades immediately ahead, both the dollar cost and energy costs of operating "smart" typewriters, telecopiers, audio and video links, and home-size computer consoles will plummet,

---

* Satellites slash the cost of long-distance transmission, bringing it so near the zero mark per signal that engineers now speak of "distance-independent" communications. Computer power has multiplied exponentially and prices have dropped so dramatically that engineers and investors alike are left gasping. With fiber optics and other new breakthrough technologies in the wings, it is clear that still further cost reductions lie ahead—per unit of memory, per processing step, and per signal transmitted.

still further increasing the relative advantage of moving at least some production out of the large central workshops that dominated the Second Wave era.

All these mounting pressures toward telecommuting will intensify as intermittent gas shortages, odd-even days, long lines at the fuel pump, and perhaps rationing disrupt and delay normal commuting, further jacking up its cost in both social and economic terms.

To this we can add even more pressures tending in the same direction. Corporate and government employers will discover that shifting work into the home—or into local or neighborhood work centers as a halfway measure—can sharply reduce the huge amounts now spent for real estate. The smaller the central offices and manufacturing facilities become, the smaller the real estate bill, and the smaller the costs of heating, cooling, lighting, policing, and maintaining them. As land, commercial and industrial real estate, and the associated tax load all soar, the hope of reducing and/or externalizing these costs will favor the farming-out of work.

The transfer of work and the reduction of commuting will also reduce pollution and therefore the tab for cleaning it up. The more successful environmentalists become at compelling companies to pay for their own pollution, the more incentive there will be to shift to low-polluting activities, and therefore from large-scale, centralized workplaces to smaller work centers or, better yet, into the home.

Beyond this, as environmentalists and conservation-minded citizens groups battle against the destructive effects of the auto, and oppose road and highway construction, or succeed in banning cars from certain districts, they unwittingly support the transfer of work. The net effect of their efforts is to force up the already high cost and personal inconvenience of transport as against the low cost and convenience of communication.

When environmentalists discover the ecological disparities between these two alternatives, and as the shift of work to the home begins to look like a real option, they will throw their weight behind this important decentralist move and help coax us into the civilization of the Third Wave.

Social factors, too, support the move to the electronic cottage. The shorter the workday becomes, the longer the commuting time in relationship to it. The employee who hates to spend an hour getting to and from the job in order to spend eight hours working may very well refuse to invest the same commuting time if the hours spent on the job are cut. The higher the ratio of commuting time to working time, the more irrational, frustrating, and absurd the process of shuttling back and forth. As resistance to commuting rises, employers will indirectly have to increase the premium paid to workers in the big, centralized work locations, as against those willing to take less pay for less travel time, inconvenience, and cost. Once again there will be greater incentive to transfer work.

Finally, deep value changes are moving in the same direction. Quite apart from the growth of privatism and the new allure of small-city and rural life, we are witnessing a basic shift in attitude toward the family unit. The nuclear family, the standard, socially approved family form throughout the Second Wave period, is clearly in crisis. We shall explore the family of the future in the next chapter. For now, we need only note that in the United States and Europe—wherever the transition out of the nuclear family is most advanced— there is a swelling demand for action to glue the family unit together again. And it is worth observing that one of the things that has bound families tightly together through history has been shared work.

Even today one suspects that divorce rates are lower among couples who work together. The electronic cottage raises once more on a mass scale the possibility of husbands and wives, and perhaps even children, working together as a unit. And when campaigners for family life discover the possibilities inherent in the transfer of work to the home we may well see a rising demand for political measures to speed up the process—tax incentives, for example, and new conceptions of workers' rights.

During the early days of the Second Wave era, the workers' movement fought for a "Ten Hour Day," a demand that would have been almost incomprehensible during the First Wave period. Soon we may see the rise of movements demanding that all work that *can* be done at home *be* done at home. Many workers will insist on that option as a right. And, to the degree that this relocation of work is seen as strengthening family life, their demand will receive strong support from people of many different political, religious, and cultural persuasions.

The fight for the electronic cottage is part of the larger super-struggle between the Second Wave past and the Third Wave future, and it is likely to bring together not merely technologists and corporations eager to exploit the new technical possibilities but a wide range of other forces—environmentalists, labor reformers of a new style, and a broad coalition of organizations, from conservative churches to radical feminists and mainstream political groups—in support of what may well be seen as a new, more satisfactory future for the family. The electronic cottage may thus emerge as a key rallying point of the Third Wave forces of tomorrow.

THE HOME-CENTERED SOCIETY

If the electronic cottage were to spread, a chain of consequences of great importance would flow through society. Many of these consequences would please the most ardent environmentalist or techno-rebel, while at the same time opening new options for business entrepreneurship.

Community Impact: Work at home involving any sizeable fraction of the population could mean greater community stability—a goal that now seems beyond our reach in many high-change regions. If employees can perform some or all of their work tasks at home, they do not have to move every time they change jobs, as many are compelled to do today. They can simply plug into a different computer.

This implies less forced mobility, less stress on the individual, fewer transient human relationships, and greater participation in community life. Today when a family moves into a community, suspecting that it will be moving out again in a year or two, its members are markedly reluctant to join neighborhood organizations, to make deep friendships, to engage in local politics, and to commit themselves to community life generally. The electronic cottage could help restore a sense of community belonging, and touch off a renaissance among voluntary organizations like churches, women's groups, lodges, clubs, athletic and youth organizations. The electronic cottage could mean more of what sociologists, with their love of German jargon, call *gemeinschaft*.

Environmental Impact: The transfer of work, or any part of it, into the home could not only reduce energy requirements, as suggested above, but could also lead to energy decentralization. Instead of requiring highly concentrated amounts of energy in a few high-rise offices or sprawling factory complexes, and therefore requiring highly centralized energy generation, the electronic cottage system would spread out energy demand and thus make it easier to use solar, wind, and other alternative energy technologies. Small-scale energy generation units in each home could substitute for at least some of the centralized energy now required. This implies a decline in pollution as well, for two reasons: first, the switch to renewable energy sources on a small-scale basis eliminates the need for high-polluting fuels, and second, it means smaller releases of highly concentrated pollutants that overload the environment at a few critical locations.

Economic Impact: Some businesses would shrink in such a system, and others proliferate or grow. Clearly, the electronics and computer and communications industries would flourish. By contrast, the oil companies, the auto industry, and commercial real estate developers would be hurt. A whole new group of small-scale computer stores and information services would spring up; the postal service, by contrast, would shrink. Papermakers would do less well; most service industries and white-collar industries would benefit.

At a deeper level, if individuals came to own their own electronic terminals and equipment, purchased perhaps on credit, they would become, in effect, independent entrepreneurs rather than classical employees—meaning, as it were, increased ownership of the "means of production" by the worker. We might also see groups of home-workers organize themselves into small companies to contract for their services or, for that matter, unite in cooperatives that jointly own the machines. All sorts of new relationships and organizational forms become possible.

Psychological Impact: The picture of a work world that is increasingly dependent upon abstract symbols conjures up an overcerebral work environment that is alien to us and, at one level, more impersonal than at present. But at a different level, work at home suggests a deepening of face-to-face and emotional relationships in both the home and the neighborhood. Rather than a world of purely vicarious human relationships, with an electric screen interposed between the individual and the rest of humanity, as imagined in many science fiction stories, one can postulate a world divided into two sets of human relationships—one real, the other vicarious—with different rules and roles in each.

No doubt we will experiment with many variations and halfway measures. Many people will work at home part-time and outside the home as well. Dispersed work centers will no doubt proliferate. Some people will work at home for months or years, then switch to an outside job, and then perhaps switch back again. Patterns of leadership and management will have to change. Small firms would undoubtedly spring up to contract for white-collar tasks from larger firms and take on specialized responsibilities for organizing, training, and managing teams of homeworkers. To maintain adequate liaison among them, perhaps such small companies will organize parties, social occasions, and other joint holidays, so that the members of a team get to know one another face-to-face, not merely through the console or keyboard.

Certainly not everyone can or will (or will want to) work at home. Certainly we face a conflict over pay scales and opportunity cost. What happens to the society when an increased amount of human interaction on the job is vicarious while face-to-face, emotion-to-emotion interaction intensifies in the home? What about cities? What happens to the unemployment figures? What, in fact, do we mean by the terms "employment" and "unemployment" in such a system? It would be naïve to dismiss such questions and problems.

But if there are unanswered questions and possibly painful difficulties, there are also new possibilities. The leap to a new system of production is likely to render irrelevant many of the most intractable problems of the passing era. The misery of feudal toil, for example, could not be alleviated within the system of feudal agriculture. It was not eliminated by peasant revolts, by altruistic nobles, or by religious utopians. Toil remained miserable until it was altered entirely by the arrival of the factory system, with its own strikingly different drawbacks.

In turn, the characteristic problems of industrial society—from unemployment to grinding monotony on the job, to overspecialization, to the callous treatment of the individual, to low wages—may, despite the best intentions and promises of job enlargers, trade unions, benign employers, or revolutionary workers' parties, be wholly unresolvable within the framework of the Second Wave production system. If such problems have remained for 300 years, under both capitalist and socialist arrangements, there is cause to think they may be inherent in the mode of production.

The leap to a new production system in both manufacturing and the white-collar sector, and the possible breakthrough to the electronic cottage, promise to change all the existing terms of debate, making obsolete most of the issues over which men and women today, argue, struggle, and sometimes die.

We cannot today know if, in fact, the electronic cottage will become the norm of the future. Nevertheless, it is worth recognizing that if as few as 10 to 20 percent of the work force as presently defined were to make this historic transfer over the next 20 to 30 years, our entire economy, our cities, our ecology, our family structure, our values, and even our politics would be altered almost beyond our recognition.

It is a possibility—a plausibility, perhaps—to be pondered.

It is not possible to see in relationship to one another a number of Third Wave changes usually examined in isolation. We see a transformation of our technological system and our energy base into a new *techno-sphere*. This is occurring at the same time that we are de-massifying the mass media and building an intelligent environment, thus revolutionizing the *info-sphere* as well. In turn, these two giant currents flow together to change the deep structure of our production system, altering the nature of work in factory and office and, ultimately, carrying us toward the transfer of work back into the home.

By themselves, such massive historical shifts would easily justify the claim that we are on the edge of a new civilization. But we are simultaneously restructuring our social life as well, from our family ties and friendships to our schools and corporations. We are about to create, alongside the Third Wave techno-sphere and info-sphere, a Third Wave *sociosphere* as well.

17 ≋

FAMILIES OF THE FUTURE

During the Great Depression of the 1930's millions of men were thrown out of work. As factory doors clanged shut against them, many plunged into extremes of despair and guilt, their egos shattered by the pink layoff slip.

Eventually unemployment came to be seen in a more sensible light—not as the result of individual laziness or moral failure but of giant forces outside the individual's control. The maldistribution of wealth, myopic investment, runaway speculation, stupid trade policies, inept government—these, not the personal weakness of laid-off workers, caused unemployment. Feelings of guilt were, in most cases, naïvely inappropriate.

Today, once more, egos are breaking like eggshells against the wall. Now, however, the guilt is associated with the fracture of the family rather than the economy. As millions of men and women clamber out of the strewn wreckage of their marriages they, too, suffer agonies of self-blame. And once more, much of the guilt is misplaced.

When a tiny minority is involved, the crack-up of their families may reflect individual failures. But when divorce, separation, and other forms of familial disaster overtake millions at once in many countries, it is absurd to think the causes are purely personal.

The fracture of the family today is, in fact, part of the general crisis of industrialism—the crack-up of all the institutions spawned by the Second Wave. It is part of the ground-clearing for a new Third Wave socio-sphere. And it is this

208

traumatic process, reflected in our individual lives, that is altering the family system beyond recognition.

Today we are told repeatedly that "the family" is falling apart or that "the family" is our Number One Problem. President Jimmy Carter declares, "It is clear that the national government should have a pro-family policy. . . . There can be no more urgent priority." Substitute preachers, prime ministers, or the press, and the pious rhetoric comes out very much the same. When they speak of "the family," however, they typically do *not* mean the family in all its luxuriant variety of possible forms, but one particular type of family: the Second Wave family.

What they usually have in mind is a husband-breadwinner, a wife-housekeeper, and a number of small children. While many other family types exist, it was this particular family form—the nuclear family—that Second Wave civilization idealized, made dominant, and spread around the world.

This type of family became the standard, socially approved model because its structure perfectly fitted the needs of a mass-production society with widely shared values and lifestyles, hierarchical, bureaucratic power, and a clear separation of home life from work life in the marketplace.

Today, when the authorities urge us to "restore" the family it is this Second Wave nuclear family they usually have in mind. By thinking so narrowly they not only misdiagnose the entire problem, they reveal a childish naïveté about what steps would actually be required to restore the nuclear family to its former importance.

Thus the authorities frantically blame the family crisis on everything from "smut peddlers" to rock music. Some tell us that opposing abortion or wiping out sex education or resisting feminism will glue the family back together again. Or they urge courses in "family education." The chief United States government statistician on family matters wants "more effective training" to teach people how to marry more wisely, or else a "scientifically tested and appealing system for selecting a marriage partner." What we need, say others, are more marriage counselors or even more public relations to give the family a better image! Blind to the ways in which historical waves of change influence us, they come up with well-intentioned, often inane proposals that utterly miss the target.

*   *   *

THE PRO-NUCLEAR CAMPAIGN

If we really want to restore the nuclear family to its former dominance, there *are* things we could do. Here are a few:

1) Freeze all technology in its Second Wave stage to maintain a factory-based, mass-production society. Begin by smashing the computer. The computer is a greater threat to the Second Wave family than all the abortion laws and gay rights movements and pornography in the world, for the nuclear family *needs* the mass-production system to retain its dominance, and the computer is moving us beyond mass production.

2) Subsidize manufacture and block the rise of the service sector in the economy. White-collar, professional, and technical workers are less traditional, less family-oriented, more intellectually and psychologically mobile than blue-collar workers. Divorce rates have risen along with the rise in service occupations.

3) "Solve" the energy crisis by applying nuclear and other highly centralized energy processes. The nuclear family fits better in a centralized than a decentralized society, and energy systems heavily affect the degree of social and political centralization.

4) Ban the increasingly de-massified media, beginning with cable television and cassette, but not overlooking local and regional magazines. Nuclear families work best where there is a national consensus on information and values, not in a society based on high diversity. While some critics naïvely attack the media for allegedly undermining the family, it was the mass media that idealized the nuclear family form in the first place.

5) Forcibly drive women back into the kitchen. Reduce the wages of women to the absolute minimum. Strengthen, rather than relax, all union seniority provisions to assure that women are further disadvantaged in the labor force. The nuclear family has no nucleus when there are no adults left at home. (One could, of course, achieve the same effect by reversing matters, permitting women to work while compelling men to stay home and rear the children.)

6) Simultaneously slash the wages of young workers to make them more dependent, for a longer time, on their families—and thus less psychologically independent. The nu-

clear family is further denuclearized when the young leave parental control to go to work.

7) Ban contraception and research into reproductive biology. These make for the independence of women and for extramarital sex, a notorious loosener of nuclear ties.

8) Cut the standard of living of the entire society to pre-1955 levels, since affluence makes it possible for single people, divorced people, working women, and other unattached individuals to "make it" economically on their own. The nuclear family needs a touch of poverty (not too much, not too little) to sustain it.

9) Finally, re-massify our rapidly de-massifying society, by resisting all changes—in politics, the arts, education, business, or other fields—that lead toward diversity, freedom of movement and ideas, or individuality. The nuclear family remains dominant only in a mass society.

In short, this is what a pro-family policy would have to be if we insist on defining family as nuclear. If we truly wish to restore the Second Wave family, we had better be prepared to restore Second Wave civilization as a whole—to freeze not only technology but history itself.

For what we are witnessing is not the death of the family as such, but the final fracture of the Second Wave family system in which all families were supposed to emulate the idealized nuclear model, and the emergence in its place of a diversity of family forms. Just as we are de-massifying our media and our production, we are de-massifying the family system in the transition to a Third Wave civilization.

NON-NUCLEAR LIFE-STYLES

The coming of the Third Wave, of course, does not mean the end of the nuclear family any more than the coming of the Second Wave meant the end of the extended family. It means, rather, that the nuclear family can no longer serve as the ideal model for society.

The little-appreciated fact is that, at least in the United States where the Third Wave is most advanced, most people *already* live outside the classical nuclear family form.

If we define the nuclear family as a working husband, a housekeeping wife, and two children, and ask how many Americans actually still live in this type of family, the answer is astonishing: 7 percent of the total United States population. Ninety-three percent of the population do not fit this ideal Second Wave model any longer.

Even if we broaden our definition to include families in which both spouses work or in which there are fewer or more than two children, we find the vast majority—as many as two thirds to three quarters of the population—living *outside* the nuclear situation. Moreover, all the evidence suggests that nuclear households (however we choose to define them) are still shrinking in number as other family forms rapidly multiply.

To begin with, we are witnessing a population explosion of "solos"—people who live alone, outside a family altogether. Between 1970 and 1978 the number of persons aged fourteen to thirty-four who lived alone nearly tripled in the United States—rising from 1.5 million to 4.3 million. Today, a fifth of all households in the United States consists of a person living solo. Nor are all these people losers or loners, forced into the solo life. Many deliberately choose it, at least for a time. Says a legislative aide to a Seattle councilwoman, "I would consider marriage if the right person came along, but I would not give up my career for it." In the meantime she lives alone. She is part of a large class of young adults who are leaving home earlier but marrying later, thus creating what census specialist Arthur Norton says is a "transitional living phase" that is "becoming an acceptable part of one's life cycle."

Looking at an older slice of the population, we find a large number of formerly married people, often "between marriages," living on their own and, in many cases, decidedly liking it. The growth of such groups has created a flourishing "singles" culture and a much publicized proliferation of bars, ski lodges, travel tours, and other services or products designed for the independent individual. Simultaneously, the real estate industry has come up with "singles only" condominia, and has begun to respond to a need for smaller apartments and suburban homes with fewer bedrooms. Almost a fifth of all home buyers in the United States today are single.

We are also experiencing a headlong growth in the number of people living together without bothering about legal formalities. This group has more than doubled in the past decade, according to United States authorities. The practice has become so common that the United States Department of Housing and Urban Development has overthrown tradition and changed its rules to permit such couples to occupy public housing. The courts, meanwhile, from Connecticut to California, are wrestling with the legal and property complications that spring up when such couples "divorce." Etiquette columnists write about which names to use in addressing partners, and "couple counseling" has sprouted as a new professional service alongside marriage counseling.

THE CHILD-FREE CULTURE

Another significant change has been the growth in the number of those consciously choosing what is coming to be known as a "child-free" life-style. According to James Ramey, senior research associate at the Center for Policy Research, we are seeing a massive shift from "child-centered" to "adult-centered" homes. At the turn of the century there were few singles in society, and relatively few parents lived very long after their youngest child left the home. Thus most households were, in fact, child-centered. By contrast, as early as 1970 in the United States only one in three adults lived in a home with children under eighteen.

Today organizations are springing up to promote the child-free life, and a reluctance to have children is spreading in many industrial nations. In 1960 only 20 percent of "evermarried" American women under age thirty were child-free. By 1975 this had shot up to 32 percent—a 60 percent jump in fifteen years. A vocal organization, the National Alliance for Optional Parenthood, has arisen to protect the rights of the childless and to combat pronatalist propaganda.

A similar organization, the National Association for the Childless, has sprouted in Britain, and many couples across Europe are also deliberately choosing to remain childless. In Bonn, West Germany, for example, Theo and Agnes Rohl, both in their mid-thirties, he a city official, she a secretary, say, "We don't think we'll have children . . ." The Rohls are modestly affluent. They own a small home. They manage a vacation trip to California or Southern France now and then. Children would drastically alter their way of life. "We're used to our life-style the way it is," they say, "and we like being independent." Nor is this reluctance to bear children a sign of capitalist decadence. It is present in the Soviet Union, too, where many young Russian couples echo the sentiments of the Rohls and explicitly reject parenthood—a fact that worries Soviet officialdom in view of the still-high birth rates among several non-Russian national minorities.

Turning now to those *with* children, the breakdown of the nuclear family is even more sharply evidenced in the spectacular increase in single-parent families. So many divorces, breakups, and separations have occurred in recent years— mainly in nuclear families—that today a staggering one-in-seven American children is raised by a single parent, and the number is even higher—one in four—in urban areas.*

The increase in such households has brought a growing recognition that, despite severe problems, a one-parent household can, under certain circumstances, be better for the child than a nuclear household continually torn by bitter strife. Newspapers and organizations now serve single parents and are heightening their group consciousness and political clout.

Nor, once again, is the phenomenon purely American. In Britain today nearly one family in ten is headed by a single parent—nearly a sixth of them headed by men—and one-parent households form what *New Society* magazine calls "the fastest growing group in poverty." A London-based organization, the National Council for One-Parent Families, has sprung up to champion their cause.

In Germany, a housing association in Cologne has constructed a special block of apartments for such families and provided them with day-time child care so the parents can work. And in Scandinavia a network of special welfare rights has grown up to support these families. The Swedes, for example, give one-parent households first crack at nursery and day-care facilities. In both Norway and Sweden, in fact, it is sometimes possible for a single-parent family to enjoy a higher standard of living than that of the typical nuclear family.

A challenging new form of family has arisen in the meantime that reflects the high rate of remarriage after divorce. In *Future Shock* I identified this as the "aggregate family," in which two divorced couples with children remarry, bringing the children of both marriages (and the adults as well) into a new, expanded family form. It is now estimated that 25 percent of American children are, or will soon be, members of such family units. According to Davidyne Mayleas, such units, with their "poly-parents," may be the mainstream family form of tomorrow. "We're into economic polygamy," says Mayleas—meaning that the two merged family units

---

* The total is also fed by out-of-wedlock births and by adoptions by single women and (increasingly) single men.

typically transfer money back and forth in the form of child support or other payments. The spread of this family form, she reports, has been accompanied by a rising incidence of sexual relations between parents and nonblood-related children.

The technologically advanced nations today are honeycombed with a bewildering array of family forms: Homosexual marriages, communes, groups of elderly people banding together to share expenses (and sometimes sex), tribal groupings among certain ethnic minorities, and many other forms coexist as never before. There are contract marriages, serial marriages, family clusters, and a variety of intimate networks with or without shared sex, as well as families in which mother and father live and work in two different cities.

Even these family forms barely hint at the even richer variety bubbling under the surface. When three psychiatrists—Kellam, Ensminger, and Turner—attempted to map the "variations of families" found in a single poor black neighborhood in Chicago, they identified "no less than 86 different combinations of adults," including numerous forms of "mother-grandmother" families, "mother-aunt" families, "mother-stepfather families," and "mother-other" families.

Faced with this veritable maze of kinship arrangements, even fairly orthodox scholars have come around to the once radical view that we are moving out of the age of the nuclear family and into a new society marked by diversity in family life. In the words of sociologist Jessie Bernard, "The most characteristic aspect of marriage in the future will be precisely the array of options available to different people who want different things from their relationships with one another."

The frequently asked question, "What is the future of the family?" usually implies that as the Second Wave nuclear family loses its dominance some other form will replace it. A more likely outcome is that during Third Wave civilization no single form will dominate the family mix for any long period. Instead we will see a high variety of family structures. Rather than masses of people living in uniform family arrangements, we shall see people moving through this system, tracing personalized or "customized" trajectories during the course of their lives.

Again, this does not mean the total elimination or "death" of the nuclear family. It merely means that from now on the nuclear family will be only one of the many socially accepted and approved forms. As the Third Wave sweeps in, the family system is becoming de-massified right along with the production system and the information system in society.

"HOT" RELATIONSHIPS

Given this flowering of a multiplicity of family forms, it is too early to tell which will emerge as significant styles in a Third Wave civilization.

Will our children live alone for many years, perhaps decades? Will they go childless? Will we retire into old-age communes? What about more exotic possibilities? Families with several husbands and one wife? (That could happen if genetic tinkering lets us preselect the sex of our children, and too many parents choose boys.) What about homosexual families raising children? The courts are already debating this issue. What about the potential impact of cloning?

If each of us moves through a trajectory of family experiences in our lives, what will the phases be? A trial marriage, followed by a dual-career marriage with no children, then a homosexual marriage *with* children? The possible permutations are endless. Nor, despite the cries of outrage, should any of these be regarded as unthinkable. As Jessie Bernard has put it, "There is literally nothing about marriage that anyone can imagine that has not in fact taken place. . . . All these variations seeemed quite natural to those who lived with them."

Which specific family forms vanish and which ones proliferate will depend less on pulpit-pounding about the "sanctity of the family" than on the decisions we make with respect to technology and work. While many forces influence family structure—communication patterns, values, demographic changes, religious movements, even ecological shifts—the linkage between family form and work arrangements is particularly strong. Thus, just as the nuclear family was promoted by the rise of the factory and office work, any shift *away* from the factory and office would also exert a heavy influence on the family.

It is impossible, in the space of a single chapter, to spell out all the ways in which the coming changes in the labor force and in the nature of work will alter family life. But one change is so potentially revolutionary, and so alien to our experience, it needs far more attention than it has received so far. This is, of course, the shift of work out of the office and factory and back into the home.

Assume for a moment that twenty-five years from now 15 percent of the work force is employed part- or full-time in the home. How would working at home change the quality of our personal relationships or the meaning of love? What would life be like in the electronic cottage?

Whether the work-at-home task is programming a computer, writing a pamphlet, monitoring distant manufacturing processes, designing a building, or typing electronic correspondence, one immediate change is clear. Relocating work into the home means that many spouses who now see each other only a limited number of hours each day would be thrown together more intimately. Some, no doubt, would find this prolonged proximity hateful. Many others, however, would find their marriages saved and their relationships much enriched through shared experience.

Let us visit several electronic cottages to see how people might adapt to so fundamental a change in society. Such a tour would no doubt reveal a wide diversity of living and working arrangements.

In some houses, perhaps the majority, we might well find couples dividing things up more or less conventionally, with one person doing the "job-work" while the other keeps house—he, perhaps, writing programs while she looks after the kids. The very presence of work in the home, however, would probably encourage a sharing of both job-work and housekeeping. We would find many homes, therefore, in which man and wife split a single full-time job. For example, we might find both husband and wife taking turns at monitoring a complex manufacturing process on the console screen in the den, four hours on, four hours off.

Down the street, by contrast, we would likely discover a couple holding not one, but two quite different jobs, with each spouse working separately. A cellular physiologist and a CPA might each work at his or her craft. Even here, however, with the jobs differing sharply in character, there is still likely to be some sharing of problems, some learning of each other's work vocabulary, some common concerns and conversation relating to work. It is almost impossible under such conditions for the work life of an individual to be strictly segregated from personal life. By the same token, it is next to impossible to freeze one's mate out of a whole dimension of one's existence.

Right next door (continuing our survey) we could well come upon a couple holding two different jobs but sharing *both*, the husband working as a part-time insurance planner and part-time as an architect's assistant, with the wife doing the same work on alternating shifts. This arrangement would provide more varied, and therefore more interesting, work for both.

In such homes, whether one or several jobs are shared, each partner necessarily learns from the other, participates in the problem-solving, engages in complex give-and-take, all of which cannot help but deepen intimacy. Forced proximity, it goes without saying, does not guarantee happiness. The extended family units of the First Wave era, which were also economic production units, were hardly models of interpersonal sensitivity and mutual psychological support. Such families had their own problems and stresses. But there were few uncommitted or "cooled out" relationships. Working together assured, if nothing else, tight, complex, "hot" personal relationships—a committedness many people envy today.

In short, the spread of work-at-home on a large scale could not only affect family structure but transform relationships within the family. It could, to put it simply, provide a common set of experiences and get marriage partners talking to one another again. It could shift their relationships along the spectrum from "cool" to "hot." It could also redefine love itself and bring with it the concept of Love Plus.

LOVE PLUS

We saw how, as the Second Wave progressed, the family unit transferred many of its functions to other institutions—education to the school, care of the ill to hospitals, and so on. This progressive stripping away of the functions of the family unit was accompanied by the rise of romantic love.

A First Wave person looking for a mate might properly have asked "Is my proposed spouse a good worker? A good healer? A good teacher for the children to come? Can we work together compatibly? Will she (or he) carry a full load or prove to be a shirker?" Peasant families actually asked "Is she strong, good at bending and lifting, or is she sickly and weak?"

As the functions of the family were hived off during the Second Wave era, those questions changed. The family was no longer a combination of production team, school, field hospital, and nursing home. Instead, its psychological functions became more important. Marriage was supposed to supply companionship, sex, warmth, and support. Soon this shift in the functions of the family was reflected in new criteria for choosing a mate. They were summed up in the single word *love*. It was love, the popular culture assured us, that makes the world go round.

Of course, real life seldom lived up to romantic fiction. Class, social status, and income continued to play a role in the choice of a mate. But all such considerations were supposed to be secondary to Love with a capital L.

Tomorrow's rise of the electronic cottage may very well overthrow this single-minded logic. Those who look ahead to working at home with a spouse, instead of spending the main part of their waking lives away, are likely to take more into consideration than simple sexual and psychological gratification—or social status, for that matter. They may begin to insist on Love Plus—sexual and psychological gratification *plus* brains (as their grandfathers once favored brawn), love *plus* conscientiousness, responsibility, self-discipline, or other work-related virtues. We may—who knows?—hear some John Denver of the future croon lyrics like:

> I love your eyes, your cherry lips,
> the love that always lingers,
> your way with words and random blips,
> your skilled computer fingers.

More seriously, one can imagine at least some families of the future taking on additional functions rather than shedding them, and serving as a multipurpose, rather than a narrowly specialized, social unit. With such a change the criteria for marriage, the very definition of love would be transformed.

THE CAMPAIGN FOR CHILD LABOR

Children, meanwhile, would also be likely to grow up differently in the electronic cottage, if for no other reason than that they would actually see work taking place. First Wave children, from their first blink of consciousness, saw their parents at work. Second Wave children, by contrast—at least in recent generations—were segregated in schools and divorced from real work life. Most today have only the foggiest notion of what their parents do or how they live while at work. One possibly apocryphal story makes the point: An executive decides to bring his son to his office one day and to take him out to lunch. The boy sees the plushly carpeted office, the indirect lighting, the elegant reception room. He sees the fancy expense-account restaurant with its obsequious waiters and exorbitant prices. Finally, picturing their home and unable to restrain himself, the boy blurts out: "Daddy, how come you're so rich and we're so poor?"

The fact is that children today—especially affluent children—are totally divorced from one of the most important dimensions of their parents' lives. In an electronic cottage kids not only observe work, they may, after a certain age, engage in it themselves. Second Wave restrictions on child labor—originally well-intentioned and necessary, but now largely an anachronistic device to keep young people out of the crowded job market—become more difficult to enforce in the home setting. Certain forms of work, indeed, might be specifically designed for youngsters and even integrated with their education. (Anyone who underestimates the capacity of even very young people to understand and cope with sophisticated work has not run into the fourteen- or fifteen-year-old boys who serve, probably illegally, as "salesmen" in California computer stores. I have had kids with braces still on their teeth explain the intricacies of home computing to me.)

The alienation of youth today flows in large measure from being forced to accept a nonproductive role in society during an endlessly prolonged adolescence. The electronic cottage would counteract this situation.

In fact, integrating young people into work in the electronic cottage may offer the only real solution to the problems of high youth unemployment. This problem will grow increasingly explosive in many countries in the years ahead, with all the attendant evils of juvenile crime, violence, and psychological immiseration, and cannot be solved within the framework of a Second Wave economy except by totalitarian means—drafting young people, for example, for war or forced service. The electronic cottage opens an alternative way to bring youth back into socially and economically productive roles, and we may see, before long, political campaigns *for*, rather than against, child labor, along with struggles over the necessary measures to protect them against gross economic exploitation.

THE ELECTRONIC EXPANDED FAMILY

Beyond this, one can easily imagine the work-at-home household becoming something radically different: an "electronic expanded family."

Perhaps the most common family form in First Wave societies was the so-called extended family, which brought several generations together under the same roof. There were also "expanded families" which, in addition to the core members, included an unrelated orphan or two, an apprentice or additional farm hand, or others. One can likewise picture the work-at-home family of tomorrow inviting an outsider or two to join it—for example, a colleague from the husband's or wife's firm, or perhaps a customer or supplier engaged in related work, or, for that matter, a neighbor's child who wants to learn the trade. One can foresee the legal incorporation of such a family as a small business under special laws designed to foster the commune-cum-corporation or the cooperative. For many the household would become an electronic expanded family.

It is true that most of the communes formed in the 1960's and 1970's fell rapidly apart, seeming to suggest that communes, as such, are inherently unstable in high-technology societies. A closer look reveals, however, that the ones that disintegrated most rapidly were those organized primarily for psychological purposes—to promote interpersonal sensitivity, to combat loneliness, to provide intimacy, or the like. Most had no economic base and saw themselves as utopian experiments. The communes that have succeeded over time—and some have—are, by contrast, those that have had a clear external mission, an economic base, and a practical, rather than purely utopian, outlook.

An external mission welds a group together. It may, indeed, provide the necessary economic base. If this external mission is to design a new product, to handle the "electronic paper work" for a hospital, to do the data processing for an insurance company department, to set up the scheduling for a commuter airline, to prepare catalogs, or to operate a technical information service, the electronic commune of tomorrow may, in fact, turn out to be a quite workable and stable family form.

Moreover, since such electronic expanded families would not be designed as a rebuke to everyone else's life-style or for demonstration purposes but rather as an integral part of the main wiring of the economic system, the chances for their survival would be sharply improved. Indeed, we may find expanded households linking up to form networks. Such networks of expanded families could supply some needed business or social service, cooperating to market their work or setting up their own version of a trade association to represent them. Internally, they might or might not share sex across marriage lines. They might or might not be heterosexual. They might be childless or child-ful.

In brief, what we see is the possible resurrection of the expanded family. Today some 6 percent of American adults live in ordinary extended families. One might easily imagine a doubling or tripling of this number in the next generation, with some units expanding to include outsiders. This would be no trivial event but a movement involving millions in the United States alone. For community life, for patterns of love and marriage, for the reconstitution of friendship networks, for the economy and the consumer marketplace, as well as for our psyches and personality structure, the rise of the electronic expanded family would be momentous.

This new version of the extended family is not presented here as inevitable, not as better or worse than some other type of family, but simply as one example of the many new family forms likely to find viable niches in the complex social ecology of tomorrow.

PARENTAL MALPRACTICE

This rich diversity of family forms won't come into being without pain and anguish. For any change in family structure also forces change in the roles we live. Every society, through its institutions, creates its own architecture of roles or social expectations. The corporation and trade union between them more or less defined what was expected of workers and bosses. Schools fixed the respective roles of teachers and pupils. And the Second Wave family allocated the roles of breadwinner, housekeeper, and child. As the nuclear family goes critical, so to speak, the roles associated with it begin to shiver and crack—with excruciating personal impact.

From the day that Betty Friedan's bombshell book, *The Feminine Mystique,* launched the modern feminist movement in many nations, we have seen a painful struggle to redefine the roles of men and women in terms appropriate to a post-nuclear-family future. The expectations and the behavior of both sexes have shifted with respect to jobs, legal and financial rights, household responsibilities, and even sexual performance. "Now," writes Peter Knobler, editor of *Crawdaddy*, a rock music magazine, "a guy's got to contend with women breaking all the rules. . . . Many regulations need breaking," he adds, "but that doesn't make it much easier."

Roles are shaken by the battle over abortion, for instance, as women insist that they—not politicians, not priests, not doctors or even husbands—have a right to control their bodies. Sexual roles are further blurred as homosexuals demand and partially win "gay rights." Even the role of the child in society is changing. Suddenly advocates spring up to lobby for a Children's Bill of Rights.

Courts are swamped by cases involving role redefinition, as alternatives to the nuclear family multiply and gain acceptability. Do unmarried spouses have to share their property after they break up? Can a couple legally pay a woman to bear a child for them by artificial insemination? (A British court said no—but for how long?) Can a lesbian be a "good mother" and retain custody of her child after a divorce? (An American court says yes.) What is meant by being a good parent? Nothing underlines the changing role structure more than the lawsuit filed in Boulder, Colorado, by an angry twenty-four-year-old named Tom Hansen. Parents can make mistakes, Hansen's lawyers argued, but they must be held legally—and financially—responsible for the results. Thus Hansen's court action claimed $350,000 in damages on an unprecedented legal ground: parental malpractice.

EASING INTO TOMORROW

Behind all this confusion and turmoil, a new Third Wave family system is coalescing, based on a diversity of family forms and more varied individual roles. This de-massification of the family opens many new personal options. Third Wave civilization will not try to stuff everyone willy-nilly into a single family form. For this reason the emergent family system could free each of us to find his or her own niche, to select or create a family style or trajectory attuned to individualized needs.

But before anyone can perform a celebratory dance, the

agonies of transition must be dealt with. Caught in the
crack-up of the old, with the new system not yet in place,
millions find the higher level of diversity bewildering rather
than helpful. Instead of being liberated, they suffer from
overchoice and are wounded, embittered, plunged into a sor-
row and loneliness intensified by the very multiplicity of their
options.

To make the new diversity work for us instead of against
us, we will need changes on many levels at once, from morality and taxes to employment practices.

In the field of values we need to begin removing the unwarranted guilt that accompanies the breakup and restructuring of families. Instead of exacerbating unjustified guilt, the
media, the church, the courts, and the political system should
be working to lower the guilt level.

The decision to live outside a nuclear family framework
should be made easier, not harder. Values change more
slowly, as a rule, than social reality. Thus we have not yet developed the ethic of tolerance for diversity that a de-massified
society will both require and engender. Raised under Second
Wave conditions, firmly taught that one kind of family is
"normal" and others somehow suspect, if not "deviant," vast
numbers remain intolerant of the new variety in family styles.
Until that changes, the pain of transition will remain unnecessarily high.

In economic and social life, individuals cannot enjoy the
benefits of widened family options so long as laws, tax codes,
welfare practices, school arrangements, housing codes, and
even architectural forms all remain implicitly biased toward
the Second Wave family. They take little account of the
special needs of women who work, of men who stay home to
take care of their children, of bachelors and "spinsters"
(hateful term!), or of between-marrieds, or "aggregate
families," or widows living alone or together. All such groupings have been subtly or openly discriminated against in
Second Wave societies.

Even while it piously praised housekeeping, Second Wave
civilization denied dignity to the person performing that task.
Housekeeping is productive, indeed crucial, work, and needs
to be recognized as part of the economy. To assure the enhanced status of housekeeping, whether done by women or
by men, by individuals or by groups working together, we
will have to pay wages or impute economic value to it.

In the out-of-the-home economy, employment practices in

many places still are based on the obsolete assumption that the man is the primary breadwinner and the wife a supplemental, expendable earner, instead of a fully independent participant in the labor market. By easing seniority requirements, by spreading flextime, by opening part-time opportunities, we not only humanize production, we adapt it to the needs of a multistyle family system. Today there are many indications that the work system is beginning to accommodate itself to the new diversity of family arrangements. Shortly after Citibank, one of the largest banks in the United States, began to promote women to managerial jobs, it found that its male executives were marrying their new colleagues. The bank had a long-standing rule barring the employment of couples. It had to change that rule. According to *Business Week*, the "company couple" is now flourishing with benefits both for company and for family life.

It is likely that before long we will go far beyond such minor adaptations. We may see demands not merely for the hiring of "company couples" but of whole families to work together as a production team. Because this was inefficient in the Second Wave factory doesn't mean it is necessarily inappropriate today. No one knows how such policies would work out but, as in other family matters, we ought to encourage, perhaps even publicly fund, small-scale experiments.

Such measures could help us ease our way into tomorrow, minimizing for millions the pain of transition. But whether painful or not, a new family system is emerging to supplant the one that characterized the Second Wave past. This new family system will be a core institution in the novel sociosphere taking shape alongside the new techno-sphere and info-sphere. It is part of the act of social creation by which our generation is adapting to and constructing a new civilization.

18

THE CORPORATE
IDENTITY CRISIS

The big corporation was the characteristic business organization of the industrial era. Today several thousand such behemoths, both private and public, bestride the earth, producing a large proportion of all the goods and services we buy.

Seen from the outside they present a commanding appearance. They control vast resources, employ millions of workers, and they deeply influence not merely our economies but our political affairs as well. Their computers and corporate jets, their unmatched ability to plan, to invest, to execute projects on a grand scale, make them seem unshakably powerful and permanent. At a time when most of us feel powerless, they appear to dominate our destinies.

Yet that is not the way they look from the inside, to the men (and a few women) who run these organizations. Indeed, many of our top managers today feel quite as frustrated and powerless as the rest of us. For exactly like the nuclear family, the school, the mass media, and the other key institutions of the industrial age, the corporation is being hurled about, shaken and transformed by the Third Wave of change. And a good many top managers do not know what has hit them.

KABUKI CURRENCY

The most immediate change affecting the corporation is the crisis in the world economy. For three hundred years Second Wave civilization worked to create an integrated global marketplace. Periodically these efforts were set back by wars,

226

depressions, or other disasters. But each time the world economy recovered, emerging larger and more closely integrated than before.

Today a new crisis has struck. But this one is different. Unlike all previous crises during the industrial era, it involves not only money but the entire energy base of the society. Unlike the crises of the past, it brings inflation and unemployment simultaneously, not sequentially. Unlike those of the past, it is directly linked to fundamental ecological problems, to an entirely new species of technology, and to the introduction of a new level of communications into the production system. Finally, it is not, as Marxists claim, a crisis of capitalism alone, but one that involves the socialist industrial nations as well. It is, in short, the general crisis of industrial civilization as a whole.

The upheaval in the world economy threatens the survival of the corporation as we know it, throwing its managers into a wholly unfamiliar environment. Thus from the end of World War II until the early 1970's the corporation functioned in a comparatively stable environment. Growth was the key word. The dollar was king. Currencies remained stable for long periods. The postwar financial structure laid in place at Bretton Woods by the capitalist industrial powers, and the COMECON system created by the Soviets, seemed solid. The escalator to affluence was still ascending, and economists were so confident of their ability to predict and control the economic machine that they spoke casually about "fine tuning" it.

Today the phrase evokes only derisive snorts. The President wisecracks that he knows a Georgia fortune-teller who is a better forecaster than the economists. A former Secretary of the Treasury, W. Michael Blumenthal, says that "the economics profession is close to bankruptcy in understanding the present situation—before or after the fact." Standing in the tangled wreckage of economic theory and the rubble of the postwar economic infrastructure, corporate decision-makers face rising uncertainties.

Interest rates zigzag. Currencies gyrate. Central banks buy and sell money by the carload to damp the swings, but the gyrations only grow more extreme. The dollar and the yen perform a Kabuki dance, the Europeans promote their own new currency (quaintly named the "ecu"), while Arabs frantically off-load billions of dollars worth of American paper. Gold prices break all records.

While all of this is occurring, technology and communications restructure world markets, making transnational production both possible and necessary. And to facilitate such operations, a jet-age money system is taking form. A global electronic banking network—impossible before the computer and satellite—now instantaneously links Hong Kong, Manila, or Singapore with the Bahamas, the Cayman Islands, and New York.

This sprawling network of banks, with its Citibanks and Barclays, its Sumitomos and Narodnys, not to mention Crédit Suisse and the National Bank of Abu Dhabi, creates a balloon of "stateless currency"—money and credit outside the control of any individual government—which threatens to blow up in everyone's face.

The bulk of this stateless currency consists of Eurodollars—dollars outside the United States. In 1975, writing about the accelerated growth of Eurodollars, I warned that this new currency was a wild card in the economic game. "Here the 'Euros' contribute to inflation, there they shift the balance of payments, in another place they undermine the currency—as they stampede from place to place" across national boundaries. At that time there were an estimated 180 billion such Eurodollars.

By 1978 a panicky *Business Week* was reporting on "the incredible state" of the international finance system and the 180 billion had mushroomed into some 400 billion dollars worth of Eurodollars, Euromarks, Eurofrancs, Euroguilders, and Euroyen. Bankers dealing with the supranational currency were free to issue unlimited credit and—not being required to hold any cash reserves—were able to lend out at bargain-basement rates. Today's estimates put the Eurocurrency total as high as a trillion dollars.

The Second Wave economic system in which the corporation grew up was based on national markets, national currencies, and national governments. This nation-based infrastructure, however, is utterly unable to regulate or contain the new transnational and electronic "Eurobubble." The structures designed for a Second Wave world are no longer adequate.

Indeed, the entire global framework that stabilized world trade relations for the giant corporations is rattling and in danger of coming apart. The World Bank, the International Monetary Fund, and the General Agreement on Tariffs and Trade are all under heavy attack. Europeans scramble to bolt together a new structure to be controlled by them. The "less developed countries" on one side, and the Arabs brandishing their petrodollars on the other, clamor for influence in the financial system of tomorrow and speak of creating their own counterparts to the IMF. The dollar is dethroned, and jerks and spasms rip through the world economy.

All this is compounded by erratic shortages and gluts of energy and resources; by rapid changes in the attitudes of consumers, workers, and managers; by rapidly shifting imbalances of trade; and above all by the rising militancy of the non-industrial world.

This is the volatile, confusing environment in which today's corporations struggle to operate. The managers who run them have no wish to relinquish corporate power. They will battle for profits, production, and personal advancement. But faced with soaring levels of unpredictability, with mounting public criticism and hostile political pressures, our most intelligent managers are questioning the goals, structure, responsibility, the very *raison d'être* of their organizations. Many of our biggest corporations are experiencing something analogous to an identity crisis as they watch the once stable Second Wave framework disintegrate around them.

THE ACCELERATIVE ECONOMY

This corporate identity crisis is intensified by the speed at which events are moving. For the very speed of change introduces a new element into management, forcing executives, already nervous in an unfamiliar environment, to make more and more decisions at a faster and faster pace. Response times are honed to a minimum.

At the financial level the speed of transactions is accelerating as banks and other financial institutions computerize. Some banks even relocate geographically to take advantage of time zone differences. Says *Euromoney,* the international bankers' journal, "Time zones can be used as a competitive edge."

In this hotted-up environment, the big corporations are driven almost willy-nilly to invest and borrow in various currencies not on an annual, a ninety-day, or even a seven-day basis, but literally on an overnight or minute-to-minute basis. A new corporate officer has appeared in the executive suite—the "international cash manager," who remains plugged into the worldwide electronic casino twenty-four hours a day, searching for the lowest interest rates, the best currency bargains, the fastest turnaround.*

In marketing, a similar acceleration is evident. "Marketers must respond quickly in order to insure survival for tomorrow," declares *Advertising Age*, reporting that "Network TV programmers . . . are accelerating their decisions on killing new TV series that show rating weaknesses. No more waiting six or seven weeks, or a season. . . . Another example: Johnson & Johnson learns that Bristol-Myers is determined to undersell J&J's Tylenol . . . Does J&J adopt a wait-and-see attitude? No. In an amazingly short time, it moves to cut Tylenol's prices in the stores. No more weeks or months for procrastination." The very prose is breathless.

In engineering, in manufacture, in research, in sales, in training, in personnel, in every department and branch of the corporation the same quickening of decision-making can be detected.

And once more we see a parallel process, though less advanced, in the socialist industrial nations. COMECON, which used to revise its prices every five years when it issued its five-year plan, has been forced to revise its prices annually in an attempt to keep up with the faster pace. Before long it will be six months, then even less.

The results of this generalized speedup of the corporate metabolism are multiple: shorter product life-cycles, more leasing and renting, more frequent buying and selling, more ephemeral consumption patterns, more fads, more training time for workers (who must continually adjust to new procedures), more frequent changes in contracts, more negotiations and legal work, more pricing changes, more job turnover, more dependence on data, more *ad hoc* organization—all of it exacerbated by inflation.

The result is a high-stakes, high-adrenaline business environment. Under these escalating pressures it is easy to see why so many businessmen, bankers, and corporate executives wonder what exactly they are doing and why. Brought up with Second Wave certainties, they see the world they knew tearing apart under the impact of an accelerating wave of change.

---

* Nor is this function trivial. Like farmers who make more from selling land than from growing food, some major corporations are making more profit—or racking up greater losses—from currency and financial manipulation than from actual production.

THE DE-MASSIFIED SOCIETY

Even more mystifying and upsetting for them is the crack-up of the industrial mass society in which they were trained to operate. Second Wave managers were taught that mass production is the most advanced and efficient form of production . . . that a mass market wants standardized goods . . . that mass distribution is essential . . . that "masses" of uniform workers are basically all alike and can be motivated by uniform incentives. The effective manager learned that synchronization, centralization, maximization, and concentration are necessary to achieve his goals. And in a Second Wave environment these assumptions are basically correct.

Today, as the Third Wave strikes, the corporate manager finds all his old assumptions challenged. The mass society itself, for which the corporation was designed, is beginning to de-massify. Not merely information, production, and family life, but the marketplace and the labor market as well are beginning to break into smaller, more varied pieces.

The mass market has split into ever-multiplying, ever-changing sets of mini-markets that demand a continually expanding range of options, models, types, sizes, colors, and customizations. Bell Telephone, which once hoped to put the same black telephone in every American home—and very nearly succeeded—now manufactures some one thousand combinations or permutations of telephone equipment from pink, green, or white phones to phones for the blind, phones for people who have lost the use of their larynx, and explosion-proof phones for construction sites. Department stores, originally designed to massify the market, now sprout "boutiques" under their roofs, and Phyllis Sewell, a vice president of Federated Department Stores, predicts that "we will be going into greater specialization . . . with more different departments."

The fast-increasing variety of goods and services in the high-technology nations is often explained away as an attempt by the corporation to manipulate the consumer, to invent false needs, and to inflate profits by charging a lot for trivial options. No doubt, there is truth to these charges. Yet something deeper is at work. For the growing differentiation of goods or services also reflects the growing diversity of actual needs, values, and life-styles in a de-massified Third Wave society.

This rising level of social diversity is fed by further divisions in the labor market, as reflected in the proliferation of new occupations, especially in the white-collar and service fields. Newspaper want ads clamor for "Vydec Secretary" or "Mini-computer Programmer," while at a conference on the service professions I watched a psychologist list 68 new occupations from consumer advocate, public defender, and sex therapist to psycho-chemotherapist and ombudsman.

As our jobs become *less* interchangeable, people do too. Refusing to be treated as interchangeable, they arrive at the workplace with an acute consciousness of their ethnic, religious, professional, sexual, subcultural, and individual differences. Groups that throughout the Second Wave era fought to be "integrated" or "assimilated" into mass society now refuse to melt their differences. They emphasize instead their unique characteristics. And Second Wave corporations, still organized for operation in a mass society, are still uncertain how to cope with this rising tide of diversity among their employees and customers.

Though sharply evident in the United States, social de-massification is progressing rapidly elsewhere as well. In Britain, which once regarded itself as highly homogeneous, ethnic minorities, from Pakistanis, West Indians, Cypriots, and Ugandan Asians to Turks and Spaniards now intermingle with a native population itself becoming more heterogeneous. Meanwhile, a tidal influx of Japanese, American, German, Dutch, Arab, and African visitors leave in their wake American hamburger stands, Japanese tempura restaurants, and signs in store windows that read "Se Habla Espanol."

Around the world, ethnic minorities reassert their identities and demand long-denied rights to jobs, income, and advancement in the corporation. Australian Aborigines, New Zealand Maoris, Canadian Eskimos, American Blacks, Chicanos, and even Oriental minorities once regarded as politically passive are on the move. From Maine to the Far West, Native Americans assert "Red Power," demand the restoration of tribal lands, and dicker with the OPEC countries for economic and political support.

Even in Japan, long the most homogeneous of the industrial nations, the signs of de-massification are mounting. An uneducated convict overnight emerges as spokesman for the small minority of Ainu people. The Korean minority grows restless, and sociologist Masaaki Takane of Sophia University says, "I have been haunted by an anxiety . . . Japanese society today is quickly losing its unity and its disintegrating."

In Denmark scattered street fights break out between Danes and immigrant workers and between leather-jacketed motorcyclists and long-haired youth. In Belgium the Walloons, the Flemish, and the Bruxelloises reactivate ancient, indeed preindustrial, rivalries. In Canada Quebec threatens to secede, corporations padlock their headquarters in Montreal, and English-speaking executives throughout the country take crash courses in French.

The forces that made mass society have suddenly been thrown into reverse. Nationalism in the high-technology context becomes regionalism instead. The pressures of the melting pot are replaced by the new ethnicity. The media, instead of creating a mass culture, de-massify it. In turn all these developments parallel the emerging diversity of energy forms and the advance beyond mass production.

All these interrelated changes create a totally new framework within which the production organizations of society, whether called corporations or socialist enterprises, will function. Executives who continue to think in terms of the mass society are shocked and confused by a world they no longer recognize.

REDEFINING THE CORPORATION

What deepens the identity crisis of the corporation still further is the emergence, against this already unsettling background, of a worldwide movement demanding not merely modest changes in this or that corporate policy but a deep redefinition of its purposes.

In the United States, writes David Ewing, an editor of the *Harvard Business Review,* "public anger at corporations is beginning to well up at a frightening rate." Ewing cites a 1977 study by a research affiliate of the Harvard Business School whose findings, he says, "sent tremors throughout the corporate world." The study revealed that about half of all consumers polled believe they are getting worse treatment in the marketplace than they were a decade earlier; three fifths say that products have deteriorated; over half mistrust product guarantees. Ewing quotes a worried businessman as saying, "It feels like sitting on a San Andreas fault."

Worse yet, Ewing continues, "growing numbers of people are not simply disenchanted, irritated or angry, but . . . irrationally and erratically afraid of new technologies and business ventures."

According to John C. Biegler, an executive of Price Waterhouse, one of the giant blue-chip accounting firms, "public confidence in the American corporation is lower than at any time since the Great Depression. American business and the accounting profession are being called on the carpet for a kind of zero-based rejustification of just about everything we do. . . . Corporate performance is being measured against new and unfamiliar norms."

Similar tendencies are visible in Scandinavia, Western Europe, and even, *sotto voce,* in the socialist industrial nations. In Japan, as Toyota's official magazine puts it, "A citizens' movement of a type never before seen in Japan is gradually gathering momentum, one that criticizes the way corporations disrupt everyday life."

Certainly corporations have come under scorching attack at other times in their history. Much of today's clamor of complaint, however, is crucially different and arises from the emerging values and assumptions of Third Wave civilization, not the dying industrial past.

Throughout the Second Wave era corporations have been seen as economic units, and the attacks on them have essentially focused on economic issues. Critics assailed them for underpaying workers, overcharging customers, forming cartels to fix prices, making shoddy goods, and a thousand other economic transgressions. But no matter how violent, most of these critics accepted the corporation's self-definition: they shared the view of the corporation as an inherently economic institution.

Today's corporate critics start from a totally different premise. They attack the artificial divorce of economics from politics, morality, and the other dimensions of life. They hold the corporation increasingly responsible, not merely for its economic performance but for its side effects on everything from air pollution to executive stress. Corporations are thus assailed for asbestos poisoning, for using poor populations as guinea pigs in drug testing, for distorting the development of the non-industrial world, for racism and sexism, for secrecy and deception. They are pilloried for supporting unsavory regimes or political parties, from the fascist generals in Chile and the racists in South Africa to the Communist party in Italy.

What is at issue here is not whether such charges are justified—all too often they are. What is far more important is the concept of the corporation they imply. For the Third Wave brings with it a rising demand for a new kind of institution altogether—a corporation no longer responsible simply for making a profit or producing goods but for simultaneously contributing to the solution of extremely complex ecological, moral, political, racial, sexual, and social problems.

Instead of clinging to a sharply specialized economic function, the corporation, prodded by criticism, legislation, and its own concerned executives, is becoming a multipurpose institution.

A PENTAGON OF PRESSURES

The redefinition is not a matter of choice but a necessary response to five revolutionary changes in the actual conditions of production. Changes in the physical environment, in the lineup of social forces, in the role of information, in government organization, and in morality are all pounding the corporation into a new, multi-faceted, multipurposeful shape.

The first of these new pressures springs from the biosphere.

In the mid-1950's, when the Second Wave reached its mature stage in the United States, world population stood at only 2.75 billion. Today it is over 4 billion. In the mid-1950's the earth's population used a mere 87 quadrillion Btu of energy a year. Today we use over 260 quadrillion. In the mid-50's, our consumption of a key raw material like zinc was only 2.7 million metric tons a year. Today it is 5.6 million.

Measured any way we choose, our demands on the planet are escalating wildly. As a result the biosphere is sending us alarm signals—pollution, desertification, signs of toxification in the oceans, subtle shifts in climate—that we ignore at the risk of catastrophe. These warnings tell us we can no longer organize production as we did during the Second Wave past.

Because the corporation is the main organizer of economic production, it is also a key "producer" of environmental impacts. If we want to continue our economic growth—indeed if we wish to survive—the managers of tomorrow will have to assume responsibility for converting the corporation's environmental impacts from negatives into positives. They will assume this added responsibility voluntarily or they will be compelled to do so, for the changed conditions of the biosphere make it necessary. The corporation is being transformed into an environmental, as well as an economic, institution—not by do-gooders, radicals, ecologists, or government bureaucrats, but by a material change in the relationship of production to the biosphere.

The second pressure springs from a little-noticed change in the social environment in which the corporation finds itself. That environment is now far more organized than before. At one time each firm operated in what might be termed an underorganized society. Today the socio-sphere, especially in the United States, has leaped to a new level of organization. It is packed with a writhing, interacting mass of well-organized, often well-funded, associations, agencies, trade unions, and other groupings.

In the United States today, some 1,370,000 companies interact with well over 90,000 schools and universities, 330,000 churches, and hundreds of thousands of branches of 13,000 national organizations, plus countless purely local environmental, social, religious, athletic, political, ethnic, and civic groups, each with its own agenda and priorities. It takes 144,-000 law firms to mediate all these relationships!

In this densely crowded socio-sphere, every corporate action has repercussive impacts not merely on lonely or helpless individuals but on organized groups, many of them with professional staffs, a press of their own, access to the political system, and resources with which to hire experts, lawyers, and other assistance.

In this finely strung socio-sphere, corporate decisions are closely scrutinized. "Social pollution" produced by the corporation in the form of unemployment, community disruption, forced mobility, and the like is instantly spotted, and pressures are placed on the corporation to assume far greater responsibility than ever before for its social, as well as economic, "products."

A third set of pressures reflects the changed info-sphere. Thus, the de-massification of society means that far more information must be exchanged between social institutions—including the corporation—to maintain equilibrial relationships among them. Third Wave production methods further intensify the corporation's hunger for information as raw material. The firm thus sucks up data like a gigantic vacuum cleaner, processes it, and disseminates it to others in increasingly complex ways. As information becomes central to production, as "information managers" proliferate in industry, the corporation, by necessity, impacts on the informational environment exactly as it impacts on the physical and social environment.

The new importance of information leads to conflict over the control of corporate data—battles over disclosure of more information to the public, demands for open accounting (of oil company production and profit figures, for example), more pressures for "truth in advertising," or "truth in lending." For in the new era, "information impacts" become as serious a matter as environmental and social impacts, and the corporation is seen as an information producer as well as an economic producer.

A fourth pressure on the corporation arises from politics and the power-sphere. The rapid diversification of society and the acceleration of change are everywhere reflected in a tremendous complexification of government. The differentiation of society is mirrored in the differentiation of government, and each corporation must therefore interact with more and more specialized units of government. These units, badly coordinated and each with its own priorities, are, moreover, in a perpetual turmoil of reorganization.

Jayne Baker Spain, a senior vice-president of Gulf Oil, has pointed out that as recently as ten or fifteen years ago, "There was no EPA. There was no EEOC. There was no ERISSA. There was no OSHA. There was no ERDA. There was no FEA." All these and many other government agencies have sprouted up since then.

Every company thus finds itself increasingly ensnarled in politics—local, regional, national, or even transnational. Conversely, every important corporate decision "produces" at least indirect political effects along with its other output, and is increasingly held responsible for them.

Finally, as Second Wave civilization wanes and its value system shatters, a fifth pressure arises, affecting all institutions—including the corporation. This is a heightened moral pressure. Behavior once accepted as normal is suddenly reinterpreted as corrupt, immoral, or scandalous. Thus the Lockheed bribes topple a government in Japan. Olin Corporation is indicted for shipping arms to South Africa. Gulf Oil's chairman is forced to resign in the wake of a bribery scandal. The reluctance of Distillers Company in Britain to repay the victims of Thalidomide adequately, the failures of McDonnell Douglas with respect to the DC-10—all trigger tidal waves of moral revulsion.

The ethical stance of the corporation is increasingly seen as having a direct impact on the value system of the society, just as significant to some as the corporation's impact on the physical environment or the social system. The corporation is increasingly seen as a "producer" of moral effects.

These five sweeping changes in both the material and non-material conditions of production make untenable the Second Wave school-book notion that a corporation is nothing but an economic institution. Under the new conditions the corporation can no longer operate as a machine for maximizing some economic function—whether production or profit. The very definition of "production" is being drastically expanded to include the side, as well as the central, effects, the long-range as well as the immediate effects, of corporate action. Put simply, every corporation has more "products" (and is now held responsible for more) than Second Wave managers ever had to consider—environmental, social, informational, political, and moral, not just economic products.

The purpose of the corporation is thus changed from singular to plural—not just at the level of rhetoric or public relations but at the level of identity and self-definition as well.

In corporation after corporation we can expect to see an internal battle between those who cleave to the single-purpose corporation of the Second Wave past and those who are ready to cope with the Third Wave conditions of production and to fight for the multipurpose corporation of tomorrow.

THE MULTIPURPOSE CORPORATION

Those of us brought up in Second Wave civilization have a difficult time thinking of institutions in this way. We find it hard to think of a hospital as having economic as well as medical functions, a school as having political as well as educational functions—or a corporation as having powerful non-economic or "trans-economic" functions. That recently retired exemplar of Second Wave thinking, Henry Ford II, insists that the corporation "is a specialized instrument designed to serve the economic needs of society and is not well equipped to serve social needs unrelated to its business operations." But while Ford and other defenders of the Second Wave resist the redefinition of the production organization, many firms are, in fact, altering both their words and their policies.

Lip service and public relations rhetoric often substitute for real change. Fancy promotional brochures proclaiming a new era of social responsibility very often camouflage a robber-baron rapacity. Nevertheless, a fundamental "paradigm shift"—a reconceptualization—of the structure, goals, and responsibilities of the corporation is taking place in response to new pressures brought by the Third Wave. The signs of this change are numerous.

Amoco, a leading oil company, for example, states that "it is the policy of our company, with respect to plant locations, to supplement the routine economic evaluation with a detailed exploration of the social consequences. . . . We look at many factors, among them the impact on the physical environment, the impact on public facilities . . . and the impact on local employment conditions, particularly with respect to minorities." Amoco continues to weight economic considerations most heavily, but it assigns importance to other factors as well. And where alternative locations are similar in economic terms but "different in terms of the social impact," these social factors can prove decisive.

In the event of a merger proposal, the directors of Control Data Corporation, a top U.S. computer manufacturer, explicitly take into account not merely financial or economic considerations but "all relevant" factors—including the social effects of the merger and its impact on employees and the communities in which Control Data operates. And while other companies have been racing into the suburbs, Control Data has deliberately built its new plants in inner city areas of Washington, St. Paul, and Minneapolis, to help provide employment for minorities and to help revive urban centers. The corporation states its mission as "improving the quality, equality, and potential of people's lives"—*equality* being an unorthodox goal for a corporation.

In the United States, the advancement of women and non-whites has become a long overdue matter of national policy, and some companies go so far as to reward their managers financially for meeting "affirmative action" targets. At Pillsbury, a leading food company, each of its three product groups must present not only a sales plan for the following year but a plan relating to the hiring, training, and promotion of women and minority group members. Executive incentives are linked to the attainment of these social goals. At AT&T

all managers are evaluated annually. Fulfillment of affirmative action objectives counts as part of a positive appraisal. At Chemical Bank in New York, 10 to 15 percent of a branch manager's job performance appraisal is based on her or his social performance—sitting on community agency boards, making loans to not-for-profit organizations, hiring and upgrading minorities. And at the Gannett chain of newspapers, chief executive Allen Neuharth brusquely tells editors and local publishers that "a major portion" of their bonuses will "be determined on the basis of progress in these . . . programs."

Similarly, in many top corporations we see a distinct upgrading of the status and influence of executives concerned with the environmental consequences of corporate behavior. Some now report directly to the president. Other companies have set up special committees on the board of directors to define the new corporate responsibilities.

This social responsiveness of the corporation is not all substance. Says Rosemary Bruner, director of community affairs at Hoffmann-LaRoche's American subsidiary, "Some of this is pure public relations, of course. Some is self-serving. But much of it actually does reflect a changed perception of corporate functions." Grudgingly, therefore, driven by protests, lawsuits, and fear of government action as well as by more laudable motives, managers are beginning to adapt to the new conditions of production and are accepting the idea that the corporation has multiple purposes.

MANY BOTTOM LINES

The multipurpose corporation that is emerging demands, among other things, smarter executives. It implies a management capable of specifying multiple goals, weighting them, interrelating them, and finding synergic policies that accomplish more than a single goal at a time. It requires policies that optimize not for one, but for several variables simultaneously. Nothing could be further from the single-minded style of the traditional Second Wave manager.

Moreover, once the need for multiple goals is accepted we are compelled to invent new measures of performance. Instead of the single "bottom line" on which most executives have been taught to fixate, the Third Wave corporation requires attention to multiple bottom lines—social, environmental, informational, political, and ethical bottom lines—all of them interconnected.

Faced with this new complexity, many of today's managers are taken aback. They lack the intellectual tools necessary for Third Wave management. We know how to measure the profitability of a corporation, but how do we measure or evaluate the achievement of non-economic goals? Price Waterhouse's John C. Biegler says, managers "are being asked to account for corporate behavior in areas where no real standards of accountability have been established—where even the language of accountability has yet to be developed."

This explains today's efforts to develop a new language of accountability. Indeed, accounting itself is on the edge of revolution and is about to explode out of its narrowly economic terms of reference.

The American Accounting Association, for example, has issued reports of a "Committee on Non-Financial Measures of Effectiveness" and of a "Committee on Measures of Effectiveness for Social Programs." So much work is being done along these lines that each of these reports lists nearly 250 papers, monographs, and documents in its bibliography.

In Philadelphia, a consulting firm called the Human Resources Network is working with twelve major U.S. corporations to develop cross-industry methods for specifying what might be called the "trans-economic" goals of the corporation. It is trying to integrate these goals into corporate planning and to find ways of measuring the company's trans-economic performance. In Washington, meanwhile, the Secretary of Commerce, Juanita Kreps, raised a storm of controversy by suggesting that the government itself should prepare a "Social Performance Index," which she described as a "mechanism companies could use to assess their performance and its social consequences."

Parallel work is under way in Europe. According to Meinolf Dierkes and Rob Coppock of the Berlin-based International Institute for Environment and Society, "Many large and medium-sized companies in Europe have been experimenting with [the social report] concept. . . . In the Federal Republic of Germany, for example, about 20 of the largest firms now publish social reports regularly. In addition, more than a hundred others draw up social reports for internal management purposes."

Some of these reports are no more than puff—accounts of the corporation's "good works," carefully overlooking controversial problems like pollution. But others are remarkably open, objective, and tough. Thus a social report issued by the giant Swiss food firm, Migros-Genossenschafts-Bund self-critically confesses that it pays women less than men, that many of its jobs are "extremely boring," and that its nitrous dioxide emissions have risen over a four-year period. Says the company's managing director, Pierre Arnold, "It takes courage for an enterprise to point out the differences between its goals and its actual results."

Companies like STEAG and the Saarbergwerke AG have pioneered the effort to relate company expenditures to specific social benefits. Less formally, companies like Bertelsmann AG, the publisher; Rank Xerox GmbH, the copier firm; and Hoechst AG, the chemical manufacturer, have radically broadened the kind of social data they make available to the public.

A much more advanced system is employed by companies in Sweden and Switzerland and by Deutsche Shell AG in Germany. The latter, instead of publishing an annual report, now issues what it calls an *Annual and Social Report* in which both economic and trans-economic data are interrelated. The method used by Shell, termed "goal accounting and reporting" by Dierkes and Coppock, stipulates concrete economic, environmental, and social goals for the corporation, spells out the actions taken to achieve them, and reports the expenditures allocated to them.

Shell also lists five overall corporate goals—only one of which is to achieve a "reasonable return on investment"—and specifically states that each of the five goals, economic and non-economic, must "carry the same weight" in corporate decision-making. The goal accounting method forces companies to make their trans-economic objectives explicit, to specify time periods for their attainment, and to open this up to public review.

On a broader theoretical level, Trevor Gambling, professor of accounting at the University of Birmingham in the United Kingdom, in a book called *Societal Accounting* has called for a radical reformulation of accounting that begins to integrate the work of economists and accountants with that of the social scientists who have developed social indicators and methods of social accounting.

In Holland the Dean of the Graduate School of Management in Delft, Cornelius Brevoord, has designed a set of multidimensional criteria for monitoring corporate behavior. This is made necessary, he suggests, by deep value changes in the society, among them the change from "an economic production orientation" in society to "a total well-being orientation." Similarly, he notes a shift from "functional specialization to an interdisciplinary approach." Both these changes strengthen the need for a more rounded concept of the corporation.

Brevoord lists 32 different criteria by which a corporation must measure its effectiveness. These range over its relationships with consumers, shareholders, and unions to those with ecology organizations and its own management. But, he points out, even these 32 are only "a few" of the parameters along which the emerging corporation of the future will test itself.

With the Second Wave economic infrastructure in a shambles, with change accelerating as de-massification spreads, with the biosphere sending danger signals, with the level of organization in society rising, and the informational, political, and ethical conditions of production changing, the Second Wave corporation is obsolete.

What is happening, therefore, is a thoroughgoing reconceptualization of the meaning of production and of the institution that, until now, has been charged with organizing it. The result is a complex shift to a new-style corporation of tomorrow. In the words of William Halal, professor of management at American University, "Just as the feudal manor was replaced by the business corporation when agrarian societies were transformed into industrial societies, so too should the older model of the firm be replaced by a new form of economic institution. . . ." This new institution will combine economic and trans-economic objectives. It will have multiple bottom lines.

The transformation of the corporation is part of the larger transformation of the socio-sphere as a whole, and this in turn parallels the dramatic changes in the techno-sphere and info-sphere. Taken together, they add up to a massive historical shift. But we are not merely altering these giant structures. We are also changing the way ordinary people, in their daily lives, behave. For when we change the deep structure of civilization, we simultaneously rewrite all the codes by which we live.

19

DECODING THE NEW RULES

In millions of middle-class homes a ritual drama is enacted: the recently graduated son or daughter arrives late for dinner, snarls, flings down the want ads, and proclaims the nine-to-five job a degrading sham and a shuck. No human being with even a shredlet of self-respect would submit to the nine-to-five regimen.

Enter parents:

The father, just returned from his own nine-to-five job, and the mother, exhausted and depressed from paying the latest batch of bills, are outraged. They have been through this before. Having seen good times and bad, they suggest a secure job with a big corporation. The young person sneers. Small companies are better. No company is best of all. An advanced degree? What for? It's all a terrible waste!

Aghast, the parents see their suggestions dismissed one after another. Their frustration mounts until, at last, they utter the ultimate parental cry: "When are you going to face the real world?"

Such scenes are not limited to affluent homes in the United States or even Europe. Japanese corporate moguls mutter in their saké about the swift decline of the work ethic and corporate loyalty, of industrial punctuality and discipline among the young. Even in the Soviet Union middle-class parents face similar challenges from the youth.

Is this just another case of *épater les parents*—the traditional generational conflict? Or is there something new here? Can it be that young people and their parents are simply not talking about the same "real world"?

The fact is that what we are seeing is not merely the classical confrontation of romantic youth and realistic elders. Indeed, what was once realistic may no longer be. For the basic code of behavior, containing the ground rules of social life, is changing rapidly as the onrushing Third Wave arrives.

We saw earlier how the Second Wave brought with it a "code book" of principles or rules that governed everyday behavior. Such principles as synchronization, standardization, or maximization were applied in business, in government, and in a daily life obsessed with punctuality and schedules.

Today a countercode book is emerging—new ground rules for the new life we are building on a de-massified economy, on de-massified media, on new family and corporate structures. Many of the seemingly senseless battles between young and old, as well as other conflicts in our classrooms, boardrooms, and political backrooms are, in fact, nothing more than clashes over which code book to apply.

The new code book directly attacks much of what the Second Wave person has been taught to believe in—from the importance of punctuality and synchronization to the need for conformity and standardization. It challenges the presumed efficiency of centralization and professionalization. It compels us to reconsider our conviction that bigger is better and our notions of "concentration." To understand this new code, and how it contrasts with the old one, is to understand instantly many of the otherwise confusing conflicts that swirl around us, exhausting our energies and threatening our personal power, prestige, or paycheck.

THE END OF NINE-TO-FIVE

Take the case of the frustrated parents. Second Wave civilization, as we saw, synchronized daily life, tying the rhythms of sleep and wakefulness, of work and play, to the underlying throb of machines. Raised in this civilization, the parents take for granted that work must be synchronized, that everyone must arrive and work at the same time, that rush-hour traffic is unavoidable, that meal times must be fixed, and that children must, at an early age, be indoctrinated with time-consciousness and punctuality. They cannot understand why their offspring seem so annoyingly casual about keeping appointments and why, if the nine-to-five job (or other fixed-schedule job) was good enough in the past, it should suddenly be regarded as intolerable by their children.

The reason is that the Third Wave, as it sweeps in, carries with it a completely different sense of time. If the Second Wave tied life to the tempo of the machine, the Third Wave challenges this mechanical synchronization, alters our most basic social rhythms, and in so doing frees us from the machine.

Once we understand this, it comes as no surprise that one of the fastest-spreading innovations in industry during the 1970's was "flextime"—an arrangement that permits workers, within predetermined limits, to choose their own working hours. Instead of requiring everyone to arrive at the factory gate or the office at the same time, or even at pre-fixed staggered times, the company operating on flextime typically sets certain core hours when everyone is expected to show up, and specifies other hours as flexible. Each employee may choose which of the flexible hours he or she wishes to spend working.

This means that a "day person"—a person whose biological rhythms routinely awaken him or her early in the morning—can choose to arrive at work at, say, 8:00 A.M., while a "night person," whose metabolism is different, can choose to start working at 10:00 or 10:30 A.M. It means that an employee can take time off for household chores, or to shop, or to take a child to the doctor. Groups of workers who wish to go bowling together early in the morning or late in the afternoon can jointly set their schedules to make it possible. In short, time itself is being de-massified.

The flextime movement began in 1965 when a woman economist in Germany, Christel Kämmerer, recommended it as a way to bring more mothers into the job market. In 1967 Masserschmitt-Bölkow-Blohm, the "Deutsche Boeing," discovered that many of its workers were arriving at work worn out from fighting rush-hour traffic. Management gingerly experimented by allowing 2,000 workers to go off the rigid eight-to-five schedule and to choose their own hours. Within two years all 12,000 of its employees were on flextime and some departments had even given up the requirements for everyone to be there during core time.

In 1972 *Europa* magazine reported that ". . . in some 2,-000 West German firms, the national concept of rigid punctuality has vanished beyond recall. . . . The reason is the introduction of *Gleitzeit*"; i.e., "sliding" or "flexible" hours. By 1977 fully a fourth of the West German work force, more than 5,000,000 employees in all, were on one or another form of flextime, and the system was being used by 22,000 companies with an estimated 4,000,000 workers in France, Finland, Denmark, Sweden, Italy, and Great Britain. In Switzerland, 15 to 20 percent of all industrial firms had switched to the new system for all or part of their work force.

Multinational firms (a major force for cultural diffusion in today's world) soon began exporting the system from Europe. Nestlé and Lufthansa, for example, introduced it to their operations in the United States. By 1977, according to a report prepared for the American Management Association by Professor Stanley Nollen and consultant Virginia Martin, 13 percent of all U.S. companies were using flexible hours. Within a few years, they forecast, the number will reach 17 percent, representing more than 8,000,000 workers. Among the American firms trying out flextime systems are such giants as Scott Paper, Bank of California, General Motors, Bristol-Myers, and Equitable Life.

Some of the more moss-backed trade unions—preservers of the Second Wave status quo—have hesitated. But individual workers, by and large, see flextime as a liberating influence. Says the manager of one London-based insurance firm: "The young married women were absolutely rapturous about the change-over." A Swiss survey found that fully 95 percent of affected workers approve. Thirty-five percent—men more than women—say they now spend more time with the family.

One Black mother working for a Boston bank was on the verge of being fired because—although a good worker in other respects—she was continually turning up late. Her poor attendance record reinforced racist stereotypes about the "unreliability" and "laziness" of Black workers. But when her office went on flextime she was no longer considered late. It turned out, reported sociologist Allen R. Cohen, "that she'd been late because she had to drop her son in a day-care center and could just never get to the office by starting time."

Employers, for their part, report higher productivity, reduced absenteeism, and other benefits. There are, of course, problems, as with any innovation, but according to the AMA survey only 2 percent of the companies trying it have gone back to the old rigid time structure. One Lufthansa manager summed it up succinctly: "There's no such thing now as a punctuality problem."

THE SLEEPLESS GORGON

But flextime, while widely publicized, is only a small part of the general restructuring of time that the Third Wave carries with it. We are also seeing a powerful shift toward increased night work. This is occurring not so much in the traditional manufacturing centers like Akron or Baltimore, which have always had a lot of workers on night shifts, but in the rapidly expanding services and in the advanced, computer-based industries.

"The modern city," declares the French newspaper *Le Monde*, "is a Gorgon that never sleeps and in which . . . a growing proportion of the citizens work outside the [normal] diurnal rhythms." Across the board in the technological nations the number of night workers now runs between 15 and 25 percent of all employees. In France, for example, the percentage has soared from only 12 in 1957 to 21 by 1974. In the United States the number of full-time night workers jumped 13 percent between 1974 and 1977; the total, including part-timers, reached 13.5 million.

Even more dramatic has been the spread of part-time work—and the active preference for it expressed by large numbers of people. In the Detroit area an estimated 65 percent of the total work force at the J. L. Hudson department stores consists of part-timers. Prudential Insurance employs some 1,600 part-timers in its U.S. and Canadian offices. In all, there is now one voluntary part-time worker for every five full-timers in the United States, and the part-time work force has been growing twice as fast as the full-time force since 1954.

So far has this process advanced that a 1977 study by researchers at Georgetown University suggested that in the future almost all jobs could be part-time. Entitled *Permanent Part-Time Employment: The Manager's Perspective,* the study covered 68 corporations, more than half of which already used part-timers. Even more noteworthy is the fact that the percentage of *unemployed* workers who want only part-time work has doubled in the past twenty years.

The opening up of part-time jobs is particularly welcomed by women, by the elderly and semi-retired, and by many young people who are willing to settle for a smaller paycheck in return for time to pursue their own hobbies, sports, or religious, artistic, or political interests.

What we see, therefore, is a fundamental break with Second Wave synchronization. The combination of flextime, part-time, and night work means that more and more people are working outside the nine-to-five (or any fixed schedule) system, and that the entire society is shifting to round-the-clock operations.

New consumer patterns, meanwhile, directly parallel changes in the time structure of production. Note, for instance, the proliferation of all-night supermarkets. "Will the 4 A.M. shopper, long considered a hallmark of California kookiness, become a regular feature of life in the less flamboyant East?" asks *The New York Times.* The answer is a resounding "Yes!"

A spokesman for a supermarket chain in the eastern United States says his company will keep its stores open all night because "people are staying up later than they used to." The *Times* feature writer spends a night at a typical store and reports on the varied customers who take advantage of the late hours: a truck driver whose wife is ill shops for his family of six, a young woman on her way to a postmidnight date pops by to purchase a greeting card, a man up late with a sick daughter rushes in to buy her a toy banjo and stops to pick up a hibachi as well, a woman drops by after her ceramics class to do the week's shopping, a motorcyclist roars up at 3:00 A.M. to buy a deck of cards, two men straggle in at dawn on their way to go fishing. . . .

Mealtimes are also affected by these changes and are similarly desynchronized. People do not all eat at the same time, as most of them once did. The rigid three-meal-a-day pattern is broken as more and more fast-food shops spring up, serving billions of meals at all hours. Television watching changes, too, as programmers devise shows specifically aimed at "urban adults, night workers, and just plain insomniacs." Banks, meanwhile, give up their celebrated "bankers' hours."

Manhattan's giant Citibank runs television commercials for its new automated banking system: "You are about to witness the dawn of a revolution in banking. This is Citibank's new twenty-four-hour service . . . where you can do most of your everyday banking anytime you want. So if Don Slater wants to check his balance at the crack of dawn, he can do it. And Brian Holland can transfer money from savings into checking anytime he wants to. . . . You know and I know that life doesn't stop at three P.M. Monday to Friday. . . . The Citi never sleeps."

If, therefore, we look across the board at the way our society now treats time, we find a subtle but powerful shift away from the rhythms of the Second Wave and toward a new temporal structure in our lives. In fact, what is happening is a de-massification of time that precisely parallels the de-massification of other features of social life as the Third Wave sweeps in.

SCHEDULE-A-FRIEND

We are only just beginning to feel the social consequences of this restructuring of time. For example, while the increasing individualization of time patterns certainly makes work less onerous, it also can intensify loneliness and social isolation. If friends, lovers, and family all work at different hours, and new services are not laid in place to help them coordinate their personal schedules, it becomes increasingly difficult for them to arrange face-to-face social contact. The old social centers—the neighborhood pub, the church clambake, the school prom—are losing their traditional significance. In their place, new Third Wave institutions must be invented to facilitate social life.

One can, for example, easily imagine a new computerized service—call it "Pers-Sched" or "Friend-Sched"—that not only reminds you of your own appointments but stores the schedules of various friends and family members so that each person in the social network can, by pushing a button, find out where and when his or her friends and acquaintances will be, and can make arrangements accordingly. But far more significant social facilitators will be needed.

The de-massification of time has other consequences, too. Thus we can already begin to see its effects in transportation. The Second Wave insistence on rigid, mass work schedules brought with it the characteristic rush-hour crush. The de-massification of time redistributes traffic flows in both space and time.

In fact, one crude way to judge just how far the Third Wave has advanced in any community is to look at the traffic flows. If the peak hours are still heavily accented, and if all the traffic moves one way in the morning and reverses itself in the evening, Second Wave synchronization still prevails. If traffic flows all day long, as it does in an increasing number of cities, and moves in all directions, rather than merely back and forth, it is safe to assume that Third Wave industries have taken root, that service workers far outnumber manufacturing workers, that flextime has begun to spread, that part-time and night work are prevalent, and that all-night services—superettes, banks, gas stations, and restaurants—will not be far behind.

The shift toward more flexible and personalized schedules also reduces energy costs and pollution by leveling out peak loads. Electric utilities in a dozen states are now using "time-of-day" pricing for industrial and residential customers to discourage energy use during traditional peak hours, while Connecticut's Department of Environmental Protection has urged companies to institute flextime as a means of complying with federal environmental requirements.

These are among the most obvious implications of the time shift. As the process continues to unfold in the years and decades ahead, we will see far more powerful and as yet unimagined consequences. The new time patterns will affect our daily rhythms in the home. They will affect our art. They will affect our biology. For when we touch on time we touch on all of human experience.

COMPUTERS AND MARIJUANA

These Third Wave rhythms spring from deep psychological, economic, and technological forces. At one level they arise from the changed nature of the population. People today—more affluent and educated than their parents and faced with more life choices—simply refuse to be massified. The more people differ in terms of the work they do or the products they consume, the more they demand to be treated as individuals—and the more they resist socially imposed schedules.

But at another level the new, more personalized Third Wave rhythms can be traced to a wide range of new technologies moving into our lives. Video cassettes and home video recording, for example, make it possible for televiewers to tape programs off the air and view them at times of their own choosing. Writes columnist Steven Brill, "Within the next two or three years television will probably stop dictating the schedules of even the worst tube addicts." The power of the great networks—the NBCs, the BBCs or NHKs—to synchronize viewing is coming to an end.

The computer, too, is beginning to recast our schedules

and even our conceptions of time. Indeed it is the computer which has made flextime possible in large organizations. At its simplest it facilitates the complex interweaving of thousands of personalized, flexible schedules. But it also alters our communications patterns in time, permitting us to access data and exchange it both "synchronously" (i.e., simultaneously) and "asynchronously."

What that means is illustrated by the growing number of computer users who are today engaged in "computer conferencing." This permits a group to communicate with one another through terminals in their homes or offices. Some 660 scientists, futurists, planners, and educators today in several countries conduct lengthy discussions of energy, economics, decentralization, or space satellites with one another through what is known as the Electronic Information Exchange System. Teleprinters and video screens in their homes and offices provide a choice of either instant or delayed communication. Many time zones apart, each user can choose to send or retrieve data whenever it is most convenient. A person can work at 3:00 A.M. if he or she feels like it. Alternatively, several can go on line at the same time if they so choose.

But the computer's effect on time goes much deeper, influencing even the way we think about it. The computer introduces a new vocabulary (with terms like "real-time," for example) that clarifies, labels, and reconceptualizes temporal phenomena. It begins to replace the clock as the most important timekeeping or pace-setting device in society.

Computer operations take place so rapidly that we routinely process data in what might be termed "subliminal time"—intervals far too short for the human senses to detect or for human neural response times to match. We now have computer-operated microprinters capable of turning out 10-000 to 20,000 lines per minute—more than 200 times faster than anyone can read them, and this is still the slowest part of computer systems. In twenty years computer scientists have gone from speaking in terms of milliseconds (thousandths of a second) to nanoseconds (billionths of a second) —a compression of time almost beyond our powers to imagine. It is as though a person's entire working life of, say 80,000 paid hours—2,000 hours per year for forty years—could be crunched into a mere 4.8 minutes.

Beyond the computer we find other technologies or products that also move in the direction of de-massifying time. Mood-influencing drugs (not to speak of marijuana) alter the perception of time within us. As far more sophisticated mood drugs appear it is likely that, for good or for ill, even our interior sense of time, our experience of duration, will become further individualized and less universally shared.

During Second Wave civilization machines were clumsily synchronized to one another, and people on the assembly line were then synchronized to the machines, with all the many social consequences that flowed from this fact. Today, machine synchronization has reached such exquisitely high levels, and the pace of even the fastest human workers is so ridiculously slow by comparison, that full advantage of the technology can be derived not by coupling workers to the machine but only by decoupling them from it.

Put differently, during Second Wave civilization, machine synchronization shackled the human to the machine's capabilities and imprisoned all of social life in a common frame. It did so in capitalist and socialist societies alike. Now, as machine synchronization grows more precise, humans, instead of being imprisoned, are progressively freed.

One of the psychological consequences of this is a change in the very meaning of punctuality in our lives. We are moving now from an across-the-board punctuality to selective or situational punctuality. Being on time—as our children perhaps dimly sense—no longer means what it used to mean.

Punctuality, as we saw earlier, was not terribly important during First Wave civilization—basically because agricultural work was not highly interdependent. With the coming of the Second Wave one worker's lateness could immediately and dramatically disrupt the work of many others in factory or office. Hence the enormous cultural pressure to assure punctuality.

Today, because the Third Wave brings with it personalized instead of universal or massified schedules, the consequences of being late are less clear. To be late may inconvenience a friend or co-worker, but its disruptive effects on production, while still potentially severe in certain jobs, are less and less obvious. It is harder—especially for young people—to tell when punctuality is really important and when it is demanded out of mere force of habit, courtesy, or ritual. Punctuality remains vital in some situations but, as the computer spreads and people are permitted to plug into and out of round-the-clock cycles at will, the number of workers whose effectiveness depends on it decreases.

The result is less pressure to be "on time" and the spread

of more casual attitudes toward time among the young. Punctuality, like morality, becomes situational.

In short, as the Third Wave moves in, challenging the old industrial way of doing things, it changes the relationship of the entire civilization to time. The old mechanical synchronization that destroyed so much of the spontaneity and joy of life and virtually symbolized the Second Wave is on its way out. The young people who reject the nine-to-five regime, who are indifferent to classical punctuality, may not understand why they behave as they do. But time itself has changed in the "real world," and along with it we have changed the ground rules that once governed us.

THE POST-STANDARDIZED MIND

The Third Wave does more than alter Second Wave patterns of synchronization. It attacks another basic feature of industrial life: standardization.

The hidden code of Second Wave society encouraged a steamroller standardization of many things—from values, weights, distances, sizes, time, and currencies to products and prices. Second Wave businessmen worked hard to make every widget identical, and some still do.

Today's savviest businessmen, as we have seen, know how to customize (as opposed to standardize) at lowest cost, and find ingenious ways of applying the latest technology to the individualization of products and services. In employment the numbers of workers doing identical work grows smaller and smaller as the variety of occupations increases. Wages and fringe benefits begin to vary more from worker to worker. Workers themselves become more different from one another, and since they (and we) are also consumers, the differences immediately translate into the marketplace.

The shift away from traditional mass production thus is accompanied by a parallel de-massification of marketing, merchandising, and of consumption. Consumers begin to make their choices not only because a product fulfills a specific material or psychological function but also because of the way it fits into the larger configuration of products and services they require. These highly individualized configurations are transient, as are the life-styles they help to define. Consumption, like production, becomes configurational. Post-standardized production brings with it post-standardized consumption.

Even prices, standardized during the Second Wave period, begin to be less standard now, since custom products require custom pricing. The price tag for an automobile depends on the particular package of options selected; the price of a hi-fi set similarly depends on the units that are plugged together and on how much work the buyer wishes to do; the prices of aircraft, offshore oil rigs, ships, computers, and other high-technology items vary from one unit to the next.

In politics we see similar trends. Our views are increasingly non-standard as consensus breaks down in nation after nation and thousands of "issue groups" spring up, each fighting for its own narrow, often temporary, set of goals. In turn, the culture itself is increasingly de-standardized.

Thus we see the breakup of the mass mind as the new communications media described in Chapter Thirteen come into play. The de-massification of the mass media—the rise of mini-magazines, newsletters, and small scale, often Xeroxed, communications along with the coming of cable, cassette, and computer—shatters the standardized image of the world propagated by Second Wave communications technologies, and pumps a diversity of images, ideas, symbols, and values into society. Not only are we using customized products, we are using diverse symbols to customize our view of the world.

Art News summarized the views of Dieter Honisch, director of the National Gallery in West Berlin: "What is admired in Cologne may not be accepted in Munich and a Stuttgart success may not impress the Hamburg public. Ruled by sectional interests, the country is losing its sense of national culture."

Nothing underlines this process of cultural de-standardization more crisply than a recent article in *Christianity Today*, a leading voice of conservative Protestantism in America. The editor writes, "Many Christians seem confused by the availability of so many different translations of the Bible. Older Christians did not face so many choices." Then comes the punch line. "*Christianity Today* recommends that no version should be the 'standard.'" Even within the narrow bounds of Biblical translation, as in religion generally, the notion of a single standard is passing. Our religious views, like our tastes, are becoming less uniform and standardized.

The net effect is to carry us away from the Huxleyan or Orwellian society of faceless, de-individualized humanoids that a simple extension of Second Wave tendencies would suggest and, instead, toward a profusion of life-styles and more highly individualized personalities. We are watching the rise of a "post-standardized mind" and a "post-standardized public."

This will bring its own social, psychological, and philosophical problems, some of which we are already feeling in the loneliness and social isolation around us, but these are dramatically different from the problems of mass conformity that exercised us during the industrial age.

Because the Third Wave is not yet dominant even in the most technically advanced nations, we continue to feel the tug of powerful Second Wave currents. We are still completing some of the unfinished business of the Second Wave. For example, hard-cover book publishing in the United States, long a backward industry, is only now reaching the stage of mass-merchandising that paperback publishing and most other consumer industries attained more than a generation ago. Other Second Wave movements seem almost quixotic, like the one that urges us at this late stage to adopt the metric system in the United States to bring American measurements into conformity with those used in Europe. Still others derive from bureaucratic empire building, like the effort of Common Market technocrats in Brussels to "harmonise" everything from auto mirrors to college diplomas—"harmonisation" being the current gobbledygook for industrial-style standardization.

Finally, there are movements aimed at literally turning back the clock—like the back-to-basics movement in United States schools. Legitimately outraged by the disaster in mass education, it does not recognize that a de-massified society calls for new educational strategies, but seeks instead to restore and enforce Second Wave uniformity in the schools.

Nevertheless, all these attempts to achieve uniformity are essentially the rearguard actions of a spent civilization. The thrust of Third Wave change is toward increased diversity, not toward the further standardization of life. And this is just as true of ideas, political convictions, sexual proclivities, educational methods, eating habits, religious views, ethnic attitudes, musical taste, fashions, and family forms as it is of automated production.

An historic turning point has been reached, and standardization, another of the ruling principles of Second Wave civilization, is being replaced.

THE NEW MATRIX

Having seen how swiftly we are moving away from industrial-style synchronization and standardization, it should surprise no one that we are also rewriting other sections of the social code.

We saw earlier that, while all societies need some measure of both centralization and decentralization, Second Wave civilization was heavily biased toward the former and against the latter. The Great Standardizers who helped build industrialism marched hand in hand with the Great Centralizers, from Hamilton and Lenin down to Roosevelt.

Today a sharp swing in the opposite direction is evident. New political parties, new management techniques, and new philosophies are springing up that explicitly attack the centralist premises of the Second Wave. Decentralization has become a hot political issue from California to Kiev.

In Sweden a coalition of largely decentralist small parties drove the centralist Social Democrats from power after 44 years in office. Struggles over decentralization and regionalism have shaken France in recent years, while across the Channel and to the north the Scottish Nationalists now include a wing committed to "radical economic decentralization." Similar political movements can be identified elsewhere in Western Europe, while in New Zealand a still-small Values Party has sprouted, demanding "an expansion of the functions and autonomy of local and regional government . . . with a consequent reduction in the functions and size of central government."

In the United States, too, decentralism has picked up support, and supplies at least some of the fuel for the tax revolt that is, for good or for ill, surging across the country. On the municipal level, too, decentralism gains force, with local politicos demanding "neighborhood power." Activist, neighborhood-based groups are proliferating, from ROBBED (Residents Organized for Better and Beautiful Environmental Development) in San Antonio, to CBBB (Citizens to Bring Broadway Back) in Cleveland and the People's Firehouse in Brooklyn. Many see the central government in Washington as the source of local ills rather than the potential cure.

According to Monsignor Geno Baroni, himself a former neighborhood and civil rights activist and now the Assistant Secretary for Neighborhoods in the U.S. Department of Housing and Urban Development, such small, decentralized groups reflect the breakdown of machine politics and the inability of big government to cope with the wide diversity of local conditions and people. Says *The New York Times*, neighborhood activists are winning "victories in Washington and across the country."

The decentralist philosophy is being spread, moreover, in schools of architecture and planning, from Berkeley to Yale in the United States to the Architectural Association in London, where students are, among other things, exploring new technologies for environmental control, solar heating, or urban agriculture with the aim of making communities partially self-sufficient in the future. The impact of these young planners and architects will be increasingly felt in the years to come as they move into responsible positions.

More important, however, the term "decentralization" has also become a buzzword in management, and large companies are racing to break their departments down into smaller, more autonomous "profit centers." A typical case was the reorganization of Esmark, Inc., a huge company with operations in the food, chemical, oil, and insurance industries.

"In the past," declared Esmark's chairman, Robert Reneker, "we had an unwieldly business. . . . The only way we could develop coordinated effort was to divide it into bite-size bits." The result: an Esmark cut into 1,000 different "profit centers," each one largely responsible for its own operations.

"The net effect," said *Business Week*, "is to lift the routine decision-making from Reneker's shoulders. Decentralization is evident everywhere but in Esmark's financial controls."

What is important is not Esmark—which has probably reorganized itself more than once since—but the general tendency it illustrates. Hundreds, perhaps thousands, of companies are also in the process of continual reorganization, decentralizing, sometimes overshooting and swinging back, but gradually, over time, reducing centralized control over their day-to-day operations.

At an even deeper level, large organizations are changing the authority patterns that underpinned centralism. The typical Second Wave firm or government agency was organized around the principle of "one man, one boss." While an employee or an executive might have many subordinates, he or she would never report to more than a single superior. This principle meant that the channels of command all went to the center.

Today it is fascinating to watch that system crack under its own weight in the advanced industries, in the services, the professions, and many government agencies. The fact is, growing multitudes of us today have more than a single boss.

In *Future Shock* I pointed out that big organizations were increasingly honeycombed by temporary units like task forces, interdepartmental committees, and project teams. I termed this phenomenon "ad-hocracy." Since then, many large companies have moved to incorporate these transient units into a radically new formal structure called "matrix organization." Instead of centralized control, matrix organization employs what is known as a "multiple command system."

Under this arrangement, each employee is attached to a department and reports to a superior in customary fashion. But he or she is also assigned to one or more teams for jobs that can't be done by a single department. Thus a typical project team may have people from manufacturing, from research, sales, engineering, finance, and from other departments as well. The members of this team all report to the project leader as well as to a "regular" boss.

The result is that vast numbers of people today report to one boss for purely administrative purposes and another (or a succession of others) for practical get-the-work-done purposes. This system lets employees give attention to more than one task at a time. It speeds up the flow of information and avoids their looking at problems through the narrow slit of a single department. It helps the organization respond to different, quickly changing circumstances. But it also actively subverts centralized control.

Spreading from such early users as General Electric in the United States and Skandia Insurance in Sweden, the matrix-style organization is now found in everything from hospitals and accounting firms to the U.S. Congress (where all sorts of new, semiformal "clearinghouses" and "caucuses" are springing up across committee lines). Matrix, in the words of Professors S. M. Davis of Boston University and P. R. Lawrence of Harvard, "is not just another minor management technique or a passing fad . . . it represents a sharp break . . . matrix represents a new species of business organization."

And this new species is inherently less centralized than the old one-boss system that characterized the Second Wave era.

Most important, we are also radically decentralizing the economy as a whole. Witness the rising power of small regional banks in the United States as against that of the handful of traditional "money market" giants. (As industry becomes more geographically dispersed, firms that previously had to rely on "money center" banks have increasingly turned to the regionals. Says Kenneth L. Roberts, president of First American, a Nashville bank, "The future of U.S. banking no longer lies with the money market banks.") And as with the banking system, so too with the economy itself.

The Second Wave gave rise to the first truly national markets and the very concept of a national economy. Along with these came the development of national tools for economic management—central planning in the socialist nations, central banks and national monetary and fiscal policies in the capitalist sector. Today both these sets of tools are failing—to the mystification of the Second Wave economists and politicians who try to manage the system.

Although the fact is only dimly appreciated as yet, national economies are swiftly breaking down into regional and sectoral parts—subnational economies with distinctive and differing problems of their own. Regions, whether the Sun Belt in the United States, the Mezzogiorno in Italy, or Kansai in Japan, instead of growing more alike as they did during the industrial era, are beginning to diverge from one another in terms of energy requirements, resources, occupational mix, educational levels, culture, and other key factors. Moreover, many of these subnational economies have now reached the scale of national economies only a generation ago.

Failure to recognize this accounts in good measure for the bankruptcy of government efforts to stabilize the economy. Every attempt to offset inflation or unemployment through nationwide tax rebates or hikes, or through monetary or credit manipulation, or through other uniform, undifferentiated policies, merely aggravates the disease.

Those who attempt to manage Third Wave economies with such centralized Second Wave tools are like a doctor who arrives at a hospital one morning and blindly prescribes the same shot of Adrenalin for all patients—regardless of whether they have a broken leg, a ruptured spleen, a brain tumor, or an ingrown toenail. Only disaggregated, increasingly decentralized economic management can work in the new economy, for it, too, is becoming progressively decentralized at the very moment it seems most global and uniform.

All these anti-centralist tendencies—in politics, in corporate or government organization, and in the economy itself (reinforced by parallel developments in the media, in the distribution of computer power, in energy systems, and in many other fields)—are creating a wholly new society and making yesterday's rules obsolete.

SMALL-WITHIN-BIG IS BEAUTIFUL

Many other sections of the Second Wave social code are also being drastically rewritten as the Third Wave arrives. Thus Second Wave civilization's obsessive emphasis on maximization is also under sharp attack. Never before have advocates of Bigger Is Better been so assailed by advocates of Small Is Beautiful. It was only in the 1970's that a book with that title could have become an influential, worldwide best seller.

Everywhere we are seeing a dawning recognition that there are limits to the much-vaunted economies of scale and that many organizations have exceeded those limits. Corporations are now actively searching for ways to reduce the size of their work units. New technologies and the shift to services both sharply reduce the scale of operation. The traditional Second Wave factory or office, with thousands of people under a single roof, will be a rarity in the high-technology nations.

In Australia, when I asked the president of an auto company to describe the auto plant of the future, he spoke with utter conviction, saying, "I would never, ever again build a plant like this one with seven thousand workers under the same roof. I would break it into small units—three hundred or four hundred in each. The new technologies now make this possible." I have since heard similar sentiments from the presidents or chairmen of companies producing food and many other products.

Today, we are beginning to realize that neither big *nor* small is beautiful, but that appropriate scale, and the intelligent meshing of both big *and* small, is most beautiful of all. (This was something that E. F. Schumacher, author of *Small Is Beautiful*, knew better than some of his more avid followers. He once told friends that, had he lived in a world of small organizations, he would have written a book called *Big Is Beautiful*.)

We are also beginning to experiment with new forms of organization that combine the advantages of both. For example, the rapid spread of franchising in the United States, Britain, Holland, and other countries is often a response to capital shortage or tax quirks and can be criticized on various grounds. But it represents a method for rapidly creating small units and linking them together in larger systems, with varying degrees of centralization or decentralization. It is an attempt to mesh large- and small-scale organizations.

Second Wave maximization is on its way out. Appropriate scale is in.

Society is also taking a hard look at Second Wave specialization and professionalism. The Second Wave code book put experts on a towering pedestal. One of its basic rules was "Specialize to succeed." Today, in every field, including politics, we see a basic change in attitude toward the expert. Once regarded as the trustworthy source of neutral intelligence, specialists have been dethroned from public approval. They are increasingly criticized for pursuing their own self-interest and for being incapable of anything but tunnel vision. We see more and more efforts to restrain the power of the expert by adding laymen to decision-making bodies—in hospitals, for example, and many other institutions.

Parents demand the right to influence school decisions, no longer content to leave them to professional educators. After studying citizen political participation a few years ago, a task force in the state of Washington concluded, in a statement that summed up the new attitude, "You don't have to be an expert to know what you want!"

Second Wave civilization encouraged yet another principle: concentration. It concentrated money, energy, resources, and people. It poured vast populations into urban concentrations. Today this process, too, has begun to turn around. We see increasing geographical dispersal instead. At the level of energy, we are moving from a reliance on concentrated deposits of fossil fuels to a variety of more widely dispersed forms of energy and we are seeing numerous experiments aimed at "de-concentrating" the populations of schools, hospitals, and mental institutions.

In short, one could move systematically through the entire code book of Second Wave civilization—from standardization to synchronization right on down to centralization, maximization, specialization, and concentration—and show, item by item, how the old ground rules that governed our daily lives and our social decision-making are in the process of being revolutionized as Third Wave civilization sweeps in.

THE ORGANIZATION OF THE FUTURE

Earlier we saw that when all the Second Wave principles were put to work in a single organization the result was a classical industrial bureaucracy: a giant, hierarchical, permanent, top-down, mechanistic organization, well designed for making repetitive products or repetitive decisions in a comparatively stable industrial environment.

Now, however, as we shift to the new principles and begin to apply them together, we are necessarily led to wholly new kinds of organizations for the future. These Third Wave organizations have flatter hierarchies. They are less top-heavy. They consist of small components linked together in temporary configurations. Each of these components has its own relationships with the outside world, its own foreign policy, so to speak, which it maintains without having to go through the center. These organizations operate more and more around the clock.

But they are different from bureaucracies in another fundamental respect. They are what might be called "dual" or "poly" organizations, capable of assuming two or more distinct structural shapes as conditions warrant—rather like some plastic of the future that will change shape when heat or cold is applied but spring back into a basic form when the temperature is in its normal range.

One might imagine an army that is democratic and participatory in peace time but highly centralized and authoritarian during war, having been organized, in the first place, to be capable of both. We might use the analogy of a football team whose members are not merely capable of rearranging themselves in T formation and numerous other arrangements for different plays but who, at the sound of a whistle, are equally capable of reassembling themselves as a soccer, baseball, or basketball squad, depending upon the game being played. Such organizational players need to be trained for instant adaptation, and they must feel comfortable in a wider repertoire of available organizational structures and roles.

We need managers who can operate as capably in an open-door, free-flow style as in a hierarchical mode, who can work in an organization structured like an Egyptian pyramid as well as in one that looks like a Calder mobile, with a few thin managerial strands holding a complex set of nearly autonomous modules that move in response to the gentlest breeze.

We do not yet have a vocabulary for describing these organizations of the future. Terms like *matrix* or *ad hoc* are inadequate. Various theorists have suggested different words. Advertising man Lester Wunderman has said, "Ensemble groups, acting as intellectual commandos, will . . . begin to replace the hierarchial structure." Tony Judge, one of our most brilliant organization theorists, has written extensively about the "network" character of these emerging organizations of the future, pointing out, among other things, that "the network is not 'coordinated' by anybody; the participating bodies coordinate themselves so that one may speak of 'auto-coordination.'" Elsewhere he has described them in terms of Buckminster Fuller's "tensegrity" principles.

But whatever terms we use, something revolutionary is happening. We are participating not merely in the birth of new organizational forms but in the birth of a new civilization. A new code book is taking form—a set of Third Wave principles, fresh ground-rules for social survival.

It is hardly any wonder that parents—still mainly tied to the industrial-era code book—find themselves in conflict with children who, aware of the growing irrelevance of the old rules, are uncertain, if not blindly ignorant, of the new ones. They and we alike are caught between a dying Second Wave order and the Third Wave civilization of tomorrow.

THE RISE
OF THE PROSUMER

Giant historical shifts are sometimes symbolized by minute changes in everyday behavior. One such change—its significance all but overlooked—occurred early in the 1970's when a new product began invading the pharmacies of France, England, Holland, and other European countries. The new product was a do-it-yourself pregnancy test kit. Within a few years an estimated 15 to 20 million such kits had been sold to European women. Soon ads in American newspapers were clamoring: "Pregnant? The sooner you know, the better." When Warner-Lambert, an American firm, introduced the kit under its brand name it found the response "overwhelmingly good." By 1980 millions of women on both sides of the Atlantic were routinely performing for themselves a task previously carried out for them by doctors and laboratories.

They were not the only ones sidestepping the physician. According to *Medical World News*, "Self-care—the idea that people can and should be more medically self-reliant—is a fast rolling new bandwagon. . . . Across the land, ordinary people are learning to handle stethoscopes and blood pressure cuffs, administer breast self-examinations and Pap smears, even carry out elementary surgical procedures."

Today mothers are taking throat cultures. Schools offer courses on everything from foot care to "instant pediatrics." And people are checking their own blood pressure in coin-operated machines located in more than 1,300 shopping centers, airports, and department stores in the United States.

As recently as 1972 few medical instruments were sold to non-physicians. Today a growing share of the instrument market is destined for the home. Sales of otoscopes, ear-cleaning devices, nose and throat irrigators, and specialized convalescent products are all booming, as individuals take on more responsibility for their own health, reduce the number of visits to the doctor, and cut short their hospital stays.

On the surface all this might seem no more than a fad. Yet this rush to treat one's own problems (instead of paying someone else to do so) reflects a substantial change in our values, in our definition of illness, and in our perception of body and self. Even this explanation, however, diverts attention from a still larger meaning. To appreciate the truly historic significance of this phenomenon, we need to glance briefly backward.

THE INVISIBLE ECONOMY

During the First Wave most people consumed what they themselves produced. They were neither producers nor consumers in the usual sense. They were instead what might be called "prosumers."

It was the industrial revolution, driving a wedge into society, that separated these two functions, thereby giving birth to what we now call producers and consumers. This split led to the rapid spread of the market or exchange network—that maze of channels through which goods or services, produced by you, reach me and vice versa.

Earlier I argued that, with the Second Wave, we went from an agricultural society based on "production for use"—an economy of prosumers, as it were—to an industrial society based on "production for exchange." The actual situation was more complicated, however. For just as a small amount of production for exchange—i.e., for the market—existed during the First Wave, there continued to be a small amount of production for self-use during the Second.

A more revealing way of thinking about the economy, therefore, is to think of it as having two sectors. Sector A comprises all that unpaid work done directly by people for themselves, their families, or their communities. Sector B comprises all the production of goods or services for sale or swap through the exchange network or market.

Seen this way, we can now say that during the First Wave, Sector A—based on production for use—was enormous, while Sector B was minimal. During the Second Wave the reverse was true. In fact, the production of goods and services for the market mushroomed to such an extent that Second Wave economists virtually forgot the existence of Sector A. The very word "economy" was defined to exclude all forms of work or production not intended for the market, and the prosumer became invisible.

This meant, for example, that all the unpaid work done by women in the home, all the cleaning, scrubbing, child-rearing, the community organizing, was contemptuously dismissed as "non-economic," even though Sector B—the visible economy —could not have existed without the goods and services produced in Sector A—the invisible economy. If no one were at home minding the children there would be no next generation of paid workers for Sector B, and the system would fall of its own weight.

Can anyone imagine a functional economy, let alone a highly productive one, without workers who, as children, have been toilet trained, taught to speak, and socialized into the culture? What would happen to the productivity of Sector B if the workers flowing into it lacked even these minimal skills? Though ignored by Second Wave economists, the fact is that the productivity of each sector depends heavily on the other.

Today, as Second Wave societies suffer their terminal crisis, politicians and experts still bandy about economic statistics based entirely on Sector B transactions. They worry about declining "growth" and "productivity." Yet so long as they continue to think in Second Wave categories, so long as they ignore Sector A and regard it as outside the economy— and so long as the prosumer remains invisible—they will never be able to manage our economic affairs.

For if we look closely we find the beginnings of a fundamental shift in the relationship of these two sectors or forms of production to one another. We see a progressive blurring of the line that separates producer from consumer. We see the rising significance of the prosumer. And beyond that, we see an awesome change looming that will transform even the role of the market itself in our lives and in the world system.

All this takes us back to the millions of people who are beginning to perform for themselves services hitherto performed for them by doctors. For what these people are really doing is shifting some production from Sector B to Sector A, from the visible economy that the economists monitor to the phantom economy they have forgotten.

They are "prosuming." And they are not alone.

OVEREATERS AND WIDOWS

In Britain in 1970, a Manchester housewife named Katherine Fisher, after suffering for years from a desperate fear of leaving her own home, founded an organization for others with similar phobias. Today that organization, The Phobics Society, has many branches and is one of thousands of new groups cropping up in many of the high-technology nations to help people deal directly with their own problems—psychological, medical, social, or sexual.

In Detroit, some 50 "bereavement groups" have sprung up to aid people suffering from grief after the loss of a relative or friend. In Australia an organization called GROW brings together former mental patients and "nervous persons." GROW now has chapters in Hawaii, New Zealand, and Ireland. In 22 states an organization called Parents of Gays and Lesbians is in formation to help those with homosexual children. In Britain, Depressives Associated has some 60 chapters. From Addicts Anonymous and the Black Lung Association to Parents Without Partners and Widow-to-Widow, new groups are forming everywhere.

Of course, there is nothing new about people in trouble getting together to talk out their problems and learn from one another. Nonetheless, historians can find little precedent for the wildfire speed with which the self-help movement is spreading today.

Frank Riessman and Alan Gartner, co-directors of the New Human Services Institute, estimate that in the United States alone there are now over 500,000 such groupings—about one for every 435 in the population—with new ones forming daily. Many are short-lived, but for each one that disappears several seem to take its place.

These organizations vary widely. Some share the new suspicion of specialists and attempt to work without them. They rely entirely on what might be termed "cross-counseling"—people swapping advice based on their own life experience, as distinct from receiving traditional counseling from the professionals. Some see themselves as providing a support system for people in trouble. Others play a political role, lobbying for changes in legislation or tax regulations. Still others have a quasi-religious character. Some are intentional communities whose members not only meet but actually live together.

Such groups are now forming regional, even transnational linkages. To the extent that professional psychologists, social workers, or doctors are involved at all, they increasingly undergo a role change, shifting from the role of impersonal expert who is assumed to know best to that of listener, teacher, and guide who works with the patient or client. Existing voluntary or nonprofit groups—originally organized for the purpose of helping others—are similarly struggling to see how they fit in with a movement based on the principle of helping oneself.

The self-help movement is thus restructuring the sociosphere. Smokers, stutterers, suicide-prone people, gamblers, victims of throat disease, parents of twins, overeaters, and other such groupings now form a dense network of organizations that mesh with the emerging Third Wave family and corporate structures.

But whatever their significance for social organization, they represent a basic shift from passive consumer to active prosumer, and they thus hold economic meaning as well. Though ultimately dependent on the market and still intertwined with it, they are transferring activity from Sector B of the economy to Sector A, from the exchange sector to the prosumption sector. Nor is this burgeoning movement the only such force: Some of the richest and largest corporations in the world are also—for their own technological and economic reasons—accelerating the rise of the prosumer.

THE DO-IT-YOURSELFERS

In 1956 the American Telephone & Telegraph Company, creaking under the burden of exploding communications demand, began introducing new electronic technology that made it possible for callers to direct-dial their long-distance calls. Today it is even possible to direct-dial many overseas calls. By punching in the appropriate numbers, the consumer took on a task previously done for him by the operator.

In 1973–74 the oil squeeze triggered by the Arab embargo sent gasoline prices soaring. Giant oil companies reaped bonanza profits, but local filling-station operators had to fight a desperate battle for economic survival. To cut costs many introduced self-service fuel pumps. At first these were an oddity. Newspapers wrote funny feature stories about the motorist who tried to put the fuel hose into the car radiator. Soon, however, the sight of consumers pumping their own gas became a commonplace.

Only 8 percent of U.S. gas stations were on a self-service basis in 1974. By 1977 the number reached nearly 50 percent. In West Germany, of 33,500 service stations some 15 percent had shifted to self-service by 1976, and this 15 percent accounted for 35 percent of all the gasoline sold. Industry experts say that it will soon be 70 percent of the total. Once more the consumer is replacing a producer and becoming a prosumer.

The same period saw the introduction of electronic banking, which not only began to break down the pattern of "banker's hours" but also increasingly eliminated the teller, leaving the customer to perform operations previously done by the bank staff.

Getting the customer to do part of the job—known to economists as "externalizing labor cost"—is scarcely new. That's what self-service supermarkets are all about. The smiling clerk who knew the stock and went and got it for you was replaced by the push-it-yourself shopping cart. While some customers lamented the good old days of personal service, many liked the new system. They could do their own searching and they wound up paying a few cents less. In effect, they were paying themselves to do the work the clerk had previously done.

Today this same form of externalization is occurring in many other fields. The rise of discount stores, for example, represents a partial step in the same direction. Clerks are far and few between; the customer pays a bit less but works a bit harder. Even shoe stores, in which a supposedly skilled clerk was long regarded as a necessity, are moving to self-service, shifting work to the consumer.

The same principle can be found elsewhere, too. As Caroline Bird has written in her perceptive book, *The Crowding Syndrome*, "More things come knocked down for supposedly easy assembly at home . . . and during the Christmas season shoppers in some of the proudest old New York stores have to make out sales slips for clerks unable or unwilling to write."

In January 1978 a thirty-year-old government worker in

Washington, D.C., heard strange noises emanating from his refrigerator. The customary thing to do in the past was to call in a mechanic and pay him to fix it. Given the high cost and the difficulty of getting a repairman at a convenient hour, Barry Nussbaum read the instructions that came with his refrigerator. On it he discovered an 800 telephone number that he could use to call the manufacturer—Whirlpool Corporation of Benton Harbor, Michigan—free of charge.

This was the "Cool-Line" set up by Whirlpool to help customers with service problems. Nussbaum called. The man at the other end then "talked him through" a repair, explaining to Nussbaum exactly which bolts to remove, which sounds to listen for and—later—what part would be needed. "That guy," says Nussbaum, "was super-helpful. He not only knew what I needed to do, he was a great confidence builder." The refrigerator was fixed in no time.

Whirlpool has a bank of nine full-time and several part-time advisers, some of them former service field men, who wear headsets and take such calls. A screen in front of them instantly displays for them a diagram of whatever product is involved (Whirlpool makes freezers, dishwashers, air-conditioners, and other appliances in addition to refrigerators) and permits them to guide the customer. In 1978 alone Whirlpool handled 150,000 such calls.

The Cool-Line is a rudimentary model for a future system of maintenance that permits the homeowner to do much of what a paid outside mechanic or specialist once did. Made possible by advances that have driven down the cost of long-distance telephoning, it suggests future systems that might actually display step-by-step fix-it-yourself instructions on the home television screen as the adviser speaks. The spread of such systems would reserve the repair mechanic only for major tasks, or turn the mechanic (like the doctor or social worker) into a teacher, guide, and guru for prosumers.

What we see is a pattern that cuts across many industries—increasing externalization, increasing involvement of the consumer in tasks once done for her or him by others—and once again, therefore, a transfer of activity from Sector B of the economy to Sector A, from the exchange sector to the prosumption sector.

All of this pales by comparison with what we see when we look at the dramatic changes that have hit other parts of the do-it-yourself industry. Do-it-yourselfers have always put-

tered away at fixing cracked windowpanes, broken light
fixtures, or chipped flagstones. Nothing new about that. What's
changed—and changed astonishingly—is the relationship between the do-it-yourselfer and the professional builder, carpenter, electrician, plumber, or what have you.

As recently as ten years ago in the United States only 30
percent of all electric power tools were sold to do-it-yourselfers; 70 percent went to carpenters or other professional
craftsmen. In a short ten years those figures have been reversed: Today only 30 percent are sold to professionals; fully
70 percent are bought by consumers who, more and more,
are doing-it-themselves.

An even more significant milestone, according to Frost &
Sullivan, a leading industrial research firm, was passed in the
United States between 1974 and 1976, when "for the first
time, more than half of all building materials . . . were purchased directly by homeowners rather than by contractors doing work for them." And this did not include an additional
$350,000,000 spent by the home craftsman for jobs costing
under $25.

While overall expenditures for building materials rose 31
percent during the first half of the seventies, those bought by
do-it-yourself homeowners rose over 65 percent—more than
twice as fast. The change, declares the F & S report, is "both
dramatic and continuing."

Another Frost & Sullivan study speaks of the "skyrocketing"
growth of such expenditures and underscores the value shift
toward self-sufficiency. "Where working with one's hands was
looked down upon (at least by the middle class) it is now a
sign of pride. People doing their own work are proud of it."

Schools, universities, and publishers are busy offering an
avalanche of how-to courses and books. Says *U.S. News &
World Report:* "Both rich and poor are caught up in the
boom. In Cleveland, home-repair instruction is offered in
public-housing projects. In California, owner-installed saunas,
spas and decks are popular."

In Europe, too, the so-called "DIY revolution" is under
way—with a few variations based on national temperament.
(German and Dutch do-it-yourselfers tend to treat their projects very soberly, set high standards, and equip themselves
carefully. Italians, by contrast, are just beginning to discover
the DIY movement, many older husbands insisting that it is
degrading to do the work themselves.)

Once more the reasons are multiple. Inflation. The difficulty of getting a carpenter or plumber. Shoddy work. Expanded leisure. All these play a part. A more potent reason, however, is what might be called the Law of Relative Inefficiency. This holds that the more we automate the production of goods and lower their per-unit cost, the more we increase the relative cost of handcrafts and nonautomated services. (If a plumber gets $20 for a one-hour house call and $20 will buy one hand calculator, his price, in effect, goes up substantially when the same $20 will buy several hand calculators. Relative to the cost of other goods, his price has risen several times over.)

For such reasons, we must expect the price of many services to continue their skyrocketing climb in the years ahead. And as these prices soar, we can expect people to do more and more for themselves. In short, even without inflation, the Law of Relative Inefficiency would make it increasingly "profitable" for people to produce for their own consumption, thus transferring further activity from Sector B to Sector A of the economy, from exchange production to prosumption.

OUTSIDERS AND INSIDERS

To glimpse the long-range future of this development, we need to look not only at services, but at goods. And when we do we find that here, too, the consumer is increasingly being drawn into the production process.

Thus eager manufacturers today recruit—even pay—customers to help design products. This is not merely true in industries that sell direct to the public—food, soap, toiletries, et cetera—but even more so in the advanced industries like electronics where de-massification is most rapid.

"We've been most successful when we have worked closely with one or two customers," says the manager of Texas Instruments' planning system. "To go off and study an application by ourselves and then try to come up with a standard product in that market has not been successful."

Indeed, Cyril H. Brown of Analog Devices, Inc. divides all products into two kinds: "inside-out" products and "outside-in" products. The latter are defined not by the manufacturer but by the potential customer, and these outsider products, according to Brown, are ideal. The more we shift toward advanced manufacture, and the more we de-massify and customize production, the stronger the customer's involvement in the production process must necessarily grow.

Today members of Computer-aided Manufacturing International (CAM-I) are hard at work classifying and coding parts and processes to permit the full automation of production. The prospect is still no more than a glint in the eye of such experts as Professor Inyong Ham of Penn State's Department of Industrial and Manufacturing Systems Engineering, but ultimately a customer will be able to feed his or her specifications into a manufacturer's computer directly.

The computer will not only design the product the customer wants, Professor Ham explains, but select the manufacturing processes to be used. It will assign the machines. It will sequence the necessary steps from, say, milling or grinding right down to painting. It will write the necessary programs for the subcomputers or numerical control devices that will run the machines. And it may even feed in an "adaptive control" that will optimize these various processes for both economic and environmental purposes.

In the end, the consumer, not merely providing the specs but punching the button that sets this entire process in action, will become as much a part of the production process as the denim-clad assembly-line worker was in the world now dying.

While such a customer-activated manufacturing system is still some distance off, at least some of the hardware already exists. Thus, at least in theory, the computer-run laser gun used in the garment industry and described in Chapter Fifteen could, if linked by telephone to a personal computer, permit a customer to feed in his or her various dimensions, select appropriate cloth, and then actually activate the laser cutter—without leaving his or her own home.

Robert H. Anderson, head of the Information Services Department at the RAND Corporation and a leading expert on computerized manufacture, explains it this way: "The most creative thing a person will do 20 years from now is to be a very creative consumer . . . Namely, you'll be sitting there doing things like designing a suit of clothes for yourself or making modifications to a standard design, so the computers can cut one for you by laser and sew it together for you by numerically controlled machine. . . .

"You really could, because of the computers, take your specs and turn them into a car. They will, of course, have programmed within them all the federal safety regulations and all the physics of the situation so they won't let you get too far out of bounds."

And if to this we now add the possibility that many people may soon be working at home anyway in the electronic cottages of tomorrow, we begin to imagine a significant change in the "tools" available to the consumer. Many of the same electronic devices we will use in the home to do work for pay will also make it possible to produce goods or services for our own use. In this system the prosumer, who dominated in First Wave societies, is brought back into the center of economic action—but on a Third Wave, high-technology basis.

In short, whether we look at self-help movements, do-it-yourself trends, or new production technologies, we find the same shift toward a much closer involvement of the consumer in production. In such a world, conventional distinctions between producer and consumer vanish. The "outsider" becomes an "insider," and even more production is shifted from Sector B of the economy to Sector A where the prosumer reigns.

As this occurs we begin—glacially at first but then, perhaps, with accelerating speed—to alter that most fundamental of our institutions: the market.

PROSUMER LIFE-STYLES

The willing seduction of the consumer into production has staggering implications. To understand why, it helps to remember that the market is premised on precisely the split between producer and consumer that is now being blurred. An elaborate market was not necessary when most people consumed what they themselves produced. It only became necessary when the task of consumption was separated from that of production.

Conventional writers define the market narrowly as a capitalist, money-based phenomenon. Yet the market is merely another word for an exchange network, and there have been (and still are) many different kinds of exchange networks. In the West the most familiar to us is the profit-based, capitalist market. But there are also socialist markets—exchange networks through which the goods or services produced by Ivan Ivanovich in Smolensk are traded for goods or services turned out by Johann Schmidt in East Berlin. There are markets based on money—but also markets based on barter. The market is neither capitalist nor socialist. It is a direct, inescapable consequence of the divorce of producer from consumer. Wherever this divorce occurs the market arises. And wherever the gap between consumer and producer narrows, the entire function, role, and power of the market is brought into question.

The rise of prosuming today, therefore, begins to change the role of the market in our lives.

It is too early to know where this subtle but significant thrust is taking us. Certainly the market is not going to go away. We are *not* going to go back to premarket economies. What I have called Sector B—the exchange sector—is not going to shrivel up and vanish. We will, for a long time to come, continue to be heavily dependent upon the market.

Nevertheless, the rise of prosuming points strongly toward a fundamental change in the relationships between Sector A and Sector B—a set of relationships that Second Wave economists have until now virtually ignored.

For prosuming involves the "de-marketization" of at least certain activities and therefore a sharply altered role for the market in society. It suggests an economy of the future unlike any we have known—an economy that is no longer lopsidedly weighted in favor of either Sector A or Sector B. It points to the emergence of an economy that will resemble neither First Wave nor Second Wave economies, but will, instead, fuse the characteristics of both into a new historic synthesis.

The rise of the prosumer, powered by the soaring cost of many paid services, by the breakdown of Second Wave service bureaucracies, by the availability of Third Wave technologies, by the problems of structural unemployment, and by many other converging factors, leads to new work-styles and life arrangements. If we permit ourselves to speculate, bearing in mind some of the shifts described earlier—such as the move toward de-synchronization and part-time paid work, the possible emergence of the electronic cottage, or the changed structure of family life—we can begin to discern some of these life-style changes.

Thus we are moving toward a future economy in which very large numbers never hold full-time paid jobs, or in which "full-time" is redefined, as it has been in recent years, to mean a shorter and shorter workweek or work year. (In

Sweden, where a recent law guaranteed all workers five weeks of paid vacation regardless of age or length of service, a normal work year was considered to be 1840 hours. In fact, absenteeism has run so high that a more realistic average per worker is 1600 hours per year.)

Large numbers of workers already do paid work for what averages out to only three or four days a week, or they take six months or a year off to pursue educational or recreational goals. This pattern may well grow stronger as two-paycheck households multiply. More people in the paid labor market—higher "labor participation rates," as the economists put it—may very well go with reduced hours per worker.

This casts the whole question of leisure into a new light. Once we recognize that much of our so-called leisure time is, in fact, spent producing goods and services for our own use—prosuming—then the old distinction between work and leisure falls apart. The question is not work versus leisure, but paid work for Sector B versus unpaid, self-directed, and self-monitored work for Sector A.

In the Third Wave context new life-styles based half on production for exchange, half on production for use, become practical. Such life-styles were, in fact, common in the early days of the industrial revolution among farm populations who were slowly being absorbed into the urban proletariat. For a long transitional period millions of people worked part-time in factories and part-time on the land, growing their own food, buying some of their necessities, making the rest. This pattern still prevails in many parts of the world—but usually on a technologically primitive basis.

Imagine this life pattern—but with twenty-first century technology for goods and food production, as well as immensely enhanced self-help methods for the production of many services. Instead of a dress pattern, for example, tomorrow's prosumer might well buy a cassette with a program on it that will drive a "smart" electronic sewing machine. Even the clumsiest househusband, with such a cassette, could make his own custom-fitted shirts. Mechanically inclined tinkerers could do more than tune up their autos. They could actually half-build them.

We saw that it may become possible some day for the customer to program his or her own specifications into the auto manufacturing process via computer and telephone. But there is another way in which the consumer, even now, can participate in producing an auto.

A company called Bradley Automotive already offers a "Bradley GT kit" that lets you "put together your own luxurious sports car." The prosumer who buys the partly preassembled kit mounts the fiberglass body on a Volkswagen chassis, connects the engine wires, sets up the steering, plugs in the seats, and so on.

One can easily picture a generation brought up on part-time paid work as the norm, eager to use their own hands, equipped with many cheap mini-technologies in the home, forming a sizable segment of the population. Half in the market, half out, working intermittently rather than all year round, taking a year off now and then, they might well earn less—but compensate by supplying their own labor for many tasks that now cost money, thus mitigating the effects of inflation.

America's Mormons offer another clue to possible future life-styles. Many Mormon stakes—a stake corresponds to, say, a Catholic diocese—own and operate their own farms. Members of the stake, including urban members, spend some of their free time as volunteer farmers growing food. Most of the produce is not sold but stored for emergency use or distributed to Mormons in need. There are central canning plants, bottling facilities, and grain elevators. Some Mormons grow their own food and take it to the cannery. Others actually buy fresh vegetables at the supermarket, then take them to the local cannery.

Says a Salt Lake City Mormon, "My mother will buy tomatoes and can them. Her relief 'society,' the women's auxiliary society, will have a day and they'll all go and can tomatoes for their own use." Similarly, many Mormons not only contribute money to their church but actually perform volunteer labor—construction work, for example.

None of this is to suggest that we are all going to become members of the Mormon church, or that it will be possible in the future to re-create on a wide scale the social and community bonds one finds in this highly participatory yet theologically autocratic group. But the principle of production for self-use, either by individuals or by organized groups, is likely to spread farther.

Given home computers, given seeds genetically designed for urban or even apartment agriculture, given cheap home tools for working plastic, given new materials, adhesives, and membranes, and given free technical advice available over the telephone lines, with instructions perhaps flickering on the

TV or computer screen, it becomes possible to create life-styles that are more rounded and varied, less monotonous, more creatively satisfying, and less market-intensive than those that typified Second Wave civilization.

It is still too early to know how far this shift of activity from exchange in Sector B to prosumption in Sector A will go, how the balance between these sectors will vary from country to country, and which particular life-styles will actually emerge from it. What is certain, however, is that any significant change in the balance between production for use and production for exchange will set off depth charges under our economic system and our values as well.

THIRD WAVE ECONOMICS

Is it possible that the much-bewailed decline of the Protestant work ethic is linked to this shift from production for others to production for self? Everywhere we see the decay of the industrial ethos that promoted hard work. Western executives mutter darkly about this "English disease" which is supposed to reduce us all to penury if we do not cure it. "Only the Japanese still work hard," they say. But I have heard top leaders of Japanese industry say that their labor force is suffering from the same infection. "Only the South Koreans work hard," they say.

Yet the very people who are supposedly unwilling to work hard on the job are often the same people who are, in fact, working hard off the job—laying bathroom tile, weaving carpets, lending their time and talents to a political campaign, attending self-help meetings, sewing, growing vegetables in the garden, writing short stories, or remodeling the attic bedroom. Can it be that the driving motivation that powered the expansion of Sector B is now being channeled into Sector A—into prosuming?

The Second Wave brought with it more than steam engines and mechanical looms. It brought with it an immense characterological change. Today we can still see this shift occurring among populations moving from First Wave to Second Wave societies—like the Koreans, for example, who are still busy expanding Sector B at the expense of Sector A.

By contrast, in the mature Second Wave societies reeling under the impact of the Third Wave—as production moves back to Sector A and the consumer is drawn back into the production process—another characterological shift begins. Later on we will explore this fascinating change. For now we need only bear in mind that the structure of personality itself is likely to be heavily influenced by the rise of prosumption.

Nowhere, however, are the changes wrought by the rise of the prosumer likely to be more explosive than in economics. Economists, instead of training all their guns on Sector B, will have to develop a new, more wholistic conception of an economy—will have to analyze what happens in Sector A as well and learn how the two parts relate to one another.

As the Third Wave has begun to restructure the world economy, the economics profession has been savagely attacked for its inability to explain what is happening. Its most sophisticated tools, including computerized models and matrices, seem to tell us less and less about how the economy really works. Indeed, many economists themselves are concluding that conventional economic thought, both Western and Marxist, is out of touch with a fast-changing reality.

One key reason may be that, more and more, changes of great significance lie outside Sector B—i.e., outside the entire exchange process. To bring economists back in touch with reality Third Wave economists will need to develop new models, measures, and indices for describing processes in Sector A and will have to rethink many root assumptions in the light of the rise of the prosumer.

Once we recognize that powerful relationships link the measured production (and productivity) in Sector B and the unmeasured production (and productivity) in Sector A, the invisible economy, we are compelled to redefine these terms. As early as the mid-1960's, economist Victor Fuchs of the National Bureau of Economic Research sensed the problem, pointing out that the rise of services made traditional measures of productivity obsolete. Declared Fuchs: "The knowledge, experience, honesty, and motivation of the consumer affects service productivity."

But even in these words the "productivity" of the consumer is still seen only in terms of Sector B—only as a contribution to production for exchange. There is no recognition as yet that actual production also takes place in Sector A—that goods and services produced for oneself are quite real, and that they may displace or substitute for goods and services turned out in Sector B. Conventional production figures, especially GNP figures, will make less and less sense until we explicitly expand them to include what happens in Sector A.

An understanding of the rise of the prosumer also helps bring the concept of cost into sharper focus. Thus we gain powerful insights once we recognize that the effectiveness of the prosumer in Sector A can lead to higher or lower costs to companies or government agencies operating in Sector B.

For example, high rates of alcoholism, absenteeism, nervous breakdowns, and mental disorder in the work force all add to the "cost of doing business" as measured conveniently in Sector B. (Alcoholism alone has been estimated to cost American industry $20 billion in production time a year. In Poland or the Soviet Union, where this disease is, if anything, more widespread, the comparable figures must be even more appalling.) To the degree that self-help groups alleviate such problems in the work force, they reduce these operating costs. The efficiency of prosumption thus affects the efficiency of production.

Subtler factors also influence the cost of production in business. How literate or articulate are the workers? Do they all speak the same language? Can they tell time? Are they culturally prepared for the job? Do the social skills learned in family life add to or detract from their competence? All these character traits, attitudes, values, skills, and motivations necessary for high productivity in Sector B, the exchange sector, are produced or, more accurately, prosumed in Sector A. The rise of the prosumer—the reintegration of the consumer into production—will force us to look far more closely at such interrelationships.

The same powerful change will compel us to redefine efficiency. Today, in determining efficiency, economists compare alternative ways of producing the same product or service. They seldom compare the efficiency of producing it in Sector B as against that of prosuming it in Sector A. Yet this is precisely what millions of people—supposedly innocent of economic theory—are doing. They are finding that, once a certain level of money income is assured, it may be more profitable, economically as well as psychologically, to prosume than to earn more cash.

Nor do economists or businessmen systemically track the negative effects of Sector B efficiency on Sector A—as for example when a company demands extremely high mobility of its executives and causes a wave of stress-related illness, family breakdown, or increased alcohol intake as a result. We may very well find that what appears to be inefficient in conventional Sector B terms is, in fact, tremendously efficient when we look at the whole economy and not just part of it.

To make sense, "efficiency" must refer to secondary, not merely first order, effects, and to both sectors of the economy, not just one.

What about concepts like "income," "welfare," "poverty," or "unemployment"? If a person lives half-in and half-out of the market system, which products, tangible or intangible, are to be regarded as part of his or her income? How meaningful are income figures at all in a society in which prosuming may account for much of what the average person has?

How do we define welfare in such a system? Should welfare recipients work? If so, should all this work necessarily be in Sector B? Or should welfare recipients be encouraged to prosume?

What is the real meaning of unemployment? Is a laid-off auto worker who puts a new roof on his house, or overhauls his car, unemployed in the same sense as one who sits idly at home watching football on television? The rise of the prosumer forces us to question our entire way of looking at the twin problems of unemployment, on the one hand, and bureaucratic waste and featherbedding, on the other.

Second Wave societies have attempted to cope with unemployment, for example, by resisting technology, closing off immigration, creating labor exchanges, increasing exports, decreasing imports, setting up public works programs, cutting back on work hours, attempting to increase labor mobility, deporting whole populations, and even waging war to stimulate the economy. Yet the problem becomes more complex and difficult every day.

Can it be that the problems of labor supply—both gluts and shortages—can *never* be satisfactorily solved within the framework of a Second Wave society, whether capitalist or socialist? By looking at the economy as a whole, rather than focusing exclusively on one part of it, can we frame the problem in a new way that helps us solve it?

If production occurs in both sectors, if people are busy producing goods and services for themselves in one sector and for others in a different sector, how does this affect the argument over a guaranteed minimum income for all? Typically, in Second Wave societies income has been inextricably linked to work for the exchange economy. But are not prosumers also "working," even if they are not part of the market or are only partially in it? Should not a man or woman who stays home and rears a child, thereby contributing to the productivity of Sector B through his or her efforts in Sector A, receive some income, even if he or she does not hold down a paid job in Sector B?

The rise of the prosumer will decisively alter all our economic thinking. It will also shift the basis of economic conflict. The competition between worker-producers and manager-producers will no doubt continue. But it will shrink in importance as prosuming increases and we move farther into Third Wave society. In its place new social conflicts will arise.

Battles will flare over which needs will be met by which sector of the economy. Struggles will sharpen, for example, over licensing, building codes, and the like, as Second Wave forces attempt to hold on to jobs and profits by preventing prosumers from moving in. Teachers' unions typically fight to keep parents out of the classroom with all the zeal of building tradesmen fighting to preserve obsolete building codes. Yet just as a number of health problems (like those deriving from overeating, lack of exercise, or smoking, for example) cannot be solved by doctors alone but require instead the active participation of the patient, so a number of educational problems cannot be resolved without the parent. The rise of the prosumer changes the entire economic landscape.

Thus all these effects will be intensified and the entire world economy changed by a massive historical fact now staring us in the face—which seems to have gone unnoticed by Second Wave economists and thinkers. This last towering fact sets into perspective all we have so far read in this chapter.

THE END OF MARKETIZATION

What has gone almost unnoticed is not merely a change in the patterns of participation in the market but, even more fundamentally, the completion of the entire historical process of market-building. This turning point is so revolutionary in its implications, yet so subtle, that capitalist and Marxist thinkers alike, lost in their Second Wave polemics, have scarcely noticed its signs. It fits into neither of their theories and thus has remained undetectable by them.

The human race has been busy constructing a worldwide exchange network—a market—for at least 10,000 years. In the past 300 years, ever since the Second Wave began, this process has roared forward at very high speed. Second Wave civilization "marketized" the world. Today—at the very moment when prosuming begins to rise again—this process is coming to an end.

The immense historical meaning of this cannot be appreciated unless we are clear about what a market or exchange network is. It helps to imagine it as a pipeline. When the industrial revolution burst forth on the earth, launching the Second Wave, very few people on the planet were tied into the money system. Trade existed but only the peripheries of society were touched by it. The various networks of jobbers, distributors, wholesalers, retailers, bankers, and other elements of the trade system were small and rudimentary—providing only a few narrow pipelines through which goods and money might flow.

For 300 years we poured earth-cracking energies into building this pipeline. It was accomplished in three ways. First the merchants and mercenaries of Second Wave civilization spread around the globe, inviting or coercing new populations to enter the market—to produce more and prosume less. Self-sufficient African tribesmen were induced or compelled to grow cash crops and dig copper. Asian peasants who once grew their own food were put to work on plantations instead, tapping rubber trees to put tires on automobiles. Latin Americans began growing coffee for sale in Europe and the United States. With each such development the pipeline was built or further elaborated and more and more populations drawn into dependence on it.

The second way in which the market expanded was through the increasing "commoditization" of life. Not only were larger populations enmeshed *in* the market but more and more goods and services were designed *for* the market, requiring a continual enlargement of the "channel capacity" of the system—a widening, as it were, of the diameter of the pipes.

Finally, the market expanded in another way. As society and the economy grew more complex, the number of transactions required for, say, a single bar of soap to pass from producer to consumer multiplied. The more intermediaries, the more ramified the maze of channels or pipes became. This growing elaborateness of the system was itself a form of further development, like the addition of still more special tubes and valves to a pipeline.

Today all these forms of market expansion are reaching their outer limits. Few populations still remain to be brought into the market. Only a handful of the remotest people remain untouched by the market. Even the hundreds of millions of subsistence farmers in poor countries are at least partially integrated into the market and the accompanying money system.

What remains, therefore, is a mopping-up operation at best. The market can no longer expand by engulfing vast new populations.

The second form of expansion is still at least theoretically possible. With imagination, we can still, no doubt, think up additional services or goods to to sell or barter. But it is precisely here that the rise of the prosumer becomes significant. The relationships between Sector A and Sector B are complex, and many of the activities of prosumers depend on the purchase of materials or tools from the market. But the rise of self-help, in particular, and the de-marketization of many goods and services suggests that here, too, the end of the process of marketization may be in sight.

Lastly, the increasing elaborateness of the "pipeline"—the growing complexity of distribution, the interpolation of more and more middlemen—also appears to be reaching a point of no return. The costs of exchange itself, even as conventionally measured, are now outrunning the costs of material production in many fields. At some point this process reaches a limit. Computers, meanwhile, and the emergence of a prosumer-activated technology both point to smaller inventories and simplified, rather than more complex, chains of distribution. Once again, therefore, the evidence points to the end of the process of marketization, if not in our time, then soon after.

If our "pipeline project" is nearing completion, what might this mean for our work, our values, and our psyches? A market, after all, does not consist of the steel or shoes or cotton or canned food that flows through it. The market is the structure through which such goods and services are routed. Moreover, it is not simply an economic structure. It is a way of organizing people, a way of thinking, an ethos, and a shared set of expectations (e.g., the expectation that goods purchased will indeed be delivered). The market is thus as much a psychological structure as an economic reality. And its effects far transcend economics.

By systematically interrelating billions of people to one another, the market produced a world in which no one had independent control over his or her destiny—no person, no nation, no culture. It brought with it the belief that integration into the market was "progressive" while self-sufficiency was "backward." It spread vulgar materialism and the belief that economics and economic motivation were the primary forces in human life. It fostered a view of life as a succession of contractual transactions, and of society as bound together by the "marriage contract" or the "social contract." Marketization thus shaped the thoughts and values, as well as the actions, of billions and set the tone of Second Wave civilization.

It took an enormous investment of time, energy, capital, culture, and raw materials to create a situation in which a purchasing agent in South Carolina could do business with an unseen and unknown clerk in South Korea—each with his or her own abacus or computer, each with an internalized image of the market, each with a set of expectations about the other, each performing certain predictable acts because both have been life-trained to play certain prespecified roles, each part of a giant global system involving millions, indeed billions, of others.

One might plausibly argue that the construction of this elaborate structure of human relationships, and its explosive diffusion around the planet, was the single most impressive achievement of Second Wave civilization, dwarfing even its spectacular technological achievements. The step-by-step creation of this essentially sociocultural and psychological structure for exchange (quite apart from the torrent of goods and services that flowed through it) can be likened to the building of the Egyptian pyramids, the Roman aqueducts, the Chinese wall, and the medieval cathedrals, combined and multiplied a thousandfold.

This grandest construction project of all history, the laying into place of the tubes and channels through which much of the economic life of civilization pulsed and flowed, gave Second Wave civilization everywhere its inner dynamism and propulsive thrust. Indeed, if this now dying civilization can be said to have had a mission at all, it was to marketize the world.

Today that mission is all but fulfilled.

The heroic age of market-building is over—to be replaced by a new phase in which we merely maintain, renovate, and update the pipeline. We will undoubtedly have to redesign important pieces of it to accommodate radically increased flows of information. The system will increasingly depend on electronics, biology, and new social technologies. This, too, will no doubt require resources, imagination, and capital. But compared with the exhausting effort of Second Wave marketization, this renewal program will absorb a far smaller fraction of our time, energy, capital, and imagination. It will use less, not more, hardware and fewer, not more, people than the original process of construction. However complex conversion proves to be, marketization will no longer be the central project of the civilization.

The Third Wave will therefore produce history's first "trans-market" civilization.

By trans-market I do not mean a civilization without exchange networks—a world thrown back into small, isolated, completely self-sufficient communities unable or unwilling to trade with one another. I do not mean a move backward. By "trans-market" I mean a civilization that is dependent on the market but is no longer consumed by the need to build, extend, elaborate, and integrate this structure. A civilization able to move on to a new agenda—precisely because the market has already been laid in place.

And just as no one living in the sixteenth century could have imagined how the growth of the market would change the world's agenda in terms of technology, politics, religion, art, social life, law, marriage, or personality development—so too it is extremely difficult for us today to envision the long-range effects of the end of marketization.

Yet these are likely to radiate into every cranny of our children's lives, if not our own. The marketization project exacted a price. Even in purely economic terms this price was enormous. As the productivity of the human race rose during the past three hundred years, a significant part of that productivity—in both sectors—was set aside and allocated to the market-building project.

With the basic construction task now virtually complete, the enormous energies previously poured into building the world market system become available for other human purposes. From this fact alone will flow a limitless array of civilizational changes. New religions will be born. Works of art on a hitherto unimagined scale. Fantastic scientific advances. And, above all, wholly new kinds of social and political institutions.

What is at stake today is more than capitalism or social-

ism, more than energy, food, population, capital, raw
material, or jobs; what is at stake is the role of the market in
our lives and the future of civilization itself.

This, at its core, is what the rise of the prosumer is about.

Change in the deep-structure of the economy is part of the
same wave of interrelated changes now striking our energy
base, our technology, our information system, and our family
and business institutions. These are intertwined, in turn, with
the way we view the world. And in this sphere, too, we are
undergoing an historic upheaval. For the entire world view of
industrial civilization—indust-reality—is now being revolutionized.

———————————

≈≈≈ 21

THE
MENTAL
MAELSTROM

Never before have so many people in so many countries—
even educated and supposedly sophisticated people—been so
intellectually helpless, drowning, as it were, in a maelstrom of
conflicting, confusing, and cacophonous ideas. Colliding
visions rock our mental universe.

Every day brings some new fad, scientific finding, religion,
movement, or manifesto. Nature worship, ESP, holistic medicine, sociobiology, anarchism, structuralism, neo-Marxism,
the new physics. Eastern mysticism, technophilia. technopho-
bia, and a thousand other currents and crosscurrents sweep
across the screen of consciousness, each with its scientific
priesthood or ten-minute guru.

We see a mounting attack on establishment science. We see
a wildfire revival of fundamentalist religion and a desperate
search for something—almost anything—to believe in.

Much of this confusion is actually the result of an intensifying cultural war—the collision of an emerging Third Wave
culture with the entrenched ideas and assumptions of industrial society. For just as the Second Wave engulfed traditional
views and spread the belief system I call indust-reality, so today we see the beginnings of a philosophical revolt aimed at
overthrowing the reigning assumptions of the past 300 years.
The key ideas of the industrial period are being discredited,
discounted, superseded, or subsumed into much larger and
more powerful theories.

The core beliefs of Second Wave civilization did not win
acceptance during the past three centuries without a bitter
struggle. In science, in education, in religion, in a thousand

fields, the "progressive" thinkers of industrialism fought against the "reactionary" thinkers who reflected and rationalized agricultural societies. Today it is the defenders of industrialism who have their backs against the wall as a new, Third Wave culture begins to take form.

THE NEW IMAGE OF NATURE

Nothing illustrates this clash of ideas more clearly than our changing image of nature.

In the past decade a worldwide environmental movement has sprung up in response to fundamental, potentially dangerous changes in the earth's biosphere. And this movement has done more than attack pollution, food additives, nuclear reactors, highways, and hair-spray aerosols. It has also forced us to rethink our dependency on nature. As a consequence, instead of conceiving ourselves as engaged in a bloody war with nature, we are moving toward a fresh view that emphasizes symbiosis or harmony with the earth. We are shifting from an adversary to a nonadversary posture.

At the scientific level, this has led to thousands of studies aimed at understanding ecological relationships so that we can soften our impacts on nature or channel them in constructive ways. We have just begun to appreciate the complexity and dynamism of these relationships and to reconceptualize society itself in terms of recycling, renewability, and the carrying capacity of natural systems.

All this is mirrored in a corresponding shift of popular attitudes toward nature. Whether we examine opinion surveys or the lyrics of pop songs, the visual imagery in advertising or the content of sermons, we find evidence of a heightened, though often romantic, regard for nature.

City dwellers by the millions yearn for the countryside, and the Urban Land Institute reports a significant population shift toward rural areas. Interest in natural foods and natural childbirth, in breastfeeding, biorhythms, or body care has boomed in recent years. And public suspicion of technology is so widespread that even the most single-minded pursuers of GNP today pay at least lip service to the idea that nature must be protected, not raped—that the adverse side effects of technology on nature must be anticipated and prevented, not simply ignored.

Because our power to damage it has escalated, the earth now is regarded as far more fragile than Second Wave civilization suspected. At the same time, it is seen as a diminishing dot in a universe that grows larger and more complex with every passing moment.

Since the Third Wave began some 25 years ago, scientists have developed a whole battery of new tools for probing nature's most distant reaches. In turn these lasers, rockets, accelerators, plasmas, fantastic photographic capabilities, computers, and colliding-beam devices have burst our conception of what surrounds us.

We are now looking at phenomena that are bigger, smaller, and faster by orders of magnitude than any we examined during the Second Wave past. Today we are probing phenomena that are as tiny as 1/1,000,000,000,000,000th of a centimeter in an explorable universe whose edge lies at least 100,000,000,000,000,000,000,000,000 miles away. We are studying phenomena so short-lived that they occur in 1/10,000,000,- 000,000,000,000,000th of a second. By contrast, our astronomers and cosmologists tell us the universe is some 20,000,000,000 years old. The sheer scale of explorable nature has burst beyond yesterday's wildest assumptions.

Moreover, in this swirling vastness, we are told, the earth may not be the only inhabited sphere. Says astronomer Otto Struve, "the vast number of stars that must possess planets, the conclusions of many biologists that life is an inherent property of certain types of complicated molecules or aggregates of molecules, the uniformity throughout the universe of the chemical elements, the light and heat emitted by solar-type stars, and the occurrence of water not only on the earth but on Mars and Venus, compel us to revise our thinking" and consider the possibility of extraterrestrial life.

This doesn't mean little green humanoids. And it doesn't mean (or not mean) UFOs. But by suggesting that life is not unique to the earth, it further alters our perception of nature and our place in it. Since 1960, scientists have been listening in the dark, hoping to detect signals from some distant intelligence. The United States Congress has held hearings on "The Possibility of Intelligent Life Elsewhere in the Universe." And the Pioneer 10 spacecraft, as it streaked into interstellar space carried with it a pictorial greeting to extraterrestrials.

As the Third Wave dawns, our own planet seems much smaller and more vulnerable. Our place in the universe seems less grandiose. And even the remote possibility that we are not alone gives us pause.

Our image of nature is not what it used to be.

DESIGNING EVOLUTION

Neither is our image of evolution—or, for that matter, evolution itself.

Biologists, archaeologists, and anthropologists, attempting to unravel the mysteries of evolution, similarly find themselves in a bigger and more complex world than previously imagined and are discovering that laws once regarded as universal in application are actually special cases.

Says the Nobel Prize-winning geneticist François Jacob, "Since Darwin, biologists have gradually developed a . . . chart of the mechanism of evolution, called natural selection. On that basis attempts have often been made to portray all evolution—cosmic, chemical, cultural, ideological, social—as governed by a similar selection mechanism. But such understandings seem doomed, inasmuch as the rules change at every plane."

Even on the biological plane, rules once thought to apply across the board are in question. Thus scientists are being forced to ask whether all biological evolution is a response to variation and natural selection or whether, at the molecular level, it may depend instead on an accumulation of variations which result in "genetic drift" without the operation of Darwinian natural selection. Says Dr. Motoo Kimura of the National Institute of Genetics in Japan, evolution at the molecular level appears to be "quite incompatible with the expectations of neo-Darwinism."

Other long held assumptions are being shaken as well. Biologists have told us that *eukaryotes* (human beings and most other forms of life) are ultimately descended from simpler cells called *prokaryotes* (among which are bacteria and algae). Fresh research is now undermining that theory, leading to the unsettling notion that the simpler life forms may have descended from the more complex.

Furthermore, evolution is supposed to favor adaptations that enhance survival. Yet we are now finding striking examples of evolutionary developments that seem to confer long-term benefit—at the cost of short-term disadvantage. Which does evolution favor?

Then there is the startling news from, of all places, the Grant Park Zoo in Atlanta, where the chance mating of two species of ape with two quite different sets of chromosomes has produced the first known hybrid ape. Even though researchers are unsure whether the hybrid will be fertile, her bizarre genetics lend support to the idea that evolution may occur in leaps and bounds as well as through the accretion of small changes.

Indeed, instead of seeing evolution as a smooth process, many of today's life scientists and archaeologists are studying the "theory of catastrophes" to explain "gaps" and "jumps" in the multiple branches of the evolutionary record. Others are studying small changes that may have been amplified through feedback into sudden structural transformations. Heated controversies divide the scientific community over every one of these issues.

But all such controversies are dwarfed by a single history-changing fact.

One day in 1953 at Cambridge in England a young biologist, James Watson, was sitting in the Eagle pub when his colleague, Francis Crick, ran excitedly in and announced to "everyone within hearing distance that we had found the secret of life." They had. Watson and Crick had unraveled the structure of DNA.

By 1957, as the first stirrings of the Third Wave were being felt, Dr. Arthur Kornberg learned how DNA reproduces itself. Since then, as one popular summary describes the sequence, "We have cracked the DNA code . . . We have learned how DNA transmits its instructions to the cell . . . We have analyzed chromosomes to determine genetic function . . . We have synthesized a cell . . . We have fused cells from two different species . . . We have isolated pure human genes . . . We have 'mapped' genes . . . We have synthesized a gene . . . We have changed the heredity of a cell." Today genetic engineers in laboratories around the world are capable of creating entirely novel life forms. They have endrun evolution itself.

Second Wave thinkers conceived of the human species as the culmination of a long evolutionary process; Third Wave thinkers must now face the fact that we are about to become the *designers* of evolution. Evolution will never look the same.

Like the concept of nature, evolution too is in the process of being drastically reconceptualized.

THE PROGRESS TREE

With Second Wave ideas about nature and evolution both changing, it is hardly surprising that we are also sharply re-evaluating Second Wave ideas about progress. The industrial period was characterized, as we saw earlier, by a facile optimism that saw each scientific breakthrough or "new improved product" as evidence of an inevitable advance toward human perfection. Since the mid-1950's, when the Third Wave began battering Second Wave civilization, few ideas have taken as rough a beating as this cheery creed.

The "beats" of the fifties and the hippies of the sixties made pessimism about the human condition, not optimism, a pervasive cultural theme. These movements did much to replace knee-jerk optimism with knee-jerk despair.

Soon pessimism became positively chic. Hollywood movies of the 1950's and 1960's, for example, replaced the jut-jawed heroes of the 1930's and 1940's with alienated antiheroes—rebels without a cause, stylish gunmen, dope pushers with charm, angst-ridden motorcyclists, and hard, inarticulate (but soulful) punks. Life was a game nobody won.

Fiction, drama, and art also took on a graveyard hopelessness in many Second Wave nations. By the early fifties, Camus had already defined the themes that countless novelists would subsequently pursue. A British critic summed these up as: "Man is fallible, political theories are relative, automatic progress is a mirage." Even science fiction, once filled with utopian adventures, turned bitter and pessimistic, generating countless poor imitations of Huxley and Orwell.

Technology, instead of being portrayed as the engine of progress, increasingly appeared as a juggernaut destroying both human freedom and the physical environment. For many environmentalists, indeed, "progress" became a dirty word. Weighty volumes poured into the bookshops, bearing titles like *The Stalled Society, The Coming Dark Age, In Danger of Progress,* or *The Death of Progress.*

As Second Wave society lurched into the seventies, The Club of Rome report on *The Limits to Growth* set a funereal tone for much of the decade that followed, with its projections of catastrophe for the industrial world. Upheavals, unemployment, and inflation, intensified by the oil embargo of 1973, added to the spreading pall of pessimism and the rejection of the idea of inevitable human progress. Henry Kissinger spoke in Spenglerian accents about the decline of the

West—sending yet another *frisson* of fear down a good many spines.

Whether such despair was, or is, justified remains for each reader to decide. One thing is clear, however: the notion of inevitable single-track progress, another pillar of indust-reality, found fewer takers as the end of Second Wave civilization loomed closer.

Today there is a fast-spreading recognition around the world that progress can no longer be measured in terms of technology or material standard of living alone—that a society that is morally, aesthetically, politically, or environmentally degraded is not an advanced society, no matter how rich or technically sophisticated it may be. In short, we are moving toward a far more comprehensive notion of progress— progress no longer automatically achieved and no longer defined by material criteria alone.

We are also less inclined to think of societies as moving along one track, each society traveling automatically from one cultural way-station to the next, one more "advanced" than another. There may be many branch lines, as it were, rather than a single roadbed, and societies may be able to achieve comprehensive development in a variety of ways.

We are beginning to think of progress as the flowering of a tree with many branches extending into the future, the very variety and richness of human cultures serving as a measure. In this light, today's shift toward a more diverse, de-massified world may itself come to be seen as an important forward leap—analogous to the tendency toward differentiation and complexity so common in biological evolution.

Whatever happens next, it is unlikely that the culture will ever again return to the naïve, unilinear, Pollyannaish progressivism that characterized and inspired the Second Wave era.

The past decades, therefore, have witnessed a forced reconceptualization of nature, evolution, and progress alike. These concepts, however, were in turn based on still more elemental ideas—our assumptions about time, space, matter, and causality. And the Third Wave is dissolving even these assumptions—the intellectual glue that held Second Wave civilization together.

●   ●   ●

THE FUTURE OF TIME

Each emerging civilization brings with it not merely changes in how people handle time in daily life but also changes in their mental maps of time. The Third Wave is redrawing these temporal maps.

Second Wave civilization, from Newton on, assumed that time ran along a single line from the mists of the past into the most distant future. It pictured time as absolute, uniform throughout all parts of the universe, and independent of matter and space. It assumed that each moment, or chunk of time, was the same as the next.

Today, according to John Gribbin, an astrophysicist-turned-science-writer, "Sober scientists with impeccable academic credentials and years of research experience calmly inform us that . . . time isn't something that flows inexorably forward at the steady pace indicated by our clocks and calendars, but that it can be warped and distorted in nature, with the end product being different depending on just where you are measuring it from. At the ultimate extreme, supercollapsed objects—black holes—can negate time altogether, making it stand still in their vicinity."

By the turn of the century Einstein had already proved that time could be compressed and stretched, and had dynamited the notion that time is absolute. He put forth the now classic case of the two observers and the railroad track, which went more or less like this:

A man standing alongside a railroad track sees two bolts of lightning strike at the same time—one at the far north end of the track, the other at the south. The observer is mid-way between the two. A second fellow is sitting in a high-speed train rocketing northward along the track. As he passes the observer outside he, too, sees the bolts of lightning. But to him the two flashes do not appear as simultaneous. Because the train is speeding him away from one and toward the other, the light from one reaches him sooner than the light from the other. To the man on the moving train it appears that the northern flash occurs first.

While in daily life the distances are so small and the speed of light so fast that the difference would be unnoticeable, the example dramatized Einstein's point: that the chronological order of events—what comes first, second, or later in time—depends upon the velocity of the observer. Time is not absolute, but relative.

This is a long way from the kind of time on which classical physics and indust-reality were based. Both took for granted that "before" or "after" had a fixed meaning independent of any observer.

Today physics is both exploding and imploding. Every day its practitioners hypothesize—or find—new elementary particles or astrophysical phenomena, from quarks to quasars, with amazing implications, some of which are forcing additional changes in our conceptions of time.

At one end of the scale, for example, black holes appear to punctuate the skies, sucking into themselves everything, including light itself, straining—if not smashing—the laws of physics. These dark maelstroms, we are told, terminate in "singularities" into which energy and matter simply vanish. Physicist Roger Penrose has even posited the existence of "wormholes" and "white holes" through which the lost energy and matter are spewed into another universe—whatever that might mean.

A single moment in the vicinity of a black hole, it is believed, might be the equivalent of eons on earth. Thus if some Interstellar Mission Control were to send a spaceship to explore a black hole, we might have to wait a million years for the ship to arrive. Yet because of gravitational distortion in the vicinity of the black hole, not to mention the effects of velocity, the ship's clock would show the passage of only a few minutes or seconds.

When we leave the vast heavens and enter the world of microscopic particles or waves, we find similarly puzzling phenomena. At Columbia University Dr. Gerald Feinberg has even hypothesized particles called *tachyons* that move faster than light and for which—according to some of his colleagues—time moves backward.

The British physicist J. G. Taylor tells us: "The microscopic notion of time is very different from the macroscopic." Another physicist, Fritjof Capra, puts it more simply. Time, he says, is "flowing at different rates in different parts of the universe." Increasingly, therefore, we cannot even speak of "time" in the singular; there appear to be alternative and plural "times" operating under different rules in different parts of the universe or universes we inhabit. All of which knocks the props from under the Second Wave idea of universal linear time—without substituting ancient notions of cyclical time.

At precisely the same moment, therefore, that we are radically restructuring our social uses of time—by introducing flextime on the job, by decoupling workers from the mechanical conveyor, and in the other ways described in Chapter Nineteen—we are also fundamentally reformulating our theoretical images of time. And while these theoretical discoveries seem at the moment to have no practical application to daily life, the same was true of those seemingly speculative chalk marks on the blackboard—the formulas that led ultimately to the smashing of the atom.

SPACE TRAVELERS

Many of these changes in our conception of time also blast holes in our theoretical understanding of space, since the two are tightly interwoven. But we are altering our image of space in more immediate ways as well.

We are changing the actual spaces in which all of us live, work, and play. How we get to work, how far and how frequently we travel, where we live—all these influence our experience of space. And all these are changing. In fact, as the Third Wave arrives we enter a new phase in humanity's relationship to space.

The First Wave, which spread agriculture around the world, brought with it, as we saw earlier, permanent farming settlements in which most people lived out their entire lives within a few miles of their birthplace. Agriculture introduced a stay-put, spatially intensive existence, and fostered intensely local feelings—the village mentality.

Second Wave civilization, by contrast, concentrated huge populations in great cities and, because it needed to draw resources from afar and to distribute goods at a distance, it bred mobile people. The culture it produced was spatially extensive and city- or nation- rather than village-centered.

The Third Wave alters our spatial experience by dispersing rather than concentrating population. While millions of people continue to pour into urban areas in the still-industrializing parts of the world, all the high-technology countries are already experiencing a reversal of this flow. Tokyo, London, Zurich, Glasgow, and dozens of other major cities are all losing population while middle-sized or smaller cities are showing gains.

The American Council of Life Insurance declares: "Some urban experts believe that the major U.S. city is a thing of the past." *Fortune* magazine reports that "transportation and commuication technology has cut the cords that bound big corporations to the traditional headquarters cities." And *Business Week* entitles an article "The Prospect of a Nation With No Important Cities."

This redistribution of and de-concentration of population will, in due time, alter our assumptions and expectations about personal as well as social space, about acceptable commuting distances, about housing density, and many other things.

In addition to such changes, the Third Wave also appears to be generating a new outlook that is intensely local, yet global—even galactic. Everywhere we find a new concentration on "community" and "neighborhood," on local politics and local ties at the same time that large numbers of people—often the same ones who are most locally oriented—concern themselves with global issues and worry about famine or war 10,000 miles away.

As advanced communications proliferate and we begin to shift work back into the electronic cottage, we will encourage this new dual focus, breeding large numbers of people who remain reasonably close to home, who migrate less often, who travel more perhaps for pleasure but far less often for business—while their minds and messages range across the entire planet and into outer space as well. The Third Wave mentality combines concern for near and far.

We are also rapidly adopting more dynamic and relativistic images of space. I have in my office several large blowups of satellite and U-2 photographs of New York City and the surrounding area. The satellite photos look like fantastically beautiful abstractions, the sea a deep green, the coastline detailed against it. The U-2 photos show the city in infrared, and in such exquisite detail that the Metropolitan Museum and even individual planes parked on the ramps at La Guardia Airport are clearly visible. Referring to the planes at La Guardia, I asked a NASA official if, by further enlarging the photos, one could actually see the stripes or symbols painted on the wings. He looked at me with amused tolerance and corrected me. "The rivets," he replied.

But we are no longer limited to exquisitely refined still pictures. Professor Arthur H. Robinson, a cartographer at the University of Wisconsin, says that within a decade or so satellites will permit us to look at a living map—an animated display—of a city or a country and watch the activities on it as they take place.

When this happens the map will no longer be a static representation but a movie—indeed an X ray in motion, since it will show not merely what is on the surface of the earth but also reveal, layer by layer, what lies below the surface and above it at each level of altitude. It will provide a sensitive, continually changing image of terrain and our relationships to it.

Some map makers, meanwhile, are rebelling against the conventional world map seen in every Second Wave classroom. Since the industrial revolution the most commonly used map of the world has been based on Mercator's projection. While this type of map is convenient for ocean navigation, it wildly distorts the scale of land surfaces. A quick look at your handy atlas will—if it uses a Mercator map—show Scandinavia as larger than India, even though the latter is actually almost three times larger.

Hot controversy rages among map makers over a new projection developed by Arno Peters, a German historian, to show land surfaces in proper proportion to one another. Peters charges that the distortions of the Mercator map have fostered the arrogance of the industrial nations and made it difficult for us to see the non-industrialized world in proper political, as well as cartographic, perspective.

"Developing countries have been cheated with regard to their surface and their importance," Peters contends. His map, strange to the European or American eye, shows a shrunken Europe, a flattened and squashed Alaska, Canada, and Soviet Union, and a much elongated South America, Africa, Arabia, and India. Sixty thousand copies of the Peters map have been distributed in the non-industrial countries by the Weltmission, a German evangelical mission and other religious organizations.

What this controversy underscores is the recognition that there is no single "right" map, but merely different images of space that serve different purposes. In the most literal sense the arrival of the Third Wave brings a new way of looking at the world.

WHOLISM AND HALFISM

These deep changes in our views of nature, evolution, progress, time, and space begin coming together as we move from a Second Wave culture that emphasized the study of things in isolation from one another to a Third Wave culture that emphasizes contexts, relationships, and wholes.

In the early fifties, at almost precisely the same time that biologists were breaking the genetic code, communications theorists and engineers at the Bell Labs, computer specialists at IBM, physicists at Britain's Post Office Laboratory, and specialists at Le Centre National de Récherche Scientifique in France, also began a period of intense and exciting work.

Drawing on "operations research" conducted during World War II, but advancing far beyond it, this work gave birth to the automation revolution and a whole new phylum or species of technology that underpins Third Wave production in factory and office. Along with the hardware, however, came a new way of thinking. For a key product of the automation revolution was the "systems approach."

Whereas Cartesian thinkers emphasized the analysis of components, often at the expense of context, systems thinkers stressed what Simon Ramo, an early advocate of systems theory, called a "total, rather than a fragmentary, look at problems." Emphasizing the feedback relationships among subsystems and the larger wholes formed by these units, systems thinking has had a pervasive cultural impact since the mid-1950's when it first began to seep out of the laboratories. Its language and concepts have been employed by social scientists and psychologists, by philosophers and foreign policy analysts, by logicians and linguists, by engineers and administrators.

But the advocates of systems theory are not the only ones in the past decade or two who have urged a more integrative way of looking at problems.

The revolt against narrow overspecialization also received a boost from the environmental campaigns of the 1970's, as ecologists increasingly discovered the "web" of nature, the interrelatedness of species, and the wholeness of ecosystems. "Non-environmentalists tend to want to separate things into components and to solve one thing at a time," wrote Barry Lopez in *Environmental Action.* By contrast, "Environmentalists tend to see things quite differently. . . . Their instinct is to balance the whole, not to solve a single part." The ecological approach and the systems approach overlapped and shared the same thrust toward synthesis and the integration of knowledge.

In universities, meanwhile, more and more calls were heard for interdisciplinary thinking. While departmental barriers still block the cross-fertilization of ideas and the integration of information in most universities, this demand for inter- or multi-disciplinary work is now so widespread it has an almost ritual quality.

These changes in intellectual life were mirrored elsewhere in the culture as well. Eastern religions, for example, had long had a tiny fringe following among the European middle classes, but it was not until the disintegration of industrial society began in earnest that thousands of Western young people began lionizing Indian swamis, jamming the Astrodome to hear a 16-year-old guru, listening to ragas, opening Hindu-style vegetarian restaurants, and dancing down Fifth Avenue. The world, they suddenly chanted, was not broken into Cartesian chips: it was a "oneness."

In the field of mental health, psychotherapists searched for ways to cure the "whole person" by employing gestalt therapy. A gestalt explosion erupted that saw the establishment of gestalt therapists and institutes throughout the United States. The goal of this activity, according to psychotherapist Frederick S. Perls, was "to increase human potential through the process of integration" of the individual's sensory awareness, perceptions, and relationships with the outside world.

In medicine, a "holistic health" movement has sprung up based on the notion that the well-being of the individual depends on an integration of the physical, the spiritual, and the mental. Mixing quackery with serious medical innovation, the movement gained enormous strength in the late 1970's.

"A few years ago," reports *Science*, "it would have been unthinkable for the federal government to lend its sponsorship to a conference on health that featured such topics as faith healing, iridology, acupressure, Buddhist meditation, and electromedicine." Since then there has been "a virtual explosion of interest in alternative healing methods and systems, all of which go under the name of holistic health."

With so much activity, on so many different levels, it is hardly surprising that the terms "wholism" or "holism" should have crept into the popular vocabulary. Today they are used almost indiscriminately. A World Bank expert calls for "a holistic understanding of . . . urban shelter." A research group in the United States Congress demands long-range "holistic" studies. A curriculum expert claims to employ "holistic reading and scoring" in teaching school children to write. And a Beverly Hills beauty gym offers "holistic exercise."

Each of these movements, fads, and cultural currents is different. But their common element is clear. All of them represent an attack on the assumption that the whole can be understood by studying the parts in isolation. Their thrust is summed up in the words of philosopher Ervin Laszlo, a leading systems theorist: we are "part of an interconnected system of nature, and unless informed 'generalists' make it their business to develop systematic theories of the patterns of interconnection, our short-range projects and limited controllabilities may lead us to our own destruction."

This attack on the fragmentary, on the partial and analytic has grown so fierce, in fact, that many fanatic "holists" blithely forget the parts in their pursuit of the ineffable whole. The result is not wholism at all but yet another fragmentation. Their wholism is halfism.

More thoughtful critics, however, seek to balance Second Wave analytic skills with a much greater emphasis on synthesis. This idea was perhaps most clearly expressed by ecologist Eugene P. Odum in urging his colleagues to combine wholism with reductionism—to look at whole systems as well as their parts. "As components . . . are combined to produce larger functional wholes," he declared when he and his more famous brother, Howard, jointly won the Prix de l'Institut de la Vie, "new properties emerge that were not present or not evident at the next level below. . . .

"This is not to say that we abandon reductionist science, since a great deal of good has resulted for mankind from this approach," but that the time has come to give equal backing to studies of "large-scale integrated systems."

Taken together, systems theory, ecology, and the generalized emphasis on wholistic thinking—like our changing conceptions of time and space—are part of the cultural attack on the intellectual premises of Second Wave civilization. That attack reaches its culmination, however, in the emerging new view of why things happen as they do: the new causality.

THE COSMIC PLAYROOM

Second Wave civilization gave us the comfortable assurance that we knew (or at least could know) what caused things to happen. It told us that every phenomenon occupied a unique, determinable location in space and time. It told us that the same conditions always produced the same results. It told us that the entire universe consisted, so to speak, of cue sticks and billiard balls—causes and effects.

This mechanistic view of causality was—and still is—extremely useful. It helps us cure disease, build giant skyscrapers, design ingenious machines, and assemble huge organizations. Yet, powerful as it is in explaining phenomena that work like simple machines, it has proved far less satisfactory in explaining phenomena like growth, decay, sudden breakthroughs to new levels of complexity, big changes that suddenly fizzle out or, conversely, those tiny—often chance—events that occasionally mushroom into giant, explosive forces.

Today the Newtonian pool table is being shoved into a corner of the cosmic playroom. Mechanistic causality is seen as a special case applying to some but not all phenomena, and scholars and scientists all over the world are piecing together a new view of chance and causation more in keeping with our rapidly changing views of nature, evolution, and progress, of time, space, and matter.

The Japanese-born epistemologist Magoroh Maruyama, the French sociologist Edgar Morin, information theorists like Stafford Beer and Henri Laborit, and many others are providing clues to how causation works in nonmechanical systems that live, die, grow, and undergo both evolution and revolution. The Belgian Nobel Prize-winner, Ilya Prigogine, offers us a staggering synthesis of the ideas of order and chaos, chance and necessity, and how these relate to causation.

In part, the emerging Third Wave causality arises from a key concept of systems theory: the idea of feedback. A classical example used to illustrate this notion is the home thermostat that maintains room temperature at an even level. The thermostat turns on the furnace, then monitors the resulting temperature rise. When the room is warm enough, it turns the furnace off. When the temperature falls, it senses this change in its environment and flicks the furnace on again.

What we see here is a feedback process that preserves equilibrium, damping down or suppressing change when it threatens to exceed a given level. Called "negative feedback," its function is to maintain stability.

Once negative feedback was defined and explored by information theorists and systems thinkers in the late 1940's and early 1950's, scientists began looking for examples or analogues of it. And with rising excitement, they found similar stability-protecting systems in every field from physiology (for example, the processes by which the body maintains its temperature) to politics (as in the way an "establishment" damps out dissent when it goes beyond an acceptable level). Negative feedback seemed to be at work all around us, causing things to retain their equilibrium or stability.

By the early 1960's, however, critics like Professor Maruyama began to note that too much attention was being paid to stability and not enough to change. What was needed, he argued, was more research on "positive feedback"—processes that do not suppress change but amplify it, do not maintain stability but challenge it, sometimes even overwhelming it. Positive feedback, Maruyama emphasized, can take a small deviation or "kick" in the system and magnify it into a giant structure-threatening shudder.

If the first kind of feedback was change-reducing or "negative," here was a whole class of processes that were change-amplifying or "positive," and both needed equal attention. Positive feedback could illuminate causation in many previously puzzling processes.

Because positive feedback breaks stability and feeds on itself, it helps explain vicious circles—and virtuous ones. Imagine the thermostat again, but with its sensor or its trigger mechanism reversed. Every time the room got warm, the thermostat, instead of shutting *off* the furnace, would click it *on,* forcing the temperature to hotter and hotter levels. Or imagine the game of Monopoly (or, for that matter, the game of real-life economics) in which the more money a player has, the more property he or she can buy, which means more rental income and therefore more money with which to buy property. Both are examples of positive feedback at work.

Positive feedback helps explain any process that is self-excitatory—like the arms race, for example, in which every time the U.S.S.R. builds a new weapon the U.S. builds a bigger one, which then motivates the U.S.S.R. to build yet another one . . . to the point of global insanity.

And when we put negative and positive feedback together and see how richly these two different processes interplay in complex organisms, from the human brain to an economy, startling insights emerge. Indeed, once we as a culture recognize that any truly complex system—whether a biological organism, a city, or the international political order—is likely to have within it both change amplifiers and change reducers, positive as well as negative feedback loops interacting with one another, we begin to glimpse a whole new level of complexity in the world with which we are dealing. Our understanding of causation is advanced.

Yet another leap in understanding occurs when we further recognize that these change reducers and amplifiers are not necessarily built into biological or social systems from the beginning; they may be absent at first, then grow into place, as it were, sometimes as a result of what amounts to chance. A stray event can thus trigger a fantastic chain of unexpected consequences.

This tells us why change is so often hard to track and extrapolate, so filled with surprise. It is why a slow, steady process can suddenly convert into an explosive change, or vice versa. And this in turn explains why similar starting conditions may lead to sharply dissimilar outcomes—an idea alien to the Second Wave mentality.

The Third Wave causality that is gradually taking shape pictures a complex world of mutually interacting forces, a world filled with astonishment, with change amplifiers as well as reducers and many other elements as well—not just billiard balls clacking predictably and endlessly against one another on the cosmic pool table. It is a world far stranger than simple Second Wave mechanisms suggested.

Is everything predictable in principle, as Second Wave mechanical causality implied? Or are things inherently, unavoidably unpredictable, as critics of mechanism have insisted? Are we governed by chance or necessity?

Third Wave causality has exciting new things to say about this ancient contradiction as well. In fact, it helps us escape at last from the either/or trap that for so long has pitted determinists against anti-determinists—necessity against chance. And this may be its most important philosophical breakthrough.

THE TERMITE LESSON

Dr. Ilya Prigogine and his teams of co-workers at the Free University of Brussels and the University of Texas at Austin have struck directly at Second Wave assumptions by showing how chemical and other structures leap to higher stages of differentiation and complexity through a combination of chance and necessity. It is for this work that Prigogine was awarded the Nobel Prize.

Born in Moscow, brought to Belgium as a child, and fascinated since youth by the problems of time, Prigogine was puzzled by a seeming contradiction. On the one hand, there was the physicist's belief in entropy—that the universe is running down and that all organized patterns must eventually decay. On the other, there was the biologist's recognition that life itself is organization and that we are continually giving rise to higher and higher, more and more complex organization. Entropy pointed in one direction, evolution in another.

This led Prigogine to ask how higher forms of organization come into being, and to years of research in chemistry and physics in pursuit of the answer.

Today Prigogine points out that in any complex system, from the molecules in a liquid to the neurons in a brain or the traffic in a city, the parts of the system are always undergoing small-scale change: they are in constant flux. The interior of any system is quivering with fluctuation.

Sometimes, when negative feedback comes into play, these fluctuations are damped out or suppressed and the equilibrium of the system maintained. But, where amplifying or positive feedback is at work, some of these fluctuations may be tremendously magnified—to the point at which the equilibrium of the entire system is threatened. Fluctuations arising in the outside environment may hit at this moment and further amplify the mounting vibration—until the equilibrium of the whole is destroyed and the existing structure is smashed.*

Whether the result of the runaway internal fluctuations or of external forces, or both, this breakup of the old equilibrium often results not in chaos or breakdown, but in the creation of a wholly new structure at a higher level. This new structure may be more differentiated, internally interactive, and complex than the old one, and needs more energy and matter (and perhaps information and other resources) to sustain itself. Speaking mainly about physical and chemical reactions, but occasionally calling attention to social analogues, Prigogine calls these new, more complex systems "dissipative structures."

---

* It is illuminating to think of the economy in these terms. Supply and demand are maintained in equilibrium by various feedback processes. Unemployment, if intensified by positive feedback and not offset by negative feedback elsewhere in the system, can threaten the stability of the whole. Outside fluctuations—such as oil price hikes—may converge to make the internal swings and fluctuations wilder, until the equilibrium of the whole system is shattered.

He suggests that evolution itself may be seen as a process leading toward increasingly complex and diversified biological and social organisms, through the emergence of new, higher-order dissipative structures. Thus, according to Prigogine, whose ideas have political and philosophical resonance as well as purely scientific meaning, we develop "order out of fluctuation" or, as the title of one of his lectures expresses it, "Order out of Chaos."

This evolution, however, cannot be planned or predetermined in a mechanistic fashion. Until quantum theory came along, many leading Second Wave thinkers believed that chance played little or no role in change. The starting conditions of a process predetermined its outcome. Today in subatomic physics, for example, it is widely believed that chance dominates change. In recent years many scientists, like Jacques Monod in biology, Walter Buckley in sociology, or Maruyama in epistemology and cybernetics, have begun to fuse these opposites.

Prigogine's work not only combines chance and necessity but actually stipulates their relationship to one another. In brief, he strongly suggests that at the precise point at which a structure "leaps" to a new stage of complexity, it is impossible, in practice and even in principle, to predict which of many forms it will take.* But once a pathway has been chosen, once the new structure comes into being, determinism dominates once more.

In one colorful example he describes how termites create their highly structured nests out of apparently unstructured activity. They begin by crawling about a surface in random fashion, stopping here and there to deposit a bit of "goo." These deposits are distributed by chance, but the substance contains a chemical attractant so that other termites are drawn to it.

In this way, the goo begins to collect in a few places, gradually building up into a pillar or wall. If these buildups are isolated, work stops. But if by chance they are near one another, an arch results that then becomes the basis for the complex architecture of the nest. What begins with random activity turns into highly elaborate nonrandom structures. We see, as Prigogine puts it, "the spontaneous formation of coherent structures." Order out of chaos.

---

* This presumably goes for the leap from Second Wave to Third Wave civilization as well as for chemical reactions.

All this strikes hard at the old causality. Prigogine sums it up: "The laws of strict causality appear to us today as limiting situations, applicable to highly idealized cases, nearly as caricatures of the description of change . . . The science of complexity . . . leads to a completely different view."

Instead of being locked into a closed universe that functioned like a mechanical clock, we find ourselves in a far more flexible system in which, as he says, "there is always the possibility of some instability leading to some new mechanism. We really have an 'open universe.' "

As we move beyond Second Wave causal thinking, as we begin to think in terms of mutual influence, of amplifiers and reducers, of system breaks and sudden revolutionary leaps, of dissipative structures and the fusion of chance and necessity—in short, as we take off our Second Wave blinders—we emerge blinking into a wholly new culture, the culture of the Third Wave.

This new culture—oriented to change and growing diversity—attempts to integrate the new view of nature, of evolution and progress, the new, richer conceptions of time and space, and the fusion of reductionism and wholism, with a new causality.

Indust-reality, which once seemed so powerful and complete, so all-encompassing an explanation of how the universe and its components fitted together, turns out now to have been immensely useful. But its claims to universality are shattered. The super-ideology of the Second Wave will be seen, from the vantage point of tomorrow, to have been as provincial as it was self-serving.

The decay of the Second Wave thought system leaves millions of people grasping desperately for something to hold on to—anything, from Texas Taoism to Swedish Sufism, from Philippine faith healing to Welsh witchcraft. Instead of constructing a new culture appropriate to the new world, they attempt to import and implant old ideas appropriate to other times and places or to revive the fanatic faiths of their own ancestors who lived under radically different conditions.

It is precisely the collapse of the industrial era mind-structure, its growing irrelevance in the face of the new technological, social, and political realities, that gives rise to today's facile search for old answers, and to the continual stream of pseudo-intellectual fads that pop up, flash, and consume themselves at high speed.

In the very midst of this spiritual supermarket, with its depressing razzmatazz and religious fakery, a positive new culture is being seeded—one appropriate to our time and place. Powerful new integrative insights are beginning to emerge, new metaphors for understanding reality. It is possible to glimpse the earliest beginnings of a new coherence and elegance as the cultural debris of industrialism is swept away by history's Third Wave of change.

The super-ideology of Second Wave civilization that is now crumbling was reflected in the way industrialism organized the world. An image of nature based on discrete particles was mirrored in the idea of discrete, sovereign nation-states. Today, as our image of nature and matter change, the nation-state itself is being transformed—another step on the path toward a Third Wave civilization.

THE CRACK-UP OF THE NATION

At a time when the flames of nationalism burn fiercely around the world—when national liberation movements proliferate in places like Ethiopia and the Philippines, when tiny islands like Dominica in the Caribbean or Fiji in the South Pacific declare their nationhood and send delegates to the United Nations—a strange thing is happening in the high-technology world: instead of new nations arising, old ones are in danger of coming apart.

As the Third Wave thunders across the earth, the nation-state—the key political unit of the Second Wave era—is being squeezed by viselike pressures from above and below.

One set of forces seeks to transfer political power downward from the nation-state to subnational regions and groups. The others seek to shift power upward from the nation to transnational agencies and organizations. Together they are leading toward a crack-up of the high-technology nations into smaller and less powerful units, as a look around the world quickly reveals.

ABKHAZIANS AND TEXICANS

It is August 1977. Three hooded men sit at a makeshift table, a lantern at one end, a guttering candle at the other, a flag draped across its middle. On the flag: an angry man's face with a swirling headband, and the letters FLNC. Peering through their eye-slits, the men tell their story to a huddle of newsmen who have been brought blindfolded to the rendez-

311

vous. The hooded ones announce that they are responsible for the bombing of the Serra-di-Pigno television repeater station—the only Corsican source of French telecasts. They want Corsica to secede from France.

Seething because Paris traditionally looked down its nose at them and because the French government had done little to develop their island economy, Corsicans were angered anew when units of the French Foreign Legion were shipped to bases in Corsica after the Algerian war. The locals were further outraged when the government gave the *pieds noirs*—ex-colonials from Algeria—subsidies and special rights to settle in Corsica. Settlers arrived in hordes and promptly bought up many of the island's vineyards (the main industry, apart from tourism), leaving the Corsicans to feel even more like strangers on their own island. Today France has a small-scale Northern Ireland brewing on its Mediterranean island.

At the opposite end of the country, too, long-simmering separatist sentiments have flared up in recent years. In Brittany, with high unemployment and some of the lowest wage scales in France, the separatist movement has widespread popular support. It is split into rival parties and has a terrorist arm whose members have been arrested for bombing public buildings including the palace at Versailles. Meanwhile Paris is beset with demands for cultural and regional autonomy in Alsace and Lorraine, parts of the Languedoc, and other sections of the country.

Across the Channel, Britain confronts comparable, though less violent, pressures from the Scots. In the early 1970's, talk about Scottish nationalism was regarded as a joke in London. Today, with North Sea oil providing the potential for Scotland's independent economic development, the issue is not funny at all. While a move to create a separate Scottish assembly was defeated in 1979, pressures for autonomy run deep. Long irked by government policies that favored the economic development of the South, Scottish nationalists now charge that their own economy is poised for a takeoff, and that the sluggish British economy is dragging them down.

They demand more control over their oil. They also seek to supplant their depressed steel and shipbuilding industries with new ones based on electronics and other advanced industries. Indeed, while Britain is torn with controversy over whether to go ahead with plans for a state-backed semiconductor industry, Scotland is already, after California and

Massachusetts, the third largest assembler of integrated circuits in the world.

Elsewhere in Britain separatist pressures are evident in Wales, and tiny autonomist movements are even surfacing in Cornwall and Wessex, where local regionalists demand home rule, their own legislative assembly, and a transition out of backward industry into high technology.

From Belgium (where tension among the Walloons, the Flemish and the Bruxelloises is rising) to Switzerland (where a split-away group recently won a fight for their own canton in the Jura) to West Germany (where Sudeten Germans are demanding the right to return to their original homeland in nearby Czechoslovakia) to the South Tyrolese in Italy, the Slovenes in Austria, the Basques and Catalans in Spain, the Croatians in Yugoslavia, and dozens of lesser known groups, all of Europe is feeling a relentless buildup of centrifugal pressures.

On the other side of the Atlantic, Canada's internal crisis over Quebec is not yet over. The election of the Quebecois separatist premier, René Lévesque, the flight of capital and business from Montreal, the heightened bitterness between French-speaking and English-speaking Canadians have created the real possibility of national disintegration. Former Prime Minister Pierre Trudeau, fighting to preserve national unity, warned that "if certain centrifugal tendencies fulfill themselves, we will have permitted this country either to break up or to become so divided that its existence and its ability to act as one nation will have been destroyed." Quebec, moreover, is not the only source of divisive pressures. Perhaps equally important, though less well known abroad, is the swelling chorus of separatist or autonomist voices in oil-rich Alberta.

Across the Pacific, nations like Australia and New Zealand display similar tendencies. In Perth a mining magnate named Lang Hancock has charged that mineral-rich Western Australia is compelled to pay artificially high prices for eastern Australia's manufactured wares. Among other things, Western Australia claims that it is politically underrepresented in Canberra; that, in a country of vast distances, airfares are rigged against her; and that national policies discourage foreign investment in the West. The gold-lettered sign outside Lang Hancock's office reads "Western Australia Secession Movement."

Meanwhile New Zealand has its own troubles with breakaways. The South Island's hydroelectric power provides much of the whole country's energy needs, but, say the South Islanders—who comprise roughly a third of the total population—they receive little for it and industry continues to depart for the North. At a recent meeting chaired by the mayor of Dunedin, a movement was born to declare the South Island independent.

What we see, across the board, are widening fissures threatening to crack nation-states apart. Nor are such pressures absent in the two giants—the U.S.S.R. and the United States.

It is difficult for us to imagine the actual breakup of, say, the Soviet Union, as the dissident historian Andrei Amalrik once forecast. But Soviet authorities have jailed Armenian nationalists for a 1977 bombing of the Moscow metro, and since 1968 an underground National Unification Party has campaigned for reunification of Armenian lands. Similar groups exist in other Soviet republics. In Georgia thousands of marching demonstrators have forced the government to make Georgian the official language of the republic, and foreign travelers in the Tbilisi airport have been startled to hear a Moscow-bound flight announced as a flight to "the Soviet Union."

Indeed, while the Georgians were demonstrating against the Russians, the Abkhazians—a minority group within Georgia—were meeting in their capital of Sukhumi to demand their own independence from the Georgians. So serious were these demands and the mass meetings held in three cities that heads rolled among Communist party officials, and Moscow, to placate the Abkhazians, announced a $750-million development plan for them.

It is impossible to gauge the full intensity of separatist sentiment in various parts of the U.S.S.R. But the nightmare of multiple secession movements must haunt the authorities. If war were to break out with China, or a series of uprisings suddenly exploded in Eastern Europe, Moscow might well face open secessionist or autonomist revolts in many of its republics.

Most Americans can hardly conceive of circumstances that would tear the Untied States apart. (Neither could most Canadians as recently as a decade ago.) But sectionalist pressures are steeply on the rise. In California today, a best-selling underground novel visualizes the Northwest seceding from America by threatening to detonate nuclear mines in New York and Washington. Other secession scenarios also make the rounds. Thus a report prepared for Kissinger while he was still national security adviser discussed the possible breakaway of California and the Southwest to form Spanish-speaking or bilingual geographical entities—"Chicano Quebecs." Letters to the editor speak of re-attaching Texas to Mexico to form a mighty oil power called Texico.

At a hotel newsstand in Austin not long ago I bought a copy of *Texas Monthly* which sharply criticized Washington's "gringo" policy toward Mexico, adding, "In recent years it seems we have had more in common with our old enemies in Mexico City than with our leaders in Washington. . . . The Yankees have been stealing our oil since Spindletop . . . so Texans should be least surprised by Mexico's attempt to avoid the same kind of economic imperialism."

On that same newsstand I also purchased a prominently displayed bumper sticker. It consisted of the Texas star and a single word: Secede.

Such talk may be quite farfetched, yet the plain fact is that throughout the United States, as in the other high-technology countries, national authority is being tested and sectional pressures are mounting. Leaving aside the rising potential for separatism in Puerto Rico and Alaska, or the demands of Native Americans for recognition as a sovereign nation, we can trace widening cleavages among the continental states themselves. According to the National Conference of State Legislatures, "There is a second civil war taking place in America. The conflict pits the industrial Northeast and Midwest against the sunbelt states of the South and Southwest."

A leading business publication speaks of the "Second War Between the States," and declares that "disparate economic growth is pushing the regions toward a sharp conflict." The same bellicose language is used by bristling governors and officials from the South and West who refer to what is happening as the "economic equivalent of the civil war." Infuriated by White House energy proposals, these officials, according to *The New York Times*, have "pledged everything short of secession from the Union to save oil and natural gas supplies for the region's growing industrial base."

Widening cleavages also divide the Western states themselves. Says Jeffery Knight, legislative director of Friends of the Earth, "Western states see themselves increasingly as energy colonies of states like California."

Then there were the much-publicized bumper stickers that

sprouted in Texas, Oklahoma, and Louisiana during the
heating-oil shortages of the mid-1970's and declared: "Let the
Bastards Freeze in the Dark." The thinly veiled implication
of secession could also be found in the wording of an ad
placed in *The New York Times* by the state of Louisiana. It
urged the reader to "Consider an America without Louisiana."

Midwesterners today are being advised to stop "chasing
smoke-stacks," to move to more advanced industry, and to
start thinking like regionalists, while Northeastern governors
are organizing themselves to defend that region's interests.
The public mood was hinted at in a full-page ad placed by a
Coalition to Save New York. The ad charged that "New
York Is Being Raped" by federal policies and that "New
Yorkers can fight back."

What does all this belligerent talk around the world, not to
mention the protests and violence, add up to? The answer is
unmistakable: potentially explosive internal stresses within
the nations spawned by the industrial revolution.

Some of these stresses obviously arise from the energy
crisis and the need to shift from a Second Wave to a Third
Wave energy base. Others can be traced to conflicts over the
transition from a Second Wave to a Third Wave industrial
base. In many places we are also witnessing, as suggested in
Chapter Nineteen, the growth of subnational or regional
economies that are as large, complex, and internally differentiated as national economies were a generation ago. These
form the economic launching pad for separatist movements
or drives for autonomy.

But whether taking the form of open secessionism, of
regionalism, bilingualism, home-rulism, or decentralism, these
centrifugal forces also gain support because national governments are unable to respond flexibly to the rapid de-massification of society.

As the mass society of the industrial era disintegrates under the impact of the Third Wave, regional, local, ethnic, social, and religious groups grow less uniform. Conditions and
needs diverge. Individuals, too, discover or reassert their differences.

Corporations typically meet this problem by introducing
more variety into their product lines and by a policy of
aggressive "market segmentation."

National governments, by contrast, find it difficult to customize their policies. Locked into Second Wave political and bureaucratic structures, they find it impossible to treat each region or city, each contending racial, religious, social, sexual, or ethnic group differently, let alone to treat each citizen as an individual. As conditions diversify, national decision-makers remain ignorant of fast-changing local requirements. If they try to identify these highly localized or specialized needs, they wind up deluged with overdetailed, indigestible data.

Pierre Trudeau, caught in the struggle against Canadian secessionism, put it clearly as early as 1967 when he argued: "You can't have an operative, operating system of federal government if one part of it, province or state, is in a very important special status, if it has a different set of relationships toward the central government than the other provinces."

In consequence, national governments in Washington, London, Paris, or Moscow continue, by and large, to impose uniform, standardized policies designed for a mass society on increasingly divergent and segmented publics. Local and individual needs are forgotten or ignored, causing the flames of resentment to reach white heat. As de-massification progresses, we can expect separatist or centrifugal forces to intensify dramatically and threaten the unity of many nation-states.

The Third Wave places enormous pressures on the nation-state from below.

FROM THE TOP DOWN

At the same time, we see equally powerful fingers clawing at the nation-state from above. The Third Wave brings new problems, a new structure of communications, and new actors on the world stage—all of which drastically shrink the power of the individual nation-state.

Just as many problems are too small or localized for national governments to handle effectively, new ones are fast arising that are too large for any nation to cope with alone. "The nation state, which regards itself as absolutely sovereign, is obviously too small to play a real role at the global level," writes the French political thinker, Denis de Rougement. "No one of our 28 European states can any longer by itself assure its military defense and its prosperity, its technological resources, . . . the prevention of nuclear wars and of ecological catastrophes." Nor can the United States, the Soviet Union, or Japan.

Tightened economic linkages between nations make it virtually impossible for any individual national government today to manage its own economy independently or to quarantine inflation. The ever-swelling bubble of Euromoney, for example, as suggested earlier, is beyond the power of any individual nation to regulate. National politicians who claim their domestic policies can "halt inflation" or "wipe out unemployment" are either naïve or lying, since most economic infections are now communicable across national boundaries. The economic shell of the nation-state is now increasingly permeable.

Furthermore, national borders that can no longer contain economic flows are even less defensible against environmental forces. If Swiss chemical plants dump wastes into the Rhine, the pollution flows through Germany, through Holland, and ultimately into the North Sea. Neither Holland nor Germany can, by itself, guarantee the quality of its own waterways. Oil tanker spills, air pollution, inadvertent weather modification, the destruction of forests, and other activities often involve side effects that sweep across national borders. Frontiers are now porous.

The new global communications system further opens each nation to penetration from the outside. Canadians have long resented the fact that some 70 U.S. television stations along the border telecast programs to Canadian audiences. But this Second Wave form of cultural penetration is minor compared with that made possible by Third Wave communications systems based on satellites, computers, teleprinters, interactive cable systems, and dirt cheap ground stations.

"One way to 'attack' a nation," writes United States Senator George S. McGovern, "is to restrain the flow of information—cutting off contact between the headquarters and overseas branches of a multinational firm . . . building information walls around a nation. . . . A new phrase is entering the international lexicon—'information sovereignty.'"

Yet it is questionable how effectively national borders can be sealed off—or for how long. For the shift toward a Third Wave industrial base requires the development of a highly ramified, sensitive, wide open "neural network" or information system, and attempts by individual nations to dam up data flows may interfere with, rather than accelerate, their own economic development. Moreover, each technological breakthrough provides yet another way to penetrate the nation's outer shell.

All such developments—the new economic problems, the new environmental problems, and the new communications technologies—are converging to undermine the position of the nation-state in the global scheme of things. What's more, they come together at precisely the moment when potent new actors appear on the world scene to challenge national power.

THE GLOBAL CORPORATION

The best-publicized and most powerful of these new forces is the transnational or, more commonly, the multinational corporation.

What we have seen in the past 25 years is an extraordinary globalization of production, based not merely on the export of raw materials or finished manufactured goods from one country to another, but on the organization of production across national lines.

The transnational corporation (or TNC) may do research in one country, manufacture components in another, assemble them in a third, sell the manufactured goods in a fourth, deposit its surplus funds in a fifth, and so on. It may have operating affiliates in dozens of countries. The size, importance, and political power of this new player in the global game has skyrocketed since the mid-1950's. Today at least 10,000 companies based in the non-communist high-technology nations have affiliates outside their own countries. Over 2,000 have affiliates in six or more host countries.

Of 382 major industrial firms with sales over $1 billion, fully 242 had 25 percent or more "foreign content" measured in terms of sales, assets, exports, earnings, or employment. And while economists disagree wildly on how to define and evaluate (and therefore classify and count) these corporations, it is clear that they represent a crucial new factor in the world system—and a challenge to the nation-state.

To glimpse their scale, it helps to know that on a given day in 1971 they held $268 billion in short-term liquid assets. This, according to the International Trade Subcommittee of the United States Senate, was "more than twice the total of all international monetary institutions in the world on the same date." The total *annual* U.N. budget, by comparison, represented less than 1/268 or 0.0037 of that amount.

By the early 1970's, General Motors' annual sales revenue was larger than the Gross National Product of Belgium or Switzerland. Such comparisons led economist Lester Brown, president of the Worldwatch Institute, to note that "It was once said that the sun never set on the British Empire. Today the sun does set on the British Empire, but not on the scores of global corporate empires including those of IBM, Unilever, Volkswagen and Hitachi."

Exxon alone has a tanker fleet 50 percent larger than that of the Soviet Union. The East-West specialist Josef Wilczynski, an economist at the Royal Military College of Australia, once whimsically pointed out that in 1973 "The proceeds from the sales" of only ten of these transnational corporations would have been "enough to give the 58,000,000 members of the Communist Parties in all the 14 Socialist countries a six-month holiday at the American standard of living."

While typically thought of as a capitalist invention, the fact is that some 50 "socialist transnationals" operate through the COMECON countries, laying pipelines, making chemicals and ball bearings, extracting potash and asbestos, and running ship lines. Moreover, socialist banks and financial institutions—ranging from the Moscow Narodny Bank to the Black Sea and Baltic General Insurance Company—do business in Zurich, Vienna, London, Frankfurt, or Paris. Some Marxist theorists now regard the "internationalization of production" as necessary and "progressive." In addition, of the 500 Western-based, privately owned TNCs whose sales in 1973 exceeded $500 million, fully 140 had "significant commercial dealings" with one or more of the COMECON countries.

Nor are the TNCs only based in the rich nations. The 25 countries in the Latin American Economic System recently moved to create transnationals of their own in the fields of agri-business, low-cost housing, and capital goods. Philippine-based companies are developing deepwater ports in the Persian Gulf, and Indian transnationals are building electronics plants in Yugoslavia, steel mills in Libya, and a machine tool industry in Algeria. The rise of the TNC alters the position of the nation-state on the planet.

Marxists tend to see national governments as handmaidens of corporate power, and therefore stress the commonality of interests between the two, yet the TNCs very often have their own interests that run counter to those of their "home" nations, and vice versa.

"British" TNCs have violated British embargos. "American" TNCs have violated U.S. regulations concerning the Arab boycott of Jewish firms. During the OPEC embargo the transnational oil companies rationed deliveries between countries according to their own, not national, priorities. National loyalties fade quickly when opportunities present themselves elsewhere, so that TNCs transfer jobs from country to country, escape environmental rules, and play off host countries against one another.

"For the past few centuries," Lester Brown has written, "the world has been neatly divided into a set of independent, sovereign nation-states. . . . With the emergence of literally hundreds of multinational or global corporations, this organization of the world into mutually exclusive political entities is now being overlaid by a network of economic institutions."

In this matrix, the power that once belonged exclusively to the nation-state when it was the only major force operating on the world scene is, at least in relative terms, sharply reduced.

Indeed, transnationals have already grown so large that they have taken on some of the features of the nation-state itself—including their own corps of quasi-diplomats and their own highly effective intelligence agencies.

"The multinationals' intelligence needs . . . are not much different from those of the United States, France or any other country. . . . Indeed, any discussion of the intelligence battles among the CIA, KGB, and their satellite agencies will be incomplete if it doesn't describe the increasingly important roles played by the apparats of Exxon, Chase Manhattan, Mitsubishi, Lockheed, Phillips and others," writes Jim Hougan in *Spooks,* an analysis of the private intelligence agencies.

Sometimes cooperating with their "home" nation, sometimes exploiting it, sometimes executing its policies, sometimes using it to execute their own, the TNCs are neither all good nor all bad. But with their ability to shunt billions back and forth instantly across national boundaries, their power to deploy technology and to move relatively quickly, they have often outflanked and outrun national governments.

"It is not just, or even mainly, a question of whether international companies can circumvent particular regional laws and regulations," writes Hugh Stephenson in a study of the impact of TNCs on the nation-state. "It is that our whole framework of thought and reaction is found in the . . . concept of the sovereign nation state [while] international corporations are rendering this notion invalid."

In terms of the global power system, the rise of the great transnationals has reduced, rather than strengthened, the role of the nation-state at precisely the time when centrifugal pressures from below threaten to part it at the seams.

THE EMERGING "T-NET"

Though they are the best known, the transnational corporations are not the only forces on the global stage. We are witnessing, for example, the rise of transnational trade union groupings—the mirror image, as it were, of the corporations. We are also seeing a growth of religious, cultural, and ethnic movements that flow across national lines and link up with one another. We observe an antinuclear movement whose demonstrations in Europe draw protesters together from several countries at a time. We also are witnessing the emergence of transnational political party groupings. Thus Christian Democrats and Socialists alike speak of forming themselves into "Europarties" that transcend individual national boundaries—a move accelerated by the creation of the European Parliament.

Paralleling these developments, meanwhile, is a rapid proliferation of nongovernmental transnational associations. Such groups devote themselves to everything from education to ocean exploration, sports to science, horticulture to disaster relief. They range from the Oceania Football Confederation to the International Red Cross, the International Federation of Small and Medium-Sized Commercial Enterprises, and the International Federation of Women Lawyers. In aggregate, such "umbrella" organizations or federations represent millions of members and tens of thousands of branches in many countries. They reflect every conceivable shade of political interest or lack of interest.

In 1963 some 1,300 such organizations operated across national lines. By the mid-1970's the number had doubled to 2,600. The total is expected to zoom to 3,500—4,500 by 1985 —with a new one springing up approximately every three days.

If the United Nations is the "world organization," these

less visible groups form, in effect, a "second world organization." Their aggregate budgets in 1975 amounted to a mere $1.5 billion—but this is only a tiny fraction of the resources controlled by their subordinate units. They have their own "trade association"—the Brussels-based Union of International Associations. They relate to one another vertically, with local, regional, national, and other groupings coming together under the transnational organization. They also relate horizontally through a dense mesh of consortia, working groups, interorganizational committees, and task forces.

So dense are these transnational ties that, according to a study by the Union of International Associations, there were an estimated 52,075 identifiable, interlocking relationships and cross-linkages among 1,857 such groups in 1977. And this number is soaring upward, too. Literally thousands of transnational meetings, conferences, and symposia bring the members of these different groupings into contact with one another.

Though still relatively underdeveloped, this fast-growing transnational network (or T-Net) adds yet another dimension to the emerging Third Wave world system. Even this does not complete the picture, however.

The nation-state's role is still further diminished as nations themselves are forced to create supranational agencies. Nation-states fight to retain as much sovereignty and freedom of action as they can. But they are being driven, step by step, to accept new constraints on their independence.

European countries, for example, grudgingly but inevitably have been driven to create a Common Market, a European parliament, a European monetary system, and specialized agencies like CERN—the European Organization for Nuclear Research. Richard Burke, the Common Market's tax commissioner, brings pressure to bear on member nations to alter their domestic tax policies. Agricultural and industrial policies once determined in London or Paris are hammered out in Brussels. Members of the European Parliament actually ram through an $840-million increase in the EEC budget over the objections of their national governments.

The Common Market is perhaps the prime example of the gravitation of power to a supranational agency. But it is not the only example. We are, in fact, seeing a population explosion of such inter-governmental organizations (or IGOs) —groupings or consortia of three or more nations. They range from the World Meteorological Organization and the International Atomic Energy Agency to the International Coffee Organization or the Latin American Free Trade Association, not to mention OPEC. Today such agencies are needed to coordinate global transport, communications, patents, and work in dozens of other fields from rice to rubber. And the number of such IGOs has also doubled, shooting up from 139 in 1960 to 262 in 1977.

Through these IGOs, the nation-state seeks to cope with larger than national problems, while retaining maximum decisional control at the national level. Bit by bit, however, a steady gravitational shift occurs as more decisions are transferred to—or constrained by—these larger than national organizational entities.

From the rise of the transnational corporation to the population explosion of transnational associations to the creation of all these IGOs, we see a set of developments all moving in the same direction. Nations are less and less able to take independent action—they are losing much of their sovereignty.

What we are creating is a new multilayered global game in which not merely nations but corporations and trade unions, political, ethnic, and cultural groupings, transnational associations and supranational agencies are all players. The nation-state, already threatened by pressures from below, finds its freedom of action constrained, its power displaced or diminished, as a radically new global system takes form.

PLANETARY CONSCIOUSNESS

The shrinkage of the nation-state reflects the appearance of a new-style global economy that has emerged since the Third Wave began its surge. Nation-states were the necessary political containers for nation-sized economies. Today the containers have not only sprung leaks, they have been made obsolete by their own success. First, there is the growth within them of regional economies that have attained a scale once associated with national economies. Second, the world economy to which they gave rise has exploded in size and is taking on strange new forms.

Thus the new global economy is dominated by the great transnational corporations. It is serviced by a ramified banking and financial industry that operates at electronic speeds. It breeds money and credit no nation can regulate. It moves toward transnational currencies—not a single "world money" but a variety of currencies or "meta-currencies," each based on a "market basket" of national currencies or commodities. It is torn by a world-scale conflict between resource suppliers and users. It is riddled with shaky debt on a hitherto unimaginable scale. It is a mixed economy, with private capitalist and state-socialist enterprises forming joint ventures and working side by side. And its ideology is not laissez faire or Marxism, but globalism—the idea that nationalism is obsolete.

Just as the Second Wave created a slice of the population that had larger than local interests and became the base for nationalist ideologies, so the Third Wave gives rise to groups with larger than national interests. These form the base of the emerging globalist ideology sometimes called "planetary consciousness."

This consciousness is shared by multinational executives, long-haired environmental campaigners, financiers, revolutionaries, intellectuals, poets, and painters, not to mention members of the Trilateral Commission. I have even had a famous U.S. four-star general assure me that "the nation-state is dead." Globalism presents itself as more than an ideology serving the interests of a limited group. Precisely as nationalism claimed to speak for the whole nation, globalism claims to speak for the whole world. And its appearance is seen as an evolutionary necessity—a step closer to a "cosmic consciousness" that would embrace the heavens as well.

In sum, therefore, at every level, from economics and politics to organization and ideology, we are witnessing a devastating attack, from within and without, on that pillar of Second Wave civilization: the nation-state.

At the exact historical moment when many poor countries are desperately fighting to establish a national identity because nationhood in the past was necessary for successful industrialization, the rich countries, racing beyond industrialism, are diminishing, displacing, or derogating the role of the nation.

We can expect the next decades to be torn by struggle over the creation of new global institutions capable of fairly representing the prenational as well as the postnational peoples of the world.

MYTHS AND INVENTIONS

No one today, from the experts in the White House or the Kremlin to the proverbial man in the street, can be sure how the new world system will shake out—what new kinds of institutions will arise to provide regional or global order. But it is possible to dispel several popular myths.

The first of these is the myth propagated by such films as *Rollerball* and *Network*, in which a steely-eyed villain announces that the world is, or will be, divided up and run by a group of transnational corporations. In its most common form this myth pictures a single worldwide Energy Corporation, a single Food Corporation, a single Housing Corporation, a single Recreation Corporation, and so forth. In a variant, each of these is seen as a department of an even larger mega-corporation.

This simplistic image is based on straight-line extrapolations from Second Wave trends: specialization, maximization, and centralization.

Not only does this view fail to take into account the fantastic diversity of of real life conditions, the clash of cultures, religions, and traditions in the world, the speed of change, and the historic thrust now carrying the high-technology nations toward de-massification; not only does it naïvely presuppose that such needs as energy, housing, or food can be neatly compartmentalized; it ignores the fundamental changes now revolutionizing the structure and purpose of the corporation itself. It is based, in short, on an obsolete, Second Wave image of what a corporation is and how it is structured.

The other, closely related fantasy pictures a planet run by a single, centralized World Government. This is usually imagined as an extension of some existing institution or government—a "United States of the World," a "Planetary Proletarian State," or simply the United Nations writ large. Again the thinking is based on simplistic extensions of Second Wave principles.

What appears to be emerging is neither a corporation-dominated future nor a global government but a far more complex system similar to the matrix organizations we saw springing up in certain advanced industries. Rather than one or a few pyramidal global bureaucracies, we are weaving nets or matrices that mesh different kinds of organizations with common interests.

We may, for example, see the emergence over the next decade of an Oceans Matrix, composed not solely of nation-states but of regions, cities, corporations, environmental organizations, scientific groups, and others with an interest in the sea. As changes occur new groupings would emerge and plug into the matrix, while others would drop out. Similar organizational structures may well emerge—are, in some sense, already emerging—to deal with other issues: a Space Matrix, a Food Matrix, a Transport Matrix, an Energy Matrix, and the like, all flowing into and out of one another, overlapping and forming a messily open, rather than a neatly closed, system.

In short, we are moving toward a world system composed of units densely interrelated like the neurons in a brain rather than organized like the departments of a bureaucracy.

As this happens, we can expect a tremendous struggle to break out within the United Nations over whether that organization shall remain a "trade association of nation-states" or whether other types of units—regions, perhaps religions, even corporations or ethnic groups—should be represented in it.

As nations are torn apart and restructured, as TNCs and other new factors move onto the global scene, as instabilities and the threats of war erupt, we shall be called upon to invent wholly new political forms or "containers" to bring a semblance of order to the world—a world in which the nation-state has become, for many purposes, a dangerous anachronism.

23

GANDHI WITH SATELLITES

"Convulsive shudders" . . . "unexpected uprising" . . . "wild swings" . . . The headline writers search frantically for terms to describe what they perceive as mounting world disorder. The Islamic uprising in Iran stuns them. The sudden reversal of Maoist policies in China, the collapse of the dollar, the new militancy of the poor countries, outbreaks of rebellion in El Salvador or Afghanistan are all seen as startling, random, unconnected events. The world, we are told, is careening toward chaos.

Yet much that appears anarchic is not. The eruption of a new civilization on the earth could not but shatter old relationships, overthrow regimes, and send the financial system spiraling. What seems like chaos is actually a massive realignment of power to accommodate the new civilization.

We will look back on today as the twilight of Second Wave civilization, and be saddened by what we see. For as it came to a close, industrial civilization left behind a world in which one quarter of the species lived in relative affluence, three quarters in relative poverty—and 800,000,000 in what the World Bank terms "absolute" poverty. Fully 700,000,000 people were underfed and 550,000,000 illiterate. An estimated 1,200,000,000 human beings remained without access to public health facilities or even safe, drinkable water, as the industrial age ended.

It left behind a world in which some 20 to 30 industrialized nations depended on the hidden subsidies of cheap energy and cheap raw materials for much of their economic success. It left a global infrastructure—the International

Monetary Fund, GATT, the World Bank, and COME-CON—which regulated trade and finance for the benefit of the Second Wave powers. It left many of the poor countries with one-crop economies twisted to serve the needs of the rich.

The rapid emergence of the Third Wave not only foreshadows the end of the Second Wave imperium, it also explodes all our conventional ideas about ending poverty on the planet.

THE SECOND WAVE STRATEGY

Ever since the late 1940's a single dominant strategy has governed most efforts to reduce the gap between the world's rich and poor. I call this the Second Wave strategy.

This approach starts with the premise that Second Wave societies are the apex of evolutionary progress and that, to solve their problems, all societies must replay the industrial revolution essentially as it happened in the West, the Soviet Union, or Japan. Progress consists of moving millions of people out of agriculture into mass production. It requires urbanization, standardization, and all the rest of the Second Wave package. Development, in brief, involves the faithful imitation of an already successful model.

Scores of governments in country after country have, in fact, tried to carry out this game plan. A few, like South Korea or Taiwan, where special conditions prevail, appear to be succeeding in establishing a Second Wave society. But most such efforts have met with disaster.

These failures in one impoverished country after another have been blamed on a mind-bending multiplicity of reasons. Neo-colonialism. Bad planning. Corruption. Backward religions. Tribalism. Transnational corporations. The CIA. Going too slowly. Going too fast. Yet, whatever the reasons, the grim fact remains that industrialization according to the Second Wave model has flopped far more frequently than it has succeeded.

Iran offers only the most dramatic case in point.

As late as 1975 a tyrannical Shah boasted he would make Iran into the most advanced industrial state in the Middle East by pursuing the Second Wave strategy. "The Shah's builders," reported *Newsweek*, "toiled over a glorious array of mills, dams, railroads, highways and all the other trimmings of a full-fledged industrial revolution." In June 1978 international bankers were still scrambling to lend billions at hairthin interest rates to the Persian Gulf Shipbuilding Corporation, to the Mazadern Textile Company, to Tavanir, the state-owned power utility, to the steel complex at Isfahan and the Iran Aluminium Company, among others.

While this buildup was supposedly turning Iran into a "modern" nation, however, corruption ruled Teheran. Conspicuous consumption aggravated the contrast between rich and poor. Foreign interests—mainly, but not exclusively, American—had a field day. (A German manager in Teheran was paid a third more than he could have earned at home, but his employees worked for one tenth a German worker's pay-packet.) The urban middle class existed as a tiny island within a sea of misery. Apart from oil, fully two thirds of all the goods produced for the market were consumed in Teheran by one tenth the country's population. In the countryside, where income was barely a fifth of that in the city, the rural masses continued to live under revolting and repressive conditions.

Nurtured by the West, attempting to apply the Second Wave strategy, the millionaires, generals, and hired technocrats who ran the Teheran government conceived of development as a basically economic process. Religion, culture, family life, sexual roles—all these would take care of themselves if only the dollar signs were got right. Cultural authenticity meant little because, steeped in indust-reality, they saw the world as increasingly standardized rather than moving toward diversity. Resistance to Western ideas was simply dismissed as "backward" by a cabinet 90 percent of whose members had been educated at Harvard, Berkeley, or European universities.

Despite certain unique circumstances—like the combustive mixture of oil and Islam—much of what happened in Iran was common to other countries pursuing the Second Wave strategy. With some variation, much the same might be said of dozens of other poverty-stricken societies from Asia and Africa to Latin America.

The collapse of the Shah's regime in Teheran has sparked a widespread debate in other capitals from Manila to Mexico City. One frequently asked question has to do with the pace of change. Was the pace too accelerated? Did the Iranians suffer from future shock? Even with oil revenues, can governments create a large enough middle class rapidly enough to avoid revolutionary upheaval? But the Iranian tragedy and the substitution of an equally repressive theocracy for the Shah's regime compel us to question the very root premises of the Second Wave strategy.

Is classical industrialization the only path to progress? And does it make any sense to imitate the industrial model at a time when industrial civilization itself is caught in its terminal agonies?

THE BROKEN SUCCESS MODEL

So long as the Second Wave nations remained "successful"—stable, rich, and getting richer—it was easy to look upon them as a model for the rest of the world. By the late 1960's, however, the general crisis of industrialism had exploded.

Strikes, blackouts, breakdowns, crime, and psychological distress spread throughout the Second Wave world. Magazines did cover pieces on "why nothing works any more." Energy and family systems shook. Value systems and urban structures crumbled. Pollution, corruption, inflation, alienation, loneliness, racism, bureaucratism, divorce, mindless consumerism, all came under savage attack. Economists warned of the possibility of a total collapse of the financial system.

A global environmental movement, meanwhile, warned that pollution, energy, and resource limits might soon make it impossible for even the existing Second Wave nations to continue normal operations. Beyond this, it was pointed out, even if the Second Wave strategy did, miraculously, work in the poor nations, it would turn the entire planet into a single giant factory and wreak ecological havoc.

Gloom descended on the richest nations as the general crisis of industrialism deepened. And suddenly millions around the world asked themselves not merely if the Second Wave strategy could work but why anyone would want to emulate a civilization that was itself in the throes of such violent disintegration.

Another startling development also underminded the belief that the Second Wave strategy was the only path from rags to riches. Always implicit in this strategy was the assumption that "first you 'develop,' then you grow rich"—that affluence was the result of hard work, thrift, the Protestant Ethic, and a long process of economic and social transformation.

However, the OPEC embargo and the sudden flood of petro-dollars into the Middle East stood this Calvinist notion on its pointed head. Within mere months unexpected billions spewed, splashed, and spumed into Iran, Saudi Arabia, Kuwait, Libya, and other Arab countries, and the world saw seemingly limitless wealth *preceding*, rather than following, transformation. In the Middle East, it was the money that produced the drive to "develop," rather than "development" that produced the money. Nothing like that, on so vast a scale, had ever happened before.

Meanwhile, competition among the rich nations themselves was heating up. "With South Korean steel being used at California construction sites, television sets from Taiwan being marketed in Europe, tractors from India being sold in the Middle East and . . . China emerging dramatically as a major potential industrial force, concern is mounting over how far developing economies will undercut established industries in the advanced nations of Japan, the United States and Europe," wrote a Tokyo correspondent for *The New York Times*.

Striking French steelworkers, as one might expect, put it more colorfully. They called for an end to "the massacre of industry" and protesters occupied the Eiffel Tower. In one after another of the older industrial nations, Second Wave industries and their political allies attacked the "export of jobs" and policies that spread industrialization to the poorer countries.

In short, doubts mushroomed on all sides as to whether the much-trumpeted Second Wave strategy could—or even should work.

THE FIRST WAVE STRATEGY

Faced by the failures of the Second Wave strategy, rocked by angry demands by the poor countries for a total overhaul of the global economy, and deeply worried about their own future—the rich nations in the 1970's began to hammer out a new strategy for the poor.

Almost overnight many governments and "development agencies," including the World Bank, the Agency for International Development, and the Overseas Development Council, switched to what can only be called a First Wave strategy.

This formula is almost a carbon copy reverse of the Second Wave strategy: Instead of squeezing the peasants and forcing them into the overburdened cities, it calls for a new emphasis on rural development. Instead of concentrating on cash crops for export, it urges food self-sufficiency. Instead of striving blindly for higher GNP in the hopes that benefits will trickle down to the poor, it calls for resources to be channeled directly into "basic human needs."

Instead of pushing for labor-saving technologies, the new approach stresses labor-intensive production with low capital, energy, and skill requirements. Instead of building giant steel mills or large-scale urban factories, it favors decentralized, small-scale facilities designed for the village.

Turning Second Wave arguments upside down, the advocates of the First Wave strategy were able to show that many industrial technologies were a disaster when transferred to a poor country. Machines broke down and went unrepaired. They needed high-cost, often imported raw materials. Trained labor was in short supply. Hence, the new argument ran, what was needed were "appropriate technologies." Sometimes called "intermediate," "soft," or "alternative," these would lie, as it were, "between the sickle and the combine harvester."

Centers for the development of such technologies soon sprang up all over the United States and Europe—the Intermediate Technology Development Group founded in 1965 in Britain serving as an early model. But the developing countries, too, created such centers and began pouring out low-scale technological innovations.

The Mochudi Farmers Brigade in Botswana, for example, has developed an ox- or donkey-drawn device that can be used for plowing, planting, and spreading fertilizer in single or double row cultivation. The Department of Agriculture in Gambia has adopted a Senegalese tool-frame which can be used with a single moldboard plow, a groundnut lifter, a seeder, and a ridger. In Ghana work is going forward on a pedal-driven rice thresher, a screw press for spent brewer's grain, and an all-wood squeezer to extract water from banana fiber.

The First Wave strategy has been applied on a much broader basis as well. Thus in 1978 the new government of India, still reeling from oil and fertilizer price hikes and from disappointment with the Second Wave strategies followed by

Nehru and Indira Gandhi, actually banned further expansion of its mechanized textile industry and urged increased production of fabrics on handlooms instead of power looms. The intent was not merely to increase employment but to retard urbanization by favoring rural cottage industry.

There is much about this new formula that admittedly makes excellent sense. It confronts the need to slow down the massive migration to the cities. It aims to make the villages—where the bulk of the world's poor dwell—more livable. It is sensitive to ecological factors. It stresses the use of cheap local resources rather than expensive imports. It challenges conventional, all-too-narrow definitions of "efficiency." It suggests a less technocratic approach to development, taking local custom and culture into account. It emphasizes improving the conditions of the poor rather than passing capital through the hands of the rich in the hopes that some will trickle down.

Yet after all due credit is given, the First Wave formula remains just that—a strategy for ameliorating the worst of First Wave conditions without ever transforming them. It is a Band-Aid, not a cure, and it is perceived in exactly these terms by many governments around the world.

Indonesian President Suharto expressed a widely held view when he charged that such a strategy "may be the new form of imperialism. If the West contributes only to small-scale grassroots projects, our plight may be alleviated somewhat but we will never grow."

The sudden love affair with labor-intensivity is also subject to the charge that it is self-serving for the rich. The longer the poor countries remain under First Wave conditions, the fewer competitive goods they are likely to shove onto an overloaded world market. The longer they stay down on the farm, so to speak, the less oil, gas, and other scarce resources they will siphon off, and the weaker and less troublesome they will remain politically.

There is also, built deep into the First Wave stragegy, a paternalistic assumption that while other factors of production need to be economized, the time and energy of the laborer needn't be—that unrelieved backbreaking toil in the fields or rice paddies is fine—so long as it is done by somebody else.

Samir Amin, director of the Institute of African Economic Development and Planning, sums up many of these views, saying that labor-intensive techniques have suddenly been rendered attractive, "thanks to a medley of hippie ideology, return to the myth of the golden age and the noble savage, and criticism of the reality of the capitalist world."

Worse yet, the First Wave formula dangerously de-emphasizes the role of advanced science and technology. Many of the technologies now being promoted as "appropriate" are even more primitive than those available to the American farmer of 1776—closer by far to the sickle than to the harvester. When American and European farmers began to employ more "appropriate technology" 150 years ago, when they shifted from wooden to steel harrow teeth or to the iron plow, they did not turn their back on the world's accumulated knowledge of engineering and metallurgy—they seized it.

At the Paris Exposition of 1855, according to a contemporary account, newly-invented threshing machines were dramatically demonstrated. "Six men were set to threshing with flails at the same moment that the different machines commenced operations, and the following were the results of an hour's work:

"Six threshers with flails .... 36 liters of wheat
Belgian threshing machine .... 150 liters of wheat
French threshing machine .... 250 liters of wheat
English threshing machine .... 410 liters of wheat
American threshing machine ...... 740 liters of wheat"

Only those who have never spent years at grueling manual labor can lightly brush aside machinery that, as early as 1855, could thresh grain 123 times faster than a man.

Much of what we now call "advanced science" was developed by scientists in rich countries to solve the problems of the rich countries. Precious little research has been addressed to the everyday problems of the world's poor. Nonetheless, any "development policy" that begins by blinding itself to the potentials of advanced scientific and technological knowledge condemns hundreds of millions of desperate, hungry, toiling peasants to perpetual degradation.

In some places, and at certain times, the First Wave strategy can improve life for large numbers of people. Yet there is painfully little evidence to show that any sizable country can ever produce enough, using premechanized First Wave methods, to invest in change. Indeed, a mass of evidence suggests the exact opposite.

By dint of heroic effort, Mao's China—which invented and

tried out basic elements of the First Wave formula—almost, but not quite, managed to prevent famine. This was a towering achievement. But by the late sixties, the Maoist emphasis on rural development and backyard industry had gone as far as it could go. China had reached a dead end.

For the First Wave formula, by itself, is ultimately a recipe for stagnation and is no more applicable to the entire range of poor countries than the Second Wave strategy.

In a world of exploding diversity we shall have to invent scores of innovative strategies and stop looking for models either in the industrial present—or in the preindustrial past. It is time we began to look at the emergent future.

THE THIRD WAVE QUESTION

Must we remain forever trapped between two obsolete visions? I have deliberately caricatured these alternative strategies to sharpen the differences. In real life, few governments can afford to follow abstract theories, and we find many attempts to combine elements of both strategies. Yet the rise of the Third Wave strongly suggests that we no longer need to Ping-Pong back and forth between these two formulas.

For the arrival of the Third Wave drastically alters everything. And while no theory emanating from the high-technology world, whether capitalist or Marxist in bias, is going to solve the problems of the "developing world," and no existing models are wholly transferable, a strange new relationship is springing up between First Wave societies and the fast-forming Third Wave civilization.

More than once we have seen naïve attempts to "develop" a basically First Wave country by imposing on it highly incongruous Second Wave forms—mass production, mass media, factory-style education. Westminster-style parliamentary government, and the nation-state, to name a few—without recognizing that for these to operate successfully, traditional family and marriage customs, religion, and role structures would all have to be crushed, the entire culture ripped up by its roots.

By astonishing contrast, Third Wave civilization turns out to have many features—decentralized production, appropriate scale, renewable energy, de-urbanization, work in the home, high levels of prosumption, to name just a few—that actually resemble those found in First Wave societies. We are seeing something that looks remarkably like a dialectical return.

This is why so many of today's most startling innovations arrive with a comet's tail of trace memories. It is this eerie sense of *déjà vu* which accounts for the fascination with the rural past that we find in the most rapidly emergent Third Wave societies. What is so striking today is that First and Third Wave civilizations seem likely to have more in common with each other than with Second Wave civilization. They are, in short, congruous.

Will this strange congruity make it possible for many of today's First Wave countries to take on some of the features of Third Wave civilization—without swallowing the whole pill, without totally surrendering their culture or first passing through the "stage" of Second Wave development? Will it, in fact, be easier for some countries to introduce Third Wave structures than to industrialize in the classical manner?

Is it now possible, moreover, as it was not in the past, for a society to attain a high material standard of living without obsessively focusing all its energies on production for exchange? Given the wider range of options brought by the Third Wave, cannot a people reduce infant mortality and improve life span, literacy, nutrition, and the general quality of life without surrendering its religion or values and necessarily embracing the Western materialism that accompanies the spread of Second Wave civilization?

Tomorrow's "development" strategies will come not from Washington or Moscow or Paris or Geneva but from Africa, Asia, and Latin America. They will be indigenous, matched to actual local needs. They will not overemphasize economics at the expense of ecology, culture, religion, or family structure and the psychological dimensions of existence. They will not imitate any outside model. First Wave, Second Wave or, for that matter, Third.

But the ascent of the Third Wave places all our efforts in a new perspective. For it provides the world's poorest nations, as well as the richest, with wholly new opportunities.

SUN, SHRIMP, AND CHIPS

The surprising congruence between many of the structural features of First Wave and Third Wave civilizations suggests that it may be possible in the decades ahead to combine elements of past and future into a new and better present.

Take, for example, the issue of energy.

With all the talk about an energy crisis in the countries transitioning into Third Wave civilization, it is often forgotten that First Wave societies are facing an energy crisis of their own. Starting from an extremely low base, what kind of energy systems should they create?

Certainly they need big centralized fossil-fuel-based power plants of the Second Wave type. But in many of these societies, as the Indian scientist Amulya Kumar N. Reddy has shown, the most urgent need is for decentralized energy in the countryside rather than vast, centralized supplies for the cities.

The family of a landless Indian peasant now spends about six hours a day merely finding the firewood it needs for cooking and heating. Another four to six hours are spent bringing water from a well, and a similar amount to graze cattle, goats, or sheep. "Since such a family cannot afford to hire labour and cannot buy labour-saving gadgets, its only rational response is to have at least three children to satisfy its energy needs," says Reddy, pointing out that rural energy "may prove an excellent contraceptive."

Reddy has studied rural energy needs and concluded that the requirements of a village can easily be met by a tiny, cheap bio-gas plant that uses human and animal waste from the village itself. He has gone on to demonstrate that many thousands of such units would be far more useful, ecologically sound, and economical than a few giant, centralized generating plants.

Precisely this reasoning lies behind bio-gas research and installation programs in countries from Bangladesh to Fiji. India already has 12,000 plants in operation and has targeted for 100,000 units. China plans to have 200,000 family-size bio-gas plants at work in Szechuan. Korea has 29,450 and hopes to reach a total of 55,000 by 1985.

Just outside New Delhi, the prominent futurist writer and businessman, Jagdish Kapur, has turned ten arid, miserably unproductive acres into a world-renowned model "solar farm" with a bio-gas plant. The farm now produces enough grains, fruits, and vegetables to feed his family and employees as well as tons of food to sell at a profit to the marketplace.

The Indian Institute of Technology, meanwhile, has

designed a ten-kilowatt solar plant for village use to provide electricity for lighting homes, operating water pumps, and powering community television or radio sets. In Madras in Tamil Nadu, the authorities have installed a solar-powered desalinization plant. And Central Electronics near New Delhi has set up a demonstration home using photovoltaic solar cells to produce electricity.

In Israel molecular biologist Haim Aviv has proposed a joint Egyptian-Israeli agro-industrial project in the Sinai. Using Egyptian water and Israel's advanced irrigation technology, it would be possible to grow cassava or sugar cane, which in turn could be converted into ethanol for use in car fuel. His plan calls for sheep and cattle to be fed on the sugar cane by-products and for paper plants to make use of the cellulose wastes, creating an integrated ecological cycle. Similar projects, Aviv suggests, could be built in parts of Africa, Southeast Asia, and Latin America.

The energy crisis which is part of the breakdown of Second Wave civilization is generating many new ideas for both centralized and decentralized, large-scale and small-scale energy production in the poorer regions of the planet. And there is a clear parallel between some of the problems facing First Wave and emergent Third Wave societies. Neither can rely on energy systems designed for the Second Wave era.

What about agriculture? Once again, the Third Wave leads us in unconventional directions. At the Environmental Research Lab in Tucson, Arizona, shrimp are being grown in long troughs in greenhouses, right alongside cucumbers and lettuce—with the shrimp waste recycled to fertilize the vegetables. In Vermont experimenters are raising catfish, trout, and vegetables in a similar manner. The water in the fish tank collects solar heat and releases it at night to keep temperatures up. Again, the fish waste is used to fertilize the vegetables.

In Massachusetts, at the New Alchemy Institute chickens are being raised atop the fish tank. Their droppings fertilize algae, which the fish then eat. These are only three of countless examples of innovation in food production and food processing—many of which have special, exciting relevance for today's First Wave societies.

A forecast of 20-year trends in world food supply prepared by the Center for Futures Research (CFR) at the University of Southern California suggests, for example, that several key developments are likely to slash, rather than increase, the need for artificial fertilizers. According to the CFR study, chances are nine out of ten that by 1996 we will have cheap controlled-release fertilizer which will reduce the need for nitrogenous fertilizer by 15 percent. There is a substantial likelihood that nitrogen-fixing grains will also be available by then, further reducing demand.

The report regards as "virtually certain" new grain varieties which produce higher yields per acre on non-irrigated land—with gains as high as 25 to 50 percent. It suggests that "trickle-drip" irrigation systems, with decentralized wind-powered wells and water distributed by draft animals, could substantially increase yields while cutting year-to-year fluctuations in the harvest.

Furthermore, it tells of forage grass that, because it needs only minimal water, could double the livestock carrying capacity of arid regions; of a potential 30 percent jump in non-grain yields in tropical soils as a result of a better understanding of nutrient combinations; of breakthroughs in pest control that will cut crop losses drastically; of new low-cost water pumping methods; of the control of the tsetse fly, which would open up vast new regions to livestock farming; and many other advances.

On a longer time-scale, one can imagine much of agriculture devoted to "energy farms"—the cultivation of crops for energy production. Ultimately we may see the convergence of weather modification, computers, satellite monitoring, and genetics to revolutionize the world's food supply.

While such possibilities put no food in a hungry peasant's belly today, First Wave governments must consider these potentials in their long-range agricultural planning, and must search for ways to combine, as it were, the hoe and the computer.

New technologies, associated with the shift to Third Wave civilization, also open fresh possibilities. The late futurist John McHale and his wife and colleague, Magda Cordell McHale, in their excellent study *Basic Human Needs*, concluded that the emergence of super-advanced biotechnologies hold great promise for transforming First Wave societies. Such technologies include everything from ocean farming to the use of insects and other organisms for productive work, the processing of cellulose wastes into meat via microorganisms, and the conversion of plants like euphorbia into sulphur-free fuel. "Green medicine"—the manufacture of pharmaceuticals from previously unknown or under-utilized plant life—also holds high potential for many First Wave countries.

Advances in other fields also cast doubt on traditional development thinking. An explosive issue facing many First Wave countries is massive unemployment and underemployment. This has triggered a global debate between First Wave and Second Wave advocates. One side argues that mass-production industries do not use enough labor, and that the emphasis in development should be placed on smaller-scale, more technologically primitive factories that use more people and less capital and energy. The other side urges the introduction of precisely the Second Wave industries now moving out of the most technologically advanced nations—steel, auto, shoes, textiles, and the like.

But rushing off to build a Second Wave steel mill may be the equivalent of constructing a buggy-whip factory. There may be strategic or other reasons to build a mill but, with wholly new composite materials many times stronger, stiffer, and lighter than aluminum, with transparent materials that are as strong as steel, with reinforced plastic mortar to replace galvanized water pipes, how long before the demand for steel peaks and production capacity is excessive? According to Indian scientist M. S. Iyengar, such advances may "make the linear expansion in steel and aluminium production redundant." Perhaps, instead of seeking loans or foreign investment to build steel capability, the poorer countries ought to be preparing now for the "materials age"?

The Third Wave brings more immediate possibilities as well. Ward Morehouse of the Research Policy Program, University of Lund, Sweden, argues that the poor nations should be looking beyond First Wave small-scale industry or Second Wave centralized, large-scale industry, and should focus instead on one of the key industries of the emerging Third Wave: microelectronics.

"Over emphasis on labor-intensive technology with low productivity could become a trap for poor countries," Morehouse writes. Pointing out that productivity is rising spectacularly in the computer chip industry, he argues that "it is certainly an advantage to capital-poor developing countries to get greater output per unit of capital invested."

More important, however, is the compatibility between Third Wave technology and existing social arrangements.

Thus, Morehouse says, the great product diversity in microelectronics means that "developing countries can take a basic technology and adapt it more easily to suit their own social requirements or raw materials. Microelectronic technology lends itself to decentralization of production."

This also means reduced population pressures on the big cities, and the rapid miniaturization in this field cuts transportation costs as well. Best of all, this form of production has low energy requirements, and the growth of the market is so rapid—and the competition so keen—that even though rich nations attempt to monopolize these industries they are unlikely to succeed.

Morehouse is not alone in pointing out how the most advanced Third Wave industries dovetail with the needs of the poor countries. Says Roger Melen, Associate Director of Stanford University's Integrated Circuit Laboratory: "The industrial world moved everybody into the cities for production, and now we're moving the factories and work forces back into the country, but many nations have never really switched from a 17th century agrarian economy, including China. It now appears they can integrate new manufacturing techniques into their society without moving entire populations."

If this is so, the Third Wave offers a fresh technological strategy for the war on want.

The Third Wave throws the need for transportation and communication into a new perspective as well. At the time of the industrial revolution, roads were a prerequisite for social, political, and economic development. Today an electronic communications system is necessary. It was once thought that communications were the outgrowth of economic development. Now, says John Magee, president of Arthur D. Little, the research firm, this "is an outmoded thesis . . . telecommunications is more of a precondition than a consequence."

Today's plummeting cost of communications suggests the substitution of communications for many transport functions. It may be far cheaper, more energy-conserving, and more appropriate in the long run to lay in an advanced communications network than a ramified structure of costly roads and streets. Clearly, road transport is needed. But to the degree that production is decentralized, rather than centralized, transport costs can be minimized without isolating villages from one another, from the urban areas, or from the world at large.

That more and more leaders of First Wave countries are aware of the importance of communications is clear from the fight they are waging for a redistribution of the world's electronic spectrum. Because the Second Wave powers developed telecommunications early, they have captured control of the available frequencies. The U.S. and the U.S.S.R. alone use up 25 percent of the available shortwave broadcasting spectrum, and a bigger chunk of the more sophisticated parts of the spectrum.

This spectrum, however, like the ocean floor and the planet's breathable air, belongs—or should belong—to everyone, not just a few. Thus many of the First Wave countries insist the spectrum is a limited resource and want to be assigned a share of it—even if at the moment they lack the equipment to use it. (They assume they can "rent out" their part until such time as they are ready to use it themselves.) Facing resistance from both the U.S. and the U.S.S.R., they call for a "New World Information Order."

The larger issue they face, however, is internal: how to divide their limited resources between telecommunications and transport. It is the same question that the most technically sophisticated of nations also must confront. Given low-cost ground stations, computerized kibbutz-size irrigation systems, perhaps even ground sensing devices, and super-cheap computer terminals for village use and cottage industry, it may be possible for First Wave societies to avoid some of the enormous expenditure for heavy transport that the Second Wave nations had to bear. Such ideas no doubt sound utopian today. But the time will soon be on us when they are commonplace.

Not long ago, Indonesian President Suharto pressed the tip of a traditional sword against an electronic push button and thereby inaugurated a satellite communications system aimed at linking the parts of the Indonesian archipelago together—much as the railroads with their golden spike linked the two coasts of America a century ago. In so doing, he symbolized the new options that the Third Wave presents to countries seeking transformation.

Developments like these in energy, agriculture, technology, and communications suggests something even deeper—whole new societies based on the fusion of past and future, of First Wave and Third Wave.

One can begin to picture a transformation strategy based on the development of both low-stream, village-oriented, capital-cheap, rural industries and certain carefully selected, high-stream technologies, with an economy zoned to protect or promote both.

Jagdish Kapur has written: "A new balance has now to be struck between" the most advanced science and technology available to the human race and "the Gandhian vision of the idyllic green pastures, the village republics." Such a practical combination, Kapur declares, requires a "total transformation of the society, its symbols and values, its system of education, its incentives, the flow of its energy resources, its scientific and industrial research and a whole lot of other institutions."

Yet an increasing number of long-range thinkers, social analysts, scholars, and scientists believe that just such a transformation is now under way, carrying us toward a radical new synthesis: Gandhi, in short, with satellites.

THE ORIGINAL PROSUMERS

Implied in this approach is another synthesis at an even deeper level. This involves the entire economic relationship of people to the market—irrespective of whether that market is capitalist or socialist in form. It forces us to question how much of any individual's total time and labor should be devoted to production and how much to prosumption—i.e., how much to working for pay in the marketplace as against working for self.

Most First Wave populations have already been drawn into the money system. They have been "marketized." But while the wretched money income earned by the world's poorest people may be vital to their survival, production for exchange provides only part of their income; prosumption provides the rest.

The Third Wave encourages us to look at this situation, too, in a fresh way. In country after country millions are jobless. But is full employment in these societies a realistic goal? What combination of policies can possibly, within our lifetime, provide full-time jobs for all these surging millions? Is the very notion of "unemployment" itself a Second Wave concept, as hinted at by the Swedish economist Gunnar Myrdal?

The problem, writes Paul Streeten of the World Bank, is "not 'unemployment,' which is a Western concept that presupposes modern sector wage employment, labor markets, labor exchanges and scoial security payments. . . . The problem [is] rather, unremunerative, unproductive work of the poor, particularly of the rural poor." The remarkable rise of the prosumer in the affluent nations today, a striking phenomenon of the Third Wave, leads us to question the deepest assumptions and goals of most Second Wave economists.

Perhaps it is a mistake to emulate the industrial revolution in the West, which saw the transfer of most economic activity out of Sector A (the prosumer sector) and into Sector B (the market sector).

Perhaps prosumption needs to be seen as a positive force, rather than a regrettable holdover from the past.

Perhaps what is needed for most people is part-time employment for wages (possibly with some transfer payments) plus imaginative new policies aimed at making their prosumption more "productive." Indeed, linking these two economic activities more intelligently to one another may be the missing key to survival for millions.

Practically speaking, this might mean providing "capital tools for prosumption"—just as the rich countries now do. In the affluent countries we see a fascinating synergy springing up between the two sectors, with the marketplace providing powerful capital tools for use by the prosumer: everything from washing machines to handdrills to battery testers. Misery in the poor countries is often so extreme that to speak of washing machines or power tools seems, at first glance, wildly out of place. Yet is there no analogue here for societies moving beyond First Wave civilization?

The French architect-planner Yona Friedman reminds us that the world's poor do not necessarily want jobs—they want "food and a roof." The job is only a means to this end. But one can often grow one's own food and build one's own roof, or at least contribute to that process. Thus in a paper for UNESCO, Friedman has argued that governments should encourage what I have called prosumption by relaxing certain land laws and building codes. These make it hard (often, indeed, impossible) for squatters to build or improve their own housing.

He strongly urges governments to remove these obstacles and to help people supply their own housing, offering them "assistance in organization, the provision of some materials otherwise difficult to obtain . . . and, if possible, site development"—i.e., water or electricity. What Friedman and others are beginning to say is that anything that helps the individual prosume more effectively may be just as important as production measured in conventional GNP terms.

To increase the "productivity" of the prosumer, governments need to focus scientific and technological research on prosumption. But even now they could, at remarkably low cost, provide simple hand tools, community workshops, trained craftsmen or teachers, limited communications facilities and, where possible, power generation equipment—plus favorable propaganda or moral support for those who invest "sweat equity" in building their own homes or improving their bits of land.

Second Wave propaganda today unfortunately conveys to even the world's most remote and poorest people the idea that the things they make themselves are inherently inferior to the worst mass-produced junk. Rather than teaching people to despise their own efforts, to value Second Wave products and downgrade what they themselves create, governments should be offering prizes for the best or most imaginative self-built homes and goods, the most "productive" prosumption. The knowledge that even the world's richest people are increasingly prosuming may help change attitudes among the very poorest. For the Third Wave casts into a dramatic new light the entire relationship of market to nonmarket activities in all the societies of the future.

The Third Wave also raises non-economic and non-technological concerns to primary importance. It makes us look at education, for example, with fresh eyes. Education, everyone agrees, is central to development. But what kind of education?

When the colonial powers introduced formal education into Africa, India, and other parts of the First Wave world, they transplanted either factory-style schools or set up miniature, tenth-rate imitations of their own elite schools. Today Second Wave education models are being questioned everywhere. The Third Wave challenges the Second Wave notion that education necessarily takes place in a classroom. Today we need to combine learning with work, political struggle, community service, and even play. All our conventional assumptions about education need to be re-examined both in the rich countries and the poor.

Is literacy, for example, an appropriate goal? If so, what does literacy mean? Does it mean both reading and writing? In a provocative paper for the Nevis Institute, a futures research center in Edinburgh, the eminent anthropologist Sir Edmund Leach has argued that reading is easier to learn and more useful than writing, and that not everyone needs to learn to write. Marshall McLuhan has spoken of a return to an oral culture more in keeping with many First Wave communities. Speech recognition technology opens incredible new vistas. New, extremely cheap communications "buttons" or tiny tape recorders built into simple agricultural equipment may ultimately be able to give oral instructions to illiterate farmers. In the light of these, even the definition of functional literacy requires fresh thinking.

Finally, the Third Wave encourages us to look behind conventional Second Wave assumptions with respect to motivation as well. Better nutrition is likely to raise the entire level of intelligence and functional competence among millions of children—at the same time that it increases drive and motivation.

Second Wave people often speak of the passivity and lack of motivation of, say, an Indian villager or a Colombian peasant. Leaving aside the demotivating effects of malnutrition, intestinal parasites, climate, and oppressive political control, might not a part of what seems like lack of motivation be an unwillingness to tear up one's home, family, and life in the present in return for the dubious hope of a better life many years down the road? So long as "development" means the superimposition of a totally alien culture on an existing one, and so long as actual improvements seem impossibly beyond reach, there is every reason to hang on to the little one has.

Because many features of Third Wave civilization are consonant with those of First Wave civilization, whether in China or Iran, they imply the possibility of change with less, not more, disruption, pain, and future shock. And they therefore may strike at the roots of what we have called demotivation.

And so, not merely in the fields of energy or technology, agriculture or economics, but in the very brain and behavior of the individual, the Third Wave brings the potential for revolutionary change.

THE STARTING LINE

The emerging Third Wave civilization does not provide a ready-made model for emulation. Third Wave civilization is itself not yet fully formed. But for the poor as well as the rich it opens novel, perhaps liberating, possibilities. For it calls attention not to the weaknesses, poverty, and misery of the First Wave world, but to some of its inherent strengths. The very features of this ancient civilization that seem so backward from the standpoint of the Second Wave appear as potentially advantageous when measured against the template of the advancing Third Wave.

The congruity of these two civilizations must, in the years ahead, transform the way we think about the relations between rich and poor on the planet. Samir Amin, the economist, speaks of the "absolute necessity" of breaking out of the "false dilemma: modern techniques copied from the West of today, or old techniques corresponding to conditions in the West a century ago." This is precisely what the Third Wave makes possible.

The poor as well as the rich are crouched at the starting line of a new and startlingly different race into the future.

≈≈≈≈ 24

CODA: THE GREAT CONFLUENCE

We are no longer where we stood a decade ago, dazzled by changes whose relationships to one another were unknown. Today, behind the confusion of change, there is a growing coherence of pattern: the future is taking shape.

In a great historical confluence, many raging rivers of change are running together to form an oceanic Third Wave of change that is gaining momentum with every passing hour.

This Third Wave of historical change represents not a straight-line extension of industrial society but a radical shift of direction, often a negation, of what went before. It adds up to nothing less than a complete transformation at least as revolutionary in our day as industrial civilization was 300 years ago.

Furthermore, what is happening is not just a technological revolution but the coming of a whole new civilization in the fullest sense of that term. Thus, if we briefly look back over the ground we have covered, we find profound and frequently parallel changes at many levels simultaneously.

Every civilization operates in and on the biosphere, and reflects or alters the mix of populations and resources. Every civilization has a characteristic techno-sphere—an energy base linked to a production system which in turn is linked to a distribution system. Every civilization has a socio-sphere consisting of interrelated social institutions. Every civilization has an info-sphere—channels of communication through which necessary information flows. Every civilization has its own power-sphere.

Every civilization, in addition, has a set of characteristic relationships with the outside world—exploitative, symbiotic, militant or pacific. And every civilization has its own super-ideology—a kit of powerful cultural assumptions that structure its view of reality and justify its operations.

The Third Wave, it should now be apparent, is bringing revolutionary and self-reinforcing changes at all these different levels at once. The consequence is not merely the disintegration of the old society but the creation of foundations for the new.

Often, as Second Wave institutions crash about our heads, as crime mounts, as nuclear families fracture, as once reliable bureaucracies sputter and malfunction, as health delivery systems crack and industrial economies wobble dangerously, we see only the decay and breakdown around us. Yet social decay is the compost bed of the new civilization. In energy, technology, family structure, culture, and many other fields, we are laying into place the basic structures that will define the main features of that new civilization.

In fact, we can now for the first time identify these main features and even, to some extent, the interrelationships among them. Encouragingly, the embryonic Third Wave civilization we find is not only coherent and workable in both ecological and economic terms, but—if we put our minds to it—could be made more decent and democratic than our own.

In no way is this to suggest inevitability. The period of transition will be marked by extreme social disruption, as well as wild economic swings, sectional clashes, secession attempts, technological upsets or disasters, political turbulence, violence, wars, and threats of war. In a climate of disintegrating institutions and values, authoritarian demagogues and movements will arise to seek, and possibly attain, power. No intelligent person can be smug about the outcome. The clash of two civilizations presents titanic dangers.

Yet the odds lie not with destruction but with ultimate survival. And it is important to know where the main thrust of change is taking us—what kind of world is likely if we manage to avoid the worst of the short-term perils that lie before us. Briefly then, what kind of society is taking form?

* * *

TOMORROW'S BASICS

Third Wave civilization, unlike its predecessor, must (and will) draw on an amazing variety of energy sources—hydrogen, solar, geothermal, tidal, biomass, lightning discharges, ultimately perhaps advanced fusion power, as well as other energy sources not yet imagined in the 1980's. (While some nuclear plants will no doubt continue to operate, even if we suffer a succession of disasters worse than Three Mile Island, nuclear will, on the whole, turn out to have been a costly and dangerous digression.)

The transition to the new diverse energy base will be erratic in the extreme, with a staccato succession of gluts, shortages, and lunatic price swings. But the long-term direction seems clear enough—a shift from a civilization based heavily on a single source of energy to one based more securely on many. Ultimately we see a civilization founded once more on self-sustaining, renewable rather than exhaustible energy sources.

Third Wave civilization will rely on a far more diversified technological base as well, springing from biology, genetics, electronics, materials science, as well as on outer space and under-the-sea operations. While some new technologies will require high energy inputs, much Third Wave technology will be designed to use less, not more, energy. Nor will Third Wave technologies be as massive and ecologically dangerous as those of the past. Many will be small in scale, simple to operate, with the wastes of one industry predesigned for recycling into primary materials for another.

For Third Wave civilization, the most basic raw material of all—and one that can never be exhausted—is information, including imagination. Through imagination and information, substitutes will be found for many of today's exhaustible resources—although this substitution, once more, will all too frequently be accompanied by drastic economic swings and lurches.

With information becoming more important than ever before, the new civilization will restructure education, redefine scientific research and, above all, reorganize the media of communication. Today's mass media, both print and electronic, are wholly inadequate to cope with the communications load and to provide the requisite cultural variety for survival. Instead of being culturally dominated by a few mass media, Third Wave civilization will rest on inter-active, de-massified media, feeding extremely diverse and often highly personalized imagery into and out of the mind-stream of the society.

Looking far ahead, television will give way to "indi-video"—narrow-casting carried to the ultimate: images addressed to a single individual at a time. We may also eventually use drugs, direct brain-to-brain communication, and other forms of electrochemical communication only vaguely hinted at until now. All of which will raise startling, though not insoluble, political and moral problems.

The giant centralized computer with its whirring tapes and complex cooling systems—where it still exists—will be supplemented by myriad chips of intelligence, embedded in one form or another in every home, hospital, and hotel, every vehicle and appliance, virtually every building-brick. The electronic environment will literally converse with us.

Despite popular misconceptions, this shift toward an information-based, highly electronic society will still further reduce our need for high-cost energy.

Nor must this computerization (or, more properly, informationalization) of society mean a further depersonalization of human relationships. As we shall see in the next chapter, people will still hurt, cry, laugh, take pleasure in each other, and play—but they will do all these in a much altered context.

The fusion of Third Wave energy forms, technologies, and information media will speed revolutionary changes in the way we work. Factories are still being built (and in some parts of the world they will continue to be built for decades to come), but the Third Wave factory already bears little resemblance to those we have known until now, and—in the rich nations—the number of people in factory jobs will continue to plummet.

In Third Wave civilization the factory will no longer serve as a model for other types of institutions. Nor will its primary function be that of mass production. Even now the Third Wave factory produces de-massified—often customized—end products. It relies on advanced methods such as wholistic or "presto" production. It will ultimately use less energy, waste less raw material, employ fewer components, and demand far more design intelligence. Most significantly, many of its machines will be directly activated not by workers but at a distance, by consumers themselves.

Those who do work in Third Wave factories will perform

far less brutalizing or repetitive work than those still trapped in Second Wave jobs. They will not be paced by mechanical conveyor belts. Noise levels will be low. Workers will come and go at hours convenient for them. The actual workplace will be far more humane and individualized, often with flowers and greenery sharing the space with machines. Within fixed limits, payment and fringe benefit packages will be increasingly tailored to individual preference.

Third Wave factories will increasingly be found outside the giant urban metropolises. They are also likely to be much smaller than those of the past, with smaller organizational units as well, each enjoying a greater degree of self-management.

Similarly, the Third Wave office will no longer resemble the office of today. A key ingredient of office work—paper— will be substantially (though not wholly) replaced. The chattering banks of typewriters will fall silent. The file cabinets will shrink away. The role of the secretary will be transfigured as electronics eliminates many old tasks and opens new opportunities. The sequential movement of papers back and forth across many desks, the endlessly repetitious typing of columns of numbers—all this will become less important and the making of discretionary decisions more important, and more widely shared.

To operate these factories and offices of the future, Third Wave companies will need workers capable of discretion and resourcefulness rather than rote responses. To prepare such employees, schools will increasingly shift away from present methods still largely geared to producing Second Wave workers for highly repetitive work.

The most striking change in Third Wave civilization, however, will probably be the shift of work from both office and factory back into the home.

Not all jobs can, will, or should be carried out in people's homes. But as low-cost communications are substituted for high-cost transportation, as we increase the role of intelligence and imagination in production, further reducing the role of brute force or routine mental labor, a significant slice of the work force in Third Wave societies will perform at least part of its work at home, factories remaining only for those who must actually handle physical materials.

This gives us a clue to the institutional structure of Third Wave civilization. Some scholars have suggested that, with the increasing importance of information, the university will replace the factory as the central institution of tomorrow. This notion, however, which comes almost exclusively from academics, is based on the provincial assumption that only the university can, or does, house theoretical knowledge. It is little more than a professorial wish-fulfillment fantasy.

Multinational executives, for their part, see the executive suite as the pivot of tomorrow. The new profession of "information managers" pictures their computer rooms as the center of the new civilization. Scientists look to the industrial research laboratory. A few remaining hippies dream of restoring the agricultural commune to the center of a neo-medieval future. Others may nominate the "gratification chambers" of a leisure-drenched society.

My own nomination, for reasons outlined earlier, is none of these. It is, in fact, the home.

I believe the home will assume a startling new importance in Third Wave civilization. The rise of the prosumer, the spread of the electronic cottage, the invention of new organizational structures in business, the automation and de-massification of production, all point to the home's re-emergence as a central unit in the society of tomorrow—a unit with enhanced rather than diminished economic, medical, educational, and social functions.

Yet it is unlikely that *any* institution—not even the home—will play as central a role as the cathedral or the factory did in the past. For the society is likely to be built around a network rather than a hierarchy of new institutions.

This suggests also that the corporations (and the socialist production organizations) of tomorrow will no longer tower over other social institutions. In Third Wave societies, corporations will be recognized as the complex organizations they are, and will pursue multiple goals simultaneously—not just profit or production quotas. Instead of focusing on a single bottom line, as many of today's managers have been trained to do, the shrewd Third Wave manager will watch over (and will be held personally responsible for) multiple "bottom lines."

Executive paychecks and bonuses will gradually come to reflect this new multi-functionality, as the corporation, either through voluntary means or because it is compelled to, becomes more responsive to what today are regarded as non-economic and hence largely irrelevant factors—ecological, political, social, cultural, and moral.

Second Wave conceptions of efficiency—usually based on

the ability of the corporation to foist its indirect costs off on the consumer or the taxpayer—will be recast to take account of hidden social, economic, and other costs which often, indeed, translate into deferred economic costs as well. "Econo-think"—a characteristic deformation of the Second Wave manager—will be less common.

The corporation—like most other organizations—will also undergo drastic restructuring as the ground rules of Third Wave civilization come into play. Instead of a society synchronized to the tempo of the assembly line, a Third Wave society will move to flexible rhythms and schedules. Instead of the mass society's extreme standardization of behavior, ideas, language, and life-styles, Third Wave society will be built on segmentation and diversity. Instead of a society that concentrates population, energy flows, and other features of life, Third Wave society will disperse and de-concentrate. Instead of opting for maximum scale on the "bigger is better" principle, Third Wave society will understand the meaning of "appropriate scale." Instead of a highly centralized society, Third Wave society will recognize the value of much decentralized decision-making.

Such changes imply a striking shift away from standard old-fashioned bureaucracy, and the emergence in business, government, the schools, and other institutions of a wide variety of new-style organizations. Where hierarchies remain they will tend to be flatter and more transient. Many new organizations will do away with the old insistence on "one man, one boss"—all of which suggests a work world in which more people share temporary decisional power.

All the societies moving through the transition to the Third Wave face deepening short-term unemployment problems. From the 1950's on, vast increases in white-collar and service work absorbed millions of workers laid off by the shrinking manufacturing sector. Today, as white-collar work is in its turn automated, there is serious question as to whether further expansion of the conventional service sector can take up the slack. Some countries mask the problem through featherbedding, enlarging public and private bureaucracies, exporting excess workers, and the like. But the problem remains insoluble within the framework of Second Wave economies.

This helps explain the significance of the coming fusion of producer and consumer—what I have called the rise of the prosumer. Third Wave civilization brings with it the reemergence of a huge economic sector based on production for use rather than for exchange, a sector based on do-it-for-yourself rather than do-it-for-the-market. This dramatic turn-about, after 300 years of "marketization," will both demand and make possible radically fresh thinking about all our economic problems, from unemployment and welfare to leisure and the role of work.

It will also bring with it a changed appreciation of the role of "housework" in the economy, and subsequent fundamental changes in the role of women, who still comprise the vast majority of houseworkers. The powerful surge of marketization across the earth is cresting, with many as yet unimaginable consequences for future civilizations.

Third Wave people, meanwhile, will adopt new assumptions about nature, progress, evolution, time, space, matter, and causation. Their thinking will be less influenced by analogies based on the machine, more shaped by concepts like process, feedback, and disequilibrium. They will be more aware of the discontinuities that flow directly out of continuities.

A host of new religions, new conceptions of science, new images of human nature, new forms of art will arise—in far richer diversity than was possible or necessary during the industrial age. The emerging multiculture will be torn by turmoil until new forms of group conflict resolution are developed (present-day legal systems are unimaginative and woefully inadequate for a high diversity society).

The increasing differentiation of society will also mean a reduced role for the nation-state—until now a major force for standardization. Third Wave civilization will be based on a new distribution of power in which the nation, as such, is no longer as influential as it once was, while other institutions—from the transnational corporation to the autonomous neighborhood or even city-state—assume greater significance.

Regions will gain greater power as national markets and economies fracture into pieces, some of which are already larger than the national markets and economies of the past. New alliances may spring up based less on geographical nearness than on common cultural, ecological, religious, or economic affinities, so that a region in North America may develop closer ties with a region in Europe or Japan than with its own next-door neighbor or—eventually—its own national government. Tying this all together will be not a unitary world government but a dense network of new transnational organizations.

Outside the rich nations, the non-industrial three quarters of humanity will struggle against poverty with new tools, no longer blindly attempting to imitate Second Wave society nor satisfied with First Wave conditions. Radical new "development strategies" will arise, reflecting the special religious or cultural character of each region and consciously geared to minimizing future shock.

No longer ruthlessly tearing up their own religious traditions, family structure, and social life in the hope of creating a mirror image of industrial Britain, Germany, the U.S. or, for that matter, the U.S.S.R., many countries will attempt to build on their past, noting the congruence between certain features of First Wave society and those only now re-emerging (on a high-technology basis) in the Third Wave countries.

THE CONCEPT OF PRACTOPIA

What we see here are the outlines, therefore, of a wholly new way of life, affecting not only individuals but the planet as well. The new civilization sketched here can hardly be termed a utopia. It will be agitated by deep problems, some of which we will explore in the remaining pages. Problems of self and community. Political problems. Problems of justice, equity, and morality. Problems with the new economy (and especially the relationship between employment, welfare, and prosumption). All these and many more will arouse fighting passions.

But Third Wave civilization is also no "anti-utopia." It is not *1984* writ large or *Brave New World* brought to life. Both these brilliant books—and hundreds of derivative science fiction stories—paint a future based on highly centralized, bureaucratized, and standardized societies, in which individual differences are eradicated. We are now heading in exactly the opposite direction.

While the Third Wave carries with it deep challenges for humanity, from ecological threats to the danger of nuclear terrorism and electronic fascism, it is not simply a nightmarish linear extension of industrialism.

We glimpse here instead the emergence of what might be called a "practopia"—neither the best nor the worst of all possible worlds, but one that is both practical and preferable to the one we had. Unlike a utopia, a practopia is not free of disease, political nastiness, and bad manners. Unlike most utopias, it is not static or frozen in unreal perfection. Nor is it reversionary, modeling itself on some imagined ideal of the past.

Conversely, a practopia does not embody the crystalized evil of a utopia turned inside out. It is not ruthlessly antidemocratic. It is not inherently militarist. It does not reduce its citizens to faceless uniformity. It does not destroy its neighbors and degrade its environment.

In short, a practopia offers a positive, even a revolutionary alternative, yet lies within the range of the realistically attainable.

Third Wave civilization, in this sense, is precisely that: a practopian future. One can glimpse in it a civilization that makes allowance for individual difference, and embraces (rather than suppresses) racial, regional, religious, and subcultural variety. A civilization built in considerable measure around the home. A civilization that is not frozen in amber but pulsing with innovation, yet which is also capable of providing enclaves of relative stability for those who need or want them. A civilization no longer required to pour its best energies into marketization. A civilization capable of directing great passion into art. A civilization facing unprecedented historical choices—about genetics and evolution, to choose a single example—and inventing new ethical or moral standards to deal with such complex issues. A civilization, finally, that is at least potentially democratic and humane, in better balance with the biosphere and no longer dangerously dependent on exploitative subsidies from the rest of the world. Hard work to achieve, but not impossible.

Flowing together in grand confluence, today's changes thus point to a workable countercivilization, an alternative to the increasingly obsolete and unworkable industrial system.

They point, in a word, to practopia.

THE WRONG QUESTION

Why is this happening? Why is the old Second Wave suddenly unworkable? Why is this new civilizational tide rushing in to collide with the old?

Nobody knows. Even today, 300 long years after the fact, historians cannot pin down the "cause" of the industrial revolution. As we have seen, each academic guild or philosophical school has its own preferred explanation. The technological determinists point to the steam engine, the ecologists to the destruction of Britain's forests, the economists to fluctuations in the price of wool. Others emphasize religious or cultural changes, the Reformation, the Enlightenment, and so on.

In today's world, too, we can identify many mutually causal forces. Experts point to the rising demand for exhaustible supplies of petroleum, and mushrooming growth of world population, or the escalated threat of global pollution as key forces for structural change on a planetary scale. Others point to the incredible advances in science and technology since the end of World War II and to the social and political changes trailing in their wake. Still others emphasize the awakening of the non-industrial world and the ensuing political upheavals that threaten our life lines of cheap energy and raw materials.

One can cite striking value changes—the sexual revolution, the youth upheaval of the 1960's, the swiftly shifting attitudes toward work. One might single out the arms race which has greatly accelerated certain types of technological change. Alternatively, one might look for the cause of the Third Wave in the cultural and epistemological changes of our time—perhaps as profound as those wrought by the Reformation and Enlightenment combined.

We could, in short, find scores, even hundreds of streams of change feeding into the grand confluence, all of them interrelated in mutually causal ways. We could find amazing positive feedback loops in the social system, vastly accelerating and amplifying certain changes, as well as negative loops that suppress other changes. We could find, in this period of turbulence, analogies to the grand "leap" described by scientists like Ilya Prigogine, by which a simpler structure, in part by chance, suddenly breaks through to a wholly new level of complexity and diversity.

What we cannot find is "the" cause of the Third Wave in the sense of a single independent variable or link that pulls the chain. Indeed, to ask what "the" cause is may be the wrong way of phrasing the question or even the wrong question altogether. "What is the cause of the Third Wave?" may be a Second Wave question.

To say this is not to discount causation but to recognize its complexity. Nor does it suggest historical inevitability. Second Wave civilization may be shattered and unworkable, but that does not mean that the Third Wave civilization pictured here must necessarily take form. Any number of forces could radically change the outlook. War, economic collapse, ecological catastrophe come immediately to mind. While no one can stop the latest historical wave of change, necessity and chance are both at work. This, however, does not mean we cannot influence its course. If what I have said about positive feedback is correct, often a little "kick" to the system can bring about large-scale changes.

The decisions we take today, as individuals, groups, or governments, can deflect, divert, or channel the racing currents of change. Each people will react differently to the challenges posed by the super-struggle that pits advocates of the Second Wave against those of the Third. Russians will respond one way, Americans another, Japanese, Germans, French, or Norwegians in still other ways, and countries are likely to grow more different from one another rather than more alike.

Within countries the same is true. Little changes can trigger large consequences—in corporations, schools, churches, hospitals, and neighborhoods. And this is why, despite everything, people—even individuals—still count.

This is especially true because the changes that lie ahead are the consequences of conflict, not automatic progression. Thus in every one of the technologically advanced nations, backward regions struggle to complete their industrialization. They attempt to protect their Second Wave factories and the jobs based on them. This places them in frontal conflict with regions that are already far advanced in building the technological base for Third Wave operations. Such battles tear society apart, but they also open many opportunities for effective political and social action.

The super-struggle now being waged in every community between the people of the Second Wave and the people of the Third Wave does not mean that other struggles lose their importance. Class conflict, racial conflict, the conflict of young and old against what I have elsewhere called "the imperialism of the middle-aged," the conflict among regions, sexes, religions—all these continue. Some, indeed, will be sharpened. But all of them are shaped by, and subordinated to, the super-struggle. It is the super-struggle that most basically determines the future.

Meanwhile, two things cut through everything as the Third Wave thunders in our ears. One is the shift toward a higher level of diversity in society—the de-massification of mass society. The second is acceleration—the faster pace at which historical change occurs. Together these place tremendous strains on individuals and institutions alike, intensifying the super-struggle as it rages about us.

Accustomed to coping with low diversity and slow change, individuals and institutions suddenly find themselves trying to cope with high diversity and high-speed change. The cross-pressures threaten to overload their decisional competence. The result is future shock.

We are left with only one option. We must be willing to reshape ourselves and our institutions to deal with the new realities.

For that is the price of admission to a workable and decently humane future. To make the necessary changes, however, we must take a totally fresh and imaginative look at two blazing issues. Both are crucial to our survival, yet all but ignored in public discussion: the future of personality and the politics of the future.

To which we now turn . . .

CONCLUSION

25

THE NEW PSYCHO-SPHERE

A new civilization is forming. But where do *we* fit into it? Don't today's technological changes and social upheavals mean the end of friendship, love, commitment, community, and caring? Won't tomorrow's electronic marvels make human relationships even more vacuous and vicarious than they are today?

These are legitimate questions. They arise from reasonable fears, and only a naïve technocrat would brush them lightly aside. For if we look around us we find widespread evidence of psychological breakdown. It is as though a bomb had gone off in our communal "psycho-sphere." We are, in fact, experiencing not merely the breakup of the Second Wave techno-sphere, info-sphere, or socio-sphere but the crack-up of its psycho-sphere as well.

Throughout the affluent nations the litany is all too familiar: rising rates of juvenile suicide, dizzyingly high levels of alcoholism, widespread psychological depression, vandalism, and crime. In the United States, emergency rooms are crowded with "potheads," "speed freaks" and "Quaalude kids," "coke sniffers" and "heroin junkies," not to mention people having "nervous breakdowns."

Social work and mental health industries are booming everywhere. In Washington a President's Commission on Mental Health announces that fully one fourth of all citizens in the United States suffer from some form of severe emotional stress. And a National Institute of Mental Health psychologist, charging that almost no family is free of some form of

mental disorder, declares that "psychological turbulence . . .
is rampant in an American society that is confused, divided
and concerned about its future."

It is true that spongy definitions and unreliable statistics
make such sweeping generalizations suspect, and it is doubly
true that earlier societies were scarcely models of good mental
health. Yet something *is* terribly wrong today.

There is a harassed, knife-edge quality to daily life. Nerves
are ragged, and—as the scuffles and shootings in subways or
on gas queues suggest—tempers are barely under hair-trigger
control. Millions of people are terminally fed up.

They are, moreover, increasingly hassled by an apparently
swelling army of heavy breathers, kooks, flakes, weirdos, and
psychos whose antisocial behavior is frequently glamorized by
the media. In the West at least, we see a pernicious romanticization of insanity, a glorification of the "cuckoo nest" in-
mate. Best-sellers proclaim that madness is a myth, and a
literary journal springs up in Berkeley dedicated to the notion
that "Madness, Genius and Sainthood all lie in the same
realm, and should be given the same name and prestige."

Meanwhile, millions of individuals search frantically for
their own identities or for some magic therapy to re-integrate
their personalities, provide instant intimacy or ecstasy, or lead
them to "higher" states of consciousness.

By the late 1970's a human potential movement, spreading
eastward from California, had spawned some 8,000 different
"therapies" consisting of odds and ends of psychoanalysis,
Eastern religion, sexual experimentation, game playing, and
old-time revivalism. In the words of one critical survey,
"these techniques were neatly packaged and distributed coast
to coast under names like Mind Dynamics, Arica, and Silva
Mind Control. Transcendental Meditation was already being
peddled like speed reading; Scientology's Dianetics had been
mass-marketing its own popular therapy since the fifties. At
the same time, America's religious cults got into the swing,
fanning out quietly across the country in massive fund-raising
and recruitment drives."

More important than the growing human-potential industry
is the Christian evangelical movement. Appealing to poorer
and less educated segments of the public, making sophisticated use of high-powered radio and television, the "born
again" movement is ballooning in size. Religious hucksters,
riding its crest, send their followers scrambling for salvation
in a society they picture as decadent and doomed.

This wave of malaise has not struck all parts of the technological world with equal force. For this reason, readers in Europe and elsewhere may be tempted to shrug it off as a largely American phenomenon, while in the United States itself some still regard it as just another manifestation of California's fabled flakiness.

Neither view could be further from the truth. If psychic distress and disintegration are most strikingly evident in the United States, and especially California, it merely reflects the fact that the Third Wave has arrived a bit earlier than elsewhere, causing Second Wave social structures to topple sooner and more spectacularly.

Indeed, a kind of paranoia has settled over many communities, and not just in the United States. In Rome and Turin, terrorists stalk the streets. In Paris, and even in once peaceful London, muggings and vandalism increase. In Chicago, elderly people are afraid to walk the streets after dark. In New York, schools and subways crackle with violence. And back in California, a magazine offers its readers a supposedly practical guide to "handguns and gun courses, attack-trained dogs, burglar alarms, personal-safety devices, self-defense courses and computerized security systems."

There is a sick odor in the air. It is the smell of a dying Second Wave civilization.

THE ATTACK ON LONELINESS

To create a fulfilling emotional life and a sane psychosphere for the emerging civilization of tomorrow, we must recognize three basic requirements of any individual: the needs for community, structure, and meaning. Understanding how the collapse of Second Wave society undermines all three suggests how we might begin designing a healthier psychological environment for ourselves and our children in the future.

To begin with, any decent society must generate a feeling of community. Community offsets loneliness. It gives people a vitally necessary sense of belonging. Yet today the institutions on which community depends are crumbling in all the techno-societies. The result is a spreading plague of loneliness.

From Los Angeles to Leningrad, teen-agers, unhappy married couples, single parents, ordinary working people, and the elderly, all complain of social isolation. Parents confess that their children are too busy to see them or even to telephone. Lonely strangers in bars or launderettes offer what one sociologist calls "those infinitely sad confidences." Singles' clubs and discos serve as flesh markets for desperate divorcees.

Loneliness is even a neglected factor in the economy. How many upper-middle-class housewives, driven to distraction by the clanging emptiness of their affluent suburban homes, have gone into the job market to preserve their sanity? How many pets (and carloads of pet food) are bought to break the silence of an empty home? Loneliness supports much of our travel and entertainment business. It contributes to drug use, depression, and declining productivity. And it creates a lucrative "lonely-hearts" industry that purports to help the lonely locate and lasso Mr. or Ms. "Right."

The hurt of being alone is, of course, hardly new. But loneliness is now so widespread it has become, paradoxically, a shared experience.

Community demands more than emotionally satisfying bonds between individuals, however. It also requires strong ties of loyalty between individuals and their organizations. Just as they miss the companionship of other individuals, millions today feel equally cut off from the institutions of which they are a part. They hunger for institutions worthy of their respect, affection, and loyalty.

The corporation offers a case in point.

As companies have grown larger and more impersonal and have diversified into many disparate activities, employees have been left with little sense of shared mission. The feeling of community is absent. The very term "corporate loyalty" has an archaic ring to it. Indeed, loyalty to a company is considered by many a betrayal of self. In *The Bottom Line*, Fletcher Knebel's popular novel about big business, the heroine snaps to her executive husband: "Company loyalty! It makes me want to vomit."

Except in Japan, where the lifetime employment system and corporate paternalism still exist (though for a shrinking percentage of the labor force), work relationships are increasingly transient and emotionally unsatisfying. Even when companies make an effort to provide a social dimension to employment—an annual picnic, a company-sponsored bowling team, an office Christmas party—most on-the-job relationships are no more than skin-deep.

For such reasons, few today have any sense of belonging to

something bigger and better than themselves. This warm participatory feeling emerges spontaneously from time to time during crisis, stress, disaster, or mass uprising. The great student strikes of the sixties, for example, produced a glow of communal feeling. The antinuclear demonstrations today do the same. But both the movements and the feelings they arouse are fleeting. Community is in short supply.

One clue to the plague of loneliness lies in our rising level of social diversity. By de-massifying society, by accentuating differences rather than similarities, we help people individualize themselves. We make it possible for each of us more nearly to fulfill his or her potential. But we also make human contact more difficult. For the more individualized we are, the more difficult it becomes to find a mate or a lover who has precisely matching interests, values, schedules, or tastes. Friends are also harder to come by. We become choosier in our social ties. But so do others. The result is a great many ill-matched relationships. Or no relationships at all.

The breakup of mass society, therefore, while holding out the promise of much greater individual self-fulfillment, is at least for the present spreading the pain of isolation. If the emergent Third Wave society is not to be icily metallic, with a vacuum for a heart, it must attack this problem frontally. It must restore community.

How might we begin to do this?

Once we recognize that loneliness is no longer an individual matter but a public problem created by the disintegration of Second Wave institutions, there are plenty of things we can do about it. We can begin where community usually begins—in the family, by expanding its shrunken functions.

The family, since the industrial revolution, has been progressively relieved of the burden of its elderly. If we stripped this responsibility from the family, perhaps the time has come to restore it partially. Only a nostalgic fool would favor dismantling public and private pension systems, or making old people completely dependent on their families as they once were. But why not offer tax and other incentives for families—including non-nuclear and unconventional families—who look after their own elderly instead of farming them out to impersonal old-age "homes." Why not reward, rather than economically punish, those who maintain and solidify family bonds across generational lines?

The same principle can be extended to other functions of the family as well. Families should be encouraged to take a larger—not smaller—role in the education of the young. Parents willing to teach their own children at home should be aided by the schools, not regarded as freaks or lawbreakers. And parents should have more, not less, influence on the schools.

At the same time much could be done by the schools themselves to create a sense of belonging. Instead of grading students purely on individual performance, some part of each student's grade could be made dependent on the performance of the class as a whole or some team within it. This would give early and overt support to the idea that each of us has responsibility for others. With a bit of encouragement, imaginative educators could come up with many other, better ways to promote a sense of community.

Corporations, too, could do much to begin building human ties afresh. Third Wave production makes possible decentralization and smaller, more personal work units. Innovative companies might build morale and a sense of belonging by asking groups of workers to organize themselves into minicompanies or cooperatives and contracting directly with these groups to get specific jobs done.

This breakup of huge corporations into small, self-managed units could not merely unleash enormous new productive energies but build community at the same time.

Norman Macrae, deputy editor of *The Economist*, has suggested that "Semi-autonomous teams of perhaps six to 17 people, who choose to work together as friends, should be told by market forces what module of output will be paid for at what pay rates per unit of output, and then should increasingly be allowed to produce it in their own way."

Indeed, continues Macrae, "those who devise successful group friendship cooperatives will do a lot of social good, and perhaps will deserve some subsidies or tax advantages." (What is particularly interesting about such arrangements is that one could create cooperatives within a profit-making corporation or, for that matter, profit-making companies within the framework of a socialist production enterprise.)

Corporations could also look hard at their retirement practices. Ejecting an elderly worker all at once not only deprives the individual of a regular, full-size paycheck, and takes away what society regards as a productive role, but also truncates many social ties. Why not more partial retirement plans, and programs that assign semi-retired people to work for under-staffed community services on a volunteer or part-pay basis?

Another community-building device might draw retired people into fresh contact with the young, and vice versa. Older people in every community could be appointed "ad-junct teachers" or "mentors," invited to teach some of their skills in local schools on a part-time or volunteer basis or to have one student, let's say, regularly visit them for instruc-tion. Under school supervision, retired photographers could teach photography, car mechanics how to repair a recalci-trant engine, bookkeepers how to keep books, and so on. In many cases a healthy bond would grow up between mentor and "mentee" that would go beyond instruction.

It is not a sin to be lonely and, in a society whose struc-tures are fast disintegrating, it should not be a disgrace. Thus a letter writer to the *Jewish Chronicle* in London asks: "Why does it seem 'not quite nice' to go to groups where it is per-fectly obvious that the reason that everyone is there is to meet people of the opposite sex?" The same question would apply to singles' bars, discos, and holiday resorts.

The letter points out that in the *shtetls* of Eastern Europe the institution of *shadchan* or matchmaker served a useful purpose in bringing marriageable people together, and that dating bureaus, marriage services, and similar agencies are just as necessary today. "We should be able to admit openly that we need help, human contact and a social life."

We need many new services—both traditional and innova-tive—to help bring lonely people together in a dignified way. Some people now rely on "lonely-hearts" ads in the magazines to help them locate a companion or mate. Before long we can be sure local or neighborhood cable television services will be running video ads so prospective partners can actually see each other before dating. (Such programs, one suspects, will have enormously high ratings.)

But should dating services be limited to providing romantic contacts? Why not services—or places—where people might come simply to meet and make a friend, as distinct from a lover or potential mate? Society needs such services and, so long as they are honest and decent, we should not be embar-rassed to invent and use them.

* * *

TELECOMMUNITY

At the level of longer-term social policy we should also move rapidly toward "telecommunity." Those who wish community restored should concentrate attention on the socially fragmenting impact of commuting and high mobility. Having written in detail about this in *Future Shock*, I will not retrace the argument. But one of the key steps that can be taken toward building a sense of community into the Third Wave is the selective substitution of communication for transportation.

The popular fear that computers and telecommunications will deprive us of face-to-face contact and make human relations more vicarious is naïve and simplistic. In fact, the reverse might very well be the case. While some office or factory relationships might be attenuated, bonds in the home and the community could well be strengthened by these new technologies. Computers and communications can help us create community.

If nothing else, they can free larger numbers of us to give up commuting—the centrifugal force that disperses us in the morning, throws us into superficial work relationships, while weakening our more important social ties in the home and community. By making it possible for large numbers of people to work at home (or in close-by neighborhood work centers), the new technologies could make for warmer, more bonded families and a closer, more finely grained community life. The electronic cottage may turn out to be the characteristic mom-and-pop business of the future. And it could lead, as we have seen, to a new work-together family unit involving children (and sometimes even expanded to take in outsiders as well).

It is not unlikely that couples who spend a lot of time working together in the home during the day will want to go out in the evening. (Today the more typical pattern is for the commuter to collapse on returning home and refuse to set foot outside.) As communications begin to replace commuting, we can expect to see a lively proliferation of neighborhood restaurants, theaters, pubs, and clubs, a revitalization of church and voluntary group activity—all or mostly on a face-to-face basis.

Nor, for that matter, are all vicarious relationships to be despised. The issue is not simply vicariousness, but passivity and powerlessness. For a shy person or an invalid, unable to leave home or fearful about meeting people face to face, the emerging info-sphere will make possible interactive electronic contact with others who share similar interests—chess players, stamp collectors, poetry lovers, or sports fans—dialed up instantly from anywhere in the country.

Vicarious though they may be, such relationships can provide a far better antidote to loneliness than television as we know it today, in which the messages all flow one way and the passive receiver is powerless to interact with the flickering image on the screen.

Communications, selectively applied, can serve the goal of telecommunity.

In short, as we build a Third Wave civilization there are many things we can do to sustain and enrich, rather than destroy, community.

THE HEROIN STRUCTURE

The reconstruction of community, however, must be seen as only a small part of a larger process. For the collapse of Second Wave institutions also breaks down structure and meaning in our lives.

Individuals need life structure. A life lacking in comprehensible structure is an aimless wreck. The absence of structure breeds breakdown.

Structure provides the relatively fixed points of reference we need. That is why, for many people, a job is crucial psychologically, over and above the paycheck. By making clear demands on their time and energy, it provides an element of structure around which the rest of their lives can be organized. The absolute demands imposed on a parent by an infant, the responsibility to care for an invalid, the tight discipline demanded by membership in a church or, in some countries, a political party—all these may also impose a simple structure on life.

Faced with an absence of visible structure, some young people use drugs to create it. "Heroin addiction," writes psychologist Rollo May, "gives a way of life to the young person. Having suffered under perpetual purposelessness, his structure now consists of how to escape the cops, how to get the money he needs, where to get his next fix—all these give him a new web of energy in place of his previous structureless world."

The nuclear family, socially imposed schedules, well-defined roles, visible status distinctions, and comprehensible lines of authority—all these factors created adequate life structure for the majority of people during the Second Wave era.

Today the breakup of the Second Wave is dissolving the structure in many individual lives before the new structure-providing institutions of the Third Wave future are laid into place. This, not merely some personal failing, explains why for millions today daily life is experienced as lacking any semblance of recognizable order.

To this loss of order we must also add the loss of meaning. The feeling that our lives "count" comes from healthy relationships with the surrounding society—from family, corporation, church, or political movement. It also depends on being able to see ourselves as part of a larger, even cosmic, scheme of things.

The sudden shift of social ground rules today, the smudging of roles, status distinctions, and lines of authority, the immersion in blip culture and, above all, the breakup of the great thought-system, indust-reality, have shattered the world-image most of us carry around in our skulls. In consequence, most people surveying the world around them today see only chaos. They suffer a sense of personal powerlessness and pointlessness.

It is only when we put all this together—the loneliness, the loss of structure, and the collapse of meaning attendant on the decline of industrial civilization—that we can begin to make sense of some of the most puzzling social phenomena of our time, not the least of which is the astonishing rise of the cult.

THE SECRET OF THE CULTS

Why do so many thousands of apparently intelligent, seemingly successful people allow themselves to be sucked into the myriad cults sprouting today in the widening cracks of the Second Wave system? What accounts for the total control that a Jim Jones was able to exercise over the lives of his followers?

It is loosely estimated today that some 3,000,000 Americans belong to about 1,000 religious cults, the largest of which bear names like the Unification Church, the Divine

Light Mission, the Hare Krishna, and the Way, each of which has temples or branches in most major cities. One of them alone, Sun Myung Moon's Unification Church, claims 60,000 to 80,000 members, publishes a daily newspaper in New York, owns a fish-packing plant in Virginia, and has many other money-creating enterprises. Its mechanically cheerful fund raisers are a common sight.

Nor are such groups confined to the United States. A recent sensational lawsuit in Switzerland called international attention to the Divine Light Center in Winterthur. "The cults and sects and communities . . . are most numerous in the United States because America is, in this matter, too, 20 years ahead of the rest of the world," says the London *Economist*. "But they are to be found in Europe, west and east, and in many other places." Just why is it that such groups can command almost total dedication and obedience from their members? Their secret is simple. They understand the need for community, structure, and meaning. For these are what all cults peddle.

For lonely people, cults offer, in the beginning, indiscriminate friendship. Says an official of the Unification Church: "If someone's lonely, we talk to them. There are a lot of lonely people walking around." The newcomer is surrounded by people offering friendship and beaming approval. Many of the cults require communal living. So powerfully rewarding is this sudden warmth and attention that cult members are often willing to give up contact with their families and former friends, to donate their life's earnings to the cult, to forego drugs and even sex in return.

But the cult sells more than community. It also offers much-needed structure. Cults impose tight constraints on behavior. They demand and create enormous discipline, some apparently going so far as to impose that discipline through beatings, forced labor, and their own forms of ostracism or imprisonment. Psychiatrist H. A. S. Sukhdeo of the New Jersey School of Medicine, after interviewing survivors of the Jonestown mass suicide and reading the writings of members of the Peoples Temple, concludes: "Our society is so free and permissive, and people have so many options to choose from that they cannot make their own decisions effectively. They want others to make the decision and they will follow."

A man named Sherwin Harris, whose daughter and ex-wife were among the men and women who followed Jim Jones to death in Guyana, has summed it up in a sentence. "This is an example," Harris said, "of what some Americans will subject themselves to in order to bring some structure into their lives."

The last vital product marketed by the cults is "meaning." Each has its own single-minded version of reality—religious, political, or cultural. The cult possesses the sole truth and those living in the outside world who fail to recognize the value of that truth are pictured as either misinformed or Satanic. The message of the cult is drummed into the new member at all-day, all-night sessions It is preached incessantly, until he or she begins to use its terms of reference, its vocabulary, and—ultimately—its metaphor for existence. The "meaning" delivered by the cult may be absurd to the outsider. But that doesn't matter

Indeed, the exact, pinned-down content of the cult message is almost incidental. Its power lies in providing synthesis, in offering an alternative to the fragmented blip culture around us. Once the framework is accepted by the cult recruit, it helps organize much of the chaotic information bombarding him or her from the outside. Whether or not that framework of ideas corresponds to outer reality, it provides a neat set of cubbyholes in which the member can store incoming data. It thereby relieves the stress of overload and confusion. It provides not truth, as such, but order, and thus meaning.

By giving the cult member a sense that reality is meaningful—and that he or she must carry that meaning to outsiders—the cult offers purpose and coherence in a seemingly incoherent world

The cult, however, sells community, structure, and meaning at an extremely high price: the mindless surrender of self. For some, no doubt, this is the only alternative to personal disintegration. But for most of us the cult's way out is too costly.

To make Third Wave civilization both sane and democratic, we need to do more than create new energy supplies or plug in new technology. We need to do more than create community. We need to provide structure and meaning as well. And once again there are simple things we can do to get started.

LIFE-ORGANIZERS AND SEMI-CULTS

At the very simplest and most immediate level, why not

create a cadre of professional and paraprofessional "life-organizers"? For example, we probably need fewer psychotherapists burrowing mole-like into id and ego, and more people who can help us, even in little ways, to pull our daily lives together. Among the most widely heard don't-you-believe-it phrases in use today are: "Tomorrow I'll get myself organized" or "I'm getting my act together."

Yet structuring one's life under today's conditions of high social and technological turmoil is harder and harder to do. The breakup of normal Second Wave structures, the overchoice of life-styles, schedules, and educational opportunities—all, as we have seen, increase the difficulty. For the less affluent, economic pressures impose high structure. For the middle class, and especially their children, the reverse is true. Why not recognize this fact?

Some psychiatrists today perform a life-organizing function. Instead of years on the couch, they offer practical assistance in finding work, locating a girl or boyfriend, budgeting one's money, following a diet, and so forth. We need many more such consultants, structure-providers, and we need feel no shame about seeking their services.

In education, we need to begin paying attention to matters routinely ignored. We spend long hours trying to teach a variety of courses on, say, the structure of government or the structure of the amoeba. But how much effort goes into studying the structure of everyday life—the way time is allocated, the personal uses of money, the places to go for help in a society exploding with complexity? We take for granted that young people already know their way around our social structure. In fact, most have only the dimmest image of the way the world of work or business is organized. Most students have no conception of the architecture of their own city's economy, or the way the local bureaucracy operates, or the place to go to lodge a complaint against a merchant. Most do not even understand how their own schools—even universities—are structured, let alone how much structures are changing under the impact of the Third Wave.

We also need to take a fresh look at structure-providing institutions—including cults. A sensible society should provide a spectrum of institutions, ranging from those that are freeform to those that are tightly structured. We need open classrooms as well as traditional schools. We need easy-come-easy-go organizations as well as rigid monastic orders (secular as well as religious).

Today the gap between the total structure offered by the cult and the seemingly total structurelessness of daily life may well be too wide.

If we find the complete subjugation demanded by many cults to be repellent, we should perhaps encourage the formation of what might be called "semi-cults" that lie somewhere between structureless freedom and tightly structured regimentation. Religious organizations, vegetarians, and other sects or groupings might actually be encouraged to form communities in which moderate to high structure is imposed on those who wish to live that way. These semi-cults might be licensed or monitored to assure that they do not engage in physical or mental violence, embezzlement, extortion, or other such practices, and could be set up so that people in need of external structure can join them for a six-month or one-year hitch—and then leave without pressure or recriminations.

Some people might find it helpful to live within a semi-cult for a time, then return to the outside world, then plug back into the organization for a time, and so forth, alternating between the demands of high, imposed structure and the freedom offered by the larger society. Should this not be possible for them?

Such semi-cults also suggest the need for secular organizations that lie somewhere between the freedom of civilian life and the discipline of the army. Why not a variety of civilian service corps, perhaps organized by cities, school systems, or even private companies to perform useful community services on a contract basis, employing young people who might live together under strict disciplinary rules and be paid army-scale wages. (To bring these paychecks up to the prevailing minimum wage, corps members might receive supplementary vouchers good for university tuition or training.) A "pollution corps," a "public sanitation corps," a "paramedic corps," or a corps designed to assist the elderly—such organizations could yield high dividends for both community and individual.

In addition to providing useful services and a degree of life-structure, such organizations could also help bring much-needed meaning into the lives of their members—not some spurious mystical or political theology but the simple ideal of service to community.

Beyond all such measures, however, we shall need to integrate personal meaning with larger, more encompassing world views. It is not enough for people to understand (or think they understand) their own small contributions to society. They must also have some sense, even if inarticulate, of how they fit into the larger scheme of things. As the Third Wave arrives we will need to formulate sweeping new integrative world views—coherent syntheses, not merely blips—that tie things together.

No single world view can ever capture the whole truth. Only by applying multiple and temporary metaphors can we gain a rounded (if still incomplete) picture of the world. But to acknowledge this axiom is not the same as saying life is meaningless. Indeed, even if life *is* meaningless in some cosmic sense, we can and often do construct meaning, drawing it from decent social relations and picturing ourselves as part of a larger drama—the coherent unfolding of history.

In building Third Wave civilization, therefore, we must go beyond the attack on loneliness. We must also begin providing a framework of order and purpose in life. For meaning, structure, and community are interrelated preconditions for a livable future.

In working toward these ends, it will help to understand that the present agony of social isolation, the impersonality, structurelessness, and sense of meaninglessness from which so many people suffer are symptoms of the breakdown of the past rather than intimations of the future.

It will not be enough, however, for us to change society. For as we shape Third Wave civilization through our own daily decisions and actions, Third Wave civilization will in turn shape us. A new psycho-sphere is emerging that will fundamentally alter our character. And it is to this—the personality of the future—that we next turn.

26

THE PERSONALITY OF
THE FUTURE

As a novel civilization erupts into our everyday lives we are
left wondering whether we, too, are obsolete. With so many
of our habits, values, routines, and responses called into question, it is hardly surprising if we sometimes feel like people of
the past, relics of Second Wave civilization. But if some of us
are indeed anachronisms, are there also people of the future
among us—anticipatory citizens, as it were, of the Third
Wave civilization to come? Once we look past the decay and
disintegration around us, can we see the emerging outlines of
the personality of the future—the coming, so to speak, of a
"new man"?

If so, it would not be the first time *un homme nouveau*
was supposedly detected on the horizon. In a brilliant essay,
André Reszler, director of the Center for European Culture,
has described earlier attempts to forecast the coming of a
new type of human being. At the end of the eighteenth century there was, for example, the "American Adam"—man
born anew in North America, supposedly without the vices
and weaknesses of the European. In the middle of the twentieth century, the new man was supposed to appear in Hitler's
Germany. Nazism, wrote Hermann Rauschning, "is more
than a religion; it is the will to create the superman." This
sturdy "Aryan" would be part peasant, part warrior, part
God. "I have seen the new man," Hitler once confided to
Rauschning. "He is intrepid and cruel. I stood in fear before
him."

The image of a new man (few ever speak of a "new
woman," except as an afterthought) also haunted the Com-

munists. The Soviets still speak of the coming of "Socialist Man." But it was Trotsky who rhapsodized most vividly about the future human. "Man will become incomparably stronger, wiser and more perceptive. His body will become more harmonious, his movements more rhythmical, his voice more melodious. His ways of life will acquire a powerfully dramatic quality. The average man will attain the level of an Aristotle, of a Goethe, of a Marx."

As recently as a decade or two ago, Frantz Fanon heralded the coming of yet another new man who would have a "new mind." Che Guevara saw his ideal man of the future as having a richer interior life. Each image is different.

Yet Reszler persuasively points out that behind most of these images of the "new man" there lurks that familiar old fellow, the Noble Savage, a mythic creature endowed with all sorts of qualities that civilization has supposedly corrupted or worn away. Reszler properly questions this romanticization of the primitive, reminding us that regimes which set out consciously to foster a "new man" have usually brought totalitarian havoc in their wake.

It would be foolish, therefore, to herald yet once more the birth of a "new man" (unless, now that the genetic engineers are at work, we mean that in a frightening, strictly biological sense). The idea suggests a prototype, a single ideal model that the entire civilization strains to emulate. And in a society moving rapidly toward de-massification, nothing is more unlikely.

Nevertheless, it would be equally foolish to believe that fundamentally changed material conditions of life leave personality or, more accurately, social character, unaffected. As we change the deep structure of society, we also modify people. Even if one believed in some unchanging human nature, a commonly held view I do not share, society would still reward and elicit certain character traits and penalize others, leading to evolutionary changes in the distribution of traits in the population.

The psychoanalyst Erich Fromm, who has perhaps written best about social character, defines it as "that part of their character structure that is common to most members of the group." In any culture, he tells us, there are widely shared traits that make up the social character. In turn, social character shapes people so that "their behavior is not a matter of conscious decision as to whether or not to follow the social pattern, but one of *wanting to act as they have to act* and at the same time finding gratification in acting according to the requirements of the culture."

What the Third Wave is doing, therefore, is not creating some ideal superman, some new heroic species stalking through our midst, but producing dramatic changes in the traits distributed through society—not a new man but a new social character. Our task, therefore, is not to hunt for the mythic "man" but for the traits most likely to be valued by the civilization of tomorrow.

These character traits do not simply arise from (or reflect) outside pressures on people. They spring from the tension that exists between the inner drives or desires of many individuals and the outer drives or pressures of the society. But, once formed, these shared character traits play an influential role in the economic and social development of the society.

The coming of the Second Wave, for example, was accompanied by the spread of the Protestant Ethic with its emphasis on thrift, unremitting toil, and the deferral of gratification—traits which channeled enormous energies into the tasks of economic development. The Second Wave also brought changes in objectivity-subjectivity, individualism, attitudes toward authority, and the ability to think abstractly, to empathize and to imagine.

For peasants to be machined into an industrial work force, they had to be given the rudiments of literacy. They had to be educated, informed, and molded. They had to understand that another way of life was possible. Large numbers of people were needed, therefore, with the capacity to imagine themselves in a new role and setting. Their minds had to be liberated from the proximate present. Thus, just as to some extent it had to democratize communications and politics, industrialism was also forced to democratize the imagination.

The result of such psychocultural changes was a changed distribution of traits—a new social character. And today we are once more at the edge of a similar psychocultural upheaval.

The fact that we are racing away from Second Wave Orwellian uniformity makes it difficult to generalize about the emerging psyche. Here, even more than elsewhere in dealing with the future, we can only speculate.

Nevertheless, we *can* point to powerful changes that are likely to influence psychological development in Third Wave society. And this leads us to fascinating questions, if not conclusions. For these changes affect child-rearing, education, adolescence, work, and even the way we form our own self-images. And it is impossible to change all these without deeply altering the entire social character of the future.

GROWING UP DIFFERENT

To begin with, the child of tomorrow is likely to grow up in a society far less child-centered than our own.

The "graying" or aging of the population in all high-technology countries implies greater public attention to the needs of the elderly and a correspondingly reduced focus on the young. Furthermore, as women develop jobs or careers in the exchange economy, the traditional need to channel all their energies into motherhood is diminished.

During the Second Wave, millions of parents lived out their own dreams through their children—often because they could reasonably expect their children to do better socially and economically than they themselves had done. This expectation of upward mobility encouraged parents to concentrate enormous psychic energies on their children. Today many middle-class parents face agonizing disillusionment as their children—in a far more difficult world—move down, rather than up, the socio-economic scale. The likelihood of surrogate fulfillment is evaporating.

For these reasons, the baby born tomorrow is likely to enter a society no longer obsessed with—perhaps not even terribly interested in—the needs, wants, psychological developments, and instant gratification of the child. If so, the Dr. Spocks of tomorrow will urge a more structured and demanding childhood. Parents will be less permissive.

Nor, one suspects, will adolescence be as prolonged and painful a process as it is today for so many. Millions of children are being brought up in single-parent homes, with working mothers (or fathers) squeezed by an erratic economy, and with less of the luxury and time available to the flower child generation of the 1960's.

Others, later on, are likely to be reared in work-at-home or electronic-cottage families. Just as in many Second Wave families built around a mom-and-pop business, we can expect the children of tomorrow's electronic cottage to be drawn directly into the family's work tasks and given growing responsibility from an early age.

Such facts suggest a shorter childhood and youth but a more responsible and productive one. Working alongside adults, children in such homes are also likely to be less subject to peer pressures. They may well turn out to be the high achievers of tomorrow.

During the transition to the new society, wherever jobs remain scarce, Second Wave labor unions will undoubtedly fight to exclude young people from the job market outside the home. Unions (and teachers, whether unionized or not) will lobby for ever-longer years of compulsory or near-compulsory schooling. To the extent that they succeed, millions of young people will continue to be forced into the painful limbo of prolonged adolescence. We may, therefore, see a sharp contrast between young people who grow up fast because of early work responsibilities in the electronic cottage and those who mature more slowly outside.

Over the long pull, however, we can expect education also to change. More learning will occur outside, rather than inside, the classroom. Despite the pressure from unions, the years of compulsory schooling will grow shorter, not longer. Instead of rigid age segregation, young and old will mingle. Education will become more interspersed and interwoven with work, and more spread out over a lifetime. And work itself—whether production for the market or prosumption for use in the home—will probably begin earlier in life than it has in the last generation or two. For just such reasons, Third Wave civilization may well favor quite different traits among the young—less responsiveness to peers, less consumption-orientation, and less hedonistic self-involvement.

Whether this is so or not, one thing is certain. Growing up will be different. And so will the resultant personalities.

THE NEW WORKER

As the adolescent matures and enters the job arena, new forces come into play on his or her personality, rewarding some traits and punishing or penalizing others.

Throughout the Second Wave era, work in the factories and offices steadily grew more repetitive, specialized, and time-pressured, and employers wanted workers who were obedient, punctual, and willing to perform rote tasks. The corresponding traits were fostered by the schools and rewarded by the corporation.

As the Third Wave cuts across our society, work grows less, not more, repetitive. It becomes less fragmented, with each person doing a somewhat larger, rather than smaller, task. Flextime and self-pacing replace the old need for mass synchronization of behavior. Workers are forced to cope with more frequent changes in their tasks, as well as a blinding succession of personnel transfers, product changes, and reorganizations.

What Third Wave employers increasingly need, therefore, are men and women who accept responsibility, who understand how their work dovetails with that of others, who can handle ever larger tasks, who adapt swiftly to changed circumstances, and who are sensitively tuned in to the people around them.

The Second Wave firm frequently paid off for plodding bureaucratic behavior. The Third Wave firm requires people who are less pre-programmed and faster on their feet. The difference, says Donald Conover, general manager of Corporate Education for Western Electric, is like that between classical musicians who play each note according to a predetermined, pre-set pattern, and jazz improvisers who, once having decided what song to play, sensitively pick up cues from one another and, on the basis of that, decide what notes to play next.

Such people are complex, individualistic, proud of the ways in which they differ from other people. They typify the de-massified work force needed by Third Wave industry.

According to opinion researcher Daniel Yankelovich, only 56 percent of U.S. workers—mainly the older ones—are still motivated by traditional incentives. They are happiest with strict work guidelines and clear tasks. They do not expect to find "meaning" in their work.

By contrast, as much as 17 percent of the work force already reflects newer values emerging from the Third Wave. Largely young middle-managers, they are, declares Yankelovich, the "hungriest for more responsibility and more vital work with a commitment worthy of their talent and skills." They seek meaning along with financial reward.

To recruit such workers, employers are beginning to offer individualized rewards. This helps explain why a few advanced companies (like TRW Inc., the Cleveland-based high-technology firm) now offer employees not a fixed set of fringe benefits but a smorgasbord of optional holidays, medical benefits, pensions, and insurance. Each worker can tailor a package to his or her own needs. Says Yankelovich, "There is no one set of incentives with which to motivate the full spectrum of the work force." Moreover, he adds, in the mix of rewards for work, money no longer has the same motivating power it once did.

No one suggests these workers don't want money. They certainly do. But once a certain income level is reached they vary widely in what they want. Additional increments of money no longer have their former impact on behavior. When the Bank of America in San Francisco offered assistant vice-president Richard Easley a promotion to a branch only 20 miles away, Easley refused to accept the carrot. He didn't want to commute. A decade ago, when *Future Shock* first described the stress of job mobility, only an estimated 10 percent of employees resisted a corporate move. The number has jumped to between a third and a half, according to Merrill Lynch Relocation Management, Inc., even though moves are often accompanied by a fatter-than-usual raise. "The balance has definitely shifted away from saluting the company and marching off to Timbuctu toward a greater emphasis on family and life-style," says a vice-president of the Celanese Corporation. Like the Third Wave corporation, which must respond to more than profit, the employee, too, has "multiple bottom lines."

Meanwhile, the most ingrained patterns of authority are also changing. In Second Wave firms every employee has a single boss. Disputes among employees are taken to the boss to be resolved. In the new matrix organizations the style is entirely different. Workers have more than one boss at a time. People of different rank and different skills meet in temporary, "ad-hocratic" groups. And in the words of Davis and Lawrence, authors of a standard text on the subject: "Differences . . . are resolved without a common boss readily available to arbitrate. . . . The assumption in a matrix is that this conflict can be healthy . . . differences are valued and people express their views even when they know that others may disagree."

This system penalizes workers who show blind obedience. It rewards those who—within limits—talk back. Workers who seek meaning, who question authority, who want to exercise discretion, or who demand that their work be socially responsible may be regarded as troublemakers in Second Wave industries. But Third Wave industries cannot run without them.

Across the board, therefore, we are seeing a subtle but profound change in the personality traits rewarded by the economic system—a change which cannot help but shape the emerging social character.

THE PROSUMER ETHIC

It is not just child-rearing, education, and work that will influence personality development in Third Wave civilization. Even deeper forces are playing on tomorrow's psyche. For there is more to the economy than jobs or paid work.

I suggested earlier that we might conceive of the economy as having two sectors, one in which we produce goods for exchange, the other in which we do things for ourselves. One is the market or production sector, the other the prosumer sector. And each has its own psychological effects on us. For each promotes its own ethic, its own set of values, and its own definition of success.

During the Second Wave the vast expansion of the market economy—both capitalist and socialist—encouraged an acquisitive ethic. It gave rise to a narrowly economic definition of personal success.

The advance of the Third Wave, however, is accompanied, as we have seen, by a phenomenal increase in self-help and do-it-yourself activity, or prosumption. Beyond mere hobbyism, this production for use is likely to assume greater economic significance. And as it comes to occupy more of our time and energy, it too begins to shape lives and mold social character.

Instead of ranking people by what they own, as the market ethic does, the prosumer ethic places a high value on what they do. Having plenty of money still carries prestige. But other characteristics count, too. Among these are self-reliance, the ability to adapt and survive under difficult conditions, and the ability to do things with one's own hands—whether to build a fence, to cook a great meal, to make one's own clothes, or to restore an antique chest.

Moreover, while the production or market ethic praises singlemindness, the prosumer ethic calls for roundedness instead. Versatility is "in." As the Third Wave brings production for exchange and production for use into a better balance in the economy, we begin to hear a crescendo of demands for a "balanced" way of life.

* * *

This shift of activity from the production sector to the prosumption sector also suggests the coming of another kind of balance into people's lives. Growing numbers of workers engaged in producing for the market spend their time dealing with abstractions—words, numbers, models—and people known only slightly, if at all.

For many, such "headwork" can be fascinating and rewarding. But it is often accompanied by the sense of being dissociated—cut off, as it were, from the down-to-earth sights, sounds, textures, and emotions of everyday existence. Indeed, much of today's glorification of handcrafts, gardening, peasant or blue-collar fashions, and what might be called "truck-driver chic" may be a compensation for the rising tide of abstraction in the production sector.

By contrast, in prosumption we usually deal with a more concrete, immediate reality—in firsthand contact with things and people. As more people divide their time, serving as part-time workers and part-time prosumers, they are in a position to enjoy the concrete along with the abstract, the complementary pleasures of both headwork and handwork. The prosumer ethic makes handwork respectable again, after 300 years of being looked down upon. And this new balance, too, is likely to influence the distribution of personality traits.

Similarly, we have seen that with the rise of industrialism, the spread of highly interdependent factory work encouraged men to become objective, while staying home and working at low-interdependency tasks promoted subjectivity among women. Today, as more women are drawn into jobs producing for the marketplace, they too are increasingly objectivized. They are encouraged to "think like a man." Conversely, as more men stay home, undertaking a greater share of the housework, their need for "objectivity" is lessened. They are "subjectivized."

Tomorrow, as many Third Wave people divide their lives between working part-time in big, interdependent companies or organizations and working part-time for self and family in small autonomous, prosuming units—we may well strike a new balance between objectivity and subjectivity in both sexes.

Instead of finding a "male" attitude and a "female" attitude, neither of them well-balanced, the system may reward people who are healthily able to see the world through both perspectives. Objective subjectivists—and vice versa.

In short, with the rising importance of prosumption to the

overall economy, we touch off another racing current of psychological change. The combined impact of basic changes in production and prosumption, added to the deep changes in child-rearing and education, promises to remake our social character at least as dramatically as the Second Wave did 300 years ago. A new social character is cropping up in our very midst.

In fact, even if every one of these insights were to prove mistaken, if every one of the shifts we are beginning to see were to reverse itself, there is still one final, giant reason to expect an eruption in the psycho-sphere. That reason is summed up in the two words "communications revolution."

THE CONFIGURATIVE ME

The link between communications and character is complex, but unbreakable. We cannot transform all our media of communication and expect to remain unchanged as a people. A revolution in the media must mean a revolution in the psyche.

During the Second Wave period, people were bathed in a sea of mass-produced imagery. A relatively few centrally produced newspapers, magazines, radio and television broadcasts, and movies fed what critics termed a "monolithic consciousness." Individuals were continually encouraged to compare themselves to a relatively small number of role models, and to evaluate their life-styles against a few preferred possibilities. In consequence, the range of socially approved personality styles was relatively narrow.

The de-massification of the media today presents a dazzling diversity of role models and life-styles for one to measure oneself against. Moreover, the new media do not feed us fully formed chunks, but broken chips and blips of imagery. Instead of being handed a selection of coherent identities to choose among, we are required to piece one together: a configurative or modular "me." This is far more difficult, and it explains why so many millions are desperately searching for identity.

Caught up in that effort, we develop a heightened awareness of our own individuality—of the traits that make us unique. Our self-image thus changes. We demand to be seen as, and treated as, individuals, and this occurs at precisely the time when the new production system requires more individualized workers.

Beyond helping us to crystallize what is purely personal in us, the new communications media of the Third Wave turn us into producers—or rather prosumers—of our own self-imagery.

The German poet and social critic Hans Magnus Enzensberger has noted that in yesterday's mass media the "technical distinction between receivers and transmitters reflects the social division of labor into producers and consumers." Throughout the Second Wave era this meant that professional communicators produced the messages *for* the audience. The audience remained powerless to respond directly to, or to interact with, the message senders.

By contrast, the most revolutionary feature of the new means of communication is that many of them are interactive—permitting each individual user to make or send images as well as merely to receive them from the outside. Two-way cable, video cassette, cheap copiers and tape recorders, all place the means of communication into the hands of the individual.

Looking ahead, one can imagine a stage at which even ordinary television becomes interactive, so that instead of merely watching some Archie Bunker or Mary Tyler Moore of the future, we are actually able to talk to them and influence their behavior in the show. Even now, the Qube cable system makes it technologically possible for viewers of a dramatic show to call on the director to speed up or slow down the action or to choose one story ending over another.

The communications revolution gives us each a more complex image of self. It differentiates us further. It speeds the very process by which we "try on" different images of self and, in fact, accelerates our movement through successive images. It makes it possible for us to project our image electronically to the world. And nobody fully understands what all this will do to our personalities. For in no previous civilization have we ever had such powerful tools. We increasingly own the technology of consciousness.

The world we are fast entering is so remote from our past experience that all psychological speculations are admittedly shaky. What is absolutely clear, however, is that powerful forces are streaming together to alter social character—to elicit certain traits, to suppress others, and in the process to transform us all.

As we move beyond Second Wave civilization we are doing more than shifting from one energy system to another, or from one technological base to the next. We are revolutionizing inner space as well. In the light of this, it would be absurd to project the past upon the future—to picture the people of Third Wave civilization in Second Wave terms.

If our assumptions are even partially correct, individuals will vary more vividly tomorrow than they do today. More of them are likely to grow up sooner, to show responsibility at an earlier age, to be more adaptable, and to evince greater individuality. They are more likely than their parents to question authority. They will want money and will work for it—but, except under conditions of extreme privation, they will resist working for money alone.

Above all, they seem likely to crave balance in their lives— balance between work and play, between production and prosumption, between headwork and handwork, between the abstract and the concrete, between objectivity and subjectivity. And they will see and project themselves in far more complex terms than any previous people.

As Third Wave civilization matures, we shall create not a utopian man or woman who towers over the people of the past, not a superhuman race of Goethes and Aristotles (or Genghis Khans or Hitlers) but merely, and proudly, one hopes, a race—and a civilization—that deserves to be called human.

No hope for such an outcome, no hope for a safe transition to a decent new civilization is possible, however, until we face one final imperative: the need for political transformation. And it is this prospect—both terrifying and exhilarating—that we explore in these final pages. The personality of the future must be matched by a politics of the future.

27

THE
POLITICAL
MAUSOLEUM

It is impossible to be simultaneously blasted by a revolution in energy, a revolution in technology, a revolution in family life, a revolution in sexual roles, and a worldwide revolution in communications without also facing—sooner or later—a potentially explosive political revolution.

All the political parties of the industrial world, all our congresses, parliaments, and supreme soviets, our presidencies and prime ministerships, our courts and our regulatory agencies, and our layer upon geological layer of government bureaucracy—in short, all the tools we use to make and enforce collective decisions—are obsolete and about to be transformed. A Third Wave civilization cannot operate with a Second Wave political structure . .

Just as the revolutionaries who created the industrial age could not govern with the leftover apparatus of feudalism, so today we are faced once more with the need to invent new political tools. This is the political message of the Third Wave.

THE BLACK HOLE

Today, although its gravity is not yet recognized, we are witnessing a profound crisis not of this or that government but of representative democracy itself, in all its forms. In one country after another, the political technology of the Second Wave is sputtering, groaning, and malfunctioning dangerously.

In the United States we find an almost total paralysis of political decision-making in connection with the life-and-death questions facing society. Fully six years after the OPEC embargo, despite its sledgehammer impact on the economy, despite its threat to independence and even military security, despite interminable congressional study, despite repeated re-organization of the bureaucracy, despite passionate presidential pleas, the U.S. political machinery still spins helplessly on its axis, unable to produce anything remotely resembling a coherent energy policy.

This policy vacuum is not unique. The United States also has no comprehensive (or comprehensible) urban policy, environmental policy, family policy, technology policy. It does not even have—if we listen to critics abroad—a discernible foreign policy. Nor would the American political system have the capacity to integrate and prioritize such policies even if they did exist. This vacuum reflects so advanced a breakdown in decision-making that President Carter, in a wholly unprecedented speech, was forced to condemn the "paralysis . . . stagnation . . . and drift" of his own government.

This collapse of decision-making is, however, not the monopoly of one party or one president. It has been deepening since the early 1960's, and reflects underlying structural problems that no president—Republican or Democrat—can overcome within the framework of the present system. These political problems have destabilizing effects on the other main social institutions such as the family, the school, and the corporation.

Dozens of laws with immediate impact on family life cancel and contradict one another, worsening the family crisis. The educational system was flooded with construction funds at precisely the moment when school-age population began to plummet, thus provoking an orgy of useless school building, followed by a cutoff of funds when they are most desperately needed for other purposes. Corporations, meanwhile, are compelled to operate in a political environment so volatile that they literally cannot tell from one day to the next what government expects of them.

First, Congress demands that General Motors and the other auto manufacturers install catalytic converters on all new cars in the interests of a cleaner environment. Then, after GM spends $300 million on converters and signs a $500-million ten-year contract for the precious metals needed for their manufacture, the government announces that cars with catalytic converters emit 35 times more sulphuric acid than cars without them.

At the same time, a runaway regulatory machine generates an increasingly impenetrable mesh of rules—45,000 pages of complex new regulations a year. Twenty-seven different government agencies monitor some 5,600 federal regulations that pertain to the manufacture of steel alone. (Thousands of additional rules apply to the mining, marketing, and transport operations of the steel industry.) A leading pharmaceutical firm, Eli Lilly, spends more time filling out government forms than doing heart-disease and cancer research. A single report from Exxon, the oil company, to the Federal Energy Agency runs 445,000 pages—the equivalent of a thousand volumes!

This mandarin complexity weighs the economy down, while the jerky, on-again-off-again responses of government decision-makers add to the prevailing sense of anarchy. The political system, erratically zigzagging from day to day, greatly complicates the struggle of our basic social institutions for survival.

Nor is this decisional breakdown a purely American phenomenon. Governments in France, Germany, Japan, and Britain—not to mention Italy—exhibit similar symptoms, as do those in the Communist industrial nations. And in Japan, a prime minister declares: "We increasingly hear about the worldwide crisis of democracy. Its problem-solving capability, or the so-called governability of a democracy, is being challenged. In Japan, too, parliamentary democracy is on trial."

The political decision-making machinery in all those countries is increasingly strained, overworked, overloaded, drowned in irrelevant data, and faced with unfamiliar perils. What we are seeing, therefore, are government policy makers unable to make high priority decisions (or making them very badly) while they chase frenziedly about making thousands of lesser, often trivial, ones.

Even when important decisions are extruded they usually come too late, and seldom accomplish what they are designed to do. "We've solved every problem with legislation," says one hard-pressed British lawmaker. "We've passed seven acts against inflation. We've eliminated injustice numerous times. We've solved the ecology problem. Every problem has been solved countless times by legislation. But the problems remain. Legislation doesn't work."

An American TV announcer, reaching into the past for an analogy, puts it differently: "Right now I feel the nation is a stagecoach with the horses running headlong, and a guy trying to pull in the reins, and they are not responding."

This is why so many people—including those in high office—feel so powerless. A leading American senator privately tells me of his deep frustration and the feeling that he cannot accomplish anything useful. He questions the ruin of his family life, the frantic pace of his existence, the long hours, hectic travel, endless conferences, and perpetual pressure. He asks, "Is it worth it?" A British M.P. poses the same question, adding that "the House of Commons is a museum piece—a relic!" A top White House official complains to me that even the President, supposedly the most powerful man in the world, feels impotent. "The President feels as though he is shouting into the telephone—with nobody at the other end."

This deepening breakdown of the ability to make timely and competent decisions changes the deepest power relationships in society. Under normal, nonrevolutionary circumstances, the elites in any society use the political system to reinforce their rule and further their ends. Their power is defined by the ability to make certain things happen, or to prevent certain things from happening. This presupposes, however, their ability to predict and control events—it assumes that when they yank on the reins, the horses will stop.

Today the elites can no longer predict the outcomes of their own actions. The political systems through which they operate are so antiquated and creaky, so outraced by events, that even when closely "controlled" by the elites for their own benefit, the results often backfire.

This does not mean, one hastens to add, that the power lost by the elites has accrued to the rest of society. Power is not transferred; it is increasingly randomized, so that no one knows from moment to moment who is responsible for what, who has real (as distinct from nominal) authority, or how long that authority will last. In this seething semi-anarchy, ordinary people grow bitterly cynical not merely about their own "representatives" but—more ominously—about the very possibility of being represented at all.

As a result, the Second Wave "reassurance ritual" of voting begins to lose its power. Year by year, American voting participation decreases. In the 1976 presidential election fully 46 percent of eligible voters stayed home, meaning that a president was elected by roughly one quarter of the electorate—in reality only about one eighth of the total population of the country. More recently, pollster Patrick Caddell found that only 12 percent of the electorate still felt that voting matters at all.

Similarly, political parties are losing their drawing power. In the period 1960–1972 the number of "independents" unaffiliated with any party in the United States shot up 400 percent, making 1972 the first time in more than a century that the number of independents equaled the membership of one of the major parties.

Parallel tendencies are apparent elsewhere, too. The Labour Party, which governed Britain until 1979, has atrophied to the point at which, in a country of 56,000,000 people it is lucky if it can claim 100,000 active members. In Japan the *Yomiuri Shimbun* reports that "voters have little faith in their governments. They feel detached from their leaders." A wave of political disenchantment sweeps Denmark. Asked why, a Danish engineer speaks for many when he says, "Politicians appear useless in stopping the trends."

In the Soviet Union, writes the dissident author Victor Nekipelov, the last decade has seen "ten years of deepening chaos, militarization, catastrophic economic disorder, increases in the cost of living, insufficient basic food products, increases in crime and drunkenness, corruption and thieving, but above all of an uncontrollable drop in prestige of the present leadership in the eyes of the people."

In New Zealand, the vacuity of mainstream politics prompted one protester to change his name to Mickey Mouse and enter himself as a candidate. So many others did likewise—adopting names like Alice in Wonderland—that Parliament rushed through a law banning anyone from running for office if he or she had legally changed a name within six months prior to an election.

More than anger, citizens are now expressing revulsion and contempt for their political leaders and government officials. They sense that the political system, which should serve as a steering wheel or stabilizer in a change-tossed, runaway society, is itself broken, spinning and flapping out of control.

Thus when a team of political scientists investigated Washington, D.C., recently to find out "who runs this place?" they came up with a simple, crushing answer. Their report, published by the American Enterprise Institute, was summed up by Professor Anthony King of the University of Essex in Britain: "The short answer . . . would have to be, 'No one. Nobody is in charge here.'"

Not just in the United States but in many of the Second Wave countries being battered by the Third Wave of change, there is a spreading power vacuum—a "black hole" in society.

PRIVATE ARMIES

The dangers implicit in this power vacuum can be gauged by glancing briefly backward at the mid-1970's. Then, as energy and raw material flows faltered in the wake of the OPEC embargo, as inflation and unemployment spurted, as the dollar plunged and Africa, Asia, and South America began to demand a new economic deal, signs of political pathology flared in one after another of the Second Wave nations.

In Britain, celebrated as the home of tolerance and civility, retired generals began to recruit private armies to impose order, and a resurgent fascist movement, the National Front, fielded candidates in some 90 parliamentary constituencies. Fascists and left-wingers came close to fighting a massed battle in the London streets. In Italy the fascists of the left, the Red Brigades, escalated their reign of kneecapping, kidnapping, and assassination. In Poland, the government's attempt to hike food prices to keep up with inflation brought the country to the edge of revolt. In West Germany, wracked by terrorist murders, a jittery establishment rushed through a series of McCarthyite laws to suppress dissent.

It is true that these signs of political instability receded as the industrial economies partially (and temporarily) recovered in the late 1970's. Britain's private armies never came into play. The Red Brigades, after killing Aldo Moro, appeared for a time to pull back for regrouping. A new regime took over smoothly in Japan. The Polish government made an uneasy peace with its rebels. In the United States, Jimmy Carter, who won office by running against "the system" (and then embraced it), managed to hang on by his fingernails despite a disastrous decline in popularity.

Nevertheless, these evidences of instability must make us wonder whether existing Second Wave political systems in each of the industrial nations can survive the next round of crises. For the crises of the 1980's and 1990's are likely to be even more severe, disruptive, and dangerous than those just past. Few informed observers believe the worst is over, and ominous scenarios abound.

If turning off the oil spigots for a few weeks in Iran could cause violence and chaos on gas lines in the United States, what is likely to happen, not only in the U.S., when the present rulers of Saudi Arabia are kicked off the throne? Is it likely that this tiny clique of ruling families, who control 25 percent of the world's oil reserves, can cling to power indefinitely, while intermittent warfare rages between North and South Yemen nearby, and their own country is destabilized by floods of petrodollars, immigrant workers, and radical Palestinians? Just how wisely will the shell-shocked (and future-shocked) politicians in Washington, London, Paris, Moscow, Tokyo, or Tel Aviv respond to a coup d'état, a religious upheaval, or a revolutionary uprising in Riyadh—let alone to the sabotage of the oil fields at Ghawar and Abqaiq?

How would these same overworked, nervously twitching Second Wave political leaders, East and West, respond if, as Sheikh Yamani predicts, frogmen were to sink a ship or mine the waters of the Strait of Hormuz, thereby blocking half the oil shipments on which the world depends for survival? It is scarcely reassuring to look at a map and note that Iran, barely able to maintain domestic law and order, sits on one bank of that strategically vital, all too narrow channel.

What happens, asks another chilling scenario, when Mexico begins in earnest to exploit *its* oil—and faces a sudden, overpowering influx of petro-pesos? Will its ruling oligarchy have the desire, much less the technical skills, to distribute the bulk of that new wealth to Mexico's malnourished and long-suffering peasantry? And can it do so rapidly enough to prevent today's low-level guerrilla activity there from exploding into a full-scale war on the doorstep of the United States? If such a war were to break out, how would Washington respond? And how would the huge population of Chicanos in the ghettos of Southern California or Texas react? Can we expect even semi-intelligent decisions about crises of such magnitude, given today's disarray in Congress and the White House?

Economically, will governments already incapable of managing macro-economic forces be able to cope with even wilder swings in the international money system, or with its complete breakdown? With currencies hardly under control, the Eurocurrency bubble still expanding unchecked, and consumer, corporate, and government credit ballooning, can anyone look forward to economic stability in the years ahead? Given skyrocketing inflation and unemployment, a credit crash, or some other economic catastrophe, we may yet see private armies in action.

Finally, what happens when, among the myriad religious cults now flowering, some spring up to organize for political purposes? As the major organized religions splinter under the de-massifying impact of the Third Wave, armies of self-ordained priests, ministers, preachers, and teachers are likely to appear—some with disciplined, perhaps even paramilitary, political followings.

In the United States, it is not hard to imagine some new political party running Billy Graham (or some facsimile) on a crude "law-and-order" or "anti-porn" program with a strong authoritarian streak. Or some as yet unknown Anita Bryant demanding imprisonment for gays or "gay-symps." Such examples provide only a faint, glimmering intimation of the religio-politics that may well lie ahead, even in the most secular of societies. One can imagine all sorts of cult-based political movements headed by Ayatollahs named Smith, Schultz, or Santini.

I am not saying these scenarios will necessarily materialize. They could all turn out to be farfetched. But if these don't, we must assume that other dramatic crises *will* erupt, even more dangerous than those just past. And we must face the fact that our present crop of Second Wave leaders is grotesquely unprepared to cope with them.

In fact, because our Second Wave political structures are even more deteriorated today than they were in the 1970's, we must assume that governments will be less competent, less imaginative, and less farsighted in dealing with the crises of the 1980's and 1990's than they were in the decade just past.

And this tells us that we must re-examine, from the roots up, one of our most deeply held and dangerous political illusions.

THE MESSIAH COMPLEX

The Messiah Complex is the illusion that we can somehow save ourselves by changing the man (or woman) on top.

Watching Second Wave politicians stumble and flail drunkenly at the problems arising from the emergence of the Third Wave, millions of people, spurred on by the press, have arrived at a single, simple, easy-to-understand explanation of our woes: the "failure of leadership." If only a messiah would appear on the political horizon and put things back together again!

This craving for a masterful, macho leader is voiced today by even the most well-meaning of people as their familiar world crumbles, as their environment grows more unpredictable and their hunger for order, structure, and predictability increases. Thus we hear, as Ortega y Gasset put it during the 1930's when Hitler was on the march, "a formidable cry, rising like the howling of innumerable dogs to the stars, asking for someone or something to take command."

In the United States, the President is violently condemned for "lack of leadership." In Britain, Margaret Thatcher is elected because she offers at least the illusion of being "the Iron Lady." Even in the Communist industrial nations, where leadership is anything but timid, the pressure for still "stronger leadership" is intensifying. In the U.S.S.R., a novel appears that baldly glorifies Stalin's ability to draw the "necessary political conclusions." The publication of *Victory* by Alexander Chakovsky is seen as part of a "restalinization" drive. Little pictures of Stalin sprout on windshields, in homes, hotels, and kiosks. "Stalin on the windshield today," writes Victor Nekipelov, author of *Institute of Fools,* "is an upsurge from below . . . a protest, however paradoxical, against the present disintegration and lack of leadership."

As a dangerous decade opens, today's demand for "leadership" strikes at a moment when long-forgotten dark forces are stirring anew in our midst. *The New York Times* reports that in France, "after more than three decades in hibernation, small but influential right-wing groups are again seeking the intellectual limelight, expounding theories on race, biology and political elitism discredited by the defeat of Fascism in World War II."

Prating of Aryan racial supremacy, and violently anti-American, they control a major journalistic outlet in *Le Figaro*'s weekly. They argue that the races are born unequal and should be kept that way by social policy. They lace their arguments with references to E. O. Wilson and Arthur Jensen to lend supposedly scientific color to their virulently antidemocratic biases.

Across the globe in Japan, my wife and I not long ago spent 45 minutes in a massive traffic pile-up watching a procession of trucks crawl by, bearing uniformed and helmeted political toughs, chanting and flinging their fists skyward to protest some government policy. Our Japanese friends tell us these proto-storm troopers are linked to the mafia-like *yakuza* gangs and are financed by powerful political figures eager to see a return to prewar authoritarianism.

Each of these phenomena in turn has its "left" counterpart—terrorist gangs who mouth the slogans of socialist democracy but are prepared to impose their own brand of totalitarian leadership on society with Kalashnikovs and plastic bombs.

In the United States, among other unsettling signs, we see the rebirth of unabashed racism. Since 1978 a resurgent Ku Klux Klan has burned crosses in Atlanta; ringed the city hall of Decatur, Alabama, with armed men; fired shots at Black churches and a synagogue in Jackson, Mississippi; and shown signs of renewed activity in twenty-one states from California to Connecticut. In North Carolina, Klansmen who are also avowed Nazis have killed five left-wing anti-Klan activists.

In short, the surge of demand for "stronger leadership" coincides precisely with the recrudescence of highly authoritarian groups who hope to profit from the breakdown of representative government. The tinder and the spark are coming perilously close to one another.

This intensifying cry for leadership is based on three misconceptions, the first of which is the myth of authoritarian efficiency. Few ideas are more widely held than the notion that dictators, if nothing else, "make the trains run on time." Today so many institutions are breaking down and unpredictability is so rife that millions of people would willingly trade some freedom (someone else's, preferably) to make their economic, social, and political trains run on time.

Yet strong leadership—and even totalitarianism—has little to do with efficiency. There is not much evidence to suggest that the Soviet Union today is efficiently run, though its leadership is assuredly "stronger" and more authoritarian than that in the United States, France, or Sweden. Apart from the military, the secret police, and a few other functions vital to the perpetuation of the regime, the U.S.S.R. is, by all accounts—including many in the Soviet press—a sloppy ship indeed. It is a society crippled by waste, irresponsibility, inertia, and corruption—in short, by "totalitarian inefficiency."

Even Nazi Germany, so marvelously efficient at wiping out Poles, Russians, Jews and other "non-Aryans," was anything but efficient in other ways. Raymond Fletcher, a member of the British Parliament who was educated in Germany and has remained a close observer of German social conditions, reminds us of a forgotten reality:

"We think of Nazi Germany as a model of efficiency. In fact, Britain was better organized for war than the Germans. In the Ruhr, the Nazis continued to turn out tanks and armored personnel carriers well after they no longer could find rail transport to take them away. They used their scientists very poorly. Of 16,000 inventions of military significance made during the war, few ever actually got into production because of the prevailing inefficiency. The Nazi intelligence agencies wound up spying on each other, while British intelligence was superb. While the British were organizing everyone to contribute wrought iron fences and saucepans to the war effort, the Germans were still producing luxury goods. While the British drafted women early on, the Germans didn't. Hitler himself was a paragon of indecision. The Third Reich as an example of military or industrial efficiency is a ludicrous myth."

It takes more than strong leadership, as we shall see, to make the trains run on time.

The second fatal fallacy in the cry for strong leadership is its unspoken assumption that a style of leadership that worked in the past will work in the present or future. We are continually dredging up images from the past when we think about leadership—Roosevelt, Churchill, de Gaulle. Yet different civilizations require vastly different leadership qualities. And what is strong in one may be inept and disastrously weak in another.

During First Wave, peasant-based civilization, leadership typically derived from birth, not achievement. A monarch needed certain limited practical skills—the ability to lead men in combat, the shrewdness to play off his barons against one another, the cleverness to consummate an advantageous marriage. Literacy and broad powers of abstract thought were not among the basic requirements. Moreover, the leader was typically free to exercise sweeping personal authority in the most capricious, even whimsical fashion, unchecked by constitution, legislature, or public opinion. If approval was needed, it was only from a small coterie of nobles, lords, and ministers. The leader able to mobilize this support was "strong."

The Second Wave leader, by contrast, dealt in impersonal

and increasingly abstract power. He had many more decisions to make on a far wider variety of matters, from manipulating the media to managing the macro-economy. His decisions had to be implemented through a chain of organizations and agencies whose complex relationships to one another he understood and orchestrated. He had to be literate and capable of abstract reasoning. Instead of a handful of barons, he had to play off a complex array of elites and sub-elites. Moreover, his authority—even if he were a totalitarian dictator—was at least nominally constrained by constitution, legal precedent, party political requirements, and the force of mass opinion.

Given these contrasts, the "strongest" First Wave leader plunged into a Second Wave political framework would have appeared even more weak, confused, erratic, and inept than the "weakest" Second Wave leader.

Similarly today, as we race into a new stage of civilization, Roosevelt, Churchill, de Gaulle, Adenauer (or for that matter, Stalin)—the "strong" leaders of industrial societies—would be as out of place and inept as Mad King Ludwig in the White House. The search for seemingly decisive, jut-jawed, sharply opinionated leaders—whether Kennedys, Connallys, or Reagans, Chiracs or Thatchers—is an exercise in nostalgia, a search for a father- or mother-figure based on obsolete assumptions. For the "weakness" of today's leaders is less a reflection of personal qualities than it is a consequence of the breakdown of the institutions on which their power depends.

In fact, their seeming "weakness" is the exact result of their increased "power." Thus, as the Third Wave continues to transform society, raising it to a much higher level of diversity and complexity, all leaders become dependent on increasing numbers of people for help in making and implementing decisions. The more powerful the tools at a leader's command—supersonic fighters, nuclear weapons, computers, telecommunications—the more, not less, dependent the leader becomes.

This is an unbreakable relationship because it reflects the rising complexity on which power today necessarily rests. This is why the American President can sit next to the nuclear push button, which gives him the power to pulverize the planet, and still feel as helpless as though there were "nobody at the other end" of his telephone line. Power and powerlessness are opposite sides of the same semiconductor chip.

The emerging civilization of the Third Wave demands, for

these reasons, a wholly new type of leadership. The requisite qualities of Third Wave leaders are not yet entirely clear. We may well find that strength lies not in a leader's assertiveness but precisely in his or her ability to listen to others; not in bulldozer force but in imagination; not in megalomania but in a recognition of the limited nature of leadership in the new world.

The leaders of tomorrow may well have to deal with a far more decentralized and participatory society—one even more diverse than today's. They can never again be all things to all people. Indeed, it is unlikely that one human being will ever embody all the traits required. Leadership may well prove to be more temporary, collegial, and consensual.

Jill Tweedie, in a perceptive column in *The Guardian*, has sensed this shift. "It is easy to criticize . . . Carter," she wrote. "It is possible he was (is?) a weak and vacillating man. . . . But it is also just possible . . . that Jimmy Carter's major sin is his tacit recognition that, as the planet shrinks, the problems . . . are so general, so basic and so interdependent that they cannot be solved, as once problems were, by one man or one Government's initiative." In short, she suggests, we are moving painfully toward a new kind of leader not because someone thinks this is a good thing but because the nature of the problems make it necessary. Yesterday's strong man may turn out to be tomorrow's 90-pound weakling.

Whether or not this proves to be the case, there is one final, even more damning flaw in the argument that some political messiah is needed to save us from disaster. For this notion presupposes that our basic problem is personnel. And it isn't. Even if we had saints, geniuses, and heroes in charge, we would still be facing the terminal crisis of representative government—the political technology of the Second Wave era.

THE WORLD WEB

If choosing the "best" leader were all we had to worry about, our problem could be solved within the framework of the existing political system. In fact, however, the problem cuts far deeper. In a nutshell, leaders—even the "best"—are crippled because the institutions they must work through are obsolete.

Our political and governmental structures, to begin with,

were designed at a time when the nation-state was still coming into its own. Each government could make more or less independent decisions. Today, as we have seen, this is no longer possible, though we retain the myth of sovereignty. Inflation has become so transnational a disease that not even Mr. Brezhnev or his successor can prevent the contagion from crossing the border. The Communist industrial countries, even though partially severed from the world economy and rigidly controlled from within, are dependent upon external sources for oil, food, technology, credit, and other necessities. In 1979 the U.S.S.R. was forced to hike many consumer prices. Czechoslovakia doubled the price of fuel oil. Hungary staggered its consumers by boosting the price of electricity 51 percent. Each decision in one country forces problems or calls for responses from the next.

France builds a nuclear reprocessing plant at Cap de la Hague (which is closer to London than the British Windscale reactor) at a place where radioactive dust or gas, if released, would be wafted toward Britain by the prevailing winds. Mexican oil spills imperil the Texas coastline 500 miles away. And if Saudi Arabia or Libya raises or lowers petroleum production quotas, it has immediate or long-range effects on the ecology of many nations.

In this tightly wired web national leaders lost much of their effectiveness no matter what rhetoric they employ or sabers they rattle. Their decisions typically trigger costly, unwanted, frequently dangerous repercussions at both the global and the local level. The scale of government and the distribution of decision-making authority are hopelessly wrong for today's world.

This, however, is only one of the reasons why existing political structures are obsolete.

THE INTER-WEAVE PROBLEM

Our political institutions also reflect an out-of-date organization of knowledge. Every government has ministries or departments devoted to discrete fields such as finance, foreign affairs, defense, agriculture, commerce, post office, or transportation. The United States Congress and other legislative bodies have committees similarly set aside to deal with problems in these fields. What no Second Wave government— even the most centralized and authoritarian—can solve is the inter-weave problem: how to integrate the activities of all these units so they can produce orderly, wholistic programs instead of a mishmash of contradictory and self-canceling effects.

If there is one thing we should have learned in the past few decades, it is that all social and political problems are interwoven—that energy, for example, affects economics, which in turn affects health, which in turn affects education, work, family life, and a thousand other things. The attempt to deal with neatly defined problems in isolation from one another—itself a product of the industrial mentality—creates only confusion and disaster. Yet the organizational structure of government mirrors precisely this Second Wave approach to reality.

This anachronistic structure leads to interminable jurisdictional power struggles, to the externalization of costs (each agency attempting to solve its own problems at the expense of another), and to the generation of adverse side effects. This is why each attempt by government to cure a problem leads to a rash of new problems, often worse than the original one.

Governments typically attempt to solve this inter-weave problem through further centralization—by naming a "czar" to cut through the red tape. He makes changes, blind to their destructive side effects—or he piles on so much additional red tape himself that he is soon dethroned. For centralization of power no longer works. Another desperation measure is the creation of innumerable interdepartmental committees to coordinate and review decisions. The result, however, is the construction of yet another set of baffles and filters through which decisions have to pass—and a further complexification of the bureaucratic labyrinth. Our existing governments and political structures are obsolete because they view the world through Second Wave lenses.

In turn, this aggravates another problem.

THE DECISIONAL SPEEDUP

Second Wave governments and parliamentary institutions were designed to make decisions at a leisurely pace, suited to a world in which it might take a week for a message to travel from Boston or New York to Philadelphia. Today if an Ayatollah seizes hostages in Teheran or coughs in Qom, officials in Washington, Moscow, Paris, or London may have to respond with decisions within minutes. The extreme speed of change catches governments and politicians off guard and contributes to their sense of helplessness and confusion, as the press makes plain. "Only three months ago," writes *Advertising Age*, "the White House was telling consumers to shop hard before spending their bucks. Now the government is going all out to prod consumers into spending more freely." Oil experts foresaw the petroleum price explosion, reports *Aussenpolitik*, the German foreign policy journal, but "not the speed of developments." The 1974–1975 recession hit U.S. policy makers with what *Fortune* magazine terms "stunning speed and severity."

Social change, too, is accelerating and putting additional pressure on the political decision-makers. *Business Week* declares that in the United States, "as long as the migration of industry and population was gradual . . . it helped to unify the nation. But within the past five years the process has burst beyond the bounds that can be accommodated by existing political institutions."

The politicians' own careers have accelerated, often catching them by surprise. As recently as 1970 Margaret Thatcher forecast that, within her lifetime, no woman would ever be appointed to a high Cabinet post in the British government. In 1979 she herself was the Prime Minister.

In the United States, Jimmy Who? shot into the White House in a matter of months. What's more, although a new president does not take office until the January following the election, Carter became the de facto president immediately. It was Carter, not the out-going Ford, who was battered with questions about the Middle East, the energy crisis, and other issues almost before the ballots were counted. The lame-duck Ford instantaneously became, for practical purposes, a dead duck, because political time is now too compressed, history moving too fast to permit the traditional delays.

Similarly, the "honeymoon" with the press that a new president once enjoyed was truncated in time. Carter, even before inauguration, was blasted for his Cabinet selections and forced to withdraw his choice for head of the CIA. Later, less than halfway through the four-year term, the insightful political correspondent Richard Reeves was already forecasting a short career for the President because "instant communications have telescoped time so much that a four-year Presidency today produces more events, more troubles, more information, than any eight-year Presidency did in the past."

This hotting up of the pace of political life, reflecting the generalized speedup of change, intensifies today's political and governmental breakdown. Put simply, our leaders—forced to work through Second Wave institutions designed for a slower society—cannot churn out intelligent decisions as fast as events require. Either the decisions came too late or indecision takes over.

For example, Professor Robert Skidelsky of the School for Advanced International Studies, Johns Hopkins University, writes, "Fiscal policy has been virtually unusable because it takes too long to get appropriate measures through Congress, even when a majority exists." And this was written in 1974, long before the energy stalemate in America entered its sixth interminable year.

The acceleration of change has overpowered the decisional capacity of our institutions, making today's political structures obsolete, regardless of party ideology or leadership. These institutions are inadequate not only in terms of scale and structure but in terms of speed as well. And even this is not all.

THE COLLAPSE OF CONSENSUS

As the Second Wave produced a mass society, the Third Wave de-massifies us, moving the entire social system to a much higher level of diversity and complexity. This revolutionary process, much like the biological differentiation that occurs in evolution, helps explain one of today's most widely noted political phenomena—the collapse of consensus.

From one end of the industrial world to the other we hear politicians lamenting the loss of "national purpose," the absence of the good old "Dunkirk spirit," the erosion of "national unity," and the sudden, bewildering proliferation of high-powered splinter groups. The latest buzzword in Washington is "single issue group," referring to the political organizations springing up by the thousands, usually around what each perceives as a single burning issue: abortion, gun control, gay rights, school busing, nuclear power, and so on. So diverse are these interests at both the national and local levels that politicians and officials can no longer keep track of them.

Mobile-home owners organize to fight for county zoning changes. Farmers battle power transmission lines. Retired people mobilize against school taxes. Feminists, Chicanos, strip miners, and anti–strip miners organize, as do single parents and anti-porn crusaders. A midwest magazine even reports formation of an organization of "gay Nazis"—an embarrassment, no doubt, to both the heterosexual Nazis and the Gay Liberation Movement.

Simultaneously, national mass organizations are having trouble holding together. Says a participant at a conference of voluntary organizations, "Local churches are not following the national lead any more." A labor expert reports that instead of a single unified political drive by the AFL-CIO, affiliated unions are increasingly mounting their own campaigns for their own ends.

The electorate is not merely breaking into splinters. The splinter groups themselves are increasingly transitory, springing up, dying out, turning over more and more rapidly, and forming a yeasty, hard-to-analyze flux. "In Canada," says one government official, "we now assume the life-span of the new voluntary organizations will be six to eight months. There are more groups and they are more ephemeral." In this way, acceleration and diversity combine to create a totally new kind of body politic.

These same developments also sweep into oblivion our notions about political coalitions, alliances, or united fronts. In a Second Wave society a political leader could glue together half a dozen major blocs, as Roosevelt did in 1932, and expect the resulting coalition to remain locked in position for many years. Today it is necessary to plug together hundreds, even thousands, of tiny, short-lived special interest groups, and the coalition itself will prove short-lived as well. It may cleave together just long enough to elect a president, then break apart again the day after election, leaving him without a base of support for his programs.

This de-massification of political life, reflecting all the deep trends we have discussed in technology, production, communications, and culture, further devastates the politicians' ability to make vital decisions. Accustomed to juggling a few well-organized and clearly organized constituencies, they suddenly find themselves besieged. On all sides, countless new constituencies, fluidly organized, demand simultaneous attention to real but narrow and unfamiliar needs.

Specialized demands flood in to legislatures and bureaucracies through every crack, with every mailbag and messenger, over the transom and under the door. This tremendous pile-up of demands leaves no time for deliberation. Furthermore, because society is changing at an accelerating pace and a decision delayed may be far worse than no decision at all, everyone demands instant response. Congress, as a result, is kept so busy, according to Representative N. Y. Mineta, a California Democrat, that "guys meet each other coming and going. It doesn't allow for a coherent train of thought."

Circumstances differ from country to country, but what does *not* differ is the revolutionary challenge posed by the Third Wave to obsolete Second Wave institutions—too slow to keep up with the pace of change and too undifferentiated to cope with the new levels of social and political diversity. Designed for a much slower and simpler society, our institutions are swamped and out of synch. Nor can this challenge be met by merely tinkering with the rules. For it strikes at that most basic assumption of Second Wave political theory: the concept of representation.

Thus the rise of diversity means that, although our political systems are theoretically founded on majority rule, it may be impossible to form a majority even on issues crucial to survival. In turn, this collapse of consensus means that more and more governments are *minority* governments, based on shifting and uncertain coalitions.

The missing majority makes a mockery of standard democratic rhetoric. It forces us to question whether, under the convergence of speed and diversity, any constituency can ever be "represented." In a mass industrial society, when people and their needs were fairly uniform and basic, consensus was an attainable goal. In a de-massified society, we not only lack national purpose, we also lack regional, statewide, or citywide purpose. The diversity in any congressional district or parliamentary constituency, whether in France or Japan or Sweden, is so great that its "representative" cannot legitimately claim to speak for a consensus. He or she cannot represent the general will for the simple reason that there is none. What, then, happens to the very notion of "representative democracy"?

To ask this question is not to attack democracy. (We shall shortly see how the Third Wave opens the way to an enriched and enlarged democracy.) But it makes one fact inescapably plain: not only our Second Wave institutions but the very assumptions on which they were based are obsolete.

Built to the wrong scale, unable to deal adequately with transnational problems, unable to deal with interrelated problems, unable to keep up with the accelerative drive, unable to cope with the high levels of diversity, the overloaded, obsolete political technology of the industrial age is breaking up under our very eyes.

THE DECISIONAL IMPLOSION

Too many decisions, too fast, about too many strange and unfamiliar problems—not some imagined "lack of leadership"—explain the gross incompetence of political and governmental decisions today. Our institutions are reeling from a decisional implosion.

Working with out-of-date political technology, our capacity for effective governmental decision-making is deteriorating rapidly. "When all the decisions had to be made in the White House," wrote William Shawcross in *Harper's* magazine, discussing the Nixon-Kissinger Cambodian policy, "there was little time for considering fully any one of them." In fact, the White House is so squeezed for decisions—on everything from air pollution, hospital costs, and nuclear power to the elimination of hazardous toys (!)—that one presidential adviser confided to me, "We are all suffering from future shock here!"

Nor are the executive agencies much better off. Each department is crushed under the mounting decision load. Each is compelled to enforce countless regulations and to generate vast numbers of decisions daily, under tremendous accelerative pressures.

Thus, a recent investigation of the U.S. National Endowment for the Arts found that its council spent all of four and a half minutes considering each class of grant applications. "The number of applications . . . have far outstripped the ability of the NEA to make quality decisions," the report declared.

Few good studies of this decisional logjam exist. One of the best is Trevor Armbrister's analysis of the 1968 *Pueblo* incident involving the capture of a U.S. spy ship by the North Koreans and a dangerous showdown between the two countries. According to Armbrister, the Pentagon official who performed the "risk evaluation" on the *Pueblo* mission, and approved it, had only a few hours to appraise the risks of 76 different proposed military missions. The official subsequently refused to estimate how much time he had actually spent considering the *Pueblo*.

But, in a revealing quote cited by Armbrister, a Defense Intelligence Agency official explained: "The way it probably worked . . . is that he got the book on his desk one morning at nine o'clock with orders to return it by noon. That book is the size of a Sears, Roebuck catalogue. It would be a physical impossibility for him to study each mission in detail." Nevertheless, under the pressure of time, the risk on the *Pueblo* mission was termed "minimal." On average, if the DIA agent is correct, each military mission evaluated that morning received less than two and a half minutes' consideration. No wonder things don't work.

Pentagon officials, for example, have lost track of $30 billion in foreign weapons orders and do not know whether this reflects colossal errors in accounting, or a failure to bill the purchasers for the full amounts due, or whether the money was dribbled away on other things entirely. This multibillion-dollar bungle, according to a Department of Defense comptroller, has the "lethal potential of a loose cannon rolling around our deck." He confesses, "The sad fact is that we don't really know how big this [confusion] really is. It will probably be five years before we'll be able to sort [it all] out." And if the Pentagon, with its computers and surefire information systems, is becoming too large and complex to manage properly, as may well be the case, what about the government as a whole?

The old decision-making institutions increasingly mirror the disarray in the outside world. Carter adviser Stuart Eizenstat speaks of "the fragmentation of society into interest groups" and the corresponding "fragmentation of congressional authority into subgroups." Faced with this new situation, a president can no longer easily impose his will on Congress.

Traditionally, an incumbent president could cut a deal with half a dozen elderly and powerful committee chairmen, and expect them to deliver the votes necessary to approve his legislative program. Today congressional committee chairmen and women can no more deliver the votes of the junior members of Congress than the AFL-CIO or the Catholic Church can deliver the votes of their followers. Unfortunate as it may seem to old-timers and hard-pressed presidents, people—including members of Congress—are doing more of their own thinking, and taking orders less submissively. All this makes it impossible, however, for Congress, as presently structured, to devote sustained attention to any issue or to respond quickly to the nation's needs.

Referring to the "frenetic schedule," a report by the Congressional Clearinghouse on the Future summarizes the situation vividly: "Increasing complexity and speed-of-light crises, such as votes in one week on gas deregulation, Rhodesia, the Panama Canal, a new Department of Education, food stamps, AMTRAK authorization, solid waste disposal, and endangered species, are turning Congress, once a center for careful and thoughtful debate . . . into the laughing stock of the nation."

Obviously, political processes vary from one industrial country to the next, but similar forces are at work on all of them. "The United States is not the only country that seems confused and stagnant," declares *U.S. News & World Report.* "Take a look at the Soviet Union. . . . No response to U.S. nuclear-arms-control proposals. Long delays in negotiating trade agreements with both socialist and capitalist nations. Confused treatment of French President Giscard d'Estaing during a state visit. Indecision over the Mideast policy. Contradictory calls for West Europe's Communists to confront and cooperate with home governments. . . . Even in a one-party system it is almost impossible to project firm policies—or respond quickly on complex issues."

In London a member of Parliament tells us that central government is "grossly overloaded," and Sir Richard Marsh, a former Cabinet minister, now head of the British Newspaper Publishers Association, declares that "the Parliamentary structure has remained relatively unchanged over the past 250 years and it's just not geared to the sort of managerial decision-making necessary today. . . . The whole thing is totally ineffectual," he says, and the "Cabinet is not much better."

What about Sweden, with its shaky coalition government barely able to resolve the nuclear issue that has torn the country apart for nearly a decade? Or Italy, with its terrorism and recurrent political crises—unable even to form a government for six months?

What we confront is a new and menacing truth. The political shudders and crises we face cannot be solved by leaders—strong or weak—so long as those leaders are compelled to operate through inappropriate, broken down, overloaded institutions.

A political system must not only be able to make and enforce decisions; it must operate on the right scale, it must be able to integrate disparate policies, it must be able to make decisions at the right speed, and it must both reflect and respond to the diversity of society. If it fails on any of these points it courts disaster. Our problems are no longer a matter of "left-wing" or "right-wing," "strong leadership" or "weak." The decision system itself has become a menace.

The truly astonishing fact today is that our governments continue to function at all. No corporation president would try to run a large company with a table of organization first sketched by the quill pen of some eighteenth-century ancestor whose sole managerial experience consisted of running a farm. No sane pilot would attempt to fly a supersonic jet with the antique navigation and control instruments available to Blériot or Lindbergh. Yet this is approximately what we are trying to do politically.

The rapid obsolescence of our Second Wave political systems, in a world bristling with nuclear weapons and poised delicately on the edge of economic or ecological collapse, creates an extreme threat for the entire society—not merely for the "outs" but for the "ins," not merely for the poor but for the rich, and for the non-industrial parts of the world as well. For the immediate danger to all of us lies not so much in the calculated uses of power by those who have it, as in the uncalculated side effects of decisions ground out by politico-bureaucratic decision machines so dangerously anachronistic that even the best of intentions can eventuate in murderous outcomes.

Our so-called "contemporary" political systems are copied from models invented before the advent of the factory system—before canned food, refrigeration, gaslight, or photography, before the Bessemer furnace or the introduction of the typewriter, before the invention of the telephone, before Orville and Wilbur Wright took wing, before the automobile and the airplane shrunk distance, before radio and television began working their alchemy on our minds, before Auschwitz industrialized death, before nerve gas and nuclear missiles, before computers, copying machines, birth control pills, transistors, and lasers. They were designed in an intellectual world that is almost unimaginable—a world that was pre-Marx, pre-Darwin, pre-Freud and pre-Einstein.

This, then, is the single most important political issue facing us: the obsolescence of our most basic political and governmental institutions.

As we are jolted by crisis after crisis, aspiring Hitlers and Stalins will crawl from the wreckage and tell us that the time has come to solve our problems by throwing away not only our obsolete institutional hulks but our freedom as well. As we race into the Third Wave era, those of us who want to expand human freedom will not be able to do so by simply defending our existing institutions. We shall—like America's founding parents two centuries ago—have to invent new ones.

28

TWENTY-FIRST
CENTURY
DEMOCRACY

To the Founding Parents:

You are the revolutionists dead. You are the men and
women, the farmers, merchants, artisans, lawyers, printers,
pamphleteers, shopkeepers, and soldiers who together created
a new nation on the distant shores of America. You include
the fifty-five who came together in 1787 to hammer out, during a broiling summer in Philadelphia, that astonishing
document called the Constitution of the United States. You
are the inventors of a future that became my present.

That piece of paper, with the Bill of Rights added in 1791,
is clearly one of the stunning achievements of human history.
I, like so many others, am continually forced to ask myself
how you managed—how you were able, in the midst of bitter
social and economic turmoil, under the most immediate
pressures—to muster so much awareness of the emerging future. Listening to the distant sounds of tomorrow, you sensed
that a civilization was dying and a new one was being born.

I conclude you were driven to it—were compelled, carried
along by the tidal force of events, fearing the collapse of an
ineffectual government paralyzed by inappropriate principles
and obsolete structures.

Seldom has so majestic a piece of work been done by men
of such sharply divergent temperaments—brilliant, antago-
nistic, and egotistic men—men passionately committed to
diverse regional and economic interests, yet so upset and
outraged by the terrible "inefficiencies" of an existing government as to draw together and propose a radically new one
based on startling principles.

Even now these principles move me, as they have moved countless millions around the planet. I confess it difficult for me to read certain passages of Jefferson or Paine, for example, without being brought to the edge of tears by their beauty and meaning.

I want to thank you, the revolutionary dead, for having made possible for me a half-century of life as an American citizen under a government of laws, not men, and particularly for that precious Bill of Rights, which has made it possible for me to think, to express unpopular views, however foolish or mistaken at times—indeed, to write what follows without fear of suppression.

For what I now must write can all too easily be misunderstood by my contemporaries. Some will no doubt regard it as seditious. Yet it is a painful truth I believe you would have quickly grasped. For the system of government you fashioned, including the very principles on which you based it, is increasingly obsolete, and hence increasingly, if inadvertently, oppressive and dangerous to our welfare. It must be radically changed and a new system of government invented—a democracy for the twenty-first century.

You knew, better than we today, that no government, no political system, no constitution, no charter or state is permanent, nor can the decisions of the past bind the future forever. Nor can a government designed for one civilization cope adequately with the next.

You would have understood, therefore, why even the Constitution of the United States needs to be reconsidered, and altered—not to cut the federal budget or to embody this or that narrow principle, but to expand its Bill of Rights, taking account of threats to freedom unimagined in the past, and to create a whole new structure of government capable of making intelligent, democratic decisions necessary for our survival in a new world.

I come with no easy blueprint for tomorrow's constitution. I mistrust those who think they already have the answers when we are still trying to formulate the questions. But the time has come for us to imagine completely novel alternatives, to discuss, dissent, debate, and design, from the ground up, the democratic architecture of tomorrow.

Not in a spirit of anger or dogmatism, not in a sudden impulsive spasm, but through the widest consultation and peaceful public participation, we need to join together to reconstitute America.

You would have understood this need. For it was one of your generation—Jefferson—who, in mature reflection, declared: "Some men look at constitutions with sanctimonious reverence and deem them like the ark of the covenant, too sacred to be touched. They ascribe to the men of the preceding age a wisdom more than human, and suppose what they did to be beyond amendment. . . . I am certainly not an advocate for frequent and untried changes in laws and constitutions . . . But I also know that laws and institutions must go hand in hand with the progress of the human mind. . . . As new discoveries are made, new truths disclosed, and manners and opinions change with the change of circumstances, institutions must advance also, and keep pace with the times."

For this wisdom, above all, I thank Mr. Jefferson, who helped create the system that served us so well for so long, and that now must, in its turn, die and be replaced.

Alvin Toffler
Washington, Connecticut

An imaginary letter . . . Surely in many nations there must be others who, given the opportunity, would express similar sentiments. For the obsolescence of many of today's governments is not some secret I alone have discovered. Nor is it a disease of America alone.

The fact is that building a new civilization on the wreckage of the old involves the design of new, more appropriate political structures in many nations at once. This is a painful yet necessary project that is mind-staggering in scope and will no doubt take decades to complete.

In all likelihood it will require a protracted battle to radically overhaul—or even scrap—the United States Congress, the Central Committees and Politburos of the Communist industrial states, the House of Commons and the House of Lords, the French Chamber of Deputies, the Bundestag, the Diet, the giant ministries and entrenched civil services of many nations, the constitutions and court systems—in short, much of the unwieldy and increasingly unworkable apparatus of supposedly representative governments.

Nor will this wave of political struggle stop at the national level. Over the months and decades ahead, the entire "global law machine"—from the United Nations at one end to the local city or town council at the other—will eventually face a mounting, ultimately irresistible, demand for restructuring.

All these structures will have to be fundamentally altered,

not because they are inherently evil, nor even because they are controlled by this or that class or group, but because they are increasingly unworkable—no longer fitted to the needs of a radically changed world.

This task will involve multimillions of people. If this radical overhaul is rigidly resisted it may well trigger bloodshed. How peaceful the process turns out to be will depend on many factors, therefore—on how flexible or intransigent the existing elites prove to be, on whether the change is accelerated by economic collapse, on whether or not external threats and military interventions occur. Clearly the risks are great.

Yet the risks of *not* overhauling our political institutions are even greater, and the sooner we begin, the safer we all will be.

To build workable governments anew—and to carry out what may well be the most important political task of our lifetimes—we will have to strip away the accumulated clichés of the Second Wave era. And we will have to rethink political life in terms of three key principles.

Indeed, these may well turn out to be the root principles of the Third Wave governments of tomorrow.

MINORITY POWER

The first, heretical principle of Third Wave government is that of minority power. It holds that majority rule, the key legitimating principle of the Second Wave era, is increasingly obsolete. It is not majorities but minorities that count. And our political systems must increasingly reflect that fact.

Expressing the beliefs of his revolutionary generation, it was Jefferson, once again, who asserted that governments must behave with "absolute acquiescence in the decisions of the majority." The United States and Europe—still at the dawn of the Second Wave era—were just beginning the long process that would turn them eventually into industrial mass societies. The concept of majority rule perfectly fitted the needs of these societies.

Today, as we have seen, we are leaving industrialism behind and rapidly becoming a de-massified society. In consequence it is growing increasingly difficult—often impossible—to mobilize a majority or even a governing coalition. This is why Italy for six months and the Netherlands for five have gone without governments altogether. In the United States, says political scientist Walter Dean Burnham of the Massachusetts Institute of Technology, "I don't see the basis for any positive majority on anything today."

Because their legitimacy depended on it, Second Wave elites always claimed to speak on behalf of the majority. The United States government was "of . . . by . . . and for the people." The Soviet Communist Party spoke for the "working class." Mr. Nixon claimed to represent America's "Silent Majority." And in the United States today, neo-Conservative intellectuals attack the demands of newly vocal minorities like Blacks, feminists, or Chicanos, and claim to speak for the interests of the great, solid, moderate, middle-of-the-road majority.

Headquartered in the great universities of the Northeast and think tanks in Washington, seldom setting foot in places like Marietta, Ohio, or Salina, Kansas, academic neo-Conservatives apparently regard "Middle America" as a great, unwashed, uniform "mass" of more or less ignorant, anti-intellectual blue-collar hardhats and white-collar suburbanites. Yet these groups are far less uniform or monochromatic than they appear to intellectuals and politicians at a distance. Consensus is just as hard to find in Middle America as elsewhere—at best it is flickering, intermittent, and limited to a very few issues. The neo-Conservatives may well be cloaking their anti-minority policies in the mantle of a mythical, rather than real, majority.

Indeed, the very same is true at the other end of the political spectrum. In many Western European countries, socialist and communist parties claim to speak for the "working masses." Yet the farther we move beyond industrial mass society, the less tenable the Marxist assumptions. For both masses and classes lose much of their significance in the emerging Third Wave civilization.

In place of a highly stratified society, in which a few major blocs ally themselves to form a majority, we have a configurative society—one in which thousands of minorities, many of them temporary, swirl and form highly novel, transient patterns, seldom coalescing into a 51 percent consensus on major issues. The advance of Third Wave civilization thus weakens the very legitimacy of many existing governments.

The Third Wave also challenges all of our conventional assumptions about the relationship of majority rule to social justice. Here too, as in so many other matters, we are watching a startling historic flip-flop. Throughout the era of

Second Wave civilization the fight for majority rule was humane and liberating. In still-industrializing countries, like South Africa today, it remains so. In Second Wave societies, majority rule almost always meant a fairer break for the poor. For the poor *were* the majority.

Today, however, in countries shaken by the Third Wave, precisely the opposite is often the case. The truly poor no longer necessarily have numbers on their side. In a good many countries they—like everyone else—have become a minority. And barring economic holocaust, they will remain so.

Not only is majority rule, therefore, no longer adequate as a legitimating principle, it is no longer necessarily humanizing or democratic in societies moving into the Third Wave.

Second Wave ideologues routinely lament the breakup of mass society. Rather than seeing in this enriched diversity an opportunity for human development, they attack it as "fragmentation" and "Balkanization" and attribute it to the aroused "selfishness" of minorities. This trivial explanation substitutes effect for cause. For the rising activism of minorities is not the result of a sudden onset of selfishness; it is, among other things, a reflection of the needs of a new system of production which requires for its very existence a far more varied, colorful, open, and diverse society than any we have ever known.

The implications of this fact are enormous. It means, for example, that when the Russians try to suppress the new diversity, or cork up the political pluralism that comes with it, they actually (to use their own jargon) "fetter the means of production"—they slow down the economic and technological transformation of society. And we in the noncommunist world face the same choice: we can either resist the thrust toward diversity, in a futile last-ditch effort to save our Second Wave political institutions, or we can acknowledge diversity and change those institutions accordingly.

The former strategy can only be implemented by totalitarian means and must result in economic and cultural stagnation; the latter leads toward social evolution and a minority-based twenty-first-century democracy.

To reconstitute democracy in Third Wave terms, we need to jettison the frightening, but false, assumption that increased diversity automatically brings increased tension and conflict in society. Indeed, the exact reverse can be true. Conflict in society is not only necessary, it is, within limits, desirable. But if one hundred men all desperately want the same brass ring, they may be forced to fight for it. On the other hand, if each of the hundred has a different objective, it is far more rewarding for them to trade, cooperate, and form symbiotic relationships. Given appropriate social arrangements, diversity can make for a secure and stable civilization.

It is the lack of appropriate political institutions today that unnecessarily sharpens conflict between minorities to the knife-edge of violence. It is the lack of such institutions that makes minorities intransigent. It is the absence of such institutions that makes the majority harder and harder to find.

The answer to these problems is not to stifle dissent or to charge minorities with selfishness (as though the elites and their experts are not similarly self-interested). The answer lies in imaginative new arrangements for accommodating and legitimating diversity—new institutions that are sensitive to the rapidly shifting needs of changing and multiplying minorities.

The rise of a de-massified civilization brings to the surface deep, unsettling questions about the future of majority rule and the entire mechanistic system of voting to express preferences. Some day, future historians may look back on voting and the search for majorities as an archaic ritual engaged in by communicational primitives. Today, however, in a dangerous world, we cannot afford to delegate total power to anyone, we cannot surrender even the weak popular influence that exists under majoritarian systems, and we cannot allow tiny minorities to make vast decisions that tyrannize all other minorities.

This is why we must drastically revise the crude Second Wave methods by which we pursue the elusive majority. We need new approaches designed for a democracy of minorities—methods whose purpose is to reveal differences rather than to paper them over with forced or fake majorities based on exclusionary voting, sophistic framing of the issues, or rigged electoral procedures. We need, in short, to modernize the entire system so as to strengthen the role of diverse minorities yet permit them to form majorities.

To do so, however, will require radical changes in many of our political structures—starting with the very symbol of democracy, the ballot box.

In Second Wave societies, voting to determine the popular will provided an important source of feedback for the ruling elites. When conditions for one reason or another became in-

tolerable for the majority, and 51 percent of the voters registered their pain, the elites could, at a minimum, shift parties,
alter policies, or make some other accommodation.

Even in yesterday's mass society, however, the 51 percent
principle was a decidedly blunt, purely quantitative instrument. Voting to determine the majority tells us nothing about
the quality of people's views. It can tell us how many people,
at a given moment, want X, but not how badly they want it.
Above all, it tells us nothing about what they would be
willing to trade off for X—crucial information in a society
made up of many minorities.

Nor does it signal us when a minority feels so threatened,
or attaches such life-and-death significance to a single issue,
that its views should perhaps receive more than ordinary
weight.

In a mass society these well-known weaknesses of majority
rule were tolerated because, among other things, most minorities lacked strategic power to disrupt the system. In today's
finely wired society, in which all of us are members of minority groups, that is no longer true.

For a de-massified Third Wave society the feedback systems of the industrial past are entirely too crude. Thus we
will have to use voting, and the polls, in a radically new way.

Instead of seeking simpleminded yes-or-no votes, we need
to identify potential trade-offs with questions like: "If I give
up my position on abortion, will you give up yours on defense spending or nuclear power?" or "If I agree to a small
additional tax on my personal income next year, to be ear-
marked for your project, what will you offer in return?"

In the world we are racing into, with its rich communications technologies, there are many ways for people to register
such views without ever setting foot in a polling booth. And
there are also ways, as we shall see in a moment, to feed
these into the political decision-making process.

We may also want to de-rig our voting laws to eliminate
anti-minority biases. There are many ways to do this. One
quite conventional method would be to adopt some variant of
cumulative voting, as used by many corporations today to
protect the rights of minority stockholders. Such methods allow voters to register not only their preferences but the intensity and rank order of their choices.

We shall almost certainly have to discard our obsolete
party structures, designed for a slowly changing world of
mass movements and mass merchandising, and invent tem-

porary modular parties that service changing configurations of minorities—plug-in/plug-out parties of the future.

We may need to appoint "diplomats" or "ambassadors" whose job is not to mediate between countries but between minorities within each country. We may have to create quasi-political institutions to help minorities—whether professional, ethnic, sexual, regional, recreational, or religious—to form and break alliances more quickly and easily.

We may, for instance, need to provide arenas in which different minorities, on a rotating, perhaps even random basis, are brought together to trade problems, negotiate deals, and resolve disputes. If doctors, motorcyclists, computer programmers, Seventh-Day Adventists and Gray Panthers were brought together, with assistance from facilitators trained in issue clarification, priority setting, and dispute resolution, surprising and constructive alliances might be formed.

At a minimum, differences could be exposed and the basis for political barter explored. Such measures will not (and should not) eliminate all conflict. But they can elevate social and political strife to a more intelligent, potentially constructive level—especially if they are linked to long-range goal setting.

Today the very complexity of issues inherently provides a greater variety of bargainable points. Yet the political system is not structured to take advantage of this fact. Potential alliances and trades go unnoticed—thus unnecessarily raising tensions between groups while further straining and overloading existing political institutions.

Finally, we may well need to empower minorities to regulate more of their own affairs, and encourage them to formulate long-range goals. We might, for example, help the people in a specific neighborhood, in a well-defined subculture, or in an ethnic group, to set up their own youth courts under the supervision of the state, disciplining their own young people rather than relying on the state to do so. Such institutions would build community and identity, and contribute to law and order, while relieving the overburdened government institutions of unnecessary work.

We may, however, find it necessary to go far beyond such reformist measures. To strengthen minority representation in a political system designed for a de-massified society, we may even eventually have to elect at least some of our officials in the oldest way of all: by drawing lots. Thus some people have seriously suggested choosing members of the legislature or parliament of the future the way we choose jury members or armies today.

Theodore Becker, professor of law and political science at the University of Hawaii, asks, "Why is it that important life and death decisions can be made by the people serving on . . . juries, but decisions on how much money should be spent on child care centers and defense spending are reserved for their 'representatives'?"

Charging that the existing political arrangements systematically shortchange minorities, Becker, a constitutional authority, reminds us that while nonwhites make up some 20 percent of the American population, they held (in 1976) only 4 percent of the seats in the House of Representatives and only 1 percent in the Senate. Women, who comprise over 50 percent of the population, held only 4 percent of the seats in the House—and none in the Senate. Poor people, young people, smart but inarticulate people, and many other groups are similarly disadvantaged. Nor is this merely true of the United States. In the Bundestag only 7 percent of the seats are held by women, and similar biases are evident in many other governments as well. Such gross distortions cannot but blunt the sensitivity of the system to the needs of underrepresented groups.

Says Becker, "Between 50 and 60 percent of the American Congress should be chosen at random from the American people in much the same way they are pressed into military service through drafts when they are deemed necessary." Startling as the suggestion is at first blush, it forces us to consider seriously whether randomly chosen representatives would (or could) do worse than those chosen through today's methods.

If we let ourselves imagine freely for the moment, we can come up with many other surprising alternatives. Indeed, we now have the techniques necessary to choose far more truly representative samples than the jury system or the draft, with their preferential exclusions, ever did. We can build an even more innovative congress or parliament of the future—and do it, paradoxically, with less disturbance of tradition.

We don't have to pick a group of people by lot and literally trundle them off, like so many Mr. Smiths, to Washington, London, Bonn, Paris, or Moscow. We could, if we chose, keep our elected representatives, allowing them, however, to cast only 50 percent of the votes on any issue, while turning the other 50 percent of the votes over to a random sample of the public.

By using computers, advanced telecommunications, and polling methods, it has become simple not only to select a random sample of the public but to keep updating that sample from day to day and to provide it with up-to-the-minute information on the issues at hand. When a law is needed, the full complement of traditionally elected representatives, meeting together in the traditional way, under the Capitol dome or in Westminster, or in the Bundeshaus or the Diet building, could deliberate and discuss, amend and frame the legislation.

But when the time for decision arrived, the elected representatives would cast only 50 percent of the votes, while the current random sample—who are not in the capital but geographically dispersed in their own homes or offices—would electronically cast the remaining 50 percent. Such a system would not merely provide a more representative process than "representative" government ever did, but would strike a devastating blow at the special interest groups and lobbies who infest the corridors of most parliaments. Such groups would have to lobby the people—not just a few elected officials.

Going even further, one might conceive of voters in a district electing not a single individual as their "representative" but, in fact, a random sample of the population. This random sample could "serve in Congress" directly—as though it were a person—its opinions statistically tallied into votes. Or it could choose a single individual, in turn, to "represent" *it*, instructing him or her how to vote. Or . . .

The permutations offered by the new communications technologies are endless and extraordinary. Once we recognize that our present institutions and constitutions are obsolete and we begin searching for alternatives, all sorts of breathtaking political options, never before possible, suddenly open up to us. If we are to govern societies racing into the twenty-first century, we ought to at least consider the technologies and conceptual tools made available to us by the twentieth.

What is important here are not these specific suggestions. By working at it together, we can no doubt come up with far better ideas, easier to implement, less drastic in design. What is important is the general path we choose to travel. We can fight a losing battle to suppress or submerge today's burgeoning minorities, or we can reconstitute our political systems to accommodate the new diversity. We can continue to use the crude, bludgeonlike tools of Second Wave political systems, or we can design sensitive new tools for a minority-based democracy of tomorrow.

As the Third Wave de-massifies the old Second Wave mass society, its pressures, I believe, will dictate that choice. For if politics were "pre-majoritarian" during the First Wave, and "majoritarian" during the Second, they are likely to be "mini-majoritarian" tomorrow—a fusion of majority rule with minority power.

SEMI-DIRECT DEMOCRACY

The second building-block of tomorrow's political systems must be the principle of "semi-direct democracy"—a shift from depending on representatives to representing ourselves. The mixture of the two is semi-direct democracy.

The collapse of consensus, as we have already seen, subverts the very concept of representation. Without agreement among the voters back home, whom does the representative really "represent"? At the same time, legislators have come to rely increasingly on staff support and on outside experts for advice in shaping the laws. British M.P.s are notoriously weak *vis-à-vis* the Whitehall bureaucracy because they lack adequate staff support, thus shifting more power away from Parliament to the unelected civil service.

The United States Congress, in an effort to counterbalance the influence of the executive bureaucracy, has created its own bureaucracy—a Congressional Budget Office, an Office of Technology Assessment, and other necessary agencies and appendages. Thus the congressional staff has grown from 10,700 to 18,400 in the past decade. But this has merely transferred the problem from extramural to intramural. Our elected representatives know less and less about the myriad measures on which they must decide, and are compelled to rely more and more on the judgment of others. The representative no longer even represents him- or herself.

More basically, parliaments, congresses, or assemblies were places in which, theoretically, the claims of rival minorities could be reconciled. Their "representatives" could make trade-offs for them. With today's antiquated, blunt-edged political tools, no legislator can even keep track of the many grouplets he or she nominally represents, let alone broker or trade effectively for them. And the more overloaded the American Congress or the German Bundestag or the Norwegian Storting becomes, the worse this situation grows.

This helps explain why single-issue political pressure groups become intransigent. Seeing limited opportunity for sophisticated trading or reconciliation through Congress or the legislatures, their demands on the system become non-negotiable. The theory of representative government as the ultimate broker collapses too.

The breakdown of bargaining, the decision crunch, the worsening paralysis of representative institutions mean, over the long term, that many of the decisions now made by small numbers of pseudo-representatives may have to be shifted back gradually to the electorate itself. If our elected brokers can't make deals for us, we shall have to do it ourselves. If the laws they make are increasingly remote from or unresponsive to our needs, we shall have to make our own. For this, however, we shall need new institutions and new technologies as well.

The Second Wave revolutionaries who invented today's basic represento-kit institutions were well aware of the possibilities of direct as against representative democracy. There were traces of direct, do-it-yourself democracy in the French revolutionary constitution of 1793. American revolutionists knew all about New England town halls and small-scale organic consensus formation. In Europe later on, Marx and his followers frequently invoked the Paris Commune as a model of citizen participation in the making and execution of the laws. But the shortcomings and limitations of direct democracy were also well-known—and, at that time, more persuasive.

"In *The Federalist* two objections to such an innovation were raised," write McCauley, Rood, and Johnson, authors of a proposal for a National Plebiscite in the United States. "First, direct democracy allowed for no check or delay on temporary and emotional public reactions. And second, the communications of that day could not handle the mechanics."

These are legitimate problems. How would a frustrated and inflamed American public in the mid-1960's, for example, have voted on whether or not to drop a nuclear bomb on Hanoi? Or a West German public, furious at the Baader-Meinhof terrorists, on a proposal to set up camps for "sympathizers"? What if Canadians had held a plebiscite over

Quebec the week after René Lévesque took power? Elected representatives are presumed to be less emotional and more deliberative than the public.

The problem of overemotional public response, however, can be overcome in various ways, such as requiring a cooling-off period or second vote before implementation of major decisions taken via referendum or other forms of direct democracy.

One imaginative approach is suggested by an actual program carried out by the Swedes in the mid-1970's when the government called upon the public to participate in the formulation of a national energy policy. Recognizing that most citizens lacked adequate technical knowledge of the various energy options, from solar or nuclear or geothermal, the government created a ten-hour course on energy and invited any Swede who took it, or an equivalent course, to make formal recommendations to the government.

Simultaneously, trade unions, adult education centers, and parties from one end of the political spectrum to the other all created their own ten-hour courses. It was hoped that as many as 10,000 Swedes would participate. To everyone's surprise, some 70,000 to 80,000 flocked to discussions in homes and community facilities—the equivalent (on the American scale) of some 2,000,000 citizens trying to think together about a national problem. Similar systems could easily be employed to cancel out the objections to "overemotionalism" in referenda or other forms of direct democracy.

The other objection can also be met. For the old communication limitations no longer stand in the way of expanded direct democracy. Spectacular advances in communications technology open, for the first time, a mind-boggling array of possibilities for direct citizen participation in political decision-making.

Not long ago, I had the pleasure of keynoting an historic event—the world's first "electronic town hall"—over the Qube cable TV system in Columbus, Ohio. Using this interactive communications system, residents of a small Columbus suburb actually took part via electronics in a political meeting of their local planning commission. By pushing a button in their living rooms they were able to vote instantly on proposals relating to such practical issues as local zoning, housing codes, and proposed highway construction. They were able not only to vote yes or no but to participate in the discussion and speak up on the air. They were even able, by

push button, to tell the chairperson when to move on to the
next point on the agenda.

This is only the first, most primitive indication of tomorrow's potential for direct democracy. Using advanced computers, satellites, telephones, cable, polling techniques, and
other tools, an educated citizenry can, for the first time in
history, begin making many of its own political decisions.

The issue is not either/or. It is not a question of direct democracy *versus* indirect, representation by self *versus*
representation by others.

For both systems have advantages, and there are highly
creative, as yet underutilized, ways to combine direct citizen
participation with "representation" into a new system of
semi-direct democracy.

We might, for example, decide to hold a referendum on a
controversial issue like nuclear development, as California
and Austria have already done. Instead of turning the ultimate decision over directly to the voters, however, we might
still want a representative body—Congress for example—to
debate and ultimately decide the issue.

Thus if the public voted pro-nuclear, a certain predesignated "bundle" of votes could be delivered to the pro-nuclear
advocates in Congress. They might, on the strength of the
public response, be given an automatic "edge" of 10 percent
or 25 percent in Congress itself, depending on the strength of
the pro vote in the plebescite. In this way, there is no purely
automatic implementation of the citizens' wishes, but these
wishes do carry some specific weight. This is a variation of
the National Plebescite proposal mentioned above.

Many other imaginative arrangements can be invented to
combine direct and indirect democracy. Right now members
of Congress and most other parliaments or legislatures set up
their own committees. There is no way for citizens to force
lawmakers to create a committee to deal with some neglected
or highly controversial issue. But why couldn't voters be empowered directly, through petition, to compel a legislative
body to set up committees on topics the public—not the lawmakers—deems important?

I hammer away at these "blue-sky" proposals not because I
unhesitatingly favor them but merely to underscore the more
general point: There are powerful ways to open and democratize a system that is now near breakdown and in which
few, if any, feel adequately represented. But we must begin
thinking outside the worn grooves of the past 300 years. We

can no longer solve our problems with the ideologies, the models, or the left-over structures of the Second Wave past.

Fraught with uncertain implications, such novel proposals warrant careful local experimentation before we apply them on a broad scale. But however we may feel about this or that suggestion, the old objections to direct democracy are growing weaker at precisely the time that the objections to representative democracy are growing stronger. Dangerous or even bizarre as it may seem to some, semi-direct democracy is a moderate principle that can help us design workable new institutions for the future.

DECISION DIVISION

Opening the system to more minority power and allowing citizens to play a more direct role in their own governance are both necessary, but carry us only part of the way. The third vital principle for the politics of tomorrow is aimed at breaking up the decisional logjam and putting decisions where they belong. This, not simply reshuffling leaders, is the antidote to political paralysis. I call it "decision division."

Some problems cannot be solved on a local level. Others cannot be solved on a national level. Some require action at many levels simultaneously. Moreover, the appropriate place to solve a problem doesn't stay put. It changes over time.

To cure today's decision logjam resulting from institutional overload, we need to divide up the decisions and reallocate them—sharing them more widely and switching the site of decision-making as the problems themselves require.

Today's political arrangements violate this principle wildly. The problems have shifted, but the decisional power hasn't. Thus, too many decisions are still concentrated, and the institutional architecture is most elaborate at the national level. By contrast, not enough decisions are being made at the transnational level, and the structures needed there are radically underdeveloped. In addition, too few decisions are left for the subnational level—regions, states, provinces, and localities, or non-geographical social groupings.

Many of the problems that national governments are grappling with are, as we saw earlier, simply beyond their grasp—too big for any individual government. We desperately need, therefore, to invent imaginative new institutions at the transnational level to which many decisions can be transferred. We cannot, for example, expect to cope with the far-reaching power of the transnational corporation—itself a rival of the nation-state—through strictly national legislation. We need new transnational arrangements to establish, and if need be enforce, codes of corporate conduct on the global level.

Take the issue of corruption. American corporations selling abroad are badly hurt by U.S. anti-bribery laws because other governments permit, indeed encourage, their manufacturers to bribe foreign customers. Similarly, multinational companies pursuing responsible environmental policies will continue to face unfair competition from firms that do not, so long as there is no adequate infrastructure at the transnational level.

We need transnational food stockpiles and "hot spot" disaster-relief organizations. We need new global agencies to provide early warnings of impending crop failures, to level out swings in the price of key resources, and to control the wildfire spread of the arms trade. We need consortia and teams of nongovernmental organizations to attack various global problems.

We need far better agencies to regulate out-of-control currencies. We shall need alternatives to—or complete transformations of—the IMF, the World Bank, COMECON, NATO, and other such institutions. We shall have to invent new agencies to spread the advantages and limit the side effects of technology. We must speed the construction of strong transnational agencies for governing outer space and the oceans. We shall have to overhaul the ossified, bureaucratic United Nations from the ground floor up.

At the transnational level, we are as politically primitive and underdeveloped today as we were at the national level when the industrial revolution began 300 years ago. By transferring some decisions "up" from the nation-state, we not only make it possible to act effectively at the level where many of our most explosive problems lie, but simultaneously reduce the decision burden at the overloaded center—the nation-state. Decision division is essential.

But moving decisions up the scale is only half the task. It is also clearly necessary to move a vast amount of decision-making downward from the center.

Again the issue is not "either/or" in character. It is not decentralization versus centralization in some absolute sense. The issue is rational reallocation of decision-making in a system that has overstressed centralization to the point at which new information flows are swamping the central decision-makers.

Political decentralization is no guarantee of democracy—quite vicious localist tyrannies are possible. Local politics are frequently even more corrupt than national politics. Moreover, much that passes for decentralization—Nixon's government reorganization, for example—is a kind of pseudo-decentralization for the benefit of the centralizers.

Nevertheless, with all these cavils, there is no possibility of restoring sense, order, and management "efficiency" to many governments without a substantial devolution of central power. We need to divide the decision load and shift a significant part of it downward.

This is not because romantic anarchists want us to restore "village democracy" or because angry affluent taxpayers want to cut back on welfare services to the poor. The reason is that any political structure—even with banks of IBM 370 computers—can handle only so much information and no more, can produce only a certain quantity and quality of decisions, and that the decisional implosion has now pushed governments beyond this breakpoint.

Moreover, the institutions of government must correlate with the structure of the economy, the information system, and other features of the civilization. Today, little noticed by conventional economists, we are witnessing a fundamental decentralization of production and economic activity. Indeed, it may well be that the basic unit is no longer the national economy.

What we are seeing, as I have already stressed, is the emergence of very large, more and more cohesive regional sub-economies within each national economy. These sub-economies are increasingly different from one another, with sharply divergent problems. One may be suffering from unemployment, another from labor shortages. Wallonia in Belgium protests the shift of industry to Flanders; the Rocky Mountain states refuse to become "energy colonies" of the West Coast.

Uniform economic policies stamped out in Washington, Paris, or Bonn have radically different impacts on these sub-economies. The same national economic policy that aids one region or industry increasingly damages others. For this reason, a great deal of economic policy making must be denationalized and decentralized.

At the corporate level, we not only see efforts at internal

decentralization (witness a recent meeting of 280 of General Motors' top executives who spent two days talking about how to break up bureaucratic patterns and move more decisions out from the center), but also an actual geographical decentralization as well. *Business Week* reports a "geographical tilt of the U.S. economy, as more companies build plants and move offices to less readily accessible parts of the country."

All this reflects, in part, a gigantic shift of information flows in society. We are, as noted earlier, undergoing a fundamental decentralization of communications, as the power of the central networks wanes. We are seeing a stunning proliferation of cable, cassette, computers, and private electronic mail systems, all pushing in the same decentralist direction.

It is not possible for a society to decentralize economic activity, communications, and many other crucial processes without also, sooner or later, being compelled to decentralize government decision-making as well.

All this demands more than cosmetic changes in existing political institutions. It implies massive battles over control of budgets, taxes, land, energy, and other resources. Decision division will not come easily—but it is absolutely unavoidable in country after overcentralized country.

So far we have looked at decision division as a way to break the bottleneck, to unfreeze the political system so it can function again. But there is far more here than greets the eye. For application of this principle does more than reduce the decision load of national governments. In a fundamental way, it changes the very structure of elites, bringing them into conformity with the needs of the emerging civilization.

THE EXPANDING ELITES

The concept of "decision load" is crucial to any understanding of democracy. All societies require a certain quantity and quality of political decisions in order to function. Indeed, each society has its own unique decision structure. The more numerous, varied, frequent, and complex the decisions required to run it, the heavier its political "decision load." And the way this load is shared fundamentally influences the level of democracy in society.

In preindustrial societies, where the division of labor was rudimentary and change was slow, the number of political or administrative decisions actually required to keep things running was minimal. The decision load was small. A tiny, semi-educated, unspecialized ruling elite could more or less run things without help from below, carrying the entire decision load by itself.

What we now call democracy burst forth only when the decision load suddenly swelled beyond the capacity of the old elite to handle it. The arrival of the Second Wave, bringing expanded trade, a greater division of labor, and a leap to a whole new level of complexity in society, caused the same kind of decision implosion in its time that the Third Wave is causing today.

As a result, the decisional capabilities of the old ruling groups were overwhelmed, and new elites and sub-elites had to be recruited to cope with the decision load. Revolutionary new political institutions had to be designed for that purpose.

As industrial society developed, becoming ever more complex, its integrating elites, the "technicians of power," were in their turn continually compelled to recruit new blood to help them carry the expanding decision load. It was this invisible but inexorable process that drew the middle class more and more into the political arena. It was this expanded need for decision-making that led to an ever-wider franchise and created more niches to be filled from below.

Many of the bitterest political battles in Second Wave countries—the struggle of American Blacks for integration, of British trade unionists for equal educational opportunity, of women for their political rights, the hidden class warfare in Poland or the Soviet Union—concerned the distribution of these new slots in the elite structures.

At any given time, however, there was a definite limit to how many additional people could be absorbed into the governing elites. And this limit was essentially fixed by the size of the decision load.

Despite the Second Wave society's meritocratic pretensions, therefore, whole subpopulations were screened out on racist, sexist, and similar grounds. Periodically, whenever the society jumped to a new level of complexity and the decision load swelled, the excluded groups, sensing the new opportunities, would intensify their demand for equal rights, the elites would open the doors a bit wider, and the society would experience what seemed like a wave of further democratization.

If this picture is even roughly correct, it tells us that the extent of democracy depends less on culture, less on Marxist class, less on battlefield courage, less on rhetoric, less on political will, than on the decision load of any society. A heavy load will ultimately have to be shared through wider democratic participation. So long as the decision load of the social system expands, therefore, democracy becomes not a matter of choice but of evolutionary necessity. The system cannot run without it.

What all this further suggests is that we may well be on the edge of another great democratic leap forward. For the very implosion of decision-making now overwhelming our presidents, prime ministers, and governments unlocks—for the first time since the industrial revolution—exciting prospects for a radical expansion of political participation.

THE COMING SUPER-STRUGGLE

The need for new political institutions exactly parallels our need for new family, educational, and corporate institutions as well. It is deeply wired into our search for a new energy base, new technologies, and new industries. It reflects the upheaval in communications and the need to restructure relationships with the non-industrial world. It is, in short, the political reflection of accelerating changes in all these different spheres.

Without seeing these connections, it is impossible to make sense of the headlines around us. For today the single most important political conflict is no longer between rich and poor, between top-dog and underdog ethnic groups, or even between capitalist and communist. The decisive struggle today is between those who try to prop up and preserve industrial society and those who are ready to advance beyond it. This is the super-struggle for tomorrow.

Other, more traditional conflicts between classes, races, and ideologies will not vanish. They may even—as suggested earlier—grow more violent, especially if we undergo large-scale economic turbulence. But all these conflicts will be absorbed into, and play themselves out within, the super-struggle as it rages through every human activity from art and sex to business and balloting.

This is why we find *two* political wars raging around us simultaneously. At one level, we see a politics-as-usual clash of Second Wave groups battling each other for immediate gain. At a deeper level, however, these traditional Second

Wave groups cooperate to oppose the new political forces of the Third Wave.

This analysis explains why our existing political parties, as obsolete in structure as in ideology, seem so much like blurry mirror images of one another. Democrats and Republicans, as well as Tories and Labourites, Christian Democrats and Gaullists, Liberals and Socialists, Communists and Conservatives, are all—despite their differences—parties of the Second Wave. All of them, while jockeying for power within it, are basically committed to preserving the dying industrial order.

Put differently, the most important political development of our time is the emergence in our midst of two basic camps, one committed to Second Wave civilization, the other to Third. One is tenaciously dedicated to preserving the core institutions of industrial mass society—the nuclear family, the mass education system, the giant corporation, the mass trade union, the centralized nation-state, and the politics of pseudorepresentative government. The other recognizes that today's most urgent problems, from energy, war, and poverty to ecological degradation and the breakdown of familial relationships, can no longer be solved within the framework of an industrial civilization.

The lines between these two camps are not yet sharply drawn. As individuals, most of us are divided, with a foot in each. Issues still appear murky and unconnected to one another. In addition, each camp is composed of many groups pursuing their own narrowly perceived self-interest, without any overarching vision. Nor does either side have a monopoly on moral virtue. There are decent people ranged on both sides. Nevertheless, the differences between these two subsurface political formations are enormous.

The defenders of the Second Wave typically fight against minority power; they scoff at direct democracy as "populism"; they resist decentralization, regionalism, and diversity; they oppose efforts to de-massify the schools; they fight to preserve a backward energy system; they deify the nuclear family, pooh-pooh ecological concerns, preach traditional industrial-era nationalism, and oppose the move toward a fairer world economic order.

By contrast, the forces of the Third Wave favor a democracy of shared minority power; they are prepared to experiment with more direct democracy; they favor both transnationalism and a fundamental devolution of power. They call for a crack-up of the giant bureaucracies. They demand a renewable and less centralized energy system. They want to legitimate options to the nuclear family. They fight for less standardization, more individualization in the schools. They place a high priority on environmental problems. They recognize the necessity to restructure the world economy on a more balanced and just basis.

Above all, while the Second Wave defenders play the conventional political game, Third Wave people are suspicious of all political candidates and parties (even new ones), and sense that decisions crucial to our survival cannot be made within the present political framework.

The Second Wave camp still includes a majority of the nominal power-holders in our society—politicians, businessmen, union leaders, educators, the heads of the mass media—although many of them are deeply troubled by the inadequacies of the Second Wave world view. Numerically, the Second Wave camp undoubtedly still claims the unthinking support of most ordinary citizens as well, despite fast-spreading pessimism and disillusionment in their ranks.

The advocates of the Third Wave are more difficult to characterize. Some head up major corporations while others are zealous anticorporate consumerists. Some are worried environmentalists; others are more concerned with the issues of sexual roles, family life, or personal growth. Some focus almost exclusively on the development of alternative energy forms; others are mainly excited by the democratic promise of the communications revolution.

Some are drawn from the Second Wave "right," others from the Second Wave "left"—free marketeers and libertarians, neo-socialists, feminists, and civil rights activists, former flower children and the straightest of straight-arrows. Some are long-time activists in the peace movement; others have never marched or demonstrated for anything in their lives. Some are devoutly religious, others diehard atheists.

Scholars may debate at length over whether or not so seemingly formless a group constitutes a "class," or whether, if so, it is the "new class" of educated information-workers, intellectuals, and technicians. Surely many of those in the Third Wave camp are college-educated, middle-class people. Surely many are directly engaged in the production and dissemination of information, or in the services, and, by twisting the term, one could probably call them a class. Yet to do so obscures more than it reveals.

For among the key groups pressing toward the de-massification of industrial society are relatively uneducated ethnic minorities, many of whose members hardly fit the picture of the attaché-case-carrying knowledge-worker.

How does one characterize women struggling to break out of confining roles in Second Wave society? How, moreover, does one describe the fast-expanding millions in the self-help movement? And what about many of the "psychologically oppressed"—the millions of victims of the epidemic of loneliness, the broken families, the single parents, the sexual minorities—who do not fit neatly into the notion of class? Such groups come from virtually all the ranks and occupations of society, yet are important sources of strength for the Third Wave movement.

Indeed even the term *movement* can be misleading—partly because it implies a higher level of shared consciousness than so far exists, partly because Third Wave people properly mistrust all the mass movements of the past.

Nevertheless, whether they comprise a class, a movement, or simply a changing configuration of individuals and transient groups, all of them share a radical disillusionment with the old institutions—a common recognition that the old system is now broken beyond repair.

The super-struggle between these Second and Third Wave forces, therefore, cuts like a jagged line across class and party, across age and ethnic groups, sexual preferences and subcultures. It reorganizes and religns our political life. And, instead of a harmonious, classless, conflict-free, non-ideological future society, it points toward escalating crises and deep social unrest in the near-term future. Pitched political battles will be waged in many nations, not merely over who will benefit from what is left of industrial society but over who participates in shaping, and ultimately controlling, its successor.

This sharpening super-struggle will decisively influence the politics of tomorrow and the very form of the new civilization. It is as a partisan in this super-struggle, aware or unwitting, that each of us plays a role. That role can be either destructive or creative.

A DESTINY TO CREATE

Some generations are born to create, others to maintain a civilization. The generations who launched the Second Wave of historic change were compelled, by force of circumstance, to be creators. The Montesquieus, Mills, and Madisons invented most of the political forms we still take for granted. Caught between two civilizations, it was their destiny to create.

Today in every sphere of social life, in our families, our schools, our businesses and churches, in our energy systems and communications, we face the need to create new Third Wave forms, and millions of people in many countries are already beginning to do so. Nowhere, however, is obsolescence more advanced or more dangerous than in our political life. And in no field today do we find less imagination, less experiment, less willingness to contemplate fundamental change.

Even people who are daringly innovative in their own work—in their law offices or laboratories, their kitchens, classrooms, or companies—seem to freeze up at any suggestion that our Constitution or political structures are obsolete and in need of radical overhaul. So frightening is the prospect of deep political change, with its attendant risks, that the status quo, however surrealistic and oppressive, suddenly seems like the best of all possible worlds.

Conversely we have in every society a fringe of pseudorevolutionaries, steeped in obsolete Second Wave assumptions, for whom no proposed change is radical enough. Archaeo-Marxists, anarcho-romantics, right-wing fanatics, armchair guerrillas, and honest-to-God terrorists, dreaming of totalitarian technocracies or medieval utopias. Even as we speed into a new historical zone, they nurse dreams of revolution drawn from the yellowed pages of yesterday's political tracts.

Yet what lies ahead as the super-struggle intensifies is not a replay of any previous revolutionary drama—no centrally directed overthrow of the ruling elites by some "vanguard party" with the masses in tow; no spontaneous, supposedly cathartic, mass uprising triggered by terrorism. The creation of new political structures for a Third Wave civilization will not come in a single climactic upheaval, but as a consequence of a thousand innovations and collisions at many levels in many places over a period of decades.

This does not rule out the possibility of violence along the way to tomorrow. The transition from First Wave to Second Wave civilization was one long blood-drenched drama of wars, revolts, famines, forced migrations, coups d'état, and calamities. Today the stakes are much higher, the time shorter, the acceleration faster, the dangers even greater.

Much depends on the flexibility and intelligence of today's

elites, sub-elites and super-elites. If these groups prove to be as shortsighted, unimaginative, and frightened as most ruling groups in the past, they will rigidly resist the Third Wave and thereby escalate the risks of violence and their own destruction.

If, by contrast, they flow with the Third Wave, if they recognize the need for a broadened democracy, they in fact can join in the process of creating a Third Wave civilization, just as the most intelligent First Wave elites anticipated the coming of a technologically based industrial society and joined in its creation.

Most of us know, or sense, how dangerous a world we live in. We know that social instability and political uncertainties can unleash savage energies. We know what war and economic cataclysm mean, and we remember how often totalitarianism has sprung from noble intentions and social breakdown. What most people seem to ignore, however, are the positive differences between present and past.

Circumstances differ from country to country, but never in history have there been so many reasonably educated people, collectively armed with so incredible a range of knowledge. Never have so many enjoyed so high a level of affluence, precarious perhaps, yet ample enough to allow them time and energy for civic concern and action. Never have so many been able to travel, to communicate, and to learn so much from other cultures. Above all, never have so many had so much to gain by guaranteeing that the necessary changes, though profound, be made peacefully.

Elites, no matter how enlightened, cannot by themselves make a new civilization. The energies of whole peoples will be required. But those energies are available, waiting to be tapped. Indeed if we, particularly in the high-technology countries, took as our explicit goal for the next generation the creation of wholly new institutions and constitutions, we could release something far more powerful even than energy: the collective imagination.

The sooner we begin to design alternative political institutions based on the three principles described above—minority power, semi-direct democracy, and decision division—the better our chances for a peaceful transition. It is the attempt to block such changes, not the changes themselves, that raises the level of risk. It is the blind attempt to defend obsolescence that creates the danger of bloodshed.

This means that to *avoid* violent upheaval we must begin

now to focus on the problem of structural political obsolescence around the world. And we must take this issue not merely to the experts, the constitutionalists, lawyers, and politicians, but to the public itself—to civic organizations, trade unions, churches, to women's groups, to ethnic and racial minorities, to scientists and housewives and businessmen.

We must, as a first step, launch the widest public debate over the need for a new political system attuned to the needs of a Third Wave civilization. We need conferences, television programs, contests, simulation exercises, mock constitutional conventions to generate the broadest array of imaginative proposals for political restructuring, to unleash an outpouring of fresh ideas. We should be prepared to use the most advanced tools available to us, from satellites and computers to video-disc and interactive television.

No one knows in detail what the future holds or what will work best in a Third Wave society. For this reason we should think not of a single massive reorganization or of a single revolutionary, cataclysmic change imposed from the top, but of thousands of conscious, decentralized experiments that permit us to test new models of political decision-making at local and regional levels in advance of their application to the national and transnational levels.

But, at the same time, we must also begin to build a constituency for similar experimentation—and radical redesign—of institutions at the national and transnational levels as well. Today's widespread disillusionment, anger, and bitterness against the world's Second Wave governments can either be whipped into fanatic frenzy by demagogues calling for authoritarian leadership or it can be mobilized for the process of democratic reconstruction.

By launching a vast process of social learning—an experiment in anticipatory democracy in many nations at once—we can head off the totalitarian thrust. We can prepare millions for the dislocations and dangerous crises that lie before us. And we can place strategic pressure on existing political systems to accelerate the necessary changes.

Without this tremendous pressure from below, we should not expect many of today's nominal leaders—presidents and politicians, senators and central committee members—to challenge the very institutions that, no matter how obsolete, give them prestige, money, and the illusion, if not the reality, of power. Some unusual, far-seeing politicians or officials will lend their early support to the struggle for political transformation. But most will move only when the demands from outside are irresistible or when the crisis is already so advanced, and so close to violence, that they see no alternative.

The responsibility for change, therefore, lies with us. We must begin with ourselves, teaching ourselves not to close our minds prematurely to the novel, the surprising, the seemingly radical. This means fighting off the idea-assassins who rush forward to kill any new suggestion on grounds of its impracticality, while defending whatever now exists as practical, no matter how absurd, oppressive, or unworkable it may be. It means fighting for freedom of expression—the right of people to voice their ideas, even if heretical.

Above all, it means starting this process of reconstruction now, before the further disintegration of existing political systems sends the forces of tyranny jackbooting through the streets, and makes impossible a peaceful transition to Twenty-first Century Democracy.

If we begin now, we and our children can take part in the exciting reconstitution not merely of our obsolete political structures, but of civilization itself.

Like the generation of the revolutionary dead, we have a destiny to create.

ACKNOWLEDGMENTS

In writing *The Third Wave* I have drawn on several streams of information. The first and most conventional comes from the reading of books, journals, newspapers, reports, documents, magazines, and monographs from many countries. The second has its source in interviews with change-makers around the world. I have visited them in their laboratories, executive suites, schoolrooms, and studios, and they have been generous with their time and ideas. They range from family experts and physicists to Cabinet members and prime ministers.

Finally, in traveling I have relied on what I trust is an alert eye and ear. Often, firsthand experience or chance conversation sheds a revealing light on abstraction. A taxi driver in a Latin American capital told me more than all his government's cheery statistics: When I asked him why his people were not doing something to protest a soaring inflation rate, he simply imitated the stuttering of a machine gun.

It is clearly impossible for me to thank individually all those who have been helpful. However, three friends, Donald F. Klein, Harold L. Strudler, and Robert I. Weingarten, have taken the trouble to read the entire manuscript and offer perceptive criticism and advice.

In addition, Lea Guyer Gordon and Eleanor Nadler Schwartz, who are certainly among the best and and most professional editorial researchers, fact-checked the completed manuscript to weed out inaccuracies. Mrs. Schwartz stayed through the final, harried days to give good-humored, beyond-the-call-of-duty assistance during preparation of the manuscript for the publisher. Special thanks, too, are owed to Betsy Cenedella of William Morrow for her excellent round-the-clock copyreading and correction. Finally, to Karen Toffler, who helped format the conceptual entries in the index and committed them to the computer/word processor during the long, late hours of the night.

Needless to say, I alone remain responsible for any errors that may have crept into these pages, despite our best efforts to avoid them.

NOTES

Bracketed [ ] *numbers indicate items listed in the accompanying Bibliography. Thus, in the Notes [1] will stand for the first item in the Bibliography:* Boucher, François. *20,000 Years of Fashion.*

PAGE	CHAPTER ONE
9	On the origins of agriculture see Cipolla, [103], p. 18.
9	For various terms used to describe the emerging society see Brzezinski, [200], and Bell, [198]. Bell traces the term "post-industrial" back to its use by an English writer named Arthur J. Penty in 1917. For Marxist terminology see [211].
10	I wrote of "super-industrial civilization" in [502] and [150].
13	Tribes without agriculture are described in, among other sources, Niedergang, [95]; also Cotlow, [74].

	CHAPTER TWO
22	For sea trade see [504], p. 3. Geoffrey Blainey's perceptive book analyzes the effects of isolation and great continental distances on the development of Australia.
22	Greek factories are noted briefly in [237], p. 40.
22	On early oil drilling see [155], p. 30.
22	Ancient bureaucracies are described in [17], Vol. 1, p. 34.
22	The Alexandrian steam engine is mentioned in a chapter by Ralph Linton in [494], p. 435; also, Lilley, [453], pp. 35–36.

22	On pre-industrial civilization, see [171], p. 15.
23	On Japan's Meiji Era: [262], p. 307.
25	Estimates of Europe's horse and oxen population are in [244], p. 257.
25	Newcomen's steam engine is described in Lilley, [453], p. 94, and Cardwell, [433], p. 69.
26	Vitruvius is quoted in [171], p. 23.
26	Precision instruments: [438], Preface and Introduction.
26	The role of machine tools is discussed in [237], p. 41.
27	Early trade is colorfully pictured in [259], pp. 64–71.
27	Advances in mass distribution are described in [29], p. 85. For the rise of the A&P chain, see pp. 159 and 162.
28	On early multigenerational households see [191], Vol. 1, p. 64.
28	The immobility of the agricultural family is described in [508], p. 196.
29	Andrew Ure is quoted in [266], pp. 359–360.
29	Nineteenth-century schooling in the U.S. is discussed in [528], pp. 450–451.
29	The increasing length of the school year is from *Historical Statistics of the United States*, p. 207.
29	For compulsory schooling see [528], p. 451.
29	The mechanics' declaration is quoted in [492], p. 391.
30	Dewing is from [14], p. 15.
30	The number of U.S. corporations before 1800 is cited in [101], p. 657.
30	The immortality of corporations was established by Chief Justice John Marshall in *Dartmouth College v. Woodward*, 4 Wheat. 518, 4 L.Ed. 629 (1819).
30	Socialist corporations are the subject of a paper by Leon Smolinski in *Survey* (London), Winter 1974.
30	In the socialist industrial nations of Eastern Europe, as in the Soviet Union, the dominant form is the so-called "production enterprise"—more accurately described as the "socialist corporation." The production enterprise is typically owned by the state rather than by private investors, and it is subject to direct political controls in the framework of a planned economy. But, like the capitalist corporation, its prime functions are to concentrate capital and organize mass production. Moreover, like its capitalist counterparts, it shapes the lives of its employees; it exerts informal but powerful political influence; it creates a new managerial elite; it relies on bureaucratic administrative methods; it rationalizes production. Its position in the social order was—and is—no less central.
32	The evolution of the orchestra is described in Sachs, [7], p. 389, and in Mueller, [6].

33   Postal history is the subject of Zilliacus's book, [56]; see p. 21.

33   Edward Everett's paean to the Post Office is in [385], p. 257.

33   The world avalanche of mail is described in [41], p. 34. See also the *UNESCO Statistical Yearbook* for 1965, p. 482.

34   On the telephone and telegraph, see Singer, [54], pp. 18–19. Also, Walker, [268], p. 261.

34   Telephone statistics are from [39], p. 802.

35   Servan-Schreiber is quoted from [52], p. 45.

36   An account of utopian socialism is found in [476], Chapter 8.

CHAPTER THREE

38   The role of the market is discussed in Polanyi's seminal work, [115], p. 49.

38   The Tlatelolco marketplace is vividly pictured in [246], p. 133.

38   The pepper merchant's comments are found in [259], pp. 64–71.

38   Braudel is from his magnificent work [245], Vol. 1, pp. 247, 425.

39   On the fusion of production and consumption, see [265], p. 30.

39   The social and political role of the consumer is brilliantly explored in Horace M. Kallen's forgotten work, [61], p. 23.

42   I am indebted to my friend Bertrand de Jouvenel for the observation that the same person is pulled in opposite psychological directions by the roles of worker and consumer.

44   On objectivity-subjectivity: the idea was first suggested to me by a reading of Zaretsky [196].

CHAPTER FOUR

47   Theodore Vail's story is in [50]. Vail was a formidable figure whose career tells much about early industrial development.

47   Frederick Winslow Taylor's influence is described in Friedmann, [79], and Dickson, [525]. Also, the Taylor Collection, Stevens Institute of Technology. Lenin's view of Taylorism is from [79], p. 271.

47   Standardized intelligence testing is described in [527], pp. 226–227.

48   On the repression of minority languages, see Thomas, [290], p. 31. Also "Challenge to the Nation-State," *Time* (European edition), October 27, 1975.

48   The French Revolution's actions with respect to the metric system and a new calendar are described in Morazé, [260], pp. 97–98; and Klein, [449], p. 117.

48   Privately minted money and the standardization of currency are from [144], pp. 10, 33.

48   On one-price policy see [29].

49   *The Advantages of the East India Trade* is cited in [138], Vol. I, p. 330.

49   Adam Smith's well-known observations about the pin maker are in [149], pp. 3–7.

      Smith attributed the startling increase in productivity to the increased dexterity developed by the worker who specialized, to the time saved by not switching from task to task, and to the improvements that the specialized worker could make in his or her tools. But Smith clearly recognized what lay at the heart of things: the market. Without a market to connect producer to consumer, who would need or want 48,000 pins a day? And, Smith continued, the bigger the marketplace the more specialization could be expected.

      Smith was right.

50   Henry Ford's cool calculations are from his autobiography [442], pp. 108–109.

50   The number of occupations is from the *Dictionary of Occupational Titles* published by the U.S. Department of Labor, 1977.

50   Lenin: from Christman, [474], p. 137.

51   The synchronizing role of work songs is from [8], p. 18.

52   E. P. Thompson's quote is from "Time, Work-Discipline, and Industrial Capitalism," *Past and Present* (London), No. 38.

53   Stan Cohen made this observation in a review of David J. Rothman's book *The Discovery of the Asylum*, in *New Society* (London), February 7, 1974.

54   European auto production figures are from [126], p. 3917.

54   Concentration of the aluminum, cigarette, and breakfast food industries is from Standard & Poor's *Industry Surveys*, 1978, 1979. Concentration in the beer industry is from "New Survival Plan for Olympia Beer," *The New York Times*, May 15, 1979.

54   German industrial concentration is documented in [126], p. 3972.

54   The concentrative process in industry produced its mirror image in the labor movement. As unions in many countries faced larger and larger monopolies and trusts they, too, consolidated. After the turn of the century the Industrial Workers of the World—the so-called Wobblies—expressed the concentrative drive in a campaign for what they called "O.B.U."—One Big Union.

54   For concentration as seen by Marxists, see Leon M. Herman, "The Cult of Bigness in Soviet Economic Planning," [126], p. 4349 +.
        This paper includes a well-known quotation from the American socialist Daniel De Leon who, at the close of the last century, argued that "the ladder by which humanity has risen to civilization is the progression in the methods of production, the growing power of the productive instruments. The trust occupies the very top of this ladder. The social storm of our times rages precisely around the trust. The capitalist class is trying to retain it for its own exclusive use. The middle class is trying to break it up, thereby delaying the course of civilization. The proletariat will set for itself the goal to preserve it, improve it, and make it accessible to everyone."

54   The N. Lelyukhina article is reprinted in [126], p. 4362+.

55   The Matsushita song is quoted from "The Japanese Dilemma" by Willard Barber, *Survey* (London), Autumn 1972.

55   AT&T's employee figures are from [39], p. 702.
        French work force statistics are in [126], p. 3958.
        On Soviet concentration and Stalin's "gigantomania," see [126], pp. 4346–4352.
        As this is written, the Soviets are racing to complete the world's biggest truck-manufacturing installation, which will require a whole new city of 160,000 with a complex of plants and conveyors extending over forty square miles, an area nearly twice the size of Manhattan island. The truck complex is described in Hedrick Smith's vivid report, [484], pp. 58, 59, 106, and 220. Smith says the Soviets "have a Texan's love for exaggerated bigness that outdoes the American love of bigness, much as the Soviet national economic growth ethic has surpassed the now-shaken American faith in the automatic blessings of economic growth."

56   With respect to the pursuit of GNP, an amusing fantasy suggests that women undertake to do each other's housework and pay each other for it. If every Susie Smith paid every Barbara Brown one hundred dollars

a week for caring for her home and children, while receiving an equivalent amount for providing the same services in return, the impact on the Gross National Product would be astounding. If 50 million American housewives engaged in this nonsense transaction it would add about 10 percent to the U.S. GNP overnight.

57   Capitalization of American plants in 1850 and railroads' management innovations are from Alfred D. Chandler, Jr. and Stephen Salisbury, "Innovations in Business Administration," in [454], pp. 130, 138–141.

57   On the case for a strong central government see [389], p. 20.

58   In his book *The Imperial Presidency* [398], Schlesinger says, "It must be said that historians and political scientists, this writer among them, contributed to the rise of the presidential mystique."

58   Governments' response to political protest is in [482], pp. 189–190.

58   Marx is quoted from Christman, [474], p. 359; Engels, p. 324.

59   The rise of central banking in Britain, France, and Germany is chronicled by Galbraith in [127], pp. 31–35 and 39–41.

59   Hamilton's struggle to create a national bank is recounted in [254], p. 187.

CHAPTER FIVE

63   Blumenthal is quoted in Korda [22], p. 46.

63   The rise of the integrational elite in the socialist nations is the subject of a vast literature. For Lenin's views see [480], pp. 102–105; Trotsky is from [475], p. 30, and [487], pp. 138, 249; Djilas was jailed for his *The New Class*, [332]; Tito's own complaint about technocracy is in "Social Stratification and Sociology in the Soviet Union" by Seymour Martin Lipset and Richard B. Dobson, in *Survey* (London), Summer 1973.

Since James Burnham's pathbreaking book, *The Managerial Revolution* [330], appeared in 1941, a whole literature has sprung up describing the climb to power of this new elite of integrators. See *Power Without Property* by A. A. Berle, Jr. In *The New Industrial State*, John Kenneth Galbraith further elaborated the idea, coining the term "technostructure" to describe the new elite.

CHAPTER SIX

71   For Newton's synthesis, see [433], p. 48.
71   De La Mettrie is quoted from *Man a Machine*, [302], p. 93.
71   Adam Smith on the economy as a system is from "Operating Rules for Planet Earth" by Sam Love, in *Environmental Action*, November 24, 1973; Smith's quote is from his posthumously published work [148], p. 60.
71   Madison is quoted from [388].
71   For Jefferson see [392], p. 161.
71   Lord Cromer is cited in [96], p. 44.
71   On Lenin, see [480], p. 163. Trotsky is quoted from [486], pp. 5, 14.
73   Bihari's remark is from his book [347], pp. 102–103.
73   For V. G. Afanasyev see [344], pp. 186–187.
74   The number of elected public officials is given in [334], p. 167.

CHAPTER SEVEN

79   The Abaco take-over attempt is described in "The Amazing New-Country Caper" by Andrew St. George, in *Esquire,* February 1975.
80   Finer is from "The Fetish of Frontiers," in *New Society* (London), September 4, 1975.
80   On patchwork of small communities in empires, see Braudel, [245], Vol. 2, Chapter IV. Also Bottomore, [490], p. 155.
80   Voltaire's complaint is cited in Morazé, [260], p. 95.
81   On Germany's 350 mini-states: [285], p. 13.
81   Various definitions of the nation-state are from [277], pp. 19 and 23.
81   Ortega: [341], p. 171.
82   For the dates of the early railroads see [55], p. 13.
83   Morazé: [260], p. 154.
83   For Mazlish see [454], p. 29.

CHAPTER EIGHT

85   Foodstuffs from abroad: [119], p. 11.
85   Chamberlain and Ferry are quoted in Birnie, [100], pp. 242–243.
86   On Dervishes and other victims of the machine gun see John Ellis's first-rate monograph, [436].

86   Re Ricardo on specialization [77], Introduction, pp.
          xii–xiii.
87   The value of world trade is from [119], p. 7.
89   The margarine story is told by Magnus Pyke in [461],
          pp. 7 +.
90   On the enslavement of the Amazonian Indians see Cot-
          low, [74], pp. 5–6. The subject is treated in greater
          detail in Bodard, [70].
90   Woodruff is quoted from [119], p. 5.
91   On European political control: [497], p. 6.
91   World trade between 1913 and 1950 is described in
          [109], pp. 222–223.
92   Creation of the IMF: [109], p. 240.
92   For U.S. gold holdings and World Bank loans to less
          developed countries, see [87], pp. 63, 91.
94   On Lenin's views, see [89]; also Cohen, [73], pp. 36,
          45–47. The Lenin arguments and the Senin quote are
          from [146], pp. 22–23.
94   The political struggle in China today can be seen as a
          conflict over whether it, too, should make or buy.
          One side, loosely called the radicals, favors self-suffi-
          ciency and internal development; the other favors
          wide trade with the outside world. The notion of self-
          sufficiency will attract greater attention among non-
          industrial nations as they increasingly come to
          recognize the hidden costs of entering into an inte-
          grated world economy constructed to serve the needs
          of the Second Wave nations.
95   On Soviet purchases of Guinean bauxite see "Success
          Breeds Success," in *The Economist*, December 2,
          1978; Soviet purchases from India, Iran, and Afghan-
          istan are detailed in "How Russia Cons the Third
          World," in *To the Point* (Sandton, Transvaal, South
          Africa), February 23, 1979. This South African
          news-weekly, despite its evident bias, provides heavy
          coverage of the Third World, especially Africa.
95   For Soviet imperialism, see also Edward Crankshaw in
          [80], p. 713.
95   Sherman is quoted from [147], pp. 316–317.
95   For a report on COMECON, see "COMECON Blues"
          by Nora Beloff, in *Foreign Policy*, Summer 1978.

CHAPTER NINE

100   On our "dominion" over nature, see Clarence J.
          Glacken, "Man Against Nature: An Outmoded
          Concept," in [162], pp. 128–129.
100   For Darwin and for early theories of evolution, see Hy-

man, [306], pp. 26–27, 56. On social Darwinism: pp. 432–433.

101   Views on progress of Liebniz, Turgot, et al. are examined by Charles Van Doren in [184], General Introduction.

102   Heilbroner is quoted from [234], p. 33.

103   Time measurement units are described in "Time, Work-Discipline, and Industrial Capitalism," by E. P. Thompson in *Past and Present*, Number 38. See also Cardwell, [433], p. 13.

104   The adoption of Greenwich Mean Time is described in [519], p. 115.

104   Buddhist and Hindu views of time are examined in [509], p. 248.

104   For Needham on cyclical time in the East see [515], p. 47.

104   Whitrow from [520], p. 18.

105   The use of space by pre–First Wave civilization is described by Morrill in [514], pp. 23–24.

106   On peasant hut location, see "The Shaping of England's Landscape" by John Patten, in *Observer Magazine* (London), April 21, 1974.

106   Hale is quoted from [252], p. 32.

107   The differing lengths of a rood are from [449], pp. 65–66.

107   For navigation prizes, refer to Coleman, [506], pp. 103–104.

107   On the metric system: [449], pp. 116, 123–125.

108   Clay's observations are from [505], pp. 46–47.

108   The S-curve patterns are described by John Patten in *Observer Magazine*, cited above.

109   On people seen as part of nature, see Clarence J. Glacken in [162], p. 128.

109   For Democritus' atomism see Munitz, [310], p. 6; Asimov, [427], Vol. 3, pp. 3–4; and Russell, [312], pp. 64–65.

109   Mo Ching and Indian atomism are from Needham, [455], pp. 154–155.

110   For atomism as a minority view: [312], pp. 72–73.

110   Descartes: [303], p. 19.

110   Dubos is quoted from [159], p. 331.

112   On Aristotle see Russell, [312], p. 169.

112   The yin and yang: Needham, [456], pp. 273–274.

112   Newton is quoted from his "Fundamental Principles of Natural Philosophy" in [310], p. 205.

113   Laplace is from Gellner, [305], p. 207.

113   Holbach is quoted in Matson [309], p. 13.

CHAPTER TEN

116 On the industrial revolution in Europe see Williams, [118]; Polanyi, [115]; and Lilley, [453].

117 The place of accounts in a process of social development is described by D. R. Scott in [145].

118 For 'First and Second Wave smells: [420], pp. 125–131.

118 Old manners are in Norbert Elias's remarkable *The Civilizing Process*, [250], pp. 120, 164.

119 First Wave communities as social "cesspools" are described in Hartwell, [107], and Hayek, [108].

119 Vaizey is from "Is This New Technology Irresistible?" in the *Times Educational Supplement* (London), January 5, 1973.

120 The Larner review appeared in *New Society* (London), January 1, 1976.

124 American Management Association survey summarized in [33], pp. 1–2.

CHAPTER ELEVEN

128 For educational test scores, see "Making the Grade: More Schools Demand A Test of Competency for Graduating Pupils," *The Wall Street Journal*, May 9, 1978.

128 On remarriage rates: *Social Indicators 1976*, U.S. Department of Commerce report, p. 53.

128 Counterfeminists are described in "Anti-ERA Evangelist Wins Again," *Time*, July 3, 1978.

128 Conflict between homosexuals and Anita Bryant is reported in "How Gay Is Gay?," *Time*, April 23, 1979.

CHAPTER TWELVE

131 Rathbone's decision on oil prices, and the formation of OPEC are described in [168], Chapter 8.

132 Nuclear plants at Seabrook and Grohnde: [163], pp. 7, 88.

132 Two thirds of the world's energy supply from oil and gas, based on [160], p. 17.

133 On shrinking oil reserves, see "The Oil Crisis is Real This Time," *Business Week*, July 30, 1979.

133 Coal gasification and liquefaction plants are critically described in Commoner, [157], pp. 67–68. See also

"A Desperate Search for Synthetic Fuels," *Business Week*, July 30, 1979.

134   Government subsidies for atomic power are described in [157], p. 65.

134   On terrorism and other dangers involving plutonium, see Thomas Cochran, Gus Speth, and Arthur Tamplin, "Plutonium: An Invitation to Disaster," in [166], p. 102; also Commoner, [157], p. 96.

134   Carr is from [153], p. 7.

135   Texas Instruments' work on photovoltaic cells is described in "Energy: Fuels of the Future," *Time*, June 11, 1979. Role of Solarex is in "The New Business of Harnessing Sunbeams" by Edmund Faltermayer, in *Fortune*, February 1976. See also Energy Conversion Devices in "A New Promise of Cheap Solar Energy," *Business Week*, July 18, 1977.

135   On Soviets in the tropopause: [153], p. 123.

135   Geothermal power developments are described in "The Coming Energy Transition" by Denis Hayes, in *The Futurist*, October 1977.

135   Wave power in Japan is from "Waking Up to Wave Power," *Time*, October 16, 1978.

135   Southern California Edison's power tower: "Energy: Fuels of the Future," *Time*, June 11, 1979.

135   Hydrogen power developments are summarized in "Can Hydrogen Solve Our Energy Crisis?" by Roger Beardwood, in the *Telegraph Sunday Magazine* (London), July 29, 1979.

136   "Redox" is described in "Washington Report," *Product Engineering*, May 1979.

136   On superconductivity see "Scientists Create a Solid Form of Hydrogen," *The New York Times*, March 2, 1979.

136   For a brief discussion of the implications of Tesla waves see *Omni* interview with Alvin Toffler, November 1978.

139   On the transition from Second Wave to Third Wave industries see "The Cross of Lorraine," *Forbes*, April 16, 1979. Britain's nationalized coal, rail, and steel industries are discussed in "The Grim Failure of Britain's Nationalized Industries" by Robert Ball, in *Fortune*, December 1975. *Strukturpolitik* is from "How Schmidt Is Using His Economic Leverage," *Business Week*, July 24, 1978.

140   Rolls-Royce ad was placed by CW Communications, Newton, Mass., in *Advertising and Publishing News*, September 1979.

140   The scope of the home computer business in the spring of 1979 can be judged by *Micro Shopper: The Mi-*

crocomputer Guide, published by MicroAge Whole-sale, Tempe, Ariz. See also "Plugging in Everyman," *Time*, September 5, 1977.

141   Fiber optics in the communications industry are described in "Lightbeams in Glass—Slow Explosion Under the Communications Industry" by Robin Lanier, in *Communications Tomorrow*, November 1976. Fiber optics in the telephone business and the comparison with copper are from an interview with Donald K. Conover, General Manager, Corporate Education, Western Electric Co., Hopewell, N.J.

141   *Science* is quoted from its issue of March 18, 1977.

142   On space shuttle program: "The Shuttle Opens the Space Frontier to U.S. Industry," *Business Week*, August 22, 1977.

142   Urokinase information supplied by Abbott Laboratories, North Chicago, Ill.; Von Puttkamer is quoted in "The Industrialization of Space," *Futurics*, Fall 1977.

142   TRW's identification of alloys is described in "Industry's New Frontier in Space" by Gene Bylinsky, in *Fortune*, January 29, 1979.

143   For Brian O'Leary's studies and the Princeton conferences, see G. K. O'Neill, *Newsletter on Space Studies* June 12, 1977.

143   On protein from the sea, the threatened extinction of marine life, and aquaculture: "The Oceans: World Breadbasket or Breakdown?" by Robert M. Girling, in *Friends Magazine*, February 1977.

144   Raymond is quoted in John P. Craven, "Tropical Oceania: The Newest World," *Problems of Journalism*: Proceedings of the 1977 Convention of the American Society of Newspaper Editors, 1977, p. 364.

144   Minerals in the sea: "Oceanic Mineral Resources" by John L. Mero, in *Futures*, December 1968. See also "The Sea-Bed" by P. N. Ganapati, in *Seminar* (New Delhi), May 1971; and "The Oceans: Wild West Scramble for Control," *Time*, July 29, 1974; and "Seabed Mining Consortia Hope to Raise the Political Anchor," *The Financial Times* (London), August 7, 1979.

144   Drugs from the sea are described in a brochure from the Roche Research Institute of Marine Pharmacology, Dee Why, N.S.W., Australia.

145   For ocean platform technology see "Floating Cities," in *Marine Policy*, July 1977.

145   D. M. Leipziger speaks of "homesteaders" and the "common heritage" argument in "Mining the Deep Seabed," *Challenge*, March-April 1977.

147   On genetics: Howard and Rifkin, [446]; also "Industry

Starts To Do Biology With Its Eyes Open," *The Economist* (London), December 2, 1978.

147   National policies for control of genetic research are outlined in *Draft Information Document on Recombinant DNA*, May 1978, Scientific and Technical Committee of the North Atlantic Assembly.

147   Cetus' president is quoted from [446], p. 190.

147   Official Soviet policy is from *Socialism: Theory and Practice*, a Soviet monthly digest of the theoretical and political press, January 1976.

149   The report to the National Science Foundation, Lawless, [452].

150   On Luddite revolts against machines, see [453], p. 111.

152   The antinuclear campaigns are described in "Crusading Against the Atom," *Time*, April 25, 1977, and "Nuclear Power: The Crisis in Europe and Japan," *Business Week*, December 25, 1978.

152   Appropriate technology is reviewed in [425]; see also Harper and Boyle, [444].

152   An example of the new interest in the airship is the brochure of Aerospace Developments, London; also "Lighter-Than-Air Transport: Is the Revival for Real?" by James Wargo, in *New Engineer*, December 1975.

CHAPTER THIRTEEN

158   Newspaper circulation figures from American Newspaper Publishers Association.

158   On percentage of Americans who read newspapers see 1972 and 1977 *General Social Surveys*, by the National Opinion Research Center, University of Chicago. Newspaper circulation losses are reported in "Newspapers Challenged as Never Before," *Los Angeles Times*, November 26, 1976; see also "Time Inc. Buys Washington Star; It Will Pay Allbritton $20 Million," *The New York Times*, February 4, 1978. For Britain's experience with newspapers see "Newspaper Sales" by Tom Forester, in *New Society* (London), October 16, 1975.

159   Decline in mass magazine circulations detailed in *The Gallagher Report* Supplement to its issue of August 22, 1977.

159   On the proliferation of regional and special-interest magazines, see *Folio* magazine, December 1977.

160   Richard Reeves is quoted from "And Now a Word from God . . ." *Washington Star*, June 2, 1979.

160   Teen-age radio habits are covered in *Radio Facts*, published by Radio Advertising Bureau, New York.

161   CB radio: "Citizens Band: Fad or Fixture" by Leonard M. Cedar in *Financial World*, June 1, 1976. Actual number of CBs in use in 1977, from Radio Research Report, published by the Radio Advertising Bureau, New York. Denial that CB has cut into radio listenership is in press release dated June 20, 1977, from CBS Radio Network. See also Marsteller survey reported in *Broadcasting*, August 15, 1977.

161   *Time*: "The Year That Rain Fell Up," in its issue of January 9, 1978.

162   NBC: "Webs Nailed for 'Stupidity'; Share Seen Dipping 50%" by Peter Warner, in *The Hollywood Reporter*, August 15, 1979.

162   On the expansion of cable TV, see "Cable TV: The Lure of Diversity," *Time*, May 7, 1979; see also *Media Decisions*, January 1978.

164   Satellite distribution of programming is described in "New Flexibility in Programming Envisioned Resulting from Upsurge in Satellite Distribution" by John P. Taylor, in *Television/Radio Age*, February 27, 1978.

164   John O'Connor is quoted from his "TV on the Eve of Drastic Change," *The New York Times*, November 13, 1977.

CHAPTER FOURTEEN

168   Stages of computer development outlined in an interview with Harvey Poppel, March 27, 1978.

169   Expenditures for distributed processing are from International Data Corporation, Stamford, Conn.

169   On rise of personal computers, note "The Electronic Home: Computers Come Home" by Lee Edson, in *The New York Times Magazine*, September 30, 1979.

169   Cost of home computers: "TI Gets Set to Move Into Home Computers," *Business Week*, March 19, 1979.

169   "The Source" is described in materials supplied by Telecomputing Corporation of America, McLean, Va.; also interview with Marshall Graham, vice-president, marketing, October 12, 1979.

170   "Fred the House" appeared in the *Micro Shopper*, published by MicroAge, Tempe, Ariz., Spring 1979.

172   For the "Laws of Robotics," see Isaac Assimov's classic [426].

173   Speech recognition technology is discussed in "Computers Can Talk to You," *The New York Times*, Au-

gust 2, 1978. For companies working on voice data entry see *Random-Access Monthly*, May 1979, a publication of Dean Witter Reynolds Inc., New York. Forecasts about talking computers are evaluated in "Speech Is Another Microelectronics Conquest," *Science*, February 16, 1979.

174 "Weave problems" are described in [462], p. 113.

CHAPTER FIFTEEN

181 For figures on the decline of the manufacturing sector in high-technology nations see the International Labor Organization's *Yearbook of Labour Statistics*, 1961, 1965, 1966, 1975.

181 On manufacturing being farmed out to developing countries, read "Vast Global Changes Challenge Private-Sector Vision" by Frank Vogl, in *Financier*, April 1978; also John E. Ullman, "Tides and Shallows," in [12], p. 289.

182 De-massified production is described in Jacobs, [448], p. 239. Also: "Programmable Automation: The Bright Future of Automation" by Robert H. Anderson, in *Datamation*, December 1972; and A. E. Kobrinsky and N. E. Kobrinsky, "A Story of Production in the Year 2000," in Fedchenko, [205], p. 64.

182 For high-volume goods as percentage of all manufactured goods see "Computer-controlled Assembly" by James L. Nevins and Daniel E. Whitney, in *Scientific American*, February 1978.

182 Short run of one-of-a-kind production is described in "When Will Czechoslovakia Become an Underdeveloped Country" reprinted from the Palach Press, London, in *Critique* (Glasgow), a Journal of Soviet Studies and Socialist Theory, Winter 1976-77. Also, "New Programmable Control Aims at Smaller Tasks," *American Machinist*, September 1976; "The Computer Digs Deeper Into Manufacturing," *Business Week*, February 23, 1976; and "In the Amsterdam Plant, The Human Touch" by Ed Grimm, in *Think*, August 1973.

182 Short-run production in Europe is covered in "Inescapable Problems of the Electronic Revolution," *The Financial Times* (London), May 13, 1976; and "Aker Outlook," *Northern Offshore* (Oslo), November 1976.

183 Pentagon production runs are analyzed in Robert H. Anderson and Nake M. Kamrany, *Advanced Computer-Based Manufacturing Systems for Defense Needs*, published by the Information Sciences Insti-

tute, University of Southern California, September 1973.

183 Japanese car production methods described in correspondence from Jiro Tokuyama, Nomura Research Institute of Technology & Economics, Tokyo, June 14, 1974.

183 Anderson quote is from an interview with author.

185 Canon AE-1 camera: see Report of First Quarter and Stockholders Meeting, Texas Instruments, 1977.

187 On the number of information transactions and the rise in office costs see Randy J. Goldfield. "The Office of Tomorrow *Is* Here Today!" Special Advertising Section, *Time*, November 13, 1978.

187 Employment effects of office automation are discussed in "Computer Shock: The Inhuman Office of the Future" by Jon Stewart, in *Saturday Review*, June 23, 1979.

188 Micronet's paperless office is described in "Firms Sponsor Paperless Office," *The Office*, June 1979; and in "Paperless Office Plans Debut," *Information World*, April 1979.

190 Alternatives to the postal system are discussed in "Another Postal Hike, and Then—," *U.S. News & World Report*, May 29, 1978.

190 The growth of the pre-electronic postal system finally peaked in the mid-1970s. *U.S. News & World Report* on December 29, 1975, noted: "The volume of mail handled by the Postal Service declined in the last fiscal year for the first time in history. The decline—about 830,000,000 pieces of mail last year—is expected to continue and possibly accelerate." The paper-based Post Office—that prototypical Second Wave institution—had finally reached its limits.

190 Satellite Business Systems is described in a "Special Report" by Drs. William Ginsberg and Robert Golden, prepared for Shearson Hayden Stone, New York.

190 Vincent Giuliano is quoted from interview with author.

192 Goldfield on "para-principals" is based on interview with author.

192 Office automation and the seven-nation study are covered in "The Coming of the Robot Workplace," *The Financial Times* (London), June 14, 1978.

CHAPTER SIXTEEN

198 Work at home, in companies like United Airlines and McDonald's, is covered in "A Way to Improve Office's Efficiency: Just Stay at Home," *The Wall Street Journal*, December 14, 1976.

198   Harvey Poppel is quoted from an interview with the author and from his unpublished forecast, "The Incredible Information Revolution of 1984."

198   Latham is cited from [54], p. 30.

198   Changes in white-collar work are discussed in "The Automated Office" by Hollis Vail, in *The Futurist*, April 1978.

198   Institute for the Future findings are reported in Paul Baran, *Potential Market Demand for Two-Way Information Services to the Home 1970–1990*, published by the Institute for the Future, Menlo Park, Calif., 1971.

199   Computer programming at home is described in "Fitting Baby Into the Programme," *The Guardian* (Manchester), September 9, 1977.

199   "People huddled around a computer" is drawn from "Communicating May Replace Commuting," *Electronics*, March 7, 1974.

199   Michael Koerner cited in [26], Vol. I, p. 240.

200   For the Nilles group halfway-house model see *Electronics*, March 7, 1974, cited above.

200   The key study on substitution of communications for commuting is [49].

CHAPTER SEVENTEEN

209   The chief government statistician on family matters, Dr. 1977.

209   Carter is quoted from "Right Now," *McCall's*, May Paul Glick of the U.S. Census Bureau, is quoted from Dr. Israel Zwerling, "Is Love Enough to Hold a Family Together?" *Cincinnati Horizons*, December 1977.

212   Percent of U.S. population in classical nuclear families is from U.S. Department of Labor, Bureau of Labor Statistics, Special Labor Force Report 206, "Marital and Family Characteristics of the Labor Force in March 1976," *Monthly Labor Review*, June 1977.

212   People living alone are described in "Today's Family— Something Different," *U.S. News & World Report*, July 9, 1979; also "Trend to Living Alone Brings Economic and Social Change," *The New York Times*, March 20, 1977; and "The Ways 'Singles' Are Changing U.S.," *U.S. News & World Report*, January 31, 1977.

212   Rise in unwed couples reported in "Unwed Couples Liv-

ing Together Increase by 117%," *The Washington Post*, June 28, 1979; see also "H.U.D. Will Accept Unmarried Couples for Public Housing," *The New York Times*, May 29, 1977.

213   On courts wrestling with unwed couples' "divorces": "How to Sue Your Live-in Lover," by Sally Abrahms in *New York*, November 13, 1978; also, "Unmarried Couples: Unique Legal Plight," *Los Angeles Times*, November 13, 1977.

213   Etiquette and "couple counseling" is from " 'Living in Sin' Is In Style," *The National Observer*, May 30, 1977.

213   Ramey is quoted from the November-December 1975 newsletter of the National Organization for Non-Parents, now renamed the National Alliance for Optional Parenthood.

213   Childless couples are described in "In New German Attitude on Family Life, Many Couples Decide to Forgo Children," *The New York Times*, August 25, 1976; also "Marriage and Divorce, Russian Style— 'Strange Blend of Marx and Freud,' " *U.S. News & World Report,* August 30, 1976.

214   On children in single-parent households, see [194], p. 1.

214   To show how demography, technology, and other forces influence the family is not to say the family is a passive element in society, merely reacting or adapting to changes elsewhere in the system. It is also an active force. But the impact of outside events on the family—war, for example, or technological change— is often immediate, while the impact of the family on society may be long delayed. The real impact of the family is not felt until its children grow up and take their place in society.

214   The rise of one-parent households in Britain, Germany, and Scandinavia is reported in "The Contrasting Fortunes of Europe's One-parent Families," *To The Point International* (Sandton, Transvaal, South Africa), August 23, 1976.

214   "Aggregate family" is identified in [502], pp. 248–249.

214   Davidyne Mayleas is quoted from "About Women: The Post-Divorce 'Poly-Family,' " *Los Angeles Times*, May 7, 1978.

215   The rich variety of family arrangements is explored in "Family Structure and the Mental Health of Children" by Sheppard G. Kellam, M.D., Margaret E. Ensminger, M.A., and R. Jay Turner, Ph.D., in the *Archives of General Psychiatry* (American Medical Association), September 1977.

215   Jessie Bernard on family diversification is quoted from [187], pp. 302 and 305.

223   For press coverage of woman hired for artificial insemination in Britain see "Astonishing Plan Says the Judge," *Evening News* (London), June 20, 1978. Also, "Woman Hired to Have a Child," *The Guardian* (Manchester), June 21, 1978.

223   Lesbian child-custody rights are discussed in "Judge Grants a Lesbian Custody of 3 Children," *The New York Times*, June 3, 1978; also, "Victory for Lesbian in Child Custody Case," *San Francisco Chronicle*, April 12, 1978.

223   "Parental malpractice" suit is covered by "Son Sues Folks for Malpractice," *Chicago Tribune*, April 28, 1978.

225   On company couples as a phenomenon in business, see "The Corporate Woman: 'Company Couples' Flourish," *Business Week*, August 2, 1976.

CHAPTER EIGHTEEN

227   Carter and Blumenthal are quoted in " 'I Don't Trust Any Economists Today' " by Juan Cameron, in *Fortune*, September 11, 1978.

227   On the "ecu," see André M. Coussement, "Why the Ecu Still Isn't Quite Real," *Euromoney*, October 1979.

228   The rise of Eurocurrencies and the global electronic banking network are described in "Stateless Money: A New Force on World Economies," *Business Week*, August 21, 1978; John B. Caouette, "Time Zones and the Arranging Centre," *Euromoney*, July 1978; and "Clash over Stateless Cash," *Time*, November 5, 1979.

228   Eurodollars were discussed by the author in [150], p. 11.

229   COMECON, centered on the Soviet Union, has its own interrelated troubles. In an unprecedented move Erich Honecker, East Germany's Communist head of state, not long ago blasted COMECON's rules as "one-sided and short-sighted," warning Moscow that "nobody has the right to halt the production of East German products." (See *Forbes*, March 20, 1978.) The U.S.S.R. economy itself has split into four distinct and conflicting segments—a Third Wave, high-technology military segment forever clamoring for bigger budgets; a hopelessly backward Second Wave segment that is riddled with mismanagement and shortages as it attempts to meet rising consumer demands; and an even more backward and malplanned agricultural seg-

ment beset with intractable problems of its own. Beneath all of these stands a shadowy fourth segment—a "phantom economy" based on payoffs, graft, and corruption, without which many of the operations in the other three segments would grind to a halt.

Greatly dependent upon infusions of technology and capital from the global economy (and susceptible to its illnesses), the socialist industrial nations are also caught up in forces larger than they can control. Poland, for example, Ping-Pongs back and forth between inflation-induced food price hikes and angry worker protests. Having borrowed $13 billion from the West, it stands poised on the knife-edge of bankruptcy and pleads with its creditors to stretch out the terms of loan repayment. The other socialist economies are similarly beginning to de-massify and their productive organizations, too, are caught up in the enormous wave of change.

On corruption in the U.S.S.R., see Smith, [484], p. 86 et seq. The U.S.S.R.'s dependence on other countries for technology and capital is discussed in "Rollback, Mark II" by Brian Crozier, in *National Review*, June 8, 1978. Poland's food and worker problems are reported in "Poland: Meat and Potatoes," *Newsweek*, January 2, 1978; its financial problems are treated in "Poland's Creditors Watch the Ripening Grain" by Alison Macleod, in *Euromoney*, July 1978.

229 The *Euromoney* quote is from its article, "Time Zones and the Arranging Center," cited above.

229 The international cash manager's role is described in "Stateless Money: A New Force on World Economies," *Business Week*, August 21, 1978.

229 Acceleration in marketing and television are discussed in Editorial Viewpoint," in *Advertising Age*, October 13, 1975.

230 COMECON's price revisions are noted in "L'inflation se généralise," *Le Figaro* (Paris), March 4, 1975.

230 The British economist Graham Hutton, in a paper for the Institute of Economic Affairs, writes that "as our inflation has accelerated, so all government and business longer-term indebtedness is forced to get younger and shorter . . . velocity of circulation rises faster; time-periods for even three-year contracts ahead have to be re-worded to build-in the expected inflation-rate of *acceleration*; wage bargains become quicker and shorter." "Inflation and Legal Institutions," in [129], p. 120.

232 Canada's Eskimos: "Eskimos Seek Fifth of Canada as Province," *The New York Times*, February 28, 1976.

232   Indian demands are reported in "Settlement of Indian Land Claim in Rhode Island Could Pave Way for Resolving 20 Other Disputes," *The Wall Street Journal*, September 13, 1978; and "A Backlash Stalks the Indians," *Business Week*, September 11, 1978.

232   On Ainu minority in Japan see "Ainu's Appeal Printed in Book," *Daily Yomiuri* (Tokyo), November 15, 1973. On Koreans: "Rightists Attack Korean Office; Six Arrested," *Daily Yomiuri* (Tokyo), September 4, 1975.

233   David Ewing is quoted from "The Corporation As Public Enemy No. 1," *Saturday Review*, January 21, 1978.

234   John C. Biegler is quoted from "Is Corporate Social Responsibility a Dead Issue?" *Business and Society Review*, Spring 1978.

237   Jayne Baker Spain: "The Crisis in the American Board: A More Muscular Contributor," audiotape produced by AMACOM, a division of the American Management Associations, 1978.

237   Olin indicted: see Olin Shareholder Quarterly and Annual Meeting Report, May 1978.

237   On Thalidomide, see "A Scandal Too Long Concealed," *Time*, May 7, 1979.

238   Henry Ford II is quoted from "Is Corporate Social Responsibility a Dead Issue?" *Business and Society Review*, Spring 1978.

239   Control Data's policies are described in "The Mounting Backlash Against Corporate Takeovers" by Bob Tamarkin, in *Forbes*, August 7, 1978; and the company's "Mission Statement," 1978.

240   Allen Neuharth is quoted from "The News Mogul Who Would Be Famous" by David Shaw, in *Esquire*, September 1979.

240   Rosemary Bruner is quoted from interview with author.

240   On the corporation's multiple purposes see "The New Corporate Environmentalists," *Business Week*, May 28, 1979; also, "MCSI: The Future of Social Responsibility" by George C. Sawyer, in *Business Tomorrow*, June 1979.

241   The American Accounting Association reports are described in [16], p. 13.

241   Juanita Kreps' suggestion is reported in "A Bureaucratic Brainstorm" by Marvin Stone, in *U.S. News & World Report*, January 9, 1978.

242   The giant Swiss food firm and the quote from Pierre Arnold are from "When Businessmen Confess Their Social Sins," *Business Week*, November 6, 1978.

242   On social reports of European companies see "Europe

Tries the Corporate Social Report" by Meinolf Dierkes and Rob Coppock, in *Business and Society Review*, Spring 1978.

243   Cornelius Brevoord is quoted from "Effective Management in the Future" in [12].

243   William E. Halal's remarks are from his "Beyond R.O.I.," *Business Tomorrow*, April 1979.

CHAPTER NINETEEN

246   Flextime has generated a large literature. Among the sources used here are: "Workers Find 'Flextime' Makes for Flexible Living," *The New York Times*, October 15, 1979; "Flexible Work Hours a Success, Study Says," *The New York Times*, November 9, 1977; "The Scheme That's Killing The Rat-Race Blues" by Robert Stuart Nathan, in *New York*, July 18, 1977; "Work When You Want To," *Europa* magazine, April 1972; "Flexing Time" by Geoffrey Sheridan, in *New Society* (London), November 1972; and Kanter, [529].

248   The increase in night work is described in "Le Sommeil du Travailleur de Nuit," *Le Monde* (Paris), December 14, 1977; and in Packard, [500], Chapter 4.

248   The growth in numbers of part-time workers is covered in "In Permanent Part-Time Work, You Can't Beat the Hours" by Roberta Graham, in *Nation's Business*, January 1979; see also "Growing Part-Time Work Force Has Major Impact on Economy," *The New York Times*, April 12, 1977.

249   The Citibank television commercial is quoted from a transcript provided by the advertising agency, Wells, Rich, Greene, Inc., New York.

251   On service workers outnumbering manufacturing workers, see [63], p. 3.

251   Time-of-day utilities pricing is reported in "Environmentalists Are Split Over Issue of Time-of-Day Pricing of Electricity," *The Wall Street Journal*, October 5, 1978.

251   Connecticut's advocacy of flextime is from "Your (Flex) Time May Come" by Frank T. Morgan, in *Personnel Journal*, February 1977.

251   Impact of video recorders on televiewing is analyzed in "Will Betamax Be Busted?" by Steven Brill, in *Esquire*, June 20, 1978.

252   Computer conferencing is described from author's experience; materials supplied by the Electronic Information Exchange System, New Jersey Institute of

Technology, Newark, N.J.; and from *Planet News*, December 1978, a publication of Infomedia Corporation, Palo Alto, Calif.

254   Varying wages and fringe benefit packages are examined in "Companies Offer Benefits Cafeteria-Style," *Business Week*, November 13, 1978.

255   For trends in German art see Dieter Honisch, "What Is Admired in Cologne May Not Be Appreciated in Munich," *Art News*, October 1978.

256   On the mass merchandising of hard-cover books, refer to "Just A Minute, Marshall McLuhan" by Cynthia Saltzman, in *Forbes*, October 30, 1978.

257   On decentralization in Kiev see [478], p. 67.

257   The defeat of Sweden's Socialist government is reported in "Swedish Socialists Lose to Coalition After 44-Year Rule," *The New York Times*, September 20, 1976.

257   Scottish nationalists' policies are analyzed in [370], p. 14.

257   New Zealand's Values Party program was laid out in Values Party, *Blueprint for New Zealand*, 1972.

257   The rise of neighborhood power is tracked in "Cities Big and Small Decentralize in Effort to Relieve Frustrations," *The New York Times*, April 29, 1979; and "Neighborhood Planning: Designing for the Future," *Self-Reliance*, published by the Institute for Local Self-Reliance, Washington, D.C., November 1976.

257   On ROBBED and other neighborhood groups note "Activist Neighborhood Groups Are Becoming a New Political Force," *The New York Times*, June 18, 1979.

258   U.S. Senator Mark Hatfield (R., Ore.) once introduced a bill designed to revive neighborhood and community government by permitting a local resident to donate up to 80 percent of his federal income tax to a duly organized local neighborhood government.

258   Esmark's reorganization was described in "Esmark Spawns A Thousand Profit Centers," *Business Week*, August 3, 1974; see also Esmark annual report, 1978.

259   Author's description of "Ad-hocracy" is from [502], Chapter 7.

259   Matrix organizations are described in [13].

260   The surprising growth of regional banks is detailed in "The Fancy Dans at the Regional Banks," *Business Week*, April 17, 1978.

262   Franchising is discussed in "The Right Way to Invest in Franchise Companies," by Linda Snyder, in *Fortune*, April 24, 1978; also, U.S. Department of Commerce, Industry and Trade Administration, *Franchising in the Economy 1976–1978*. For franchising in Holland:

letter to author from G. G. Abeln, Secretariat, Nederlandse Franchise Vereniging, Rotterdam.

262   An early report on the dispersal of population was "Cities: More People Moving Out Than In, New Census Confirms," *Community Planning Report*, Washington, D.C., November 17, 1975.

264   Lester Wunderman is quoted from *The Village Voice*, August 14, 1978.

264   Anthony J. N. Judge is quoted from "Networking: The Need for a New Concept," *Transnational Associations* (Brussels), No. 172, 1974; and "A Lesson in Organization From Building Design—Transcending Duality Through Tensional Integrity: Part I," *Transnational Associations*, No. 248, 1978.

CHAPTER TWENTY

265   The rise of self-help health services is documented in "Doctoring Isn't Just for Doctors" by Robert C. Yeager, in *Medical World News*, October 3, 1977.

265   Blood pressure machines: "Medical Robot: A Slot Machine for Blood Pressure," *Time*, October 10, 1977.

266   Boom in sales of medical instruments: "The Revolution in Home Health Care" by John J. Fried, in *Free Enterprise*, August 1978.

268   On self-help organizations: Interview with Dr. Alan Gartner, co-director, New Human Services Institute. Also, "Bereavement Groups Fill Growing Need," *Los Angeles Times*, November 13, 1977; and various issues of the *Self-Help Reporter*, published by the National Self-Help Clearinghouse, New York.

268   More than 500,000 self-help groups cited by Gartner and Riessman, [58], p. 6. Riessman and Gartner have done some of the most useful work on the service economy. Their 1974 book [59], is indispensable.

270   Introduction of self-service gasoline pumps: "Save on Gasoline: Pump It Yourself," *Washington Star*, June 6, 1975. Also, "Now, the No-Service Station," *Time*, August 22, 1977; "Business Around the World," *U.S. News & World Report*, February 9, 1976.

270   Customers doing bank tellers' work: "Tellers Work 24-Hour Day, and Never Breathe a Word," *The New York Times*, May 14, 1976.

270   Stores shifting to self-service: "Futureshock/Store Service: The Pressure on Payroll Overload," *Chain Store Age*, September 1975. Also: "Marketing Observer," *Business Week*, November 9, 1974.

270   Caroline Bird from [489], p. 109.

271   Whirlpool "Cool-Line" material supplied by Warren
      Baver, manager of customer relations, Whirlpool Cor-
      poration, Benton Harbor, Michigan.

272   Sales of power tools: "Tools for the Home: Do-It-Your-
      self Becomes a National Pastime" by John Ingersoll,
      in *Companion*, September 1977. Also, "Psychograph-
      ics: A Market Segmentation Study of the D-I-Y Cus-
      tomer," *Hardware Retailing*, October 1978.

272   The Frost & Sullivan data is from *Study of the Market
      for Home Improvement and Maintenance Products*,
      1976; *Home Center & Associated Home Improvement
      Products Market*, 1978; and *The Do-It-Yourself
      Market in the E.E.C. Countries*, 1978, Frost & Sul-
      livan, New York.

272   *U.S. News & World Report*: "A Fresh Surge in Do-It-
      Yourself Boom," issue of April 23, 1979.

273   The Texas Instruments manager and Cyril Brown are
      quoted from "Top Management Develops Strategy
      Aimed at Penetrating New Markets," *Electronics*, Oc-
      tober 25, 1978.

274   Professor Inyong Ham, from interview with author.

274   Robert Anderson is quoted from interview with author.

276   One interesting implication of the rise of the prosumer
      is a change in what might be termed the "market in-
      tensivity" of daily life. Are some societies more in-
      volved with market activities than others? One way to
      measure this is to see how people spend their time. In
      the mid-1960's sociologists in a dozen countries
      studied how urban people spent their hours. The
      "time-budget" researchers divided daily life into
      thirty-seven different kinds of activity, from working
      and watching television to eating, sleeping, or visiting
      friends.

         Without pretending to be at all scientific about it,
      I loosely lumped these thirty-seven activities into three
      categories: those that seemed to me the most "market-
      intense," those that are not, and those that lie some-
      where in between.

         For example, the time we spend working for pay,
      shopping in a department store, or commuting to our
      jobs is clearly more "market-intense" than the time
      we spend watering geraniums in the window box,
      playing fetch with the family dog, or chatting with
      the neighbors over the back fence.

         Similarly, some activities, while not done for
      market purposes, are nevertheless so commercialized
      as to lie in between. (Packaged travel tours, ski week-
      ends, even some get-away-from-it-all camping, involve

so much purchased paraphernalia, so many paid-for services, and so many economic transactions as to represent a modified form of shopping.)

Using these crude categories I reviewed the time-budget studies. I promptly discovered that some life-styles—and some societies—are more "market-intense" than others.

For instance, Americans in forty-four cities spent, on average, only 36 percent of their waking hours in market-connected activity. The remaining 64 percent of their waking hours were spent cooking, laundering, gardening, eating, brushing their teeth, studying, praying, reading, volunteering in community organizations, watching TV, chatting, or simply resting.

A similar pattern turned up in Western Europe: the average Frenchman spent an equivalent amount of waking hours in market-connected activity. For the Belgian it was a little more—38 percent. For the West German a little less—34 percent.

Ironically, as soon as we move eastward geographically and "leftward" politically, numbers begin to climb. In East Germany, the most technologically advanced of the Communist countries, the average person spent 39 percent of his or her day in market-connected activity. In Czechoslovakia the figure rose to 42 percent. In Hungary 44 percent. And in the Soviet Union it hit 47 percent.

It turns out, therefore, that mainly because of longer working hours but for other reasons as well, the life-style of the ordinary citizen was more market-intensive in Pskov than in its American counterpart. Despite socialist ideology, more of the average person's daily life was wrapped up in buying, selling, and exchanging goods, services and, indeed, labor itself.

277   Sweden's work year and absenteeism: "Shorter Hours of Work" by Birger Viklund, in *Arbetsmiljö International — 78.*

278   The Bradley GT Kit is described in materials supplied by the company: Bradley Automotive Division of Thor Corporation, Edina, Minnesota.

280   Fuchs is quoted in "How Does Self-Help Work?" by Frank Riessman, in *Social Policy*, September/October 1976.

282   How earlier societies coped with unemployment is described in [106].

285   A note on barter and money: The rise of the prosumer compels us to rethink the future of barter, too. Barter

is becoming big business these days. It is not limited to small transactions between individuals, swapping a used sofa, let's say, for some auto repair services, or exchanging legal services for dental care. (Large numbers of people are discovering that barter can help them avoid taxes.) Barter is becoming more important in the world economy, too, as countries and corporations—uncertain about the fast-changing relationships between hard and soft currencies—swap oil for jet fighters, coal for electricity, Brazilian iron ore for Chinese oil. Such barter is a form of exchange and therefore fits within Sector B.

But much of what self-help groups do can be characterized as a form of psychic barter—the swapping of life experiences and advice. And the housewife's traditional role can be interpreted as the barter of her services for goods earned by a working husband. Are her services part of Sector A or Sector B? Third Wave economists will begin to sort out such questions—for until they do it will become increasingly impossible to understand the real economy in which we live, as distinct from the Second Wave economy now fading into history.

Similarly, we need to ask about the future of money. Money supplanted barter in the past partly because it was so difficult to keep track of complex swaps involving many different units of measurement. Money radically simplified record keeping. The growing availability of computers, however, makes it easier to record extremely complex trades and therefore makes money, as such, less essential. Again, we have scarcely begun to think about such things. The rise of the prosumer, its relationship to barter, and the new technology will combine to make us think about old issues in new ways.

CHAPTER TWENTY-ONE

290   Urban Land Institute report summary in "Rural U.S. Growing Faster Than Cities," International *Herald Tribune*, August 4–5, 1979.

291   Lasers, rockets, etc.: "Contemporary Frontiers in Physics" by Victor F. Weisskopf, in *Science*, January 19, 1979.

291   Struve is quoted in "Negotiating with Other Worlds" by Michael A. G. Michaud, in *The Futurist*, April 1973.

291   Listening for signals: Sullivan, [468], p. 204.

292 François Jacob from his article "Darwinism Reconsidered," *Atlas World Press Review*, January 1978.

292 "Genetic drift" and Dr. Motoo Kimura's comments are from "The Neutral Theory of Molecular Evolution," *Scientific American*, November 1979.

292 On *eukaryotes* and *prokaryotes*: "What Came First?" *The Economist*, July 28, 1979.

293 The Grant Park Zoo apes: "Ape Hybrid Produced," *Daily Telegraph* (London), July 28, 1979. Also, "Old Evolutionary Doctrines Jolted by a Hybrid Ape," *The New York Times*, July 29, 1979.

293 The evolutionary record: Warshofsky, [470], pp. 122–125. Also, Jantsch and Waddington, [180], Introduction.

293 The discovery of the structure of DNA is described by Watson in [471].

293 Kornberg's discovery and the "populary summary": [446], pp. 24–26.

294 The British critic is S. Beynon John, "Albert Camus," in [5], p. 312.

294 Club of Rome Report: [165], pp. 23–24.

296 Second Wave view of time: Whitrow, [520], pp. 100–101; also, G. J. Whitrow, "Reflections on the History of the Concept of Time," in [510], pp. 10–11.

296 Gribbin, from [512], pp. xiii and xiv.

297 Black holes: "Those Baffling Black Holes," *Time*, September 4, 1978; "The Wizard of Space and Time" by Dennis Overbye, in *Omni*, February 1979. Also Warshofsky, [470], pp. 19–20.

297 *Tachyons:* [304], pp. 265–266.

297 Taylor is cited from his article, "Time in Particle Physics," in [510], p. 53.

297 For Capra see [300], p. 52.

297 Alternative and plural times: John Archibald Wheeler, "Frontiers of Time," lecture given at the International School of Physics, "Enrico Fermi," Varenna, Italy, summer 1977.

298 Cities losing population: "Rush to Big Cities Slowing Down: Poll," *Daily Yomiuri* (Tokyo), July 9, 1973; "Exploding Cities," *New Society* (London), July 5, 1973; "Swiss Kaleidoscope," *Swiss Review of World Affairs*, April 1974.

298 The American Council of Life Insurance report is "Changing Residential Patterns and Housing," *TAP Report 14*, Fall 1976.

299 *Fortune* is quoted from "Why Corporations Are on the Move" by Herbert E. Meyer, May 1976.

299   Arthur Robinson: "A Revolution in the Art of Map-making," *San Francisco Chronicle*, August 29, 1978.

300   The Arno Peters map is described in "The Peters World Map: Is It an Improvement?" by Alexander Dorozynski, in *Canadian Geographic*, August/September 1978.

301   Simon Ramo is cited from [311], p. vi.

301   Barry Lopez's article ran in the March 31, 1973, issue of *Environmental Action*.

302   Frederick S. Perls is quoted from his "Gestalt Therapy and Human Potentialities," in [418], p. 1.

302   The holistic health movement is discussed in "Holistic Health Concepts Gaining Momentum" by Constance Holden, in *Science*, June 2, 1978.

302   The World Bank expert is Charles Weiss, Jr., "Mobilizing Technology for Developing Countries," *Science*, March 16, 1979.

303   Laszlo is quoted in [308], p. 161.

303   Eugene P. Odum: "The Emergence of Ecology as a New Integrative Discipline," *Science*, March 25, 1977.

304   Maruyama is cited from his much-quoted paper, "The Second Cybernetics: Deviation-Amplifying Mutual Causal Processes," *American Scientist*, June 1963, pp. 164–179, 250–256.

        In "New Movements in Old Traps" published in *Futurics*, Fall 1977, pp. 59–62, Maruyama presents a critical typology of current epistemologies, comparing them in terms of such variables as causality, logic, perception, ethics, and cosmology. He has also analyzed the systemic implications of differentiation in "Heterogenistics and Morphogenetics" in *Theory and Society*, Vol. 5, No. 1, pp. 75–96, 1978.

306   The exposition on Prigogine is based on interviews and private correspondence with the author, as well as [458].

308   The termite colony is described in Ilya Prigogine, "Order Through Fluctuation: Self-Organization and Social System," in [180].

308   Prigogine is quoted from his paper, *From Being to Becoming*, published by the University of Texas Center for Statistical Mechanics and Thermodynamics, Austin, Texas, April 1978.

        See also: "Time, Structure, and Fluctuations," *Science*, September 1, 1978; "Order Out of Chaos" by I. Prigogine, Center for Statistical Mechanics and Thermodynamics, University of Texas at Austin and Faculté des Sciences, Université Libre de Bruxelles; and *La Nouvelle Alliance*, Ilya Prigogine and Isabelle Stengers (Paris: Gallimard, 1979).

CHAPTER TWENTY-TWO

312   On Corsican and other separatists: "Fissionable Particles of State," *Telegraph Sunday Magazine* (London), June 11, 1978; also "Europe's Passionate Separatists," San Francisco *Sunday Examiner & Chronicle,* October 8, 1978.

312   Scottish assembly: "Home-Rule Plan Suffers Setback in British Votes," *The New York Times,* March 3, 1979.

312   Pressures for autonomy run deep in Scotland: "The Devolution Pledges Which Will Not Go Away," *The Guardian* (Manchester), July 28, 1979.

313   Welsh nationalism: "Welsh Nationalists, Rebuffed, Fight Fiercely for Their Language," *The New York Times,* November 6, 1979.

313   Regional problems in Belgium: "Belgium: New Government Rides the Tiger," *To The Point* (Sandton, Transvaal, South Africa), October 27, 1978.

313   Sudeten Germans: "Germany's Palestinians," *Newsweek,* June 2, 1975.

313   South Tyrolese: "Conflict Within a Community" by Frances Pinter, in *New Society* (London), March 22, 1973.

313   Slovenes, Basques, Catalans, and Croatians: "How Unhappy Minorities Upset Europe's Calm," *U.S. News & World Report,* January 31, 1977.

313   Pierre Trudeau is quoted from "Language Dispute is Termed Threat to Canada's Unity," *The New York Times,* October 26, 1976.

313   Autonomy movement in Alberta: "Western Canadians Plan Own Party," *The New York Times,* October 15, 1974; also "Canada, a Vast, Divided Nation, Gets Ready for a Crucial Election," *The New York Times,* May 16, 1979.

313   Western Australia's secession movement: "How the West May Be Lost," *The Bulletin* (Sydney), January 26, 1974.

314   Amalrik's forecast is from [472].

314   Armenian nationalists: "Armenia: The USSR's Quiet Little Hotbed of Terror," *San Francisco Examiner,* October 9, 1978.

314   Georgians and Abkhazians: "Georgian and Armenian Pride Lead to Conflicts With Moscow," *The New York Times,* June 27, 1978. Abkhazian minority's demands: "Dispute in Caucasus Mirrors Soviet Ethnic Mosaic," *The New York Times,* June 25, 1978.

314   The underground novel in California: [275].

315   Report for Kissinger was prepared by Professor Arthur Corwin, Director of the Cooperative Study for Mexican Migration.

315   *Texas Monthly* is quoted from "Portillo's Revenge" by John Bloom, in the magazine's issue of April 1979.

315   Puerto Rican separatism has produced an extensive newspaper literature; see, for example, "F.A.L.N. Organization Asks Independence for Puerto Rico," *The New York Times*, November 9, 1975.

315   For Alaskan separatism see "Alaska Self-Determination," *Reason*, September 1973.

315   Native Americans asking for a sovereign state: "Black Elk Asks Young Americans: Recognize Indians as Sovereign Nation," *The Colorado Daily* (Boulder), October 18, 1974; also, "American Indian Council Seeks U.N. Accreditation," *The New York Times*, January 26, 1975.

315   The National Conference of State Legislatures is quoted from "America's Regional Economic War," *State Legislatures*, July/August 1976.

315   The "economic equivalent of civil war" is from "Coal and Oil States, Upset by Carter Plan, Prepare for 'Economic War' Over Energy," *The New York Times*, April 27, 1977.

315   Jeffrey Knight: "After Setbacks—New Tactics in Environmental Crusade," *U.S. News & World Report*, June 9, 1975.

316   "Let the Bastards Freeze in the Dark": editorial by Philip H. Abelson in *Science*, November 16, 1973.

316   Midwesterners urged to stop "chasing smokestacks": "Midwest, U.S. Heartland, Is Found Losing Economic Vitality," The *Cleveland Plain Dealer*, October 9, 1975.

316   Northeastern governors organize: "Playing Poorer Than Thou: Sunbelt v. Snowbelt in Washington," *Time*, February 13, 1978.

317   Pierre Trudeau in 1967 is quoted from Shaw [287], p. 51.

317   Denis de Rougement is quoted from the *Bulletin* of the Swiss Credit Bank, Zurich, May 1973.

318   Senator McGovern is quoted from his article "The Information Age," *The New York Times*, June 9, 1977.

319   Statistics on transnational corporations are from *Supplementary Material on the Issue of Defining Transnational Corporations*, a Report of the Secretariat to the Commission on Transnational Corporations, U.N. Economic and Social Council (UNESCO), March 23, 1979.

319   The extremely rapid spread of these TNCs may have al-

ready peaked, according to research by Prof. Brent Wilson of the University of Virginia. (Wilson shows that many large companies, in such low-technology industries as leather goods, apparel, textile, and rubber, are actually selling off foreign subsidiaries.) But this is not true for the very high-technology industries. See "Why the Multinational Tide Is Ebbing," by Sanford Rose, in *Fortune*, August 1977.

319   On relative scale of transnational corporations and U.N.: testimony by Alvin Toffler before the U.S. Senate Committee on Foreign Relations; see [294], p. 265. Also reprinted as "The USA, the UN and Transnational Networks," in *International Associations* (Brussels), No. 593, 1975.

320   General Motors' sales revenue and Lester Brown: [272], pp. 214–216.

320   Exxon's tanker fleet: see Wilczynski, [297], p. 40.

320   Communist Party members on a holiday: [297], p. 40.

320   Socialist transnationals: [297], pp. 134–145.

320   Western-based TNCs and their transactions with COMECON countries: [297], p. 57.

320   TNCs from non-industrialized nations: "The Rise of Third World Multinationals" by David A. Heenan and Warren J. Keegan, in *Harvard Business Review*, January–February 1979.

321   British TNCs violating British embargoes: "BP Confesses It Broke Sanctions and Covered Up," *Sunday Times* (London), August 27, 1978; also "Oil Chiefs Bust Sanctions," *The Observer* (London), June 25, 1978; and Rhodesia (Oil Sanctions Inquiry), House of Commons *Hansard*, pp. 1184–1186, December 15, 1978.

321   Violation of U.S. regulations regarding the Arab boycott: *Boycott Report: Developments and Trends Affecting the Arab Boycott*, issued by the American Jewish Congress, New York, February 1979.

321   Transnational oil companies favoring their own priorities: [168], p. 312 +.

321   Lester Brown is from [272], p. 222.

321   TNC intelligence: see [390].

321   Hugh Stephenson: [289], p. 3.

322   Numbers of international organizations: [294], p. 270. See also [298].

323   Transnational organizations and IGOs from author's interview with A. J. N. Judge, Union of International Associations, Brussels.

323   Common Market's tax commissioner: see "An EEC Flea in Russia's Ear," *The Economist* (London), January 13, 1979.

323   Agricultural and industrial policies made in Brussels: "Farmer Solidarity Increase in Europe," *The New York Times*, October 6, 1974.

323   Increase in the EEC budget rammed through: "A Wintry Chill in Brussels," *The Economist*, January 20, 1979.

325   Trilateral Commission: "Oil Supplies 'Could Meet Demand Until Early 1990's,' " *Financial Times* (London), June 16, 1978.

CHAPTER TWENTY-THREE

328   Figures on poverty, health, nutrition, and literacy are from Robert S. McNamara, addresses to the Board of Governors of the World Bank, September 24, 1973, and September 26, 1977.

329   Industrialization in Iran: "Iran's Race for Riches," *Newsweek*, March 24, 1975.

330   For interest rates and loans to projects and companies in Iran, see "Iranian Borrowing: The Great Pipeline Loan Will Be Followed by Many More" by Nigel Bance, in *Euromoney*, June 1978.

330   German manager's pay: "Iran: A Paradise in a Powder Keg" by Marion Dönhoff, in *Die Zeit* (Hamburg), October 10, 1976.

330   Percentage of Iran's goods consumed by one tenth of the population: "Regime of the Well-Oiled Gun" by Darryl D'Monte, in *Economic & Political Weekly* (India), January 12, 1974, extracted in *Iran Research* (London), January 1975.

330   Rural income in Iran: Introduction to special section, "Iran: The Lion That Stopped Roaring," *Euromoney*, June 1978.

330   Though it caught Washington policy makers and international bankers off guard, the collapse of the Shah was not wholly unexpected to those who followed the flow of "unofficial" information coming out of Iran. As early as January 1975, fully four years before his overthrow, Bulletin No. 8 of *Iran Research*, a freely circulated left-wing publication, reported that the movement to topple the Shah had reached "a higher stage in the revolutionary struggle." The report detailed armed actions against the regime, the bombing of the Irana Tile Factory, the assassination of the "notorious owner of the Jahan Chit factories," the escape of political prisoners with the aid of their guard. It printed the message of an Air Force lieutenant calling upon his "military brothers" to "take off this

shameful uniform and take up a guerilla gun." Above
all, it reported and praised the latest *Fatva* or procla-
mation of the exiled Ayatollah Khomeini in which he
urged intensification of the drive against the regime.

332   *The New York Times* article is "Third World Industrial-
        izes, Challenging the West . . ." in the issue of Feb-
        ruary 4, 1979.

332   French steelworkers: "Steel's Convulsive Retreat in Eu-
        rope" by Agis Salpukas, in *The New York Times In-
        ternational Economic Survey*, February 4, 1979.

333   "Between the sickle and the combine harvester" is from
        "Second Class Capitalism" by Simon Watt, in *Under-
        currents* (Reading, Berkshire), October-November,
        1976.

333   The Intermediate Technology Development Group and
        examples of appropriate technology are from *Appro-
        priate Technology in the Commonwealth: A Direc-
        tory of Institutions*, published by the Food Production
        and Rural Development Division of the Common-
        wealth Secretariat, London.

334   India's reversion to First Wave methods: "India Goes
        Back to Using the Handloom," *Financial Times*
        (London), June 20, 1978.

334   Suharto is quoted by Mohammad Sadli, the Indonesian
        minister of mines, in "A Case Study in Disillusion:
        U.S. Aid Effort in India," *The New York Times*, June
        25, 1974.

334   Samir Amin is quoted from [66], pp. 592–593.

335   Threshing contest in 1855: [101], pp. 303–304.

338   Reddy on energy is quoted from his background paper,
        Simple Energy Technologies for Rural Families,
        prepared for the UNICEF Seminar on Simple Tech-
        nology for The Rural Family, Nairobi, June 1976.

338   For bio-gas programs see: "Integrated Microbial Tech-
        nology for Developing Countries: Springboard for
        Economic Progress" by Edgar J. DaSilva, Reuben
        Olembo, and Anton Burgers, in *Impact*, April-June
        1978. Also: "Fuels from Biomass: Integration with
        Food and Materials Systems" by E. S. Lipinsky, and
        "Solar Energy for Village Development" by Norman
        L. Brown and James W. Howe, both in *Science*, Feb-
        ruary 10, 1978.

339   Technology in India: "India Developing Solar Power
        for Rural Electricity," *The New York Times*, May 11,
        1979.

339   Haim Aviv's proposal is described in "Envisions Israel-
        Egypt Joint Food-Fuel Project," New York *Post*, April
        14, 1979.

339   Environmental Research Lab in Tucson: "Powdered

Martinis and Other Surprises Coming in the Future," *The New York Times*, January 10, 1979.

339   Vermont catfish experiment and the New Alchemy Institute: "Future Farming" by Alan Anderson, Jr., in *Omni*, June 1979.

339   The twenty-year food forecasts of the Center for Futures Research at U.S.C. are in the report, *Neither Feast nor Famine: A Preliminary Report of the Second Twenty Year Forecast*, by Selwyn Enzer, Richard Drobnick, and Steven Alter.

340   John McHale and Magda Cordell McHale from [91], pp. 188–190.

341   M. S. Iyengar is quoted from his paper, *Post-Industrial Society in the Developing Countries*, presented to the Special Conference on Futures Research in Rome, 1973.

341   Ward Morehouse, "Microelectronic Chips to Feed the Third World" by Stephanie Yanchinski, in *New Scientist* (London), August 9, 1979.

342   Roger Melen: *San Francisco Chronicle*, January 31, 1979.

342   John Magee is quoted from *The New World Information Order*, a report by George Kroloff and Scott Cohen to the Senate Committee on Foreign Relations, November 1977.

343   Suharto's sword: "Asia's Communications Boom: The Promise of Satellite Technology," *Asiaweek* (Hong Kong), November 24, 1978.

344   Jagdish Kapur is quoted from his lecture, "India—2000 A.D.: A Framework for Survival," presented to the India International Centre, New Delhi, January 17, 1974.

345   Myrdal's discussion of unemployment is found in [94] p. 961.

345   A note here on the distinction between what I call "prosuming" and what some development economists term the "informal sector." An intense debate has arisen over this informal economy which springs up within many of the world's poor countries. In it, desperate millions attempt to eke out a living by doing odd jobs, peddling, street hustling, making furniture, driving, shining shoes, doing small-scale construction and other tasks. Some economists believe the existence of this sector is positive, since it opens a channel through which people make the transition into the formal economy. Other economists insist the informal economy merely locks people into permanent misery.

Whichever view proves correct, this informal sector is properly characterized as "petty commodity production" in the sense that it is part of the market economy. For this reason, it differs fundamentally from what I have called the "prosumer sector," which is based on production for use instead. The informal sector fits into what, in my terminology, is Sector B—production for exchange—not Sector A—production for use, which I call prosumption.

345 Streeten of the World Bank is quoted from his paper, *Development Ideas in Historical Perspective: The New Interest in Development* (n.d.).

345 Yona Friedman is quoted from his paper *No-Cost Housing*, presented to a meeting of UNESCO, November 14–18, 1977.

346 Some World Bank projects do emphasize self-help or sweat-equity approaches. See, for example, "The Bank and Urban Poverty" by Edward Jaycox, in *Finance & Development*, September 1978. Director of the Bank's Urban Projects Department, Jaycox points out another implication of the sweat-equity approach: "Because the beneficiaries are expected to pay the costs [in the form of their labor], it often becomes not only desirable but essential that they participate in the decisions in planning and implementing the project." Prosuming, indeed, implies a higher degree of self-determination than production.

347 Leach: *Literacy*, A Nevis Institute Working Paper, Edinburgh, 1977.

347 Marshall McLuhan discusses oral culture in [46], p. 50.

348 Samir Amin is quoted from [66], p. 595.

CHAPTER TWENTY-FOUR

(No notes are required for this chapter.)

CHAPTER TWENTY-FIVE

365 President's Commission on Mental Health, and National Institute of Mental Health cited in [409], p. 6.

366 "Madness, Genius and Sainthood": "The Marketplace," *PENewsletter*, October 1974.

366 Eight thousand therapies: [404], p. 11.

366 The critical survey: [404], p. 56.

367 California magazine: "In Guns We Trust" by Karol Greene and Schuyler Ingle, in *New West*, April 23, 1979.

368 Popular novel: [21], p. 377.

370 Norman Macrae is quoted from his excellent article,

"The Coming Entrepreneurial Revolution," *The Economist*, December 25, 1976.

371 Matchmaker: *Jewish Chronicle*, June 16, 1978.

372 Re: *Future Shock*, see [502], chapter 5.

373 Rollo May's comment is from [414], p. 34.

374 On cults, see [404], pp. 12, 16, and 35.

374 Unification Church businesses: "Gone Fishing," *Newsweek*, September 11, 1978.

375 Divine Light Center lawsuit: "Cuckoo Cult," *Time*, May 7, 1979.

375 The Unification Church official is quoted in "Honor Thy Father Moon" by Berkeley Rice, in *Psychology Today*, January 1976.

375 Dr. Sukhdeo is quoted in "Jersey Psychiatrist, Studying the Guyana Survivors, Fears Implications for U.S. Society From Other Cults" by Jon Nordheimer, in *The New York Times*, December 1, 1978.

375 Sherwin Harris is quoted in "I Never Once Thought He Was Crazy" by Jon Nordheimer, in *The New York Times*, November 27 1978.

CHAPTER TWENTY-SIX

380 Reszler's essay is "L'homme nouveau': espérance et histoire," *Cadmos* (Geneva), Winter 1978.

381 Fromm is quoted from [406], p. 304; and from [407], p. 77.

385 Conover is quoted from an interview with author.

386 Flexible fringe benefits are described in "Companies Offer Benefits Cafeteria-Style," *Business Week*, November 13, 1978.

386 Reluctance of employees to move: "Mobile Society Puts Down Roots," *Time*, June 12, 1978.

386 Matrix is described in [13], p. 104.

390 For Enzensberger, see [42], p. 97.

CHAPTER TWENTY-SEVEN

393 President Carter is quoted from his address to the country on energy problems, text in *The New York Times*, July 16, 1979.

394 General Motors' experience with catalytic converters was covered in "Why Don't We Recall Congress for Defective Parts?" by Robert I. Weingarten, in *Financial World*, March 26, 1975.

394 Forty-five thousand pages of new regulations a year: *Regulatory Failure III* (Washington, D.C.: National Association of Manufacturers, April 1978), p. A-2.

394   Steel industry: advertisement of Bethlehem Steel, *Time*,
       June 26, 1978.

394   Eli Lilly and government forms: "The Day the Paper
       Stopped" by Robert Bendiner, *The New York Times*,
       March 16, 1977.

394   Exxon report to the FEA: Michael C. Jensen and
       William H. Meckling, *Can the Corporation Survive?*
       (Rochester, N.Y.: University of Rochester Graduate
       School of Management, May 1976), p. 2.

394   On political paralysis: French voters speak of the politi-
       cal "freeze" or the "blockage of politics." A former
       prime minister, Michel Debré, sees a "crisis of the re-
       gime." See Flora Lewis's report, "Life's Not Bad, but
       French Foresee Disaster," *The New York Times*,
       November 17, 1979.

394   The Japanese prime minister Takeo Miki is quoted in
       "Fragility of Democracy Stirs Japanese Anxiety" by
       Richard Halloran in *The New York Times*, Novem-
       ber 9, 1975.

396   Election statistics for 1976 are from: Election Research
       Center, *America Votes 12* (Washington, D. C.: Con-
       gressional Quarterly, 1977), and Bureau of the Cen-
       sus, U.S. Department of Commerce.

396   Independent voters: "As the Parties Decline" by Freder-
       ick G. Dutton, in *The New York Times*, May 8,
       1972.

396   Decline of the Labour Party: "How Labour Lost Its
       Legions," by Dr. Stephen Haseler, in *Daily Mail* (Lon-
       don), August 9, 1979.

396   Japanese quote from *The Daily Yomiuri* (Tokyo), De-
       cember 28, 1972.

396   Victor Nekipelov: from "Here a Stalin There a Stalin
       Everywhere a Stalin Stalin," *The New York Times*,
       August 14, 1979.

396   New Zealand politics: "NZ Elections Give Rise to a
       Time Like Alice" by Christopher Beck, in *The Asian*,
       November 22, 1972.

396   The American Enterprise Institute report is cited by
       "TRB" in "Who's in Charge in Washington? No
       One's in Charge There," Philadelphia *Inquirer*, March
       3, 1979.

397   Private armies in Britain: "Thunder From the Right,"
       Newsweek, August 26, 1974; also "Phantom Major
       Calls up an Anti-Chaos Army" by John Murchie, in
       the *Daily Mirror* (London), August 23, 1974.

397   Red Brigades: See Curtis Bill Pepper, "The Possessed,"
       New York Times Magazine, February 18, 1979.

397   Anti-terrorism laws in West Germany: *Keesing's Con-
       temporary Archives* (London: Longman Group, 1979),

pp. 29497–8; "Scissors in the Head" by David Zane Mairowitz, in *Harper's*, May 1978; "Germany Passes Tough Terrorist Law," Indianapolis *Star*, April 14, 1978; "West Germany's Private Watch on Political Morals" by James Fenton, in *The Guardian* (Manchester), June 19, 1978.

397   Aldo Moro: "Roman Outrage," *Time*, May 14, 1979.

398   Instability in Saudi Arabia: "External Threats to Saudi Stability," *Business Week*, February 12, 1979.

398   Sheikh Yamani: "Relax and Enjoy a Drive" by Julian Snyder, in *International Moneyline*, August 11, 1979.

400   Publication of *Victory*: Michael Simmons, "Literary Victory for Stalin in Russia," *The Guardian* (Manchester), August 4, 1979.

400   Resurgence of the right wing in France: "Rightist Intellectual Groups Rise in France" by Jonathan Kandell, in *The New York Times*, July 8, 1979; and "The New Right Raises Its Voice," *Time*, August 6, 1979. Also William Pfaff column, International *Herald Tribune*, August 3, 1979.

401   The recrudescence of the Ku Klux Klan: "Violent Klan Group Gaining Members" by Wayne King, in *The New York Times*, March 15, 1979; also "Vengeance for Raid Seen as Motive for 4 Killings at Anti-Klan March," *The New York Times*, November 5, 1979; and "Prosecutor in Klan-Protest Killings Terms 12 Suspects Equally Guilty," *The New York Times*, November 7, 1979.

401   Totalitarian inefficiency: "What Does Russia Want?" by Robin Knight, in *U.S. News & World Report*, July 16, 1979.

402   Fletcher quote: Interview with author.

404   Jill Tweedie: "Why Jimmy's Power Is Purely Peanuts," *The Guardian* (Manchester), August 2, 1979.

405   Price increases in Czechoslovakia and Hungary: "Inflation Exists," *The Economist*, July 28, 1979.

407   The *Advertising Age* article is: Stanley E. Cohen, "President's Economic Switch Puts Emphasis on Spending," January 20, 1975.

407   Oil experts: See Helmut Bechtaldt, "The Diktat of the Oil Millions," *Aussenpolitik*, Third Quarter, 1974.

407   Speed of economic change: *Fortune* is quoted from "Business Roundup," January 1975.

407   Margaret Thatcher's clouded crystal ball is noted in John Cunningham, "Guardian Women," *The Guardian* (Manchester), July 31, 1979.

408   Richard Reeves is quoted from his article "The Next Coming of Teddy," *Esquire*, May 9, 1978.

408   Robert Skidelsky is cited in "Keynes and Unfinished Business," *The New York Times,* December 19, 1974.

409   Gay Nazis: "Out of Focus" column in *Focus/Midwest,* Vol. 10, No. 66.

409   Labor's political drives: A. H. Raskin, "Mr. Labor: 'Ideology is Baloney,'" book review of Joseph C. Goulden's biography of George Meany, *The New York Times,* October 23, 1972.

410   Representative Mineta is quoted in "The Great Congressional Power Grab," *Business Week,* September 11, 1978.

411   The *Harper's* magazine article is William Shawcross, "Dr. Kissinger Goes to War," May 1979.

411   Decision overload exists even in the arts bureaucracy: "The National Endowment for the Arts Grows Up" by Malcolm N. Carter, in *Art News,* September 1979.

412   For Pentagon decision-making see Armbrister, [379] pp. 191–2. The reference to seventy-six as the number of missions the Pentagon officer had to review is from Armbrister interview with author.

412   Multibillion dollar bungle: "The Case of the Misplaced $30 Billion," *Business Week,* July 24, 1978.

412   Stuart Eizenstat is quoted in "The Great Congressional Power Grab," *Business Week,* September 11, 1978.

413   Congress: see report by The Congressional Clearinghouse on the Future and the Congressional Institute for the Future, Washington, D.C., July 1979.

413   Soviet decision paralysis: "Worldgram," *U.S. News & World Report,* November 24, 1975.

413   The Member of Parliament is Gerald T. Fowler, quoted in "Devolution Will Ease Load at Whitehall, Minister Says" by Trevor Fishlock, in *The Times* (London), January 16, 1976.

413   Sir Richard Marsh is quoted in his article "Why Westminster Can't Take Business Decisions," *Industrial Management* (Wembley, Middlesex), July 1979.

413   On Italy's political crisis: "Italy Seeks a Government," *Financial Times* (London), August 3, 1979; also "Italy's Coalition Gets a Vote of Approval in Parliament" by Henry Tanner, in *The New York Times,* August 12, 1979.

CHAPTER TWENTY-EIGHT

416   On the Constitutional Convention see Flexner [387], p. 117.

418   Jefferson is quoted from [392], pp. 32, 67.

420   Burnham: "A Disenchanted Electorate May Stay Home
       in Droves," *The New York Times,* February 1, 1976.

420   Silent majority: [391], p. 410

421   South Africa: See interview with Roelof Frederik "Pik"
       Botha in Starcke [378], p. 68.
           South Africa is characterized as "still industrializ-
       ing," even though it has an advanced technological
       base, because important sectors of its population are
       still outside the industrial system. As in Brazil, Mex-
       ico, India, and other such countries, an island of quite
       developed industrialism exists in the middle of prein-
       dustrial conditions.

425   Becker from [380], pp. 183–185.

427   Growth of the Congressional staff: "Proxmire's Well-
       Placed Jab" by Marvin Stone, in *U.S. News & World
       Report,* September 10, 1979.

428   On traces of direct democracy in the French revolution-
       ary constitution: [347], p. 18.

428   Marx invoking the Paris Commune is from [347], p.
       61.

428   Federalist objections to direct democracy: See Clark
       McCauley, Omar Rood and Tom Johnson, "The Next
       Democracy," in the World Future Society *Bulletin,*
       November-December 1977.

429   René Lévesque taking power: "Business Has the Jitters
       in Quebec" by Herbert E. Meyer, in *Fortune,* October
       1977.

430   Nuclear referendum in California: "Atomic Reaction:
       Voters in California Weigh Pros and Cons of Nuclear
       Energy," *Wall Street Journal,* March 1, 1976.

433   Wallonia protests the shift of industry to Flanders:
       "Wallonia," *Financial Times Survey* (London), May
       12, 1976.

433   Western states as energy colonies: "After Setbacks—
       New Tactics in Environmental Crusade," *U.S. News &
       World Report,* June 9, 1975.

434   Geographical tilt from "Corporate Flying: Changing
       the Way Companies Do Business," *Business Week,*
       February 6, 1978.

435   The decision load concept leads to the dismal suspicion
       that, regardless of political struggle, any given deci-
       sion load will be borne by the fewest people capable
       of handling it—that a small number of people will al-
       ways succeed in monopolizing decision-making power,
       until they are overwhelmed by a decisional implosion
       and are simply no longer able to carry the load them-
       selves.

BIBLIOGRAPHY

Since articles, scientific and scholarly papers, and specialized reports are fully described in the accompanying Notes, this listing is limited to books and to a small number of monographs and proceedings. I have grouped the entries under a few headings.

ARTS

[1]   Boucher, François. *20,000 Years of Fashion.* (New York: Harry N. Abrams, 1968.)

[2]   Harling, Robert, ed. *The Modern Interior.* (New York: St. Martin's Press, 1964.)

[3]   Hauser, Arnold. *The Social History of Art* (4 vols.), trans. Stanley Godman. (New York: Alfred A. Knopf, Vintage Books, 1951.)

[4]   Klingender, Francis D. *Art and the Industrial Revolution,* ed. Arthur Elton. (London: Paladin, 1972.)

[5]   Kostelanetz, Richard, ed. *On Contemporary Literature.* (New York: Avon, 1974.)

[6]   Mueller, John H. *The American Symphony Orchestra.* (Bloomington: Indiana University Press, 1951.)

[7]   Sachs, Curt. *The History of Musical Instruments.* (New York: W. W. Norton, 1940.)

[8]   Thomson, George. *Marxism and Poetry.* (New York: International Publishers, 1946.)

BUSINESS/MANAGEMENT/ORGANIZATION THEORY

[9]   Adams, T. F. M., and N. Kobayashi. *The World of Japanese Business.* (Tokyo: Kodansha International, 1969.)

[10]   Anthony, William P. *Participative Management.* (Reading, Mass.: Addison-Wesley, 1978.)

[11]   Beer, Stafford. *Brain of the Firm: The Managerial Cybernetics of Organization.* (London: Allen Lane, The Penguin Press, 1972.)

[12]   Benton, Lewis, ed. *Management for the Future.* (New York: McGraw-Hill, 1978.)

[13]   Davis, Stanley M., and Paul R. Lawrence. *Matrix.* (Reading, Mass.: Addison-Wesley, 1977.)

[14]   Dewing, Arthur S. *Financial Policy of Corporations,* Vols. I and II, 5th edition. (New York: Ronald Press, 1953.)

[15]   Drucker, Peter F. *The Concept of the Corporation.* (New York: New American Library, Mentor, 1964.)

[16]   Gambling, Trevor. *Societal Accounting.* (London: George Allen & Unwin, 1974.)

[17]   Gross, Bertram M. *The Managing of Organizations: The Administrative Struggle,* Vols. I and II. (New York: Free Press Macmillan, 1964.)

[18]   Gvishiani, D. *Organisation and Management: A Sociological Analysis of Western Theories,* trans. Robert Daglish and Leonid Kolesnikov. (Moscow: Progress Publishers, 1972.)

[19]   Janger, Allen R. *Corporate Organization Structures: Service Companies.* (New York: Conference Board, 1977.)

[20]   Kahn, Herman, ed. *The Future of the Corporation.* (New York: Mason & Lipscomb, 1974.)

[21]   Knebel, Fletcher. *The Bottom Line.* (New York: Pocket Books, 1975.)

[22]   Korda, Michael. *Power! How To Get It, How To Use It.* (New York: Ballantine Books, 1975.)

[23]   Labor Research Association. *Billionaire Corporations.* (New York: International Publishers, 1954.)

[24]   Lawrence, Paul R., and Jay W. Lorsch. *Developing Organizations: Diagnosis and Action.* (Reading, Mass.: Addison-Wesley, 1969.)

[25]   Moore, Wilbert E. *The Conduct of the Corporation.* (New York: Random House, Vintage Books, 1962.)

[26]   Newman, Peter C. *The Canadian Establishment,* Vol. I. (Toronto: McClelland and Stewart-Bantam, Seal Books, 1977.)

[27]   Pattee, Howard H., ed. *Hierarchy Theory: The Challenge of Complex Systems.* (New York: George Braziller, 1973.)

[28]   Roy, Robert H. *The Cultures of Management.* (Baltimore: Johns Hopkins University Press, 1977.)

[29]   Scull, Penrose, and Prescott C. Fuller. *From Peddlers to Merchant Princes.* (Chicago: Follett, 1967.)

[30] Sloan, Alfred P., Jr. *My Years With General Motors.*
      (New York: MacFadden-Bartell, 1965.)

[31] Stein, Barry A. *Size, Efficiency, and Community Enter-
      prise.* (Cambridge, Mass.: Center for Community
      Economic Development, 1974.)

[32] Tannenbaum, Arnold S., et al. *Hierarchy in Organiza-
      tions.* (San Francisco: Jossey-Bass Publishers, 1974.)

[33] Tarnowieski, Dale. *The Changing Success Ethic: An
      AMA Survey Report.* (New York: Amacom, 1973.)

[34] Toffler, Alvin. *Social Dynamics and the Bell System.* Re-
      port to the American Telephone & Telegraph Co.

[35] Van der Haas, Hans. *La Mutation de L'Entreprise Eu-
      ropéenne,* trans. Pierre Rocheron. (Paris: Éditions
      Robert Laffont, L'Usine Nouvelle, 1971.)

[36] Yoshino, M. Y. *Japan's Managerial System: Tradition
      and Innovation.* (Cambridge, Mass.: MIT Press,
      1968.)

COMMUNICATIONS

[37] Aranguren, J. L. *Human Communication,* trans. Frances
      Partridge. (New York: McGraw-Hill, World Univer-
      sity Library, 1967.)

[38] Baran, Paul. *Potential Market Demand for Two-Way
      Information Services to the Home, 1970–1990.*
      (Menlo Park, Cal.: Institute for the Future, 1971.)

[39] *Bell System Statistical Manual 1940–1969.* American
      Telephone & Telegraph Co., Corporate Results Analy-
      sis Division. (New York, 1970.)

[40] Brunner, John. *The Shockwave Rider.* (New York: Har-
      per & Row, 1975.)

[41] Cherry, Colin. *World Communication: Threat or
      Promise?* (London: John Wiley, Wiley-Interscience,
      1971.)

[42] Enzensberger, Hans Magnus, *The Consciousness Indus-
      try: On Literature, Politics and the Media.* (New
      York: Seabury Press, Continuum, 1974.)

[43] Innis, Harold A. *The Bias of Communication.* (To-
      ronto: University of Toronto Press, 1951.)

[44] ————. *Empire and Communications,* rev. Mary Q.
      Innis. (Toronto: University of Toronto Press, 1972.)

[45] Laborit, Henri. *Decoding the Human Message,* trans.
      Stephen Bodington and Alison Wilson. (London: Al-
      lison & Busby, 1977.)

[46] McLuhan, Marshall. *Understanding Media: The Exten-
      sions of Man.* (New York: McGraw-Hill, 1965.)

[47] Martin, James. *The Wired Society.* (Englewood Cliffs,
      N.J.: Prentice-Hall, 1978.)

[48] Mathison, Stuart L., and Philip M. Walker. *Computers*

and *Telecommunications: Issues in Public Policy.* (Englewood Cliffs, N.J.: Prentice-Hall, 1970.)

[49]   Nilles, J. M., et al. *The Telecommunications-Transportation Tradeoff: Options for Tomorrow.* (New York: John Wiley, 1976.)

[50]   Paine, Albert Bigelow. *In One Man's Life.* (New York: Harper & Brothers, 1921.)

[51]   Pye, Lucian W., ed. *Communications and Political Development.* (Princeton, N.J.: Princeton University Press, 1963.)

[52]   Servan-Schreiber, Jean Louis. *Le Pouvoir d'Informer.* (Paris: Éditions Robert Laffont, 1972).

[53]   Singer, Benjamin D. *Feedback and Society: A Study of the Uses of Mass Channels for Coping.* (Lexington, Mass.: D. C. Heath, Lexington Books, 1973.)

[54]   ———, ed. *Communications in Canadian Society.* (Toronto: Copp Clark, 1972.)

[55]   Soper, Horace N. *The Mails: History, Organization and . . Methods of Payment.* (London: Keliher, Hudson and Kearns, 1946.)

[56]   Zilliacus, Laurin. *From Pillar to Post.* (London: Heinemann, 1956.)

CONSUMER/SELF-HELP/SERVICES

[57]   Friedman, Yona. *Une Utopie Réalisée.* (Paris: Musée d'Art Moderne, 1975.)

[58]   Gartner, Alan, and Frank Riessman. *Self-Help in the Human Services.* (San Francisco: Jossey-Bass Publishers, 1977.)

[59]   ———. *The Service Society and the Consumer Vanguard.* (New York: Harper & Row, 1974.)

[60]   Halmos, Paul. *The Personal Society.* (London: Constable, 1970.)

[61]   Kallen, Horace M. *The Decline and Rise of the Consumer.* (New York: Appleton-Century, 1936.)

[62]   Katz, Alfred H., and Eugene I. Bender. *The Strength In Us: Self-Help Groups in the Modern World.* (New York: Franklin Watts, New Viewpoints, 1976.)

[63]   Lewis, Russell. *The New Service Society.* (London: Longman, 1973.)

[64]   Steidl, Rose E., and Esther Crew Bratton. *Work in the Home.* (New York: John Wiley, 1968.)

DEVELOPMENT THEORY/IMPERIALISM

[65]   Alatas, Syed Hussein. *Modernization and Social Change.* (Sydney, Australia: Angus and Robertson, 1972.)

[66]   Amin, Samir. *Accumulation on a World Scale: A Critique of the Theory of Underdevelopment*, trans. Brian Pearce. (New York: Monthly Review Press, 1974.)

[67]   Aron, Raymond. *The Industrial Society: Three Essays on Ideology and Development*. (New York: Simon and Schuster, Clarion, 1967.)

[68]   Arrighi Giovanni. *The Geometry of Imperialism: The Limits of Hobson's Paradigm*, trans. Patrick Camiller. (London: NLB, 1978.)

[69]   Bhagwati, Jagdish N., ed. *The New International Economic Order: The North-South Debate*. (Cambridge, Mass.: MIT Press, 1977.)

[70]   Bodard, Lucien. *Green Hell: Massacre of the Brazilian Indians*, trans. Jennifer Monaghan. (New York: Outerbridge and Dienstfrey, 1971.)

[71]   Brown, Michael Barratt. *The Economics of Imperialism*. (Harmondsworth, Middlesex: Penguin Books, 1974.)

[72]   Brown, Richard D. *Modernization: The Transformation of American Life 1600–1865*, ed. Eric Foner. (New York: Hill and Wang, American Century, 1976.)

[73]   Cohen, Benjamin J. *The Question of Imperialism: The Political Economy of Dominance and Dependence*. (London: Macmillan, 1974.)

[74]   Cotlow, Lewis. *The Twilight of the Primitive*. (New York: Ballantine Books, 1973.)

[75]   Curtin, Philip D., ed. *Imperialism*. (New York: Walker, 1971.)

[76]   Deutsch, Karl W., ed. *Ecosocial Systems and Ecopolitics: A Reader on Human and Social Implications of Environmental Management in Developing Countries*. (Paris: UNESCO, 1977.)

[77]   Emmanuel, Arghiri. *Unequal Exchange: A Study of the Imperialism of Trade*, trans. Brian Pearce. (London: NLB, Monthly Review Press, 1972.)

[78]   Erb, Guy F., and Valeriana Kallab, eds. *Beyond Dependency: The Developing World Speaks Out*. (Washington, D.C.: Overseas Development Council, 1975.)

[79]   Friedmann, Georges. *Industrial Society: The Emergence of the Human Problems of Automation*, ed. Harold L. Sheppard. (Glencoe, Ill.: Free Press, 1955.)

[80]   Goldwin, Robert A., ed. *Readings in Russian Foreign Policy*. (New York: Oxford University Press, 1959.)

[81]   Goulet, Denis. *The Cruel Choice: A New Concept in the Theory of Development*. (New York: Atheneum, 1971.)

[82]   Harvie, Christopher, Graham Martin, and Aaron Scharf,

eds. *Industrialisation and Culture 1830–1914*. (London: Macmillan, Open University Press, 1970.)

[83] Hobsbawm, E. J. *Industry and Empire: From 1750 to the Present Day*. (Baltimore: Penguin Books, 1969.)

[84] Hoselitz, Bert F., and Wilbert E. Moore, eds. *Industrialization and Society*. Proceedings of the Chicago Conference on Social Implications of Industrialization and Technical Change, 15–22 September, 1960. (Mouton, France: UNESCO, 1963.)

[85] Howe, Susanne. *Novels of Empire*. (New York: Columbia University Press, 1949.)

[86] Hudson, Michael. *Global Fracture: The New International Economic Order*. (New York: Harper & Row, 1977.)

[87] ———. *Super Imperialism: The Economic Strategy of American Empire*. (New York: Holt, Rinehart and Winston, 1972.)

[88] Lean, Geoffrey. *Rich World, Poor World*. (London: George Allen & Unwin, 1978.)

[89] Lenin, V. I. *Imperialism, The Highest Stage of Capitalism*. (Moscow: Progress Publishers, 1975.)

[90] Lerner, Daniel. *The Passing of Traditional Society: Modernizing the Middle East*. (New York: Free Press, 1958.)

[91] McHale, John, and Magda Cordell McHale. *Basic Human Needs: A Framework for Action*. (New Brunswick, N.J.: Transaction Books, 1977.)

[92] Magdoff, Harry. *The Age of Imperialism: The Economics of U.S. Foreign Policy*. (New York: Monthly Review Press, Modern Reader, 1969.)

[93] Mathias, Peter. *The First Industrial Nation: An Economic History of Britain 1700–1914*. (London: Methuen, 1969.)

[94] Myrdal, Gunnar. *An Approach to the Asian Drama: Methodological and Theoretical*. (New York: Vintage Books, 1970.)

[95] Nidergang, Marcel. *The 20 Latin Americas*, Vols. I and II, trans. Rosemary Sheed. (Harmondsworth, Middlesex: Penguin Books, 1971.)

[96] Said, Edward W. *Orientalism*. (New York: Pantheon Books, 1978.)

[97] Schumpeter, Joseph. *Imperialism, and Social Classes: Two Essays*, trans. Heinz Norden. (New York: World, 1955.)

[98] Toynbee, Arnold. *The Industrial Revolution*. (Boston: Beacon Press, 1956.)

[99] World Bank. *Rural Development*, Sector Policy Paper. (Washington, D.C., 1975.)

ECONOMIC HISTORY

[100]   Birnie, Arthur. *An Economic History of Europe 1760–1939.* (London: Methuen, University Paperbacks, 1962.)

[101]   Bogart, Ernest L., and Donald L. Kemmerer. *Economic History of the American People.* (New York: Longmans, Green, 1942.)

[102]   Burton, Theodore E. *Financial Crises and Periods of Industrial and Commercial Depression.* (Wells, Vt.: Fraser, 1966.)

[103]   Cipolla, Carlo M. *The Economic History of World Population.* (Harmondsworth, Middlesex: Penguin Books, 1964.)

[104]   Clough, Shepard B., Thomas Moodie, and Carol Moodie, eds. *Economic History of Europe: Twentieth Century.* (New York: Harper & Row, 1968.)

[105]   Fohlen, Claude. *The Fontana Economic History of Europe,* Vol. VI, Chapter 2, *France 1920–1970,* trans. Roger Greaves. (London: Fontana, 1973.)

[106]   Garraty, John A. *Unemployment in History: Economic Thought and Public Policy.* (New York: Harper & Row, 1978.)

[107]   Hartwell, R. M., et al. *The Long Debate on Poverty: Eight Essays on Industrialization and "The Condition of England."* (London: Institute of Economic Affairs, 1973.)

[108]   Hayek, Friedrich A., ed. *Capitalism and the Historian.* (Chicago: University of Chicago Press, 1954.)

[109]   Kenwood, A. G., and A. L. Lougheed. *The Growth of the International Economy 1820–1960.* (London: George Allen & Unwin, 1971.)

[110]   Kindleberger, Charles P. *Manias, Panics, and Crashes: A History of Financial Crises.* (New York: Basic Books, 1978.)

[111]   ———. *The World in Depression 1929–1939.* (London: Allen Lane, Penguin Press, 1973.)

[112]   Le Clair, Edward E., Jr., and Harold K. Schneider, eds. *Economic Anthropology: Readings in Theory and Analysis.* (New York: Holt, Rinehart and Winston, 1968.)

[113]   Maizels, Alfred. *Growth & Trade.* (London: Cambridge University Press, 1970.)

[114]   Nove, Alec. *An Economic History of the U.S.S.R.* (Harmondsworth, Middlesex: Penguin Books, 1969.)

[115]   Polanyi, Karl. *The Great Transformation.* (Boston: Beacon Press, 1957.)

[116] Ringer, Fritz K., ed. *The German Inflation of 1923.* (New York: Oxford University Press, 1969.)

[117] Sahlins, Marshall. *Stone Age Economics.* (Chicago: Aldine-Atherton, 1972.)

[118] Williams, Glyndwr. *The Expansion of Europe in the Eighteenth Century: Overseas Rivalry, Discovery and Exploitation.* (New York: Walker, 1967.)

[119] Woodruff, William. *The Fontana Economic History of Europe,* Vol. IV, Chapter 2, *The Emergence of an International Economy 1700–1914.* (London: Fontana, 1971.)

ECONOMICS

[120] Alampiev, P., O. Bogomolov, and Y. Shiryaev. *A New Approach to Economic Integration,* trans. Y. Sdobnikov. (Moscow: Progress Publishers, 1974.)

[121] Aliber, Robert Z. *The International Money Game,* 2nd and expanded edition. (New York: Basic Books, 1976.)

[122] Balassa, Bela. *The Theory of Economic Integration.* (London: George Allen & Unwin, 1962.)

[123] Bozyk, Pawel. *Poland as a Trading Partner.* (Warsaw: Interpress Publishers, 1972.)

[124] Brittan, Samuel. *Participation Without Politics: An Analysis of the Nature and the Role of Markets.* (London: Institute of Economic Affairs, 1975.)

[125] *Concentration in American Industry.* Report of the Subcommittee on Antitrust and Monopoly to the Committee on the Judiciary, U.S. Senate. (Washington, D.C.: U.S. Government Printing Office, 1957.)

[126] *Economic Concentration.* Hearings before the Subcommittee on Antitrust and Monopoly of the Committee on the Judiciary, U.S. Senate. Parts 7 and 7A. (Washington, D.C.: U.S. Government Printing Office, 1968.)

[127] Galbraith, John Kenneth. *Money: Whence It Came, Where It Went.* (Boston: Houghton Mifflin, 1975.)

[128] Henderson, Hazel. *Creating Alternative Futures: The End of Economics.* (New York: Berkley Windhover, 1978.)

[129] *Inflation: Economy and Society.* (London: Institute for Economic Affairs, 1972.)

[130] Ivens, Michael, ed. *Prophets of Freedom and Enterprise.* (London: Kogan Page for Aims of Industry, 1975.)

[131] Kornai, János. *Anti-Equilibrium: On Economic Systems Theory and the Tasks of Research.* (Amsterdam: North-Holland, 1971.)

[132] Kuznetsov, V. I. *Economic Integration: Two Ap-*

proaches, trans. Bean Brian. (Moscow: Progress Publishers, 1976.)

[133] Leiss, William. *The Limits to Satisfaction: On Needs and Commodities.* (London: Marion Boyars, 1978.)

[134] Little, Jane Sneddon. *Euro-Dollars: The Money-Market Gypsies.* (New York: Harper & Row, 1975.)

[135] Loebl, Eugen. *Humanomics: How We Can Make the Economy Serve Us—Not Destroy Us.* (New York: Random House, 1976.)

[136] Mandel, Ernest. *Decline of the Dollar: A Marxist View of the Monetary Crisis.* (New York: Monad Press, 1972.)

[137] Marris, Robin. *The Economic Theory of "Managerial" Capitalism.* (London: Macmillan, 1967.)

[138] Marx, Karl. *Capital: A Critical Analysis of Capitalist Production,* trans. Samuel Moore and Edward Aveling, ed. Frederick Engels. (New York: International Publishers, 1939.)

[139] Mintz, Morton, and Jerry S. Cohen. *America, Inc.: Who Owns and Operates the United States.* (New York: Dell, 1972.)

[140] Pasinetti, Luigi L. *Lectures on the Theory of Production.* (London: Macmillan, 1977.)

[141] Ritter, Lawrence S., and William L. Silber. *Money,* 2nd edition. (New York: Basic Books, 1973.)

[142] Robertson, James. *Profit or People?: The New Social Role of Money.* (London: Calder & Boyars, 1974.)

[143] Röpke, Wilhelm. *Economics of the Free Society,* trans. Patrick M. Boarman. (Chicago: Henry Regnery, 1963.)

[144] Rothbard, Murray N., and I. W. Sylvester. *What is Money?* (New York: Arno Press & The New York Times, 1972.)

[145] Scott, D. R. *The Cultural Significance of Accounts.* (Columbia, Mo.: Lucas Brothers Publishers, undated.)

[146] Senin, M. *Socialist Integration.* (Moscow: Progress Publishers, 1973.)

[147] Sherman, Howard. *Radical Political Economy: Capitalism and Socialism from a Marxist-Humanist Perspective.* (New York: Basic Books, 1972.)

[148] Smith, Adam. *Essays on Philosophical Subjects,* with *An Account of the Life and Writings of the Author* by Dugald Stewart. (Dublin: Messrs. Wogan, Byrne, J. Moore, Colbert, Rice, W. Jones, Porter, and Folingsby, 1795.)

[149] ————. *The Wealth of Nations,* ed. Edwin Cannan. (New York: Random House, Modern Library, 1937.)

[150] Toffler, Alvin. *The Eco-Spasm Report.* (New York: Bantam Books, 1975.)

[151] Ward, Benjamin. *What's Wrong with Economics?* (London: Macmillan, 1972.)

ENERGY/ECOLOGY

[152] Brown, Lester R. *In the Human Interest: A Strategy to Stabilize World Population.* (New York: W. W. Norton, 1974.)

[153] Carr, Donald E. *Energy & the Earth Machine.* (New York: W. W. Norton, 1976.)

[154] *Choosing Our Environment: Can We Anticipate the Future?* Hearings before the Panel on Environmental Science and Technology of the Subcommittee on Environmental Pollution of the Committee on Public Works, U.S. Senate. Parts 2 and 3. (Washington, D.C.: U.S. Government Printing Office, 1976.)

[155] Clark, Wilson. *Energy for Survival: The Alternative to Extinction.* (Garden City, N.Y.: Doubleday, Anchor Books, 1974.)

[156] Commoner, Barry. *The Closing Circle: Nature, Man, and Technology.* (New York: Alfred A. Knopf, 1971.)

[157] ———. *The Poverty of Power: Energy and the Economic Crisis.* (New York: Bantam Books, 1977.)

[158] Dansereau, Pierre. *Inscape and Landscape.* Massey Lectures, Twelfth Series, Canadian Broadcasting Corporation. (Toronto: CBC Learning Systems, 1973.)

[159] Dubos, René. *Man Adapting.* (New Haven: Yale University Press, 1965.)

[160] *Energy: Global Prospects 1985–2000.* Report of the Workshop on Alternative Energy Strategies, sponsored by MIT (New York: McGraw-Hill, 1977.)

[161] Hayes, Denis. *The Solar Energy Timetable.* (Washington, D.C.: Worldwatch Institute, 1978.)

[162] Helfrich, Harold W., Jr., ed. *The Environmental Crisis: Man's Struggle to Live With Himself.* (New Haven: Yale University Press, 1970.)

[163] Jungk, Robert. *The New Tyranny: How Nuclear Power Enslaves Us,* trans. Christopher Trump. (New York: Grosset & Dunlap, Fred Jordan Books, 1979.)

[164] Lyons, Barrow. *Tomorrow's Birthright: A Political and Economic Interpretation of Our Natural Resources.* (New York: Funk & Wagnalls, 1955.)

[165] Meadows, Donella H., et al. *The Limits to Growth: A Report for the Club of Rome's Project on the Predicament of Mankind.* (New York: Universe Books, 1972.)

[166] Munson, Richard, ed. *Countdown to a Nuclear Morato-
       rium.* (Washington, D.C.: Environmental Action
       Foundation, 1976.)
[167] Odum, Howard T. *Environment, Power, and Society.*
       (New York: John Wiley, Wiley-Interscience, 1971.)
[168] Sampson, Anthony. *The Seven Sisters: The Great Oil
       Companies and the World They Shaped.* (New York:
       Bantam Books, 1976.)
[169] Schumacher, E. F. *Small Is Beautiful: Economics as if
       People Mattered.* (New York: Harper & Row, Peren-
       nial Library, 1973.)
[170] *Tokyo Fights Pollution: An Urgent Appeal for Reform.*
       Liaison and Protocol Section, Bureau of General Af-
       fairs, Tokyo Metropolitan Government. (Tokyo,
       1971.)
[171] Ubbelohde, A. R. *Man and Energy.* (New York:
       George Braziller, 1955.)
[172] Université de Montréal/McGill University, Conserver
       Society Project. *The Selective Conserver Society,* Vol.
       1, *The Integrating Report.* (Montreal: GAMMA,
       1976.)

EVOLUTION & PROGRESS

[173] Bury, J. B. *The Idea of Progress.* (New York: Macmil-
       lan, 1932.)
[174] Calder, Nigel. *The Life Game: Evolution and the New
       Biology.* (New York: Dell, Laurel, 1975.)
[175] Crozier, Michel. *The Stalled Society.* (New York: Vik-
       ing Press, 1973.)
[176] De Closets, François. *En Danger de Progrès.* (Paris:
       Éditions Denoël, 1970.)
[177] *Evolution and the Fossil Record: Readings from Scien-
       tific American.* (San Francisco: W. H. Freeman,
       1978.)
[178] James, Bernard. *The Death of Progress.* (New York:
       Alfred A. Knopf, 1973.)
[179] Jantsch, Erich. *Design for Evolution: Self-Organization
       and Planning in the Life of Human Systems.* (New
       York: George Braziller, 1975.)
[180] ———, and Conrad H. Waddington, eds. *Evolution and
       Consciousness: Human Systems in Transition.* (Read-
       ing, Mass.: Addison-Wesley, 1976.)
[181] Kuznetsov, B. G. *Philosophy of Optimism,* trans. Ye. D.
       Khakina and V. L. Sulima. (Moscow: Progress Pub-
       lishers, 1977.)
[182] Sorel, Georges. *The Illusions of Progress,* trans. John
       and Charlotte Stanley. (Berkeley: University of Cali-
       fornia Press, 1969.)

[183]   Vacca, Roberto. *The Coming Dark Age,* trans. J. S. Whale. (Garden City, N.Y.: Doubleday, 1973.)

[184]   Van Doren, Charles. *The Idea of Progress.* (New York: Frederick A. Praeger, 1967.)

[185]   Williams, George C. *Adaptation and Natural Selection: A Critique of Some Current Evolutionary Thought.* (Princeton, N.J.: Princeton University Press, 1966.)

FAMILY/SEX

[186]   Beard, Mary R. *Woman as Force in History: A Study in Traditions and Realities.* (New York: Macmillan, 1946.)

[187]   Bernard, Jessie. *The Future of Marriage.* (New York: Bantam Books, 1973.)

[188]   ————. *The Future of Motherhood.* (New York: Penguin Books, 1974.)

[189]   Francoeur, Robert T., and Anna K. Francoeur, eds. *The Future of Sexual Relations.* (Englewood Cliffs, N.J.: Prentice-Hall, Spectrum, 1974.)

[190]   Friedan, Betty. *The Feminine Mystique,* 10th anniversary edition. (New York: W. W. Norton, 1974.)

[191]   Ginsberg, Eli, ed. *The Nation's Children.* (New York: Columbia University Press, 1960.)

[192]   Peck, Ellen, and Judith Senderowitz, eds. *Pronatalism: The Myth of Mom & Apple Pie.* (New York: Thomas Y. Crowell, 1974.)

[193]   Rapoport, Rhona, and Robert N. Rapoport. *Dual-Career Families.* (Harmondsworth, Middlesex: Penguin Books, 1971.)

[194]   Ross, Heather L., and Isabel V. Sawhill. *Time of Transition: The Growth of Families Headed by Women.* (Washington, D.C.: Urban Institute, 1975.)

[195]   Tripp, Maggie, ed. *Woman in the Year 2000.* (New York: Arbor House, 1974.)

[196]   Zaretsky, Eli. *Capitalism, the Family and Personal Life.* (London: Pluto Press, 1976.)

FUTURE STUDIES/Forecasts

[197]   Albrecht, Paul, et al., eds. *Faith, Science and the Future.* Preparatory readings for a world conference. (Geneva: World Council of Churches, 1978.)

[198]   Bell, Daniel. *The Coming of Post-Industrial Society: A Venture in Social Forecasting.* (New York: Basic Books, 1973.)

[199]   Bonn, Anne-Marie. *La Rêverie Terrienne et l'Espace de la Modernité.* (Paris: Librairie Klincksieck, 1976.)

[200]   Brzezinski, Zbigniew. *Between Two Ages: America's*

Role in the Technetronic Era. (New York: Viking Press, 1970.)

[201] Clarkson, Stephen, ed. Visions 2020. (Edmonton, Alberta: M. G. Hurtig, 1970.)

[202] Cornish, Edward, ed. 1999 The World of Tomorrow: Selections from The Futurist. (Washington, D.C.: World Future Society, 1978.)

[203] Daglish, Robert, ed. The Scientific and Technological Revolution: Social Effects and Prospects. (Moscow: Progress Publishers, 1972.)

[204] Economic Commission for Europe. Overall Economic Perspective for the ECE Region up to 1990. (New York: United Nations, 1978.)

[205] Fedchenko, V., ed. Things to Come. (Moscow: Mir Publishers, 1977.)

[206] Ford, Barbara. Future Food: Alternate Protein for the Year 2000. (New York: William Morrow, 1978.)

[207] Gross, Bertram M. Space-Time and Post-Industrial Society. Paper presented to 1965 seminars of Comparative Administration Group of the American Society for Public Administration. Syracuse University, 1966.

[208] Harman, Willis W. An Incomplete Guide to the Future. (San Francisco: San Francisco Book Company, 1976.)

[209] Laszlo, Ervin, et al. Goals for Mankind: A Report to the Club of Rome on the New Horizons of Global Community. (New York: E. P. Dutton, 1977.)

[210] Malita, Mircea. Chronik für das jahr 2000. (Bucharest: Kriterion, 1973.)

[211] Man, Science, Technology: A Marxist Analysis of the Scientific Technological Revolution. (Prague: Academia Prague, 1973.)

[212] Maruyama, Magoroh, and Arthur Harkins, eds. Cultures Beyond the Earth. (New York: Random House, Vintage Books, 1975.)

[213] ———. Cultures of the Future. (The Hague: Mouton Publishers, 1978.)

[214] Mesarovic, Mihajlo, and Eduard Pestel. Mankind at the Turning Point: The Second Report to The Club of Rome. (New York: E. P. Dutton, Reader's Digest Press, 1974.)

[215] 1985: La France Face au Choc du Futur. Plan et prospectives, Commissariat Général du Plan. (Paris: Librarie Armand Colin, 1972.)

[216] Royal Ministry for Foreign Affairs in Cooperation with the Secretariat for Future Studies. To Choose a Future: A Basis for Discussion and Deliberations on Future Studies in Sweden, trans. Rudy Feichtner. (Stockholm: Swedish Institute, 1974.)

[217]   Sorrentino, Joseph N. *The Moral Revolution.* (New York: Manor Books, 1974.)

[218]   Spekke, Andrew A., ed. *The Next 25 Years: Crisis & Opportunity.* (Washington, D.C.: World Future Society, 1975.)

[219]   Stillman, Edmund, et al. *L'Envol de la France: Portrait de la France dans les années 80.* (Paris: Hachette Littérature, 1973.)

[220]   Tanaka, Kakuei. *Building a New Japan: A Plan for Remodeling the Japanese Archipelago.* (Tokyo: Simul Press, 1973.)

[221]   Theobald, Robert. *Habit and Habitat.* (Englewood Cliffs, N.J.: Prentice-Hall, 1972.)

[222]   *Thinking Ahead: UNESCO and the Challenges of Today and Tomorrow.* (Paris: UNESCO, 1977.)

FUTURE STUDIES/General

[223]   Ackoff, Russell L. *Redesigning the Future: A Systems Approach to Societal Problems.* (New York: John Wiley, 1974.)

[224]   Arab-Ogly, E. *In the Forecasters' Maze,* trans. Katherine Judelson. (Moscow: Progress Publishers, 1975.)

[225]   Bell, Wendell, and James A. Mau, eds. *The Sociology of the Future.* (New York: Russell Sage Foundation, 1971.)

[226]   Boucher, Wayne I., ed. *The Study of the Future: An Agenda for Research.* (Washington, D.C.: U.S. Government Printing Office, 1977.)

[227]   *Choosing Our Environment: Can We Anticipate the Future?* See [154].

[228]   Cornish, Edward, ed. *Resources Directory for America's Third Century,* Part 1, *An Introduction to the Study of the Future.* (Washington, D.C.: World Future Society, 1977.)

[229]   ———. *Resources Directory for America's Third Century,* Part 2, *Information Sources for the Study of the Future.* (Washington, D.C.: World Future Society, 1977.)

[230]   ———, et al. *The Study of the Future: An Introduction to the Art and Science of Understanding and Shaping Tomorrow's World.* (Washington, D.C.: World Future Society, 1977.)

[231]   Dickson, Paul. *The Future File: A Guide for People with One Foot in the 21st Century.* (New York: Rawson Associates, 1977.)

[232]   Emery, F. E., and E. L. Trist. *Towards a Social Ecology: Contextual Appreciation of the Future in the Present.* (London: Plenum Press, 1973.)

[233] Feinberg, Gerald. *The Prometheus Project: Mankind's Search for Long-Range Goals.* (Garden City, N.Y.: Doubleday, Anchor Books, 1969.)

[234] Heilbroner, Robert I. *The Future as History.* (New York: Grove Press, 1961.)

[235] Jouvenel, Bertrand de. *The Art of Conjecture,* trans. Nikita Lary. (New York: Basic Books, 1967.)

[236] Jungk, Robert. *The Everyman Project: Resources for a Humane Future,* trans. Gabriele Annan and Renate Esslen. (New York: Liveright, 1977.)

[237] McHale, John. *The Future of the Future.* (New York: George Braziller, 1969.)

[238] ———, and Magda Cordell McHale. *Futures Studies: An International Survey.* (New York: United Nations Institute for Training and Research, 1975.)

[239] Polak, Fred L. *The Image of the Future,* trans. Elise Boulding. (Amsterdam: Elsevier Scientific, 1973.)

[240] ———. *Prognostics.* (Amsterdam: Elsevier, 1971.)

[241] Sullivan, John Edward. *Prophets of the West: An Introduction to the Philosophy of History.* (New York: Holt, Rinehart and Winston, 1970.)

HISTORY

[242] Bloch, Marc. *Feudal Society,* Vol. 1, *The Growth of Ties of Dependence,* trans. L. A. Manyon. (Chicago: University of Chicago Press, Phoenix Books, 1964.)

[243] ———. *Feudal Society,* Vol. 2, *Social Classes and Political Organization,* trans. L. A. Manyon. (Chicago: University of Chicago Press, Phoenix Books, 1964.)

[244] Braudel, Fernand. *Capitalism and Material Life: 1400–1800,* trans. Miriam Kochan. (New York: Harper & Row, Harper Colophon Books, 1975.)

[245] ———. *The Mediterranean and the Mediterranean World in the Age of Philip II,* Vols. I and II, trans. Siân Reynolds. (New York: Harper & Row, 1973.)

[246] Collis, Maurice. *Cortés and Montezuma.* (London: Faber and Faber, 1963.)

[247] Commager, Henry Steele, ed. *Documents of American History,* 3rd edition. (New York: F. S. Crofts, 1943.)

[248] Darlington, C. D. *The Evolution of Man and Society.* (London: George Allen & Unwin, 1969.)

[249] Deane, Phyllis. *The First Industrial Revolution.* (London: Cambridge University Press, 1965.)

[250] Elias, Norbert. *The Civilizing Process: The Development of Manners,* trans. Edmund Jephcott. (New York: Urizen Books, 1978.)

[251] Glass, D. V., and D. E. C. Eversley, eds. *Population in History.* (London: Edward Arnold, 1965.)

[252] Hale, J. R. *Renaissance Europe 1480–1520.* (London: Fontana, 1971.)

[253] Hill, Christopher. *Reformation to Industrial Revolution: 1530–1780.* (Baltimore: Penguin Books, 1969.)

[254] Hofstadter, Richard, William Miller, and Daniel Aaron. *The United States: The History of a Republic,* 2nd edition. (Englewood Cliffs, N.J.: Prentice-Hall, 1967.)

[255] Huggett, Frank E. *The Past, Present and Future of Factory Life and Work: A Documentary Inquiry.* (London: Harrap, 1973.)

[256] Kirchner, Walther. *Western Civilization Since 1500.* (New York: Barnes & Noble, 1969.)

[257] Littlefield, Henry W. *History of Europe 1500–1848,* 5th edition. (New York: Barnes & Noble, 1939.)

[258] Mannix, Daniel P. *Those About to Die.* (New York: Ballantine Books, 1958.)

[259] Matthews, George T., ed. *The Fugger Newsletter.* (New York: Capricorn Books, 1970.)

[260] Morazé, Charles. *The Triumph of the Middle Classes: A Study of European Values in the Nineteenth Century.* (London: Weidenfeld and Nicolson, 1966.)

[261] Plumb, J. H. *The Growth of Political Stability in England 1675–1725.* (Harmondsworth, Middlesex: Penguin Books, 1967.)

[262] Sansom, G. B. *The Western World and Japan: A Study in the Interaction of European and Asiatic Cultures.* (New York: Random House, Vintage Books, 1973.)

[263] Segal, Ronald. *The Struggle Against History.* (New York: Bantam Books, 1973.)

[264] Stewart, Donald H. *The Opposition Press of the Federalist Period.* (Albany: State University of New York Press, 1969.)

[265] Tawney, R. H. *Religion and the Rise of Capitalism: A Historical Study.* (New York: New American Library, Mentor, 1954.)

[266] Thompson, E. P. *The Making of the English Working Class.* (New York: Vintage Books, 1963.)

[267] Turner, Frederick J. *The Significance of the Frontier in American History.* (New York: Readex Microprint, 1966.)

[268] Walker, James Blaine. *The Epic of American Industry.* (New York: Harper & Brothers, 1949.)

[269] Weber, Max. *The Protestant Ethic and the Spirit of Capitalism,* trans. Talcott Parsons. (New York: Charles Scribner's Sons, 1958.)

NATIONS/SEPARATISM/TRANSNATIONAL INSTITUTIONS

[270] Barnet, Richard J., and Ronald E. Müller. *Global Reach: The Power of the Multinational Corporations.* (New York: Simon and Schuster, 1974.)

[271] Bendix, Reinhard. *Nation-Building and Citizenship: Studies of Our Changing Social Order.* (Garden City, N.Y.: Doubleday, Anchor Books, 1969.)

[272] Brown, Lester R. *World Without Borders.* (New York: Random House, 1972.)

[273] Brown, Seyom. *New Forces in World Politics.* (Washington, D.C.: Brookings Institution, 1974.)

[274] ————, et al. *Regimes for the Ocean, Outer Space, and Weather.* (Washington, D.C.: Brookings Institution, 1977.)

[275] Callenbach, Ernest. *Ecotopia: The Notebooks and Reports of William Weston.* (New York: Bantam Books, 1977.)

[276] Cobban, Alfred. *The Nation State and National Self-Determination.* (New York: Thomas Y. Crowell, 1969.)

[277] Deutsch, Karl W. *Nationalism and Social Communication: An Inquiry into the Foundations of Nationality.* (Cambridge, Mass.: MIT Press, 1966.)

[278] Falk, Richard A. *A Study of Future Worlds.* New York: Free Press, 1975.)

[279] Fawcett, J. E. S. *The Law of Nations.* (New York: Basic Books, 1968.)

[280] *Information, Perception and Regional Policy.* Report prepared for National Science Foundation, Research Applications Directorate, RANN. (Washington, D.C.: National Science Foundation, 1975.)

[281] Kaldor, Mary. *The Disintegrating West.* (New York: Hill and Wang, 1978.)

[282] Kohn, Hans. *The Idea of Nationalism: A Study in Its Origins and Background.* (Toronto: Collier, 1944.)

[283] Lenin, V. I. *The Right of Nations to Self-Determination.* (Moscow: Progress Publishers, 1947.)

[284] Lévesque, René. *An Option for Quebec.* (Toronto: McClelland and Stewart, 1968.)

[285] Minogue, K. R. *Nationalism.* (Baltimore: Penguin Books, 1967.)

[286] Servan-Schreiber, Jean-Jacques. *Le Pouvoir Régional.* (Paris: Éditions Bernard Grasset, 1971.)

[287] Shaw, Brian. *The Gospel According to Saint Pierre.* (Richmond Hill, Ont.: Pocket Books Canada, 1969.)

[288] Smith, Anthony D. *Theories of Nationalism.* (New York: Harper & Row, Harper Torchbooks, 1971.)

[289] Stephenson, Hugh. *The Coming Clash: The Impact of*

Multinational Corporations on National States. (New York: Saturday Review Press, 1972.)

[290]   Thomas, Ned. *The Welsh Extremist.* (Talybont, Cardiganshire: Y Lolfa, 1973.)

[291]   Trudeau, Pierre Elliott. *Federalism and the French Canadians.* (Toronto: Macmillan of Canada, 1968.)

[292]   Turner, Louis. *Multinational Companies and the Third World.* (New York: Hill and Wang, 1973.)

[293]   *The United Nations and the Future.* Proceedings of UNITAR Conference on the Future, Moscow, June 10–14, 1974. (Moscow, UNITAR, 1976.)

[294]   *The United States and the United Nations.* Hearings before the Committee on Foreign Relations, U.S. Senate. (Washington, D.C.: U.S. Government Printing Office, 1975.)

[295]   Unterman, Lee D., and Christine W. Swent, eds. *The Future of the United States Multinational Corporation.* (Charlottesville: University of Virginia Press, 1975.)

[296]   Webb, Keith. *The Growth of Nationalism in Scotland.* (Glasgow: Molendinar Press, 1977.)

[297]   Wilczynski, J. *The Multinationals and East-West Relations: Towards Transideological Collaboration.* (London: Macmillan, 1976.)

[298]   *Year-Book of World Problems and Human Potential,* compiled by the Secretariats of Union of International Associations. (Brussels, 1976.)

PHILOSOPHY

[299]   Borodulina, T., ed. *K. Marx, F. Engels, V. Lenin: On Historical Materialism.* (Moscow: Progress Publishers, 1974.)

[300]   Capra, Fritjof. *The Tao of Physics: An Exploration of the Parallels Between Modern Physics and Eastern Mysticism.* (New York: Bantam Books, 1977.)

[301]   DeGreene, Kenyon B., ed. *Systems Psychology.* (New York: McGraw-Hill, 1970.)

[302]   De La Mettrie, Julien Offray. *Man a Machine,* annot. Gertrude Carman Bussey. (La Salle, Ill.: Open Court, 1912.)

[303]   Descartes, René. *Discourse on Method,* trans. John Veitch. (La Salle, Ill.: Open Court, 1962.)

[304]   Feinberg, Gerald. *What is the World Made Of?: Atoms, Leptons, Quarks, and Other Tantalizing Particles.* (Garden City, N.Y.: Doubleday, Anchor Books, 1978.)

[305]   Gellner, Ernest. *Thought and Change.* (Chicago: University of Chicago Press, 1965.)

[306]   Hyman, Stanley Edgar. *The Tangled Bank: Darwin, Marx, Frazer and Freud as Imaginative Writers.* (New York: Atheneum, 1974.)

[307]   Lewin, Kurt. *Field Theory in Social Science: Selected Theoretical Papers,* ed. Dorwin Cartwright. (New York: Harper & Row, Harper Torchbooks, 1951.)

[308]   Lilienfeld, Robert. *The Rise of Systems Theory: An Ideological Analysis.* (New York: John Wiley-Interscience, 1978.)

[309]   Matson, Floyd W. *The Broken Image: Man, Science and Society.* (New York: Doubleday, Anchor Books, 1966.)

[310]   Munitz, Milton K., ed. *Theories of the Universe: From Babylonian Myth to Modern Science.* (Glencoe, Ill.: Free Press, Falcon's Wing Press, 1957.)

[311]   Ramo, Simon. *Cure for Chaos: Fresh Solutions to Social Problems Through the Systems Approach.* (New York: David McKay, 1969.)

[312]   Russell, Bertrand. *A History of Western Philosophy.* (New York: Simon and Schuster, 1945.)

[313]   ———. *Human Knowledge: Its Scope and Limits.* (New York: Simon and Schuster, Touchstone, 1948.)

[314]   Webb, James. *The Flight from Reason.* (London: Macdonald, 1971.)

[315]   Weizenbaum, Joseph. *Computer Power and Human Reason: From Judgment to Calculation.* (San Francisco: W. H. Freeman, 1976.)

POLITICAL THEORY/General

[316]   Jacker, Corinne. *The Black Flag of Anarchy: Antistatism in the United States.* (New York: Charles Scribner's Sons, 1968.)

[317]   Johnson, Chalmers. *Revolutionary Change.* (Boston: Little, Brown, 1966.)

[318]   Jouvenel, Bertrand de. *On Power: Its Nature and the History of Its Growth,* trans. J. E. Huntington. (Boston: Beacon Press, 1962.)

[319]   Krader, Lawrence. *Formation of the State.* (Englewood Cliffs, N.J.: Prentice-Hall, 1968.)

[320]   Lenin, V. I. *The State and Revolution.* (Moscow: Progress Publishers, 1949.)

[321]   Oppenheimer, Franz. *The State,* trans. John Gitterman. (New York: Free Life Editions, 1975.)

[322]   Ortega y Gasset, José. *Man and Crisis,* trans. Mildred Adams. (New York: W. W. Norton, 1958.)

[323]   Rousseau, Jean-Jacques. *The Social Contract,* trans. Maurice Cranston. (Baltimore: Penguin Books, 1968.)

[324]   Silvert, Kalman H. *The Reason for Democracy*. (New York: Viking Press, 1977.)

[325]   Swartz, Marc J., Victor W. Turner, and Arthur Tuden, eds. *Political Anthropology*. (Chicago: Aldine-Atherton, 1966.)

POLITICAL THEORY/Elites

[326]   Barber, Bernard. *Social Stratification: A Comparative Analysis of Structure and Process*. (New York: Harcourt, Brace & World, 1957.)

[327]   Benveniste, Guy. *The Politics of Expertise*. (Berkeley, Cal.: Glendessary Press, 1972.)

[328]   Bottomore, T. B. *Elites and Society*. (New York: Basic Books, 1964.)

[329]   Brewer, Garry D. *Politicians, Bureaucrats, and the Consultant: A Critique of Urban Problem Solving*. (New York: Basic Books, 1973.)

[330]   Burnham, James. *The Managerial Revolution*. (Bloomington: Indiana University Press, 1960.)

[331]   Dimock, Marshall E. *The Japanese Technocracy: Management and Government in Japan*. (New York: Walker/Weatherhill, 1968.)

[332]   Djilas, Milovan. *The New Class: An Analysis of the Communist System*. (New York: Frederick A. Praeger, 1957.)

[333]   ———. *The Unperfect Society: Beyond the New Class*, trans. Dorian Cooke. (London: Unwin Books, 1972.)

[334]   Dye, Thomas R., and L. Harmon Zeigler. *The Irony of Democracy: An Uncommon Introduction to American Politics*, 2nd edition. (Belmont, Cal.: Duxbury Press, 1972.)

[335]   Girvetz, Harry K. *Democracy and Elitism: Two Essays with Selected Readings*. (New York: Charles Scribner's Sons, 1967.)

[336]   Gouldner, Alvin W. *The Future of Intellectuals and the Rise of the New Class*. (New York: Seabury Press, Continuum, 1979.)

[337]   Gvishiani, D. M., S. R. Mikulinsky, and S. A. Kugel, eds. *The Scientific Intelligentsia in the USSR: Structure and Dynamics of Personnel*, trans. Jáne Sayers. (Moscow: Progress Publishers, 1976.)

[338]   Keller, Suzanne. *Beyond the Ruling Class: Strategic Elites in Modern Society*. (New York: Random House, 1963.)

[339]   Lederer, Emil. *State of the Masses: The Threat of the Classless Society*. (New York: Howard Fertig, 1967.)

[340]   Meynaud, Jean. *Technocracy*, trans. Paul Barnes. (London: Faber and Faber, 1968.)

[341]   Ortega y Gasset, José. *The Revolt of the Masses.* (New York: W. W. Norton, 1957.)

[342]   Phillips, Kevin P. *Mediacracy: American Parties and Politics in the Communications Age.* (Garden City, N.Y.: Doubleday, 1975.)

[343]   Young, Michael. *The Rise of the Meritocracy 1870–2033: An Essay on Education and Equality.* (Harmondsworth, Middlesex: Penguin Books, 1961.)

POLITICAL THEORY/Representation/Participation

[344]   Afanasyev, V. G. *The Scientific Management of Society,* trans. L. Ilyitskaya. (Moscow: Progress Publishers, 1971.)

[345]   Araneta, Salvador. *The Effective Democracy For All.* (Manila: AIA, Bayanikasan Research Foundation, 1976.)

[346]   Bezold, Clement, ed. *Anticipatory Democracy: People in the Politics of the Future.* (New York: Random House, Vintage Books, 1978.)

[347]   Bihari, Ottó. *Socialist Representative Institutions,* trans. József Desényi and Imre Móra. (Budapest: Akadémiai Kiadó, 1970.)

[348]   Birch, A. H. *Representation.* (London: Macmillan, 1972.)

[349]   Crick, Bernard. *The Reform of Parliament.* (London: Weidenfeld and Nicolson, 1970.)

[350]   Finletter, Thomas K. *Can Representative Government Do the Job?* (New York: Reynal & Hitchcock, 1945.)

[351]   Haefele, Edwin T. *Representative Government and Environmental Management.* (Baltimore: Johns Hopkins University Press, 1973.)

[352]   International Labour Office. *Participation by Employers' and Workers' Organisations in Economic and Social Planning: A General Introduction.* (Geneva: ILO, 1971.)

[353]   Ionescu, Ghita, and Ernest Gellner, eds. *Populism: Its Meanings and National Characteristics.* (London: Weidenfeld and Nicolson, 1970.)

[354]   Jones, Charles O. *Every Second Year: Congressional Behavior and the Two-Year Term.* (Washington, D.C.: Brookings Institution, 1967.)

[355]   Kozak, Jan. *Without a Shot Being Fired: The Role of Parliament and the Unions in a Communist Revolution.* (London: Independent Information Centre, 1957.)

[356]   Langton, Stuart, ed. *Citizen Participation in America: Essays on the State of the Art.* (Lexington, Mass.: D. C. Heath, Lexington Books, 1978.)

[357]   Loewenberg, Gerhard, ed. *Modern Parliaments: Change or Decline?* (Chicago: Aldine-Atherton, 1971.)

[358]   Mill, John Stuart. *Utilitarianism, Liberty and Representative Government.* (New York: E. P. Dutton, 1951.)

[359]   Partridge, P. H. *Consent & Consensus.* (New York: Praeger, 1971.)

[360]   Pateman, Carole. *Participation and Democratic Theory.* (Cambridge: Cambridge University Press, 1970.)

[361]   Pitkin, Hanna Fenichel, ed. *Representation.* (New York: Atherton Press, 1969.)

[362]   Schramm, F. K., ed. *The Bundestag: Legislation in the Federal Republic of Germany.* (Bonn: E. Beinhauer, 1973.)

[363]   Spufford, Peter. *Origins of the English Parliament.* (New York: Barnes & Noble, 1967.)

POLITICS/Comparative

[364]   Berkowitz, S. D., and Robert K. Logan, eds. *Canada's Third Option.* (Toronto: Macmillan of Canada, 1978.)

[365]   Blondel, Jean. *Comparing Political Systems.* (London: Weidenfeld and Nicolson, 1973.)

[366]   Cohen, Ronald, and John Middleton, eds. *Comparative Political Systems: Studies in the Politics of Pre-industrial Societies.* (Garden City, N.Y.: Natural History Press, 1967.)

[367]   Finer, S. E. *Comparative Government.* (Harmondsworth, Middlesex: Penguin Books, 1970.)

[368]   Gorden, Morton. *Comparative Political Systems: Managing Conflict.* (New York: Macmillan, 1972.)

[369]   Hamilton, Alastair. *The Appeal of Fascism: A Study of Intellectuals and Fascism 1919–1945.* (London: Anthony Blond, 1971.)

[370]   Kennedy, Gavin, ed. *The Radical Approach: Papers on an Independent Scotland.* (Edinburgh: Palingenesis Press, 1976.)

[371]   McClelland, J. S., ed. *The French Right: From De Maistre to Maurras,* trans. Frears, Harber, McClelland, and Phillipson. (London: Jonathan Cape, 1970.)

[372]   Macridis, Roy C., and Robert E. Ward, eds. *Modern Political Systems: Europe,* 2nd edition. (Englewood Cliffs, N.J.: Prentice-Hall, 1968.)

[373]   Mosse, George L. *The Crisis of German Ideology: Intellectual Origins of the Third Reich.* (London: Weidenfeld and Nicolson, 1966.)

[374]   Parti Socialiste Unifié. *Controler Aujourd'hui pour Décider Demain,* manifeste. (Paris: Tema-Éditions, 1972.)

[375]   Russett, Bruce M. *Trends in World Politics.* (New York: Macmillan, 1965.)

[376]   Scalapino, Robert A., and Junnosuke Masumi. *Parties*

and Politics in Contemporary Japan. (Berkeley: University of California Press, 1962.)

[377] Smith, Gordon. *Politics in Western Europe: A Comparative Analysis.* (London: Heinemann Educational Books, 1972.)

[378] Starcke, Anna. *Survival: Taped Interviews With South Africa's Power Élite.* (Cape Town: Tafelberg, 1978.)

POLITICS/U.S.

[379] Armbrister, Trevor. *A Matter of Accountability: The True Story of the Pueblo Affair.* (New York: Coward-McCann, 1970.)

[380] Becker, Ted, et al. *Un-Vote for a New America: A Guide to Constitutional Revolution.* (Boston: Allyn and Bacon, 1976.)

[381] Becker, Theodore L. *American Government: Past, Present, Future.* (Boston: Allyn and Bacon, 1976.)

[382] Boorstin, Daniel J. *The Decline of Radicalism: Reflections on America Today.* (New York: Random House, 1969.)

[383] Brant, Irving. *The Bill of Rights: Its Origin and Meaning.* (New York: New American Library, Mentor, 1965.)

[384] Cullop, Floyd G. *The Constitution of the United States: An Introduction.* (New York: New American Library, Signet, 1969.)

[385] Everett, Edward. *The Mount Vernon Papers,* No. 27. (New York: D. Appleton, 1860.)

[386] Fisher, Louis. *President and Congress: Power and Policy.* (New York: Free Press, 1972.)

[387] Flexner, James Thomas. *George Washington and the New Nation (1783–1793).* (Boston: Little, Brown, 1970.)

[388] Gilpin, Henry D., ed. *The Papers of James Madison,* Vol. II. (Washington, D.C.: Langtree & O'Sullivan, 1840.)

[389] Hamilton, Alexander, John Jay, and James Madison. *The Federalist: A Commentary on the Constitution of the United States.* (New York: Random House, Modern Library.)

[390] Hougan, Jim. *Spooks: The Haunting of America—The Private Use of Secret Agents.* (New York: William Morrow, 1978.)

[391] Nixon, Richard. *The Memoirs of Richard Nixon.* (New York: Grosset & Dunlap, 1978.)

[392] Padover, Saul K., ed. *Thomas Jefferson on Democracy.* (New York: New American Library, Mentor; Copyright 1939 D. Appleton-Century.)

[393]   Paine, Thomas. *Rights of Man: Being an Answer to Mr. Burke's Attack on the French Revolution*, ed. Hypatia Bradlaugh Bonner. (London: C. A. Watts, 1937.)

[394]   Parrington, Vernon Louis. *Main Currents in American Thought: An Interpretation of American Literature from the Beginnings to 1920.* (New York: Harcourt, Brace, 1927.)

[395]   Perloff, Harvey S., ed. *The Future of the United States Government: Toward the Year 2000.* (New York: George Braziller, 1971.)

[396]   Saloma, John S., III, and Frederick H. Sontag. *Parties: The Real Opportunity for Effective Citizen Politics.* (New York: Alfred A. Knopf, 1972.)

[397]   Scammon, Richard M., and Alice V. McGillivray, eds. *America Votes 12: A Handbook of Contemporary Election Statistics.* (Washington, D.C.: Elections Research Center, Congressional Quarterly, 1977.)

[398]   Schlesinger, Arthur M., Jr. *The Imperial Presidency.* (New York: Popular Library, 1974.)

[399]   Smith, Edward Conrad, ed. *The Constitution of the United States: With Case Summaries.* (New York: Barnes & Noble, 1972.)

[400]   Steinfels, Peter. *The Neoconservatives: The Men Who Are Changing America's Politics.* (New York: Simon and Schuster, 1979.)

[401]   Tocqueville, Alexis de. *Democracy in America*, text Henry Reeve, rev. Francis Bowen, and ed. Phillips Bradley. (New York: Alfred A. Knopf, Vintage Books, 1945.)

PSYCHOLOGY

[402]   Allport, Gordon W. *Personality: A Psychological Interpretation.* (New York: Henry Holt, 1937.)

[403]   Back, Kurt W. *Beyond Words: The Story of Sensitivity Training and the Encounter Movement.* (New York: Russell Sage Foundation, 1972.)

[404]   Conway, Flo, and Jim Siegelman. *Snapping: America's Epidemic of Sudden Personality Change.* (Philadelphia: J. B. Lippincott, 1978.)

[405]   Freedman, Alfred M., M.D., Harold I. Kaplan, M.D., and Benjamin J. Sadock, M.D. *Modern Synopsis of Comprehensive Textbook of Psychiatry.* (Baltimore, Williams & Wilkins, 1972.)

[406]   Fromm, Erich. *Escape from Freedom.* (New York: Avon Library, 1965.)

[407]   ————. *The Sane Society.* (Greenwich, Conn.: Fawcett Premier, 1955.)

[408]   Gerth, Hans, and C. Wright Mills. *Character and Social Structure: The Psychology of Social Institutions.* (New York: Harcourt, Brace & World, Harbinger, 1953.)

[409]   Gross, Martin L. *The Psychological Society.* (New York: Random House, 1978.)

[410]   Gross, Ronald, and Paul Osterman, eds. *Individualism: Man in Modern Society.* (New York: Dell, Laurel, 1971.)

[411]   Hall, Calvin S., and Gardner Lindzey. *Theories of Personality,* 3rd edition. (New York: John Wiley, 1978.)

[412]   Kardiner, Abram, et al. *The Psychological Frontiers of Society.* (New York: Columbia University Press, 1945.)

[413]   Kilpatrick, William. *Identity & Intimacy.* (New York: Delacorte Press, 1975.)

[414]   May, Rollo. *Power and Innocence: A Search for the Sources of Violence.* (New York: W. W. Norton, 1972.)

[415]   Reich, Wilhelm. *The Mass Psychology of Fascism,* trans. Vincent R. Carfagno. (New York: Farrar, Straus & Giroux, 1971.)

[416]   Ruitenbeek, Hendrik M., ed., *Varieties of Personality Theory.* (New York: E. P. Dutton, 1964.)

[417]   Smirnov, Georgi. *Soviet Man: The Making of a Socialist Type of Personality,* trans. Robert Daglish. (Moscow: Progress Publishers, 1973.)

[418]   Stevens, John O., ed. *Gestalt Is—A Collection of Articles About Gestalt Therapy and Living.* (New York: Bantam Books, 1977.)

[419]   Sullivan, Harry Stack, M.D. *The Fusion of Psychiatry and Social Science.* (New York: W. W. Norton, 1964.)

[420]   Winter, Ruth. *The Smell Book.* (Philadelphia: J. B. Lippincott, 1976.)

[421]   Zurcher, Louis A., Jr. *The Mutable Self: A Self-Concept for Social Change.* (Beverly Hills, Cal.: Sage Publications, 1977.)

SCIENCE/TECHNOLOGY

[422]   Anderson, Robert H., and Nake M. Kamrany. *Advanced Computer-Based Manufacturing Systems for Defense Needs.* (Marina del Rey, Cal.: USC, Information Sciences Institute, 1973.)

[423]   *The Application of Computer Technology for Development.* United Nations, Department of Economic and Social Affairs, Second Report of the Secretary-General. (New York, 1973.)

[424]   *Appropriate Technology in the Commonwealth, A*

Directory of Institutions. Food Production & Rural Development Division, Commonwealth Secretariat. (London, 1977.)

[425]   *Appropriate Technology in the United States: An Exploratory Study.* Study conducted by Integrative Design Associates for the National Science Foundation RANN program. (Washington, D.C.: U.S. Government Printing Office, 1977.)

[426]   Asimov, Isaac. *I, Robot.* (New York: Fawcett Crest, 1950.)

[427]   ———. *Understanding Physics,* Vol. III, *The Electron, Proton, and Neutron.* (New York: New American Library, Signet, 1966.)

[428]   Baldwin, J., and Stewart Brand, eds. *Soft-Tech.* (New York: Penguin Books, 1978.)

[429]   Boorstin, Daniel J. *The Republic of Technology: Reflections on Our Future Community.* (New York: Harper & Row, 1978.)

[430]   Brand, Stewart, ed. *Space Colonies.* (New York: Penguin Books, 1977.)

[431]   Buchholz, Hans, and Wolfgang Gmelin, eds. *Science and Technology and the Future,* Parts 1 and 2. (Munich: K. G. Saur, 1979.)

[432]   Butterfield, Herbert. *The Origins of Modern Science: 1300–1800.* (New York: Free Press, 1957.)

[433]   Cardwell, D. S. L. *Turning Points in Western Technology.* (New York: Neale Watson Academic Publications, Science History Publications, 1972.)

[434]   Cross, Nigel, David Elliot, and Robin Roy, eds. *Man-Made Futures: Readings in Society, Technology and Design.* (London: Hutchinson, 1974.)

[435]   Einstein, Albert. *Ideas and Opinions,* trans. Sonja Bargmann. (New York: Dell, Laurel. Copyright Crown, 1954.)

[436]   Ellis, John. *The Social History of the Machine Gun.* (New York: Pantheon Books, 1975.)

[437]   Etzioni, Amitai. *Genetic Fix.* (New York: Macmillan, 1973.)

[438]   Farago, F. T. *Handbook of Dimensional Measurement.* (New York: Industrial Press, 1965.)

[439]   Farrington, Benjamin. *Head and Hand in Ancient Greece: Four Studies in the Social Relations of Thought.* (London: Watts, Thinker's Library, 1947.)

[440]   Feyerabend, Paul. *Against Method: Outline of an Anarchistic Theory of Knowledge.* (London: NLB, Verso, 1975.)

[441]   Fidell, Oscar H., ed. *Ideas in Science.* (New York: Washington Square Press, Reader's Enrichment, 1966.)

[442]   Ford, Henry. *My Life and Work.* (New York: Doubleday, Page, 1923.)

[443]   H. B. Maynard and Company. *Production: An International Appraisal of Contemporary Manufacturing Systems and the Changing Role of the Worker,* ed. Rolf Tiefenthal. (London: McGraw-Hill, 1975.)

[444]   Harper, Peter, and Godfrey Boyle, eds. *Radical Technology.* (New York: Pantheon Books, 1976.)

[445]   Heppenheimer, T. A. *Colonies in Space.* (Harrisburg, Pa.: Stackpole Books, 1977.)

[446]   Howard, Ted, and Jeremy Rifkin. *Who Should Play God? The Artificial Creation of Life and What It Means for the Future of the Human Race.* (New York: Dell, 1977.)

[447]   Illich, Ivan. *Tools for Conviviality.* (New York: Harper & Row, 1973.)

[448]   Jacobs, Jane. *The Economy of Cities.* (New York: Random House, 1969.)

[449]   Klein, H. Arthur. *The World of Measurements.* (New York: Simon and Schuster, 1974.)

[450]   Kranzberg, Melvin, and Carroll W. Pursell, Jr. *Technology in Western Civilization,* Vol. I. (New York: Oxford University Press, 1967.)

[451]   Kuhn, Thomas S. *The Structure of Scientific Revolutions.* (Chicago: University of Chicago Press, 1962.)

[452]   Lawless, Edward W. *Technology and Social Shock.* (New Brunswick, N.J.: Rutgers University Press, 1977.)

[453]   Lilley, Samuel. *Men, Machines and History.* (New York: International Publishers, 1966.)

[454]   Mazlish, Bruce, ed. *The Railroad and the Space Program: An Exploration in Historical Analogy.* (Cambridge, Mass.: MIT Press, 1965.)

[455]   Needham, Joseph. *Science and Civilization in China,* Vol. I, *Introductory Orientations.* (Cambridge: Cambridge University Press, 1965.)

[456]   ———. *Science and Civilization in China,* Vol. II, *History of Scientific Thought.* (Cambridge: Cambridge University Press, 1969.)

[457]   Newman, James R., ed. *What Is Science?* (New York: Washington Square Press, 1961.)

[458]   Nicolis, G., and I. Prigogine. *Self-Organization in Nonequilibrium Systems: From Dissipative Structures to Order Through Fluctuations.* (New York: John Wiley, Wiley-Interscience, 1977.)

[459]   Nikolaev, L. *Space Chemistry,* trans. Y. Nadler. (Moscow: Mir Publishers, 1976.)

[460]   O'Neill, Gerald K. *The High Frontier: Human Colonies in Space.* (New York: Bantam Books, 1978.)

[461]   Pyke, Magnus. *Technological Eating, or Where Does the Fish-Finger Point?* (London: John Murray, 1972.)

[462]   Ritner, Peter. *The Society of Space.* (New York: Macmillan, 1961.)

[463]   Schey, John A. *Introduction to Manufacturing Processes.* (New York: McGraw-Hill, 1977.)

[464]   Schofield, Robert E. *The Lunar Society of Birmingham: A Social History of Provincial Science and Industry in Eighteenth-Century England.* (Oxford: Oxford University Press, 1963.)

[465]   Sharlin, Harold I. *The Convergent Century: The Unification of Science in the Nineteenth Century.* (New York: Abelard-Schuman, 1966.)

[466]   Sorenson, James R. *Social Science Frontiers,* Vol. 3, *Social Aspects of Applied Human Genetics.* (New York: Russell Sage Foundation, 1971.)

[467]   Stine, G. Harry. *The Third Industrial Revolution.* (New York: G. P. Putnam's Sons, 1975.)

[468]   Sullivan, Walter. *We Are Not Alone: The Search for Intelligent Life on Other Worlds.* (New York: McGraw-Hill, 1964.)

[469]   U.S. Department of Labor. *Technological Change and Manpower Trends in Five Industries: Pulp and Paper/Hydraulic Cement/Steel/Aircraft and Missile/Wholesale Trade.* (Washington, D.C.: U.S. Government Printing Office, 1975.)

[470]   Warshofsky, Fred. *Doomsday: The Science of Catastrophe.* (New York: Reader's Digest Press, 1977.)

[471]   Watson, James D. *The Double Helix: A Personal Account of the Discovery of the Structure of DNA.* (New York: New American Library Signet Books, 1968.)

SOCIALISM/COMMUNISM

[472]   Amalrik, Andrei. *Will the Soviet Union Survive until 1984?* (New York: Harper & Row, Perennial Library, 1971.)

[473]   Brus, Wlodzimierz. *The Economics and Politics of Socialism: Collected Essays,* trans. Angus Walker (Chapter 3-6). (London: Routledge & Kegan Paul, 1973.)

[474]   Christman, Henry M., ed. *Essential Works of Lenin.* (New York: Bantam Books, Matrix, 1966.)

[475]   Howe, Irving. *The Basic Writings of Trotsky.* (New York: Random House, Vintage Books, 1965.)

[476]   Laidler, Harry W. *History of Socialism.* (New York: Thomas Y. Crowell, 1968.)

[477]   Marx, Karl, and Friedrich Engels. *The Communist Manifesto.* (Harmondsworth, Middlesex: Penguin Books, 1967.)

[478]   Nicolaus, Martin. *Restoration of Capitalism in the USSR.* (Chicago: Liberator Press, 1975.)

[479]   Nordhoff, Charles. *The Communistic Societies of the United States.* (New York: Schocken Books, 1965.)

[480]   Possony, Stefan T., ed. *The Lenin Reader: The Outstanding Works of V. I. Lenin.* (Chicago: Henry Regnery, Gateway, 1969.)

[481]   Revel, Jean-François. *The Totalitarian Temptation,* trans. David Hapgood. (Harmondsworth, Middlesex: Penguin Books, 1978.)

[482]   ———. *Without Marx or Jesus,* trans. J. F. Bernard. (London: Paladin, 1972.)

[483]   Smelser, Neil J., ed. *Karl Marx on Society and Social Change, with Selections by Friedrich Engels.* (Chicago: University of Chicago Press, 1973.)

[484]   Smith, Hedrick. *The Russians.* (New York: Quadrangle/New York Times, 1976.)

[485]   *Socialism Theory and Practice,* Soviet Monthly Digest of the Theoretical and Political Press, January 1976. (Moscow: Novosti Press Agency.)

[486]   Trotsky, Leon. *Political Profiles,* trans. R. Chappell. (London: New Park Publications, 1972.)

[487]   ———. *The Revolution Betrayed,* trans. Max Eastman, 5th edition. (New York: Pathfinder Press, 1972.)

[488]   Wesson, Robert G. *The Soviet State: An Aging Revolution.* (New York: John Wiley, 1972.)

SOCIOLOGY/SOCIAL THEORY

[489]   Bird, Caroline. *The Crowding Syndrome: Learning to Live with Too Much and Too Many.* (New York: David McKay, 1972.)

[490]   Bottomore, T. B. *Sociology: A Guide to Problems and Literature.* (London: George Allen & Unwin, 1962.)

[491]   Chapple, Eliot Dismore, and Carleton Stevens Coon. *Principles of Anthropology.* (New York: Henry Holt, 1942.)

[492]   Davis, Kingsley, Harry C. Bredemeier, and Marion J. Levy. *Modern American Society.* (New York: Rinehart, 1950.)

[493]   Etzioni, Amitai. *The Active Society: A Theory of Societal and Political Processes.* (New York: Free Press, 1968.)

[494]   ———, and Eva Etzioni, eds. *Social Change: Sources, Patterns, and Consequences.* (New York: Basic Books, 1964.)

[495] Greer, Colin, ed. *Divided Society: The Ethnic Experience in America.* (New York: Basic Books, 1974.)

[496] Harris, Marvin. *The Rise of Anthropological Theory: A History of Theories of Culture.* (New York: Thomas Y. Crowell, 1968.)

[497] Isaacs, Harold R. *Idols of the Tribe.* (New York: Harper & Row, 1975.)

[498] Kardiner, Abram, and Edward Preble. *They Studied Man.* (Cleveland: World Publishing, 1961.)

[499] Moore, Wilbert E. *The Professions: Roles and Rules.* (New York: Russell Sage Foundation, 1970.)

[500] Packard, Vance. *A Nation of Strangers.* (New York: David McKay, 1972.)

[501] Raison, Timothy, ed. *The Founding Fathers of Social Science.* (Harmondsworth, Middlesex: Penguin Books, 1969.)

[502] Toffler, Alvin. *Future Shock.* (New York: Bantam Books, 1971.)

TIME/SPACE

[503] Abler, Ronald, et al. *Human Geography in a Shrinking World.* (Belmont, Cal.: Duxbury Press, 1975.)

[504] Blainey, Geoffrey. *The Tyranny of Distance.* (Melbourne: Sun Books, 1971.)

[505] Clay, Grady. *Close-Up: How to Read the American City.* (New York: Praeger, 1973.)

[506] Coleman, Lesley. *A Book of Time.* (London: Longman, 1971.)

[507] Dean, Robert D., William H. Leahy, and David L. McKee, eds. *Spatial Economic Theory.* (New York: Free Press, 1970.)

[508] de Grazia, Sebastian. *Of Time, Work and Leisure.* (New York: Twentieth Century Fund, 1962.)

[509] Fraser, J. T., ed. *The Voices of Time.* (New York: George Braziller, 1966.)

[510] ———, F. C. Haber, and G. H. Müller, eds. *The Study of Time.* (New York: Springer-Verlag, 1972.)

[511] Gould, Peter, and Rodney White. *Mental Maps.* (Baltimore: Penguin Books, 1974.)

[512] Gribbin, John. *Timewarps.* (New York: Delacorte Press/Eleanor Friede, 1979.)

[513] Haggett, Peter, and Richard J. Chorley. *Network Analysis in Geography.* (New York: St. Martin's Press, 1969.)

[514] Morrill, Richard L. *The Spatial Organization of Society.* (Belmont, Cal.: Duxbury Press, 1970.)

[515] Needham, Joseph. *Time and Eastern Man,* the Henry Myers Lecture 1964, Royal Anthropological Institute

Occasional Paper No. 21. (Glasgow: Royal Anthropological Institute of Great Britain & Ireland, 1965.)

[516]   Norberg-Schulz, Christian. *Existence, Space & Architecture.* (New York: Praeger, 1971.)

[517]   Sandow, Stuart A. *Durations: The Encyclopedia of How Long Things Take.* (New York: Times Books, 1977.)

[518]   Tooley, R. V., Charles Brisker, and Gerald Roe Crone. *Landmarks of Mapmaking.* (Amsterdam: Elsevier, 1968.)

[519]   Welch, Kenneth F. *Time Measurement: An Introductory History.* (Newton Abbot, Devonshire: David & Charles, 1972.)

[520]   Whitrow, G. J. *What is Time?* (London: Thames and Hudson, 1972.)

WORK/EDUCATION

[521]   Anderson, Dennis, and Mark W. Leiserson. *Rural Enterprise and Non-farm Employment.* (Washington, D.C.: World Bank, 1978.)

[522]   Bartlett, Laile E. *New Work/New Life.* (New York: Harper & Row, 1976.)

[523]   Best, Fred, ed. *The Future of Work.* (Englewood Cliffs, N.J.: Prentice-Hall, 1973.)

[524]   Bowman, Jim, et al. *The Far Side of the Future: Social Problems and Educational Reconstruction.* (Washington, D.C.: World Future Society, 1978.)

[525]   Dickson, Paul. *The Future of the Workplace: The Coming Revolution in Jobs.* (New York: Weybright and Talley, 1975.)

[526]   Evans, Archibald A. *Flexibility in Working Life: Opportunities for Individual Choice.* (Paris: Organisation for Economic Co-operation and Development, 1973.)

[527]   Gates, Arthur I., et al. *Educational Psychology,* a revision of *Psychology for Students of Education.* (New York: Macmillan, 1942.)

[528]   Good, H. G. *A History of Western Education.* (New York: Macmillan, 1947.)

[529]   Kanter, Rosabeth Moss. *Social Science Frontiers,* Vol. 9, *Work and Family in the United States: A Critical Review and Agenda for Research and Policy.* (New York: Russell Sage Foundation, 1977.)

[530]   Poor, Riva, ed. *4 Days, 40 Hours: And Other Forms of the Rearranged Workweek.* (New York: New American Library, Mentor, 1973.)

[531]   Roberts, Paul Craig. *Alienation and the Soviet Economy: Toward a General Theory of Marxian Alienation, Organization Principles, and the Soviet*

Economy. (Albuquerque: University of New Mexico Press, 1971.)

[532] *The Shorter Work Week*. Papers delivered at the Conference on Shorter Hours of Work sponsored by the AFL-CIO. (Washington, D.C.: Public Affairs Press, 1957.)

[533] Wells, H. G. *The Work, Wealth and Happiness of Mankind*. (London: William Heinemann, 1932.)

[534] *Work in America*. Report of a special task force to the Secretary of Health, Education, and Welfare, prepared under the auspices of the W. E. Upjohn Institute for Employment Research. (Cambridge, Mass.: MIT Press, 1973.)

INDEX

519

ABOUT THE AUTHOR

A world-renowned scholar and social critic, Alvin Toffler's works are read in more than 50 countries. He has been at various times a Visiting Professor at Cornell University, a member of the faculty of the New School for Social Research, a Visiting Scholar at the Russell Sage Foundation, an Associate Editor of *Fortune* magazine—and, for five years, a factory worker. He holds five honorary doctorates in science, letters and law.

His books include *The Third Wave, The Eco-Spasm Report,* and *The Culture Consumers*. His articles have appeared in such journals as the Annals of the American Academy of Political and Social Science, as well as in such popular magazines as *Playboy* and the *Reader's Digest*. He works closely with his wife, Heidi, and is a much sought-after lecturer, speaking before leading business, government, academic and citizen's organizations around the world.

Future Shock won France's prestigious Prix du Meilleur Livre Étranger.

We Deliver!

And So Do These Bestsellers.

☐	23188	**BEVERLY HILLS DIET LIFETIME PLAN** by Judy Mazel	$3.95
☐	22661	**UP THE FAMILY TREE** by Teresa Bloomingdale	$2.95
☐	22701	**I SHOULD HAVE SEEN IT COMING WHEN** **THE RABBIT DIED** by Teresa Bloomingdale	$2.75
☐	22576	**PATHFINDERS** by Gail Sheehy	$4.50
☐	22585	**THE MINDS OF BILLY MILLIGAN** by Daniel Keyes	$3.95
☐	22981	**SIX WEEKS** by Fred Mustard	$2.95
☐	01428	**ALWAYS A WOMAN** (A Large Format Book)	$9.95
☐	22746	**RED DRAGON** by Thomas Harris	$3.95
☐	20687	**BLACK SUNDAY** by Thomas Harris	$3.50
☐	22685	**THE COSMO REPORT** by Linda Wolfe	$3.95
☐	22736	**A MANY SPLENDORED THING** by Han Suyin	$3.95
☐	20922	**SHADOW OF CAIN** by V. Bugliosi & K. Hurwitz	$3.95
☐	20230	**THE LAST MAFIOSO: The Treacherous** **World of Jimmy Fratianno**	$3.95
☐	13101	**THE BOOK OF LISTS #2** by I. Wallace, D. Wallechinsky, A. & S. Wallace	$3.50
☐	22771	**THE GREATEST SUCCESS IN THE WORLD** by Og Mandino	$2.75
☐	23271	**WHY DO I THINK I'M NOTHING WITHOUT** **A MAN?** by Dr. P. Russianoff	$3.50
☐	23296	**BH&G STEP-BY-STEP HOUSEHOLD REPAIRS** by BH&G Editors	$3.50
☐	20621	**THE PILL BOOK** by Dr. Gilbert Simon & Dr. Harold Silverman	$3.95
☐	23111	**GUINNESS BOOK OF WORLD RECORDS—** 21st ed. by McWhirter	$3.95
☐	20303	**YOU CAN NEGOTIATE ANYTHING** by Herb Cohen	$3.50
☐	23084	**THE UMPIRE STRIKES BACK** by Ron Luciano	$3.50

Buy them at your local bookstore or use this handy coupon for ordering:

Bantam Books, Inc., Dept. NFB, 414 East Golf Road, Des Plaines, Ill. 60016

Please send me the books I have checked above. I am enclosing $_____
(please add $1.25 to cover postage and handling). Send check or money order
—no cash or C.O.D.'s please.

Mr/Mrs/Miss _____

Address_____

City_____ State/Zip_____

NFB—5/83

Please allow four to six weeks for delivery. This offer expires 11/83.

BANTAM NEW AGE BOOKS

Bantam New Age Books are for all those interested in reflecting on life today and life as it may be in the future. This important new imprint features stimulating works in fields from biology and psychology to philosophy and the new physics.

☐	22689	**CREATIVE VISUALIZATION** Shatki Gawain	$3.50
☐	22511	**NEW RULES: SEARCHING FOR SELF-FULFILLMENT IN A WORLD TURNED UPSIDE DOWN** Daniel Yankelovich	$3.95
☐	22510	**ZEN IN THE MARTIAL ARTS** J. Hyams	$2.95
☐	20650	**STRESS AND THE ART OF BIOFEEDBACK** Barbara Brown	$3.95
☐	14131	**THE FIRST THREE MINUTES** Steven Weinberg	$2.95
☐	20059	**MAGICAL CHILD** Joseph Chilton Pearce	$3.95
☐	22786	**MIND AND NATURE:** A Necessary Unity Gregory Bateson	$3.95
☐	20322	**HEALTH FOR THE WHOLE PERSON** James Gordon	$3.95
☐	20708	**ZEN/MOTORCYCLE MAINTENANCE** Robert Pirsig	$3.95
☐	20693	**THE WAY OF THE SHAMAN** Michael Hamer	$3.95
☐	23100	**TO HAVE OR TO BE** Fromm	$3.50
☐	23125	**FOCUSING** Eugene Gendlin	$3.95
☐	13972	**LIVES OF A CELL** Lewis Thomas	$2.95
☐	14912	**KISS SLEEPING BEAUTY GOODBYE** M. Kolbenschlag	$3.95

Buy them at your bookstore or use this handy coupon for ordering:

Bantam Books, Inc., Dept. NA, 414 East Golf Road, Des Plaines, Ill. 60016

Please send me the books I have checked above. I am enclosing $_____ (please add $1.25 to cover postage and handling). Send check or money order —no cash or C.O.D.'s please.

Mr/Mrs/Miss_____

Address_____

City_____State/Zip_____

NA—4/83

Please allow four to six weeks for delivery. This offer expires 10/83.

<u>SAVE $2.00</u> ON YOUR NEXT BOOK ORDER!

BANTAM BOOKS
Shop-at-Home — *Catalog*

Now you can have a complete, up-to-date catalog of Bantam's inventory of over 1,600 titles—including hard-to-find books. And, you can save $2.00 on your next order by taking advantage of the <u>money-saving</u> coupon you'll find in this illustrated catalog. Choose from fiction and non-fiction titles, including mysteries, historical novels, westerns, cookbooks, romances, biographies, family living, health, and more. You'll find a description of most titles. Arranged by categoreis, the catalog makes it easy to find your favorite books and authors and to discover new ones.

So don't delay—send for this shop-at-home catalog and save money on your next book order.

Just send us your name and address and 50¢ to defray postage and handling costs.

BANTAM BOOKS, INC.
Dept. FC, 414 East Golf Road, Des Plaines, Ill. 60016

Mr./Mrs./Miss _____
(please print)

Address _____

City _____ State _____ Zip _____

Do you know someone who enjoys books? Just give us their names and addresses and we'll send them a catalog too at no extra cost!

Mr./Mrs./Miss _____

Address _____

City _____ State _____ Zip _____

Mr./Mrs./Miss _____

Address _____

City _____ State _____ Zip _____

FC—2/83